Harry C. Trexler Library
Muhlenberg College

The Japanese Enterprise System

The Japanese Enterprise System

Competitive Strategies and Cooperative Structures

W. MARK FRUIN

CLARENDON PRESS · OXFORD
1992

Oxford University Press, Walton Street, Oxford OX2 6DP

Oxford New York Toronto
Delhi Bombay Calcutta Madras Karachi
Kuala Lumpur Singapore Hong Kong Tokyo
Nairobi Dar es Salaam Cape Town
Melbourne Auckland Madrid

and associated companies in
Berlin Ibadan

Oxford is a trade mark of Oxford University Press

Published in the United States
by Oxford University Press Inc., New York

British Library Cataloguing in Publication Data
Data available

Library of Congress Cataloging in Publication Data
Fruin, W. Mark. 1943–
The Japanese enterprise system: competitive strategies and
cooperative structures/W. Mark Fruin.
p. cm.
Includes bibliographical references and index.
1. Corporations—Japan—History.   2. Industrial organization—
Japan—History.   3. Enterpreneurship—Japan—History.   I. Title.
HD2907.F78 1991 338.7'4'0952—dc20 91—33285
ISBN 0–19–828318–0

3 5 7 9 10 8 6 4 2

Printed in Great Britain
on acid-free paper by
Bookcraft (Bath) Ltd.,
Midsomer Norton, Avon

To my parents
and for my sons

Acknowledgements

This book was a long time coming, nearly ten years. During so many years of research, writing, and reflection, institutional and personal debts have piled up, unanswered for the most part. The following inventory captures only the most obvious and important of these which, in fact, must be judged closer to assets than arrears. Institutional support came first from the Harvard Graduate School of Business Administration; and subsequently from California State University, Hayward; Osaka University; and INSEAD (the European Institute of Business Administration). The Harvard Business School, therefore, was first to see the value of this line of research and support it. My gratitude for that foresight. Foundation support came from the Social Science Research Council, the Toyota Foundation, and the National Endowment for the Humanities.

Professor Alfred D. Chandler, Jr. of the Harvard Business School was the figure who inspired this work. I was fortunate enough to spend nearly two years at Harvard working with Chandler, writing *Kikkoman: Company, Clan, and Community* (Harvard University Press, 1983) and sketching out the early ideas for this book. From the beginning of this project to its completion, Chandler advised, queried, and counseled me. Without his scholarship, wisdom, friendship, and encouragement *The Japanese Enterprise System* could not have been written.

In addition, Gary Allinson, Masahiko Aoki, Banri Asanuma, Bala Chakravarthy, William Cummings, Yves Doz, Richard L. Fruin, Jr., Michael Gerlach, Margaret B. W. Graham, Martin Kilduff, Bruce Kogut, Mitchell Koza, Toshihiro Nishiguchi, Robert Ozaki, Hugh Patrick, Thomas Roehl, Jerry Ross, Richard Scott, Masahiro Shimotani, Thomas C. Smith, Michael Smitka, Koji Taira, Christena Turner, Eleanor Westney, and Oliver E. Williamson gave generously of their time and knowledge, immeasurably improving the book's content and argument. Collegial interactions at INSEAD were most important, underscoring the importance of environment for both the quality of life and work. Mrs. Helen Varin of the Euro-Asia Centre, INSEAD, contributed valuable technical and secretarial help.

Professor Tsunehiko Yui of Meiji University was pivotal to the successful completion of the research on several occasions. I have relied heavily on his erudition for my discussions of various aspects of the Japanese enterprise system. Together, we developed lists of the largest 200 industrial firms in Japan for 1918, 1930, 1954, and 1973. The pre-war lists were immeasurably more difficult to assemble than the post-war lists. Together, we evolved a typology of enterprise features for pre-World War Two Japan. Without him, the book would have less detail, depth, and insight.

As always, however, any errors of interpretation or fact are my own. And I suspect that there are many. This is a very ambitious work in scale and scope, and I still have a lot to learn about the modern corporation and enterprise system in Japan. But writing projects have to end sometime and somewhere, and this is the time and place.

Finally, I owe much to my parents, Richard Lawrence Fruin and Gertrude Winter Fruin, and to my sons, Noah Glenn and Nathan Mark. Any voluntary, ten-year project is a labor of love. That love, mine and theirs, sustained this endeavor. Endeavor led to knowledge and knowledge to understanding.

I want to end by suggesting that families, like all institutions, have a capacity for organizational learning. My sense of history probably comes from my father, a physician but a gifted amateur historian of the American Civil War and the Austrian school of economics. My mother is the family historian, unerringly able to trace the Irish and German sides of the family. Noah, my older son, already knows more European history (and much more about computers) than I do, and Nathan, younger by five years, can recite American aviation history chapter and verse. I hope this work continues and enriches the family tradition.

W.M.F.

Palo Alto, California and Fontainebleau, France
Spring 1991

Contents

List of Figures

List of Tables

Abbreviations

BU	business unit
CNC	computer numerical controlled machine tools
FMS	flexible manufacturing system
H-Form	holding company form
JIT	just-in-time
LH	letter handling
MEI	Matsushita Electric Industrial
M-Form	multidivisional form
MITI	Ministry of International Trade and Industry
MTP	management training program
NC	numerical controlled machine tools
NEC	Nippon Electric Company
OCR	optical character recognition
OEM	original equipment manufacturer
PPC	plain paper copier
PWP	plant within a plant
QC	quality control
SBU	strategic business unit
SCAP	Supreme Command of the Allied Powers
SIC	standard industrial classification
TP	total productivity
TQC	total quality control
TWI	training within industry
U-Form	unitary form
VLSI	very large-scale integration

Introduction

I
Context for The Japanese Enterprise System

A half-century long, phenomenal economic increase has created something of a (social) science fiction: an economy, Japan's, that appears larger-than-life, a fashion for some and a phobia for others. Japan is the first and only non-Western country to have broken a two-century-long association between geography (Western Europe and North America), a particular kind of political and economic experience (industrial democracy), and international industrial prosperity (including Australia and New Zealand among the nations of the West). South Korea, Taiwan, and Singapore may be next.[1] Fashions and phobias somehow miss the point.

Japan and its Asian neighbors suggest alternative models of development, possibilities that thoroughly modern but non-Western forms of industrial capitalism may exist. As we enter the twenty-first century these possibilities have to be taken seriously. Since 1945 alternative political and economic systems contested global leadership *within* the Western world and that see-sawing balance of power confirmed a Western slant on world affairs. An emancipation of Eastern Europe and a strategic *détente* in USA–Soviet Union–European relations have ended an internecine Cold War, attendant political, economic, military, and intellectual arrangements, a Western point of view. Or have they?

Now there is an 'enigma' of Japanese power and, seemingly, peril.[2] In 1989, shortly before the thaw in US–Soviet Union relations, three times as many Americans were more worried about the economic strength of Japan than the military strength of the former Soviet Union, and in 1990 25 percent of Americans interviewed responded that their feelings towards Japan were generally unfriendly.[3] Science fiction, enigma, and peril are the popular argot of contemporary writings on Japan.

Damning Japan, or granting Japan 'other-worldliness', misses the point. Japan's economic success is unparalleled in world history. This plain but overpowering fact summons the hopes of a post-Cold War world anxious for international peace coupled with industrial progress, political stability, national security, and material well-being. But at the same time Japan's success smites these hopes because it embodies an experience rather at odds with Western experience. Less than a century ago, recall that Japan symbolized national insecurity, economic penury, political authoritarianism, and social retardation (from a Western point of view). Out of this past flows Japan's 'success'. This chimerical reversal of fortunes (and interpretations) does not sit well, now or before the end of the Cold War, and it has prompted a rich outpouring of analysis, among which this book should be included.

The impressive numbers of such studies in languages other than Japanese suggest the appreciation and apprehension with which Japan's rise to wealth and power are weighed. However, the numbers published in Japanese are even more astonishing, pointing to a curious mix of inquisitiveness, trepidation, pride, and uneasiness with which the Japanese confront their own success. Other than purely economic arguments, a good half-dozen alternative and hybrid rationales for Japan's progress are advanced. Again, the number is surprising, suggesting that what suffices for explaining the post-war performance of, say, Germany appears unconvincing for Japan.

Putting aside neo-orthodox economic expositions ('the no-miracle occurred school') and throwing out nonsensical cultural ones ('the Japanese are successful because they're Japanese'), the five most frequently offered interpretations are:

1. exegeses based on human-resource practices, especially the importance of personnel management, career development, and company-specific training in large firms;
2. institutional control and financial interrelations, the *zaibatsu*, *kigyo shudan* and *keiretsu* models of corporate development;
3. late development, technological catch-up, and the advantages of 'back-wardness' in economic development;
4. industrial policy, government–business relations, and the capitalist development state;
5. an accent on the efficiency and utility of native economic institutions.[4]

But single-factor, simple-minded constructions of a complex people and past are not persuasive. The Japanese are not a tribe, Japanese firms not a patch. No matter which school of explanation is pursued, it is necessary to come to grips with individual choice and with issues of how individual behavior and action relate to institutional and industrial patterns. My eclectic interpretation of these issues emphasizes interactions, interactions binding individuals to individuals, individuals to institutions, and institutions to other institutions within a small and rapidly changing country.

To underscore interactions and the high levels of interdependence that result, I have adopted an implicitly comparative framework—one that looks at Japanese enterprises in light of what is known about modern corporations elsewhere, primarily in the Western world and especially in the United States. The result is a strong and abiding conviction that Japanese enterprises are different, and these differences, manifested in issues of organizational size, structure, strategy, process, and performance, constitute a realm in need of explanation.

Such differences are examined through an analysis of how and why firms appeared in Japan (Chapters 2 and 3), of how firms evolved (Chapters 4 and 5), of how they are governed, emphasizing the importance of interorganizational boundaries (Chapters 1, 2, 6, 7, and 8), of variations among major types of firms (Chapters 3, 4, and 5), and of the meanings attributed to them (Chapters 2, 6, and 8).

Hence, I merge four streams of enquiry and interpretation in *The Japanese Enterprise System*. First, it is a *historical* study of how the industrial institutions of modern Japan evolved and matured. Second, it is an *organization* study of the basic forms of social and economic interaction in Japan and their interrelation. Third, it is a *development* study of how circumstances of rapid technical and economic change have shaped the Japanese business system. And, it is a *strategy* study of how Japanese managers have responded to and shaped these circumstances. This fourfold synthesis offers a model of institutional development under conditions of late economic development and private initiative that falls somewhere between a capitalist-development state and a free-market economy. Business policy rather than industrial policy is accentuated, revealing a set of robust institutions and a dynamic to activate and interrelate them, the Japanese enterprise system.

II
Content: The Japanese Enterprise System in Comparison

The Japanese enterprise system is an interorganizational system of business management and coordination. It is based on the strategic interaction and alignment of three basic forms of industrial organization—factory, firm, and interfirm network. High productivity, functional specialization, and manufacturing adaptability are hallmarks of this system and they distinguish the Japanese enterprise system from most others.

A long-term aim of my research is to grasp the place of this interorganizational system within a global history of industrial firms while, at the same time, demarcating those features of Japanese organizations that distinguish them from Western as well as from other Asian organizational forms. Ultimately such overarching goals may be traced to the scholarship of Alfred D. Chandler, Jr., the dean of American business historians and the person most responsible for the emerging synthesis on the global history of the firm. Chandler's influential book *Strategy and Structure* (1962) inspired this study, and his subsequent publications of *The Visible Hand* (1977) and *Scale and Scope* (1990), deepened my admiration for the man and his work.

As a result, this book is motivated by a search for what is different and what is not about Japanese firms in a context of world-wide industrialization. The most obvious and striking difference is found in structure. Historians and economists alike, including Alfred D. Chandler and Oliver E. Williamson, two of the leading interpreters of American industrial development, have argued that the multidivisional form (M-Form) of the modern corporation is the most innovative and efficient form of industrial organization.[5] Imagine my puzzlement as it became evident that in Japan, one of the most advanced capitalist economies in the world, the multidivisional form of organization is not so common and not so highly regarded.[6]

Quantitative and qualitative scrutiny as to why this is the case was needed. This study is based on information about the 200 largest industrial firms in Japan since 1918, plus historical and more recent writings in Japanese culled from the most prolific business press in the world. Fieldwork and interviews have extended those materials. In all instances, only the largest and most successful industrial firms have been studied. Size counts for a lot in studies of industrial organization and because of this, quite a different book would have to be written about the 400 largest industrial firms.

Following Chandler's lead, quantitative information, including rank-order data on corporate assets, capitalization, sales/revenue, number of employees, and product lines, was collected for the 200 largest Japanese industrial firms during the years 1918, 1930, 1954, 1973, and 1987: a full seventy years of corporate evolution and maturation. The data, more comprehensive, inclusive, and lengthy than any hitherto collected, buttress the description and analysis of the modern corporation and enterprise system in Japan. Data on these 1,000 firms from five bench-mark years are published in the Appendix while insights and observations from the data are interlaced throughout the book.

Note well that these are winners—the 200 largest Japanese industrial firms. Yet even these winners are dwarfed by the predominance of American firms among the world's largest industrial corporations. Of the total 401 industrial firms employing more than 20,000 persons in 1973, over half (211 or 52.6 percent) were American, 50 from the United Kingdom, 29 from Germany, 28 from Japan, and 24 from France.[7] Since 1973, however, Japanese firms have gained the most ground in this global sweepstakes and this in spite of the fact, emphasized throughout this work, that Japanese firms are relatively small and specialized in comparison with a sample of leading Western industrial firms.

Modern industrial enterprises in Japan did not appear full-blown in 1973, however, and this book also considers the antecedents to and variations on the corporation. What was most different about Japanese companies, at least those callow enterprises that appeared in the late nineteenth century, was that they tried intentionally to emulate successful Western firms. The models emulated represented best practice in various industries, so Japanese entrepreneurs were borrowing institutional practices that were already well developed legally, managerially, and technically. The corporate form of organization was imported unshorn, uncropped, as one piece in a Western weave of institutional civilization.

It became quickly apparent that Western institutions required a great deal of adaptation and adjustment to fit local circumstances. Self-consciously and with immense effort and ingenuity, relying on translated texts from Dutch, English, French, and German and on students returned from the West, the earliest Japanese industrial enterprises were founded at the close of the nineteenth century to produce foods and beverages, electrical equipment, ore, metals, spun and woven goods of silk and cotton. A large number of frankly expedient and experimental efforts were undertaken and the most successful widely copied.

This highly focused effort to transfer organizational models, managerial methods, and production and distribution technologies from the West into a fundamentally different social and economic environment reveals the tangled origins and evolution of the Japanese enterprise system. This effort, commencing in the latter half of the nineteenth century, still continues today, although Japanese firms have pulled abreast and occasionally overtaken Western companies in certain areas. However, even if Japanese firms have come very far, very fast in the last hundred years, an initiative and desire to learn from the West, to follow the best examples of enterprise practice found anywhere, and to become leading corporations in today's interdependent global world have not diminished. Japanese managers read *In Search of Excellence* with near religious fervor.[8]

It is wrong to characterize the processes of technology transfer and of late development as simple processes of imitation, repetition, and duplication. Indeed, such a characterization smacks of ethnocentrism and near-sighted prejudice. After all, when America was imitating British technology in the nineteenth century, this was called Yankee ingenuity. The art and technique of imitation need to be better understood and more appreciated.[9]

Technology transfer is anything but simple and straightforward. It encompasses problems of implementation, more formidable than merely identifying and acquiring technology. It requires openness, receptivity, flexibility, and adaptability, and these have become ingrained attitudes and values in the Japanese business community as a result of a century-long experience of zealous technology acquisition. Moreover, the alacrity with which Japanese firms learn their lessons and cultivate them as springboards to genuine invention have been underestimated. Belying notions of 'Japanese-as-imitators', high rates of technology transfer and sustained investment in human and physical resources have yielded innumerable social, technical, and organizational innovations.

A distinction between general and institution-specific technology transfer has been crucial. The long, hard pull towards national economic success was predicated on patterns of institution-specific learning, generally called organizational learning in this study, enacted and re-enacted within and between the industrial institutions of the Japanese enterprise system.[10] Acquisition, appropriation, accumulation, adaptation, and exploitation of learning, based on technology transfer, are the operational underpinnings of the system.

Paradoxically, given the genuine emulation behind Japan's success, Japanese firms are admired today by enterprises throughout the world, sometimes the very firms that Japanese companies once copied. But the paradox disappears when it is assumed that organizations and the people in them can learn, have a collective memory, and pass down values, methods, and routines to those that follow. So, in the process of transferring the corporate form to Japan, new patterns of organization and behavior were created, and these are now modeled elsewhere. The Japanese general-trading company, for example, a business intermediary that facilitates a full-range of interorganizational transactions, is consciously imitated in Jakarta, Singapore, Washington, DC, and London, notwithstanding that the first Japanese trading companies were formed to sell abroad surplus mineral and agricultural products.

Institutions can be imitated, the interaction of institutions and environments less so. A lack of enterprise strategies and structures comparable to those found in Japan in other Asian and African countries is striking. The weight of the Japanese experience for comparative studies of social and economic development falls in favor of particularistic patterns of institutional and environmental interaction. Such patterns of business development and adaptation in Japan and elsewhere, reveal each country's corporate past as well as delimit possibilities of change. In this view, a nation's comparative advantage is really corporate or institutional advantage. Patterns of organizational evolution and, ultimately, of institutional advantage define the character of the enterprise system in Japan as elsewhere.

Endings: The Japanese Corporation in Contrast

Having set out to do what so many others have already done, namely explain and interpret Japan's economic performance, what specifically recommends this study? I argue that the idea and the introduction of the corporation brought profound changes in the life and institutions of modern Japan, perhaps more profound there than anywhere else in the industrialized world. There are four reasons for this:

1. time compression and the corporation as an agent of change;
2. information and information processing as constraints on corporate growth;
3. adaptation and cooperation as managerial responses to environmental turbulence;
4. development and evolution of organizational alternatives.

First, the corporation itself was a radical agent for change. Imported and adapted to local circumstance, the corporation, nascent in the late nineteenth century, emerged strongly in the twentieth century and in doing so compressed several centuries of ongoing organizational evolution and adaptation in the West into one or two generations in Japan. This transformed forever the legal, political, social, and institutional structures and meanings of work.

As a recently derived form of cooperation, the Japanese firm was modeled on Western corporations but it combined significant elements of Japanese circumstance and culture. These include the climate of nationalistic opinion and fervor that surrounded the introduction of the modern factory and corporate systems; the potential of indigenous institutions for further educational, technological, and economic advancement; a decidedly fragmented market for manufactured products and a well-developed market for agricultural and proto-industrial goods; a highly commercialized, urbanized, and monetized, 'household-based' (*ie*) society that valued careful and canny husbanding of resources.

Second, there are organizational and informational limits to the capacity of any firm to borrow and apply new methods.[11] Information and information processing are costly. These are especially dear where behavioral, technical, and organizational differences separate giving and receiving cultures. Clearly, Meiji Japan (1868–1912) was vastly different from the West in its economic principles and social institutions. A thoroughly alien institution, like the corporation, had to blend with local circumstances, while at the same time interacting with and reordering those circumstances. The costs of information and information processing in the midst of such uncertainty pushed corporations to focus and concentrate activities. Doing one and only one thing well was the result.

After the newly established Meiji government sorted out internal differences and embarked upon an ambitious nation-building program, the economy grew notably and in spite of differences in giving and receiving circumstances, firms took root remarkably well. Wataro Kanno tallies 3,336 joint-stock companies established by 1882 and 8,612 by 1902.[12] For half a century, from 1885 to 1940, the economy averaged nearly 3.0 percent annual growth, stimulated in large part by conflict and world war: the Sino-Japanese War 1894–5, the Russo-Japanese War 1904–5, and World War One. The redoubtable growth in the first half of the twentieth century is often overlooked due to an even more extraordinary performance after World War Two. In the ten years from 1954 to 1963 alone, real national product rose more than 2.2 times, growing at an annual average rate of 9.4 percent.[13] An OECD publication puts it, 'By the conventional measures of macroeconomic performance (income growth, inflation, unemployment), Japan has out-performed all other OECD economies since entry into the Organization in 1964'.[14]

Nevertheless, during the pre-war period of economic growth, fundamental and enduring features of the institutional framework of modern capitalism were fashioned. In particular, given limitations in the capacity of organizations to absorb and apply new methods, especially in rapidly changing circumstances, a subdivision of tasks and a distribution of rewards within an alliance of cooperating (but profit-seeking) firms constituted an effective coping strategy. In Japan, as a result, processes of corporate adaptation in the midst of unpredictable social and economic change led to three basic yet different forms of industrial organization: focal factories, unitary firms, and interfirm networks.

Networks, to take an example, shifted the burden of doing business. By linking firms through cooperation, networks lowered investment levels for individual firms, reduced risk, minimized adverse selection, and lessened capital expenditures. Cooperation included a wide range of behaviors where costs were not exactly calculated or catalogued: for example, sharing physical equipment and facilities, providing market and technical information, or simply giving that extra consideration when needed. Organizational learning or the organizational capacity to change and evolve intelligently was the basis for effective cooperation.

Cooperation was related to the span of organizational control and the quality of organizational resources. That is, the larger the enterprise and the more sparsely spread its resources, the more difficult, less frequent and reliable cooperation. Recognizing these relationships more implicitly than explicitly, entrepreneurs kept firms small and specialized, with a long-term strategy of cooperation to overcome specialization's shortcomings. Cooperation made especially good sense because acquiring another firm's assets was not an alternative; shares were closely held and thinly traded.

As a consequence, the Japanese firm came to be accented by a focused structure and strategy wherein human, material, and other resources were and are concentrated within simple, functional organizations, so-called U-Form firms (unitary in that all functions contribute to the management of a single product-line), and these are linked through cooperative agreements with other similarly structured firms. Production was the main thrust of such firms because of the prominence of factories, particularly multi-function focal factories.

Especially before the Pacific War, multi-function, and often multi-product, factories were analogous, even synonymous, with U-Form firms. Ultimately, focused factories and unitary firms were and are interconnected, like the hexagonal elements of a Buckminster Fuller dome, to scores of other similarly specialized units, creating in the aggregate large, interactive networks of organizations for resource mobilization and coordination.

The cooperative approach to business was propelled by foreign technology transfer. Because Japanese firms relied almost entirely on imported technology and thus on an internal capacity to absorb foreign learning in a timely fashion, industrialization pushed enterprises to fix resources urgently in two directions: *downward* as a means to transfer Western technologies to production sites for modification according to local markets and consumer preferences, and *outward* to find and forge complementary relationships in marketing, financing, and manufacturing with other firms.

Toyota Motor, a company examined in depth in Chapter 7, built its first motor vehicles by reverse engineering various automotive subsystems from American models while it recruited dozens of outside firms to supply parts, components, and services that it could not easily provide itself. Both thrusts, downward and outward, were incrementally yet increasingly institutionalized *inward* at Toyota as it matured into a large, modern corporation after World War Two.

Third, once institutionalized pathways of economic activity—downward, outward, and inward—were forged, they were elaborated and refined in any number of ways. The augmentation and enhancement of cooperation based on organizational learning became a principal means of competition. Firms grew in tandem with one another, forging ties, extending their efforts. Cooperative alliances helped overcome firm-specific limitations, such as bounded rationality and opportunism in the language of modern economics and organization theory, which limit the rate of organizational learning and adaptation. By securing pathways of interfirm cooperation and collaboration, a firm's resources could be deepened, refined, and refocused, enhancing knowledge-building and organizational competence. Interfirm alliances became a basis for extending intrafirm capabilities, as internal resources were increasingly interconnected with those of other enterprises. In an extreme degree, intrafirm and interfirm resources co-evolved and co-mingled.

Fourth, the combination of these organizational elements in the form of an emerging enterprise system proceeded through a number of stages from the early twentieth century until recently, when the nature of the system changed again. While earlier stages of development were driven by internal or domestic concerns, since the 1980s Japanese firms have been internationalizing their operations with alacrity and diversifying their strategies on the basis of non-Japanese markets and opportunities. As a result, Japanese firms and industries are becoming more broadly based, both geographically and in terms of products, and these new directions are modifying what had been typical patterns of corporate structure, conduct, and performance.

A word of caution, therefore. The reasons for the success of the Japanese enterprise system to date will not remain constant. Indeed, the success of the system so far has been largely contingent on the enormous growth of a home market and an elaboration and intensification of corporate strategy and structure to fit domestic circumstances. Now, market forces are driving Japanese firms overseas; patterns of corporate behavior are being modified in order to compete in foreign markets. Yet in this effort it is unlikely that Japanese corporations will jettison history, an inertial guidance system that has proven so reliable and favorable in the past.

In sum, the modern corporation was a radical agent for social and economic change in Japan even while the corporation itself was altered by a dynamic interaction with an environment rather different from that in which corporations were born and bred. Japanese firms adjusted to the uncertainties of modern economic life through specialization, learning, and collaboration: internally, firms focused on functional excellence, especially in production; externally, they structured interrelations with others for product and market breadth.

By negotiating interorganizational cooperation, an extreme subdivision of tasks and a refined distribution of rewards are possible. The advantages of this highly interdependent system are adaptability and productivity, and these are found most notably in a capacity for lowering transaction costs in spite of extensive *interfirm* dependencies and in deepening focused spheres of product and process competency through innovative *intrafirm* learning.

The combination of history, organizational development, competitive interaction, and strategy, as outlined above, occurred and reoccurred in the history of major industrial firms, resulting in processes where organizational competencies, skills, and resources were held and used interdependently, even while interdependency was and is not a synonym for altruism. Moreover, pathways of cooperation were used in adaptive ways, that is in tune with changing market and technological conditions. Once patterns of interorganizational development emerged, interdependence became an accepted and emulated principle.

The process of *acting interdependently* is the most outstanding and distinctive feature of the Japanese enterprise system. This has led to a business system that values the importance of both competition and cooperation for business, in intrafirm and interfirm relations as well as in government–business relations. The core of this system is its permeable institutional boundaries—the capacity of using resources interdependently and reliably across organizational borders.

Implications

Japanese corporations are relatively small and specialized because of permeable boundaries. They allow an emphasis on production, especially on the integrated production environment of what this book calls focal factories, and on cooperative manufacturing and distributing arrangements, namely interfirm networks. Highly differentiated patterns of intrafirm resource allocation and mobilization, like those found in focal factories, and dense, durable, and intense networks of interfirm relations are singularly Japanese in many aspects. As an organizational system, discovered, reinforced, and followed by so many Japanese firms for so long, it has been elevated almost to a country-level explanation for economic growth.

The history of the system is important because so many major Japanese firms are successful. They are successful by any international measure—approaching, equaling, and occasionally surpassing Western firms in scale, profitability, and global presence. They are remarkable for their ability to combine product and process specialization at the manufacturing level, coordination in strategic planning and marketing at the corporate level, with product and market breadth at the interfirm level. Because scope at one level is related to specialization at another through permeable boundaries (the notion and practice of organizational interdependence), the enterprise system folds neatly in on itself: a business system of extreme interlocking complexity and function.

By accumulating resources and routines with integration and interdependence at every level of economic activity, the Japanese enterprise system tenders a highly articulated, organization-centered presence even while the market-place is the final arbiter of efficiency. Causality is important here. In light of the broadly based, omnibus efforts of managers to cultivate capabilities, be profitable, and be their own masters, it would be mistaken to assign too much weight to government guidance in the formation and administration of the system. Most importantly, the state did not constrain the competitive–cooperative dynamic of this inter-organizational system. The market did.

Japanese corporations are pre-eminent in Asia, especially so in the Pacific Basin, where the foci of so much economic activity is shifting. Japanese corporations capture and highlight processes of organization and technology transfer that are recasting the social and economic landscape in Asia. Japan is consciously emulated in Taiwan, South Korea, India, Singapore, Hong Kong, the Philippines, Malaysia, and Indonesia. Even in the People's Republic of China and among the socialist countries of Asia, Japan is a model of development.[15] These countries are now

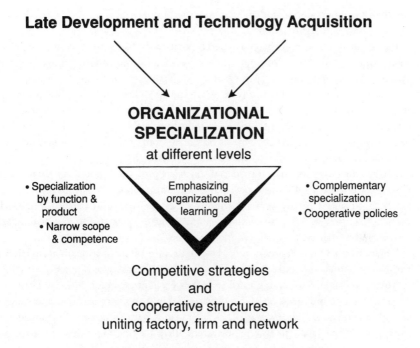

Late Development and Technology Acquisition

ORGANIZATIONAL SPECIALIZATION
at different levels

- Specialization by function & product
- Narrow scope & competence

Emphasizing organizational learning

- Complementary specialization
- Cooperative policies

Competitive strategies
and
cooperative structures
uniting factory, firm and network

FIG. I.1. *Dynamics of the Japanese Enterprise System*

attempting to do what Japan did during the last century, namely craft their economic organizations in the image of the most successful enterprises of the day. And, the more successful of these efforts in turn will become models for still later developing countries.

Japanese corporations are prototypes not only for their economic success but also for their social inventiveness. Firms have taken what was a singular Western institution with a long and particularly complex history of its own, transplanted, hybridized, and domesticated the form as their own. While the *ie* or stem household was an effective means of social and economic organization for pre-industrial Japan, it lacked the organizational repertoire of a joint-stock company for an industrial age. More than simply adapting something foreign to Japanese soil, however, the reinterpretation of the corporate form in Japan has defined a new spirit and purpose for the firm.

Learning to learn continuously as an organization is at the root of the Japanese corporate experience, and this ethic and practice are now spreading in Asia. That social innovation—the creation of a new corporate spirit and purpose—has profound material consequences of which better, cheaper, and more innovative products are only the most visible result. Employment commitment, institutional performance, and collective and personal effort are less obvious but no less real. As are the long hours, pressured lives, and institutional constraints that come with high-performance organizations.

In less than a century, the Japanese corporation has become a global model of what modern industrial firms should be. Because of this, the emergence of the modern corporation and enterprise system in Japan can no longer be regarded as merely imitative and derivative of the Western experience, and these developments are seen as both disquieting and hopeful by Westerners no less than Asians. The pre-eminence of Japanese firms in many industries globally, their salience in Asia especially, and the differences separating them from their Western counterparts, challenge our understanding of the modern corporation.

All of this suggests that the special experience of the modern corporation in Japan may require a substantial reworking of the traditional theory of the firm as it has been advanced in the West. Certainly, the structures and meanings of work defined by the values and actions joining factory, firm, and network are substantially different from that found elsewhere.

Organizational interdependence—the importance of institutional interrelations within and across corporate boundaries—owes much to the late-development effect in Japan, and hence to strategies of interfirm economies, organizational learning, and the effective mobilization and motivation of human effort under circumstances of highly constrained resources. If these conditions have so powerfully framed the emergence of the Japanese enterprise system, they may be more determinative for even later developing economies and enterprise systems. This introductory argument is summarized in Fig. I.1.

Closings

The corporation, as a major form of industrial organization and as a force for economic and social progress, has shown remarkable properties of regeneration and adaptation around the world. A case in point, Japanese companies are different from many Western counterparts in structure as well as in content yet they share basic political, economic, legal, and organizational characteristics in common. As the most evolved form of enterprise organization in Asia and the Pacific Basin, however, Japanese firms may be forging a new regional and global definition of what the corporation can be. That difference is now the subject of intense global scrutiny as Japanese companies perform so well at home and abroad.

The study of the Japanese corporation offers the chance to distinguish those features of the corporation that appear universal—true regardless of country or culture—while, at the same time, underscoring those aspects of corporate structure and strategy that may be influenced by local resources, geography, history, and circumstances. Indeed, the focused strategy of Japanese industrial firms in particular business lines is confirmed by recent American evidence as a superior form of strategic organization.[16] However, the linking of this focused strategy with structures of interfirm cooperation appears unlikely in the United States, given different historical, legal, and political circumstances.

In sum, this study seeks to distinguish between what Lance Davis and Douglass North called the *institutional environment* that gave rise to the Japanese enterprise system, that is the set of political, social, and legal ground rules that establishes a basis for production, exchange, and distribution, and the *organizational arrangements* between economic units that governs the ways in which they compete and cooperate.[17] The organizational arrangements—competitive strategies and cooperative structures—of the Japanese enterprise system advance rather persuasive examples of how to organize economic institutions for personal, social, and institutional gain, and in my opinion these lift the Japanese enterprise system beyond a particular place and time to a realm of universal significance.

NOTES

1. The economic performance of South Korea is also forcing a reconsideration of the traditional models of economic development and capitalist institutions. See Alice H. Amsden, *Asia's Next Giant* (New York: Oxford University Press, 1989).

2. In 1988 Karel van Wolferen, a Dutch journalist living in Japan, published a best-selling book titled *The Enigma of Japanese Power* (New York: Basic Books). His thesis was straightforward: no one in Japan is responsible for Japan's considerable power. Instead, the machinations of faceless technocrats in an 'insidious system' are. Van Wolferen's book found considerable favor among persons critical of Japan's success, but others found the book deplorable, even offensive.

   Van Wolferen cannot explain the workings of Japan according to Western notions of authority, decision-making, and responsibility, and because of this, the Japanese became enigmatic and worse in his prose. After twenty years of living in Japan, presumably learning Japanese and how things are 'done' in Japan, van Wolferen abandons his fate and that of 125 million Japanese to a mysterious and masterful 'system' that discounts the day-to-day, ordinary efforts of Japanese to decide their own affairs. To doubt their efforts to do so is to doubt their essential humanity and to document van Wolferen's cultural biases.

3. Media poll, *Business Week*, 7 Aug. 1989. New York Times/CBS News Poll released in Feb. 1990 and reported in the *New York Times*, 'Is the New Villain Going to be Japan? It Works on Paper', 18 June 1990, B1.

4. 'The no-miracle occurred school' is Chalmers Johnson's term. See the first chapter of his *MITI and the Japanese Miracle* (Stanford, Calif.: Stanford University Press, 1982). *MITI and the Japanese Miracle* is itself the most eloquent statement in English of the industrial-policy perspective on Japanese economic growth. However, the industrial-policy debate begins in English some twelve years earlier with Robert S. Ozaki's article, 'Japanese Views of Industrial Organization', *Asian Survey*, Oct. 1970, 872–89. Another book on the industrial-policy perspective is Daniel I. Okimoto, *Between MITI and the Market* (Stanford, Calif.: Stanford University Press, 1989). Okimoto is not so persuaded of the efficacy of top-down industrial policy.

   The debate about Japan in general begins with James Abegglen, *The Japanese Factory* (Glencoe, Ill. and New York: Free Press, 1958), and over three decades, various schools of interpretation have waxed and waned. Representative books of these various schools include K. Okochi, B. Karsh, and S. B. Levine (eds.), *Workers and Employers in Japan* (Princeton, NJ and Tokyo: Princeton University Press and University of Tokyo Press, 1973); Robert E. Cole, *Work, Mobility, and Participation* (Berkeley: University of California Press, 1979); Kazuo Koike, *Understanding Industrial Relations in Modern Japan* (New York: St. Martins Press, 1988); Gary R. Saxonhouse and Kozo Yamamura (eds.), *Law and Trade Issues of the Japanese Economy* (Seattle: University of Washington Press, 1986); Ken'ichi Imai, 'The Corporate Network in Japan', *Japanese Economic Studies*, 16 (Winter 1988); Michael Gerlach, *Alliance Capitalism* (Berkeley: University of California Press, forthcoming); and Masahiko Aoki, *Information, Incentives, and Bargaining in the Japanese Economy* (Cambridge: Cambridge University Press, 1988). A more recent contribution, itself an important work, is James C. Abegglen and George Stalk, *Kaisha: The Japanese Corporation* (New York: Basic Books, 1985).

Thomas C. Smith, *Native Sources of Japanese Industrialization, 1750–1920* (Berkeley: University of California Press, 1988), while not dealing directly with the debate, represents a stream of research that suggests one should look to Japan's internal development as a primary cause of Japan's external success.

Other notable works not fitting neatly into the above categories include: Miyohei Shinohara, 'MITI's Industrial Policy and Japanese Industrial Organization: A Retrospective Evaluation', *Developing Economies*, 14 (Dec. 1976), and id., *Industrial Growth, Trade and Dynamic Patterns in the Japanese Economy* (Tokyo: University of Tokyo Press, 1982).

Two new studies of Japanese industry are worth noting: Michael J. Smitka, *Competitive Ties: Subcontracting in Japanese Manufacturing* (New York: Columbia University Press, 1991) and Toshihiro Nishiguchi, *Strategic Dualism* (New York: Oxford University Press, forthcoming).

5. Oliver E. Williamson, *Corporate Control and Business Behavior: An Inquiry into the Effects of Organizational Form on Enterprise Behavior* (Englewood Cliffs, NJ: Prentice Hall, 1970), 175.

6. The M-Form hypothesis is coming under attack as a culture-bound argument. In particular, Cable and Dirrheimer and Cable and Yasuki have found that in Germany and Japan respectively, adoption of the M-Form model has slowed. See J. Cable and M. J. Dirrheimer, 'Hierarchies and Markets: An Empirical Test of the Multidivisional Hypothesis in West Germany', *International Journal of Industrial Organization*, 1. 43–62. J. Cable and H. Yasuki, 'Internal Organization, Business Groups and Corporate Performance: An Empirical Test of the Multidivisional Hypothesis in Japan', *International Journal of Industrial Organization*, 3 (1985), 401–20. And, Hideki Yoshihara, Akimitsa Sakuma, Hiroyuki Itami, and Tadao Kagono, *Nihon Kigyo no Takakuka Senryaku* (The Diversification of Japanese Firms) (Tokyo: Nikon Keizai Shimbun, 1981).

7. Alfred D. Chandler, Jr., *Scale and Scope* (Cambridge, Mass.: Harvard University Press, 1990), 19–20.

8. T. J. Peters and R. H. Waterman, Jr., *In Search of Excellence* (New York: Harper & Row, 1982).

9. I am grateful to Robert S. Ozaki for the insight on Yankee ingenuity. As for imitation, see Nathan Rosenberg and W. Edward Steinmueller, 'Why are Americans such Poor Imitators?' *American Economic Review*, 78/2 (May 1988), 229–34.

10. I am more specific about types and strategies of organizational learning in later chapters. There is a large and growing literature on the subject. For a step-by-step,

case-study of how Japanese organizations learn, see Bunteru Kurahara, Kiyoshi Uchimaru, and Susumu Okamoto, *Gijutsu Shudan no TQC* (TQC for Engineers) (Tokyo: Nikajiren, 1990). See (p.177) for a diagram of organizational learning process in a semiconductor-design firm covering the four areas of administration, quality assurance, technology, and ideology. This is a wonderful book about managing knowledge-intensive work in contemporary Japan.

A graphic example of organizational learning in Japanese firms comes from Dr. Toshihiro Nishiguchi who worked for Pioneer Electronic Corporation before joining the academic world and INSEAD. Toshi worked in the International Division of Pioneer. Before he was posted to London for the second time in 1982, he spent *six* weeks training his successor. This included not only a process of familiarization with the normal office routine but also an extensive number of visits to other company units and divisions as well as to outside service providers, such as shipping and warehouse agents, insurance companies, freight forwarders and handlers, and such. In addition, they traveled throughout the greater Tokyo area to visit sales outlets and when Toshi finally left for England, he gave his successor a 20-page manual with 'illustrations' (*manga*) on how to do the job. That's organizational learning! Contrast this with some Western managers who arrive in a new position, I'm told, to find no one to help them with the ropes and, unbelievably, an office devoid of any records that might offer a record of past performance.

11. This is Kenneth Arrow's perspective, admirably argued in *The Limits of Organization* (New York: W. W. Norton, 1974), esp. pp. 53–6.

12. Wataro Kanno, *Nihon Kaisha Kigyo Hasseishi no Kenkyu* (Research on the Origins of Japan's Joint-Stock Companies) (Tokyo: Keizai Hyoronsha, 1966), 14.

13. Takafusa Nakamura, *Economic Growth in Prewar Japan* (New Haven, Conn.: Yale University Press, 1983). Yoshikazu Miyazaki, 'Rapid Economic Growth in Post-War Japan', *Developing Economies*, 5/2 (1967), 329. Miyazaki contrasts Japan's 9.4 percent real annual average growth rate with a 7.4 percent rate for West Germany, 6 percent for Italy, 4.9 percent for France, 2.8 percent for the United States, and 2.5 percent for UK, during the same period.

14. OECD, *Comparative Economic Performance in OECD Nations* (Paris, 1989), 66.

15. *Nihon Keizai Shimbun*, 7 Feb. 1990: 34. In 1989, 90 percent of the 30,000 foreign students in Japanese universities came from Asia and the majority of these were Chinese.

16. Richard P. Rumelt, 'How Much Does Industry Matter?', *Strategic Management Journal*, 12/3 (Mar. 1991), 167–86. G. S. Hansen and B. Wernerfelt, 'Determinants of Firm Performance: The Relative Importance of Economic and Organizational Factors', *Strategic Management Journal*, 10/5 (Sept.–Oct. 1989).

17. *Institutional Change and American Economic Growth* (Cambridge: Cambridge University Press, 1971), 6–7. I have retained the emphasis of the original. The formulation of institutions as 'rules of the game' and organizations as 'players of the game' is restated in Douglass C. North, *Institutions, Institutional Change and Economic Performance* (Cambridge: Cambridge University Press, 1990).

1

History and the Logic of Interdependence

This is an inductive, historical study, not written to originate theory even while concepts and theories flow from the description and interpretation.[1] An integrated, long-headed perspective on the evolution of Japan's industrial structure was needed, and towards this end, the origins, emergence, and growth of large industrial firms in Japan during the last 100 years are explored and the characteristics of focal factories and interfirm networks, two corresponding organizations without which the chronicle of modern corporations in Japan would be incomplete, are explained. Like a prism, history has bent industrial organizations into a rainbow of elementary forms: factory, firm, and network, the Japanese enterprise system. The integrity and unity of this system are basic features and fundamental strengths of Japan's industrial order.

I
The Problem: Organizational Alternatives

To some extent, factories, firms, and networks are alternative ways to organize. As Oliver E. Williamson writes, 'The economic institutions of capitalism are endlessly varied'.[2] This is particularly evident where factories, firms, and networks overlap functions, such as R & D, production, purchasing, planning, and sales, and thus when *permeable boundaries* become a determining feature of the business environment (the cross-hatched area in Fig. 1.1). Permeable boundaries concede but confine transactional overlay in functions. The more overlay or redundancy in functional activities, the more factory, firm, and network represent alternatives.

Functionally postulated, factories, especially the resource-rich factories on which this book concentrates, *make* products by integrating design, development, planning, and manufacturing functions; corporations *create* manufacturing strategies to produce in volume and variety, and they *coordinate* the flows of resources between factory, firm, and network; interfirm networks *sell* as well as *make* products in tandem with factories and firms. The activities of production and distribution networks are less integrated, tightly linked, and strategic than those of focused factories and major firms.

The factory–firm–interfirm network model of industrial organization is one part empirical, one part stylized, and another part metaphorical. Typically and by comparison, Japanese industrial companies feature strong manufacturing

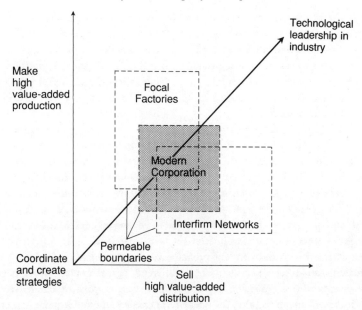

FIG. 1.1. *The Industrial Institutions of Modern Japan: A Two-Dimensional View*

capabilities (factories) and pervasive interorganizational ties (interfirm networks), though taken singly or together few firms separate cleanly into just these organizational elements. Instead, Japanese enterprises are characterized by three modal ways to organize and generally these populate the industrial economy.

In this interorganizational model, boundaries are often ill-defined because factories, firms, and networks are *not* fully nested hierarchies, telescoping neatly in graded spatial or administrative systems. So, overlap and occasional clash in functions occur. In fact, it is not conceptually obvious why some activities are typically included within the boundaries of the firm while others are excluded because factories, firms, and networks perform many of the same tasks and they interact often.[3] Some overlay is justified in the interest of effective coupling, but too much yields wasteful duplication and poor coordination.

When functions overlap or when transactional relations are not obvious, boundary-management strategies to decide where, when, and which activities should converge become key managerial concerns. Boundaries can be made more explicit but only at some cost. To ride roughshod over the independent sensibilities and ambitions of those working in factories, firms, and networks limits incentives and reduces performance. On the other hand, not to coordinate, induce, and plan is to invite middling execution and moderate performance.

In theory and as functional alternatives, organizational boundaries should be clear-cut. Buying inputs for manufacturing, for example, whether they be semi-finished or finished goods, is a purchasing department's function, producing or assembling is manufacturing's job, and selling is a sales responsibility. If markets for products are large, separate departments with similar responsibilities (and functions) are created in different regions. When functions and markets increase greatly in number as in multi-product firms, separate product divisions are established, each with its own purchasing, manufacturing, and sales departments. Factories as well as other functional units can be comfortably housed within this organizational framework.

Confusion begins when functional and locational responsibilities cut across organizational boundaries: when transactional overlay creates a potential for interactive difficulties and inefficiencies. Should sales engineering services, for example, be provided by factory or corporate personnel? This decision affects a business' structure, its accounting practices, service capabilities, and in all likelihood the quality of its service. The multidivisional corporation (M-Form firm) appeared and prospered in the United States as an answer to this confusion. Product lines were isolated administratively and assigned a full complement of managers charged with independent profit-center responsibility.

Confusion can likewise occur when different organizations evolve similar functional capabilities. Writing in 1962, the organizational theorist Herbert Simon discussed the possibility of identifying generic organizational structures within a limited number of institutional alternatives.[4] Alternatives are limited because there are few ways to perform the same task efficiently. And as task complexities increase, the numbers of critical pathways to economize on efficiency decrease.

In the course of Japan's industrial development, similar yet structure-specific ways of managing complexity evolved yielding factory, firm, and network as Simon's generic alternatives. *The Japanese Enterprise System* argues that efficient forms of economic organization can coexist in several states at once (in contrast to notions of M-Form or other kinds of firms as ideal structures), and that a deeper synergy may be obtained when transactions and interactions resonate among them.[5] The differentiation and specialization that pushed a system-specific evolution of organization at three discrete levels have their origins in particular circumstances of Japan's industrialization, most notably, an especially intense and accelerated cycle of social, economic, and technical 'late-development'. As developmental circumstances changed, the original rationale behind an organizational triad diminished. Yet patterns once established are slow to change and, in time, dissimilarities in scale, rates of change, process frequency, and intensity between factory, firm, and network became built into the industrial structure.[6] Confusion in functional and transactional relations was averted by a deep structure of organizational correspondence that sorted out relations through a systematic integration of activities at different levels of organization.

In abstract terms, the Japanese enterprise system—as an interorganizational system of factory, firm, and interfirm network—is an evolving, hierarchical, functionally differentiated, structure of economic activities existing at discrete levels of organization. As a basic structure, it is stable yet it generates both boundaries and complexity. Boundaries separate and localize behavior and events in factories, firms, and networks; complexity springs from multiple relatedness and constraints at each level of organization. All of the above—structure, process, and behavior—hinge on strategy or the human will to build, manage, and manipulate boundaries and complexity for competitive advantage.

The Solution: Organizational Interdependence

Factories, firms, and networks were less well connected formerly than they are now. Their contemporary correspondence rests on historical, axis-evolving processes of when and where to demarcate, align, and modify functional boundaries between them. In this, history is a guide to past practice and a predictor of future behavior. Institutional memory and embeddedness are the reasons why. Institutions evolve ways of doing things and once routines, protocols, and procedures are set (embedded), they are difficult to dislodge or reverse.[7] Boundary-management strategies are powerfully affected by institutional memory and embeddedness.

Because of these processes of institutional evolution wherein permeable boundaries fasten factory, firm, and network in various patterns of organizational interdependence, Japanese industrial firms can be inclined towards one of these institutional forms while not excluding the others. For example, Toyota Motor and Matsushita Electric Industrial lean towards the interfirm-network model, that is much of their production and distribution capability is parceled out among dozens or even hundreds of affiliated firms. Kao and Canon are quintessential corporations in that they internalize most functions in a unitary structure, while Hitachi, Mitsubishi Heavy Industry, and Kyowa Hakko are organized more like focal factories, giving them a bottom-heavy, production bias. Yet in the case of these companies and most other large firms, they possess functional capabilities in all areas of business. The interdependent management of these drives the Japanese enterprise system.

An Example: Toshiba and Organizational Affiliates

The Toshiba Corporation, discussed at length in Chapter 6, is a good illustration of the contemporary consequences of these patterns of institutional development. Toshiba is a major electronics/electrical-equipment producer, selling everything from integrated circuits, power turbines, space-communications satellites, to toaster and microwave ovens. In spite of this product breadth, Toshiba is a relatively small company by American standards with under 70,000 employees, considerably less than General Electric's 300,000 plus.

But Toshiba has other strengths to compensate for this apparent size mismatch.

Of Toshiba's 27 factories, at least 50 percent are focal factories (more on this in Chapter 6). Toshiba has ties to over 600 affiliated and subsidiary companies in which it holds some financial stake in about 100 (20 to 49 percent in the case of affiliates, and 50 percent or more in the case of subsidiaries). There are 53 core companies closely connected with the Toshiba Corporation, and perhaps another 50 with which Toshiba does major business, either directly or indirectly through its divisions, affiliates, and subsidiaries. As of October 1990, in spite of the large numbers of directly and indirectly connected companies, the Affiliated Companies Office of Toshiba ran with just 18 persons, attesting to the considerable autonomy and operational independence of its affiliates and subsidiaries.

These related enterprises, the actual numbers of which depend on the definitions used, are known as the Toshiba group of companies. Then, there are the 59,000 employees of the 1,300 businesses that supply Toshiba with parts, components, and sub-assemblies; Toshiba has little, if any, financial stake in them. Finally, there are periodic meetings with officers of wider enterprise groupings where Toshiba executives exchange business information, discuss economic trends, coordinate development projects, and generally share viewpoints and create visions for future directions with other executives.

The function of high-level executive associations is somewhat akin to political conventions which mobilize and articulate member interests within particular territories or constituencies. Only such groupings, usually called 'Presidents' Councils' (*shachokai*), are not so intermittent and one-sided in character as political associations; yet their existence allows for fairly rapid and effective consensus-building when high-order agreement is needed. Toshiba's *shachokai* members may sit on the Presidents' Councils of other major firms and, of course, they themselves form a core of numerous lower-level, interest-aggregation and interest-articulation groupings.

Toshiba's range of organizational correlates is not exceptional. To change focus for a moment, in the case of the Mitsui group of companies and Presidents' Councils, there are 24 companies that belong to the *nimokukai*, the inner group of top Mitsui company presidents who meet on the second Thursday of each month. But there is also the *getsuyokai* group of 62 companies that meet on Mondays and the *kohoinkai* or information group that meet once a month. Membership in groups may overlap for presidents of powerful and central Mitsui companies while presidents of less centrally positioned Mitsui companies may attend only one such meeting per month. Within Mitsui or Toshiba, of course, corporate executives hold meetings as needed with organizational subsets in order to coordinate matters particular to those groups.

At each level of organization, the Toshiba Corporation (or Mitsui or any major Japanese firm) has alliances, interfirm networks, and interorganizational assets which allow it to do much more than its 70,000 employees and 27 factories could do otherwise. These interorganizational connections, some 1,900 of them in Toshiba's case, define the way in which business is conducted; route financial, technical, and managerial information; determine marketing and sales channels;

and generally delimit the nature of business transactions and interactions. The appearance and maturation of business systems such as Toshiba's create fundamental notions and interrelations which define the nature of the enterprise system.[8]

The Practice of Interdependence

The functional and, to a lesser extent, the product and market domains of factory, firm, and network are often distinct and diverse, and they are better comprehended as being interrelated structurally and strategically. It is not so much a choice of one organizational form for all possible purposes but which one, when, under what circumstances, and for what reasons. Historical axes of structural and strategic interrelation evolve to answer these questions.

Though companies in Japan as well as elsewhere may be inclined towards one or another of these forms and their related functions, business success requires the differentiation and integration of all three within an interrelated value chain. A special and distinguishing feature of Japanese economic institutions is the degree to which these functions were organized separately, producing a countervailing need for effective integration across functions (organizations).

The starting-points were crucial: functional specialization by organization and functional integration through interorganizational correspondence. The factory system, the modern corporation, and interfirm networks appeared separately late in the nineteenth century, emerged more or less contemporaneously by World War One, and evolved interdependently thereafter. Differentiation of functions

TABLE 1.1. *Number of Product Lines: 200 Largest Industrial Firms in Japan,*
1918–1987

	Number of product lines						
	2 products[a]			3 products			Total
	within[b]	without	total	within	without	total	
1918	22	4	26	—	—	—	
1930	30	5	35	—	—	—	
1954	41	13	54	10	13	23	77
1973	35	30	65	2	3	5	70
1987	28	43	71	5	4	9	80

[a] Each product line at least 20% of total sales.
[b] Products fall *within* the same SIC classification code at the two-digit level.
Source: Office of Management and Budget, *Standard Industrial Classification Manual* (Washington, DC: US Government Printing Office, 1972).

through organizational specialization was pronounced at the outset of industrialization, while functional and strategic integration followed. Organizational consolidation of functions, as implied in a model of hierarchical administration, was not the general rule.

An elaboration and interrelation of these basic structures and strategies in the course of Japan's industrialization answer one of the most puzzling questions in economic development and organization theory: how economies of scale, scope, and transaction-cost can be realized simultaneously and fortuitously, even while resources needed to realize one depend upon another.[9] In effect, production volume, product variety, management and marketing versatility are not easily secured, especially at the same time, yet all contribute to organizational capability and to competition. The solution to this paradox is found in the specialization and coordination of the organizational triad of factory, firm, and network, the Japanese enterprise system.

Elements and Attributes of the Japanese Enterprise System

The Modern Corporation

The scope of activities pursued by Japanese manufacturing firms is often limited, while the intensity of activities within that scope is not. In contrast to comparable Western companies, Japanese firms are not widely diversified and corporate conglomerates are a rarity. Instead, the strategy is to offer a complete range of goods and services in one or a few related lines of products. This is usually termed a full-line strategy. Only 35–40 percent of Japan's largest industrial firms (far fewer in the pre-war period) produce in two or more distinct market segments, and half of this diversification effort is full-line diversification as opposed to new-product diversification (Table 1.1). This is at least 50 percent lower than leading American and European industrials.[10]

Surprisingly, in 1987 three-fifths of the largest Japanese industrials were still single- or dominant-product firms (where one product family or market segment accounts for 80 percent of total sales). Of the remaining two-fifths, half made products that were sufficiently similar to be grouped together in the same two-digit SIC classification (Fig. 1.2). In short, only one-fifth of Japan's largest industrial firms manufacture two or more major products lines that are not closely related.

Multidivisional, M-Form firms are typically related-product firms that possess a variety of assets (skills, technology, know-how) that are intangible or otherwise subject to excess capacity. When a single administrative form encompasses numerous heterogeneous products and markets, unrelated-product firms or conglomerates are the rule. In Western Europe and North America, where synergies are sought across products and markets, multidivisional structures and conglomerates are commonplace. In the case of either multidivisional or

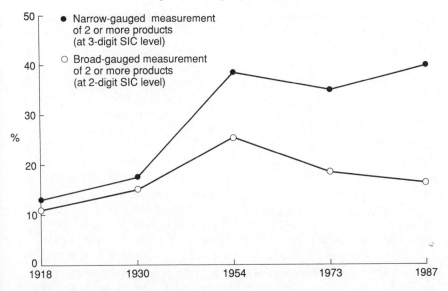

FIG. 1.2. *Number of Product Lines by Level of Measurement: 200 Largest Industrial Firms in Japan, 1918–1987*

conglomerate firms, corporate head offices are relatively large because of the need to monitor, evaluate, and coordinate the diversified activities of subordinate divisions and affiliates.

M-Form and conglomerate firms predominate among the largest Western industrials. In a sample of 127 large firms studied from 1947, for example, all had adopted M-Form structures by 1974.[11] Neither large multidivisional firms nor conglomerates are standard forms in Japan, however. Instead, modern corporations with smallish head offices staffed by professional managers concentrate on a relatively narrow range of products and markets.

The exceptional differences describing Japanese and Western corporate structures are related to interorganizational arrangements between factory, firm, and network—the architectures of industrial organization in Japan. Firms remain small and concentrated in particular market niches because focal factories excel at full product-line diversification while interfirm networks manage product and markets outside the focalized scope of single- and related-product firms (Fig. 1.3).

Interfirm Networks

While single firms are not greatly diversified in Japan, interfirm groupings typically are. Interfirm combinations, which according to the intensity of their interdependent transactions fall somewhere between the loosely coupled enterprises of a large holding company and the tightly coupled units of a multidivi-

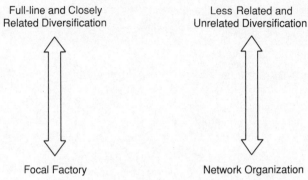

FIG. 1.3. *Diversification Strategies in Japan*

sional firm, excel in developing *interfirm* economies of scope, that is the capacity to manufacture and deliver a number of product families aggregated from the focused product lines of individual firms. As a result of the aggregation of products by specialized firms, per unit costs of production and distribution are lower than if single firms carried out similar activities.

Interfirm networks may be grouped broadly into three types: horizontal groupings of companies from a range of industries and sectors, what Japanese call *kigyo shudan*, and vertical groupings of successively smaller companies dominated by major firms at the top of an industry or *keiretsu*. In recent years task-force groupings, another type of network, bring together firms for coordinated, relatively short-lived activities. Individual firms may belong to all three types of grouping and, as a consequence, interfirm networks are extremely widespread in Japan.

Given differences in the types of interfirm networks, the nature of control, coordination, strategic intent, and action among them vary considerably. Yet the effect is the same: interfirm networks connect the resources of dozens, hundreds, and even thousands of firms in order to compete in a world where size and scale of economic activity are paramount.[12] Integration across organizations is a complement to differentiation and specialization among organizations. Interfirm coordination provides a framework for tremendous breadth in activities even while individual firms remain highly focused in their pursuits.

Focal Factories

Much of the reason for this focus may be found in the existence of multi-function manufacturing sites. A basic definition of such factories is a production site with appended planning, design, development, and process-engineering capabilities, plus an ambition to accumulate, combine, and concentrate experience for the propagation and improvement of products and processes. Focal factories exploit opportunities for *intrafirm* economies of scope by amassing and reshaping organizational capabilities in the midst of integrating product design, process development, and manufacturing. Factories with such capabilities were not at all common before World War One, increasingly so during the inter-war era, and widely present since the high-growth 1960s.

The prominence given to factories in this study turns on several factors: first, the speed with which the modern factory system spread in Japan; second, the importance of rapid and effective technology transfer for late-developing countries; third, the spatial and economic characteristics of the domestic market before World War Two; fourth, the nature of technical and strategic competition since then.

The first modern textile mill opened in 1867 and a rush to manufacture has hardly abated since. Yet before the Pacific War, demand for most industrial goods was neither stable nor predictable, markets were disordered, production and distribution poorly coordinated. In effect operational issues could not be convincingly separated from strategic issues in management.

When a firm's scope is not wide, that is when products and markets are limited, unitary firms are a logical form of organization. In such circumstances, firms may be analogous, sometimes synonymous, with factories in that a small number of factories dispersed across the landscape may operate more or less independent of head-office control by serving regional markets with nearly a full set of corporate functions. Such factories boast corporate-like attributes and demonstrate why factories can be organizational alternatives to firms and networks.

The position of focal factories was enhanced by functional specialization along the value chain. Pre-war factories could be even more pivotal and corporate head offices less so because of the role of related enterprises in interfirm networks. Specialized trading companies, for example, might assume purchasing, sales, and marketing functions. Affiliated transportation and distribution companies could move and store factory output. The provision of such functions, normally tasks for corporate-planning staffs, was conducted instead by discrete yet interdependent organizations.

In the post-war period, especially since the oil shocks of the mid-1970s, accelerating product competition, escalating process complexity, and an unrelenting swell of technology have made robust, multi-function factories into a strategic necessity. These manufacturing sites create competitive advantage by fusing intrafirm and interfirm capabilities for product development, manufacturing, and marketing.[13] Yet, as timely product design and development have become paramount, factory autonomy has been lessened by a growth in corporate and divisional-level control and by a fuller elaboration of national transportation and communication systems. The result is a diminution of factories' administrative independence but a simultaneous spurring of manufacturing's functional importance. Since technology-driven firms can be only as successful as their manufacturing operations, a continuing salience of focused factories for single- and dominant-product firms seems assured.

The pervasive ties binding large and small firms in Japan are also part of this interorganizational system. Typically, small firms are specialized in the provision of particular production and distribution services mobilized through product strategies executed and coordinated by large firms. Working in concert, small firms, focal factories and interfirm networks augment the well-tuned resources of Japanese corporations to orchestrate an enterprise system with depth as well as breadth.

A factory-centered approach to industrial organization gives corporations an intensity and richness of manufacturing excellence that is renowned world-wide. The integration of business activities through well-managed factories and closely coordinated interfirm networks provides Japanese companies a formidable range of complementary resources for potentially unending business activities. In some ways, focal factories function as an analogue for backward integration while interfirm alliances may represent a kind of forward integration. In either case, however, it is the coordination of business activities through and within the organizational prism of factory, firm, and network that distinguishes the institutional foundations of Japan's industrial economy.

This combination is a highly unusual one. It happens in Japan because of the 'permeable boundaries' that interrelate factory, firm, and network. The arguments, historical as well as theoretical, that are marshalled herein to explain permeable boundaries are highly eclectic because it is difficult, if not impossible, to understand why the Japanese enterprise system arose as it did based on single-factor explanations. Thus, I am less interested in the affinity of theories than in their utility and hence my eclectic and empirical approach.

National Patterns of Organization

Major Japanese companies are different from the American standard, the customary measure of firm structure and performance. They are smaller in number of employees, less integrated vertically, less diversified in product line, and less international in their activities than comparable American and leading European firms. These organizational differences are related to national differences in patterns of corporate adaptation to industrialization.

The M-Form firm did not advance as far in Japan as in the West for a number of reasons. The development of management-accounting systems in early twentieth-century North America, for example, spurred the introduction and diffusion of the multidivisional corporation. Increasingly sophisticated accounting systems allowed multi-product firms to identify company-wide financial goals and standards of evaluation. These provided incentives for corporate managers to seek profits and to fashion formulas that directed cash flows to high-yield outcomes. Such internal accounting procedures were indispensable to General Motors' impressive performance after the adoption of the multidivisional form in 1921, as they were important for the outstanding record of many M-Form firms thereafter.[14]

Large industrial firms in pre-war Japan lacked sophisticated management-accounting controls, however. Standardized accounting systems came later in the

1950s and 1960s. This, as much as anything else, may account for the longer time horizon of Japanese firms in evaluating financial performance, and it may well be connected to slower promotion ladders for executives. Without detailed financial information by which to evaluate short-term performance, managers cannot easily demonstrate the differences that they make. Managing 'by the numbers' proves impractical.

Japanese firms developed complementary organizational devices to cope with transactional complexity, environmental risk, resource dependency, and the need to separate operational and strategic activities. Interfirm networks of all sorts and multi-function manufacturing centers spread the responsibility and risk for product and market management beyond and below divisional levels. Not surprisingly, a statistical study of the adoption of the M-Form in Japan found no performance differential attributable to this organizational form.[15]

In the diversified United States firm, including conglomerates operating in unrelated industries, the profits of divisions (however legally defined) are forwarded to the corporate office while, at the same time, divisions receive their annual budget allocations. It is the corporate office of the parent company and not the top office of the operating enterprise (division or subsidiary) that determines the amount of funds available for investment in future production and distribution. Company operating units (sometimes legally independent) are administratively and financially controlled by the general or corporate offices of a parent company.

Within Japanese industrial firms, performance is frequently measured at levels below a division, most often at the factory level. In part, this is because at the divisional level, firm profitability is directly affected by the extent of interfirm dependency. Profits appear to be lower among firms enmeshed in financially linked interfirm networks, while in technology-intensive interfirm networks, like Toyota's, suppliers may earn higher rates of profitability than final assemblers. Such organizational differences prescribe the degree to which American, M-Form assessments can be applied to Japanese firms.

Accordingly, the strivings towards organizational autonomy which characterize focal factories within enterprise structures and independent firms within interfirm structures are fundamentally different from how divisions compete for resources within M-Form firms. In larger and necessarily more bureaucratic Western firms, reciprocity between divisions is diminished by a tendency to reduce complex matters of divisional interchange to balance-sheet numbers. Because financial rather than organizational values are emphasized, cost accounting and management-control systems often misrepresent the efficiency of internally managed transactions.[16] In interdivisional and interdepartmental negotiations where both sides bargain for the best deal, only one side is likely to realize much advantage.

Without a long-term sense of reciprocity and fair play, distance and distrust between divisions result. Instead of cooperation, internal competition and rivalry may gnaw at the health and well-being of organizations. Paradoxically, such intraorganizational difficulties undermine the supposed internal efficiency of multidivisional firms, whereas more specialized but hierarchically interdependent Japanese firms appear to excel in attaining competitive efficiency.[17]

Less diversified, U-Form firms like those found more typically in Japan invest more heavily in R & D than do diversified M-Form firms after controlling for size and industry effects.[18] Not only does higher investment lead to more focus in core areas of competency but it is likely to result in more frequent replenishment of core competencies as well. The combination results in long-term competitive advantage.

In the Japanese enterprise system, there are no parent headquarters to receive profits or to allocate resources. Members of an enterprise group—all legally independent companies—retain their earnings and are solely responsible for the allocation of resources for future production and distribution. The corporate offices of even the largest 'core' companies of a Japanese interfirm group are smaller, more autonomous and ambitious than widely diversified or conglomerated American firms. Competitive strategies motivate Japanese firms even while cooperative relationships with allied firms delimit markets within which competitive strategies are pursued.

It could be argued that multidivisional corporations as they have developed in North America are analogous in form and function to smaller, less integrated and diversified Japanese firms. But when major divisions of the largest American manufacturing firms are ranged according to size against comparable Japanese firms, American divisions are often larger than their Japanese counterparts.[19] Such a comparison based on size, moreover, ignores historical rationale for the development and sequencing of particular functions and capabilities in either American or Japanese firms.[20]

Moreover, size cannot be considered outside the context of structure. Because smaller, focused Japanese companies are connected with many other enterprises through interfirm alliances, small size may not be a particular disadvantage. Indeed, it may be an advantage if firms concentrate on one business or a few closely related businesses and thereby deepen their know-how, competence, and experience in a core range of activities, while, at the same time, expand and elaborate their ties of interdependence with others in order to integrate making, creating/coordinating, and selling functions. Thus, structure is not independent of strategy.

Though concentrating and deepening resources do not in themselves guarantee stellar performance, single firms pursue such goals not only to secure firm-specific benefits but also as a means of interfirm tactics and coalitional politics. Single firms rarely have sufficient breadth to complement the depth of their activities and they must lure and engage the complementary resources of other firms. In time, the best-performing firms increasingly align their resources and activities. Size, structure, and strategy come together and constitute the basis of enterprise positioning and planning.

Japanese firms follow a full-line strategy rather than a product-diversification strategy, as indicated earlier. Since World War One, nevertheless, Japanese firms have been slowly and steadily increasing the number of their product lines (as highlighted in Table 1.1). The smaller size and more focused activities have not accorded Japanese industrial firms the same scale advantages of Western, particularly American firms. Turnover studies show that American managerial hierarchies have been rather fixed in rank: firms that climbed to the front ranks of American industry are likely to stay there. First-mover advantages accrue to American firms, in large part because of their high levels of vertical integration and product/market diversification. These act as buffers against technological obsolescence and business-cycle fluctuations. Diversified, multidivisional firms excel at hedging rather than synergy.

In contrast, Japanese industrial firms have been characterized by considerable movement in size rankings and SIC distributions. They have not enjoyed the same first-mover advantages as large American companies and, as a result, net entry rates for the largest 200 Japanese industrial firms are higher.[21] The decline of the textile industry explains this in part but, more generally, it reflects late development, extreme social, political, and technological discontinuity in Japanese industrial history, and the difficulties of insulating firms from such turbulence. It also reflects the smaller size of Japanese firms.[22] Big firms in 1918 and 1930 are not likely to be big in 1973 and 1987. Entry and exit rates are high and positively correlated (see Table 1.2).

Large industrial firms that remain in the top 200 have done so with a high-risk strategy: being very good at a limited number of activities. In doing so, they accepted high levels of corporate risk derived from business-cycle instability

TABLE 1.2. *Turnover among 200 Largest Industrial Firms in Japan, 1918–1987[a]*

Period	Number	%	Years	%/Year
1918–30	70	35	12	2.92
1930–54	82	41	24	1.71
1954–73	63	32	19	1.68
1973–87	58	29	14	2.07

[a] Turnover measures companies leaving the top 200 listing because either (*a*) the amount of sales or assets for the years in question do not place them in the top 200, or (*b*) they were merged or acquired by another firm not qualifying in the top 200. Except for 1987, assets rather than sales is the measure employed. The effect of measuring sales as opposed to assets can be seen in the calculations in Table 1.4.

Sources: Ministry of Finance, *Yukashoken Hokokusho* (annual reports) with additional calculations by the author.

and product-cycle vacillations. This is especially true for firms that have clung doggedly and perilously to single- or closely related-product lines throughout their tenure at the top.

Firms with a well-articulated network of affiliate enterprises may be able to vary their product offerings by managing a portfolio of their own and others' products, thereby replenishing their product line-up. Yet this strategy risks potentially poor coordination of interfirm relations, possible ill will over product-line appropriation, and some likelihood that affiliates' products are not so different from one's own. Even so, good and reliable relations with network partners seem a principal means of reducing risk (but by no means a foolproof one) for Japanese industrial firms.

As a result of the oil shocks of the 1970s, Japanese firms have begun to broaden their product lines and thereby bring more balance to profits, earnings, and investments. This has been accomplished in part through vertical integration and product diversification but also through external diversification or through a broadening and deepening of interfirm coalitions. In either strategy, expanding business activities necessarily involves other firms and an elaboration of hierarchical, interdependent resources. Business success depends on an adroit and agile management of organizational interdependence.

It is absolutely wrong-headed to assume behavioral outcomes of organizational interdependence a priori. Because firms related to the Mitsubishi group account for 3 percent of total corporate sales in Japan, for example, it does not follow that anti-competitive and collusive behavior are the result.[23] Group membership is one of many starting-points. It is not determinative, not especially predictive, and not at all indicative of behavior. Historical and contemporary reasons may be adduced for this.

Historical Evidence for Interdependence

The interlocking organizations of factory, firm, and network appeared in Japan because industrial development occurred in an environment of extreme entrepreneurial and institutional risk and of highly constrained resources. Also, the political climate and economic milieu of an industrializing Japan were anything but favorable, and foreign firms were contentious and none too generous with their manufacturing and managerial know-how.

Information, technology, management ability, organizational know-how, and capital for production and consumption were all in short supply. In order to accommodate these constraints at the level of the firm, Japanese enterprises evolved in two directions: *downward*, to create powerful factory-level organizations for technology transfer and product development; and *outward*, to become integrated parts of a wider association of related firms, making them formidable building-blocks of macro-organizational diversity and integration. Organizational features such as these distinguish the modern corporation and enterprise system of Japan from all other industrial economies.

The concert of interdependence between factory, firm, and network suggests some of the ways in which Japanese corporations differ in structure, function, and meaning from those of the West where, for any number of reasons, such high levels of organizational interdependence have not appeared. Nor are they likely to, given the considerably different historical traditions and widely varying legal, political, and social traditions of the Western world. In Japan, permeable boundaries have resulted in distinctive modes of corporate cooperation, coordination, and competition, and this book explains the ways in which these have led to the appearance of Japan's modern corporation and enterprise system.

The process of institutionalizing interdependence was based primarily on organizational learning: enterprises discovered how to manage their own affairs amidst engaging other firms, clearing market conditions, and adjusting to competitive forces. An incremental logic inspired the process. Cascades of foreign technology-transfer pushed organizations to separate and specialize functions in order to effectively cope with and capture learning. Small changes, made more or less often, proved more effective than rapid, radical changes. As latecomers to industrialization, catching on and catching up were more important to Japanese firms than pioneering new technologies, products, and markets.

By the inter-war period between World Wars One and Two, Japanese firms came to nurture and exploit three essential business functions: making, creating/coordinating, and selling. At the outset of Japan's industrialization, however, these activities were segmented and poorly integrated. Because foreign technology-transfer was the source of invention for Japanese firms, the most pressing problem was to build factory-based organizations to transfer, adapt, and transform foreign technology. The making and creating functions were thus segregated in factories.

As for the selling function, a well-developed, pre-industrial, commercial economy had prepared the pathways of least resistance for industrial distribution; these operated in conjunction with newly established, foreign and specialty goods trading-houses. Together, old and new distribution outlets pre-empted much of the selling function for manufacturing firms. Finally, the market for industrial goods was rather limited. Markets were fragmented by bottlenecks in the transportation and financial infrastructure, local customs, and a diversity of standards, weights, and measures. In effect, firms were functionally and organizationally disaggregated early on.

An idealized representation of the course of functional integration of these functions during the twentieth century is shown below. Schematically, the degree of integration and disintegration may be exaggerated. Nevertheless, the size of the wedges and the gap between them suggest a kind of proportional separation of functions during the formative years of industrialization (Fig. 1.4).

A lack of capital for industrial investment contributed as well. Firms were unable to integrate backward or forward for lack of sufficient funds and, even if

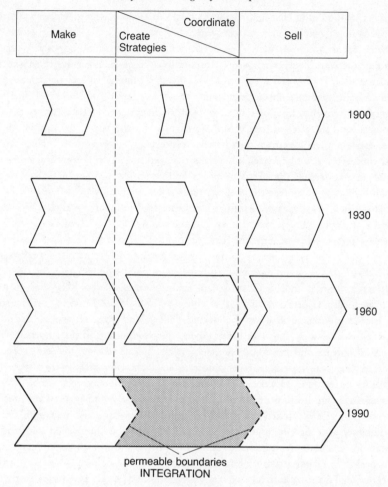

F IG . 1.4. *Stages of Functional Integration in the Japanese Enterprise System*

firms had funds to do so, an environment of heightened political and economic risk did not encourage backward or forward integration. By the early to mid-twentieth century, however, larger and more complex firms began to emerge, and as firms grew in size, gaining managerial sophistication, market experience, technological proficiency, and financial resources in the process, they began to knit together functional and organizational capabilities to make, create/coordinate, and sell products. Often the processes of integration were bolstered and reinforced by capital ties linking larger firms and smaller firms and both to the same financial institutions. Increasingly, capital, technology, personnel, and resources were committed to securing pathways of integration.

But the means to do so were not often realized in a notion of a single corporation. Instead, as Japanese firms joined activities in a functional steam—making, creating/coordinating, and selling—they did so interdependently with other firms, resulting in the functional and organizational synapses of the Japanese enterprise system. Hence, even while Japanese manufacturing firms aim for and achieve functional integration, they do not necessarily do so through a single centralized organization. The evolving model of organization appears to be one of organizational interdependence characterized by a highly developed division of labor within the value chain. So, even as large firms aim to internalize activities, they have an almost unending range of choices as to when, where, and how to do so. The choice is a strategic one resting on top management's vision, middle management's coordination of corporate resources and capabilities, and market opportunities. The result, most often in Japan, is a network form of organization where resources, capabilities, and business potential are held and husbanded in common.

Organizational Alternatives and History: National Differences

As history, the focus of this book is on longitudinal change, and as a study of corporations, it is on change mediated through organizations like Toyota Motor and the Toshiba Corporation. Also, because it is about Japanese enterprises, an explicitly cultural framework, one that emphasizes certain commonalities in Japanese world-view and values, is applied. Such commonalities include a widespread recognition of the value of learning from abroad, the need to adapt foreign ideas and institutions to fit local circumstances, the necessity of changing often in order to respond to continuous exogenous and endogenous change, and the desirability of encoding this legacy of learning and experience in an institutional form. These attitudes and convictions grow out of the Japanese historical experience—the history of a small country adjusting with difficulty and determination to the outside world—and they emerge today as basic values in a Japanese cultural framework for conducting business.

What an organization does is an expression of what is shared, valued, and promoted by those inside the organization. Expectations and attitudes about Japan's place in the world, the need for sharing resources in order to overcome obstacles, and a drive to gain international recognition, inspire the patterns of corporate development in Japan. As these values were encapsulated in the corporation, they underscored individual commitment to the corporate order; they reinforced a certain integration between individual motive, corporate strategy, and national objective; they underpinned a functional interdependence of factory, firm, and network.[24]

Quite clearly, the pioneers of industrial enterprise in Japan wanted to embody what they were learning about management, technology, production, and distribution in the corporation and to bequeath this legacy to those who came after them. It is this embodied learning, captured in the history of Japanese corporations, that holds the key to the competitiveness of Japanese industry today.[25] In general, people who worry about issues of competitiveness do not concern themselves with history because competitiveness is not a historical problem, or so they suppose.

But the Japanese study history, value history, write and read history, and in a sense, they believe in history. It represents not just the past, but the gush, spurt, and roll of life which gives meaning to the present. For most Japanese, the success of contemporary Japan cannot be separated from a century-long, dogged, continuous effort to assess and respond to external and internal changes and to make things better. In interviews at countless firms of various sizes and types, the importance of enterprise history and of recent Japanese history are constant themes. I have never heard a Japanese businessman proclaim, as Henry Ford did, that 'history is bunk'.[26]

The importance of history is a conscious and explicit part of the Japanese interpretation of themselves and of their organizations as well as a rationale for their personal and institutional actions. Ever since Samuel Smiles published *Self Help* in 1870, thousands of foreign books have been translated, read, and reread in a concerted, discerning attempt to learn from the experience of others as well as themselves. This fairly recent effort, in turn, resonates with a longer thousand-year effort to learn, adapt, use, and transform ideas and institutions from the Asian continent, mostly from China and Korea. In general, the Japanese willingly recognize their cultural debt to the Asian continent as well as to the Western world. The emphasis is on the process of using and adapting foreign ideas and institutions domestically rather than on the question of origins. Ultimately, long-established patterns of learning from and adapting to the outside world became absolutely vital in the fall-out of World War Two when almost everything material that had been realized earlier was devastated.

As a consequence, change, constant change, and the need for social and organizational adaptation and experimentation, are ingrained in Japanese culture. As an engineer for a high-technology firm in Japan told me, 'what we're doing today is less important than what we leave behind for tomorrow' ('sentan gijutsu yori mo, nokosu gijutsu'). In short, in the minds of many Japanese the past is contained in the present and the present is simply an extension of the past. In such direct and persuasive ways, history makes a difference. It makes a difference because the Japanese have a rich and fertile experience with change, especially industrial change that has required institutional innovation, and this experience has ingrained the importance of history in the minds and values of contemporary Japanese.

Yet institutions are not independent of the people who sustain them. The more powerful and pervasive institutions become, the more widely people are mobilized to support them and, concurrently, the more resources may be devoted to the process of building institutional support. Nearly simultaneously, the more broadly held assumptions and attitudes become, the more deeply rooted the institutions that rest on them. In this interactive way, commonly held values and practices that underpin the modern corporation in Japan culminated in a view of social order and public service that gained increasing credibility as the Japanese economy advanced.

The development of the modern enterprise system in Japan, to interpolate liberally from Clifford Geertz's discussion of charisma, represents a process in Japanese society where its leading ideas, such as progress, perfectibility, and solidarity, came together with its leading institutions, most notably the corporation, to create an arena in which events that vitally affected the country, nation, and culture coalesced.[27]

The history of the Japanese enterprise system is a history of how certain institutions and institutional practices have acquired widespread currency and credibility. The process of acquiring currency and credibility, strictly speaking, continues today, although the factory, firm, and network have become the accepted forms for conducting economic activities by the early twentieth century. In this sense, the historical performance of the modern corporation and its correlates has endowed the contemporary versions of these institutions with widespread authority, legitimacy, and power.

However, the more strictly local and national aspects of the chronicle of the modern corporation in Japan must be weighed against the world-wide proliferation of the corporation. For the purposes of maintaining a comparative as well as contrasting perspective on Japanese industrial organization, therefore, a framework of analysis is presented which relates differences in corporate organization and behavior to such macro-structural issues as factor endowments, to issues of timing and rates of change in the availability of endowments, to micro-structural concerns such as private and public undertakings in the disposition of endowments, as well as to cultural matters such as standards of acceptable social hierarchy, interaction, and responsibility negotiated by individuals in organizations.

National Patterns and Organizational Interdependence

In the case of Toyota, Toshiba, or any other major industrial company, specific patterns of institutional imitation, learning, and action have differentiated leading Japanese companies during the past century. It is these patterns that need to be identified, unraveled, and explained because the heightened concern with the contemporary success of Japanese business has resulted unfortunately in far more attention being paid to the immediate and short-term consequences of these patterns than to the underlying patterns themselves. Furthermore, precisely because the patterns of corporate imitation, learning, and action are rooted in the past, any convincing analysis of the logic must emphasize history along with current affairs. Japanese enterprises are consciously derived institutions with an anxious eye cast towards the West, a deft finger on the political pulse, and an insatiable appetite for results.

Within this context—new businesses forged to satisfy many different constituencies, and these, in turn, resting on a bedrock of indigenous business practices—entrepreneurs created a corporate form quite unlike anything seen heretofore in Japan. In the first place, kinship was separated from management.

Previously, the *ie* or household was the fundamental unit of business organization, be it in the countryside or city. But gradually the corporation replaced kinship with a promise of performance and administrative efficiency based on acquired rather than ascribed capabilities. Moreover, after 1900 the maturation of the joint-stock company further separated ownership from management, leading to an ever greater emphasis on knowledge, strategy, and professional management of organizational resources. These fundamental changes when coupled with an inaugural Commercial Code of 1893, which clarified the legal parameters of the firm, and with the clearly patriotic effort of most early entrepreneurs to absorb manufacturing know-how from abroad, gave impetus for a corporate form both original and distinct. Japan was the first country in Asia to adapt and reinterpret the Western form of enterprise organization in light of local circumstances.

Finally, the content was as original as the form, if one thinks of content as meaning, that is the meaning that business pioneers gave to their organizations and that those employed therein took for themselves.[28] An awareness and appreciation of such differences in form and content has bemused the managerial leadership of Japanese industrial enterprises early on. Perhaps this bemusing sense of difference, derived from the effort to combine a foreign institutional form with a domestic outlook on work, most clearly illustrates the century-long effort of Japanese firms to transfer knowledge, adapt technologies, compete for markets, and survive at home and abroad.

Japanese work cultures, in this view, are the organizational consequences of human interaction, deliberation, and effort. The process of building work cultures is a conscious, historical one characterized by socially defined models of organization and interaction. The much noted preference for conducting business through interfirm networks should not be understood in some rarified way from the evolutionary process of choosing and refining organizational forms. Different sorts of interfirm networks exist for different reasons, and thus the nature of R & D collaborative networks is different from that of supplier or sales networks. Not only are goals and thus structures different but processes, values, and assumptions differ as well.

Accordingly, the character of interorganizational and intercorporate connections is shaped by the anticipated outcomes of the association. Working together in the abstract is not the goal but getting something accomplished is. Interfirm networks and focal factories, as subsequent chapters will show, became effective solutions to problems of organizing for social and economic development, and the fact that they continue to do so highlights their continuing utility and currency.

The special circumstances which envelop the beginnings of modern industrial enterprise encourage an emphasis on the historical reasons for Japan's success. History is important in order that Japanese corporations will be better understood on their own terms and that the world-wide promise of the corporate form of organization, especially the potential contribution of the Japanese enterprise experience to that promise, may be better assayed.

II
Conceptual Bases for Organizational Interdependence

Stage Theory

The consciously imitative character of public and private institutional development in Japan since the Meiji Restoration of 1868 and the rapidity of institutional development since then have usually been described by such terms as 'follower' or 'late-developer'. That is, the Meiji Government chose to model much of its ideology, institutional framework, and programs for future development on the West. Likewise, the industrial pioneers of Meiji Japan sought to emulate the West in business structure and ideology. The lateness of Japanese development, relative to the United States and Western Europe, has been repeatedly argued by Western social scientists anxious to show the advantages (hardly ever the disadvantages) that seemingly flow from late development.[29] Interestingly, the argument is almost always advanced by Western and not Asian social scientists.

All stage theories, of course, owe a great deal to Marx's seminal work positing a predictable and sequential course to economic development, and to Weber's emphasis on the historical and cultural forces that shape political, intellectual, and industrial development. Building on these, W. W. Rostow's contribution was to emphasize a less deterministic but nevertheless sequential process of development that focused on a number of interrelated conditions and effects at each stage of development. In Rostow's case, interrelationships between economic, political, and intellectual developments were more interactive but no less sequential.

More recently, Alexander Gerschenkron suggested that there might be some possible advantages to late development, that is to beginning the process of economic development somewhat late in the game. The most notable advantages are thought to be the chance to skip over sequential-development stages by profiting from the example of others, and thereby break or supersede the orderly progression of economic development assumed by earlier theorists. Gerschenkron's theories have been applied with limited success to illuminating the process of economic development in Eastern Europe and South America but with less success elsewhere, notably Asia.

Among scholars on Japan, however, Ronald Dore has taken the late-development argument one step farther by asserting that the rapidity of Japanese development, largely under the aegis of state planning and direction, constitutes a new model of economic development—one that represents the highest stage of development and one that might be emulated by nations of both the East and West. Dore's late-development hypothesis is certainly suggestive although it tends to overemphasize the speed and ease of Japan's industrial and institutional development. Chalmers Johnson has characterized this approach as one involving developmental rather than regulatory state institutions and policies, and likewise finds this difference critical to modern Japanese economic success. However, it is important to note that other scholars of Japan, most notably E. H. Norman and his editor, John Dower, have taken an entirely opposite stance as to the benefits of late development.

Nevertheless, it is widely believed that late development permits a larger range of acquisition choices in technology, institutional design, and government policy, as well as in economic and managerial structure simply because there are more examples to follow. Conceptually, late development enables later emerging organizations to leap-frog existing institutional forms, thereby gaining higher levels of efficiency and performance. On the other hand, late development may limit the extent of implementation choices by the simple need to close the gap as quickly as possible. Also, choices to follow based on prior experience may not be so transparent.[30]

If there are broad-jumping advantages to late development, they are given equally to corporations and governments. These appear to be opportunities to scan prior and existing institutional forms, technology and engineering-process choices, managerial structures, and thereby learn from the mistakes and successes of others. Indeed, Richard Samuels in his 'politics of reciprocal consent' sees an interactive dynamic wherein late development mutually affected state and industry.[31]

All of these perspectives on late development have something to offer. The one presented here interprets late development as an enhanced opportunity for organizational learning, and posits this institutional trait as a fundamental feature of the Japanese enterprise system. From the start, Japanese managers targeted Western firms as organizations to learn from, catch up to, and, by dint of determination and effort, surpass. These attitudes remain characteristic of Japanese companies today in their continuing emphasis on history, learning, and getting ahead.

Japanese companies, in terms of the dynamics of their internal actions and external affiliations, have learned how to learn. The historical circumstances of late development have encouraged and required this, and ongoing struggles for economic and institutional survival have reinforced it. The overwhelming dependence of Japanese firms on foreign technology-transfer as well as on borrowed foreign institutional structures offer perhaps the strongest case on record anywhere of the advantages of late development. Thus, the basic strengths of the Japanese enterprise system are closely connected to the late development of the nation and the resulting opportunities for organizational learning.

It is important to recognize that decisions to shape institutions in certain ways and to take action in concert are the result of deliberations and decisions taken by individuals. The processes of making and implementing such choices are cultural ones, and accordingly work structures in Japan are not in any sense predetermined givens but are instead outcomes of an iterative historical process. The history of corporations, therefore, is a history of negotiated settlements of what should be done, when, where, by whom, and in what way.

Clearly, past negotiations are the building-blocks for later negotiations, and in this way stages of development in institutional practices are added to earlier institutional forms. As more effective and efficient methods, forms, routines are devised, there are no reasons to revert to earlier, less beneficial patterns as long as practitioners have learned the value of past practices and how to incorporate them. In this view the corporation is much more than a simple accumulation of human and organizational resources. It is the culmination of processes of planned and unplanned resource utilization and appraisal; these iterative, cumulative decisions transform corporations into learning, acting, purposeful, even 'intuitive' organizations. That is the organizational learning that has been expressed in successively more complicated stages of corporate development in Japan since the late nineteenth century.

Learning how to learn occurred in stages. In general, these stages may be characterized in the metaphor of human development as infancy, adolescence, early adulthood, and late adulthood, recognizing, all the while, that corporations are nearly as different and similar as people are, and that all such characterizations lose something of the particular in translation. The first stage appeared during the last quarter of the nineteenth century, an agitated time when the joint-stock company was being introduced into Japan. New models of work and workplace culture synthesized a ragtag amalgam of long-established urban commercial traditions, a warrior-dominated legacy of administered public works, an imperfect reading of Western commercial, legal, and corporate practices, and a large dose of historical accident and experimentation. None the less, by the turn of the century a number of 'successful' work organizations appeared with Japanese managers and workers reacting to and interacting with each other, within a Western-inspired governance and ownership structure, and with locally modified Western technology. (This is the story of Chapter 2.)

Stage two unfolds as new-style organizations increased and as techniques of management, control, production, and distribution were refined and reworked. Chronologically, this stage continues to World War One by which time the modern Japanese corporation had clearly emerged. Three generic types of modern corporation may be distinguished at this point, each characterized by its own endowment mix, type of managerial hierarchy, technologies of production and distribution, sources of capital, and geographical focus in what was still a semi-rural/semi-urban society. (Chapter 3 covers these developments.)

A third phase falls during the inter-war period from about 1920 to 1940 when an irreversible growth in urban population and treacherous economic conditions allowed large firms to get larger (by rationalizing production, raising funds through the sale of public securities, tapping into distant markets by taking advantage of expanding railroad and telegraphic systems). Smaller firms were often forced to align themselves with larger enterprises or go under. An increasing specialization and division of work through the alignment of businesses in inter-firm networks for supply of parts in production and for transportation and storage in distribution promoted transaction-cost economies. All of this was accomplished without legal, political, or organizational barriers to interfirm cooperation. Accordingly, it was a time when orthodox theories of economies of scale and scope help explain the success of some firms compared to others, and when government industrial policy altered the business environment. (Chapters 3 and 4 treat these matters in detail.)

Finally, after World War Two, a new stage unfolded as the American Occupation forces revamped the business culture and industrial structure of Japan. The Japanese economy grew faster for longer than any other economy ever has; the rate of enterprise R & D expenditure grew even faster than GNP;[32] and Japanese firms widened their product lines and found new markets, moving out of Asia in large numbers for the first time. (Chapters 5, 6 and 7.)

Beyond Stage Theory: Learning and Economic Development

In the manner suggested above, history as well as economic and organizational theories must be employed in order to understand the nature of the Japanese enterprise system. National patterns of organization appear as a result of a specific chronology of choices pursued in the context of industrialization. Late development in Japan's case underscored the importance of specialization and learning. These emerged both as outcomes of late development and as causes of high levels of interdependence that linked the institutions of the Japanese enterprise system. The effect was to emphasize a dynamic interaction of history, economics, strategy, and organization theory.

The economic and organization theories that inform this study are principally four: scale economies, economies of the learning curve, economies of scope, and transaction-cost economies. In addition, there is corporate strategy, a less codified but equally important and dynamic rationale for the achievement of Japanese firms at home and overseas. In the sense of business institutions as an embodiment of the ideas and actions of those who work within them, strategy is the underlying thrust behind economic and organizational theories of the firm.

Organizational Learning as Economic Development

The history of the enterprise system in Japan is a history of factory, firm, and network learning how to learn, as independent and interdependent organizations, not once or even twice but more or less continuously. This is the fundamental notion of organizational learning employed in this study. Repetition with intention leads to enhanced effectiveness, and this leads to higher levels of efficiency. The process regulates firm as well as interfirm performance.

Organizational learning represents a firm-specific capability to operationalize knowledge, often in conjunction with other firms. This happens in three ways, according to Hakan Hakansson. First, there is an *additive* or multi-competence *effect* when an exchange of capabilities produces a new, derived capability, such as a fortuitous joining of Firm A's IC chip and Firm B's computer architecture. Second, there is an *interactive effect* when an interplay of two or more actors results in something entirely new and desirable. In effect, new ways of using existing resources are created. Third, there is the *specialization–coordination effect* when increasing specialization of organizational resources forces interorganizational cooperation as a way to mobilize complementary resources. The third effect is really a special case of the first, raised to a higher level of integration and performance.[33]

While organizational learning has been characterized as routine-based, history-dependent, and target-oriented, such characterizations tend to view organizational learning in the short run. In the long run, organizational learning is limited only by the speed with which general knowledge can be transformed reliably into applied or firm-specific knowledge. In circumstances of nearly complete dependence on foreign technology-transfer (late development), organizational learning (the firm-specific capacity to use knowledge) accumulated operationally in Japan, more often at the level of the shop-floor rather than in corporate-level offices. Theoretical knowledge was and is of limited value. In these circumstances, organizational learning includes both 'learning-by-doing' or so-called 'experience curves' (more efficient effort as a function of accumulated output) as well as what are sometimes referred to as generalized or categorical scripts.[34]

In short, both seat-of-the-pants and formalized learning are valuable if operational practices change as a result of learning. Various kinds of learning are important because the processes of technology transfer and adaptation have been unending for late industrializers. While cost benefits from 'learning-by-doing' may eventually diminish to a point of unimportance, rapid change in product and process technologies provide ample, indeed unending, opportunities for lowering costs as a function of both learning and experience. Changes in material, product design, work flow, staffing, and sales planning can be so substantial that some argue for a reinvention of technology every time a firm embraces a new technology.[35]

For late-developing Japan, the necessities of technical experimentation, new skill development, organizational learning, flexibility and initiative in resource mobilization, and commitment have been paramount and pervasive. Knowing when and how to act in concert were obligatory. Late development enshrined learning as an organizational imperative and as organizational routine.[36] Both imperatives and routines, based on the stock and flow of organizational knowledge, were accelerated by the science-based thrust of modern life, inducing new learning, experimentation, and adaptation. Knowledge-based opportunities, more than anything else, have influenced the environment within which the Japanese enterprise system appeared.

There is a motivational increment to learning-by-doing as well. Catching up to the West was an early and long-held value underpinning organizational learning, and at some point, most likely during the 1970s, the value of learning for learning's sake, that is, a value of constantly testing the parameters of performance (a more internally generated dynamic) supplanted the historical motive of catching up based on late development (an external dynamic). Economic explanations for Japan's performance, such as economic theories of increasing returns to scale and scope, are sensible only in the context of organizational learning and competence, that is where organizations possess sufficient knowledge, capabilities, and values to act effectively in their own self-interest.[37]

The three forms of organizational learning proposed by Hakansson are concerned largely with interfirm or network learning. Other than interfirm learning, there is a vast and growing literature on how individual firms learn that also divides easily into three types: learning from others or the acquisition and adaptation of knowledge from outside (the firm); learning from experience, the educational benefits inherent in increasing returns to scale (the learning curve) and in inter-generational learning associated with product life-cycles; learning from reflection or purposeful, iterative, and intentioned efforts to set goals and attain them. In Japan the last of these is most evident in QC (Quality Control), TQC (Total Quality Control), and TP (Total Productivity) activities.

This study includes all of these forms of interfirm and intrafirm learning. At first, learning was largely *borrowed from abroad* and it was merely fitted to indigenous ways of doing things. For single firms and for firms linked together formally, as in the case of the early *zaibatsu*, the initial effort at learning was *additive*. Yet *integration* of learning occurred as firms learned how to learn, individually and in concert. This was manifest when firms adopted *scale- and scope-related strategies* of volume production and distribution from the Russo-Japanese War (1904–5).

Through integrative experience with economies of scale and scope, firms progressed to a stage of strategic incrementalism, namely a learning strategy of *reflective, goal-oriented, corporate-wide activity* implemented across-the-board in cognizance of similar but company-specific efforts under way elsewhere. The best known and most obvious of these, already mentioned, are QC, TQC, and contemporary TP activities that are predicated on step-by-step improvement in the use of firm-specific experience.

Intrafirm and interfirm learning become progressively interrelated by combining the most basic, additive types of learning with the most sophisticated modes of complementary specialization. The success of this strategy pivots on the limited specialization of single firms matched with the organizational capabilities of other firms. Hence, firm-specific competence becomes tied to the scope, accumulated effort, and complementary specialization of other firms. Some varieties of organizational learning and a proposed illustration of their interdependent character are offered in Fig. 1.5.

Economic Development as Organizational Learning

Economies of Scale. Scale economies occur as the amount of economic activities increase beyond the point of minimum efficient scale, that is beyond the point where the value of production exceeds the costs of production. Economies of scale allow firms to produce larger volumes at lower average costs than do smaller

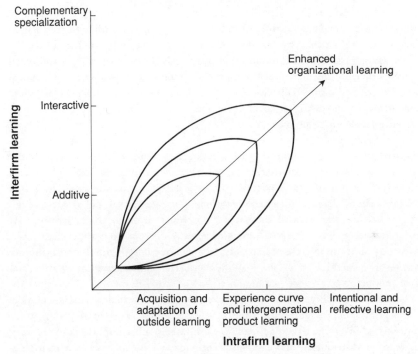

FIG. 1.5. *Varieties of Organizational Learning*

volumes. Basically, the concept holds that unit costs of production and distribution will fall as the size, quantity, and proportion of production and distribution facilities grow.

In scale economies, larger equals better in the sense that unit costs decrease in direct proportion to volume. Three different factors are thought to bring about scale economies: fixed costs; external economies; and technological factors.[38] Fixed costs refer to capital investments at various levels of production, external economies to the acquisition of production inputs, and technological factors to higher rates of throughput based on better or fuller use of plant and equipment. Each factor, alone and in combination, may contribute to scale economies.[39]

In general, technological progress is believed to be the main driving force behind increasing economies of scale because improved technology makes larger facilities and greater throughput possible. However, the size of the market provides an obvious limitation in the degree to which scale economies may be realized. Also, there are organizational limits related to firm-specific capabilities to exploit technologies and to respond effectively to market changes. The combination of these factors is expressed in the term 'minimum efficient scale', that is the relationship between 'minimum optimal scale' in a particular industry and market share.[40]

However, Alfred D. Chandler, Jr. has argued convincingly that minimal optimal scale and market share are significant only in relationship to firm-specific throughput and managerial capability. Thus, it is possible to describe certain firms as possessing the minimum efficient scale (organizational capability) to operate efficiently in their industries. In sum, economies of scale may be obtained when costs per unit of operation or output decrease in a more or less direct proportion to increasing scale of operations, up to a point where market and organizational limits intervene.[41]

Economies of Learning. Learning economies are related to scale economies, in that costs of operation are expected to fall in direct ratio to the amount of activity. However, the amount of activity is measured less in a physical sense, such as in the size of production, than in an educational sense. Costs will fall as a function of the experience accumulated in making a product or providing a service. Cost reductions flow from these accumulated effects, that is from the realization of scale economies over time. Essentially, the smarter one becomes at making and marketing something, the less costly the production and distribution processes and final product.[42]

Considered broadly, learning economies, sometimes called economies of value engineering, may occur at any time in the process of manufacture, so that improvements in product design, manufacturing, unit sub-assembly, parts delivery, or even in distribution and marketing may contribute to cost savings through learning economies. The pervasiveness of training programs, seminars, and even comic book-like, illustrated manuals to teach techniques for reducing costs and managing production, quality control, total quality control, and the like in Japan, attest to the universality of learning economies and to the importance and intensity of employee involvement with them.[43]

There are three reasons why learning economies are especially characteristic of Japanese enterprise. First, the relatively low rates of turnover in personnel, often misleadingly referred to as 'lifetime employment' but better termed 'long-term employment', ensure that what employees learn on the job is likely to stay on the job. Second, in-company education and on-the-job training are emphasized in Japan, and these have become characteristic features of large industrial firms in the post-war period. Together, in-company education and on-the-job training reinforce the meaning of work as an educational endeavor. This was especially true in light of 'how far behind' Japanese firms were in comparison with more technically and organizationally advanced Western firms. Finally, the relatively egalitarian character of rewards and the ample opportunity for participation and meaningful contribution within large post-war Japanese firms motivate employees towards learning and retaining the practical lessons of work.

The post-war popularity of quality-control circles and the delegation of much of the routine responsibility for production scheduling and layout, inventory control, and product development to shop-floor employees are two ways in which accumulated learning and know-how are captured by Japanese organizations.

For such reasons, Japanese planners expect to drive costs down as a function of manufacturing experience, and repeatedly they have been proven correct.

Economies of Scope. Economies of scope refer most often to cost savings that occur when related products and services are run through the same institutional facilities. If, for example, a two-door hardtop is manufactured in the same factory as a four-door sedan, the cost of making either unit should be lower than the combined cost of making each unit separately. In brief, increasing the number of related lines of goods run through the same set of facilities should lower the cost per transaction for all units. Economies of scope, therefore, are scale economies based on plant- or enterprise-specific economies. More recently, other sorts of economies of scope based on information, learning, technical capabilities, and managerial competencies, have received increasing attention.[44] Economies of scope based on the sharing of non-physical resources are undoubtedly as important as those based on the sharing of plant and equipment, even if it is more difficult to document the utility of these economies. (But see Chapters 5 through 8 for attempts to do so.)

The theory behind economies of scope has focused for the most part on cost savings when related production and distribution are run through a single set of facilities, a single corporation's plant and equipment, for example; the model should work equally well where cost savings are realized through joint production and distribution in common facilities and experiences. The latter point is critical in Japan where interfirm networks are common, and where economies of scope in the management of tangible as well as intangible assets provide part of the logic for organizational combinations.

Where economies of scope are potentially realizable, firms may be closely linked in production and distribution networks without mutual shareholding. Indeed, economies of scope offer a far more powerful explanation for the existence and efficacy of interfirm networks in Japan than do interpretations based on equity ownership, asset interspecificity, and other financially based criteria.[45] Moreover, because market size and technological limitations frequently stymie the realization of true economies of scale (often the case in pre-war Japan), slack capacity and know-how within firms (generated through processes of organizational learning) could be invested in realizing economies of scope. Such intrafirm as well as interfirm economies of scope may be seen in my discussion of patterns of organizational learning in Chapters 6 and 7.

Transaction-Cost Economies. Transaction-cost economies refer to the costs of making transactions between operating units. These are generally the costs of managing, that is the administrative costs of running an organization minus production costs. Oliver E. Williamson, the most outstanding economist in this tradition, writes that 'the criterion for organizing commercial transactions is assumed to be the strictly instrumental one of cost economizing'.[46]

Between firms, transaction costs may be defined contractually; within firms, they are often represented as transfer prices. In practice, differing managerial structures not only affect the costs of production and distribution but also the costs of administration. Because companies choose to staff, segment, and control their managerial hierarchies and their intercorporate relations in different ways, these choices have profound cost consequences. Transaction-cost economics stresses the *ex post* adjustments of such institutional arrangements because it assumes that private ordering can adapt organizations in order to minimize costs.[47] Thus, transaction-cost economies are consistent with learning economies because organizational structures, practices, and routines and modified in the interest of economizing on costs.

To compare Hitachi and Toshiba factories as an example, Hitachi's factories are profit centers while Toshiba's are cost centers. This means that in Hitachi's case, all costs associated with making and selling products are calculated at the level of the factory, while in Toshiba's case, only the costs of production are tallied at the factory level and other costs are balanced at the divisional and corporate level. Choices, such as these, of how to organize work affect unit and aggregate costs. Transaction-cost economies, in this sense, are the general costs that reflect the overall managerial assumptions driving economies of scale, scope, and learning.[48]

At the risk of over-simplification and with the notable exception of cotton textiles, newsprint, cement, some foods, and agricultural chemicals, scale economies were not centrally important to Japanese economic development until after World War One, and, as a consequence, economies of scope and transaction-cost economies played correspondingly larger roles. After the Pacific War, scale economies and related learning economies have become central, but they have been realized within a context of interfirm relations and corporate boundaries which were already geared to exploit economies of scope and of transaction cost. Since the oil shortages of the 1970s and the consequent lowered levels of economic growth, there are indications that a new amalgamation of enterprise interests combining elements of both economies of scale and scope within a dynamic interfirm context is emerging in Japan.

Corporate Strategy. Finally, there is the matter of corporate strategy. The strategic-management process has been characterized as the identification and implementation of patterns of resource-allocation commitments and their evaluation which, over time, define the evolution of a firm in relation to its environment. Although Japanese firms have not seemingly employed systematic long-range planning until recently, the geographical and chronological circumstances of industrial development have forced Japanese firms, like it or not, to assess continually their sources of supply, their organizational competence, the accessibility and longevity of markets, the congruence of interests between a developing state and developing enterprises, and the need to confront uncertainty with scarce resources.[49]

Japanese enterprises were required, by dint of their overwhelming reliance on derived technology and managerial methods, to appraise constantly and critically their economic position at home and abroad. This context, more than anything else, has shaped the strategy of modern Japanese corporations. A lack of resources, talent, and experience within single firms pushed Japanese companies to focus their efforts internally while they sought and secured complementary functions and assets externally. Technology transfer drove the logic of interdependence and was in time complemented by other sinew-knitting resources, such as capital, personnel, and managerial method. Competitive strategies and cooperative structures, an organizational and strategic shorthand for the Japanese enterprise system, followed.

The Japanese enterprise system appeared conclusively in response to the need to focus organizational resources in three ways: *downward* in the production function as a result of the processes of technology transfer and adaptation; *outward* in interfirm cooperative structures as a partial consequence of pre-existing and developing production, transportation, and distribution functions in the value chain; *inward* in a process of adapting Western corporate models and methods to indigenous business values and systems of social relations. The history of the Japanese enterprise system is the story of how such material and immaterial forces have intersected with factory, firm, and network, the principal institutions for accomplishing industrial work in Japan. The result is a country and corporate system which are noteworthy for their work organization and ethic, industrial structure and policies, and commitment of limited organizational resources to long-term economic growth and security.

History and the Logic of Organizational Interdependence

In the long run or from a population ecology perspective, the conditions under which enterprise and industry competition take place are likely to be idiosyncratic and in flux, especially so under conditions of late development and rapid change in social and economic circumstances. Strategic choices are necessarily taken in the midst of limited strategic alternatives. Organizational adaptation and attrition result. The former suggests incremental, piecemeal stabs in the dark, not quite random but not quite assured. The latter stresses economic efficiency, a relentless selection and elimination of less well-endowed and less well-managed enterprises.[50]

Certainly, economies of scale, scope, and transaction cost are of the latter sort. All of these assume a lot and give away very little. Rationality, efficiency, causality, optimality—are the lexicon of economic theory. Concepts of organizational learning and strategy employ such terms while they recognize human frailty beyond bounded rationality and opportunism. Choices are not perfect, trade-offs less so, and actions suffer badly.

The arguments of this work assume a certain degree of rationality and efficiency in the choices taken by Japanese managers in the long, hard climb to industrial prosperity. Competition forced this. Technology transfer and acquisition demanded this. Industry structure prompted this by mandating a strategy of aligning factory, firm, and network, resulting in a primary ordering and coordinating of economic activities. But neither competition nor managers were perfect, and

TABLE 1.3. *Why Micro-Organizational Alternatives in*
Japanese Industrial History

Value Chain	Focal Factory	Network
Functional Segmentation	XX	X
Technology Transfer	XX	X
High-Risk Environment	X	XX
Complementary Specialization	X	XX
Level of National Integration	XX	XX

X   Less important
XX   More important

individual as well as institutional choice enshrined human folly. The march to superpower status was not guaranteed.

A rush of Western technology and entrepreneurial nerve forced a flight towards what worked. Attrition and adaptation were processes of enterprise growth and change as were focus, specialization, and organizational correspondence at levels of factory, firm, and network. All of these advanced notions of efficiency and productivity that cut through a clouded maze of alternative forms, methods, techniques, and choices.

Some worked better than others, changes took hold, patterns appeared, and many starts towards an economic logic of institutions and institutional relations emerged. Government policy, moreover, tilted the playing-field in certain industries and at certain times, inducing partisanship and predispositions. Policy (both public and private) led to notions of cooperation for the purposes of securing complementary resources as well as organizational capabilities. In all cases, effective learning was the basis of survival.

As functional alternatives, managers pursued product and market strategies through the organizational forms that best fit their needs. As complementary organizations, strategic choices connected factories, firms, and networks in an enterprise system rich in form, method, and means. Some of the factors affecting the formation of Japanese industrial organizations are listed in Table 1.3. Choices to pursue these organizational forms reflected views of business and society and of institutional interaction that were widely approved and practiced. These were continually reinterpreted and reinforced and they came to reflect a cultural orientation towards business which was, at once, rooted in the past and renewed in the present. Obviously, Japanese entrepreneurs had no prescience as to the ultimate efficiency of these long-term developments. They were simply selecting and re-fining organizational patterns that were sensible, available, and efficient enough to encourage their continued practice.

In the long run, in spite of organizational variety, strategic decisions, and sensible choice few of Japan's largest industrial firms stayed large for long. Most failed or, at least, failed to remain among the largest 200 industrial firms, and so teleology was not part of the process leading to the formation of the Japanese enterprise system. Being good and being lucky were. Hence, strategy and choice urged ahead the evolution of the Japanese enterprise system in a sequence of progressive and hierarchical stages described in the next four chapters.

NOTES

1. In this work I have established some of the ways in which large industrial firms in Japan differ from their Western counterparts. History and an interactive dynamic fusing institutions and environments were some of the reasons why. Organizational interdependence was the result. Now I want to pursue questions of organizational interdependence more formally. In particular, I am interested in notions of interfirm networks as strategic groups in Japan. The former are typically described as collections of firms, rather heterogeneous in character, that cooperate for strategic advantage. The latter are groupings depicted in the strategic-management literature as firms, rather homogeneous in character, that compete in the same industry. Employing both notions should help reveal the nature of firm rivalry and competition in Japan. Note well in this regard that the very concept of strategic group in Japan is different from that found in the West. The notion refers to a group of cooperating yet heterogeneous enterprises that pursue isomorphic strategies in Japan. In the West, it indicates a group of competitors who pursue similar strategies.

   My use of the term strategic group, therefore, is unconventional. I thank Bala Chakravarthy for this point. The literature on strategic groups is explored by Karel Cool and Ingemar Dierickx, 'Strategic Groups, Rivalry and Firm Performance', mimeo, INSEAD, Mar. 1990. See also Karel Cool and D. Schendel, 'Strategic Group Formation and Performance: The Case of the U.S. Pharmaceutical Industry, 1963–1982', *Management Science*, 33/9 (Sept. 1987), 1102–24; Cool and Schendel, 'Performance Differences among Strategic Group Members', *Strategic Management Journal*, 9 (1988), 207–23.

2. *The Economic Institutions of Capitalism* (New York: Free Press, 1985), 385.

3. Probably the leading schools of interpretation concerning the scope or boundaries of the firm are resource-dependency theory and transaction-cost economics. For the former, see Jeffrey Pfeffer and Gerald Salancik, *The External Control of Organizations* (New York: Harper & Row, 1978), and Jeffrey Pfeffer, *Power in Organizations* (Cambridge, Mass.: Ballinger, 1981). For the latter, see Oliver E. Williamson, *Markets and Hierarchies: Analysis and Antitrust Implications* (New York: Free Press, 1975), and id., *Economic Institutions of Capitalism*. For a discussion of some of the differences between the two approaches, see David Ulrich and Jay Barney, 'Perspectives in Organizations: Resource Dependency, Efficiency, and Population', *Academy of Management Review*, 9 (1984), 471–81; Ian Maitland and Bob DeFillippi, 'The Scope of the Firm: An Efficiency Critique of Resource Dependency Theory', Discussion Paper No. 61, Strategic Management Research Center, University of Minnesota, Oct. 1986.

4. H. A. Simon, 'The Architecture of Complexity', *Proceedings of the American Philosophical Society*, 106 (Dec. 1962), 467–82.

5. A notion of the M-Form firm or other kinds of firms as ideal types is deeply engrained in economic and organizational writings on the firm because all theories simplify reality; the simplicity of one ideal type is most often preferred to a reality of mixed forms and muddled structures. The Japanese enterprise system model avoids extreme simplification by arguing in favor of a mixed model at the outset.

6. Ibid.; H. A. Simon, *The Sciences of the Artificial* (Cambridge, Mass.: MIT Press, 1969); Stanley N. Salthe, *Evolving Hierarchical Systems* (New York: Columbia University Press, 1985).

7. Mark Granovetter, 'Economic Action and Social Structure: The Problem of Embeddedness', *American Journal of Sociology*, 91 (Nov. 1985), 481–510.

8. A paper of mine which traces the complex nature of business transactions between the Toshiba Corporation and some of its parts suppliers is, 'Cooperation and Competition: Supplier Networks in the Japanese Electronics Industry', Center for Japanese Studies, UC Berkeley, 4 Nov. 1987. Figures on the number of related firms and the size of the Affiliated Companies Office in Toshiba were obtained through an interview with Mr. Taizo Wakayama, head of that office, in Toshiba headquarters at Hammatsucho on 5 Oct. 1990.

9. Scale and scope are, of course, the interrelated concerns of Alfred D. Chandler's latest book, *Scale and Scope* (Cambridge, Mass.: Harvard University Press, 1990). It may be argued that the Japanese enterprise system and the Western business system as described by Chandler represent different solutions to similar problems. Why such different solutions arose is the theme of this and Chandler's work.

    Producing a full line may be considered a form of diversification, one that depends primarily on expanding existing facilities and capabilities. More often and in this analysis, diversification is considered a form of enterprise growth that requires investment in new facilities and in adding new organizational capabilities. My measurement of the degree of newness is the extent to which the new products of diversification fall within or without the classification of a firm's existing products according to the US Standard Classification Code calibrated at the two-digit level of classification.

10. Vijay Mahajan, Subhash Sharma, and Richard A. Bettis, 'The Adoption of the M-Form Organization Structure: A Test of the Imitation Hypothesis', *Management Science*, 34/10 (Oct. 1988). And, Akitake Taniguchi, 'Gigyobusei soshiki no gendaikei', in Kazuichi Sakamoto (ed.), *Gijutsu Kakushin to Kigyo Kozo* (Technical Innovation and Enterprise Organization) (Kyoto: Minerva Press, 1986). Chandler's *Scale and Scope* does not exactly calculate turnover in the way that I do; however, Appendices A.4, B.4, and C.4 do indicate a high level of persistency in ranking for the major American, British, and German industrial firms. See Chandler's recounting of diversification studies by Rumelt, Channon, and Thanheiser on pp. 617–19.

11. Neil Fligstein, 'The Spread of the Multidivisional Form among Large Firms, 1919–1979', *American Sociological Review*, 50/3 (June 1985). Alfred D. Chandler's *Strategy and Structure* (Cambridge, Mass.: MIT Press, 1962) was the pioneering effort to categorize corporate structure according to a classification of strategic choices. His work was followed by a number of important studies at the Harvard Graduate School of Business Administration which applied Chandler's framework to large industrial firms in a number of nations. See Derek F. Channon, *The Strategy and Structure of British Enterprise* (Boston: Havard Business School Press, 1973); Richard Rumelt, *Strategy, Structure, and Economic Performance* (Boston: Harvard Business School, 1986); Gareth Dyas and Heinz Thanheiser, *Emerging European Enterprise* (London: Macmillan, 1976).

12. The nature of interfirm relations is not always clear, even to the Japanese. I recall a conversation overheard on the Tohoku Keihin line as the train neared Kawasaki City station on 22 Feb. 1990 around 23.45. 'Uchi no kaisha wakaran . . . nijususha no kanren kigyo aru', or 'I don't understand our company . . . we have some twenty odd related companies', implying bewilderment at how so many companies were related.

13. Much of what has been written about company culture could be applied equally well to factory culture. Focal factories have a particularly rich, what anthropologists call 'thick', culture. See Edgar H. Schein, *Organizational Culture and Leadership* (San Francisco: Jossey–Bass, 1985).

14. Mahajan, Sharma, and Bettis, 'Adoption of the M-Form'; Fligstein, 'Spread of the Multidivisional Form'. Also, H. Thomas Johnson and Robert S. Kaplan, *Relevance Lost: The Rise and Fall of Management Accounting* (Boston: Harvard Business School Press, 1987), 99.

15. J. Cable and H. Yasuki, 'Internal Organization, Business Groups and Corporate Performance: An Empirical Test of the Multidivisional Hypothesis in Japan', *International Journal of Industrial Organization*, 3 (1985), 401–20. Also, Akira Goto, 'Statistical Evidence on the Diversification of Large Japanese Firms', *Journal of Industrial Economics*, 29/3 (Mar. 1981); Minoru Harada, 'Seizogyo no Takakuka: Shogyo Fudosangyo ni Shinshutsu Sakan' (Industrial Diversification: Growing Investment in Commerce and Real Estate), *Nihon Keizai Shimbun*, 30 Mar. 1991, 28.

While a US–Japan comparison based on assets, sales, number of employees, or any single measure yields disproportionate results, various combined measures reduce differentials somewhat. For example, if sales to employee ratios are calculated on a value-added basis, then size differentials are not so large. However, even doing so, that is calculating sales per employee, results in a per capita turnover some 2 to 4 times higher for Japanese firms. These discrepancies in scale, already striking, were larger in the past when the size of the market served by Japanese firms was notably smaller than that of American firms.

TABLE 1.4. *Largest Five Firms in Selected Industries Comparison: America and Japan, 1987*

American			Japanese		
Name	Sales ($m.)	Employees	Name	Sales ($m.)[a]	Employees
Dupont	30,468	140,145	Asahi Chemical	6,108	15,595
Dow	13,377	53,100	Mitsubishi Chemical	4,984	8,751
Monsanto	7,639	49,734	Toray Industries	4,332	10,143
United Carbide	6,914	43,119	Sumitomo Chemical	4,126	7,707
Grace	5,046	39,393	Kao	3,920	6,697
AVERAGE	12,689	65,098	AVERAGE	4,694	9,779
IBM	54,217	389,348	Hitachi	23,356	76,210
Unisys	9,713	92,500	Toshiba	21,462	70,288

TABLE 1.4. *Continued*

American			Japanese		
Name	Sales ($m.)	Employees	Name	Sales ($m.)[a]	Employees
Digital Equipment	9,389	110,500	NEC	18,435	38,004
Hewlett-Packard	8,090	82,000	Mitsubishi Electric	15,633	48,562
NCR	5,641	62,000	Fujitsu	13,715	50,617
AVERAGE	17,410	147,270	AVERAGE	18,520	56,736
Occidental Petroleum	17,096	50,350	Taiyo Fishery	4,401	3,685
Kraft	11,011	46,500	Nippon Suisan	3,849	3,772
Sara Lee	9,155	92,400	Snow Brand Milk	3,685	8,213
Conagra	9,002	42,176	Ajinomoto	3,460	5,438
Beatrice	8,926	62,000	Nippon Meat Packers	3,189	3,359
AVERAGE	11,038	58,685	AVERAGE	3,717	4,893
ALCOA	7,767	55,000	Nippon Steel	17,176	61,423
LTV	7,582	48,200	NKK	8,402	25,193
Bethlehem Steel	4,621	34,400	Kobe Steel	7,807	22,741
Reynolds Metals	4,284	27,300	Kawasaki Steel	7,491	20,803
Inland Steel Industries	3,453	20,740	Sumitomo Metal Industries	7,274	23,108
AVERAGE	5,541	37,128	AVERAGE	9,630	30,654
General Motors	101,782	813,400	Toyota Motor	48,199	64,329
Ford	71,643	350,320	Nissan Motor	27,349	51,237
Chrysler	26,258	122,745	Honda	21,200	29,640
Dana	4,142	37,500	Mitsubishi Motors	14,024	22,997
Navistar International	3,530	14,918	Mazda	12,818	28,423
AVERAGE	41,471	267,777	AVERAGE	24,718	39,325

[a] $1 = 125 yen.

Sources: Ministry of Finance, *Yukashoken Hokokusho* (annual reports) with additional calculations by the author.

16. Johnson and Kaplan, *Relevance Lost*, 205.
17. Masahiko Aoki and I arrive at similar conclusions but for very different reasons. See *The Co-operative Game Theory of the Firm* (Oxford: Oxford University Press, 1984), ch. 11.
18. Robert E. Hoskisson and Michael A. Hitt, 'Strategic Control Systems and Relative R & D Investment in Large Multiproduct Firms', *Strategic Management Journal*, 9 (1988), 605–21.

19. Personal communication from Alfred D. Chandler, Jr., 19 Jan. 1990.
20. Johnson and Kaplan, *Relevance Lost*, 99.
21. Alfred D. Chandler, Jr. asserts that the first Western industrial firms to make co-ordinated investments in production and distribution functions and in a managerial hierarchy to govern and assess those investments gained first-mover advantages. In other words, they created barriers to entry for later developing firms in those industries. First-mover advantages appear less significant in Japan.
22. The effect of measuring sales as opposed to assets can be seen in Table 1.5.

TABLE 1.5. *Sensitivity Test for SIC Distribution, 200 Largest Japanese Industrial Firms, 1987*

SIC group	By assets	By sales	Asset sensitive[a]	Sales sensitive[b]
Food and beverage 20	22	25		3
Tobacco 21	1	1		
Textiles 22	3	2	1	
Apparel 23	1	0	1	
Lumber 24	2	3		1
Furniture 25	1	1		
Paper 26	9	8	1	
Printing 27	2	4		2
Chemicals 28	36	34	2	
Petroleum 29	13	13		
Rubber 30	4	5		1
Leather 31	0	0		
Stone, Clay, Glass 32	12	11	1	
Primary metals 33	19	17	2	
Fabricated metals 34	5	5		
Machinery 35	27	27		
Electrical machinery 36	15	14	1	
Transport equipment 37	17	20		3
Instruments 38	9	8	1	
Miscellaneous 39	2	2		
TOTAL	200	200		

[a] textiles, apparel, paper, chemicals, stone/clay/glass, primary metals, electrical machinery, measuring instruments.

[b] food, lumber, printing, rubber, transportation equipment.

23. According to the lead article of the *Nihon Keizai Shimbun* (Japan Economic Journal), 23 Feb. 1990, American negotiators at the opening of the Third Structural Initiatives talks between the US and Japan claimed that the 3 percent of total corporate sales garnered by members of the Mitsubishi group of companies was 'highly unusual'. Besides definitional issues with regard to determining group membership (the definitions employed by American representatives were not explained), there is little

evidence supporting the thesis that group membership, by and of itself, results in anti-competitive behavior. If so, it becomes hard to explain Mitsubishi Electric and Mitsubishi Motors' performance in their respective industries.

The next day's edition of the *Nihon Keizai Shimbun* reported Mitsubishi Trading Company's response. 'What's the significance of 3 percent?' The Chairman of the Trading Company, Mr. Mimura, was quoted as saying, 'Japanese enterprise groups are not closed.' Mitsubishi Trading claimed that the manufactured products of member companies accounted for 6 percent of its sales and that internal buying and selling within the group amounted to 16–18 percent of total sales. Representatives of the Mitsubishi group of companies stressed that these figures demonstrated how low was the degree of internal business transactions.

In the same article, representatives of Toyota Motor, another interfirm alliance, were reported as stating that transfer prices between itself and its suppliers were not inappropriately pegged and that Toyota did not exercise external control over its suppliers. *Nihon Keizai Shimbun*, 'Tomadou Gyokai', 24 Feb. 1990, 3.

24. The history of corporations in Japan, when viewed in this way, recalls the structure/agency arguments of Anthony Giddens for social theory where notions of structure and action presuppose one another, as well as the strategy/structure models of Alfred D. Chandler, Jr., where the interconnections between strategy and corporate structure for the modern American corporation are assayed. Also, it echoes the work of Mary Douglas where different institutional frameworks allow individuals to think and feel in certain ways. Anthony Giddens, *Central Problems in Social Theory* (Berkeley: University of California Press, 1983), 53, 80, 94–5. See also, Eugene F. Fama, 'Agency Problems and the Theory of the Firm', *Journal of Political Economy* (1980), 288–307; Huseyin Leblebici and Avi Fiegenbaum, 'Managers as Agents without Principles: An Empirical Examination of Agency and Constituency Perspectives', *Journal of Management*, 12/4 (1986), 485–98; Chandler, *Strategy and Structure*; Mary Douglas, *How Institutions Think* (Syracuse, NY: Syracuse University Press, 1986).

25. In *How Institutions Think*, the chapter on 'Institutions do the Classifying' offers a perfect example of the embodiment of knowledge in an organizational routine. Arthur L. Stinchcombe wrote in a similar vein in *Creating Efficient Industrial Administrations* (New York: Academic Press, 1973), esp. 20–3 on the administrative coding of causes. Also, see his 'Social Structure and Organizations', in J. March (ed.), *Handbook of Organizations* (Chicago: Rand McNally, 1965). Finally, a delightfully written but profound treatment of the whole matter can be found in Alan M. Kantrow, *The Constraints of Corporate Tradition* (New York: Harper & Row, 1987).

26. David L. Lewis, *The Public Image of Henry Ford* (Detroit: Wayne State University Press, 1976), 107, 224.

27. Clifford Geertz, *Local Knowledge* (New York: Basic Books, 1983), esp. ch. 6, 'Centers, Kings, and Charisma: Symbolics of Power', 122–3.

28. Byron K. Marshall, *Capitalism and Nationalism in Prewar Japan: The Ideology of the Business Elite, 1864–1941* (Stanford, Calif.: Stanford University Press, 1967); Johannes Hirschmeier, *The Origins of Entrepreneurship in Meiji Japan* (Cambridge, Mass.: Harvard University Press, 1964); W. Mark Fruin, *Kikkoman: Company, Clan, and Community* (Cambridge, Mass.: Harvard University Press, 1983), ch. 4.

29. The literature on late development and the resulting development consequences is long. To cite the most conspicuous only: Chalmers Johnson, *MITI and the Japanese Miracle* (Stanford, Calif.: Stanford University Press, 1982); Alexander Gerschenkron,

Economic Backwardness in Historical Perspective (Cambridge, Mass.: Harvard University Press, 1962); W. W. Rostow, *The Stages of Economic Growth* (Cambridge, Mass.: Harvard University Press, 1961). Ronald Dore, *British Factory—Japanese Factory* (Berkeley: University of California Press, 1973); John Dower (ed.), *Origins of the Modern Japanese State: Selected Writings of E. H. Norman* (New York: Pantheon Press, 1975).

30. Robert E. Cole, *Work, Mobility and Participation* (Berkeley: University of California Press, 1979).

31. Richard J. Samuels, *The Business of the Japanese State* (Ithaca, NY: Cornell University Press, 1987).

32. National Science Foundation, *The Science and Technology Resources of Japan: A Comparison with the United States* (Washington, DC: National Science Foundation 88–318, 1988), 1–8.

33. Hakan Hakansson (ed.), *Industrial Technological Development: A Network Approach* (London: Croom Helm, 1987).

34. Bala Chakravarthy and Seog K. Kwun, 'The Strategy Process: An Organizational Learning Perspective', working paper, The Carlson School of Management, University of Minnesota, 1987.

35. Peter Clark, *Anglo-American Innovation* (London: Methuen, 1987). Graham Hall and Sydney Howell, 'The Experience Curve from the Economist's Perspective', *Strategic Management Journal*, 6/6 (1985). B. Levitt and J. Marsh, 'Organizational Learning', *Annual Review of Sociology*, 14 (1988), 319. Levitt and Marsh identify a range of organizational learning types and strategies in their excellent review article.

36. Richard R. Nelson and Sidney G. Winter, *An Evolutionary Theory of Economic Change* (Cambridge, Mass.: Harvard University Press, 1982), 105.

37. Edith T. Penrose, *The Growth of the Firm*, rev. edn. (White Plains, NY: M. E. Sharpe, 1980), 260–5.

38. See F. M. Scherer, *Industrial Market Structure and Economic Performance* (Boston: Houghton Mifflin Co., 1980). George J. Stigler, *The Organization of Industry* (Chicago: University of Chicago Press, 1983), 67–94. Kenneth Arrow, *Limits of Organization* (New York: W. W. Norton, 1974).

39. The following sketch offers a simple illustration of scale economies. A bicycle manufacturer has a welding facility large enough to handle 1,000 frames per day. The cost of producing, say, an additional 200 frames at the same facility will be much less than the cost of making any portion of the frames and frame sets leading up to the daily target of 1,000. In short, gaining more production from existing facilities is less expensive than achieving comparable levels of production in new facilities.

40. Chandler, *Scale and Scope*, 734.

41. Learning economies have been modeled formally in three ways: the ability to learn a new technique; the rate of mastery of the technique; production experience with the technique. See e.g. Leonard Dudley, 'Learning and Productivity Change in Metal Products', *American Economic Review*, 62 (Sept. 1972), 662–9; Kenneth Arrow, 'The Economic Implications of Learning by Doing', *Review of Economic Studies* (1962), 155–7; and Leonard Rapping, 'Learning and World War II Production Functions', *Review of Economics and Statistics*, 47 (Feb. 1965), 81–6.

42. J. G. Abramowitz and G. A. Shotluck, Jr., 'The Learning Curve: A Technique for Planning, Measurement and Control', IBM Report No. 31.101, 1970.

43. e.g. A. Igarashi (ed.), *Kojo Kosto Daun Jiten* (A Dictionary of Factory Cost Reduction Terms) (Tokyo: Nikkan Kogyo, 1990).

44. David Teece, 'Towards an Economic Theory of the Multiproduct Firm', *Journal of Economic Behavior and Organization*, 3 (Mar. 1982), 39–63; id., 'Economies of Scope and the Scope of the Enterprise', *Journal of Economic Behavior and Organization*, 1 (Sept. 1980), 223–47; Sumantra Ghoshal, 'Global Strategy: An Organizing Framework', *Strategic Management Journal*, 8 (1987), 425–40; Megumi Suto, 'Economies of Scope in the Securities Business', *Kinyu Gakkai Hokoku*, No. 65 (1988).

45. Michael Gerlach's careful work on alliance capitalism in Japan is based on tracing the financial links and interlocking directorates that join so many of Japan's major firms. Michael Gerlach, 'Business Alliances and the Strategy of the Japanese Firm', *California Management Review*, 30 (Fall 1987), 126–42. Also see, id., *Alliance Capitalism* (Berkeley: University of California Press, forthcoming).

    While there is no doubt as to the pervasiveness of these ties, there is doubt as to the adequacy of financial ties and of interlocking directorates alone in explaining the economic performance of Japan's industrial giants. Nevertheless, in the course of Japan's economic development, close relations between industrial firms and their sources of capital should lead to lower transaction costs and lower capital costs, and these could be reflected in higher debt-to-equity ratios. Gerlach's work tracks these important relationships.

    Yet financial and directorate ties can be traced only at highly aggregated, abstracted levels of generalization. From the standpoint of explaining the coalitional networks that power firm and interfirm relations on a day-to-day basis, highly aggregated ties have limited value. But they do have value, nevertheless. The work of Nakatani Iwao and Thomas Roehl suggests that the close ties joining traditional industrial and financial firms in Japan comes at a performance cost, namely lower rates of profitability and market-share growth. See Ch. 7, nn. 41–3.

46. Williamson quoted in Chandler, *Scale and Scope*, 734 n. 3.

47. Oliver E. Williamson, 'Comparative Economic Organization: The Analysis of Discrete Structural Alternatives', mimeo, University of California, Berkeley, Mar. 1990, 14.

48. See e.g. Williamson, *Markets and Hierarchies*; id., 'The Economics of Organization: The Transaction Cost Approach', *American Journal of Sociology*, 87/3 (1981).

49. Yves Doz and Jean-Pierre Lehmann, 'The Strategic Management Process: The Japanese Example', *Bonner Zeitschrift für Japonologie*, 8 (1986).

50. This last section was inspired by James A. Robins, 'Organizational Economics: Notes on the Use of Transaction-Cost Theory in the Study of Organizations', *Administrative Science Quarterly*, 32/1 (Mar. 1987), 68–86. See also Christine Oliver for a discussion of institutional isomorphism, a debate that has some relevance for the evolution of the Japanese enterprise system. Christine Oliver, 'The Collective Strategy Framework: An Application to Competing Predictions of Isomorphism', *Administrative Science Quarterly*, 33 (1988), 543–61. My own feeling is that competing explanations of institutional isomorphism all have relevance: population-ecology perspectives early on, institutionalization perspectives in time, and strategic-choice perspectives throughout. See also Glenn R. Carroll, 'On the Organizational Ecology of Chester I. Barnard', in Oliver E. Williamson (ed.), *Organization Theory* (New York: Oxford University Press, 1990), 56–71.

2

The Institutional Environment

Major Japanese corporations are different from comparable Western firms, and they are different for historical reasons. The first of these involves timing. Japanese companies appeared quite late in the nineteenth century, yet by World War One they were already driving ahead the Japanese economy.[1] As a consequence of this later development relative to the major economies of the West, the macro- and micro-economic climate as well as the political and social milieu of institutional development were different.

The later development of modern public and private institutions in Japan has given them a highly reflexive quality. That is, as institutions, they embody a rather self-conscious effort on the part of local leaders to pick and choose from a variety of available organizational options, and to adapt, modify, and refine these after their introduction into Japan. The Japanese navy, for example, was modeled after the British Navy while the army followed France at first and then Germany.[2] Western systems of jurisprudence, banking, education, and business incorporation were lifted from the contexts in which they were formed, transported hundreds of years and thousands of miles in time and space, recombined and reordered at the hands of Japanese statesmen, industrialists, managers, and workers.

Japanese institutions were founded on the basis of learning, choice, and action, and the openly intentional aspects of the endeavor were quite remarkable. The creation of such modern institutions assumes rather sophisticated knowledge and appreciation of Western institutions as well as careful consideration of what was possible in turn-of-the-century Japan. The adaptation and re-creation of Western models of organization, like the corporation, represent one of the most successful and systematic attempts to pick and choose, design, and mold the institutional framework of contemporary life.[3]

Although the process of institutional creation begins with human effort, will-power alone is not enough. Intention cannot replace experience, effort, and education. Suggestively, Japanese companies were behind Western firms in making products of the first industrial revolution, such as low thread-count textiles, milled foods, and iron, but, by the turn of the twentieth century as the second industrial revolution began to unfold, Japanese firms were not so obviously disadvantaged in the manufacture of mechanical and electrical machinery, a variety of chemical products, high thread-count and synthetic textiles, and transportation equipment, especially ships and rolling-stock. By the third and fourth industrial revolutions, Japanese enterprises were global leaders in high-tension steel, exotic metal alloys, micro-electronics, superconductivity, biotechnology, and space-age materials.

Thus, timing began to favor rather than hinder Japanese efforts as industrialization shifted from the first to the second industrial divide and as Japanese entrepreneurs gained experience with the possibilities of re-creating Western institutions. Indeed, catching and riding the crest of a gathering industrial wave necessitated a certain size in production units and sophistication of method. These required an initial period of experience, effort, and education followed by a period of accelerated growth culminating in a crescendo of more advanced products. Japan was a follower nation in the first industrial revolution, a representative nation of the second, and a leader by the third.

Second, the speed of industrial development in Japan has fascinated observers from the developed and developing world. As a consequence of speed, especially when it is recognized that speed embodies powerful new production and propulsion technologies, the accelerated adaptation of the modern corporate form in Japan ushered in an organizational revolution there, while corporations were more the culmination of a several-century process of organizational evolution in the West. What took three or four centuries in the West was accomplished in less than one in Japan.

The first Western corporation, the Russia or Muscovy Company, was created in England by Mary Tudor, Queen of England, in 1555, while a commercial code which defined the legal and economic characteristics of corporations in Japan was not drafted until 1893.[4] Since 1555 in the West, the corporation evolved fitfully but steadily by various legal, economic, political, and social conventions. Until the mid-nineteenth century, to be sure, corporations were used more in municipalities, universities, and utilities. Such corporations and great trading companies had political as well as economic purposes. It was not until the last half of the nineteenth century that corporations became common in commerce (except banks) and manufacturing, yet the rapid spread of the corporation thereafter was predicated on the sophisticated legal, planning, and organizational advantages that had evolved previously.

In contrast, the Japanese corporation appeared relatively late in the global history of the firm, and it emerged in conscious imitation of an already advanced Western corporation. Most importantly, it materialized in a society where, until the 1880s and 1890s, a small number of large, bureaucratic government offices were juxtaposed with a very large number of small, personalized, mostly agricultural and industrial household enterprises. In such circumstances, the corporation as a commercial and manufacturing organization had revolutionary impact.

Finally, a powerful advantage realized by the modern corporation in Japan, based on timing and speed of development, was the combination of superior organizational and technological resources. From the mid-twentieth century, size and sophistication of method were married to manufacturing technologies that promised much higher throughput, more exacting standards of production, and greater reliability. This was an especially seductive combination for government and business leaders alike, and thereby political and economic interests were united in creating a regime of comparative organizational and technological advantage.

As a result of the corporation's late appearance, conscious efforts to emulate Western corporations, plus a lack of competing indigenous institutions, two decisive advantages were imparted to modern corporations. Japanese corporations could begin on a grander scale, with more complex organization, more refined tools of accounting and production, and generally with greater organizational sophistication because there was very little interference from past organizational practices, and because Western models for organizational imitation and adaptation were already well differentiated and evolved. The pre-existing models of corporate organization in Japan, such as the bureaucratic models found in domain and *bakufu* governments or the familial models practiced everywhere in agriculture and commerce, were not well suited to profit-seeking, industrial enterprises. Traditional labor-management practices, such as the internal contracting system, disappeared within several decades of the introduction of Western models of industrial relations.[5]

By the same token, Japanese enterprises begin on a higher technological plane than would otherwise have been the case. The lateness of Japanese development, relative to the Western record, offered unusual opportunities to select among production technologies already proven in the West. Of course, industrial technology even in the late nineteenth century did not come unfettered by political and economic considerations, but none the less, Japanese industrialists were able to pick and choose production, propulsion, and power-generation technologies with a latitude and discrimination not enjoyed more recently, since the advent of twentieth-century techno-nationalism.

It is worth emphasizing that such fortune in organizational and technical choice came not once but twice. The later development of Japan offered a range of choices appropriate to the first as well as second industrial revolutions. Early success with textiles, later success with transportation equipment, such as motor vehicles, and a most recent success with electronics, are all based in part on Japan's late development. As detailed in Chapter 6, because Japanese electrical firms had not developed computers and other advanced electrical devices based on vacuum tubes, as had American and European firms, they were less deterred to move into semiconductor-driven products. The coincidence of such organizational and technical advantages underpin the emergence of factories, firms, and networks as fundamental building-blocks of Japanese industrial capitalism.

By virtue of these combined organizational and technological opportunities, plus a positive change in government policies and attitudes towards private enterprise after the Meiji Restoration of 1868, completely new models of industrial organization and manufacturing technique could become established within a surprisingly short time. The later development of Japan relative to the more advanced nations of the West offered Japanese industrialists extraordinary possibilities, as long as they were able to recognize and take advantage of them. This is what Keiichiro Nakagawa calls 'the learning industrial revolution'.[6]

Taking advantage of these opportunities defines the essence and context of corporations in Japan. Corporations appeared late, grew fast, and matured rapidly, even abruptly. This was achieved through the 'learning industrial revolution' wherein Japanese industrialists brought together traditional factors of production with the latest information on markets, technology, and method, imbuing the process of learning with a sense of urgency, ambition, and purpose. The culmination of these efforts was an organizational ethic of learning and a corporation largely unfettered by old ideas and practices.

Due to these special circumstances, the modern corporation in Japan emerged in something less than a generation, from 1885 to 1920 or so. And, in the years between 1920 and 1980, two additional forms of the corporation appeared, the large, modern corporation, and what this book calls the interdependent form of the large, modern corporation. Together, these three forms represent basic modalities of corporate structure in Japan. Thus, during the half-century of development prior to the Pacific War and several decades after that milestone, enduring and distinguishing features of corporate organization, attributes which had evolved during a period of four centuries in the West, took hold and flourished.

These elements would include such characteristics as joint-stock ownership, easily transferable ownership, limited liability, perpetual succession of corporate officers, concentration and professionalization of management, legal personality, separation of ownership and control, a standardized method of organization and operation, as well as rules and regulations concerning public and private disclosure. Most importantly, with the passage of the Commercial Code of 1893 and its subsequent revisions, business organizations were formed in compliance with state-issued acts of incorporation and they conducted business operating under legal charters. Legal instruments defined and refined the environment, both external and internal, within which modern business forms and practices could develop and progress.

As a consequence of a highly compressed cycle of industrial, legal, and social development, Japanese firms are at odds with the history and a good deal of the economic and organizational theories of the firm as they have appeared in the West. Also, there are important differences between enterprises as to structure and function, and these differences need to be understood in the context of Japanese industrial development. This chapter summarizes the historical background for the appearance and evolution of the modern corporation and enterprise system in Japan and, thereafter, a typology is presented which characterizes the major features and varieties of industrial enterprise as they emerged in Japan.

The Distinctiveness of Early Japanese Enterprise

Four reasons stand out for the rapid and distinctive rise of the modern industrial corporation and enterprise system in Japan. First, Japan was well endowed by pre-industrial standards. This vital legacy was combined with Western business practices, technologies, and standards to push economic activities to newer and higher levels. The closely held joint-stock corporation, the publicly held corporation, the public or state corporation, as well as Western forms of limited and unlimited partnership were powerful organizing tools to channel the energies of a dynamic political economy that was steadily growing during the nineteenth century. In short, Western forms of business organization were grafted on to already well-established business practices, and this substantial underpinning clouds any simplistic explanations for Japan's more recent economic development.[7]

Second, differences, more than similarities, are germane to understanding the origins of pre-war business enterprises in Japan. Modern enterprises appeared during the latter half of the nineteenth century when differences in sources of domestic and foreign technology, modes of organization and management, markets, ideologies, government relations, finances, and a wealth of other factors were extreme. Such differences were a result of the highly decentralized but well-developed commercial character of Japanese society under Tokugawa (1603–1868) and early Meiji (1868–1911) rule, the lack of consistent government industrial and fiscal policies early on, and the vastness of choices available in the methods of business activity at the time. As a result, heterogeneity in organizational form and function as well as in products and markets typify the genesis of modern business enterprises.[8]

Heterogeneity presented choices. In spite of the later development of Japan and, thus, the assumed benefits of choosing technical trajectories with hindsight, ill-conceived and wrong-headed choices were rampant. Heterogeneity minimized the damage of such choices. Heterogeneity would not disappear substantially until economic, political, and social movements which favored centralization, standardization, and uniformity appeared in the mid-twentieth century at the peak of the second industrial era. Yet, not long thereafter, a diversity of technological, managerial, and market forces associated with the third industrial revolution were again introducing heterogeneity in corporate form and function by the end of the twentieth century.

Third, the attention given to the rise of a particular class of late-nineteenth and early- to mid-twentieth century businesses, generically referred to as the *zaibatsu*, has skewed understanding and appreciation of the modern corporation and enterprise system in Japan. *Zaibatsu* enterprises were large, diversified for their day, family-owned, and sometimes family-managed businesses that were interconnected with other similarly configured enterprises through holding companies, banks, and trading companies in loosely organized pan-business federations. *Zaibatsu* enterprises appeared late in the nineteenth century and by the 1920s, networks of *zaibatsu* enterprises were well represented within Japan and, to a considerably lesser extent, outside of the country.

There is no question of the importance of *zaibatsu* enterprises before World War Two, only of the degree of that importance. Anachronistic thinking clouds our understanding of this matter for it is the contemporary significance of what are sometimes called the successors to the *zaibatsu*, *keiretsu* enterprise groups and, to a lesser extent, *kigyo shudan* groups, that causes us to overestimate their weight in the pre-war economy. I estimate their contribution to gross domestic product, compared to other types of enterprise, before the 1930s at one-quarter to one-third.[9] (This estimate sets aside for the moment complicated definitional issues concerning the degree of separation in ownership and control characterizing various *zaibatsu* groups by the 1920s.)

That is clearly important, hugely so, but nowhere near as important as the almost exclusive attention to *zaibatsu* enterprises by scholars would suggest. *Zaibatsu* enterprises, as a result, must be considered along with independent enterprises, both urban and rural, to understand the development of modern Japanese corporations in a more balanced and accurate manner. Independent enterprises, in contrast to *zaibatsu* enterprises, commanded different resources and markets, and they had distinctive modes of relationship with prefectural and national government offices and financial institutions. In the next chapter, a typology is presented for differentiating pre-war enterprises into three sorts by the structure and nature of their activities.

Finally, an effective and consistent amalgamation of business ideas and institutions from foreign and domestic sources did not evolve until after World War Two in all likelihood. In other words, the maturation of the modern corporation and enterprise system required several generations, even though the corporation was established in its earliest form by World War One. A domestic market for consumer durables and a truly international trading and manufacturing presence did not develop until the 1960s, for example. Bright, well-trained, and ambitious university graduates did not enter major corporations by the hundreds until this time; after this, their presence, in the aggregate, transformed the managerial character of industrial enterprises. Also, labor-union structures and a more egalitarian working consciousness did not effectively penetrate the workplace before the 1950s and 1960s. Capital liberalization and the globalization of products and markets did not emerge for another decade. As a result of these monumental post-war changes occurring throughout the 1950s, 1960s, and 1970s, the chronology of enterprise development before the war has been typically de-emphasized, in spite of the fact that fundamental and determining changes in all aspects of enterprise operation and management occurred before 1945.[10]

The Institutional Context of the Corporation

In order to capture the full and rich history of the corporation in Japan, during the pre-war as well as post-war periods, a framework of chronological development is presented here and in subsequent chapters which highlights the evolution of various structural and strategic features of the Japanese enterprise system. Older companies, those with a history as long as eighty to a hundred years, may have progressed through each stage of development as outlined. Others, beginning

TABLE 2.1. *A Chronology of Evolving Hierarchy: Factory, Firm, and Interfirm Network*

Time	Enterprise type	Interfirm type	Factory type
1890–1920	modern industrial enterprise	namesake groups with commercial and financial emphases	primary factory without well-developed capabilities for scale economies
1920–55	large, modern industrial enterprise	financially based, hierarchical groups with emerging/ emergent manufacturing emphasis	secondary factory with organizational capability for scale and some scope economies; functional integration via local centralization
1955–2000	interdependent, large modern industrial enterprises	task force/product focused, reciprocity-oriented, management-intensive groups	focal factory with organizational capabilities for scale, scope, learning, transaction-cost economies; decentralized coordination

later, did not necessarily recapitulate the entire institutional history of the enterprise system. A basic hypothesis of this study is that organizations can and do learn, from others and from themselves, and this attribute is clearly manifested in the evolution of later developing industrial enterprises in Japan. The successes of earlier firms had powerful demonstration effects on later developing ones.

Also, as this book asserts in almost every chapter, the corporation in Japan must be considered along with two corresponding institutions, interfirm networks and focal factories, and thus, as the corporation has evolved, so too have these interlocking organizations. For the purposes of situating the earlier and later forms of these corresponding institutions, as they have developed in conjunction with the corporation, see the schematic Table 2.1.

For such reasons—the fortuitous combination of a vigorous domestic economy with Western business institutions; the heterogeneity of business forms and functions in pre-war, especially nineteenth-century, Japan; the comparative weight of *zaibatsu* as well as non-*zaibatsu* enterprises before World War Two; and, the importance of chronology in understanding the developmental process of the Japanese enterprise system—a description and a typology of pre-war Japanese enterprise attributes are needed. This chapter offers a historical sketch of the social and economic conditions within which industrialization and the stages of corporate development occurred in Japan. In the next chapter a typology is presented which synthesizes these characteristics and provides a description and explanation of the ways in which three types of enterprises evolved.

Origins: The Emergence of a Modern Enterprise System

Pre-industrial Economy and Population

The more recent successes of Japanese business cannot be understood without appreciating Japan before Commodore Perry, that is before the Western world unceremoniously forced its way into Japan in 1853. Before Perry, at least compared to the rest of Asia and even compared with much of the Western world, Japan was already highly developed economically, rather urbanized, reasonably well administered, and culturally advanced.

Japan, like many of the Western European nations and to a much lesser extent the United States, was commercialized long before it was industrialized. For more than 250 years, during the Tokugawa era (1603–1868), the domestic economy had been commercialized, monetized, and specialized in the production and distribution of a variety of agricultural and non-agricultural goods and services.[11] Furthermore, a domestic commercial revolution was coupled with the country's thousand-year-old traditions of local and central government, regional and national culture, as well as a basic transformation of Japan's social, economic, demographic, and political systems during the Tokugawa regime. The success of Japan's jump-start industrialization was predicated on this pre-industrial progress.

In spite of the complexity of Japan's commercialized economy prior to industrialization, per capita income was considerably lower than in the leading industrial nations of the West until fairly recently (the 1970s). Ryoshin Minami estimates that per capita income at the start of modern economic development was typically two to three times lower than in the West, and that even this lower figure was realized from two to three decades later in Japan than in Western countries (see Table 2.2).

Notwithstanding that Japan's per capita income was lower than in the West (although higher than anywhere else in Asia), per capita income was concentrated in ways beneficial to the economy. An unusually large percentage of the total population was found in urban places—estimated at about 22 percent in 1750 and higher thereafter—and, as a result, unusually large shares of gross national expenditures were concentrated there.[12] In addition, Tokyo (Edo), perhaps the largest city in the world in the eighteenth century, exceeded one million inhabitants, while Osaka and Kyoto, pushed well beyond the half-million mark. Another dozen or so cities topped 100,000 and several dozens more dotted the landscape in the 40–50,000 range. So, not only was the urban population unusually large for a pre-industrial country but also it was well distributed, unlike the complete dominance of London or Paris in their lands at the same time. The widespread

TABLE 2.2. *Per Capita Income at the Start of Modern Economic Development* (1965 dollars)

Japan	$136 (in 1886)
America	$474 (in 1834–43)
Holland	$347 (in 1831–40)
Germany	$302 (in 1850–9)
France	$242 (in 1831–40)
England	$227 (in 1765–85)
Sweden	$215 (in 1861–9)

Source: Ryoshin Minami, *Nihon no Keizai Hatten* (The Economic Development of Japan) (Tokyo: Toyo Keizai Shinposha, 1981), 3.

distribution of urban places in Japan minimized the contrasts between urban and rural, a division which often characterizes patterns of social and economic development in pre-industrial and early industrial states. Also, the concentration of expenditures in an unusually well-developed system of towns gathered and accumulated economic transactions there, and this minimized the negative consequences of Japan's low per capita income. Six to seven million of Japan's pre-industrial population, out of thirty million, were in cities.

The number and distribution of urban places during the Tokugawa period encouraged the development of an elaborate network for the movement and marketing of goods between and within regions and cities. Land and water transportation routes culminated in a national system of urban places and these contributed to an already considerable volume of urban economic transactions. Retailers, wholesalers, and 'national brokers' (*nakagai*) were numerous; commerce and distribution were everywhere highly developed.[13] Marketing of agricultural and non-agricultural products existed at local, regional, and national levels, and most sales and transportation channels remained viable even after the collapse of the Tokugawa Government in 1867. An extensive infrastructure for distribution and marketing gave scope to the economy.

In addition, government policy and action, both before and increasingly after the Meiji Restoration of 1868, increased economic activity in urban areas by focusing investment there, regulating those markets, and improving the physical infrastructure as well as social-overhead capital located in urban areas. Although such government actions were not always welcomed, effective, or well considered, the cumulative result of a great deal of private economic activity occurring within an institutional framework of public as well as private design created an economic environment of unusual activity and size. In public and private ways, therefore, the negative consequences of Japan's low per capita income at the start of industrialization were partially offset.

In spite of the concentration of higher-order economic activities in cities, it is thought that much of the countryside prospered, sometimes at the expense of cities, by a steady if gradual accumulation of economic resources. By the end of the Tokugawa era, it is estimated that many farmers, tenants as well as landed, derived as much as one-half of their income from non-agricultural pursuits in commerce, transportation, and household industry; many lived comfortably, dressed and ate well, could read and write. Warriors and other urban dwellers commented with increasing disfavor on the accumulating countryside wealth although, in fact, much of the rural wealth was recycled through the system of towns.[14] Nevertheless, most warriors viewed an expanding economy with hostility and even as a disgrace: their sources of income were fixed while those of commoners were increasing in absolute as well as relative terms.

Most significantly, the concentration and growth of economic activity, income, and investment during the eighteenth and nineteenth centuries were not wiped out by a concomitant growth in population.[15] In spite of the relatively large size of the Japanese population at that time (large relative to England, France, and the United States), the press of people on resources was contained. Expansion in the agricultural and commercial economy and productivity improvements (through the use of more and better fertilizers or the enhanced efficiency of coastal shipping, for example) were not dissipated by an equal or offsetting growth in population.

Japan's pre-industrial economic development was not Malthusian in nature, in spite of occasional and violent mortality crises. Critical over-population was avoided, it appears, due to an absence of a strict religious ban on infanticide and abortion. Population control by these means provided a basis for the accumulation of wealth in stem family structures, *ie*, where descent, inheritance, and management of household matters were not determined solely by blood relations. Instead, the concept of a household as a functional grouping of persons cooperating for mutual benefit became common.

Although there was nothing akin to the modern industrial corporation during the Tokugawa period, the concept and, more importantly, the practice of business in an institutional sense was well understood and developed. The stem household, *ie*, and variations on the household theme constituted the basic unit of business administration, and such modern institutional practices as perpetual succession, decentralized forms of business organization, and functional specialization were all accommodated within the concept of a household engaged in one or several lines of commercial activity.

Thomas C. Smith's research has emphasized the social and economic pre-eminence of the household in pre-modern Japan in three ways. First, families, naturally more unified and motivated than non-kin-based economic groupings, were quicker to take advantage of productivity-enhancing methods, tools, and ideas. Second, the internal cohesion and discipline of families allowed a fuller exploitation of employment opportunities. Finally, the smaller size of family groupings widened rather than restricted possibilities for economic, social, and individual development because of the nature of wet-rice agriculture, the predominant farm crop. Wet-rice agriculture seemingly skirts the law of diminishing returns by offering consistently high returns on increasing labor inputs.[16] Also, a modified form of primogeniture practiced by Japanese farming households allowed for both the accumulation of resources within family units while, at the same time, unneeded human and material resources were released for alternative investments. The rural economy remained vigorous because of, not in spite of, the growth and proliferation of cities.

It is often argued that the concept of a household as the core of business activity continues even today, and this may be taken as evidence of the attractiveness and pervasiveness of the household analogy in Japanese business organization.[17] It is true that the obviously paternalistic content of contemporary business ideology aims to engender an emotional as well as economic identification with the firm, and this strikes a responsive chord with Tokugawa business practices. None the less, in terms of structural differentiation and functional specialization, today's enterprises owe little to former household forms of business organization.[18] In particular, there was nothing in pre-industrial or even late-nineteenth-century Japan that rivals the scale of today's businesses, compares with the sophistication of their methods of manufacture and management, or presages their personnel policies. All evidence suggests little or no institutional carry-over from pre-modern to modern business practices.[19] An ideological transfer is more likely, although the conscious linking of family imagery with modern industrial enterprise appears late, sometime after the turn of the twentieth century.

The pervasiveness of the household form and its importance as a pre-industrial business institution were well suited to the acclaimed omnipresence and omnipotence of government in business. Indeed, a prolonged economic ascent during this era may be traced largely to the frugality and diligence of rural and urban householders on the one hand, and less so to central and local government activities and policies on the other. The ability of government to exert its power over peasants, merchants, and the market-place was sporadic and uneven, and government's mastery of the economy was more legal than actual. Households prospered as a partial result.

While the direct impact of government on business was moot, the indirect impact of local, regional, and national government on business was great. Tax and transportation policies, defense and education spending, market and monetary regulation, all acted to induce a kind of government-supported infrastructure for the economic activities of individuals and households. So while the government's *de jure* authority was recognized by all who bought and sold in the market-place, government's *de facto* authority was far less impressive. Nevertheless, in spite of the periodic, piecemeal, and largely legal nature of government control in the market, lip-service to state involvement in the economy created an important and widespread precedent for later and more effective government regulation of the economy by the end of the nineteenth century.

Government claims to economic authority were often transmitted and enforced through guild and trade associations. These have a long history, even pre-dating the founding of the Tokugawa regime. But the *miyaza* (religious guilds) and *kabu-*

nakama associations (commercial monopolies) of local and regional origin, for example, which were founded before the seventeenth century, were forced to align themselves with the unquestioned authority of the Tokugawa Government after that time. New associations were likewise legitimated by central or local government imprimatur. Indeed, government encouraged such associations for they served a dual purpose of providing revenue in the form of licensing fees and commodity-specific taxes, and of regulating markets in the absence of government's ability to do so directly.

Pre-industrial Political and Social Change

Economic growth and development, population regulation, and a kind of helter-skelter management of the economy were accompanied by noteworthy political and social transformations. The Tokugawa regime (*bakufu*) was a federation of some several hundred local domains, each ruled by a *daimyo* or a lord and his retainers, and each integrated to greater or lesser degrees into regional or national political and economic systems. Politically, a weakening of the power but not so much the authority of the central government allowed scores of lesser local governments the opportunity to experiment with all sorts of economic and social changes. Local governments were able to innovate in such areas as monetary policy, fiscal incentives for growing and marketing agricultural commodities, local and regional market regulation, and general matters of political economy.

As a result of the large number of local jurisdictions (over 200) and a plethora of local initiatives, local leaders, who were uniformly from the service class of warriors, had ample opportunity to make and implement their own decisions, and to develop a taste and, occasionally, a talent for politics. Thus, on the eve of industrialization, Japan already had a class of administrators, the *bushi* or warriors, who constituted a large percentage of the population (around 6 percent), some of whom were well educated, knowledgeable about political matters, and experienced in local decision-making. Unfortunately, many warriors proved to be not particularly good businessmen.

Socially, a weakening of class distinctions within the warrior class as well as within and between other social classes allowed for considerable social mobility by the late eighteenth and early nineteenth centuries. At the same time, a loosening of controls on the movement of local populations permitted extensive geographical mobility. The combination of social and geographical mobility, albeit within the confines of a pre-industrial society, stimulated aspirations, ambitions, curiosity, and creativity.[20] Pre-industrial Japan during the Tokugawa period was anything but static, rigid, and uniform in matters of taste, life-style, and life opportunities.

In numerous other ways, Japan was changing. Intellectually, a variety of schools of philosophical and political thought competed for adherents. Many different kinds and styles of artistic activity were championed and mutually tolerated, and the most popular and unconventional of these were expressions of the urban and rural common classes. An estimated 40 percent of the population received some amount of formal education by the middle of the nineteenth century, with nearly 60 percent of men and 15 percent of women able to read, write, and do simple arithmetic.[21]

Japan was healthy, relative to other Asian and some European countries. New but limited research suggests that mortality levels and age-specific marital fertility of the registered population were on a par with or below European levels before industrialization.[22] Cities were clean and individuals had high standards of personal hygiene. Health and hygiene had much to do with Shinto's emphasis on cleanliness. Age-specific mortality data indicate an unusually vigorous and vital population.[23] Production technologies associated with the common endeavors of wet-rice agriculture, silk-spinning, and traditional shipbuilding were highly developed, and overall the technologies of production and distribution in Japan compared favorably with similar technologies employed in China and elsewhere in Asia.

In short, Japan was a country of progress in economic, political, technological, social, and cultural matters before industrialization. Yet because of the prior industrialization of some Western nations and Japan's geographical isolation from Western currents of change, Japan was a relatively backward country in firearms, global navigation, international diplomacy, and factory-based manufacturing. In these areas, Japan would have to do a lot of catching up.

But the fact that Japan did catch up and rather handily at that may be attributed in large part to the internal developments which occurred prior to industrialization. Some have referred to this as 'development before development' or as 'proto-industrialization'.[24] This is a useful distinction as long as one does not assume that pre- or proto-industrial means backward in matters of polity, economy, and society. Japan was certainly not backward, and accordingly, the outlines of a framework which favored the appearance of modern economic institutions was largely in place when the first Western businessmen and their products materialized during the latter half of the nineteenth century.

Evolution: Three Business Traditions

Three major business traditions emerge during the Tokugawa period (1603–1868) and these remain the most important lines of business development until the watershed of World War Two. These traditions were associated with national, or what would become *zaibatsu* enterprise, urban enterprise, and local enterprise. Distinctions between the last two—urban and local—begin to disappear during the inter-war period bracketed by World Wars One and Two as improving transportation, better manufacturing technology, access to core financial institutions, and a growing professionalization of management make the urban/rural dimension less salient. By the Pacific War, therefore, the tripartite division of enterprises outlined here was telescoped into a two-tiered economy of *national* firms (both new and old *zaibatsu*) and independent, generally smaller enterprises. Surprisingly enough, only one tradition, national or *zaibatsu* enterprise, has received much attention by scholars, while urban enterprise and especially rural enterprise have received far less notice than they deserve.

Onset of Industrialization

At the earliest stage of modern economic development, Japan's industries were few in number, small in size, on-again off-again in operations, and quite unsophisticated in terms of manufacturing technology. Especially in the countryside, small, seasonal, undercapitalized, handicraft ventures were common. In most cases, rural enterprises were simply household endeavors that had been expanded into something more substantial. Yet rural ventures were important because a majority of the population lived in the countryside and most of the nation's capital, human resources, and technical and business know-how were located there.

The modern enterprise system begins to emerge during the decade following the Meiji Restoration of 1868 as the government's economic stance changed from a traditional posture concerned primarily with regulation to one obsessed with development. Once internal political rivalries and external diplomatic relations were put in order, the Meiji leaders embarked on an ambitious and far-reaching reform of the political economy during the 1870s.

Actually, a number of new industrial efforts already existed, many of which were inspired by the West and financed by local and regional government bodies. Most of these ventures were still rural, because that was where resources were concentrated, and they were government-initiated for the most part because government alone could afford the costs of imported technology, buying plant and equipment, securing and training workers, and finding markets for new manufactures.[25] The first modern cotton mill employing about 200 workers was established by the Lord of Satsuma in 1867, on the advice of his secretary, Seiryu Ishikawa, a so-called Dutch scholar or specialist in foreign affairs. Three years later, the same Lord opened an even larger factory in Sakai under the direct supervision of Ishikawa.[26]

During the 1870s, the national government, continuing the practice of local lords, initiated numerous industrial endeavors in mining, transportation, communications, and manufacturing. The experiences of Hisashige Tanaka, a local inventor, entrepreneur, and government contractor, illustrates the fragile, often government-centered, character of Japan's early industrialization. Tanaka was invited to Tokyo in 1873, the national capital since the fall of the shogun five years earlier. The still-struggling Meiji Government charged Tanaka with the critical task of developing Morse telegraphic equipment. Otherwise a crucially important infrastructure of national and regional communications would be monopolized by equipment of foreign manufacture and design.

Tanaka's reputation for invention preceded him. As a youth in the Kurume

Domain on the southern island of Kyushu, Tanaka was called the 'puppet genius' for the mechanical marionettes, illumination devices, astronomically accurate, moving models of the heavens, and time-keeping mechanisms that he invented. Tanaka's mechanical aptitude was considered an oddity for most of his life, until at the age of 54, Lord Kanso Nabeshima invited him to Saga Domain where he fabricated cannon, armaments, communications equipment, and even a 60-foot steamer for the Lord. Called back to Kurume, Tanaka engineered the take-off of an armaments industry there until summoned to Tokyo in 1873.

After completing several orders for telegraphic devices from the Meiji Government, Tanaka opened Japan's first telegraphic equipment factory in July 1875, the same year that Alexander Graham Bell invented the telephone. This was the forerunner of today's immense Toshiba Corporation, although at the time, Tanaka's combined office, shop, and residence in the Shinbashi district of Tokyo measured just 80 square meters. Tanaka enjoyed three years of unending success as a designated production facility for the Ministry of Industry, until in 1878, the Government decided to put the important function of manufacturing communications equipment directly under its own control. Thereafter, Tanaka hustled orders for general-purpose machinery and communications gear until he died nearly four years later in November 1881 at the age of 82.[27]

Aside from strategically important ventures, such as arsenals, shipyards, and Tanaka's telegraphic equipment, cotton- and silk-spinning were the most common industrial investments supported by the Government. Government took the lead in these efforts because it alone could afford the sizeable and coordinated investments they required. An iron foundry, for example, demanded investment not only in smelter plant and equipment but also in road, rail, and perhaps harbor facilities, as well as in raw and intermediate materials.

At the same time, would-be industrialists watched government-sponsored efforts with fascination as they themselves experimented in limited ways with new technologies, products, and markets. But the fence-sitting ended after 1883 when the Osaka Cotton Mill was founded. This was a mammoth enterprise for its day, commanding a capital of 280,000 yen with ninety-five shareholders, 60 percent of whom were Osaka and Tokyo merchants. Only one-fifth or one-tenth the scale of contemporary Lancashire cotton mills, the Osaka Cotton Mill's 10,500 spindles were marvelous and enormous for the day. The mill ran both day and night shifts, and it showed a profit from its first year of operation. Takeo Yamanobe, an ex-samurai who trained in economics at the University of London and textile engineering at King's College, administered the mill as the 'engineering manager' (*komu-shihainin*). The advantages of engineering-oriented management and joint-stock company organization were readily apparent.[28] Across the country businessmen rushed to emulate the Osaka Cotton Mill.

A change in national leadership after 1868 brought the scrapping of traditional licensing and market-regulating agreements, and long-favored urban merchants scrambled to secure new lines of government-commissioned business. Concurrently, model factories and industrial endeavors were initiated and sometimes subsidized by the Government. The Meiji Government, in effect, assumed a dramatically activist role in promoting, cajoling, and furthering modern business. This was in sharp contrast with accepted practice during the Tokugawa era, although even then there were numerous instances of local government's encouragement of new business activities. However, by the 1870s the later industrial take-off of Japan, relative to the industrially advanced countries of Western Europe and North America, resulted in a frenzied paranoia over Japan's relative economic backwardness and in a certain degree of strategic advantage as Japan's leaders attempted to pick and choose from among the already established Western manufacturing technologies and products.

Throughout the early years of the Meiji era, the Government at both the national and prefectural levels encouraged new trade and distribution associations, generally known as *dogyo kumiai*, to help clear the way for the introduction and dissemination of Western technology, more modern management methods, commercial law, and practical education. Though the government's use and encouragement of such groups was similar in spirit to the regulatory role of business played by Tokugawa authorities, the Meiji leadership was much more direct and constructive in its efforts to stimulate the economy. For example, the Government published fairly detailed handbooks on incorporating private enterprises in 1871 and on banking in 1872 and 1876.[29] As a result of government promotion, a rush of new bank incorporations swept Japan from 1876 to 1879, doing much to diffuse the idea of joint-stock incorporation in the process. Indeed, until 1893, when a new commercial code was enacted, the Government provided a wide variety of incentives, including direct subsidies, to stimulate business starts. By the mid- to late 1870s, therefore, the Government had created a business climate which was on the whole conducive to investment, innovation, and risk-taking even though its policies were not always consistent, fair, or effective.

The Meiji Government's pioneering efforts to foster business development and its support for trade and industry, nevertheless, were not radical acts in themselves because of precedents for both sorts of activities established during the Tokugawa period. The differences were found in the overtly patriotic and nationalistic motivations of Meiji leaders and businessmen, a more rigorous business climate as a result of foreign and heightened domestic competition, and a quickened pace of market and technological opportunities. These circumstances plus a natural desire to 'catch up' quickly with the West prompted the appearance of what Alexander Gerschenkron called 'late development effects'. A few of these were:

1. a larger role for the state in economic organization,
2. more centralized and coordinated investment strategies with state planning as a critical variable,
3. closer cooperation between government and business in the establishment and management of national industries,
4. greater stress on producers' rather than consumers' goods with more production going to the state,

5. the rate of economic growth varies directly with the degree of industrial backwardness and indirectly with a slow evolution from the putting-out system to the factory system.[30]

Nevertheless, most new ventures failed for lack of capital, know-how, and/or practical experience. A sharp discontinuity in industrial technology between traditional practices and Western methods of production almost guaranteed that industrial ventures would be unsuccessful. Fortunately, a diversity of efforts and ambitions meant that failure of one or even many ventures did not scuttle the entire enterprise. This was as true for public as for private concerns which were greater in number if more limited in size than government-backed efforts. The difference was that government-initiated businesses were gauged as much by what they contributed to the public well-being as by the amount of money they made (or lost). The earliest government successes, say in the 1870s, initially came in railroad- and telegraph-construction ventures even while these efforts were quite limited in scale. None the less, railroad and telegraph lines were visually impressive, everyone understood the immense cost and effort associated with such undertakings and their strategic and economic importance. In these circumstances, normal cost–benefit considerations are not the point.

But the Meiji Government did not have deep pockets, and private capital was cautious and dispersed. Once the initial imperative for a 'rich country and strong army' diminished, the Government could ill afford many of its model factories and pet industrial projects. Showcase schemes of the 1870s were frequently auctioned off to the highest bidder in the 1880s. The separation of politics and economics, prompted by government indebtedness and, some would say, mismanagement, forced an increasing sophistication of business methods in the private sector. The denationalization of government enterprises laid the basis for an emergence of modern managerial enterprises.

None the less, even after the sell-off of government-backed ventures, modern business methods and institutions did not appear overnight. Shrewd and wary urban merchants and conservative country businessmen were content to change as little as necessary: perhaps to trade some foreign goods, to buy some railroad stock, to tinker with a new technology, such as steam power for manufacturing, or just to watch and wait. The beginnings of industrialization in Japan were not impressive, except in the number of business failures, the poor choices made and the wrong turns taken.

It is important, therefore, not to forget or to minimize the difficulties of Japan's initial run at industrialization. The eventual, powerful demonstration of Japanese economic development often obscures the difficulties encountered along the way. People inside and outside the Government were confused, precious money and resources were wasted, accomplishments of lasting substance and value were few and far between. But, most importantly, a start had been made. More accurately, many starts had been made, because the decentralized character of the economy and polity in the 1860s and 1870s meant that all over the country different sorts of people were experimenting with a variety of new and traditional business methods and models. Those not experimenting themselves were intensely curious and observant of those who were. Changes in attitude and practice were apparent.

Transition Period

This transitional period, between what had been appropriate but was still largely traditional and what was modern but not yet successful, lasted for a generation or so. Basically, the period between 1870 and 1900 was one of experimentation, innovation, and incremental progress in most industries and enterprises. It would be mistaken, therefore, to assume that Japan's early industrial development, especially that part of it falling between the introduction of the factory system and the appearance of modern management, was easy, quickly traversed, and characterized by a clear vision and a firm hand.

Accordingly, it is essential to distinguish between the beginnings of industrialization and the appearance of a modern management philosophy and practice in Japan. The fits and starts at the first phase of industrial development and even the early successes with the factory system were not synonymous or congruent with managerial capitalism, which does not appear until the debut of the modern corporation in the early twentieth century. Indeed, a modern managerial system characterized by complex, multi-unit organization, sophisticated accounting and production controls, and above all by a well-developed managerial hierarchy does not emerge until World War One or thereafter.

Critical distinctions must be raised, therefore, between the appearance of the factory system, the establishment of industrial corporations, and the full-blown arrival of what are the main subject of this book—large, modern, managerially intensive corporations. Chronologically, the factory system is in place by the late nineteenth century, the first industrial enterprises by the early twentieth century, and modern, large corporations by World War One and the inter-war period. In all cases, these distinctions relate to the size, complexity, and sophistication of the managerial hierarchies that governed production and distribution activities in industrial enterprises.

There was a sharp break in management practices with the establishment of modern corporations. Modern corporations represent a stage of development where organizational learning became paramount, that is when internalized and institutionalized routines, methods, and processes superseded idiosyncratic, expedient, and frankly entrepreneurial measures. Newer organizational forms were only weakly connected with past institutions, although there was a considerable degree of interaction and even borrowing between them. To disregard that interaction is to deny the importance of organizational learning.

Traditional practices and institutions provided an important foundation for the appearance of modern practices, and, even more importantly, it was through the clash and combination of the old and the new that alternative forms of industrial structure and strategy were created. For example, because owners of the early joint-stock companies, especially the omnipresent cotton-spinning companies, were typically merchants and former warriors, they were personally unfamiliar with Western manufacturing technology and factory-management techniques. They fought often and sometimes heatedly with overseas-trained Japanese who were hired to supervise the actual transfer and implementation of Western industrial technology into Japan after 1880.[31]

From the turn of the century, as a consequence, a considerable rift opened in factory organization between primary and secondary factories, in the terminology of this book. Primary factories were sites of production where for the first time factors of production were gathered in one location. While capital was invested and people were collected in one site, there were no real managers to systematically organize, assess, plan, and supervise production. Instead, labor contractors, job bosses, and other intermediaries in the production process held sway, and internal contracting characterized the organization and management of these primary factories. Mediation instead of management was the rule.

The interjection of managers into factories, of assembly-line methods of manufacture, and of modern management into factory organization came anywhere from the close of the nineteenth century to the first quarter of the twentieth. These developments ushered in secondary factories. A possible exception to this chronology were leading cotton-textile firms which from the late 1880s were already characterized by managerial hierarchies, emergent economies of scale, and modern accounting methods. These were well-developed functional organizations.

The early transition of cotton-textile firms may be contrasted with the deliberate, difficult, and delayed transition of most other enterprises where mobile workers, labor-gang bosses, ensconced foremen, book-trained technicians, and university graduates battled for ascendancy in the workplace. Firms failed left and right, industry shake-outs were rife. Answers were found fairly quickly or not at all.

As a result of the speed of Japan's industrial development, friction and conflict between entrenched bosses and modern-minded supervisors as well as between traditionally minded owners and technologically trained engineers, the joint-stock company in Japan moved fairly quickly to a stage where ownership and management were largely separated. By the early twentieth century in most instances, owners were retreating from active, day-to-day management, while engineers and others with a social- or natural-science education were serving increasingly as the chief officers and board members of the more successful joint-stock companies. Factories moved away from being simple sites of primary production to more technologically sophisticated and better managed sites of secondary production. In factories and firms, members of a new managerial hierarchy of engineers, technicians, bookkeepers, and personnel officers were actually making decisions and taking action though often not legally authorized to do so; however, their training, inclination, and ambition hurried them to these purposes.[32]

The Emergence of Modern Industrial Enterprise

The early retreat of owners from management had several noteworthy effects. First, there was not a prolonged period of anti-owner/anti-capitalist feeling on the part of either labor or management. An entrenched, bitter, and necessarily adversarial attitude, focused around the issue of enterprise ownership, did not sink deep roots in Japan. Second, once technically trained engineers and managers gained control of joint-stock companies, they were usually quick to liberalize enterprise finances. They had already recognized that the wherewithal provided by traditionally minded owners was insufficient for a great leap forward in the means and methods of industrial management. In order to raise sufficient financial resources, share-holding was broadened from scores to hundreds, and from hundreds to thousands. This hastened the separation of ownership and management.

Changes in tax laws further accelerated the separation. Matao Miyamoto has argued that the initial tax law of 1899 and its revisions in 1905, 1913, and 1920, created a progressive tax system in which the incidence of taxation fell most heavily on personal wealth. Joint-stock companies gained ground in part to thwart a progressive tax burden. Especially after the 1920 revision in which taxes were levied on dividends and bonuses paid to individuals, family-controlled firms adopted the joint-stock form of ownership as a means of reducing taxes.[33]

Third, an emergence of university-trained and often Western-seasoned managers transferred the locus of top decision-making and -ratification from the Board of Directors (*torishimari-yakukai*) to the lower-level Committees of Senior and Managing Executive Directors (*jomukai* and *senmukai*) which appeared after the turn of the century. Board members were often investors with little knowledge and experience in actually running a business, especially one that depended on Western method and technique. As a consequence, factory managers and general managers, without a substantial stake in the enterprise but crucial to the ongoing success of the business, were elevated to positions of authority, handsomely rewarded, and eagerly recruited. Committees of Senior and Managing Executive Directors became fulcrums of organizational power for a rising class of professional managers.[34]

Finally, once traditionally minded owners and methods of management, such as the internal-contracting system, were moved aside, engineers and technicians were frequently found on the shop-floor, directly supervising the process of technology transfer.[35] Those familiar with Western methods of manufacture, through class-room and practical experience, recognized that shop-floor personnel could not hope to cope with the theory and application of Western knowledge without super-vision, collaboration, and consultation.

Even so, due to a lack of practical experience classroom-trained engineers often overestimated the amount of time and expense that particular jobs and orders would require and they overlooked opportunities for transforming experience into learning. Yet the process of technology transfer required the adaptation of foreign technology to Japanese materials, know-how, and market circumstances. Neither engineers nor workers could make decisions independently on how and when to do so. So, once an increasingly large cadre of technically minded engineers and managers displaced initial owners and traditional foremen, patterns of technology transfer based on close cooperation between engineers, technicians, and shop-floor personnel came to describe early-twentieth-century joint-stock companies. This may be attributed, at least in part, to a late-development effect whereby theory and practice had to be joined within a relatively brief period of time.

As a result of an accelerated process of institutional development and a displacement of past practices by the latest thinking on enterprise organization, traditional labor—management practices offered weak resistance to the ongoing thrust of enterprise advance. Importantly, a reticent, disinclined, foreman class of workers did not maintain their power and authority in the workplace. Because traditional foremen, who went by such names as *oyakata*, *shoya*, and *toji*, had neither the technical nor managerial skills needed to mediate the introduction of modern production methods, they were swept aside in a rush to erect modern factories and enterprises in Japan.[36] Between 1900 and 1920 technically trained engineers were hired by the hundreds and thousands in newly emerging industrial enterprises and traditional craftsmen and labor bosses were displaced in equal or greater numbers. Without tradition-minded workers and foremen resisting change, managers and engineers devised whatever organizational structures and routines appeared promising.

As mentioned already, the first enterprises to take root and grow in Japanese soil may be classified into three generic types: *zaibatsu*, independent urban, and independent rural. As the characteristics of each are rather different, it is necessary to distinguish the strategic and structural features of each, as described and analyzed in the next chapter.

Comparative Perspectives on Organizational Forms and Attributes

Patterns of government—business relations as well as of social effects on organizational form are clearly evident in the history of the modern corporation both in Japan and in the United States. The patterns found in North America, in particular, have provided a model for corporate development world-wide because of the power and influence of American corporations and because American firms are the most studied and best understood in the world. But now, a new model, that of the Japanese enterprise system, is emerging and in the process challenging common archetypes of industrial organization and the environments within which industrial structures and strategies evolve.

A brief reflection on the interaction of environmental and organizational dynamics in the American and Japanese cases, therefore, may clarify some of the important issues underlying the American and Japanese business systems. In the United States as well as the industrialized Western world more generally, firms tend to integrate new corporate initiatives as divisions or as wholly-owned subsidiaries within the same governance structure. In either case, firms are large with many functional and product spheres of activity.

Oliver E. Williamson has called the multidivisional firm as 'American capitalism's most important single innovation in the twentieth century'.[37] It is important to recognize the exceptional circumstances that colored the society within which multidivisional corporations emerged. The following six features of the American business landscape in the nineteenth century profoundly altered the circumstances of the appearance and evolution of modern industrial enterprises in the twentieth century.

1. Immense natural wealth. There were and are few countries blessed with the natural resources of the United States, and these, it should be remembered, were almost entirely undeveloped until the beginning of the nineteenth century.

2. Absence of an entrenched commercial and government structure. In every developed country today, with the exception of the United States, Canada, New Zealand, and Australia, a pre-existing and pre-industrial commercial and government structure played a critical and formative role in the process of industrialization.

3. High per capita income combined with a rapidly growing population. At the turn of the twentieth century, the United States had achieved a remarkable and unprecedented feat: combining rapid population growth from both natural increase and immigration with the highest per capita income in the world. The result was a higher rate of growth in aggregate product in the United States than in the European countries.[38] By 1900, moreover, half of the population was concentrated in urban areas, resulting in a new age of mass consumption, production, and distribution.

4. A large and reliable market for industrial and corporate securities. By the end of the nineteenth century, financial instruments to fuel industrial growth were well accepted and widely traded. Securities and bonds were first developed to pay for road and turnpike construction (1830s and 1840s), a canal system (1840s and 1850s), and a railroad system (1850s to 1870s). With this legacy, industrial corporations could raise capital easily and safely in public stock-exchanges without relying excessively on bank credit or government capital.

5. Strategic importance of a national railway system. The railway system in the United States developed largely without government investment, management, or regulation. The lessons of speed, specialization, and coordination learned during the era of railroad expansion in the mid-nineteenth century were transferred to the management of new private industrial enterprises after that time.

6. The appearance of anti-trust and anti-monopoly legislation. In 1890 the Sherman Antitrust Act was passed by Congress. It held that all combinations in restraint of trade were illegal. After 1911 the Supreme Court adopted the

so-called 'rule of reason' whereby anti-trust laws were applied to those combinations that were thought to result in unreasonable restraint of trade. Finally in 1914 the Clayton Act and the Federal Trade Commission Act were passed to prohibit certain types of price discrimination and tying contracts, as well as to regulate holding-company activities and interlocking directorates.

While it is clear that the multidivisional form of organization, which appeared in the United States as a partial response to the circumstances outlined above, can be imitated, promoted, and transferred to very different business environments, the consequences of that transfer for resulting organizational forms must be necessarily different. Environmental conditions enveloping the emergence of the American multinational firm cannot be repeated elsewhere.[39]

Business–Government Relations in Japan: Timing and Balance

By the same token, the emergence of the modern corporation in Japan was reshaping the nature of the economy and the character of economic competition there. The legal advantages of the corporation, when coupled with the superior financial, technological, and human resources that the corporation could command, pushed aside earlier and less efficient forms of economic organization. Although household and family-based businesses would continue to be the most common institutional expression of economic activity in Japan (as elsewhere in the world), family businesses, even those adopting the corporate form, could not long compete with modern, joint-stock enterprises.

Such companies offered superior performance based on a managerial hierarchy. The essence of competition in an industrial society is managerial or administrative coordination. Coordination, in this sense, refers to planning the flows and functions associated with processes of industrial production and distribution. The culmination of coordination comes when production runs full and steady with very little inventory. This is the responsibility of management.

Cooperation, by contrast, centers on the legal, financial, political, and social environment within which industrial coordination occurs. In industrial Japan, competition flourishes to an extraordinary degree and this may be because coordination and cooperation are so widely and effectively interrelated. Each is independently valued and yet all are promoted and integrated.

Coordination defines the interactions that take place within corporate divisions, departments, and factories, between corporations, suppliers, and buyers, and, most importantly in Japan, between corporations and their close organizational correlates. This coordination defines the vital essence of enterprise and industrial development within the course of Japan's economic transformation *since* World War One. Cooperation characterizes the ties between corporations and less closely related economic institutions, such as trade associations, government–business interactions, and non-competing businesses.

Because of the forced opening of Japan by the Western powers and an imperiled quality to the development of state and enterprise, there has always been an implicit and mutual recognition that the state-championed domestic business institutions and, in return, the progress and well-being of the Japanese enterprise system promoted the national welfare. Probably the development of no other industrial nation has been distinguished by as much parity, reciprocity, and mutuality of means and ends between business and government.

Government and enterprises were newly hewn at the close of the nineteenth century; neither preceded the other in a temporal or material sense. Notwithstanding government's more public and dramatic role, agricultural and industrial enterprises grounded, funnelled, and propelled Japan's structural and strategic transformation of the economic order. In truth, government and enterprise co-evolved, and for this reason both cooperation and coordination were accorded equal weight in the emerging framework which defined the nature of competition in modern Japan.

In the United States, by contrast, large-scale business enterprise preceded comparable scale in government institutions by at least a generation. Significant managerial hierarchies appeared before the turn of the twentieth century in railroad and industrial enterprises while, at the federal level, government officers were few in number and administrative hierarchies simple and unadorned. Alfred Chandler, Jr. argues that in no other industrial country were large managerial hierarchies in private industry created so extensively and so early before the appearance of comparably large and complex hierarchies in government. Lateness of growth in big government was accompanied by suspicion towards an already daunting presence of big business. Suspicion, rivalry, and self-righteousness resulted in regulatory legislation, such as the Interstate Commerce Act of 1887 and the Sherman and Clayton Antitrust Acts of 1890 and 1914.[40]

But in Japan, the development and early transformation of government was paralleled by a comparable growth and evolution in private enterprise. In some areas of social authority and control, government activities may have preceded the development of enterprise, but in others enterprises were clearly the pioneer.[41] In particular, manufacturing corporations as private organizations could acquire and exploit most of the benefits accruing from economies of scale without government help (save the passage of general incorporation laws), unlike transportation industries where eminent domain, high capital-output ratios, and public-welfare issues were paramount.[42] Also a widespread emphasis on in-company training appears related to government's decision to emphasize universal primary schooling over higher-level education. Enterprises, by necessity, created a wide variety of on-the-job and in-company educational activities to supplement and supplant what the government offered (or failed to offer).[43]

The dynamics of government–business co-evolution were underscored by a relative equality of action and importance in rebuilding the nation following Japan's disastrous defeat in World War Two. Co-evolution in roles occurred not once but twice. At either time, government's roles were many: representative of the people, protector of the people, regulator, trouble-shooter, leader, promoter, and adviser. Yet strong political leadership and programs are ineffective without equally strong economic performance and promise. And this was the job of business, abetted and occasionally directed by government, but nevertheless the work of business and business leaders.[44]

This is not to argue that government direction, regulation, and promotion have been unimportant. Rather, it is to contend that the role of government in the economy, both directly and indirectly, has been so often emphasized that the creative, innovative, and risk-taking character of modern management has been undeservedly minimized. Government's non-involvement in the private ordering of most business transactions has been overlooked by a parochial and sometimes quarrelsome concern with a limited number and range of government activities in the private market-place. Nevertheless, the underlying points are clear: government policies have fostered cooperation while corporate strategies have favored competition.

The government, after all, can set directions, define parameters, and determine policies, yet it is in coordination with private institutions that public plans are conceived and usually carried out. Indeed the interdependencies that join factory, firm, and network are prime examples of private initiative and planning. So, a similarity in outlook and values often joins government and business in Japan regardless of which side takes the initiative in a particular endeavor.

This compatibility in goals and outcomes may be rooted in the history of Japan's encounter with the West: a common experience of nationalistic reaction to a combined Western military, political, economic, and cultural threat, in a common response that recognized and underscored the linkage between a strong polity and economy (revealed in such late-nineteenth-century slogans as *fukoku kyohei*, 'a prosperous country and strong army'), and in similar patterns of recruitment and promotion in business and government once universities and technical schools began to graduate new cohorts of future leaders for government and business.

Hoshimi Uchida's tally of employment opportunities for university and technical college graduates through 1920 finds that an overwhelming 75 percent went into industry (9,961 compared to 3,601 individuals) and that a propensity for industrial employment rather than government service was clearly evident from 1900.[45] While numbers alone do not tell the whole story, far more of Japan's best and brightest have found a home in business than in government service during the course of this century.

In large measure, finally, the unusual similarity of interests that characterize government–business relations in Japan reflect the underdeveloped nature of corporate law there. Western notions of the firm have long stressed issues of ownership, stockholders' interests, and the rights and liabilities of the corporation as a legal personality. This is in keeping with the long history of the firm in the West as well as the relatively narrow interests of owner-investors before the widespread sale of securities; these have coalesced in the excessively litigious activities of special-interest stockholders. In Japan, however, the various constituencies that combine to form the firm have not especially sought to protect or extend their special interests by legal means.[46] Indeed, the very lack of a narrowly legalistic approach to business affairs has promoted an unusually cooperative attitude between labor and management as well as between government and business in the post-World War Two era. This has facilitated the tasks of managerial coordination in a period of national reconstruction.

Towards a Modern Corporate System in Japan

The most straightforward explanation for the superiority of the modern corporation lies in its capacity to expand its resources beyond the genealogical limits inherent in family-run firms. These limits are not simply biological but are financial, managerial, educational, and informational as well.[47] Among these, however, the later development of the firm in Japan, in comparison with the Western corporation, has emphasized the importance of organizational learning, or the importance of Western knowledge and its transformation into Japanese practice. The dynamics of an enterprise system characterized by competitive strategies and cooperative structures disinclined Japanese managers towards the multidivisional model. The rapidity of technological change drove firms to entrench resources in narrow market segments, and a lack of abundant natural and financial resources prompted managers to collaborate with rather than to incorporate all but closely related businesses.

Increasing numbers of professional mangers entering Japanese enterprises propelled this dynamic interaction. They entered turn-of-the-century businesses, boasting of the best possible education, access to the latest technology, plus a willingness to marry education with experience. In family and closely held firms, where high position and rapid promotion were often linked more to ascription than achievement, the difficulties of securing large numbers of these new men forced an increasing separation of ownership and control, a liberalization of finances, and a reworking of patterns of technical and managerial recruitment and advancement. Education and information were undoubtedly the most critical resources for industrializing firms in early-twentieth-century Japan, and such intangible resources were not typically generated and replenished rapidly enough in firms where families had substantial ownership and management positions.

From this perspective, the later development of the modern corporation in Japan demanded that leading firms surmount shortages in traditional factor endowments, such as mineral resources, skilled labor, and capital, by securing superior technique and method from abroad and by applying them rapidly and effectively at home. Without the possibility of exploiting these knowledge-based late-development advantages, it is impossible to explain why Japan was resource-poor at the start of industrialization but can hardly be characterized as resource-poor today. This historic reversal has been made possible by the emergence of new forms of industrial organization and a new class of industrial managers, and not by the discovery of new mineral and material resources.

New Men, Methods, and Motivations

It is the role of entrepreneurs to coalesce resources, recombine them, and through their pioneering efforts transform capital, technique, method, and purpose. This entrepreneurial function was no less important in Japan. Because of the later development of Japan, however, government statesmen and bureaucrats played important roles in scanning, securing, and underwriting product and process technologies, selecting legal and organizational forms from abroad. Likewise, in the early Meiji period government support for 'samurai business' (*shizoku jusan*) as well as the number of government-initiated industrial ventures illustrate the importance of the Japanese state as entrepreneur.

The state also provided a strong impetus towards economic and organizational modernization through the creation of a national educational system for closing the knowledge-gap between Japan and the Western world. But given that the majority of the population was resident in the countryside or in small- to medium-sized cities, fully committed to making money on their own and for their own purposes, it is easy, too easy, to exaggerate the role of the state in Japan's economic development. Most studies of entrepreneurship in turn-of-the-century Japan place peasants in the forefront of the movement to establish, direct, and develop modern business methods and techniques.[48]

As argued earlier, family businesses suffer from built-in limitations that flow from their closely held character. Since most early industrial endeavors were of this kind, it seems likely that private entrepreneurs benefited greatly if indirectly from government encouragement, promotion, and direction of countless efforts to establish industrial enterprises in late-nineteenth-century Japan. Thus, the thrust towards more modern forms of economic organization must be understood as a combination of government promotion and policy on one hand, and a counter-vailing upsurge of private ambition and activity on the other. This volatile mixture of public and private initiative sparked modern forms of corporate enterprise with the legal, financial, organizational, and informational advantages that they enjoy. Arising in favorable circumstance and with widespread public patronage and private support, the corporation transformed and was transformed by the social and economic development of Japan.

In short, the introduction, implantation, and cultivation of newer forms of business organization were neither automatic nor haphazard, and these many efforts clashed, commingled, and transformed existing forms of business organization and practice. Both the visible hand of the state and the invisible hand of the market were at work. Statesmen, entrepreneurs, managers, engineers, technicians, workers, even enterprising peasants—all contributed by engaging in a dialectic of effort;

government leaders promoted alternative forms of business activity and cultivated an intense desire to be modern and Western as well as Japanese. The changing confluence and synthesis of thoughts and actions, especially within the context of profit-seeking private institutions, pushed organizations forward through processes of organizational adaptation and learning. Some of this could be considered strategic thinking in that internal organizational resources were consciously calibrated against opportunities in the market-place. Some of it, perhaps most of it, was less formal and more a process of repeated trial and error.

The gradual accumulation of experience and technique within joint-stock firms was reflected before long in changing structures and strategic orientations. Traditional owners gave way to university-trained managers, dexterous craftsmen were superseded by schooled technicians, workers became more skilled and integrated into coordinated production processes. At the same time, corporations grew in size and in functional and operational complexity. Corporate strategies based on economies of scale and market segmentation became viable. As the corporation acquired a kind of organizational sophistication based on effort and experience, it also gained focus in what was attempted and achieved.

Corporations concentrated energy and attention in well-defined spheres of activity, in part because the process of technology transfer demanded concentrated effort for successful learning and implementation, and in part because market conditions were not yet well sorted out. Success in uncertain markets requires more focus than would be the case otherwise. Also, choosing from among the best available techniques and methods, while an advantage of late development, demanded ever larger amounts of capital. This too demands focus. And it cannot be denied that extremely high uncertainty was associated with disengaging and transferring organization and production techniques to Japan that were originally developed for foreign firms and markets. In such circumstances, the only effective response is to narrow and limit the focus of activity, so that experience becomes the principal guide as to what works.

By the early twentieth century, Japanese firms were developing in a number of distinctly different ways, based on complex patterns of interaction and fusion, blending material and human resources, accumulating experience with foreign method and technique, and coping with local market uncertainty. Calculation, choice, change, and perhaps progress, were the order of the day. As a result, three main traditions of enterprise strategy and structure emerge as primary pathways of industrial business development through World War Two. They are the subject of the next chapter.

NOTES

1. According to Takafusa Nakamura, *Economic Growth in Pre-war Japan* (New Haven, Conn.: Yale University Press, 1983), 22, the net domestic product for secondary

industry in 1920 was 3,887 million yen. My estimate of the adjusted sales of the largest 200 industrial firms in Japan in 1918 is 2,369 million yen (from the Appendix). The adjusted figure represents a total of 1,978 million yen for 167 firms from the 1918 list where sales are known, plus the average of this group for the 33 missing values. This assumes that large corporations were not buying very much from small corporations at this time, and so relatively little double counting of transactions occurs. As a result, it can be advanced that Japan's largest industrial firms were providing over half of the value of the output in the secondary industrial sector. Using these figures, in fact, the total comes to 61 percent.

Using another source only strengthens the argument. According to Kazushi Ohkawa and Miyohei Shinohara (eds.), *Patterns of Japanese Economic Development* (New Haven, Conn.: Yale University Press, 1979), 274, the net domestic product for manufacturing and mining in 1920 was 3,218 million yen. Using this figure, the adjusted sales of the 200 largest industrial firms in 1918 would account for 74 percent of the net domestic product for secondary industry. I find this figure high. However, it seems likely that the 200 largest industrials were accounting for 60 to 70 percent of net domestic product for secondary industry by 1918; so modern industrial firms were already the driving force of the economy.

2. Eleanor Westney treats the issue of institutional emulation in the context of late development in Japan in her book, *Imitation and Innovation* (Cambridge, Mass.: Harvard University Press, 1987).

3. Some of these ideas on the making of modern institutions were culled from three lectures given by the British sociologist Anthony Giddens at Stanford University from 4–6 Apr. 1988. Unfortunately, Giddens seems to feel that what he calls modernity was a uniquely Western European phenomenon while I believe that most of his argument applies equally well to several Asian countries, particularly Japan and China. Indeed, the whole issue of reflexivity as it applies to Japanese and Chinese society before industrialization is a field of considerable academic enquiry and discussion.

4. Dow Votaw, *Modern Corporations* (Englewood Cliffs, NJ: Prentice Hall, 1965), 13.

5. A description of some of the variation in business forms and functions at the turn of the twentieth century is contained in my paper, 'Instead of Management: Internal Contracting and the Genesis of Modern Labor Relations in Japan', in Keiichiro Nakagawa and Tsunehiko Yui (eds.), *Japanese Management in Historical Perspective*, Fuji Business History Conference XV (Tokyo: University of Tokyo Press, 1989).

6. Professor Keiichiro Nakagawa's paper on the 'Learning Industrial Revolution' in Japan appears in the volume cited in the previous note.

7. There is a limited but growing literature on the varieties of early modern commercial and industrial endeavor in Japan. Its existence documents the rather well-developed economic, political, and social character of Japan prior to industrialization.

8. Some indication of this heterogeneity can be found in my essay, 'Instead of Management'. More generally, the International Business History series, some fifteen volumes strong, published by the University of Tokyo Press attests to the variety of forms and strategies characterizing Japanese business.

9. This is in line with Morikawa Hidemasa's estimates appearing in *Nihon Zaibatsu-shi* (A History of Japanese Zaibatsu) (Tokyo: Kyoiku-sha, 1978), 193–201. Morikawa's latest thinking on this and other matters relating to the pre-war *zaibatsu* will appear in a forthcoming book from Harvard University Press. According to Kamekichi Takahashi's estimates, a somewhat biased source, the big four *zaibatsu* provided a 15.2 percent

share of the nation's total paid-up social capital in 1928. Kamekichi Takahashi, *Nihon Keizai Toseiron* (The Control of the Japanese Economy) (Tokyo: Kaizosha, 1933). Cited in Nakamura, *Economic Growth in Pre-war Japan*, 208.

10. The pre-war development of Japanese enterprise is well documented e.g. in the fifteen-volume Japanese business history series published by the University of Tokyo Press. Also, the Council on East Asian Studies at Harvard University has published a series of Japanese business histories from the Harvard University Press.

11. The pioneer in this area was Thomas C. Smith who published a series of monographs on pre-industrial Japanese economic development. These included: *Political Change and Industrial Development in Japan: Government Enterprise 1868–80* (Stanford, Calif.: Stanford University Press, 1955); *The Agrarian Origins of Modern Japan* (Stanford, Calif.: Stanford University Press, 1959); and *Nakahara: Family Farming and Population in a Japanese Village, 1717–1830* (Stanford, Calif.: Stanford University Press, 1977).

12. Thomas C. Smith, 'Pre-Modern Economic Growth: Japan and the West', *Past and Present*, 60 (Aug. 1973); Gilbert Rozman, *Urban Networks in Ch'ing China and Tokugawa Japan* (Princeton, NJ: Princeton University Press, 1973).

13. Sidney Crawcour, 'The Development of a Credit System in Seventeenth-Century Japan', *Journal of Economic History*, 21 (Sept. 1961).

14. Smith, 'Pre-Modern Economic Growth'.

15. Akira Hayami, *Nihon Keizaishi e no Shikaku* (Perspectives on Japanese Economic History) (Tokyo: Toyo Keizai Shinposha, 1986); id., *Kinsei Noson no Rekishijinkogakuteki Kenkyu* (The Historical Demography of Early Modern Agricultural Villages) (Tokyo: Toyo Keizai Shinposha, 1973); Smith, *Nakahara*.

16. Thomas C. Smith, *Native Sources of Japanese Industrialization* (Stanford, Calif.: Stanford University Press, 1987), 4–5.

17. W. Mark Fruin, 'The Firm as a Family and the Family as a Firm in Japan', *Journal of Family History*, 5/4 (Winter 1980).

18. This has been well argued in the literature for some time. See Koji Taira, *Economic Development and the Labor Market in Japan* (New York: Columbia University Press, 1970); Robert E. Cole, *Japanese Blue Collar* (Berkeley: University of California Press, 1971) and his 'Permanent Employment in Japan: Facts and Fantasies', *Industrial and Labor Relations Review*, 26 (1972), 615–30; Andrew Gordon, *The Evolution of Labor Relations in Japan: Heavy Industry, 1853–1955* (Cambridge, Mass.: Harvard University Press, 1985).

19. Among the largest industrial firms in 1918 and 1930, Noda Shoyu Company represents the only major Japanese corporation that became large on the basis of an indigenous technology and represents organizational and managerial continuity from the Tokugawa era. See the Appendix and my *Kikkoman: Company, Clan and Community* (Cambridge, Mass.: Harvard University Press, 1983).

20. See W. Mark Fruin, 'Labor Migration in Nineteenth-Century Japan', Ph.D. thesis (Stanford University, 1973).

21. Ronald Dore, *Education in Tokugawa Japan* (Berkeley: University of California Press, 1965). Dore's 40 percent figure is not a literacy rate but an estimate of how many Japanese were receiving some formal schooling in the mid-nineteenth century.

22. Susan Hanley, 'Zenkogyokaki Nihon no Toshi ni Okeru Koshu Eisei', in Akira Hayami, Osamu Saito, and Shin'ya Sugiyama (eds.), *Tokugawa Shakai kara no Tenbo* (Observations from Tokugawa Society) (Tokyo: Dobunkan, 1988), 216–37.

23. Ann B. Jannetta, *Epidemics and Mortality in Early Modern Japan* (Princeton, NJ: Princeton University Press, 1987).
24. Osamu Saito, *Puroto kogyoka no jidai: Seio to Nihon no hikaku* (The Age of Proto-industrialization: Japan and the West) (Tokyo: Hyoronsha, 1985).
25. This point was first argued by Smith in *Political Change and Industrial Development in Japan*.
26. Nakagawa, 'Learning Industrial Revolution', as cited in n. 6 above.
27. Translated and adapted from Tokyo Shibaura Denki, *Toshiba Hyakunenshi* (Tokyo: Daiyamondo, 1977).
28. Nakagawa, 'Learning Industrial Revolution', 2.
29. Westney, *Imitation and Innovation*, 17.
30. *Economic Backwardness in Historical Perspective* (Cambridge, Mass.: Harvard University Press, 1962).
31. This point emerges clearly in the published papers of the 15th Fuji Business History Conference. See contributions by Nakagawa, Uchida, Daito, and Fruin, in Nakagawa and Yui (eds.), *Japanese Management in Historical Perspective*.
32. Shin'ichi Yonekawa, 'Meijiki Daiboseki Kigyo no Shokuinso' (The Managerial Class in Large Textile Firms during the Meiji Period), *Shakai Keizaishigaku* (Social Economic History) 51/4 (Fall 1986).
33. Matao Miyamoto, 'The Position and Role of Family Business in the Development of the Japanese Company System', in Akio Okochi and Shigeaki Yasuoka (eds.), *Family Business in the Era of Industrial Growth* (University of Tokyo Press, 1982), 39–94.
34. Tsunehiko Yui, 'Meiji Jidai ni okeru Juyaku Soshiki no Keisei' (The Formation of Boards of Directors during the Meiji Period), *Keiei Shigaku* (Business History), 14/1 (Winter 1979), and id., 'The Development of the Organizational Structure of Top Management in Meiji Japan', *Japanese Yearbook on Business History* (Tokyo: Japanese Business History Institute, 1984).
35. I provide some detail on this point in my paper 'Instead of Management'.
36. Fruin, *Kikkoman*. This book describes the longest labor strike in pre-war Japan and posits its outbreak as a clash between traditional methods of labor organization and management and modern requirements for high-volume production and an attendant need for direct management of the production function.
37. *Corporate Control and Business Behavior: An Inquiry into the Effects of Organizational Form on Enterprise Behavior* (Englewood Cliffs, NJ: Prentice Hall, 1970), 175.
38. Simon Kuznets, 'Notes on the Pattern of U.S. Economic Growth', in Edgar O. Edwards (ed.), *The Nation's Economic Objectives* (Chicago: University of Chicago Press, 1964). Also quoted in Alfred D. Chandler, Jr., *Scale and Scope* (Cambridge, Mass.: Harvard University Press, 1990), 736.
39. A recent article that argues for social and spatial effects on the adoption of the multidivisional form is Donald Palmer, Roger Friedland, P. Devereaux Jennings, and Melanie E. Powers, 'The Economics and Politics of Structure: The Multidivisional Form and the Large U.S. Corporation', *Administrative Science Quarterly*, 32 (Mar. 1987), 25–48.
40. Alfred D. Chandler, Jr., 'Government versus Business: An American Phenomenon', in John T. Dunlop (ed.), *Business and Public Policy* (Cambridge, Mass.: Harvard University Press, 1980).

41. W. Mark Fruin, 'Pre-Corporate and Corporate Charity in Japan: From Philanthropy to Paternalism in the Noda Soy Sauce Industry', *Business History Review*, 61/2 (Summer 1982).

42. Lance E. Davis and Douglass C. North, *Institutional Change and American Economic Growth* (Cambridge: Cambridge University Press, 1971), 250–1.

43. Solomon B. Levine and Hisashi Kawada, *Human Resources in Japanese Industrial Development* (Princeton, NJ: Princeton University Press, 1980). Much the same argument could be made in the area of social-welfare programs. In the post–World War Two era, for example, companies were compelled to offer social-welfare services precisely because government provided the bare minimum until the late 1960s.

44. Business initiatives often went and still go unheralded. The revival of the steel industry in early post-war Japan offers a celebrated example of this. See Ch. 5.

45. 'Comment on Professor Nakagawa's Paper', Fuji International Conference on Business History, 5–8 Jan. 1987.

46. Masahiko Aoki, *The Co-operative Game Theory of the Firm* (Oxford: Oxford University Press, 1986).

47. I discuss these matters in a detailed case-study of the Mogi and Takanashi Families that are behind the long history and international success of the Kikkoman Corporation. See my book *Kikkoman*.

48. Hiroshi Mannari, *The Japanese Business Leaders* (Tokyo: University of Tokyo Press, 1974).

3

Inventing the Enterprise System

The enterprise system appeared around the turn of the twentieth century when the factory system was effectively joined with a managerial hierarchy in production and distribution. It is the emerging coordination of previously independent organizations for production, management, and distribution—shop-floor, front office, and sales office—that generates the organizational innovation known as the Japanese enterprise system. The initial correspondence of factory, firm, and network was uncertain, yet their alignment was progressively adjusted and interrelated.

The exact timing of this emergence and the precise way in which production, management, sales and distribution were interrelated vary according to location, type of industry, market conditions, and patterns of ownership and control. These variations are systematically explored in this chapter by classifying such differences into three categories of generic modern enterprise: *zaibatsu* or national enterprise; independent, urban enterprise; and independent, rural enterprise.

During a half-century of economic development or from 1905 to 1955, these categorical differences gradually diminish in importance. By the initiation of the high-growth, post-Korean War era, it is possible to speak with confidence about the nature of industrial structure on a national level and of the specific capabilities of firms in those industries. Before the World Wars, especially before World War One, however, it is quite difficult to generalize in this way. For these reasons, a typology of enterprise features is offered which attempts to characterize major lines of enterprise development, while recognizing that individual firms may not fit neatly within the framework.

The prominence of focal factories in the Japanese enterprise system is closely related to relative levels of economic development, market integration, and administrative coordination during the first half of the century. As national demand was sporadic in most instances, coordination of supply and demand occurred on a local or regional basis. Textiles were an exception but one that proved the rule. Export demand required an integration of textile production and distribution capabilities that was otherwise unrivalled in Japan. More localized, piecemeal, and decentralized approaches to the market were the rule.

Modern Industrial Enterprise: A Typology

The Zaibatsu

Zaibatsu literally means 'financial group', and in the context of the development of Japanese business before World War Two, it also infers family-based control of a number of interrelated business enterprises. The classical definition of *zaibatsu*, therefore, includes the concepts of size (size, in terms of assets and employees of single firms as well as the aggregated assets and employees of a group of firms), family-based control (usually exercised through a holding company), a nucleus of financially related enterprises as well as specialized sales, marketing, and distribution companies to service the manufacturing firms in an enterprise group.[1]

Although *zaibatsu* have been compared to large industrial holding companies, such as the Société Générale of Belgium, they were quite different in origin and character.[2] The large industrial holding companies of Belgium were not family holding companies, and they originated with a mixed banking mission to hold long-term industrial assets in mining, iron, steel, and railroads and, at the same time, to engage in the activities of a commercial bank. In many instances holding companies moved beyond purely financial management and lent technical advice, commercial guidance, and industrial planning to their operating subsidiaries. *Zaibatsu*, by contrast, were family-owned holding companies that originated in non-manufacturing activities, were nearer to a closed-end investment bank than midway between a long-term credit and commercial bank, and they provided little technical and managerial advice to subsidiary operations.

In addition, it is useful to see that *zaibatsu* followed a form of diversification which allowed unrelated as opposed to related diversification to be the principal mode of business development before the 1930s. Related diversification refers to the adding of new businesses to established business lines through linkages based on technical or market-place similarities. A classical example is the Standard Oil Company of Indiana which was established to refine and distribute kerosene when kerosene was used primarily for illumination. Standard Oil became the largest company in the world when demand for alternative uses of its basic petroleum feedstock, such as gasoline, diesel, and heating oil other than kerosene, pushed it to develop impressive economies of scale in refining and distribution. The technical capability to refine kerosene gave Standard Oil the opportunity to produce and sell a host of related petroleum products.

In Japan, *zaibatsu* grew for the most part by unrelated diversification, which is to say that economies of scale in production and distribution were not the forces behind the development of national or *zaibatsu* business groupings. Eventually, the largest Japanese companies turned to product- and market-diversification strategies but these did not appear commonly until the 1960s and 1970s, unlike large American industrial firms which moved in these directions during the inter-war years.

Thus, complementarity in technology and markets did not push diversification in Japan until after World War Two. Instead, expediency drove diversification. Unrelated businesses were combined with the original economic activities of the *zaibatsu*, which were commercial and service-related for the most part. Expedient combinations gradually produced internal sinews of their own, so that some sort of technical and market cohesiveness was created in time, yet this often required decades. Thus, goodness-of-fit arguments based on organizational and technological complementarities that assume a high level of resource exchange or pooling do not satisfactorily explain the origin and evolution of most of the major business combinations dating from the late nineteenth or early twentieth centuries.

Even so, the dispersed origins of *zaibatsu* business and the initial non-manufacturing emphases produced an economic logic of interdependence. Economies of scope, that is cost reductions which accrue through joint production and distribution, were pivotal in bringing *zaibatsu* enterprises together. Briefly stated, economies of scope are possible when the costs of producing or distributing two or more products together are lower than the costs of doing so separately. The most obvious opportunities for such economies in early *zaibatsu* groupings were in areas of financing, transport, purchasing, and distribution.

Thus *zaibatsu* began as a handful of family-based businesses which grew in number and size, yielding a structure that maintained family-based control without family-based management (holding companies permitted this), and that dictated a strategy of eventually pulling together and relating a large number of firms that were not initially well matched. *Zaibatsu* appear during the last quarter of the nineteenth century, create holding-company structures with interlocking directorates and shareholding among group enterprises by the turn of the twentieth century, and rough-hew loose structures of indirect financial control over growing numbers of independently organized but strategically interrelated firms after World War One. Hidemasa Morikawa calls this last stage of development the multi-corporate system, and it could be called the highest stage of development for traditional *zaibatsu* enterprises.[3] The multi-corporate system of independently managed yet strategically interrelated firms appears during the inter-war period.

After World War Two and the dissolution of *zaibatsu* holding companies by an American-led Occupation reform movement (1945–51), the character of *zaibatsu* changed in noteworthy ways. No longer called *zaibatsu*, successors to the *zaibatsu* are often called *kigyo shudan*. *Kigyo shudan* are constellations of firms organized around a core of firms (usually a bank, trading company, and several old, large financial services and manufacturing concerns) which own sufficient numbers of shares and exercise enough strategic oversight in affiliated firms so as to induce a cooperative attitude.

Core companies, as their name implies, are at the center of planning, co-ordinating, and allocating resources for the group as a whole. Before World War Two, family holding companies were part of the core and they played a central role in controlling and integrating investment for the group as a whole. After the war, however, holding companies were disbanded by the Occupation, even while critical coordinating functions played by holding companies were clearly transferred to other enterprises.[4] The substance of coordination continued though the structure of coordination changed.

At the close of the nineteenth century when the first *zaibatsu* appeared, two distinct types arose. Those like Mitsui and Sumitomo, already boasted several centuries of history, and others, like Mitsubishi and Yasuda, were founded in the mid- to late nineteenth century. In either case, however, it is not proper to append the appellation *zaibatsu* until these débutante businesses were transformed by the purchase and imperfect integration of government-initiated ventures during the 1880s. *Zaibatsu*, including Mitsui and Sumitomo, with the full characteristics listed above did not appear until the late nineteenth century.

The reason for the appearance of the *zaibatsu* at this time was the Meiji Government's recognition that its painstaking efforts to industrialize Japan from the top down were doomed and that it must divest nearly everything industrial, except for certain sensitive/strategic enterprises, to private interests. The devolution of government-owned businesses after 1885 occasioned the formation of the *zaibatsu*, namely a collection of commercial, industrial, and service enterprises which were family-owned and, for a while, family-managed. Since the sales as well as purchases of government industrial ventures were not planned far in advance, the businesses of nascent *zaibatsu* groupings were largely unrelated at their inception. Much of the early history of the *zaibatsu* after the 1880s, as a result, was focused on efforts to create interdependence between *zaibatsu* enterprises.

Political intrigue, regional factionalism in national politics, personal favoritism, nepotism, and even bribery appear to have infected the divestiture program of the 1880s, yet the program of privatization determined much of the course and content of industrialization from the turn of the twentieth century. A lack of interdependence among *zaibatsu*-related ventures at the outset of industrialization was the result of the disarray of government–business cooperation, the confusion of the first rush towards industrialization, a failure of coordination in public and private investment, and the pell-mell character of the Government's divestiture program. Given such divisive circumstances, the unrelated character of early *zaibatsu* enterprises is hardly surprising.[5]

The next section sketches the history of the four main *zaibatsu* enterprise groups before 1945, highlighting the diversity of their origins in the nineteenth century and contrasting their strategies of growth from the early twentieth century. Besides the Big Four *zaibatsu*, there were a handful of other *zaibatsu* before the war, including Furukawa, Okura, Asano, and Fujita. They did not differ greatly from the Big Four, except in size and in degree of vertical integration and product/market diversification (they were smaller, less integrated and even less diversified). Including the larger four *zaibatsu*, it must be emphasized that *zaibatsu* enterprises originated in non-manufacturing pursuits, especially if a distinction between mining and manufacturing is rigorously applied.

Mitsui

In the case of Mitsui, government-released enterprises in the 1880s provided it with mining and manufacturing components to complement already existing strengths in commodity trading, dry-goods retailing, and money-leanding. Some of these businesses were begun as early as the seventeenth century. But it was in money-lending that Mitsui flourished; by the mid-nineteenth century, Mitsui had become a kind of private exchequer to the Government, giving it a valuable, informed position from which its other businesses could be enriched.[6]

During the late 1870s, however, Mitsui's banking services lost favor, as the central government attempted to establish its own national banking system. Moreover, Mitsui's aggressive lending activities left a number of failed or failing industrial endeavors in receivership which it could ill afford to rescue. In its own defense, Mitsui moved to strengthen its banking activities as a purely private concern, establishing the Mitsui Bank in 1876. It also consolidated its commercial broker operations under a newly formed trading company, and it acquired through competitive, if insider, bidding the Miike coal-mine, several lesser mines, and a number of manufacturing ventures that the Government had decided to dispose of.

By the end of the 1880s Mitsui was considerably more diversified than it had been a decade earlier, and, more importantly, it was less encumbered by government connections and contracts in managing those resources. As a result, Mitsui blended its traditional lines of specialized trading and banking activities with newer endeavors in banking, more generalized trading, mining, and manufacturing to create the first true *zaibatsu* by the close of the nineteenth century.[7]

Mitsui Gains Toshiba (Tokyo Shibaura Electric). Mitsui was a novice in manufacturing. Mitsui's experience with Tokyo Shibaura Electric illustrates the early difficulties Mitsui encountered as it migrated towards a strategy of integrated business operations. In the last chapter, there was brief mention of Hisashige Tanaka, the eccentric yet brilliant founder of the telegraphic-equipment venture that would ultimately become the Toshiba Corporation. After Hisashige's death in November 1881, Tanaka's adopted son assumed his father's name and business. He had been employed in the Government's efforts to manufacture communications equipment, so shifting over to his father's firm presented few difficulties for the fledgling firm, the son, or the Government.

Tanaka immediately landed a big Navy contract for underwater torpedoes as well as for other military and communications devices. To that end, he built a 2,500-square-meter plant on a site four times as large in 1882 in the Shibaura district and employed the then large workforce of 200. Five years later, 680 were engaged at the Tanaka Works.

The defense industry is notoriously cyclical and unpredictable. A new Finance Minister, Matsukata Masayoshi, sabered government spending and a rash of lean, upstart businesses brought out telephonic equipment which competed directly and favorably with Tanaka's. Hard times and competitive rivals squeezed the over-extended firm. The Tanaka Works dropped to fewer than 100 employees in 1893. Its debt to the Mitsui Bank exceeded 230,000 yen, and, most seriously, the Navy completed a major arsenal in Yokosuka and thereafter canceled many of its contracts with civilian suppliers.

On 17 November 1893, the Tanaka Works was bought by the Mitsui Bank and renamed the Shibaura Engineering Works. Raita Fujiyama was dispatched from the bank to take charge of the company. Fujiyama was a graduate of Keio University, a prominent private university in Tokyo, and a close protégé of Hikojiro Nakamigawa, also a Keio man. Nakamigawa was elevated in 1891 to managing director of Mitsui Bank at the age of 38.[8]

Fujiyama was called Nakamigawa's enforcer. Fujiyama had collected on a million-yen bad loan owed to the bank by Higashi Hongan-ji, the main temple of the largest Buddhist sect in Japan. He had foreclosed on three large silk mills which had borrowed from the failing Thirty-Third Bank of Gumma Prefecture. And, he had really made his mark by rescuing from bankruptcy the Oji Paper Company, another Mitsui company and the largest, most cost-efficient enterprise in the paper industry. Fujiyama was a managerial zealot who wanted to prove that aggressive and determined management worked in any company and industry.

Whether Fujiyama should be given the credit or whether a simple upturn in the business cycle explains more, by 1894 business was picking up. In 1894 the Shibaura Engineering Works produced its first 60-kilowatt, two-phase alternating-current generator, and in the next year, a 25-horsepower direct-current model. With these triumphs, the company established its reputation in the growing market for industrial power-equipment.

Mitsui Detaches Toshiba. In 1894 Mitsui businesses were reorganized into three groupings: banking, trading, and manufacturing. In the latter field, the Shibaura Engineering Works was the cornerstone of Mitsui's perch in the electrical-equipment industry; in 1895 the company broadened its product line by securing an order from the Kanegafuchi Spinning Company, another Mitsui affiliate, for a 1,300-horsepower steam generator, and from the Tokyo Electric Power Company for a 60-meter high, 2.7-meter diameter, earthquake-proof, power-station smokestack.

In 1896 Fujiyama left Shibaura to take over the Oji Paper Company. He was succeeded briefly by Yujiro Ono, until Ono was replaced with Genkichi Wakayama in September 1897. Wakayama was a retired naval officer, and with these naval connections he was able to secure some military contracts for the Shibaura firm in spite of the economic plummet after the Sino-Japanese War 1894–5. In November 1898 Shibaura Engineering was placed under the management of the Mitsui Mining Company in a major corporate reshuffling of the Mitsui group. Two months later, Wakayama died suddenly.

Odakuro Shigegoro, 34-year-old manager of Mitsui & Company's (the trading company) branch office in the coal-mining town of Miike, was dispatched to assume control of the Shibaura Engineering Works in July 1899. Within a year he

TABLE 3.1. *Shibaura Engineering's Product Line, 1900*

Electrical machinery	Non-electrical machinery
generators	steam engines
electromotors (direct current)	steam boilers
electric-railway equipment	earthquake-proof industrial chimneys
water power-generation equipment	railroad bridges
electric-illumination equipment	waterwheels
transformers	petroleum-drilling rigs
	oil-pressing equipment
	mining equipment
	sawmill equipment
	bundle-binding equipment
	rice-milling equipment
	overhead, freight-carrying cable equipment

fashioned a startling reorganization. Three existing departments—design, manufacturing, and administration—were folded into two: manufacturing and sales. Thus, Shibaura Engineering adopted the classic U-Form organization, structuring the company in two uniform halves: one for production and one for sales.

Under the production-half of the firm, electrical machinery, non-electrical machinery, and plant sales departments were established. A recently inaugurated shipbuilding business was dropped. A casting shop was organized to shape parts for machine tools, cranes, boilers, and other industrial equipment. The administrative side of the manufacturing business was revamped as well. New company rules and regulations were promoted with an eye to rewarding employee service, loyalty, and effort. A company savings plan, worker-injury scheme, and restrictions on overtime and night work were instituted. By the second half of 1900 the company was back in the black.

In 1900 Shibaura Engineering's product line covered a broad range of electrical and non-electrical machinery. The main items in each are shown in Table 3.1. It is important to recognize that most of these products were manufactured strictly according to customer needs and specifications. Shibaura Engineering was not yet in the mass-production business, and indeed, no Japanese electrical-equipment firm was. In this sense, the firm was not tied to long production runs and any sort of scale economies. The resources of the firm, outside of its plant and equipment, were mostly tied up in the individual skills, experience, and know-how of its employees who could be assigned to any one of a number of tasks. This made work interesting, variegated, as well as uncertain for the employees of Shibaura Engineering. It also stamped the industrial character of Shibaura Engineering's production sites. They were rough-and-ready works where almost anything, within limits of course, could and would be made.

The outbreak of the Russo-Japanese War (1904–5) put those talents and people to full use. The demand for electric power-generating and power-using equipment escalated sharply. Small, steam-based, electric power stations gave way to larger, hydroelectric generating plants. Shibaura's steam engines and boilers, electric generators, transformers, dynamos, electromotors, and illumination equipment were all back-ordered.

Shibaura Engineering's success should not be simply ascribed to Mitsui's good management. Although Mitsui ventured into three different manufacturing lines by the early twentieth century—buying or founding three silk-reeling factories, initiating four cotton-spinning mills, and taking over one electrical-machinery plant (Tanaka Electric/Shibaura Electric Works)—many of these manufacturing efforts failed, and mostly they failed for a lack of good management. Mitsui blundered by not making the new concerns independent or, at least, semi-independent of holding-company and trading-company control. Instead manufacturing ventures were run more as in-house branches than separate divisions. Accordingly, they did not keep their own capital-based accounting records, they did not have more than a handful of managers assigned to them, and they had very few specialized staff functions.[9] They were organized, in the language of this book, as primary factories.

As one after another reeling or spinning factories floundered, Mitsui gradually loosened head-office control and allowed manufacturing ventures to become more like independent divisions. This meant giving them greater managerial authority and autonomy, and bolstering the number of line and staff specialists. The head office and central companies of the Mitsui group did not have core managerial skills that could be moved at will to rescue failing private-sector firms. The strategic success of Kanebo Spinning, Oji Paper, and Shibaura Electric was rooted in the decision to separate them from, rather than integrate them with, the Mitsui *omoto-kata* or head office. They all became major independent companies between 1910 and 1920.

Hence, their operational advance was related to hands-on management of development and production capabilities, garnered, husbanded, and improved, at increasingly well-run manufacturing sites. They prospered in proportion to their managerial independence. Fortunately, an expansion of demand for high-capacity, high-voltage power equipment during World War One guaranteed the wisdom of this separation for Shibaura Electric. As for the other manufacturing operations, Mitsui's successful move into textiles production during the inter-war era was predicated on the operational capabilities of individual firms reinforced by the strategic resource capabilities of the group. The order of this progression was important.

Sumitomo

Sumitomo's pre-nineteenth-century business base was copper mining, ore processing, metals smelting, and the brokering of metals commodities in the West–East trade between Osaka and Tokyo. In copper trading, Sumitomo was a favored merchant of the Tokugawa Government, operating from its Besshi copper mine on Shikoku island, the most productive copper mine in the country. These strengths became the basis for Sumitomo's rapid expansion in the modern manufacture of metals, chemicals, dyes, and machinery after Western methods of mining and manufacturing were introduced and after a more effective distribution system for the sale of Sumitomo products, both within and without Japan, was established.[10]

Sumitomo purchased only government enterprises related to mining and metals production and because of this, Sumitomo enjoyed a relatively high level of interrelation among its various businesses by the turn of the twentieth century. Ores dug in its mines were processed in its refineries, forged, cast, and fashioned in its shops. However, Sumitomo ran these interrelated activities more as shops than as separate business entities which is to say that the authority of the Sumitomo holding company was paramount. Product-in-progress at each step in an integrated mining and manufacturing operation was passed along without exploring possibilities for new business opportunities.

As a consequence, the Sumitomo holding company retained full ownership over a relatively small number (twenty-one) of subsidiaries until the mid-1930s. While professional managers were placed in subsidiaries, they were not allowed much functional autonomy and managerial discretion. The Sumitomo family exercised control through personnel policies as well as through financial means: managers were dispatched from the holding company to subsidiaries as a means to implement policy changes; managers were rotated more frequently among Sumitomo subsidiaries than was the case for Mitsui and Mitsubishi; the holding company kept systematic albeit simple financial and accounting records of subsidiaries until the second decade of the twentieth century.[11]

As a result of holding-company control, the main lines of Sumitomo business—copper and iron mining, smelting and refining, iron manufacture, and electric-wire fabrication—did not grow much in size and scale of activity. The managerial ranks of Sumitomo businesses were sparse and frequently reshuffled (compared with Mitsui and Mitsubishi *zaibatsu*), and Sumitomo organization practices exaggerated an already pronounced weight of the family holding company in all business matters. In fact, there was only one set of sales offices for Sumitomo's half-dozen product lines until the 1920s.

Mitsubishi

Unlike Mitsui and Sumitomo's hoary origins, Mitsubishi and Yasuda, the other two top *zaibatsu*, appeared relatively late—in the middle of the nineteenth century. They succeeded at first as government agents in one venture or another, but given the precarious underpinnings of successive governments from the 1850s to the 1880s, Mitsubishi and Yasuda did not free themselves of an uncertain government dependency until the last two decades of the century.

Mitsubishi's start came as a government agent for the sale of Tosa Domain's products. Yataro Iwasaki, a leading samurai representing Tosa in Nagasaki and Osaka at end of the Tokugawa regime, acquired Tosa's assets in Osaka in 1872, primarily ships and warehouse facilities. The lease of these ships to the government during the Taiwan Expedition in 1874 gave the newly formed firm a much needed boost, and continued government demand for the transportation of mail and of tax revenues in the form of rice proved crucial to the first Mitsubishi venture.[12]

During the 1870s Mitsubishi grew wealthy and powerful through government protection, patronage, and subsidy. Because of its favored position, Mitsubishi Steamship Company (later renamed Mitsubishi Mail Steamship Company) could block foreign steamship companies that wanted to open scheduled coastal shipping runs in Japanese waters, and instead, offered its own network of domestic and overseas shipping lines by the end of the decade. Secure in the commercial shipping industry, Mitsubishi moved into marine insurance, ship repairs, coal mining, and banking. In order to better handle these expanding lines of business activity, Mitsubishi adopted a Western-style accounting system in 1876, and this system was later adapted and upgraded with so much success that it was little different from the internal-accounting system used until the 1970s. Mitsubishi's involvement in manufacturing, it should be noted, comes entirely after the turn of the century (mostly after World War One), with the result that its industrial base has concentrated in the manufacture of products of the so-called second industrial revolution, namely machinery and heavy industry as opposed to textiles, light industry, and iron production.

In order to manage these diverse business interests in shipping, maritime insurance, coal and ore mining, banking, and manufacturing, Yataro Iwasaki hired hundreds of technical and general university graduates to knit together the plurality of Mitsubishi holdings. Large numbers of university graduates translated into a fair degree of managerial independence and authority for Mitsubishi enterprises. Other companies, such as Asahi Glass, Nihon Kogaku, Kirin Beer, and Mitsubishi Paper, unrelated to the original Mitsubishi interests in mining, metals, and shipping, were added to the Mitsubishi group of companies by World War One. By 1917–18 most Mitsubishi businesses were separated from the holding company as independent companies although they were still very much under the strategic control of the family holding company. But by the end of the 1920s they had gained managerial independence and authority for the most part.[13]

The specification of corporate relations between holding company and subsidiaries was ably laid out in company regulations newly adopted in 1918. The appointment of corporate officers and the payment of their salaries, for example, were the responsibility of subsidiaries. While subsidiary capital was raised through the holding company, profit and losses associated with the management of capital were shouldered by subsidiaries. Fiscal and personnel decisions, taken locally, had to be communicated centrally to the holding company. In short, subsidiaries were independent in day-to-day operations as long as long-range decisions were taken in conjunction with the holding company.[14]

The evolution of the Mitsubishi *zaibatsu* from a tightly held, private concern, through an initial separation of independent operations under holding-company control, to a full-fledged corporate group with strategic and operational management, can be observed in Fig. 3.1.

Yasuda

The Yasuda *zaibatsu* appeared late in the Tokugawa period and it rested almost entirely on the talents of one man, Zenjiro Yasuda. He started as a independent money-changer in Edo (Tokyo) in 1863, opened his own money-changing premises in 1866, became a government-designated dealer in exchanging old coins for new in 1867, and acted in behalf of the new Meiji Government after 1868 in the circulation of new paper currency. By 1876, less than fifteen years after he made his start, Yasuda opened the Third National Bank, a quasi-public-funded bank, and in 1880 the Yasuda Bank, an unlimited partnership. In tandem, the two banks laid the foundations of the Yasuda *zaibatsu* which were largely in the areas of finance and banking.[15]

In 1903, for example, the Yasuda holding company and Yasuda Bank held shares in twelve banks, three insurance companies, eight railroad lines, two steamship lines, and four other firms, only two of which, Shimono Hemp and Kumamoto Spinning, were manufacturers. Transportation-related investments burgeoned at the time of the Russo-Japanese War (1904–5), so that Yasuda held shares in seventeen railroad lines. Manufacturing investments picked up noticeably at the same time. By 1910, 60 percent of Yasuda Bank's portfolio was invested in manufacturing, with Kanebo Spinning, Teikoku Hemp, Nihon Oil, and Nihon Seido Ammonia Fertilizer, among the more important holdings. None the less, Yasuda remained a financially oriented group relative to Mitsui, Sumitomo, and Mitsubishi, and when it ventured outside of banking and insurance, most of its investments were in transportation, storage, power generation, and not manufacturing.[16]

Strategy and Structure of the *Zaibatsu*

In sum, *zaibatsu* firms first clustered around the activities of transportation (shipping), energy production (coal mining and later electric power-generation), and finance (banking and insurance). Later Mitsubishi moved into shipbuilding, Mitsui into paper production and electrical equipment, and Sumitomo into chemicals. It must be underscored that these efforts came later. Manufacturing was grafted on to shipping, banking, and mining. Non-manufacturing ventures gave an early and weighty importance to financial and commercial matters and, as a result, many of the structural and strategic features of early *zaibatsu* enterprises, such as family control, holding-company dominance, and the pre-eminence of financial and commercial interests over manufacturing, continued well into the twentieth century.

Mitsubishi Goshi Company 1916

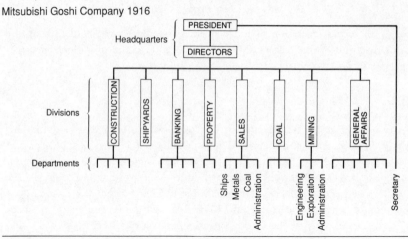

Headquarters { PRESIDENT / DIRECTORS

Divisions: CONSTRUCTION, SHIPYARDS, BANKING, PROPERTY, SALES, COAL, MINING, GENERAL AFFAIRS

Departments {

Ships, Metals, Coal, Administration — Engineering, Exploration, Administration — Secretary

Mitsubishi Goshi Company 1919

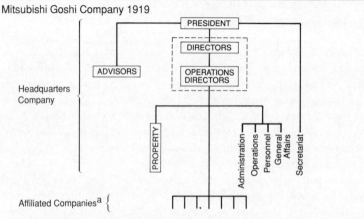

Headquarters Company {

PRESIDENT

ADVISORS

DIRECTORS / OPERATIONS DIRECTORS

PROPERTY — Administration, Operations, Personnel, General Affairs, Secretariat

Affiliated Companies[a] {

Mitsubishi Goshi Company 1926

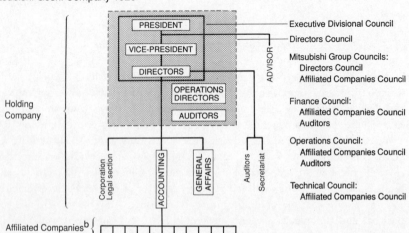

Holding Company {

PRESIDENT
VICE-PRESIDENT
DIRECTORS
OPERATIONS DIRECTORS
AUDITORS
ADVISOR

Corporation Legal section, ACCOUNTING, GENERAL AFFAIRS — Auditors, Secretariat

Affiliated Companies[b] {

Executive Divisional Council
Directors Council

Mitsubishi Group Councils:
  Directors Council
  Affiliated Companies Council

Finance Council:
  Affiliated Companies Council
  Auditors

Operations Council:
  Affiliated Companies Council
  Auditors

Technical Council:
  Affiliated Companies Council

Until World War One or thereabouts, *zaibatsu* groupings were slow to develop a strategy of organizational integration and management centralization based on the concept of economies in scale in manufacturing. Instead, economies of scope in non-manufacturing activities, especially banking, insurance, shipping, and other commercial areas, were accentuated. This strategy acted to reduce the cost per transaction of converting raw materials into intermediate goods and then, in some but not all cases, turning these into final products. As the steps in this process are many and as numerous ancillary services and activities, like shipping, warehousing, freight and marine insurance, credit financing, and the like, are involved in delivering final products, the dispersed and loosely linked character of early *zaibatsu* was well suited to strategies that sought to exploit interfirm economies of scope. When *zaibatsu* (as opposed to new *zaibatsu*, *shinko zaibatsu*, discussed in the next chapter) do move in the direction of scale-sensitive industries, they often did so in intermediate product markets, leaving the final goods' market to others.

The early *zaibatsu* strategy hinges on the effectiveness, not the volume, of interfirm transactions. Nevertheless, if shipping, warehousing, freight handling, and other steps in the value chain are not well articulated, costs climb quickly. Common ownership and management policies among *zaibatsu* enterprises facilitated the mobilization of interfirm resources without prohibitively high transaction costs. Common ownership and management did not guarantee efficacy, however.

Economies of scale appeared, of course, but only as wartime demand peaked in the second decade of the century by which time Japanese enterprises had seemingly acquired enough technical know-how to produce at high minimum efficient scale (MES). This does *not* assume that MES for Japanese producers was the same as for Western producers, only that certain minimal levels of throughput are needed for MES-threshold effects.[17]

Demand grew quickly during the wartime period, at home but especially in overseas markets cut off from European suppliers, driving firms to compete on the basis of cost, a production strategy that is viable only when increasing returns to scale are possible. In the case of either economies of scale or scope, a centralized *zaibatsu* strategy culminating in strong holding-company ownership and control retards the appearance and development of managerial independence in *zaibatsu*

FIG. 3.1. *Evolution of the Structure of the Mitsubishi* Zaibatsu

Mitsubishi Goshi Company 1916

Mitsubishi Goshi Company 1919[a]

Mitsubishi Company 1926[b]

[a] Affiliated companies: Mitsubishi Shipbuilding, Mitsubishi Steel, Mitsubishi Warehouse, Mitsubishi Trading, Mitsubishi Mining, Mitsubishi Marine Insurance, and Mitsubishi Bank.

[b] Affiliated companies: Mitsubishi Heavy Industry, Mitsubishi Warehousing, Mitsubishi Trading, Mitsubishi Mining, Mitsubishi Bank, Mitsubishi Electric, Mitsubishi Trust, Mitsubishi Property, Mitsubishi Steel, Mitsubishi Oil, Nippon Industrial Chemicals, and Mitsubishi Insurance.

TABLE 3.2. *Structure and Strategy of* Zaibatsu *Enterprises before World War One*

	Strategy
Interfirm relations	evolving vertical and horizontal integration within holding-company control
Marketing	specialized sales and trading companies within group for marketing and distribution
Mode of competition	oligopolistic rivalry with other *zaibatsu* focusing on economies of scope
Finance	internal capital accumulation, intergroup banking and shareholding, coordinated through family holding company control
	Structure
Ownership	closed-family ownership of strategic assets through holding company and bank control
Management	key positions within major *zaibatsu* firms held by professional managers after 1900
Administrative coordination	development of some specialized functions, such as cost accounting, applied research, and executive-support functions after 1900
Government relations	close government–business relations with encouragement and subsidy of *zaibatsu* projects; development–state relations

operating units. Without independence, the processes of managerial mediation that underlie the coordination, planning, and scheduling implied by economies of scale and scope, are less likely to appear.

The Table 3.2 summarizes and generalizes what has been said about the early history of the *zaibatsu*.

Non-*Zaibatsu* Enterprises

Independent, Urban Enterprises

Increasing numbers of independent, urban entrepreneurs entered the market for Western goods during the last quarter of the nineteenth century. They made three sorts of goods for the most part: simple, light industrial products which depended on the density of urban demand, such as ceramic wares, fabricated metal goods, paper, food, and beverages; intermediate goods produced in volume, such as cotton thread and textiles for export, cement, and agricultural fertilizers; more technologically complex and mostly custom-ordered goods, such as wall clocks, factory machinery, electrical motors, and generators. The last were needed especially for the expansion of urban public services, like power transmission, street lighting, trolley and rail lines.

Hattori Seiko. The Seiko (Hattori Seiko) Company, one of the best-known contemporary Japanese firms, had its start as an independent urban enterprise in the late nineteenth century. In 1892 Kentaro Hattori, in cooperation with two others, began to produce wall clocks for sale. In this enterprise, they relied on metal casting and smithing techniques refined during the Tokugawa period, while the latest watchmaking methods and designs were carried back to Japan by young apprentices dispatched overseas, mostly to Switzerland.[18] Amalgamations of form and function like this, often Rube Goldberg-like affairs, fell somewhere in between indigenous tools and techniques and imported concepts, designs, and know-how. They were the rule in virtually every start-up enterprise.

In 1893 Hattori's attentions were divided between the manufacture of large wall clocks for which he used a 7-horsepower steam engine for cutting and shaping parts, while he fashioned casings for pocket watches and imported the movements. By 1895, with three years' brief experience under his kimono sash, the ambitious Hattori was shipping his clocks to China, and in 1896 Hattori succeeded in producing cylinder-escapement watches, sold under the brand name 'Timekeeper'.[19] During the next five years, Hattori expanded the product line to include pocket watches, nickel-plated alarm clocks, and table clocks. In 1917 Hattori's enterprise was incorporated with a capitalization of 5 million yen, which was increased immediately to 10 million yen in the next year.[20] This level of capitalization did not land Seiko among the largest 200 industrial firms in 1918, although continued aggressive expansion of the product line catapulted Seiko into the 104th position by 1930 (see Appendix).

In addition to Western-inspired goods, like Hattori's watches and clocks, more traditional goods, such as pharmaceuticals and seasonings, were produced in volume for the first time using Western factory technology. These goods were distributed in the main by traditional 'wholesalers' (*tonya* and *toi'ya*), which were well organized and fairly efficient in the distribution of such goods. Products of this sort were branded by the distributor rather than by the manufacturer and, as a result, marketing power was severed from manufacturing capability. Product advertising was not emphasized at the point of sale.

Takeda Chemical Industries. Takeda Chemical Industries, Japan's largest pharmaceutical company, provides a case in point. Takeda began in Osaka in 1781 as an importer of Chinese medicines. These were imported in bulk, repackaged, and resold under various brand names by Takeda and other wholesalers of traditional medicines. With the opening of Japan in the late nineteenth century, Takeda expanded its business by adding Western medicines in 1871 to its inventory of marketed rather than manufactured goods.[21]

At the close of the nineteenth century with a war-induced shortage of medicines during the Sino-Japanese War, Takeda initiated the manufacture of medical and pharmaceutical preparations in Japan. In 1907 a product and quality-inspection department opened in the Nakatsu district of Osaka. By 1909 Takeda was manufacturing 20 different pharmacological preparations under Western license, and in 1914 it produced aspirin by a method of its own invention. Indeed, when World War One interrupted the orderly importation of medicines from overseas, Takeda upgraded its production inspection and control department into a research laboratory, and Jiro Takeda, family scion and student in the Pharmacology Department of the University of Tokyo was appointed its first Director.[22] New home-grown medications and preparations soon followed. Takeda burgeoned with research, production, inspection, and control departments in 1918 but had no sales or traffic offices of its own.

Other than pharmaceutical and medicinal products, manufacturers branded and advertised goods which did not fit easily into the traditional pattern of distribution or which producers purposely kept out of that system. Such makers relied on Western technology for manufacturing but consciously chose non-traditional means for distribution. Enterprises in this group include Kirin beer (the 89th largest industrial firm in 1918), pharmaceuticals from the Hoshi Pharmaceutical Company (No. 165 in 1918), paints and varnishes from Dai-Nihon Paint, alcoholic beverages from the Suntory (Kotobukiya) Company, and milled grains from Nihon Seifun (No. 73 in 1918).

Kirin Beer. Kirin beer is especially interesting because Kirin is the only company founded by foreigners which has continued successfully (under Japanese ownership) to the present day. Established in Yokohama as the Japan Beer Company in 1889, the precursor of Kirin was actually a Hong Kong registered company operating in Japan. In order to make and sell beer from a base in the foreign enclave in Yokohama, the company opened the first private glass-bottle factory in Japan in 1889 and from that date until 1927, Kirin beer, the company's brand name, was distributed solely by Meidi-ya, a Yokohama-based Western dry-goods wholesaler and retailer which remains a favored grocery for affluent Japanese and Westerners residing in greater Tokyo today.[23]

Thomas Glover of Nagasaki (and of Madame Butterfly fame) sat on the Board of Directors of the Japan Beer Company and, at the same time, was one of the principal advisers to Yataro Iwasaki, the head of the burgeoning Mitsubishi empire.[24] The importance of men like Glover in enterprises like Kirin cannot be overemphasized: from the last two decades of the nineteenth century until the first decade of the twentieth, they were actively transmitting Western business forms and practices to Japan. In fact, official business accounts were kept in English until World War One in both the Japan Beer Company and the Nagasaki Shipyard, highlighting the importance of foreign managers, methods, and models of organization well into the twentieth century.

Apparently, Glover recommended the purchase of the Japan Beer Company to Iwasaki, and in 1907 the company became part of the Mitsubishi group even though Meidi-ya continued to distribute Kirin for another twenty years. The purchase by Iwasaki should remove Kirin from our category of independent, urban enterprises except that Kirin was already well established as Japan's second largest beer-brewing company in 1907. The main change to Kirin's operations upon

Iwasaki's acquisition was to shift its purchases of German hops and barley to the Mitsubishi Trading Company.[25]

In 1927 Kirin began it own sales department as it moved towards a strategy of high-volume production and distribution during a period of excess capacity in the industry. (This was much like Noda Shoyu at the same time as the next section relates.) Although nominally part of the Mitsubishi group, Kirin Beer operated independently with a representative from Meidi-ya sitting on the Board since 1927. Kirin Beer introduced its famous lemon drink in 1928 in a move to diversify its position in the food and beverage industry.[26]

In the case of independent, urban enterprises, like Hattori, Takeda, and Kirin, the men who were legally and formally in charge of these enterprises were rarely the men who actually ran them. It was highly unusual that wealthy and politically connected men were also experienced in management and manufacturing. Instead, the chief executives and officers of most early industrial firms were closer to capitalists than managers, while the general managers and technical specialists on their staffs were more akin to managers than owners. Often, chief executive and other executive officers served simultaneously as directors of several companies, further diminishing their managerial role.

However, the separation of ownership from management was hardly complete. Most enterprises remained closely held and managerially immature. A gifted or, at least, determined amateur with proper financial backing could pilot the ventures. Separation of ownership from management would come after World War One.

The most important category of independent enterprises, textile firms, are treated later in this chapter. For now, it should be noted that the earliest textile factories were located in the countryside and in small cities. During the second and third decades of the twentieth century, textile mills grew greatly in number and size and came to be located increasingly in cities. Thus, textile firms straddle two of the three categories of enterprises discussed here, independent-urban and independent-rural.

The attributes and characteristics of independent, urban enterprises in the early twentieth century in Japan are abridged for ease of understanding in Table 3.3.

Independent, Rural Enterprises

The initial pattern of predominately rural industrialization made it possible to expand non-farm employment in the countryside without displacing large numbers of countryside people. This occurred, in part, because many of the early manufactured products were traditional ones which had been made in the countryside in small-scale, labor-intensive operations from the middle of the Tokugawa period. Household industry was practiced extensively, and in some areas accounted for as much as half or more of all household income. Thus, continuity and expansion in non-farm employment were the basis for Japan's early industrialization, a point that cannot be overemphasized in explaining the emergence of Japan's modern economy.

TABLE 3.3. *Structure and Strategy of Independent, Urban Enterprises before World War One*

	Strategy
Interfirm relations	specialization in a single product/market with non-existent or limited interfirm ties
Marketing	dependence on traditional and new wholesalers as well as trading firms
Mode of competition	price competition based on evolving economies of scale
Finance	city banks and stock issue on regional exchanges
	Structure
Ownership	several patterns of stock ownership: closely held, a few large blocks, or widely dispersed
Management	professional managers early on
Administrative coordination	development by 1920; specialized functions in accounting, research, planning, and marketing
Government relations	regulation by central government, encouragement by local government; representation by trade and business associations

Moreover, many of the newer, Western-inspired products that appeared in the late nineteenth century were also made in the countryside. Entrepreneurial landlords and urban merchants with an eye for rural investments, sometimes working together but more often working apart, set up small factories and shops to make items like new farming implements (the rotary cultivator-weeder and improved plows), wire brushes, kerosene lamps, and fabricated metal and wooden parts of various sorts and sizes. They also invested in local banks and railroad ventures. Occasionally, local factories were organized as subcontractors to larger scale works in the countryside or city, but generally the degree of coordination was not close and output was mostly a matter of how much time one found to work.[27]

The dual structure of many rural industries, namely a few large enterprises with many small, satellite establishments, has been proposed as advantageous to Japan's industrial development. In circumstances where minimum efficient scale was low, foreign firms with high-quality, high-cost goods cannot easily penetrate local markets.

Such quality-cost differentials are thought to allow domestic firms a critical 'window of opportunity' during which time they can accumulate technical and market know-how for producing lower-quality, lower-cost goods. Given sufficient time and learning, domestic firms will dominate local markets because of their lower costs and superior knowledge.[28] Such advantages were closely related to the existence of a dual industrial structure as long as transaction costs between functionally specialized, large and small businesses were not so high as to offset the production costs of the system.

Private investment concentrated in a handful of ventures: the spinning and weaving of cotton and silk, food and beverage production, paper manufacture, and clay/stone/glass products. Non-manufacturing investment flowed in banking, shipping, and transportation. Where, as in the case of textiles, some sort of continuous application of power to the manufacturing process was desired, water-powered machinery was common. Then, after 1880, steam-powered equipment began to appear, and about the turn of the century, electricity-powered equipment was introduced. In spite of the short transition period from water- to electricity-powered machinery, all forms of power generation as well as hybrids of the three basic types coexisted well into the twentieth century. The availability of electricity by the early twentieth century allowed all areas of Japan, all classes of Japanese, and all levels of factory-based production to run on affordable and available energy during the drive to industrialization.

Markets for initial manufactures were both rural and urban, but because the population was concentrated in the countryside, the origins as well as destinations for most goods were rural. A majority of high-income families were resident there and large numbers of small countryside towns belie simple notions of a rural/urban dichotomy. However, as the urban population burgeoned from the early twentieth century and as urban fashion and demand changed, many products made in the countryside were increasingly designed and destined for cities. In this category were gas and later electrical-lighting fixtures, Western-style paper and paper products, apparel, milled-grain goods, kitchen tools, glass, and ceramic ware.

Private efforts to industrialize did no better, perhaps worse, than government efforts, which is to say that failure as much as success characterized early manufacturing efforts. Capital investment in new ventures was low, often too low to enable enterprises to compete successfully with foreign-trade goods and traders. Since tariffs were set by international treaty at a low 5 percent *ad valorem*, local ventures in commerce and industry had to fight their way uphill against better quality, sometimes cheaper, more varied Western imports. Indeed, the influx of inexpensive, sturdy, and useful foreign imports threatened to undermine traditional agricultural and handicraft industries, threatening the continued sale of rural products by local and regional merchants and thereby endangering the social and economic fabric of the countryside.

As foreign goods rushed into Japan during the 1870s and as foreign middlemen, with their privileges, muscled into money-exchange and commodity markets, the traditional Japanese economy tottered on the edge of collapse. The situation worsened in spite of the appearance of non-tariff barriers that enterprising Japanese erected around the still limited number of foreign enclaves.[29] Deflationary policies adopted under Prime Minister Matsukata during the early 1880s exacerbated rural difficulties. A collapse in the traditional economy would release a flash flood of failures bankrupting not only time-honored ways of doing things but also newly established ventures that depended on foreign-exchange earnings in the form of tea, rice, and silk-thread exports. Failure in the countryside would undermine both the rural and urban economy.

But private, rural enterprises survived the stress-filled period of the 1870s and 1880s by relying in part on growing urban demand and by satisfying the needs of the majority of the population which still lived in the countryside. Rural manufacturers produced simple, straightforward goods that mixed, milled, wove, and processed rural raw materials for local and more distant markets. Typical products included ubiquitous textiles (rural spinning and weaving establishments tended to be smaller than those found in larger central places), silk thread, cereal milling, sugar refining, 'rice wine' (*sake*), 'soy bean paste and sauce' (*miso* and *shoyu*), vegetable and fish oils, agricultural fertilizers, cement, ceramic ware, and implements. Such goods were undifferentiated consumer goods, neither branded nor advertised. Instead, urban-based wholesalers and larger retailers packaged and branded these products, if branding was practiced at all.

Noda Shoyu (Kikkoman). There were some exceptions, of course. Kikkoman soy sauce (the 80th largest industrial firm in 1918), Noritake ceramics (158th in 1918), Nisshin grain and oil products (104th in 1918), Onoda cement (78th in 1918), and Ajinomoto seasoning (164th in 1918), were a few of the rural-manufactured goods that were packaged as well as branded in the countryside.[30] None the less, rural products were rarely distributed in cities by their makers; they were sold as undifferentiated rural products that were distributed by traditional 'wholesalers' (*tonya* or *toi'ya*). While investment in private railroad lines eased the flow of local goods to city markets at the turn of the century, it did little to disrupt well-established marketing and distribution flows that had been in place for so long.[31]

Occasionally, rural enterprises evolved rapidly into dynamic and thriving outposts of modern manufacturing. The Noda (Kikkoman) Soy Sauce Company and Onoda Cement Company are two such examples. Kikkoman soy sauce, noted earlier for packaging and branding its own product, was located a day's sail from Tokyo in the late nineteenth century. Although relatively close to its main market, Kikkoman's location in Noda City in rural Chiba Prefecture was far enough from Tokyo to prompt its management to form a cluster of related businesses to support its local manufacturing activities. Kikkoman established its own bank in 1900, a central research and development laboratory in 1904, and helped build a railroad line from Kashiwa through the town in 1911. Related enterprises like these, in turn, could be mobilized to help the company realize economies of scope in distribution and of scale in manufacturing. As soon as it was practical, during the 1910s and 1920s, hydraulic presses, steam boilers, conveyor belts, and transfer lines for bottling and canning were installed.[32] Increasing throughput was matched by expanded sales and marketing in northern and western Japan.

Onoda Cement. Onoda Cement was another example of innovative success in the countryside. Located in Yamaguchi Prefecture at the extreme southern tip of the main island of Honshu, Onoda Cement was founded by a warrior from the local

Choshu Domain. Apparently, class was more important than location in securing orders from the central government which turned frequently to Onoda Cement, more than 800 kilometers away. Many top government leaders, especially in the Army, were from Choshu.

At the turn of the century, the founder's son was dispatched to Germany to study chemistry and the company forged close relations with Mitsui Bussan, the Mitsui *zaibatsu*'s trading company, for domestic and foreign (Korea and China) transportation of their products. Yamaguchi Prefecture was an ideal export location for Northeast Asian markets. Onoda's exceptional dependence on Mitsui Bussan for distribution allowed it to deepen its functional focus on production. A countryside location was not an obvious obstacle to industrial innovation and progress.[33]

But Kikkoman and Onoda were unusually successful. Most rural enterprises were small, undercapitalized, without proficient managers, and at the mercy of well-entrenched marketing and distribution interests. Food and beverage companies, aside from textile ventures, were the most conspicuous and consistent industrial performers: Taiwan Sugar, Ensuiko Sugar, Meiji Sugar, Teikoku Sugar, Tainan Sugar, Niitaka Sugar, Dai-Nihon Salt, Minami Manshu Sugar, Taito Sugar, Settsu Oil, Kikkoman, Nisshin Flour Mills, Japan Flour Mills, Manshu Flour Mills, Nisshin Oil Products, and Nanyo Sugar. These were major country-side industrials in 1918.

Most significantly, Japan's initial products for export were more agricultural—tea, rice, and silk thread—than industrial in character, and more extractive—coal and metals mining—than value-additive in nature. It was unthinkable to package, brand, and advertise such products. The base for industrial products, especially those originating in the countryside, was narrowly defined to just a few categories of products: textiles, cement, food, and beverages.

All early enterprises in Japan—rural, urban, and *zaibatsu* alike—were ill prepared for the natural selection of industrialization. Few of the ventures begun in the nineteenth century survived long into the twentieth. Manufacturing did not contribute an important share to Japan's GNP at any point in the nineteenth century, and a century of trade deficits with the industrialized West afflicted Japan from the 1870s to 1970s. Except for the most recent two decades, the 1970s and 1980s, Japan's trade balance with the West has always been negative.

The attributes of independent, rural companies like Kikkoman and Onoda Cement in the early twentieth century are outlined in Table 3.4.

Non-Integration of Production and Distribution

A distinctive feature of modern industrial enterprises as they developed in the early twentieth century was the nearly universal separation of production and distribution. Even today, on the eve of the twenty-first century, approximately half of the value of Japan's imports and exports are handled by specialized distribution companies, the 'general-trading companies' (*sogo shosha*). Several reasons may be

TABLE 3.4. *Structure and Strategy of Independent, Rural Enterprises before World War One*

	Strategy
Interfirm relations	limited diversification and integration of unrelated enterprises
Marketing	traditional wholesalers in regional and national centers; specialty trading houses on occasion
Mode of competition	local monopoly and regional trade associations
Finance	local banks and wholesaler credit
	Structure
Ownership	closed-family ownership with holding-company control
Management	family management and ownership, with few professional managers as a consequence
Administrative coordination	later development: line and staff specialist positions and functions appear by the 1930s
Government relations	encouragement of local businesses at prefectural level with close business–government relations

offered for this basic division of labor. First, traditional products, such as food stuffs, beverages, paper, and lumber products, as outlined above had well-confirmed marketing channels developed during the Tokugawa era. After these goods were manufactured by Western methods, as was mostly the case by 1900, they continued to be sold and distributed through long-established wholesale and retail networks. Manufacturers saw little need and had few resources to devote to replacing or supplanting traditional distributors.

Second, the government's active encouragement of railroad construction and its eventual involvement in the establishment of a national railroad system were immeasurably beneficial to the development of modern commerce and industry. The construction of railroads followed existing roads for the most part, and thus the transportation revolution brought on by railroads reinforced rather than transformed existing hierarchies and networks of marketing and distribution. Greater transportation efficiency without a major reorientation of marketing arrangements gave the country a running start at industrial development. However, the integration of railroad development within an existing economic and social framework meant that railroad construction and coordination would not challenge established business forms. This had been the case in the United States but not in Japan.

Alfred D. Chandler, Jr. has insisted that the creation and consolidation of a railroad network in North America required sizeable administrative organizations—larger and more specialized by function and region than anything previously seen. These interlocking and distinguishing features resulted in the formation of managerial hierarchies composed of line and staff functionaries who pioneered entirely new sorts of administrative, accounting, and statistical procedures.[34]

In America, railroad managerial hierarchies prefigured and, in some ways, propelled the development of ever larger and more complex industrial managerial hierarchies. In the Japanese case, however, consolidation of the railway network took place under government control for the most part, although privately financed and operated lines took an initial lead in railroad construction. But most private lines failed or were failing when the Government consolidated much of the railway network in the early twentieth century.[35]

As a result, the complex administrative hierarchies which resulted from the railroad boom and consolidation in the United States did not appear in private hands in Japan. Instead, they appeared under government control, some forty years after similar developments in the United States. The appearance of private industrial enterprises employing up-to-date manufacturing technologies in Japan was not preceded by or coupled with the reorganization of distribution and transportation functions as had been the case in America.

Moreover, the focused product line strategy of Japanese industrials played into the hands of distributors. By linking markets and marketing activities, distributors could achieve economies of scope in heterogeneous products. Single-product firms rarely had the wherewithal or know-how to distribute nation-wide. It was not until the post-war boom in consumer goods that some firms joined production and distribution, witness the examples of Sony, Sharp, Casio, Kao, and Matsushita Electric Industrial. The size of post-war consumer markets, their volatility, and their profit margins prompted manufacturers to integrate forward into distribution in order to ensure market share for expanding production capabilities.

Pre-war consolidation of the railroad system under government control had beneficial consequences for the rolling-stock industry. With the exception of Kawasaki Shipyard, the largest industrial firm in 1918 and the largest of the rolling-stock makers, government specification of industry standards and government coordination of industry output boosted the number of new ventures (independent, urban enterprises) in this industry. These included Railroad Car Manufacturing (No. 71 in 1918) and Japan Rolling Stock (No. 135 in 1918). The stabilization of the industry led to spill-over effects in related machinery industries where Osaka Iron Works (No. 48 in 1930), Hitachi (No. 62 in 1930), Fujinagata Shipyard (No. 93 in 1930), and Niigata Engineering (No. 147 in 1918 and No. 156 in 1930), all benefited from government support of the railroad industry.[36]

Third, new industrial products were introduced by either piggybacking them on already established routes for traditional products, such as the case of Western medicinal and pharmaceutical preparations, or they were handled through entirely new sales and distribution companies established for this purpose. Relatively undifferentiated products tended to be handled in the former manner while more differentiated products could support the higher costs associated with specialized sales companies. Needless to say, given the distance from Western markets, relatively low standards of living, and limited growth opportunities in the Japanese market at this time, Western firms were reluctant to invest in developing shipping, storage, transportation, and sales facilities. Instead, it was natural to seek out Japanese partners or licensees for these purposes. This situation gave rise to the founding of countless specialized trading companies.

After 1900 complex, multi-tiered distribution channels were established for most industrial products. At the highest level, there were national and regional sales companies, often enjoying sole agency privileges for their exclusive product lines. One level down, within regional and local marketing systems, secondary sales agencies handled a variety of differentiated and undifferentiated product lines and categories. One more level down, in villages, towns, and urban neighborhoods, branches of secondary sales companies delivered goods to countless retail shops and markets.[37]

Trading companies are often considered a special feature of the Japanese economy, especially the mammoth general-trading companies that have come to monopolize so much of Japan's imports and exports after World War Two. Although the origins of today's general-trading companies may be traced back to the nineteenth century, few general-trading companies appeared before World War Two, if by a general-trading company one means an enterprise which has a world-wide network of offices and affiliates, which handles numerous commodities and products in a big way, and which accounts for a large share of the foreign trade in those product areas.[38]

Before World War Two, and especially before World War One, Japanese trading firms were few, small (numbering in the dozens and perhaps hundreds of employees), and limited in the numbers of commodities and products traded. They were few in number because the initial thrust occurred in rationalizing traditional industries where established distribution channels already existed. They were small because the volume of trade was small. They were limited as to the number of commodities and products they handled because each product demands a dif-ferentiated strategy of distribution, marketing, and sales. Highly differentiated approaches to the market-place are expensive, involving considerable up-front costs, like warehousing, advertising, training of sales agents and service tech-nicians, as well as after-sale costs, like replacement-parts inventory, maintenance requirements, and overhead costs. Moreover, in the case of turn-of-the-century Japan, new products and technologies came from overseas; as a consequence, there were relatively few persons with the linguistic, technical, and cultural skills necessary to negotiate successfully the introduction and support of new products and production processes. For these reasons, specialized trading companies and, eventually, general-trading companies appeared.

In brief, trading companies appeared to specialize in the distribution of products and commodities which were either not available in the traditional economy or were no longer handled and sold in traditional ways. As Japan edged into the twentieth century, more and more goods and services were of these sorts. Almost inevitably, trading companies came to occupy an increasingly important place in the economy, although their growing presence in the aggregate masks the volatility, instability, and difficulty that individual traders faced in various markets.

The specialization of trading companies was likewise related to the low levels of volume in manufacturing. Scale leads to standardization, even at comparatively low levels of increasing returns to scale. Standardization leads to price competition because products become more alike, and consumers buy similar products on the basis of dissimilar prices. But when scale-based competition is not prevalent, specialization in the distribution of products and in the provision of product-specific services becomes viable, even necessary. In this way, the scope of trading firms was related to the low levels of scale in manufacturing and distribution.

Because a series of interconnected facilities and services greatly eases the task of trading, it is obvious why certain products came to be quickly dominated by just a handful of firms. In the case of coal, for example, there is the initial complex decision of what kind of coal to buy and in what volume. Next, there are questions of shipping, storage, and delivery. Insurance, freight handling, and customs, where necessary, further complicate matters. And none of this considers the need for sales offices, technical advising at the points of origin and delivery, and overall coordination of the process of sale and distribution.

As the example of coal illustrates, certain products, by the nature of their size, cost, handling, or use characteristics, demand an entire set of interrelated facilities in order to be sold successfully. Accordingly, the investment in human and material resources to sell products, especially foreign products, could be quite considerable. It is in these sticky investment requirements that the origins of general-trading companies can be found; few traders could muster the inter-connected facilities and services needed to sell and distribute numerous products. 'Generalness' was a long time coming for *Sogo Shosha*. The reasons are found in what are called economies of scope as opposed to economies of scale.

Enterprises of Scope

There is a trade-off between economies of scope and economies of scale. The former requires coordinated interdependence among a number of related firms, none of which may depend greatly on volume manufacturing or distribution for its economic viability. The latter economies, in contrast, occur in industries and enterprises geared to volume pure and simple. In Japan before World War Two, indeed before the late 1950s, the domestic and proximate East Asian markets for volume goods were not large, and it was extremely risky to compete on the basis of economies of scale in most instances. The beneficial effects of volume are exhausted or, at least, reduced substantially at relatively low levels of production. Ship-building, diesel engine manufacture, railroad rolling-stock, and telegraph/telephone-equipment industries—core industries of pre-war Japan and typically producer-goods—were not especially geared to volume manufacturing.

Certain industries, noted earlier, were able to achieve some sort of sustainable scale economies, and these included textiles, paper, some metals production, food, cement and beverages. But most industries and enterprises were driven more by economies of scope, that is economies which emphasized joint production and distribution. An interrelated constellation of firms, each performing part of a complex production and distribution process and each joined in a mutual effort to coordinate flows and functions associated with the entire process, could reduce costs. How much they could reduce costs depends on how effectively they could coordinate interrelated activities. In any event, the cost savings realized would have to be sufficient to offset the high costs associated with small production runs and limited demand.[39]

It is in this intercorporate context that *zaibatsu* groups, new as well as old, were likely to be effective in lowering costs. A trading company associated with one of the groups, say, Mitsui & Co. founded in 1876 as an amalgamation of Kokusan Kata and Senshu Kaisha, could supply quotes on overseas prices for various raw materials and finished goods, such as raw cotton or textile machinery. The opportunity costs for accurate information without overseas offices might be rather high.

But Mitsui & Co.'s overseas offices could do a great deal more than simply provide information. By 1901 Mitsu & Co. offices were found in Shanghai, Hong Kong, Tientsin, Singapore, Surabaya, Bombay, London, and New York. A string of offices could arrange for shipping, warehousing, freight forwarding, and customs-duty clearances. These services were extended not only for the importation of raw materials into Japan but also for the export of finished goods. Such services were essentially financial and managerial in character, and when the resources of Mitsui & Co. proved insufficient, those of the mighty Mitsui Bank could be committed—for a fee, of course.

In 1901, for example, Mitsui & Co. struck a deal with Kanegafuchi Boseki, one of the largest cotton-spinning companies, wherein Kanegafuchi agreed to purchase at least 70 percent of the raw cotton it would require from Mitsui & Co., and in return Kanegafuchi contracted with Mitsui & Co. for credit financing of its raw-cotton purchases as well as for quality inspection and delivery of raw cotton to Kanegafuchi mills. Mitsui & Co. could lend on favorable terms to Kanegafuchi because Mitsui & Co. could borrow on extremely favorable terms from Mitsui Bank, the largest bank in terms of the size of deposits in pre-war Japan.

In 1906 Mitsui & Co. organized the Nippon Menpu Yushutsu Kumiai or the Association of Japanese Cotton Exporters in order to promote the export of finished cotton goods from Japan. Mitsui & Co. was clearly instrumental in creating markets at home and abroad for its broad range of services and clients. And when Mitsui & Co. was unable to service a market or promote a product, it was quick to call on other Mitsui companies for help. In addition to Mitsui Bank, major Mitsui firms were Oji Paper, Shibaura Engineering, Toyo Koatsu Industries, Toyo Menka (a specialized firm for the cotton trade), Onoda Cement, and Denki Kagaku Kogyo (Electro-Chemical Industries).[40]

Together, Mitsui & Co. and Mitsui Bank could boast an impressive equity position in 253 different companies in fourteen different industries in 1940.[41] In essence, Mitsui & Co. was far more than a trading company. It was a holding company, bank, shipping and distribution agent, marketing, and consulting company. Much the same could be said for Mitsubishi Trading Company, the other 'general' trading company in the pre-war period. Such firms leaned towards operations based on economies of scope, that is joint sourcing, shipping, manufacturing, and marketing, and thereby lowered costs per transaction of getting goods to market. By increasing the flow of activities channeled through existing facilities, trading firms could serve larger markets and maintain marginal revenues in the face of increasing marginal costs.[42]

Because the size of the pre-war market for most products was limited, transporting, processing, marketing, and distributing economies appear more important than scale economies in manufacturing (although the question of scale is more a question of appropriate size of plant than market). Textiles were exceptional in their emphasis on scale. Most industries and facilities, by contrast, emphasized economies of scope, and this was especially true among the pre-war *zaibatsu* groups of interrelated firms. Such groupings capitalized on the overseas connections of trading firms and on market-sharing agreements realized through trade-association activities and horizontal combinations in industry. Rather than having one or at most several firms emerging as clear-cut price and productivity leaders in various manufacturing industries, trade and manufacturing associations could effectively set industry standards, tacitly divide up the market, coordinate competition, and otherwise work to reduce the risks and managerial overhead which individual firms faced. This would not obviate price competition but it would reduce it.

When manufacturers are not producing at moderate-to-high levels of minimum efficient scale, the availability of goods and after-market services may become more important than price. Manufacturers compete, as a result, on the basis of advantages in shipping, transport, distribution, finance, and related services that are provided by a combination of firms. Trading companies, in particular, were important because of their well-entrenched sales network at home and overseas; their crucial role in technology transfer and in securing foreign manufacturing licenses; and their capabilities for maximizing economies of scope by carrying and moving a number of products quickly through the distribution pipeline.

As a result, until the turn of the twentieth century in a few industries and until a decade or two later in most industries, corporations in Japan were slow to develop strategies of organizational centralization and integration based on the concepts of economies of scale and product/market share. This happened only after major operating companies of *zaibatsu* enterprise groups hired large numbers of university and technical school graduates; such graduates are not thought to have figured significantly until the inter-war period, except perhaps in the case of the Mitsubishi group.[43]

Until then, holding companies provided a vehicle for wealthy families and individuals to control their investments in a growing number of operating companies. Holding companies often performed managerial functions for operating firms, yet unlike the headquarters of multidivisional corporations as described by

Chandler, holding companies did not act as a capital market to measure the performance of and allocate funds to subsidiary enterprises. Thus, Japanese holding companies were unlike the general headquarters of American firms adopting the multidivisional form during the inter-war period. They were somewhat more akin to the head offices of single-product, single-function firms which still dominated Western markets at this time, but even these U-Form firms were more complex structures, with larger managerial staffs and with more varied functions than Japanese pre-war holding companies.

In sum, manufacturing was divorced from distribution, due to the continued importance of the traditional distribution sector and to the brokering activities performed by trading companies. Also, because manufacturing activities were not solely geared towards achieving minimum efficient scale, managerial resources were not concentrated at the middle and upper-middle reaches of the firm where planning, scheduling, coordinating, and evaluating functions associated with scale economies would be normally found. Economies of scope in pre-World War One Japan led to an appearance of manufacturing firms which concentrated managerial resources in factories and at the lower levels of the firm rather than in higher level coordinating functions, and which relied on a network of interrelated firms to achieve breadth in business activities.

Enterprises of Scale

Textile firms were pre-eminent enterprises of scale, although companies producing foodstuffs, such as beer, sugar, and milled grains, as well as some paper, cement, metal, and chemical manufacturers were committed to manufacturing in volume. Ocean-going ships, while not exactly fabricated in volume, increased in number by World War One. Six of the largest twenty industrial firms in 1918 were shipyards and attendant steel producers: Kawasaki Shipyards, Mitsubishi Shipyards, Mitsubishi Steel, Japan Steel, Japan Steel Works, and Uraga Dock.

With the exception of textiles, the other scale industries were not export industries. Their growth was limited by the size of the domestic market which was not exceptionally large before the 1960s. In the case of textiles, however, Japanese manufacturers could reap scale economies in production before World War Two by exporting the bulk of their manufactures. Textile firms, therefore, became the first modern industrial enterprises with extensive managerial hierarchies and they accounted for one-quarter of the largest 200 industrial firms in 1918 and for one-third in 1930. (See Appendix as well as Table 5.1 and Fig. 5.1.)

Textile firms, nevertheless, were surprisingly simple in organization until after World War One. The usual pattern was that a large number of stockholders/owners, numbering in the dozens and sometimes hundreds, supplied money while a smaller number of managers and engineers/technicians actually ran the operations. Raw materials for processing and machines for manufacturing were imported by trading firms which normally disposed of the finished product as well. In many cases, 'regional wholesalers' (*tonya*) could substitute local manufactures for imported goods. Because raw materials and machinery were acquired in this fashion and finished goods handled in this way, textile companies were quite lean in middle-management functions.

The missing middle-management functions, such as the monitoring of markets, scheduling of inputs and outputs, timing of purchases and sales, were performed on the whole by specialized and later general-trading companies and by traditional dry-goods wholesalers. Accordingly, textile companies did not develop elaborate managerial hierarchies to plan, coordinate, schedule, and allocate, until much later, generally well into the middle of the twentieth century. Their organizational hierarchies remained comparatively simple in structure, and, unlike the organization of the textile industry in many other countries, spinning and weaving operations were not often combined. Textile firms, as a consequence, were modern enterprises, essentially the first enterprises to maximize economies of scale, but few became extended, large, modern enterprises in the way those adjectives are employed in this study.[44]

None the less, textile firms were modern because they were the first to develop an organization which combined the factory system of manufacture with a managerial hierarchy for cost control and for coordination of production and distribution. In accomplishing this, Japanese textile firms relied little upon past industrial practices. Instead they incorporated Western machinery, technology, organization, and management in new forms and new ways to achieve manufacturing economies of scale. The high-thread-count cotton textiles that began to appear at the close of the nineteenth century were quite different from what had been previously the market standard: low-thread count, low-quality goods that were made with indifferent production controls and smallish looms. High-quality thread and textiles were new products requiring close integration, careful monitoring of the steps of production, a better trained and motivated workforce, a more highly capitalized and better managed enterprise.

The choice to move away from small (2–3,000 spindles), water-powered mills which lost money in the 1860s and 1870s, to larger (more than 10,000 spindles), steam-powered mills from the 1880s, led to the development of functionally specialized, closely administered manufacturing sites that eventually included purchasing, sales, finance, engineering, power generation, transport, personnel, plant and production inspection, quality control, sanitation, industrial training, accounting, and employee recruitment.[45] Integration of these functions necessitated the creation of a class of managers who actually managed. Pioneering firms influenced strongly the direction of the industry; their success and its imitation minimized the struggles of countless others.

In 1895, for example, Sanji Muto of Kanegafuchi Spinning (now Kanebo) established a corporate office separate from the company's two factories in Tokyo and Kobe. Technical and managerial specialists, like the chief works engineer and company accountants, were assigned to the head office while operational personnel hired from universities and technical schools were assigned to functional responsibilities in the two plants. Muto even designed much of the plant and machinery for the company, establishing an engineering department in each factory to carry out his designs, and he created a labor department to coordinate the overall recruitment, training, and supervision of Kanegafuchi employees.[46] But Muto's system at Kanegafuchi was unusual for its day. Most spinning companies had not yet separated head office and factory functions, and so they had two general managers at the same site: one for production and one for purchasing and sales.

Even after textile companies became large through merger and an expansion of production facilities, there was often a remarkable decentralization of management personnel and functions. In the case of Toyobo, for example, after it acquired Settsu and Hirano Spinning Companies to become one of the largest industrial enterprises in Japan, the number of personnel located at the head office remained surprisingly small. According to the Toyobo Company history, at the end of 1914 there were a total of 36,694 personnel working for the firm. Of these, 36,215 were working at one of the far-flung Toyobo factories, leaving less than 500 persons at the head office to carry out central administrative, accounting, and personnel functions. In fact, 479 persons at Toyobo's head office in 1914 constituted only 1.3 percent of the total number of company employees.[47]

Instead of attempting to centralize administrative functions and coordinate them at the head office, factories hired large local administrative staffs. In Toyobo's case, following its amalgamation with Settsu and Hirano, the company decided not to centralize, standardize, and systematize operations in one central location under a single standard of corporate strategy and structure.[48] Instead, it integrated and coordinated activities in a decentralized way, following the model of focal factories discussed elsewhere. Toyobo's example of not centralizing operations was widely imitated, following a wave of mergers in the textile industry during the recession years of 1907–14. While some economies of scale in production may have been sacrificed by not combining facilities, offsetting benefits may have been realized in other areas, such as savings associated with the costs of capital or raw-material inputs.[49]

Conclusion: Origins and Early Evolution of the Japanese Enterprise System

The extremely rapid pace of economic development from the Russo-Japanese War of 1904–5 to the end of World War One propelled a broad spectrum of Japanese firms forward, increasing their sales, profits, organizational size and complexity. In fact the economy grew more swiftly than the capacity of most firms to internalize sufficient resources to respond effectively. In a different economy or in a different time, managers might have attempted to internalize additional functions, new products and markets within the confines of a single firm, as was the case for large M-form firms in the United States. Japanese managers did so to some degree. Firms grew larger and became more complex in form and function. But the economy expanded extremely rapidly and the capabilities of most firms were simply not adequate to respond in kind.

Finances were constrained by a lack of collateral, bank credit, and a proven securities exchange. Management was largely unequal to the tasks of simultaneously devising new methods of financial and cost-accounting control, deepening technical and engineering know-how, developing new sales and marketing channels, and deploying human and non-human resources in the most effective ways possible. Managers were too few in number and not yet experienced in running large, complex business organizations.

So firms did what they could do, namely specialize.[50] Manufacturers focused product lines, sales firms extended market and service channels, and all firms looked elsewhere for organizational connections that might allow business expansion without incurring the full costs of doing so. An enterprise system began to appear, at first slowly.

Three different pathways in the evolution of modern industrial enterprise in Japan emerged. An amalgamation of private and de-nationalized endeavors defies any easy characterization of *zaibatsu* enterprises; over time *zaibatsu* families and their holding companies sought to find and define complementary spheres of activity among many business ventures. A holding-company structure enabled families to maintain ownership in the midst of expanding activity even as the management of major operating companies, like banks, trading firms, and large manufacturing ventures, became increasingly professionalized in management and complex in organizational structure.

Independent, that is non-*zaibatsu*, enterprises were smaller, less complex in form, and less well off financially than *zaibatsu* competitors. In aggregate, however, they were more numerous, widespread, and diversified in terms of the breadth of their activities. They were also more important given their estimated two-thirds to three-quarters contribution to the nation's domestic manufactured product.

Independent, urban companies tended to be single-product firms, competing on the basis of price, with professionalized management and open financing structures from the start. Independent, rural companies, by contrast, were less focused in product line, less price competitive, and less open in matters of ownership and control. They often enjoyed significant competitive advantages based on their location. Markets for many products were still local.

No matter the forms of modern industrial enterprise, the corporation was rooted in Japanese soil by World War One. Numerous intersecting signs of its establishment were apparent. In production management, there was a shift from indirect to direct methods of management. Companies relied on their own abilities to recruit and retain workers and to manage them effectively. An advance by company-trained technicians and engineers supplemented the efforts of foremen. Managers expanded their responsibilities to include the quality, education, on-the-job training, and general well-being of workers as well as the repeatability, reproducibility, and stability of the production process.[51] This corresponds to the distinction between primary and secondary factories employed in this study.

There was both a technical and economic logic to this shift. Ever increasing numbers of university and technical school graduates were entering private enterprise. By the 1920s Hoshimi Uchida estimates that 20,000 technically trained graduates were working in government and industry, the majority in private enterprises.[52] By 1935 this number would climb to 50,000. The more complex and technically demanding products of the second industrial revolution required more and better trained engineers and managers.

By World War One, professional or salaried managers would sit on the Boards of most industrial enterprises, entrusted with not only day-to-day decisions but also strategic oversight. This was a considerable leap forward in their status and responsibilities, compared with the situation at the turn of the century, some twenty years earlier. At that time, professional managers and engineers, mostly younger and less experienced, were *not* sitting on Boards and participating in strategic decision-making. They were factory managers, production overseers, engineering specialists, but not corporate managers. At the turn of the century, the time-horizons of joint-stock companies were foreshortened; companies were often disbanded on a predetermined schedule, usually three, five, or ten years, regardless of whether or not enterprises were profitable. The more profitable the enterprise, the more likely that its shareholders sought corporate dissolution as a quick road to profits. Such attitudes were customary in the investment pools of early railroad and industrial enterprises.[53]

However, the macro-economic climate changed dramatically. The Russo-Japanese War of 1904–5 and World War One forced enterprises to shorten lead times and to promote advances in technical and production specifications; simultaneously, wartime circumstances provided unusual opportunities for companies willing and able to make a leap to higher levels of enterprise management and coordination. Increasingly the Government promoted policies of import substitution, science-based innovation, and production efficiency. In order to respond to these new and lucrative opportunities, companies hired growing numbers of scientists, engineers, and technicians. Company headquarters were moved, if necessary, to the down-town sections of Tokyo and Osaka, to be closer to government offices as well as to the banking, finance, and transportation services. Shares and debentures in the leading industrial enterprises were more widely held than previously. Companies forged close ties with other companies for doing business together on something less than an 'arms-length' basis.

As a result of this massive, extended, and largely one-way effort to catch up, streamline, transform, and propel the country and its leading institutions forward, it is possible to say that Japan was closer to the West in 1910–20 than in any other time past or present. Admittedly, this is contrary to the technological convergence argument which assumes that as nations industrialize, they become increasingly similar in organizational and behavioral patterns. However, the driving force behind the successful modernization of Japanese industry is, in fact, a threefold process: the application of knowledge to problems of organization and production, positive and numerous intrafirm/interfirm feedback loops in the technology-transfer process, and accumulated experience through organizational learning.

Obviously, similarities based on technological convergence are greatest at the point of knowledge acquisition and weakest at the point of knowledge implementation. Organizational learning is, above all, a process of institutional differentiation: to the extent that institutions depend on organizational learning, they become increasingly adept at managing change and increasingly different as a result of change. Distinctive company cultures result.

In sum, by 1920 a new form of enterprise organization, the modern corporation and its organizational correlates, interfirm networks and full-function factories, had gained a number of decisive advantages in the mobilization and management of industrial resources in Japan. Consistent with the concept of a 'learning industrial revolution', the modern corporation had been transformed into an institution of managers, engineers, technicians, and workers, organized to match and join enterprise strategy with market and technological opportunities. But it would not be until the inter-war period that modern corporations, well-articulated networks, and fully integrated factories, as we think of them—large, functionally specialized, professionally managed, organizationally complex and interrelated—would gain sufficient internal strength and sophistication to emerge clearly and powerfully as the leading economic institutions of Japan.

NOTES

1. Professor Hidemasa Morikawa, along with Professors Asajima, Yui, Yasuoka, Miyazaki, and others, have published a great deal in Japanese on the subject of *zaibatsu*, *zaibatsu* history, the connection between *zaibatsu* and *keiretsu*, and related matters. For the most part, there is agreement about the organizational characteristics of evolved *zaibatsu*, that is *zaibatsu* groups after the devolution of government ventures in the 1880s but before the separation of ownership and control in the 1920s.

2. Herman Daems, *The Holding Company and Corporate Control* (Leiden: Martinus Nijhoff, 1978), 2–9.

3. Professor Morikawa's study of *zaibatsu* enterprise groups is scheduled to appear from Harvard University Press.

4. John G. Roberts documents this pretty thoroughly for the Mitsui group of companies in *Mitsui* (Tokyo: Weatherhill, 1973). Eleanor M. Hadley, however, argues for a rather effective dissolution of *zaibatsu* control by the abolition of family holding companies and the confiscation of *zaibatsu* family wealth in *Anti-trust in Japan* (Princeton, NJ: Princeton University Press, 1970). I side with Roberts on this issue. Industrial coordination, integration, and interdependence are not based largely on financial ties in a modern industrial economy, although such ties may facilitate, buttress, and promote coordination. By the 1930s and 1940s the separation of ownership from control and the consequent professionalization of management were well advanced in *zaibatsu* interfirm groups.

5. Divestiture was not based on technological or market relatedness. It was based more on inside knowledge and politics than anything else.

6. Johannes Hirschmeier and Tsunehiko Yui (eds.), *The Development of Japanese Business*, 2nd edn. (London: George Allen & Unwin, 1981), 133–5.

7. Ibid. 227–8.

8. Ibid. 201, 225.

9. This brief history of Shibaura Engineering and its early relationship with Mitsui comes from Toyko Shibaura Denki, *Toshiba Hyakunenshi* (A Hundred Years of Toshiba) (Tokyo: Daiyamondo, 1977).

10. Hirschmeier and Yui (eds.), *Development of Japanese Business*, 198, 220.

11. Shin'ichi Yonekawa and Hideki Yoshihara, *Business History of General Trading Companies* (Tokyo: University of Tokyo Press, 1987). Tsunehiko Yui was a personal source for some of these insights concerning the nature of the Sumitomo holding company and the Sumitomo group in the pre-war period.

12. William D. Wray, *Mitsubishi and the N.Y.K., 1870–1914* (Cambridge, Mass.: Harvard University Press, 1984).

13. This is not simply my assertion but the research findings of others looking at the Mitsubishi group as well. First, Takayasu Miyakawa, Director of the Mitsubishi Research Institute and for long in charge of the Mitsubishi Archives in Tokyo, has affirmed this point. Second, scholars, including Hidemasa Morikawa, Yasuo Mishima, and Shigeaki Yasuoka, have come to a similar conclusion in their studies.

14. Mitsubishi Corporation, *Mitsubishi Shashi*, xxix (Tokyo: Tokyo University Press, 1981), 4322–3, 4487–8.

15. See Hidemasa Morikawa's history of the *zaibatsu* (in English), *Zaibatsu: The Rise and Fall of Family Enterprise Groups in Japan* (Tokyo: University of Tokyo Press, 1992). See also, Hirschmeier and Yui (eds.), *Development of Japanese Business*, 153–4.

16. Tsunehiko Yui (ed.), *Yasuda Zaibatsu* (The Yasuda Zaibatsu) (Tokyo: Nihon Keizai Shinpunsha, 1986), 118–21, 283–4, 325.

17. It is not known what the MES for various per-war Japanese industries was. It is known that factory-level economies of scale are not directly dependent on the total size of the market. Michael A. Cusumano's study, *The Japanese Automobile Industry* (Cambridge, Mass.: Harvard University Press, 1985), established this for the post-war automobile industry. A possible interpretation of this surprising fact is illustrated in Fig. 3.2 suggested by Professors Masaharu Udagawa and Hikino Takashi. MES is not uniform across markets and countries.

18. Seiko Company, *Hattori & Co.* (mimeograph in Japanese), undated.

19. Uchida Hoshimi, 'Comment on Professor Nakagawa's Paper', Fuji International Conference on Business History, 5–8 Jan. 1988.

20. Seiko Company, *Hattori & Co.* (mimeograph in Japanese), undated.

21. Probably the most complete company history in Japan is the massive two-volume history of Takeda Chemical Industries. In addition, Takeda maintains a company archive, professionally staffed. See Takeda Yakuhin Kogyo, *Takeda Yakuhin Sanbyakunenshi* (300 years of Takeda Pharmaceuticals) (1985).

22. Ibid.

23. Kirin Beer Co., *Kirin Biiru Gojunenshi* (50 years of Kirin Beer) (Tokyo: 1957).

24. Kirin Beer Co., *Kaisha Gaiyo* (Company Profile) (Tokyo, 1981).

25. Kirin Beer Co., *Kirin Biiru Gojunenshi*, 56–8.

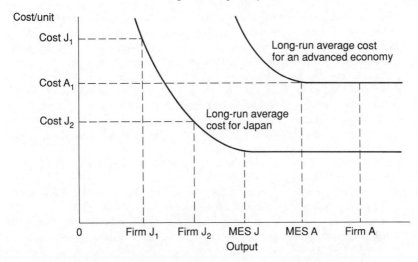

FIG. 3.2. *Minimum Efficient Scale, Unit Cost, and International Competition*

26. Kirin Beer Co., *Kaisha Gaiyo*.
27. The point has been well established for such rural industries as *sake* and *shoyu* production as well as for silk-spinning, lacquer-ware, and, depending on local circumstances, ceramics, some cotton-spinning, metals fabrication, utensils, and household goods made of wood. For cotton-spinning and weaving, see Taikichi Ito, 'Kikai kogyo no hattatsu: Tokuni menboshoku kikai kogyo no hattatsu o chushin to shite', in Arisawa Hiromi *et al.* (eds.), *Chusho Kigyo Kenkyu I: Chusho Kigyo no Hattatsu* (Research on Small- and Medium-sized Business I: The Development of Small- and Medium-sized Business) (Tokyo: Toyo Keizai Shinposha, 1960).
28. Minoru Sawai, 'The Development of Machine Industries and The Evolution of Production and Labor Management', in Keiichiro Nakagawa and Tsunehiko Yui (eds.), *Japanese Management in Historical Perspective* (Tokyo: University of Tokyo Press, 1989), 202.
29. Shin'ya Sugiyama, 'Jukyuseiki Kohanki ni okeru Higashi Ajia Seito-shijo no Kozo', in Akira Hayami, Osamu Saito, and Shin'ya Sugiyama (eds.), *Tokugawa Shakai kara no Tenbo* (Observations from Tokugawa Society) (Tokyo: Dobunkan, 1989). Sugiyama argues that local Japanese businessmen set up shipping, warehousing, and freight-handling capabilities around foreign settlements in Japan, both as a way to benefit from cross-society trading and as a way to control it.
30. W. Mark Fruin, *Kikkoman: Company, Clan, and Community* (Cambridge, Mass.: Harvard University Press, 1983); Nihon Seifun Co., *Nihon Seifun 70 Nenshi* (70 years of Nihon Seifun) (Tokyo, 1968); Nisshin Seifun, *Nisshin Seifun Kabushiki Kaisha* (70 years of Nisshin Seifun) (Tokyo, 1955).
31. Steve Erickson, 'Private Railroads in the Meiji Era: Forerunners of Modern Japanese Management?' in Nakagawa and Yui (eds.), *Japanese Management in Historical Perspective*.
32. Fruin, *Kikkoman*.

33. Ibid. Thomas C. Smith's seminal article in this regard was a stimulus to my own work; 'Pre-Modern Economic Growth: Japan and the West', *Past and Present*, 60 (Aug. 1973).

34. Based on the Nationalization Law of 1906, the Japan National Railway bought six privately owned railway companies in 1906, eleven in 1907, and still more later. After purchasing the lines, the Government set about to integrate them by reorganizing repair facilities, standardizing locomotives and rolling-stock, scheduling preventive and routine repairs, and working to monitor and streamline the flow of traffic. See Eisuke Daito, 'Industrial Training and Factory Management in Japan, 1900–1930', in Keiichiro Nakagawa and Tsunehiko Yui (eds.), *Organization and Management* (Tokyo: Japan Business History Institute, 1983), 65–6.

35. Erickson, 'Private Railroads in the Meiji Era', in Nakagawa and Yui (eds.), *Japanese Management in Historical Perspective*.

36. Minoru Sawai, 'Machine Industries and Production and Labor Management', in Nakagawa and Yui (eds.), *Japanese Management in Historical Perspective*, 200.

37. Tsunehiko Yui, 'Development Organization and International Competitiveness of Industrial Enterprises in Japan (1880–1915)', *Business and Economic History*, 2nd ser., 17 (1988), 14.

38. Kunio Yoshihara, *Sogo Shosha: The Vanguard of the Japanese Economy* (Oxford: Oxford University Press, 1981). This is Yoshihara's working definition of general-trading companies.

39. This is an argument that economies of scope can be more important than economies of scale in certain cases. Normally, economies of scope are considered as a corollary of economies of scale and, therefore, they should not exist independent of increasing returns to scale. However, where raw materials had to be sourced overseas, paid for and insured, shipped to Japan, held in storage, shipped again, processed, and then distributed, the non-manufacturing segment of the value chain is quite extended and rather more important than the manufacturing segment in determining aggregate costs. In such circumstances as these, I would argue that interfirm economies of scope should be treated separately from increasing returns to scale.

40. Roberts, *Mitsui*.

41. Yoshihara, *Sogo Shosha*, 30.

42. I want to thank Tom Roehl for clarifying my thinking on the relationship between marginal revenue and marginal costs in situations characterized by economies of scope.

43. Shin'ichi Yonekawa, 'University Graduates in Japanese Enterprises before the Second World War', *Business History*, 26/2 (July 1984), 193–218.

44. Tsunehiko Yui, 'Development, Organization, and Business Strategy of Industrial Enterprises in Japan (1915–1935)', in Shigeaki Yasuoka and Hidemasa Morikawa (eds.), *Japanese Yearbook on Business History*, 5 (Tokyo: Japan Business History Institute, 1988).

45. Matao Miyamoto, 'The Products and Market Strategies of the Osaka Cotton Spinning Company: 1883–1914', in Yasuoka and Morikawa (eds.), *Japanese Yearbook on Business History*.

46. Yui, 'Development, Organization and International Competitiveness', 8.

47. Toyobo Company, *Toyoboseki Shichijunenshi* (Osaka: Toyoboseki, 1953), 204–5, 245–6, 290–1, 347–50. Toyobo Company, *Hyakunenshi: Toyobo* (A Hundred Years of Toyobo) (Osaka: Toppan, 1986), 78, 168–70, 174–6, 178–84, 205–6, 219–21. Daido Keori, *Ito Hitosuji* (Tokyo: Bunshodo, 1960).

48. Keiichiro Nakagawa's statement at the 15th Fuji Business History Conference, 6 Jan. 1988.
49. Yui, 'Development, Organization and International Competitiveness', 16.
50. Specialization or focus is one of three generic strategies identified by Michael Porter in *Competitive Strategy* (New York: Free Press, 1980). The other two are differentiation and cost leadership. My argument is that, of the three, only specialization made sense in the early stages of Japan's industrialization. Companies could hardly succeed with one product much less several, and a strategy of cost leadership was inconceivable at the time. As companies developed their capabilities in specialized markets, they could assume a cost-leadership position, and once that strategy had been secured, differentiation strategies became possible. It is crucial to recognize the sequencing of these strategies for historical and logical reasons.
51. This is a theme that I have developed in several places and one in which I remain involved in my current research. See e.g., the chapters on labor management in *Kikkoman*; 'Instead of Management: Internal Contracting and the Genesis of Modern Labor Management', in Nakagawa and Yui (eds.), *Japanese Management in Historical Perspective*.
52. Ryoichi Iwauchi, 'The Growth of White-Collar Employment in Relation to the Education System', and Hoshimi Uchida, 'Comment' (on Iwauchi's paper), in Nakagawa and Yui (eds.), *Japanese Management in Historical Perspective*. See also, Minoru Sawai, 'Machine Industries and Production and Labor Management', in Nakagawa and Yui, (eds.), *Japanese Management in Historical Perspective*, 208–16.
53. Yui, 'Development, Organization, and Business Strategy'.

4

Defining the Enterprise System

Large Modern Corporations, 1918–1954

The twentieth-century emergence of modern corporations in Japan, detailed in the last chapter, was furthered by an elaboration and maturation of modern corporations into *large* modern corporations during the inter-war period. The passage to large and modern represents more than an increase in size, for size in this instance is a surrogate measure for institutional progress in the degree of organizational complexity, specialization, integration, and coordination. In particular, size is related to organizational interdependence. Firms became large as strategic planning and functional coordination between production (factories and networks) and distribution (firms and networks) became paramount, and so growth in one constituent element of the Japanese enterprise system signals growth and development in the others.

These processes of institutional refinement occurred as three critical conditions for the development of an industrial economy were met: first, a transportation infrastructure, dominated by railroads but buttressed by maritime shipping and surface-road expansion under government leadership, was built, standardized, and extended to the far corners of the Japanese empire. In 1906–7 the Japanese Government incorporated the Japan National Railroad and in the process acquired many private lines while at the same time standardizing existing equipment and services. From 1907 to 1916, the length of operating lines in service grew by 40 percent, men/kilometers of service by 230 percent, and tons/kilometers of freight by 350 percent.[1]

Second, the expansion and regularization of transportation systems improved access to raw-material sources as well as to markets for intermediate and finished products, pushing the flow of manufactures beyond Japan to East Asia, Southeast Asia, and even to Europe and North America. The most important new sources for raw materials were Korea, Taiwan, and Sahkalin, all war-won colonial possessions (Sino-Japanese War 1894–5 and Russo-Japanese War 1904–5). The same colonies, plus China and Southeast Asia minus Sakhalin, were Japan's best overseas markets before the Pacific War.

Third, the product mix of Japanese industry was enriched by an ongoing concentration in light industry, most importantly spun and woven textile goods, cement, food and beverages, and by a further development of the heavy industrial sector, notably organic and, later, synthetic chemicals, transportation equipment, electrical machinery, non-ferrous metals, and steel. The growth of heavy manufacturing and machinery sectors during the inter-war period diversified the economy, adding weight as well as reach to industrial output. Growth was evident in the numbers of large firms, their size as measured by assets, sales, and number of employees, and in the increasing sophistication of their production methods. (See Appendix, 1930.)

Chemicals, especially synthesized chemicals and electrochemicals, machinery (electric and non-electric), and transportation equipment are products of the second industrial revolution, so-called because England, the first industrial nation, ushered in the original products of a new industrial age, principally iron, textiles, distilled and brewed alcohols. More sophisticated products, such as those mentioned above as well as high-grade steel, gunpowder and more powerful explosives, cellulose, locomotives, steamships, automobiles, electrical motors, diesel and gasoline motors, mammoth power transformers and generators, came later with what is called the second industrial revolution. Depending on the countries in question, the first industrial revolution ranged from the late eighteenth to early nineteenth centuries while the second followed from the late nineteenth to early twentieth centuries.

Japanese corporations benefited, as late-developing industrial enterprises, from the opportunity to pick and choose from emerging as well as established manufacturing technologies and product lines of the Western world. Remember that the benefit was found primarily in the range of choices and not in the ease of application. Through the mid-1960s, in fact, fully one-third of Japanese manufacturers' expenditures on R & D went towards technology scanning and technology adaptation for local circumstances.[2]

The most advanced products for domestic adoption were those of the second industrial revolution and, more than anything else, the manufacture of these punctuates the move to large and complex corporations. Because Japanese firms lacked resources of all sorts, however, they were unable to achieve the size and economies of the Western enterprises that they emulated. Their innovativeness was to make do by finding ways to manage the complexities of industrial markets, technologies, and organizations without the resources of Western firms. A strategy of interrelating production and distribution functions through interorganizational coordination was an innovative consequence.

The demand for new production technologies, new products, and new producers accelerated dramatically at the time of the Great War. Among the major industrial nations, Japan alone was removed geographically and politically from the European conflict and, as a result, Japanese firms filled prodigious orders for virtually all combatants. As orders mounted, the scale and sophistication of Japan's industrial complex grew. The newer, twentieth-century products were more complicated to make and sell than those of the nineteenth century, and the rise of the second industrial revolution was pivotal in promoting a maturation of enterprise structure and strategy. Coupled with an enhancement of the transportation infrastructure, improved access to raw materials and markets, and with an existing manufacturing foundation in light industry, the second industrial revolution introduced more elaborate and complex forms of industrial enterprise—namely, large, modern corporations.

But the concept of the large and modern Japanese corporation is a relative one. Certainly, major industrial firms of the inter-war period were large and modern compared to what had been typical before World War One, but large and modern are still relative. The numbers of head-office and corporate-level staff rarely became as large as those of comparable American firms. In 1939, the head office of the Kureha Spinning Company, a large enterprise with fourteen factories producing natural and synthetic silk fiber, ran with no more than ten people.[3]

In terms of assets, sales, and the number of employees or product lines, Japanese firms were still smaller than the North American and European standard. In 1918, for example, only 26 out of the country's largest 200 industrial firms manufactured products in two different SIC (Standard Industrial Classification) categories (at the two-digit level of SIC measurement and where the second product line accounts for at least 20 percent of total sales), and of these, 22 firms or 85 percent were textile companies. Since big textile companies often spun thread and wove cloth, this is less product diversification than forward integration of an intermediate good towards a final product—thread to cloth.

In 1930, furthermore, only 35 of the largest 200 industrial firms made products in two different SIC categories. That is, only 17.5 percent of Japan's largest firms made products that were sufficiently different to be classified in two distinct categories at the three-digit level of classification. Of 35 enterprises, 30 were again firms where the products fell into the same SIC category at the two-digit level of measurement. Indeed, 26 of these 35 companies were textile firms, integrating spinning and weaving.

As a result, only 9 non-textile but large industrial firms in 1930 made products sufficiently different to fall into two distinctly different SIC categories at the two-digit level of measurement. That number, by the way, had not changed since 1918, although the nine firms were not the same. In both 1918 and 1930, not one of Japan's major industrial firms produced goods in three different SIC categories (as measured above), and in 1930 less than 5 percent of Japan's largest 200 industrial firms were diversified in two different SIC areas. In short, there were *no* widely diversified Japanese firms before World War Two.

Given product specialization, small market size, and the separation of production and distribution functions from the start of industrialization, the relatively small size of Japanese industrial enterprises is understandable. Product specialization at the corporate level is related to manufacturing competence at the factory level. Production focus and specialization are sensible strategies for late-developing firms that can ill afford to spread resources widely. Multi-function, focal factories mirror low levels of vertical integration and product diversification at the corporate level. They concentrate resources in one product line or, at best, in one product family for local and regional markets.

Accordingly, a need to form business alliances in order to generate complementarities in functions and activities seems logical and predictable. Resource constraints of various sorts forced Japanese industrial firms to narrow their core competencies to specific products and processes while, at the same time, managers sought functional links in purchasing, production, distribution, and marketing to ensure business survival. Thus, specialization in form and function preceded and propelled systemic interdependence. The modern corporation matured in tandem with production and distribution organizations: firm, factory, and network grew strong in their particular capabilities as they became interrelated.

Size and Organizational Complexity

Along with organizational size and complexity come much larger numbers of managers spread from top to bottom, greater differentiation in managerial functions, a need for closer integration between production and distribution, the emergence of scale economies in sectors other than textiles, more attention to applied and basic research, new accounting and managerial tools, the appearance of product and corporate advertising, and greater sophistication in head-office functions and activities. Technological and organizational issues associated with the introduction of high-speed assembly lines from about the time of World War One forced these changes. As machine tools and transfer lines to support continuous, repetitive production based on increasingly tight schedules and closely defined specifications grew in number, not only did shop-floor personnel burgeon but so did staff/line ratios, productivity, and numbers of products. In the Noda Shoyu Company, for example, as high-volume production technology was introduced, the number of managerial posts expanded sharply between 1918 and 1923 (61 to 272) and these were more centralized posts created in the interest of achieving organizational coordination (the ratio of centralized to decentralized positions jumping from 0.30 to 0.86).[4] In brief, assembly-line technology, an attendant division of labor, elongated hierarchy, and enhanced capacity for production, transformed the very nature of the firm. Enterprises grew in size, complexity, level of differentiation, and need for integration and coordination.

These developments, concentrated at the factory level because of the day-to-day adaptation of foreign technology, led ultimately to the appearance of integrated production sites encompassing an entire range of corporate functions. Resources were focused in manufacturing without allocating countervailing resources to middle or higher levels of the firm. Head offices were relatively small as were divisional and branch offices. Most matters of operational consequence were decided and executed in production facilities.

Moreover, horizontal integration furthered the concentration of resources at production sites. During the inter-war period, excess capacity and highly cyclical demand in some industries, such as cotton-spinning and weaving, paper, agricultural chemicals, and machinery, drove firms to engage in mergers and acquisitions. But, legal consolidation was not often followed by organizational centralization. Instead, the least efficient of the acquired facilities were closed or appended to regional manufacturing centers where manufacturing and managerial responsibilities were combined. The autonomy of regional manufacturing centers imparted a particular significance to focal factories as hubs of territorial administration, not unlike the largely independent activities of local manufacturing works for Krupp, Vickers, and Schneider in Europe about the same time.[5]

The concentration of assets, means, and manpower at manufacturing sites organized by product and region brought about multi-function manufacturing organizations which due to the richness of their resource mix and operational experience found themselves with slack resources from time to time. Edith Penrose asserts that enterprise growth comes about from a constant inability to have exactly the right mix of all resources. In the case of Japanese firms during the inter-war era, this happened most often in areas of manufacturing and applied technology transfer.[6]

The most notable of these underused resources was localized learning in the transfer and application of technology, that is an abundance of trial-and-error learning in the adaptation of specific technologies to particular production problems. This learning represented the accumulated experience of a nation attempting to industrialize quickly on the basis of foreign knowledge and technology. Such learning accumulated in the integrated production environments of what this book terms focal factories.

Learning was available to be generalized to new products and processes. The emergence of focal factories, one leg of the organizational triad of factory, firm, and network, promised not only economies of scale but also economies of scope to inter-war firms as they mastered how to make better and broader use of learning. There is a progression here. Organizations began with single functions, like production or purchasing. When that was mastered and when circumstances allowed, single-function organizations matured into multiple-function organizations. And these might become multi-functional in capability, if further learning and exploration occurred. In order to capture these opportunities, however, corporations had to become larger, better organized and managed, with functional excellence in many parts.

Purchasing, for example, could be an opportunity for learning. Purchasing departments were established not only to locate needed raw materials and supplies, but also to check and monitor the quality, price, terms of delivery, and uniformity of purchases as well. Such purchasing functions either had not been executed previously by manufacturing firms or they had been delegated to outside purchasing agents, such as specialized trading companies. But as companies came to employ increasingly complex production processes making more and more precise, intricate, and valuable products, firms came to rely on their own resources for buying raw and intermediate goods. The need to consolidate upstream purchasing and sourcing requirements often led to corporate reorganization.

Where firms decided not to manufacture in-house, they located and cultivated other firms to manufacture for them and, if necessary, offered them capital, equipment, and training. Not all firms necessarily moved in this direction but those choosing to make the more demanding products of the second industrial revolution almost always did so. Product and process reliability required that they bring purchasing and development capabilities in-house or, at least, near-house, and indeed, this turnabout and integration of organizational functions was one of the forces leading to the appearance of focal factories and interfirm networks.

Advances in one part of the enterprise system, represented by the creation of purchasing departments and supplier networks, affected the configuration and operation of the whole. Complexity and variety in function led to an efflorescence of the system. As firms produced higher value-added and more differentiated products, they began to perform more of their own distribution, advertising, and marketing functions or they encouraged the formation of affiliated firms with high product-specific and market-specific capabilities to perform those tasks. As manufacturing systems became more integrated internally, changes in one area or function brought about change in other areas and functions. Japanese industrial firms were developing the firm-specific capabilities and interconnections that characterize them as parts of an enterprise system.

As companies embraced more resources and capacities, the value and complexity of corporate information increased enormously. Specialists were hired in numerous sub-fields of business activity. Research laboratories were established to further company-specific knowledge in materials and manufacturing, and they were staffed by university graduates with scientific and technical backgrounds. Science-based industry made inroads and began to complement the trial-and-error tinkering that had characterized Japanese production. Technology was still imported for the most part, and Japanese firms did not abandon the emphasis on organizational learning that emanated from the technology-transfer process. Nor did they clearly separate basic and applied R & D activities. Instead, as the numbers of university and technical-school graduates in large firms grew, a gradual but progressive upgrading and strengthening of technical and research capabilities occurred. With few exceptions, central R & D laboratories—organizationally, geographically, and functionally distinct basic research centers—are a post-World War Two phenomena.

Management was increasingly professionalized, encouraging a further separation of ownership and control in large corporations, and leading to a growth of specialized knowledge in the functional sub-fields of modern management. Engineering, accounting, and management associations were forged nation-wide to represent and promote sub-fields of corporate specialization. The educational background of new company employees rose, whether these were middle-school, technical-school, and university engineering graduates or social-science and commerce graduates.

At the apex of the large modern corporation, new and clearly defined positions of great responsibility appeared. The title of *shacho* or 'company president' came into vogue. Boards of Executive Directors, where each director possessed well-delimited areas of responsibility, such as production, sales, and research, were created. Specialized staff functions, such as executive secretaries and presidential administrative assistants, proliferated. Being part of the president's staff came to be associated with power and prestige whereas a few years earlier, when general managers and chief engineers were running the first modern corporations, no one could have imagined the exalted privileges of the new breed of executives.

The Board of Directors changed its character and scope of authority. Traditionally, members of the board had been outside investors with limited knowledge and experience in management. Accordingly, as the structures of the large modern firm evolved, inside boards, usually referred to as Committees of Executive Directors, came to wield most of the decision-making power, thus supplanting Boards of Directors as the nexus of legal and day-to-day responsibility and authority.[7] As inside directors became full-time, top managers of firms, board members seconded from affiliated or allied companies lost influence, attenuating the voice of holding companies and core companies in financially linked, *zaibatsu* groups. As the knowledge, experience, and power of full-time, inside managers on boards increased, operational and a fair degree of strategic decision-making passed into their hands.

In short, large modern corporations are organizations of professionalized management where coordination between managerial functions is the key to performance. The transition from the modern corporation to the large and modern corporation epitomizes an organizational coming-of-age: large, complex, functionally variegated, multi-unit and multi-tiered, professionally administered corporations emerged strongly during the inter-war years to gain control over much of the economy. This story could be told anywhere as nations advance industrially and as enterprises grow large and complex as a consequence. What was different about the Japanese case was the rate of macro-economic growth, the successive cascades of technology transfer, and the general social, political, and economic turbulence of the environment within which large, modern corporations and their organizational correlates appeared. These forces produced corporations characterized by accelerated organizational learning, segregation of business functions in discrete organizational forms, with pressing needs to integrate organizations through managerial coordination. The Japanese enterprise system arose as a response to such forces: an organizational system with focus in production, coordination in management, and strength in numbers.

Size and Choice

An increase in corporate size was made possible in large part by the growth of the market, that is by opportunities to produce in greater volume than previously and thereby to achieve minimum economies of scale in manufacturing and distribution. Economies of scale were available in two areas: increasing returns to scale in the manufacture of a single product line, and economies of scope whereby the manufacture of a number of products in the same set of facilities results in increasing returns to scale. Per unit costs of production as well as distribution will fall to the degree that numbers of related goods can be run through the same set of facilities. Likewise, as the rate of capacity utilization climbs, overhead-costs associated with a facility or operation are spread over a wider range of products. Also, the innovative, inventive faculties of employees may be more fully exploited when they are encouraged to develop new uses for existing plant and equipment. In the case of either sort of scale economies, larger firms are thought to experience faster rates of technological change and thus greater potential for upgrading and enhancing the production process.[8] Learning and efficiency may go hand-in-hand.

Some of the reasons for the smaller size of Japanese firms, even the major ones, may be found in the smaller size of the Japanese market, but three others stand out:

1. a strategy of specializing in a relatively narrow range of products induced in all likelihood by the difficulties of transferring generalized knowledge (Western technique) into localized knowledge;
2. a preference for merger and acquisition as well as for product-line expansion which neither commandeered the resources of merged firms into unified corporate structures nor integrated new product lines into single organizational entities;
3. a proclivity for decentralizing operational autonomy to regional field offices and to multi-function production facilities. Decentralization by function and by market was practiced. The choice was to allow various facilities to run without too much integration, centralization, and coordination.

Multi-function factories in the pre-war period (but not the post-war period) may represent an institutional adaptation to cope with bureaucratic- and market-failure. A centralized, unified governance structure climaxing in corporate head-office control was not viable when markets were local, territorial administrative responsibilities considerable (after Japan's colonial expansion), and demand unpredictable. In these respects, pre-war Japan may resemble post-war China during the economic liberalization of the mid-1980s when territorial-based administrative systems were commonplace.[9]

These conditions had long-term consequences for the nature of the modern corporation. The narrow specialization of firms means that Japanese firms, even the 'large and modern ones', tend to be small by Western standards. The strategy of concentrating resources—human, capital, and technological resources—in a limited range of activities, which in turn mitigates the need for large planning staffs at the corporate level, was developed in tandem with the building of networks of affiliated firms and the concentration of resources at lower levels of organization, especially in manufacturing facilities that may be variously called lead factories, head factories, or focal factories. As a consequence, mechanisms of corporate growth, such as merger, acquisition, vertical and horizontal integration, frequently resulted in resource devolution: downward to production sites in the case of a full-line strategy and outward to allied organizations in the case of a product-diversification strategy.

Evolving Structures and Strategies

The Appearance of Product-Focused Interfirm Networks

The networks of affiliated firms which appeared during the inter-war period were mostly product focused, in contrast with politically etched and financially oriented earlier groupings. None the less, previous patterns of interfirm alliance had important demonstration effects for enterprise networks formed during the inter-war period, even though the logic of interfirm combinations changed noticeably. Also, as *zaibatsu* manufacturing firms gradually gained some measure of financial independence from holding companies, trading firms, and group banks, they often organized product focused subgroupings of their own.

Such alliances were characterized by a variety of internal rationale although, in most instances, a logic of market-focused forward or production-focused backward integration was paramount. Groups were formed to achieve economies of scale in manufacturing and to guarantee sources of supply and, less often, of distribution outlets. In periods of considerable economic and technological uncertainty, like the inter-war years, corporate liability could be minimized by segmenting business activities to legally independent entities, even while these entities cooperated in many of their business activities. In sum, each firm in a group was able to concentrate its efforts in well-defined spheres of activity, knowing that a narrow range of focus would not stymie participation in ever larger spans of interfirm activity.

According to a Ministry of Commerce and Industry study published in November 1936 but based on 1932 data, the extent of out-sourcing as a percentage of manufacturing value added was highly variable. It ranged between 5 and 65 percent. Generally, the larger the enterprise, the greater the value of in-house production as a percentage of total value added; in industries where out-sourcing was common, the level of vertical integration was correspondingly lower. In the automobile, textile-weaving, and electrical-equipment industries, at least 20 percent of the manufacturing value of all products came from suppliers. Already, before the war-induced demand surge of the Sino-Japanese (1937–45) and Pacific (1941–5) Wars, a structure of product-based supplier networks was in place, important, and, in some industries, determinative of performance.[10]

Part of the reason why large firms in these industries could reliably out-source parts of subcontract steps in the manufacturing process was the availability of skilled and semi-skilled workers in a large pool of underemployed or unemployed workers. The economic downturn following World War One and defense cuts after the Washington Conference of 1922 caused widespread layoffs among military arsenals and civilian shipbuilders. In October 1922, 5,136 non-military employees of naval arsenals were let go, and in the next year, even more were laid off.

Mitsubishi Shipyards alone dismissed 8,611 between February 1922 and June 1924. Those laid off were among the cadre of small subcontractors that became suppliers to large firms after this time. A survey of Tokyo factories published in 1932 reports that two-thirds of the 322 small iron- and metal-working shops in Tokyo were founded between 1922 and 1930.[11] Larger firms turned with increasing regularity to smaller firms to take advantage of their lower wages, technical strengths, and underemployed workers. Not surprisingly, smaller firms responded eagerly, and the seeds of a system of relational contracting took root.

While large firms were lining up a network of suppliers, they were beginning to extend benefits of long-term employment and seniority-based compensation to growing numbers of regular managerial and technical employees. That is, as Taira, Levine, Gordon, and others have argued, there is a critical institutional link between the professionalization of management, the emergence of job security, in-company training, and higher wages and performance in large firms on one hand, and the appearance of subcontracting and interfirm sourcing networks clustered around large firms, on the other.[12] Regular wage increases were limited to large-scale enterprises, especially those producing heavy industrial goods. In these companies, however, foremen were more likely than rank-and-file employees to gain seniority-compensation advantages. Sometimes, but not always, promotion and remuneration were tied to in-company training. During the 1920s internal training systems appeared in Hitachi, Karatsu Iron Works, Okumura Electric (No. 103 in 1918), Japan Rolling Stock (No. 135), Kawakita Electric Engineering (No. 49), Yasukawa, and Toyoda Automatic Loom (No. 191 in 1930).[13]

While these developments were transpiring, internal-contracting systems for mobilizing skilled and semi-skilled workers were disappearing.[14] The labor market was increasingly bifurcated into a well-paid, relatively secure minority of workers employed in large firms and a less well-paid, majority of workers in small- to medium-sized enterprises where tenure, wages, and livelihood were uncertain. The advance of production technology and the introduction of process controls created fissures within the working class along lines of education, skills, adaptability, and attitude. Those that were willing to learn, especially by experimenting with new work forms and routines were rewarded with tenure and promotion.

The Emergence of Focal Factories

Within firms, a strategy of enterprise growth based on internalizing manufacturing and management know-how, derived largely from foreign sources, dictated that resources should be consciously concentrated at the production level. Factories, especially focal factories or multi-function factories were charged with the design, planning, and manufacture of a company's most sophisticated and demanding products. Activities within factories became physically and managerially differentiated into those requiring a lot of resources in unknown amounts and those where inputs and outputs were known or, at least, relatively predictable.

Focal factories were distinguished by the range of activities occurring within their confines. Their omnibus, multi-function quality is captured in substance if not in spirit by the phrase 'plant within a plant', a Western concept that comes close to identifying some of the elements embodied in focal factories. Elements of this factory architecture incorporating localized coordination and hierarchical authority, have been described elsewhere as territorial administrative systems.[15] Focal factories duplicated locally the growing complexity in managerial functions found at the apex of the corporate hierarchy. Within focal factories, a panoply of corporate functions could be found: quality-assurance offices, marketing and sales staff, research facilities, and even personnel departments. Factory managers, like company presidents, were enveloped by a hive of clerical and technical specialists.

When focal factories tie together organizational resources on a local or territorial basis, they function as administrative hubs of geographically defined production systems. This occurs when national systems of transportation and communication are not well developed or when the cost of their use is obviously more than their value to local users; in such circumstances, it may be more efficient and certainly more convenient to invest in localizing managerial resources and functions. In Italy, Germany, and France, for example, industrial districts defined by the collaborative efforts of many local producers have proved to be highly viable and flexible alternatives to nationally organized production systems.[16] In the case of Japan, especially before the Pacific War, the role of focal factories in organizing local resources and in coordinating production and distribution systems on a territorial basis appears to have been crucial to Japan's industrial development. They also figure prominently in labor management.

Labor management is, of course, an important component of factory management anywhere, and as Japan shifted from a light to a heavy industry base during the first quarter of the twentieth century, industrial relations assumed great importance. But new demands on labor and on the management of industrial relations are only partial aspects of the story of focal factory management. Focal factories were charged not only with labor management but also with technology transfer, product and process innovation, engineering, manufacturing, cost accounting, new personnel policies, regional distribution, and sales coordination.

Such responsibilities do not belong to 'lower-level' management. Given the comprehensive functions associated with focal factory management in Japan, they are more akin to what is called middle-level management functions. In short, Japanese industrial firms typically emphasize manufacturing functions and facilities above all others. This is where the troublesome process of technology transfer is assimilated, if at all, to Japanese conditions, and this is where the consequences of organizational learning can yield competitive advantage.

As Western production technology in textiles, metals, food, machinery and beverage industries became fully transferred to Japan, major innovations appeared less and less often. Factory managers had to consider what capabilities they already had but were perhaps not fully utilizing. Large firms began to introduce process controls in manufacturing and to separate design activities from manufacturing. Firms moved beyond the point of simply making 'dead copies' or reverse engineering.[17] One way to do this was by the introduction of Taylor-like time and motion studies. Engineers showed up on or near the shop-floor in ever larger numbers, and an engineering approach to manufacturing gradually permeated the workplace.[18] Another way to do this was by creating work structures where product and process innovation were considered indivisible.

These somewhat paradoxical aims were a direct response to the need for *incremental, indigenous innovation*. They were realized by creating integrated, multi-function production sites where slack, redundancy, and organizational learning could be harnessed in the interest of cost leadership and product differentiation. It should be stressed that firms groped and stumbled towards this solution. Concentrating resources in omnibus development, planning, and production sites happened more haphazardly than strategically. Focus made sense. A vision of integrated, full-bodied production facilities did not. A number of examples illustrate these points.

In 1915, for example, Shibaura Engineering intensified its reliance on internal engineering design and development capabilities by creating six design sections: alternating-current machinery, direct-current machinery, transformers, distributors, tool design, and drafting. Hitachi merged four design sections into one integrated design department at about the same time. Process-control practices were introduced at Mitsubishi Electric in conscious imitation of what Shibaura Engineering and Hitachi were already doing in 1923.[19] Electrical-equipment firms were becoming engineering- and managerial-intensive organizations.

In the case of Mitsubishi Electric, when the company was founded in 1921, it produced heavy electric machinery primarily for ships and mining operations. Demand for producers' goods of this sort was uneven and the company sought more reliable and stable markets for its products. Electric fans were one such market. Between 1921 and 1923, the company produced 10,000 of these. Mitsubishi Electric responded to the Tokyo Earthquake of 1923 by making induction motors and controllers for the rebuilding of the Tokyo transportation system.

In order to produce goods for higher volume markets, however, Mitsubishi Electric had to reorganize its production-management capabilities. Producing standardized or semi-standardized goods, like electric fans and induction motors of various power ratings, led Mitsubishi Electric to set up a new factory for prototype development within its sprawling Kobe Works. It led as well to a broad-gauged technology-transfer agreement with the Westinghouse Company.

Prototype production is essential for making standardized goods because planning, design, production, and distribution issues must be solved before products reach the market-place in volume. Otherwise, a company and its distributors will have a lot of unsalable inventory on hand. A new facility integrating these functions was constructed in 1923 within the Kobe Works. Late in that year, an order for 1,000 induction motors was received and in the first six months of 1924, 5,000 electric fans were produced. By the end of the decade in a further differentiation of manufacturing facilities, another new plant was constructed in Nagoya for the exclusive design and production of small electric motors, transformers, heaters, and fans.[20]

Mitsubishi Electric's new strategy required not only a reorganization of its production function, creating a multi-function manufacturing center, but also a reorganization of sales and distribution functions as well. Heavy electric equipment was sold through a sales engineering force that visited customer locations and assessed production and pricing needs on site. Induction motors, railroad-engine controllers, and electric fans—all produced in some volume—were better suited to sales planning coordinated through a sales department. In 1924 a 'wholesale sales association' (*tokuyakuten*) was formed, and the first meeting of the association brought thirty-five dealers to Kobe from all the prefectures and major cities of Japan as well as Taiwan, Korea, and North China. By 1926 the number of dealers increased to forty-two and the coverage provided by these dealers in conjunction with the Mitsubishi Trading Company's offices gave Mitsubishi Electric a national and East Asian regional presence.[21]

The effect of horizontal merger on enterprise structure and strategy is also instructive in the case of Tokyo Electric. Between the end of World War One and 1932, twelve electric light-bulb makers were acquired by Tokyo Electric. Rationalization of production facilities did *not* follow. Instead, the acquired companies continued to produce light bulbs as before, and sold them either directly to Tokyo Electric or indirectly to one of four sales companies owned by Tokyo Electric. In effect, Tokyo Electric bought market share, not by the rationalization of facilities and increasing returns to scale but by buying companies. These companies continued to operate as before except that their legal and organizational status had changed, from independent firms to regional manufacturing facilities. This is congruent with the multi-function factory model and with the history of one of Tokyo Electric's factories, the Yanagicho Works, examined in depth in Chapter 6.[22]

Finally, the Fujikoshi Machine Tool Company grew rapidly in personnel and equipment from its founding in 1931 with just forty employees and twenty-two machine tools. Six years later, 1,980 employees and 771 machine tools crowded its offices and plants. To cope, the company created a functional, U-Form structure, dividing employees between either manufacturing or sales; in 1937 an eighteen-step internal promotion ladder was initiated for both manufacturing and sales personnel.[23] Factory and firm were nearly the same at Fujikoshi.

As factory organization progressed at Toshiba, Hitachi, Mitsubishi Electric, Tokyo Electric, and Fujikoshi, intrafirm developments were linked with advances outside the firm. Japanese companies embraced a strategy of business development with long-range consequences: the establishment of a core firm with well-developed product and market foci, surrounded by a complement of firms linked to the core company by supplier relationships and ties of vertical integration, nourished by a style of factory management and organization that emphasized technology transfer, organizational learning, and adaptive innovation in product and process development.

A Typology of Inter-war Enterprises

As sketched out previously, there were important differences in the enterprise system model depending upon location (rural or urban), industry, and management. These differences continued during the inter-war period, although they became less important as disparities in rural/urban infrastructure were minimized and as political and economic conditions became more uniform. Nevertheless, important differences remained until the post-war era when fundamental changes in law, transportation, communication, and education, transformed forever the institutional environment for doing business in Japan.

Zaibatsu *or National Enterprise*

The Mitsui Group. The Mitsui *zaibatsu*'s historical strength was based in trade, finance, and insurance, that is in non-manufacturing pursuits. However, beginning in the 1890s under the direction of the particularly able Hikojiro Nakamigawa, Mitsui began to invest in manufacturing activities. Nakamigawa was not related to the Mitsui family in any way, and perhaps for this reason he could venture beyond the family-based traditions that frequently hamper the growth and development of such businesses.

Nakamigawa established two cotton-spinning companies, bought one, and re-possessed another between 1890 and 1900. He also invested heavily in three manufacturing companies which became standout performers early in the twentieth century: Kanegafuchi Spinning, Oji Paper, and Shibaura Engineering Works. Even after Nakamigawa was no longer at the helm, the Mitsui group expanded its manufacturing base, buying Toyo Koatsu Industries and establishing Electro-Chemical Industries and the Japan Steel Works, all before World War One.[24]

Because of the importance of sourcing raw materials overseas as well as selling abroad, Mitsui & Co., the main trading firm for the Mitsui group, often held a direct controlling interest in a sizeable number of manufacturing ventures. During the inter-war period, the most important of these included Toyo Menka (later, separated off as an independent cotton-trading firm), Toyo Rayon, Taiwan Sugar Manufacturing, Yuasa Storage Battery Manufacturing, Onoda Cement, Kyokuto Condensed Milk, Santai Oils, Sanki Engineering, Tama Shipyard, as well as a number of joint ventures with foreign makers, such as Toyo Otis Elevator, Toyo Babcock, and Toyo Carrier Engineering. One source claims that by 1940 Mitsui & Co. held equity shares in 253 companies in fourteen different industries for a total of about 275 million yen (about 90 percent of its paid-in capital).[25]

Another example of Mitsui's move into manufacturing comes from the synthetic ammonia and agricultural fertilizer industry. When Suzuki & Co., a major independent trading company, went bankrupt in 1927, Mitsui took over its ammonia plant at Hikojima. In 1928 there were 24 white-collar workers at Hikojima, two-thirds of which were engineers, and in 1940 there were 64 white-collar workers, two-thirds of which (42 out of 64) were engineers. Since there were 550 blue-collar workers in 1940, the overall ratio of white- to blue-collar workers was 1:8.5 and the ratio of engineers to workers was 1:13. In both years, two-thirds of the white-collar employees were engineers, suggesting a relatively intensive staffing of manufacturing facilities with technical personnel.[26]

By the inter-war period the Mitsui group of companies had moved into manufacturing as well as non-manufacturing activities. However, as this happened, it became impossible to manage 2–300 companies in a single, unified system of command and governance. Interfirm equity investments in manufacturing firms held by group holding companies, banks, and trading companies did amount to fiduciary control although they did not constitute managerial control. Without intimate knowledge of the day-to-day activities of its manufacturing affiliates, non-manufacturing firms like banks and holding companies could say little about the operations, products, sales, service, or marketing of manufacturers.

Financially based interfirm alliances were significant, none the less. First, ownership carried the right to exercise some strategic voice in the overall business plan and performance of operational firms. Because ownership was divided typically among a half-dozen or more firms, however, the right to exercise strategic voice ended up most often as a right to exercise strategic vetoes. This was an important right obviously, but not one that significantly affected the day-to-day running of manufacturing firms. Strategic voice and operational control were becoming decoupled.

Second, perhaps more importantly, ownership gave the right to send outside directors to affiliated companies, creating a structure of interlocking directorates. Yet the closely knit nature of shareholding and the potential exercise of a strategic veto at the highest levels of decision-making pushed Japanese manufacturing firms towards a system of inside directorships. Instead of the 'Board of Directors' (*torishimari-yakukai*) as the locus of decision-making, Executive Director Committees, made up of the ablest managers who were promoted from *within* the firm, functioned in this way. Firms organized themselves in such a way as to be operationally autonomous even while they were strategically enmeshed in interfirm structures.[27]

Third, the principal advantage of financially based interfirm groupings was precisely in the realm of finance. Money was hard to come by. The Japanese stock market was small, undeveloped in terms of the range and sophistication of financial instruments, and highly speculative. Financing obtained through a small number of reliable and friendly firms, be it equity or debt financing, was infinitely more attractive than public offerings and underwritings. As a result, within financially linked interfirm combinations, retained earnings for companies operating within groups were often funneled back to group holding companies for re-allocation, while bank deposits, insurance premiums, and credit allowances were distributed by banks, insurance, and trading companies to operating firms within the group according to need, demand, and purpose.

In short, as *zaibatsu* groupings became larger, more managerial intensive, and interdependent in function and structure, operational control slipped more into the hands of front-line managers. Top managers retained strategic oversight and this was important no doubt, but without intimate knowledge of the intricate, day-to-day operations of independent firms in an increasingly diverse enterprise group, strategic oversight was most often exercised negatively, as a strategic veto.

The Mitsubishi Group. The Mitsubishi group of companies was likewise quick to recognize the limits of financial control when manufacturing firms face highly variable market and technological conditions. Mitsubishi-sha, the parent company for Mitsubishi endeavors, was founded in 1886. By 1893, the year of the promulgation of the new Commercial Code, it had adopted a functional department structure with five main areas of business activity: banking, mining, real estate, shipping, and trade.[28]

By 1908 the volume of business in these five areas had become so great that each of the main areas of business activity operated more or less independently, that is more or less as legally separated enterprises. Each business had its own internal regulations and procedures, was evaluated on the basis of its performance, and was legally responsible for its actions and decisions. But businesses were not yet incorporated separately. At the same time, some things were more or less uniform across Mitsubishi businesses.

In May 1908 a new structure of employment, promotion, and organizational guidelines were fixed for all Mitsubishi companies. In June 1911 a research department was established as part of the general-staff function of the Mitsubishi holding company. It was the task of the research department (later the famous Mitsubishi Research Institute) to draft suggestions for the overall organizational and strategic development of the Mitsubishi group of firms. About now, Mitsubishi took its first deliberate steps into manufacturing by moving its shipping department in the direction of shipbuilding while mining was encouraged to develop energy systems. Actually, Mitsubishi had taken over the Nagasaki Shipyard from the Government in 1884 and this could be considered its first manufacturing venture. But it operated mainly as a repair facility until World War One. Irrespective of how late Mitsubishi entered the shipbuilding business, by the 1930s, Mitsubishi was building giant battleships like the 72,000-ton *Musashi*.

The formal incorporation and separate establishment of new manufacturing ventures into autonomous enterprises did not occur until there was a change in the leadership of the Iwasaki family. Koyata Iwasaki, son of the second President of Mitsubishi, Yanosuke, became partner and was appointed Vice-President of Mitsubishi Company in 1906. Two years later, Yanosuke died, and by 1916 Koyata assumed the overall presidency of the Mitsubishi group of companies. Within two years, he separated off seven operating departments from the Mitsubishi holding company and made them independent operating units. These included Mitsubishi Shipbuilding & Engineering and Mitsubishi Iron & Steel in 1917; Mitsubishi Warehouse, Mitsubishi Mining, and Mitsubishi Trading in 1918; Mitsubishi Marine & Fire Insurance and Mitsubishi Bank in 1919. In addition, Mitsubishi Internal Combustion Engine Manufacturing (later, Mitsubishi Aircraft) and Mitsubishi Electric Manufacturing were established in 1920 and 1921 respectively.[29] During the 1930s Mitsubishi became involved with Japan Aluminum Company, Mitsubishi Oil, Japan Tar Industries (later Mitsubishi Chemical), as well as a number of smaller ventures.

By hiving off so many business activities from Mitsubishi Goshi-sha, the parent holding company, Koyata Iwasaki was purposely divorcing ownership from control. At the same time, in order to finance a growing family of firms, Koyata aggressively expanded the lending activities and commercial branch network of Mitsubishi Bank which boasted 170 branches and 7,000 employees in 1934.[30] In short, Koyata forced an administrative reorganization of the Mitsubishi Group into a holding company representing the ownership interests of the Iwasaki family on one hand, and, on the other, a number of legally independent joint-stock companies, each with its own professional management, common and preferred stock issues, strategic direction, and its own fate hanging within its own control. Indirectly, the holding company maintained some influence during the next twenty years by appointing outside chairmen to managerial duties in subsidiary firms, but in 1937, the separation of ownership and control proceeded to the point where the Mitsubishi Goshi-sha, the holding company of the Iwasaki family, itself became a joint-stock company with its shares actively bought and sold on the Tokyo Stock Exchange. (Readers may wish to refer back to the illustrations on p. 100 that trace aspects of the organization evolution of the Mitsubishi group of companies.)

The holding company invested in numerous companies and projects outside the Mitsubishi group, so that the revenues of the parent company were based only in part on the performance of Mitsubishi firms. Increasingly, Mitsubishi companies were organized in response to performance criteria, and group membership became a qualitative attribute but not a determinative one. None the less, in spite of the legal (1908) and operational (1917–20) separation of the holding company and its various subsidiaries, the degree of holding-company influence in Mitsubishi affiliates could be occasionally considerable, depending on the issues under consideration and the relative strengths of the holding company and affiliate managements. Yet, the degree of control was never fixed; it varied from company to company and from time to time.

Like Mitsui, the size, complexity, and interpenetration of the Mitsubishi group of companies made it impossible for any one man or any single command center to plan for and coordinate group activities by the 1920s. Even acting in concert, the core financial firms for the group, Mitsubishi Goshi-sha, Mitsubishi Bank, and Mitsubishi Trading, could not possibly coordinate functions across all the inter-related activities of the group. As a result, day-to-day activities were left to independent operating companies. Week-to-week and month-to-month perform-ance were monitored by representatives of core financial firms on the Boards of individual enterprises. Recall, however, that their principal role was to exercise a strategic veto, when and if that became necessary. And, of course, they could only exercise a veto based on detailed, inside information provided by the Executive Directors and middle managers of independent firms. In sum, the control of operating companies was increasingly in the hands of a professionalized manage-ment team which gathered information about complex business situations, evalu-ated the alternatives, and carried out decisions based on their product-specific administrative and functional skills.[31]

The highest level of interfirm coordination, weekly and monthly meetings of member companies in financially linked groups like Mitsubishi, brought together Presidents and Chairmen of member firms to discuss the general business climate and to assess the performance of combinations of firms within the group. Occa-sionally more substantial matters would be discussed and decided on, such as major financial decisions for the group, new business ventures, and matters concerning government and business relations. An indication of the Mitsubishi Company's efforts to tie together its expanding and diverse businesses can be seen in the founding of the Yowakai, a social club composed of members of the managerial staff of the Mitsubishi Company and eleven core companies of the group. A 1942 report writes,

The object of the club, besides affording a means of amusement, is the improvement in the health and promotion of the spirit of good-fellowship among its members, by providing opportunities for intercourse and facilities for exercise and recreation. Its ultimate aim is the development of individual character and the inculcation of the 'Mitsubishi Spirit'.[32]

In 1942 the club numbered 27,300. How eloquently the Yowakai club under-scores the search for enterprise community and the separation of ownership and control even before the Occupation reforms of the post-war years.

Independent, Urban Enterprise

The new *zaibatsu* (*shinko zaibatsu*), a collective and somewhat vague term for a variety of industrial conglomerates founded during the inter-war period are suf-ficiently different from the old *zaibatsu* to warrant extended and separate attention.

Some scholars even suggest use of a different term, new industrial concerns (*shinko konzern*), other than the new *zaibatsu* as a way to differentiate old and new *zaibatsu*.[33]

In fact, the new *zaibatsu* should not be classified as *zaibatsu* firms at all. The only structural feature that they share in common is a preference for alliance capitalism, namely the formation of constellations of related firms for the purposes of vertical integration and product diversification. But this is not necessarily a *zaibatsu* characteristic. Indeed, this book argues that growth through alliance and affiliation is a basic trait of Japanese industrial enterprises and that such strategies maximized opportunities to achieve transaction-cost economies as well as economies of scale and scope in the course of Japan's industrial development.

Although both old and new *zaibatsu* employed alliance strategies for enterprise growth, they were otherwise dissimilar. New *zaibatsu* were publicly owned because the capital requirements for firms specializing in products of the second industrial revolution were considerably greater than for firms making the earlier, less capital-intensive products of the nineteenth century. Both start-up and running costs were large for new *zaibatsu* firms, and they had precious little time for evolving internal competencies in a variety of functional areas. By necessity, they relied most often on bank debt and public issues to raise funds in spite of the volatility of security exchanges in pre-war Japan. In brief, new *zaibatsu* lacked the banks and commercial elements of the old *zaibatsu*; they specialized in products of the second industrial revolution; they were much more science and innovation driven; and, they raised a large portion of their capital through government subsidy and publicly offered securities.[34]

Until the rapid expansion of the Japanese economy from the mid-1930s, industrial enterprises relied little on debt financing. Enterprises were financed by retained earnings and by limited equity issues. But the capital requirements for firms entering the newer industrial markets of World War One were considerably greater than those of even a generation earlier, while the availability of investment funds was no less constrained. The new *zaibatsu*, without the group banks of the original *zaibatsu*, turned increasingly towards independent city banks as sources for debt financing. This introduced a pattern of high debt-to-equity ratios that colored industrial finance for the next forty years.

Because the role of old money was correspondingly less important, middle- and upper-level managers in new *zaibatsu* were in full control of their companies. They were less constrained as well by nepotistic ownership squabbles that frequently thwarted older *zaibatsu* groupings. A separation of ownership and control gave the new *zaibatsu* a decidedly more aggressive tone. They acquired smaller firms voraciously and diversified into technically advanced industries, such as electro-chemicals, trucks and automobiles, as well as non-ferrous metals.

Jun Noguchi and Nitchitsu. The career and business empire of Jun Noguchi (1873–1944) illustrate the contrast between newer and older *zaibatsu* groups. Noguchi graduated in 1896 from Tokyo Imperial University's electrical-engineering course.

For the next ten years, he continued his studies, especially in the use of electricity as a chemical catalyst, worked for the Japanese branch of Siemens, the German electrical-equipment company, travelled abroad, and held a variety of jobs.

In 1906 Noguchi established Sogi Electric, a power-generating plant on the Sogi River. With excess electricity produced in the plant, Noguchi began the manufacture of calcium carbide. Two years later, in August 1908, with capital support from Mitsubishi Bank, Noguchi founded Nippon Chisso Hiryo (Japan Nitrogenous Fertilizers) or Nitchitsu, a firm specialized in the manufacture of calcium carbide. Within a year, Noguchi upgraded the company's output from calcium carbide to ammonium sulfate, a superior but more complex product to manufacture. It would appear that Nitchitsu was the first Japanese company to produce ammonium sulfate from calcium cyanamide.[35] Already, by 1909, Noguchi had conclusively demonstrated his entrepreneurial ambition, technical virtuosity, and managerial strategy of upgrading and extending a full-line of electrochemical products. In 1918 Japan Nitrogenous Fertilizers was the 41st largest industrial firm (ranked by assets) and by 1930 it had climbed to No. 6.

After World War One, Noguchi switched Nitchitsu's basic production process for fertilizers from the cyanamide method to the newer, synthesized ammonia method. The latter method which manufactured ammonium sulfate by synthesizing ammonia under high temperature and pressure opened possibilities for making a number of related chemical products. In turn, product diversification would generate higher sales and, hopefully, greater profits. Different product lines, however, were managed by independent enterprises rather than merged under a unified organization and management.

After Noguchi opened Nitchitsu's state-of-the-art ammonium sulfate plant at Nobeoka in 1923, a subsidiary Shin'etsu Nitrogenous Fertilizer was established to produce calcium cyanamide by the old method. In 1925 Noguchi opened Chosen Chisso Hiryo, as Nitchitsu's independent subsidiary in Korea. He also joined in the founding of Chosen Hydroelectric in January 1926. Chosen Chisso and Chosen Hydroelectric were merged in 1929, and the first ammonium sulfate produced by the new firm, still called Chosen Chisso, appeared in January 1930.[36] The Military Governor of Korea required that Noguchi establish a power-generation company to transmit power to Seoul and Pyongyang. Thus, Chosen Electricity Transmission was established in 1933. In the next year, Chosen Chisso Explosives was founded to manufacture glycerine and nitric acid, while in 1935, another subsidiary, Chosen Coal Industries, was created.

In all these instances—Shin'etsu Nitrogenous Fertilizer (1923), Chosen Chisso Hiryo (1925), Chosen Hydroelectric (1926), Chosen Chisso (1929), Chosen Electricity Transmission (1933), Chosen Chisso Explosives (1934), and Chosen Coal Industries (1935)—Noguchi did not attempt to vertically integrate his enterprises and thereby reap the rich economies of scope in research, production, and distribution that were possibly available to him.[37] Part of the reason for this may be found in the economic difficulties of the time and therefore in a strategy of insulating the risks of one business from others. But part of the reason must certainly be that Noguchi was simply following standard practice for his day, namely the separation and specialization of business activities by function and product line.

Even though Nitchitsu followed an aggressive strategy of product diversification through the application and exploitation of related electrochemical technologies—a strategy already pioneered by Dupont, Nobel, American Cyanamid, and other well-known Western chemical firms—Noguchi and Nitchitsu conspicuously failed to integrate these diverse product lines in a unitary structure and to manage them according to the logic, method, and rigor of the multidivisional form. The strategy was one of product diversification but the structure was one of specialized product lines manufactured by independent (legally and managerially) firms. A kind of loose coordination among Nitchitsu's numerous holdings was affected by the power of Noguchi's personality and by periodic interfirm meetings for technical and managerial coordination. The organizational point remains the same: product/process specialization within a framework of interfirm cooperation. Economies of scope in production and consistent measures of organizational performance across different fields of business endeavor were not easily assayed in Noguchi's entrepreneurial empire.

A key element in Nitchitsu's success was that Noguchi secured most of the critical technical licenses himself. He travelled abroad and by force of his personality and through his familiarity with technical developments in the industry, he was able to bypass the intercession of trading companies in acquiring foreign licenses. This gave Nitchitsu a cost advantage over rival firms because no margin was paid to trading firms, and clearly it gave Nitchitsu a strategic advantage by staking-out favorable positions in evolving chemical technologies.

Slower moving, less entrepreneurial firms, however, forged trade associations and sought government protection from foreign competitors. Since traditional *zaibatsu* groups were strong in transportation, marine insurance, distribution, and other non-manufacturing pursuits, *zaibatsu*-related chemical firms were often content to import chemical products and sell them under license in Japan. Noguchi's Nitchitsu is representative of the so-called new *zaibatsu* which sought to develop domestic manufacturing capabilities without excessive dependence on foreign technology and to establish overseas markets in Asia in competition with Western firms based on the growth of a domestic chemical industry.[38] New *zaibatsu* were quick to diversify on the basis of technical capabilities but they were inclined to spin off and split off new ventures rather than incorporate them in a single managerial structure.

Textiles: Small is Beautiful. Textiles firms were the most numerous and managerially advanced industrial enterprises of the inter-war period. The most successful textile companies, like Kanegafuchi Spinning, Mie Spinning (Toyo Spinning), Osaka Spinning (Toyobo), Fuji Gas Spinning (Kurabo), and Kurashiki Spinning (Fujibo), were quick to establish new organizational, technical, and managerial innovations in the practice of running large, modern industrial enterprises, and their success exerted a powerful modeling effect on later developing, less advanced firms in the light-industry sector. But advances in managerial and technical method did not always occur in the context of organizational consolidation and centralization. *Accounting and The Management of Cotton Spinning*, a manual published in the early 1930s, for example, argues in favor of situating the head offices of cotton-spinning companies in one of the company's local factories. In this way, the report argues that factory managers could easily report to senior managers, located at the same site, and specialization could advance without a loss of coordination.[39]

Such arrangements were rather common. Either head-office functions were decentralized to operational sites or regional 'head offices' were established to minimize the coordination of national functions and activities. In either case, centralization was minimal and the separation of operational and strategic activities was not advanced. A number of reasons might be marshalled to explain the low levels of centralization.

First and foremost, factories were not producing for the national market but one step down or up, that is for regional or international markets. In the case of relatively undifferentiated goods like processed sugar, soy sauce, *sake*, and milled grains, markets were local and regional or, at best, on the verge of becoming national. But even in the last case, the technologies of transportation and communication did not allow for an easy and effective implementation of a national sales function. It was better to leave coordination functions to regional manufacturing sites.

Second, cost-accounting methods were not well developed and in the absence of these, consolidation and centralization on a national basis were impractical. In order to rationalize operations at multiple sites and facilities, a standard basis of cost comparison is absolutely essential. While corporate-level managers were aware of the need to standardize accounting procedures, factory managers were preoccupied with the rationalization of shop-floor practices, the adaptation and application of production technology, and the amelioration of work conditions for laborers and managers alike. Factory-level accounting procedures were idiosyncratic, reflecting the fact that centralization of functions was not advanced and that local autonomy in operations was the norm. The result was a low-profile corporation, highly decentralized, with lean middle- and upper-management structures but with elaborated local hierarchies where product and market coordination mostly occurred.[40]

Take, for example, the case of Kureha Spinning, the twenty-fourth largest industrial firm in 1954. Founded in 1888, the company does not even appear among the 200 largest industrial firms in 1930. But in 1939 it acquired Toyama Spinning (the 203rd largest firm in 1930) and three other smaller companies, bringing the total of its factories to fourteen. These were apportioned among four regional offices where production and sales for different parts of the country were coordinated. The head office had commercial, secretarial, and technical-staff sections, and ran with less than a dozen people.[41] Low levels of centralization and coordination were possible because growth by acquisition was not often followed by vertical or even horizontal integration within a single management structure. Instead, functional integration of production, sales, and finance proceeded slowly, in a piecemeal fashion, by region at first and later by product. An important reason for this was the existence of well-established regional traders and middlemen who obviated the need for companies to centralize and standardize coordinating functions. This was especially true in the spinning and weaving industries as well as in other industries, like cement, food, and beverages, which considered together account for 53 percent of the 200 largest industrial firms in 1930. In some industries, however, more centralized structures and strategies of business were evolving. Matsushita Electric Industrial and Hitachi, Ltd. were two of these in the important electrical-equipment sector.

The Origins of Matsushita Electric Industrial. Konosuke Matsushita founded Matsushita Electric Works in 1918.[42] The company's first products were socket plugs, plugs for electrical appliances, and oval bicycle lamps (from 1923); these initial products were all designed by the founder, Konosuke Matsushita.

Matsushita's bicycle lamp used a bulb and batteries, and these were far superior in sturdiness and reliability than the candle-powered or oil-burning lamps then in common use. Matsushita did not manufacture the component parts of the bicycle lamp in the beginning, though he conceived the design and developed the product as a practical bicycle accessory. However, wholesalers refused to handle Matsushita's bicycle lamp at first. So, Matsushita distributed them himself, selling directly to retail bicycle dealers who were willing to handle his lamps upon demonstration that the batteries would last for at least 30 hours. Once this was done successfully, sales of his battery-powered lamps took off.

The marketing lesson for Matsushita was that a new product in itself could not guarantee success. Unless a product could be sold, and this may require innovation in sales and marketing, it might not amount to much. So Matsushita labored to establish sales channels for his products and this effort led to the Matsushita retail store network, the largest chain among all the electrical-goods makers in Japan.

The Maturation of Matsushita. In 1927 Matsushita designed and manufactured a rectangular-shaped lamp which could be used at home and on bicycles, creating quite a stir among bicycle shops and electrical-lighting stores. In 1928 monthly production climbed to 30,000 units and by 1930 to a prodigious 50,000 units, becoming Japan's first hit product in the home electrical industry.[43] The innovative product shows Matsushita's early orientation towards volume manufacturing and distribution as a basic company policy. Other volume products—electric irons, home-heating devices, and dry-cell batteries—soon followed, and they followed the same pattern of mass manufacture and distribution. (In 1930, however, Matsushita expanded into the field of radio manufacture which was not a high-volume business but lucrative none the less.)

Thus, the main elements of Matsushita's pre-war strategy were clear by the 1930s. First, products for which Matsushita possessed no specialized in-house know-how and for which the costs of development were high, such as dry-cell batteries, vacuum tubes, and light bulbs, Matsushita bought from suppliers or made in conjunction with various manufacturing partners. Interfirm sourcing was an explicit policy and practice from the start. Toyota Motor began with the same strategy, as addressed in Chapter 7. Second, products which Matsushita made itself, such as plug sockets, battery-powered lamps, heating devices, and toasters, were scrutinized in great detail to improve their features and to enable the company to manufacture them in high volume but at low cost.

The 1929 decision to distribute (but not necessarily manufacture) a full product line brought significant changes in organization: not only was the size of the company expanded but also the management structure was clarified and improved. This was seen first in the establishment of factories for volume manufacture of specific products. In May 1929 Matsushita formed an 'Executive Committee' (*shacho-kanbu kaigi*) as the highest decision-making body in the company, and the production, sales, and general-affairs departments of *each* factory were represented on this committee.[44]

By the 1930s marketing's ascendancy and manufacturing's willingness to follow marketing's lead in exploiting markets for new products were already evident. Given that the manufacture of plug-in electrical appliances and their sales and distribution were entirely different from that of radios, in 1933 a 'multidivisional' structure wherein each main product line was a separate division within the firm was adopted. There were three divisions at the time: the radio division, the bicycle lamp and dry-cell battery division, and the plug-in electrical appliances division. In each division a sales department was formed, and regional sales offices were established in Tokyo and Nagoya to coordinate manufacturing and sales.

Considering Matsushita's size, scale, and scope, a divisional structure was more than adequate to meet its needs. And, relative to similar developments in the United States, Matsushita was hardly behind the times. Dupont and General Motors adopted the multidivisional form in 1921, and Westinghouse did so only in 1935. But Matsushita's divisions did not have the size, autonomy, and importance of GM and Dupont's divisions.[45] In 1935 Matsushita had less than one-fifth the assets and sales of GM and Dupont, and the company looked as in Table 4.1.

While some have argued that the 1918 devolution of operational autonomy to manufacturing corporations in the Mitsubishi group pre-dates the initiation of multidivisional structure by General Motors and Dupont and that Matsushita Electric Industrial's adoption of a three division, corporate structure in 1933 was not at all 'late' relative to GM and Dupont, questions of timing and origin should not be confused with those of substance and practice. Western firms, like General Motors, Dupont, and Westinghouse, being significantly larger than comparable

TABLE 4.1. *Matsushita Electric Industrial Sales by Product Line,*
1935

	Sales (1000s of yen)
Plug-in electric lighting	1,200
Electric appliances	1,200
Batteries and battery lamps	6,000
Radio sets	350
Electric motors	120
TOTAL	8,870

Capital: 1 million yen
Number of employees: 3,545

Source: Yasuo Okamoto, *Hitachi to Matsushita*, vol. 1 (Tokyo: Chuo Koronsha, 1979): 46

Japanese industrial firms, were first to move in sizeable numbers in the direction of a clearer separation of powers and responsibilities into strategic and operational spheres. The rationale for organizational change rather than the resulting organizational forms must be emphasized.

Matsushita: 1945–55. Matsushita's main products in the early 1950s were dry-cell batteries, radios, and light bulbs—all holdovers from the pre-war period. In 1949–50 Matsushita's market share for dry-cell batteries was a dominant 43–7 percent, and in radios Matsushita enjoyed, even from before the war, a substantial market share.

Before and after the war, Matsushita was not a technical innovator for the most part. It launched its products after those of its competitors. For example, it introduced its first portable radio in 1953 after other companies had done so in 1952, and it trailed Sony (Tokyo Tsushin Kogyo) in the development (1955) and sale (1956) of a transistorized radio by a year in both instances. But even though Matsushita brought its products to market late, it could garner a high market share on the strength of its national sales network encompassing scores of distributors and thousands of retail shops.

Matsushita compensated for the later launching of its products by careful product planning, skillful product differentiation, and effective marketing and advertising. These product planning and marketing skills were rather uncommon for their day. When Matsushita introduced its water-jet style of washing machine in 1954, for example, it launched four models simultaneously, each different in terms of washing capacity, price, absence or presence of timing switches, spinning features, number of washing cycles, etc. Based on its own market research, Matsushita planned different batch-size production runs for each machine, and overnight, Matsushita became the largest washing-machine maker in Japan.

Independent, Rural Enterprise

Hitachi: Emerging National Champion. Hitachi traces its origins to 1908 when Kodaira Namihei, one of the entrepreneurial engineers who flourished during the inter-war period, founded Kuhara Mining which would itself become Nippon Mining, a major non-ferrous company in the pre-war period and a top petroleum refiner in the post-war era.[46] Hitachi began, in fact, as the electrical-machinery repair shop of Kuhara Mining at the Hitachi Mine.

In June 1915 Kuhara Mining's machine shop supplied a hydraulic turbine of 10,000 hp for the Tone River Power Company's Iwashitsu power plant, and this established the importance and capabilities of the machine shop. In 1918 in a historically early effort to integrate forward on the basis of technically related, product development, Kuhara Mining opened an electric copper-wire factory at the mining town of Hitachi—copper wire being necessary for electrical power transmission and for electrical-machinery manufacture. The demand for power transmission and power-transmission equipment climbed dramatically. In 1914, for example, a 225-kilometer transmission line from Lake Inawashiro, Fukushima Prefecture, to Tokyo was completed. The 115,000-volt line, one of the highest voltages in the world at the time, was constructed as were the water wheels, generators, transformers, switches, and even insulators by foreign makers.[47] Hitachi was established to overturn the foreign domination in electrical equipment and, hence, to provide Japanese equipment of Japanese design for the Japanese market.

In 1918 Hitachi merged with another facility for the production of machinery in nearby Kameido. In 1920 Hitachi became a limited company, Hitachi, Ltd. In 1921 Hitachi took over Kasado Works, a plant making freight cars and locomotives. Following these mergers, Hitachi absorbed Kokusan Kogyo in 1937, thus extending its product line to iron and steel parts, malleable cast iron, and electric communication devices in addition to rolling-stock, electrical and mechanical machinery, power generators, and turbines.

Perhaps because of these early mergers, Hitachi localized the management of various business lines in leading facilities producing each of those goods. The Hitachi Works produced copper wire and electrical machinery, Kameido non-electric machinery, and Kasado rolling-stock. Kokusan Kogyo's numerous products were manufactured in several facilities. Hitachi's assignment of product-line responsibility to major manufacturing facilities presents an early example of the

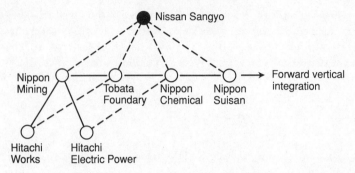

FIG. 4.1. *Nissan Industries in the 1930s: Evolving Product-Centered Group*

emergence of focal factories: a factory, created by strategic choice, with division-like product and market responsibilities.

In Japan, with a few notable exceptions like Matsushita Electric Industrial, multidivisionalization was not the answer to the increasing complexity of modern business. Instead, as in the precedent set by *zaibatsu* firms, the strategy was to form constellations of interdependent firms, joined by financial ties and integrated through business interactions. Indeed, in the absence of anti-trust legislation which prohibited such interlocking business alliances, a strategy of structured interdependence had much to recommend it. Individual business units did not become overly large and bureaucratic, the financial necessity of diluting ownership by recourse to public offerings was avoided, and firms could remain focused in energies and resources.

Hitachi exemplified such a strategy. After the corporate headquarters of Kuhara Mining was moved to Tokyo in 1918, Hitachi Limited was split off as a specialty electrical-machinery maker in 1920. Hitachi was capitalized at 10 million yen and the shares were all held by Kuhara Mining, Namihei Kodaira, business associates, friends, and relatives. They all profited handsomely when in three years' time, after the great Kanto earthquake of 1923, Hitachi was awash with orders to replace damaged and destroyed machinery. Given its location 100 kilometers north of Tokyo, Hitachi's main production facilities in Hitachi were not effected by the quake at all. Hitachi's place within the evolving Nissan business group may be represented in Fig. 4.1, where dotted lines represent financial but not product-coordination control.

By 1936 Hitachi had grown to be the equal of any of the electrical-equipment makers that were associated with *zaibatsu* groups, and, unlike them, Hitachi aimed at developing its own technology rather than relying on imported technology. Already the fourth or fifth largest electrical-equipment manufacturer in 1930 (after Shibaura Engineering, Furukawa Electric, Mitsubishi Electric, and Fuji Electric), depending on whether sales or assets are taken as the measure of size, Hitachi outpaced most of its rival firms by manufacturing a rather complete line of non-electrical machinery to complement its electrical-machinery offerings.

Hitachi's manufacturing knowledge and experience, while not without foreign elements, was developed largely on the strength of internal efforts to master the rapidly evolving electrical and precision-machining technologies of the day. Hitachi was something of a national champion in this regard, and as the economy of Japan fell under increasing military control in the latter half of the 1930s, Hitachi was asked to make telecommunications equipment, electrical parts and components, and other advanced electrical gear for the military. It is worth noting that Hitachi's in-house success with the development of electrical technologies underscored the role of factories as sites of applied R & D, product development, and multi-function manufacturing. Hitachi is famous in Japan for its factory-centered approach to organization and management, and this bottom-heavy emphasis was already apparent by the 1920s.

After the war, through the middle of the 1950s, Hitachi continued to manufacture its basic line of pre-war goods, namely industrial equipment, heavy electrical machinery, and electrical components. A decisive factor in Hitachi's early post-war recovery was the national government's program for the development of hydro-electric power. Beginning in 1951, government contracts boosted not only power-generation equipment orders but also breathed life into the construction, overhauling, transportation, and repair businesses.

In 1949 Hitachi adopted an expanded, functionally organized structure with four divisions: production, sales, finance, and general affairs. Production was organized into six departments: electrical machinery, vehicles (forklifts, etc.), electrical wire, telecommunications equipment, construction equipment, and steel products. Because each production area had its own manufacturing facilities, and because sales, research, product development, and some marketing were also localized in these facilities, the functional organization of the firm was rather pronounced in most ways. Hitachi's headquarters encompassed a rather small staff of financial, legal, and personnel specialists while factories were omnibus sites of product design, planning, manufacture, and marketing.[48]

In 1952, taking advantage of technology licensed from RCA, Hitachi opened a plant for the production of electronic tubes and parts. This would initiate a new direction for Hitachi towards smaller, lighter, and more versatile products than its traditional heavy-equipment emphasis had allowed. But the shift from heavy to light electrical devices would not gather significant force for another decade or so, and Hitachi's pre-eminence as a maker of large, heavy, electrical producer goods would not be so easily shed. (The next chapter continues this story.)

Other Independent, Rural Enterprises. Even where traditional middlemen had no role to play, such as in the newer products of the Second Industrial Revolution, corporations were typically decentralized with functional activities concentrated at integrated production sites. Dainippon Jinzo Hiryo (Dainippon Inorganic Fertilizer), for example, was the eighteenth largest industrial firm in Japan in 1930 selling nitrogenous fertilizers to a nation with nearly half of its population still in the countryside. The sales function was decentralized to factories, where production and distribution was coordinated. Factory managers were directly responsible to the company's general manager, while the production department at the corporate level supported factories with technical advice and services. In short, factories ran nearly autonomously with corporate functions subordinated to operational priorities.[49]

The autonomy and authority enjoyed by regional manufacturing centers led to strong business—government ties locally and at the prefectural level. Naturally enough, managers interacted often with local and prefectural authorities. In the case of Noda City and Noda Shoyu Company, town and county public services were planned and executed collaboratively. Similar circumstances framed government—business relations in Nada and Takarazuka Cities outside Osaka where *sake* breweries were the most important source of industrial employment, tax revenue, and local boosterism.

The main factories of Teikoku Sugar Manufacturing (Teikoku Seito), in various regions controlled other more remote production units without going through the head office.[50] Sales departments in lead factories promoted and exported sugar for themselves and their satellite factories. Again, the localization of functions to focal factories which were responsible for a variety of production and non-production functions on a regional basis is conspicuous. A few more examples from a variety of industries will reinforce the point that large, modern Japanese corporations of the inter-war period represent a considerable advance over the immature enterprises of the pre-war One era even while inter-war firms were not especially large and centralized compared to the leading Western firms of the day. Niigata Engineering (No. 156 in 1930) made diesel engines for a variety of surface and marine applications. In 1937 its four factories were specialized in different markets (petroleum equipment, rolling-stock, diesel engines, and mechanical engineering) and each factory had its own sales office in charge of trading and enquiries.[51] The head office for Niigata Engineering was correspondingly small.

Asano Cement (No. 13 in 1930) was managed from two branch offices, one for eastern another for western Japan. Each branch office had production, sales, and accounting functions. A head office existed but it had no operating sub-units. When Asano Cement acquired a number of smaller cement companies in the post-war slump of the 1920s, it attempted to centralize functions at the head office with a U-Form structure but this was later abandoned in favor of a decentralized branch office system.[52] Centralization complicated the task of being responsive to local needs which were not yet sufficiently similar to permit Asano Cement to organize and coordinate effectively at the national level. Onoda Cement, Asano's main rival, was perhaps even less centralized since it delegated most sales and distribution functions to Mitsui & Co.

Nichiro Fishery, the twenty-third largest industrial firm in 1930 and the biggest fish-processing company in Japan, had as many as 270 factories in the

1930s. These involved such activities as ice-manufacture, fish-processing and freezing. As these were spread over the Japanese islands as well as in colonial territories from Sakhalin to Taiwan, they were controlled locally with production, sales, and accounting functions carried out at each production site.[53] Again, volume production and distribution were impractical, and a devolution of authority and local specialization resulted.

Yamasa *shoyu* characterized its corporate and competitive strengths over arch-rival Noda Shoyu in 1929 in the following ways: one family and one business-ism (in contrast to Noda Shoyu's eight families and several businesses); one business and one product-ism (Noda Shoyu produced several different brands of soy sauce); one product and one brand-ism (Noda Shoyu distributed several different qualities of *shoyu*). Notwithstanding the touching simplicity of Yamasa's posture, within a dozen years it lost half of its market share to Noda Shoyu's (Kikkoman's) full-line and related business strategy.

In both Yamasa's and Kikkoman's case, however, the factory was the organizational basis for modernizing technical and managerial capabilities. Detailed statistics comparing productivity by factory (standardized for factory capacity, manpower commitment, and fermentation time) collected on a monthly basis, allowed not only for comparisons of general levels of productivity but also of relative qualities of factory-specific management. Such documents detail that the enhancement and improvement of corporate operations depended foremost on the quality of its factory management and workforce. Resources were devolved and authority delegated to factories as a primary means of strengthening corporate performance.[54]

Summary of Three Enterprise Types

Table 4.2 summarizes most of the major features of corporate development in Japan during the inter-war period along the lines of a threefold geographical/organizational typology introduced in this and the last chapter. By the post-war period, the tripartite division disappears as transportation, communication, financial, and managerial conditions become more uniform across the country, as corporations increasingly garner and exploit resources on a national basis, and as firms institutionalize the means to exploit them ever more efficiently.

Towards the Emergence of Large, Modern Enterprises

During the inter-war years in Japan, the basic mold of the Japanese corporation, a decentralized U-Form, single-product/dominant-product firm was defined. This

TABLE 4.2. *Three Types of Modern Industrial Enterprise, 1918 to 1954*

	Zaibatsu/national	Independent, urban	Independent, rural
Strategy			
Interfirm relations	increasing integration and diversification with declining holding-company control	horizontal merger, amalgamation, and cartelization	limited, mostly related diversification with strong holding-company control
Marketing	group and non-group trading companies, and related sales companies	wholesalers as exclusive agents with some trading companies	direct sales locally; urban wholesalers and trading firms
Mode of competition	oligopoly with economies of scope, emerging scale, and some scope	monopoly where makers attempt to control distribution	local monopoly, regional oligopoly, national competition
Finance	holding and trading companies' capital/group banking and independent self-financing	city banks and stock issue	holding-company capital and local banks
Structure			
Ownership	inter-group shareholding with group banks, holding and trading companies, and core companies	somewhat scattered ownership but a few large blocs controlled by firm managers	traditional family-based holding company
Management	powerful and progressive within and between group firms	established, independent and competent	developing as both owners and managers gain higher education
Administrative coordination	well established within increasingly independent firms and divisions	developed but limited to needs of U-Form enterprises	developing but constrained by unity of ownership and control
Government relations	close contact with civil government and political parties	indirect ties to individual politicians, direct ties to trade association	strong local and regional political ties; weak nationally

new organizational model was pioneered by cotton-spinning, machinery, cement, food and beverage companies as they assayed the point of balance between scale (high-volume manufacturing of few products) and scope (sizeable numbers of related products) in manufacturing within the context of a nation with limited purchasing power but well-established distribution.

The new model emphasized the importance of managerial coordination within and between firms, increased concern with technology transfer and the R & D process, volume production for projected demand, the evolution of production and labor management, and, especially, functional specialization through the evolution of decentralized but integrated production sites (focal factories) and through the creation of networks of allied firms (interfirm networks). The latter included manufacturing affiliates (ranging from independent but cooperating firms to captured subcontractors) and service-specific alliances with firms specializing in finance, transportation, distribution, advertising, and engineering.

Small, single-product/dominant-product firms sufficed even as Japanese firms grew larger because vertical integration and product diversification were not often internalized in single corporations. Instead, firms specialized in certain activities while cooperative relationships with other enterprises secured complementary assets and capabilities. Or, firms localized and integrated activities in territorial-based organizations. In either case, there was little need to separate out operational and strategic activities; corporate headquarters remained relatively small without much overall coordinating responsibility. Managerial hierarchies of the size and sophistication found in North America and Western Europe were unknown.

The speed of economic and technological change during the inter-war years encouraged institutional evolution along well-travelled pathways. Rapidity of change also made firms reluctant to grow by absorbing more activities internally. To do so was risky, as it added manpower, facilities, and bureaucratic inertia, possibly leading to entrenched structures and strategies. Joining with other firms in manufacturing and distribution alliances, however, was a means to minimize risk while taking advantage of the production and distribution resources that other firms commanded.

Moreover, where firms were financially interrelated as in the *zaibatsu* model of organization, the profits of the *group* were not necessarily reduced by alliances, especially when the highly cyclical character of business during the inter-war years is considered. As one firm prospered another might falter, but within an interfirm network, such differences in performance would be averaged out for the group as a whole. Indeed, given the incipient market for industrial goods, a strategy of maximizing interfirm economies of scope through group-driven cooperative transactions made better sense than the pursuit of internal production and allocative efficiencies through vertical integration and product diversification. From the competitive point of view, the result was much the same: medium-high entry and exit barriers were created by the formation of strategic interfirm groupings.

The advantages of interfirm networks and of focal factories as firm correlates were recognized before World War Two. In 1941 the Japanese economist, Kisou Tasugi, was writing that the degree of interfirm specialization in parts and components supply was limited only by the costs of managerial coordination and the level of technological diffusion.[55] Tasugi was observing the flourishing practice of subcontracting in machinery industries, and already, he saw interfirm networks as a fundamental feature of the Japanese economy during the first-half of the twentieth century.

The same themes are echoed by Akira Goto for the post-war period underscoring the continuity and elaboration of pre-war patterns after the war:

From the standpoint of the firm, by forming or joining a group, it can economize on the transaction costs that it would have incurred if the transaction had been done through the market, and at the same time, it can avoid the scale diseconomies or control loss which would have occurred if it had expanded internally and performed that transaction within the firm.[56]

Because the division of labor is limited by the extent of the market, a rule first articulated by Adam Smith, even the largest Japanese enterprises were not especially large by Western standards, due to the limited size of domestic and colonial overseas markets before World War Two. The limited size of the market allowed local production sites or focal factories to serve as 'territorial-based organizations', satisfying most of the local demand in the value-added chain without national integration and centralization.

Moreover, limited natural resources and a reliance on foreign manufacturing technology crippled the ability of Japanese firms to integrate backward while at the same time an entrenched, active, and interdependent (co-dependent) network of distribution firms obviated most of the need to integrate forward. So, as interfirm sourcing arrangements grew, firms aimed not to increase the number of different products that they manufactured in-house as much as they sought to increase their value-added contribution to the manufacturing process. Relatively small, specialized, and organizationally interdependent firms were the consequence.

These developments were rather specific to Japan. The markets of the industrializing West were not as constrained geographically and demographically. Western nations had each other as trading partners and for the most part they enjoyed higher standards of living, larger economies, and greater investment flows. In these countries, especially in the United States, it was pragmatic and profitable for firms to grow large by internalizing a diverse range of related- and semi-related businesses and to separate operational and strategic decision-making as a result. But few firms in Japan needed to go so far; firms were small with core activities managed through the coordination of full-function factories and interfirm networks.

These institutional arrangements worked well. Well enough, in fact, that when multidivisional organizational structures gained currency with the American Occupation of Japan, Japanese firms had to jerryrig compromise corporate forms so as to uphold the functional separation and specialization that was already so familiar. (Toshiba's post-war grapplings with the multidivisional form are recounted in Chapter 6.) Various solutions appeared, all of which sought to join production and distribution functions in some way at some level. A growing interdependence of factory, firm, and network was not easily reversed, however. Basic patterns and principles of economic organization were already in place before the traumatic wrenchings of the war and post-war eras.

NOTES

1. Eisuke Daito, 'Railroad and Scientific Management in Japan, 1900–1930', a paper given at the UC Intercampus Group in Economic History Conference, University of California, Santa Cruz, 29 Apr. 1988, 8.
2. R. E. Caves and M. Uekusa, 'Industrial Organization', in Hugh Patrick and Henry Rosovsky (eds.), *Asia's New Giant* (Washington, DC: Brookings Institution, 1976), 126.
3. Ministry of Commerce and Industry, *Kikai Kigukogyo Gaichu Jokyo Chosa*, Nov. 1936; cited by Tetsuo Minato, 'The Formation of the Japanese Subcontracting System between the Two World Wars' (in Japanese), *Aoyama Kokusai Seikeironshu*, 7 (June 1987), 93.
4. W. Mark Fruin, *Kikkoman: Company, Clan, and Community* (Cambridge, Mass.: Harvard University Press, 1983), 111–14.
5. James M. Laux, 'Managerial Structures in France', in Harold F. Williamson (ed.), *Evolution of International Management Structures* (Newark NJ: University of Delaware Press, 1975), 98.
6. Edith T. Penrose, *The Growth of the Firm*, rev. edn. (White Plains, NY: M. E. Sharpe, 1980).
7. Tsunehiko Yui, 'Meiji Jidai ni okeru Juyaku Soshiki no Keisei' (The Formation of Top Management during the Meiji Period), *Keiei Shigaku* (Business History) 14/1 (Winter 1979); id., 'The Development of the Organizational Structure of Top Management in Meiji Japan', *Japanese Yearbook on Business History* (Tokyo: Japanese Business History Institute, 1984).
8. W. Y. Oi, 'Heterogeneous Firms and the Organization of Production', *Economic Inquiry*, 21 (Apr. 1983), 147–71; Yasukichi Yasuba, 'The Evolution of Dualistic Wage Structure', in Hugh Patrick (ed.), *Japanese Industrialization and Its Social Consequences* (Berkeley: University of California Press, 1976).
9. I am thinking of China's economic development zones as territorial based administrative systems. Max Boisot and John Child, 'The Iron Law of Fiefs: Bureaucratic Failure and the Problem of Governance in the Chinese Economic Reforms', *Administrative*

Science Quarterly, 33/4 (Dec. 1988), 507–27. I am grateful to Jerry Ross for pointing out this citation and indicating its relevance to my work.

10. Minato 'Formation of the Japanese Subcontracting System', 96–7.

11. Mikio Sumiya, *Showa Kyoko* (The Showa Crisis) (Tokyo: Yuikaku, 1974), 67–73; Fruin, *Kikkoman*, 155–210.

12. Koji Taira, *Economic Development and the Labor Market in Japan* (New York: Columbia University Press, 1970); Andrew Gordon, *The Evolution of Labor Relations in Japan: Heavy Industry, 1853–1955* (Cambridge, Mass.: Harvard University Press, 1985); Solomon B. Levine and Hisashi Kawada, *Human Resources in Japanese Industrial Development* (Princeton, NJ: Princeton University Press, 1980). See also, Thomas C. Smith, 'The Right to Benevolence: Dignity and Japanese Workers, 1890–1920', *Comparative Studies in Society and History*, 26/4 (Oct. 1984), 587–613.

13. Minoru Sawai, 'The Development of Machine Industries and the Evolution of Production and Labor Management', in Keiichiro Nakagawa and Tsunehiko Yui (eds.), *Japanese Management in Historical Perspective* (Tokyo: University of Tokyo Press, 1989), 213–18.

14. W. Mark Fruin, 'Instead of Management: Internal Contracting and the Genesis of Modern Labor Relations in Japan', in Nakagawa and Yui (eds.), *Japanese Management in Historical Perspective*.

15. Boisot and Child, 'The Iron Law of Fiefs', 507–27

16. The best-known treatment of industrial districts in Italy and France appears in Michael J. Piore and Charles F. Sabel, *The Second Industrial Divide: Possibilities for Prosperity* (New York: Basic Books, 1984). For a similar treatment of Japan, inspired by Piore and Sabel, see David Friedman, *The Misunderstood Miracle* (Ithaca, NY: Cornell University Press, 1988).

17. Sawai, 'Development of Machine Industries', 214–17.

18. Ibid. 208–16.

19. Ibid. 208, 212–14.

20. Mitsubishi Electric, *Mitsubishi Denki Shashi* (A History of Mitsubishi Electric) (Tokyo: Toppan, 1982), 23–7, 30–2.

21. Mitsubishi Electric, *Kengyo Kaiko* (Reflections on Business) (Tokyo: Toppan, 1951), 305–8. Also, interview with Takayasu Miyakawa, Director, Mitsubishi Research Institute, 3 June 1981.

22. Tokyo Electric, *Tokyo Denki Gojunenshi* (50 years of Tokyo Electric) (Tokyo: Dainippon, 1940), 114–15.

23. Fujikoshi Machine Tool Company, *Fujikoshi Gojunenshi* (50 years of Fujikoshi) (Tokyo: Dainippon, 1978), 34.

24. Kunio Yoshihara, *Sogo Shosha: The Vanguard of the Japanese Economy* (Oxford: Oxford University Press, 1981), 30–5.

25. Keiichiro Nakagawa and Eisuke Daito, 'Business Management in Historical Perspective: Lifetime Employment in Japan', mimeo, 1990: 39, 49.

26. Sawai, 'Development of Machine Industries', 209–13.

27. Yui, 'Organizational Structure of Top Management in Meiji Japan'; Hidemasa Morikawa, 'Significance and Development of Middle Management in Japan', in Keiichiro Nakagawa and Tsunehiko Yui (eds.), *Organization and Management* (Proceedings of the Japan–Germany Business History Conference) (Tokyo: Japanese Business History Institute, 1983).

28. Mitsubishi Corporation, *An Outline of Mitsubishi Enterprise* (Tokyo: Dainippon Printing, 1942), 2.

29. Ibid.

30. Yoshihara, *Sogo Shosha*, 38–9.

31. Here I am following the broad outlines of Chandler's arguments appearing in *The Visible Hand* and *Scale and Scope* concerning the separation of ownership and management in Western industrial firms. As the degree of financial control exerted by Japanese holding companies does not appear to be greater than that exerted in American and German industrial firms at about the same time, an analogous argument may be made for Japan. For a detailed discussion of the American case, see David M. Kotz, *Bank Control of Large Corporations in the Unites States* (Berkeley: University of California Press, 1978).

32. Mitsubishi Corporation, *Outline of Mitsubishi Enterprise*, 4.

33. Shigeaki Yasuoka, *Zaibatsu no Keieishi* (Zaibatsu Business History) (Tokyo: Shakai Shisosha, 1990), 95.

34. Masaharu Udagawa has written the best book on the new *zaibatsu*: *Shinko Zaibatsu* (Tokyo: Nihon Keizai Shinbunsha, 1984).

35. Barbara Molony, 'Innovation and Business Strategy in the Prewar Chemical Industry', in Nakagawa and Yui (eds.) *Japanese Management in Historical Perspective*, 150–1.

36. Ibid. 155–6.

37. Ibid. 154–9.

38. Yoshitaka Suzuki, 'The Formation of Management Structure in Japanese Industrials 1920–40', lecture notes, Tohoku University, Sendai, 1983: 20.

39. Ibid. 20–30.

40. While this is not exactly Suzuki's conclusion, it is certainly mine, based in part on his data: Suzuki, 'Formation of Management Structure'. Suzuki's most recent formulation of his findings appears in *Japanese Management Structures, 1920–80* (London: Macmillan, 1991). Unfortunately, Suzuki's new book appeared after mine was already in Press.

41. Ibid. 20–30.

42. The discussion of Matsushita Electric Industrial and Hitachi Ltd. contained in this chapter and the next are drawn from Yasuo Okamoto's richly detailed and forcefully argued two-volume history of the firms: Yasuo Okamoto, *Hitachi to Matsushita* (2 vols., Tokyo: Chuo Koronsha, 1979).

43. Ibid. i. 40–5.

44. Ibid. i. 41–2.

45. Suzuki, 'Formation of Management Structure', 25.

46. Ibid. 17.

47. Yasuo, *Hitachi to Matsushita*, 15–16.

48. Hitachi Ltd., *Hitachi Seisakushoshi*, (3 vols.; Tokyo: Hitachi, 1949), preface 3–5.

49. Suzuki, 'Formation of Management Structure', 30.

50. Ibid. 31.

51. Ibid. 32.

52. Ibid. 32–3.

53. Ibid. 33–4.

54. Yamasa Shoyu Company Archive, 'Shokko Sagyo Bunryocho' (Measurements of Factory Output), handwritten (Choshi, 1923–4); id., 'Kojo Getsubetsu Moromi Motokoku-zandaka' (Monthly Production of *Moromi* by Factory), handwritten (Choshi, 1930–7);

id., 'Shoyugyo Jozo ni Tsuite' (Concerning Shoyu Fermentation), typed (Choshi, May 1929). Similar documents exist for Kikkoman at the same period.

55. Kisou Tasugi, *A Treatise on Industrial Subcontracting* (Tokyo, 1941); cited by Minato, 'Formation of the Japanese Subcontracting System'.

56. 'Business Groups in a Market Economy', *European Economic Review*, 1982, 53–70.

5

Advancing the Enterprise System

Interdependent, Large Modern Corporations, 1954 to 1987

The unprecedented post-war performance of Japanese corporations, at home and overseas, has its institutional roots in patterns of corporate development already established before World War Two. In this sense, the interdependent, large modern corporation is an elaboration and consolidation of what already characterized large modern corporations, namely an interorganizational system of factory, firm, and network. However, similarities in pre-war and post-war structures do not tell the entire story. The post-war democratization of the social structure of the firm, its patterns of ownership, management, social relations, internal communication, and especially production organization, embody a remarkable transformation of the meanings attached to work structures. Accordingly, the post-war history of the modern corporation and enterprise system in Japan encapsulates a half-century of ongoing structural adaptation reinterpreted and reinvigorated in light of new social meanings and relations.

From the standpoint of organizational structure, there are a number of reasons for judging the post-war firm as an extension rather than alteration of existing institutional patterns. First, the underlying macro-economic forces that promoted economic growth in the pre-war period continued after World War Two. These were primarily an expansion and improvement of the transportation infrastructure, especially a massive road-building program that noticeably altered the way in which people and materials moved.[1] Second, improvements in transportation when linked with the opening of markets for raw materials and finished products on a world-wide basis boosted both the volume and velocity of economic growth. Finally, an ongoing shift in industrial structure, reflected in changing patterns of SIC distribution among major industrial firms, heralded the rise of a consumer-oriented economy at home and the success of Japanese firms abroad in capturing markets for producers' and consumers' goods.

This last shift, clearly revealed in Table 5.1 and Fig. 5.1, reflects the coming-of-age of such capital-intensive, scale industries as chemicals, petroleum refining, and rubber production (motor-vehicle tires), and such scope industries as electric and non-electric machinery, business and office machines, and instruments and measuring devices. These developments signalled an end to the piecemeal character of local and regional markets that had distinguished certain sectors of the economy

TABLE 5.1. *SIC Numerical Distribution of the Largest 200 Japanese Industrial Firms*
(ranked by assets)

SIC No.	Name	1918	1930	1954	1973	1987
20	Food and beverages	32	27	26	15	22
21	Tobacco	1	1	0	0	1
22	Textiles	50	65	33	15	3
23	Apparel	1	1	1	0	1
24	Lumber	2	1	0	3	2
25	Furniture	0	0	0	0	1
26	Paper	12	7	13	8	9
27	Printing	0	2	0	2	2
28	Chemicals	20	18	26	25	36
29	Petroleum	4	2	10	19	13
30	Rubber	0	1	2	5	4
31	Leather	2	1	0	0	0
32	Stone, clay, glass	14	14	7	13	12
33	Primary metals	27	23	39	26	19
34	Fabricated metals	5	3	1	6	5
35	Machinery	4	5	9	16	27
36	Electrical machinery	8	10	9	17	15
37	Transporation equipment	13	15	21	23	17
38	Instruments	3	3	3	6	9
39	Miscellaneous	2	1	0	1	2

previously and, therefore, to the tripartite division of Japanese enterprises along geographical, structural, and strategic lines employed in earlier chapters.

Structural changes like these were prefigured during the inter-war era, and they reinforced existing patterns of structure and strategy that already delineated corporate behavior. Firms remained relatively small in size, focused in activities, and linked through networks and alliances with other enterprises in lieu of extensive vertical integration and multidivisionalization. Firms capitalized extensively on economies of scope and thus broadened their product lines measurably at the three-digit level of SIC classification, but a general product diversification at the two-digit level did not occur. Between 1954 and 1987, the number of diversified firms among the 200 largest industrial firms in Japan changed little: from 77 to 80. And 41–52 percent of diversification measured in this way, occurred within the same two-digit SIC category, continuing an emphasis on full-line production.[2] (See p. 21, for the full seventy years' calculation of product diversification in Japan.)

Instead of diversification, scale and scope economies in manufacturing were realized in multi-function, multi-product factories where sunk costs in the

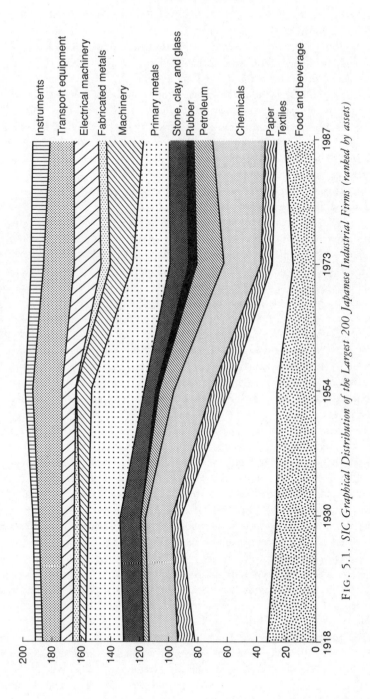

FIG. 5.1. *SIC Graphical Distribution of the Largest 200 Japanese Industrial Firms (ranked by assets)*

accumulation and application of technical learning in core product lines paid handsome dividends through enhanced speed, heightened sophistication, and reduced costs in focused product development. As a result, the number of new-product launchings within specialized product families could be significantly increased, resulting in the full product-line strategy so synonymous with the success of Japan's large industrial firms. While multi-function factories were not new to post-war Japan, the size, sophistication, and velocity of change in the post-war market allowed for considerable elaboration and extension of this institutional form. Market share competition, a widely regarded measure of corporate well-being in post-war Japan, is often a surrogate for product-development capabilities, and these capabilities are embedded in the focal-factory structure.

Also, from the standpoint of corporate strategy, the post-war macro-economic policies of industrial planning and resource allocation that have received so much attention were not new. Early and largely ineffective government efforts to guide enterprises were apparent from the 1870s and 1880s, as outlined in Chapters 2 and 3. Again, in the 1930s with the militarization of the political economy, government became heavily involved in industrial planning. Pre-war patterns of macro-economic resource allocation were continued in spirit and, more importantly, in substance during the Occupation of Japan from 1945 to 1951.

Thus, from the last quarter of the nineteenth century, government had sought to shape economic policy and performance. After the Occupation ended, during the 1950s, 1960s, 1970s, and well into the 1980s, government macro-economic policy and planning molded a political and economic landscape within which the initiatives of individual enterprises were clearly prescribed, occasionally constrained, but rarely proscribed. Such circumstances are typical of modern industrial economies everywhere.

What best distinguished Japanese macro-economic planning through the mid-1960s was the speed of economic growth in spite of government regulation. Government controls over foreign-exchange licenses, interest rates, loan requirements, tariff schedules, capital and financial markets, defined and delimited the economic environment for all corporations. Yet in comparison with the military controls imposed first by Japanese and then American macro-economic planners, the scope and degree of government control over the economy diminished rather than expanded. Government planning and Japan's economic growth may have been more coincidental than causal.

The extent and effectiveness of government regulation in the post-war period can be questioned on other grounds as well. Peter Duus has argued that big business succeeded in resisting the military's attempts before World War Two to supplant a free-market economy with a controlled one.[3] Much the same argument can be made for the post-war period. Duus believes that the new economic order of the pre-war era was little more than congeries of watered-down cartel-like industrial associations. These were more important as vehicles of liaison between business and government than as control organs over the economy. The Major Industries Control Law of 1931, while seen as a breakthrough in government control of the economy, did little to alter the structure of the economy, Duus argues. Businessmen retained command over what to produce, how to produce, when to produce, as well as how to distribute the gains from what was produced. The government's role was reduced to deciding output and price, and even these were confined to certain categories of goods only.

Skepticism as to the effectiveness of government controls during the post-war era economy is likewise warranted.[4] In the first place, businessmen were used to it by then. During the pre-war period of heightened government involvement in the economy, businessmen found ways to work around the rather clumsy efforts of government officials to legislate prices and control production. The same was often true in the post-war era of government control, especially when Occupation officials had little knowledge of the inside workings and institutional mechanisms that held the economy together.

In the conventional and popular view, the major evidence offered for the effectiveness of government control in the post-war era is a massive, 'government-induced' shift in industrial structure from light to heavy industry, from labor-intensive to capital-intensive industry. However, as the SIC distribution of Japan's major firms (ranked by assets) indicates, the shift was already underway by 1930 and well advanced by 1954. Although Japan lacked refinery and distribution capacity in the petroleum industry before and after World War Two, other heavy industrial sectors were already well developed. If SIC categories 28 (chemicals), 33 (primary metals), 35 (machinery), 36 (electrical machinery), and 37 (transportation equipment) are lumped together, by 1930, 35 percent of Japan's largest 200 industrial firms were in these product areas and 52 percent by 1954. And if the SIC shift is based on sales rather than asset ranking, the shift would be even more pronounced.[5]

If better than one-third in 1930 and one-half of Japan's major manufacturing companies in 1954 had *already* made the shift from light to heavy industry, then the effectiveness of government policy in mandating that shift may be questioned. The Occupation era ended in 1952 so that less than two years had elapsed before the 1954 bench-mark year used here. By 1973 just before the first oil shock, the count of large firms in the above SIC categories had risen by a total of three since 1954, so that 53.5 percent of Japan's largest industrial firms were now in heavy industry. Adding petroleum to the SIC list, raises the percentages from 36 percent in 1930, to 57 percent in 1954, and to 63 percent in 1973. Even at a time when the government exercised pervasive controls over the petroleum industry in energy-poor Japan, between 1954 and 1973 there was only a 6-point gain in the numbers of large industrial firms in the machinery and heavy industry categories.[6]

Shifting attention from the macro-economy to just one industry yields similar results. The steel industry offers the most celebrated (and controversial) story of government success with post-war restructuring. The standard explanation has an omniscient Ministry of International Trade and Industry (MITI), Ministry of Finance (MOF), and Bank of Japan controlling industry entry, setting production quotas, regulating capacity, and generally managing sectoral affairs.[7]

In fact, government's involvement in the steel case was quite different. In 1950 with American authorization and insistence, Japan Steel (Nittetsu), the largest steel company in Japan, was split into Yahata Steel and Fuji Steel. During the militarized 1930s and 1940s, Japan Steel had been a government-owned mill with controlled output and fixed prices. However, after de-nationalization and in the context of a changing American policy, it was unclear whether or not Japan would or could be self-sufficient in steel production; self-sufficiency aside, it was also uncertain which firms would produce what kinds of steel in what volumes.[8]

Late in 1950, Yataro Nishiyama, President of Kawasaki Steel, announced a grand scheme to build a mammoth steel plant in Chiba Prefecture. Hosai Huga, President of Sumitomo Metals and not to be outdone by Kawasaki Steel, countered with an ambitious plan to construct an equally large plant in Kanagawa Prefecture. The possibility of ruinous overcapacity in pig iron and steel production prompted Naoto Ichimada, Chairman of the Bank of Japan, to oppose publicly Sumitomo Metal's plans, triggering a contentious debate in the trade press over the proper pace and direction for Japan's economic recovery.

Finally, in 1952, after the American Occupation ended and some eighteen months after Nishiyama's startling and provocative announcement, MITI offered the first of what would become three 5-year plans to control investment, rationalize production, and coordinate output in the steel industry. In short, MITI was responding to what business had already begun.

Such stories could be repeated endlessly, and depending on a choice of stories, an ascendancy of either business or government could be argued. Suffice it to say that the quality and quantity of government–business interaction has varied over time and will continue to vary widely across industries and sectors. In raw-material processing and energy generating industries, government involvement has been substantial and ongoing, pitched towards the maintenance of a steady production of basic materials and energy for public and private uses. In producer goods, especially synthetic fibers, ferrous and non-ferrous metals, shipbuilding, and electrochemicals, government policies to control prices and output have been widely noted; however, the efficacy of such policies may be questioned even while the willingness of industry to adapt autonomously to changing market circumstances and to output control by self-regulation are manifest.

As the example of the steel industry suggests, selective promotion of particular producer goods industries certainly occurred, but there are important questions about the effects of those policies and who was responding to whom. Finally, in consumer goods industries, which the government has not generally attempted to regulate (except in a few notable instances like automobile exports), corporate independence is assumed. By focusing narrowly on government–business relations in basic industries, most Western accounts underestimate the importance of business initiative, misunderstand the institutional structures within which businesses operate and through which markets and market-regulatory processes are structured, and misread the thrust of entrepreneurial talent, ambition, and social relations within the institutional context of the Japanese enterprise system.[8]

The figures on SIC distribution before and after the war as well as the story of the post-war steel industry call into question the importance of government policies for implementing a basic shift in the post-war composition and character of Japanese industry. None the less, the figures do suggest that a shift occurred, beginning before the war as early as 1930 and continuing thereafter. And if a shift was occurring already, well before the government took the policy lead, there can be little question that businesses themselves were the force behind this conversion.

While government may have abetted the process, a change in industrial structure preceded and superseded government efforts to affect a fundamental transformation of industrial structure. Industrial policy accelerated economic restructuring and undoubtedly kept more advanced Western products off the domestic market. Industrial targeting, foreign-exchange controls, credit-allocation policies, and the like, all helped. Without industrial policy, the post-war recovery would have been slower, more uncertain, and vulnerable. But a post-war recovery would have occurred and was already occurring none the less. In this view of Japan's industrial policy and government–business relations, government's principal contribution was a macro-economic environment of low inflation rates and stable prices, while big business reciprocated with employment security, capital investment, and R & D—especially development—intensity.

Social Transformation and Shop-floor Reformation

If the effectiveness of government policies mandating economic change may be moot, the importance of enterprise policies for promoting social change in work structures and meanings cannot be doubted. The social reconstruction of the post-war corporation rests on new systems of industrial relations, manufacturing operations, and management organization that were developed from the early 1950s. In the main, these were generated and elaborated without government involvement in any direct and meaningful way but with the active involvement of many employees and most stakeholders in the Japanese enterprise system. While the new initiatives merely extended the structure of the firm in terms of such quantifiable measures as size and scope, they dramatically affected the way in which people worked in firms and thought about work. As a result they powerfully affected enterprise performance.

Since the Korean War, there has been a growing convergence in the sources of information, standards for decision-making, and nature of social agreement about how corporate profits should be measured and distributed within large firms. At the micro-organizational level, the most widely followed measure is productivity calculated in narrowly gauged product lines, and at the macro-organizational level, market share and sales volume have become the measures of a firm's long-term earning power.[9] As a result of a convergence on these standards and a growing agreement on the distribution of economic rewards measured in these ways, labor and management accord in large firms has become notably enlarged. With agreement about what is being measured and how it is being assessed, it has become much easier to decide how much is to be distributed to whom and why.

In the extreme, the convergence has been so great that the distinction between labor and management, often conceived of as an unchanging power dichotomy in the West, has become fuzzy, blurred, less and less important in large industrial firms. Work compensation and content are more a function of experience and skill than formal education or hierarchical status, particularly as the education level of employees has risen across-the-board. A broader sharing of information, a wider agreement about what the information means and how to use it have resulted in a consensual pact regarding the sources of corporate competitiveness and profitability. With this understanding, a negotiated balance between consumption and saving can be found.

To wit, the emergence of a shop-floor reformation, of a transformation of labor—management relations and of a redefinition of the meaning of work at the production level, are rooted in a decidedly new relationship between unions and managers. This occurred with the creation and emergence of enterprise or company unions in the post-war era which depended on 'active consent' strategies uniting labor and management.[10] Such strategies would have been impossible in the absence of agreement on information and incentives as a basis for labor—management bargaining.[11]

For most of the pre-war period, unions were illegal and efforts to protect the rights of workers were smothered under slogans and programs of corporate paternalism and national patriotism. The American Occupation changed all that, making unions legal once again, and giving them considerable political and economic power in the process. Upper-level managers responded initially with a barrage of measures to protect and enforce traditional managerial prerogatives. But a crescendo of nation-wide strikes and labor demonstrations from the late 1940s through the early 1950s quickly and permanently convinced companies of the inevitability of a new age of relative parity-cum-equality (joint decision-making) in labor—management relations.

The initial vehicle for joint decision-making were labor—management councils that existed in two-thirds of all unionized firms by mid-1946.[12] Council deliberations gave workers partial control of the workplace, shop-floor personnel management, calculation of wages and bonuses, and to a limited extent, therefore, of corporate strategy. While union strikes were often protracted and substantial, the most famous confrontations occurring in the Electric Power Union (Densan), Toshiba, Nissan Motors, and Mitsui's Miike Mine, differences were settled increasingly along lines established by the joint labor—management councils. That is, labor and management were becoming partners in an enterprise-based society.

By the mid-1950s unions challenged the legitimacy of a managerial hierarchy less and less, while managers recognized the eminent authority of labor in matters of production layout, work control, personnel transfers on the shop-floor, and worker compensation. The result was a gradual emergence of an 'enterprise society', namely a socially negotiated parity in the interests of labor and management in the context of a booming post-war economy. The corporation became the principal institution within which deliberations affecting national livelihood, distribution of income, and social well-being were determined. While the government debated and temporized, large companies were guaranteeing income on the basis of education, age, employment category, and attitude from the mid-1950s. Indeed, the nation waited a decade or more for comprehensive medical care and adequate unemployment compensation after these were routinely available in large companies. The large corporation became the means and measure of national development in the fullest sense possible: economic, political, and social rights and rewards were secured first in the industrial workplace. And because large firms are nodes of production and distribution networks, often of smaller-sized firms, a trickle-down or 'trickle-out' phenomenon gradually enhanced the working conditions of employees in smaller firms.

The fundamental anchor of labor—management relations in large firms in the post-war period is a guarantee of secure employment, often referred to as 'lifetime employment', for nearly all employees in the absence of any severe and drastic downturn in the employing company's competitive position. Nearly all employees means just that. All employees in large firms of more than 500 employees, save department heads and above (and certain staff employees), are union members. This means typically that somewhere around 90−5 percent of employees belong to the company union.[13] Thus, an important reason for the success of enterprise unions is their universality and inclusiveness and, as a result, the status and position of 'employees' have superseded traditional blue-collar, white-collar distinctions. Economists refer to this shift in Japan as corporate humanism, enterpriser sovereignty, and employee rights-centered corporatism.[14]

Accordingly, labor—management conflict is avoided because a company-wide union means that everyone is affected; labor—management accord is sought because nothing can be accomplished without it. In effect, employment security and unionism in the context of a long and strong tradition of corporate paternalism has created a bias in favor of managerial authority in Japan. That bias has been reinforced by the economic performance of large industrial firms during the past three to four decades.

Given a fundamental congruence in political and economic aims, the main function of unions is to protect the safety and well-being of workers while management seeks to make money for the firm. These otherwise conflicting goals are neatly resolved by a perspective that employee interests and shareholder interests are nearly identical in large Japanese firms.[15] The identity and solidarity of those interests overwhelm competing claims of corporate stakeholders. Although merger and acquisition activity may ultimately unravel employee and shareholder interests in the twenty-first century, since the mid-1950s these have been seen as mutually reinforcing in large corporations. The identity of employee and shareholder interests cannot be easily contested, given a stable core of shares that are never traded.

While employment is secure, the content and scope of work are not. Instead of a narrow specification of job content, boundaries, and design, a legacy of decades of highly charged labor–management bargaining in the West, individual job responsibilities are not often clearly specified in Japan even though few ambiguities exist in overall task design or in what should be done, when, and by whom. In practice, foremen or assistant foremen in factories and section heads or their assistants in offices assign tasks on a daily basis; they have weekly and monthly work schedules, of course, but these are modified without challenge according to daily needs. Task demarcations arise as a consequence of the natural division of labor based on employee skills. It is expected that almost everyone can do almost every task within work groups even if the acquisition of fluency with multiple tasks and functions requires considerable training and experience. In part, this explains the emphasis on in-company education and on-the-job training in Japanese firms.

The fruits of the post-war parity in labor-management relations were not immediately apparent during the 1950s, even while new practices of information-sharing, income redistribution, production reorganization, work participation, and decision-making were negotiated and renegotiated in the process of extremely rapid economic recovery. Probably the best documented of the newly negotiated work structures are quality control circles (QC) although QC circles may not neces-sarily be the most representative institutional reflection of the post-war labor–management *rapprochement*.[16] TQC (Total Quality Control) practices were introduced from the United States in 1957, both to improve the quality of products and the quality of working life. The latter emphasis may be crucial as it consciously aims to create organizational subcultures that simultaneously seek to achieve and amalgamate human and corporate goals.[17]

In some important ways, the process of work negotiation has continued throughout the post-war period although a possible interpretation might be that the shock of two oil crises ushered in a broad and lasting agreement once and for all. Oil shocks aside, the coincidence of an ongoing renegotiation of labor–management relations in the context of sustained double-digit economic growth before the mid-1970s greatly reduced the potential for conflict. A growing eco-nomic pie is more easily and readily parceled.

The consequences of renegotiation are increasingly apparent. While the Japanese firm is characterized by a finely delimited, hierarchical structure, this does not deter the horizontal flow of information within and between departments. In addition, horizontal information-exchange may result in relatively less resistance to hierarchical authority than would otherwise be the case.[18] The utility of hierarchy is found in its capability for improving safety, quality, efficiency, participation, and general performance without meting out efficiency gains according to a discriminatory notion of rewards.

It is important to recognize that Japanese firms have become increasingly competitive not by eliminating hierarchy but by elaborating hierarchy. This has occurred at all levels of the corporation but a disproportionate amount has appeared in factories and other operational facilities where a thrust towards specialization in work content combined with generalization in work skills have been especially pronounced. With an elaborated hierarchy in place, the need to continuously define one's organizational position is attenuated (more slots and levels in the organization mean less competition), and instead, one is freer to contribute and participate in the workplace.[19] A socially responsive hierarchy is the means by which work is negotiated and rewarded in large firms. It is common, therefore, to have as many as six or seven levels of hierarchy in a large factory with perhaps fewer levels between the factory and a chief executive officer in the head office.

Specialization in work content but generalization in work skills have driven the Japanese factory in the direction of 'skilling' rather than 'de-skilling' the workforce.[20] It is more cost efficient to educate and upgrade worker skills in job control, shop layout, multiple machine competency, and general communication systems, than it is to invest in complex, hardware-intensive manufacturing systems where worker skills are minimized. Such facilities are often a good deal less flexible than they are theoretically supposed to be.[21] Also, investment in 'humanware' rather than hardware pays for itself soon enough, as evidenced in shorter lead times, quicker turn-around response, more rapid and less costly product-development cycles, and a generally more effective implementation of Flexible Manufacturing Systems (FMS) in Japan. For now and the foreseeable future, hardware-dependent systems are not as flexible as 'humanware'-oriented ones, at least with human resources of the caliber and motivation found in large Japanese firms.

In terms of a model of organizational learning, the post-war reformation of industrial relations has changed the institutional context within which learning occurs. This has been accomplished through an increase in the amount and velocity of what is sometimes called localized knowledge. Localized knowledge, in distinction to generalized knowledge, is a cognitive association about the relationship between the sub-units of an organization and its environment.[22] Recent research suggests that high-tech Japanese manufacturing organizations are characterized by elevated levels of localized knowledge, due to a combination of extremely high levels of technical complexity and systemic complexity in focal factories.[23] This combination is achieved through the integration of technical, organizational, and human resources, visually apparent in a riot of shop-floor posters, banners, and other graphic materials that are hung, stretched, and plastered across Japanese factories. These visible signs bolster across-the-board efforts to harvest the benefits of organizational learning.

Localized knowledge can be measured in some abstract sense by the amount of accumulated experience, the degree of work-routine formalization, or by measuring how many employees have been on the job, for how long, doing what. It is more useful, however, to consider localized knowledge dynamically, where employees are stimulated or motivated to learn by goal-setting, problem-definition, and action. In this perspective, localized knowledge, as a form of organizational learning, can be enhanced by (1) retaining human resources in the workplace (reducing turnover); (2) enriching the learning environment by clarifying goals, motivating actors, and rewarding performance. These goals, by the way, describe important features of the focal-factory model of organization discussed in the next chapter.

Goal-setting encourages organizational members to respond more effectively to the environment and, by doing so, affect their environment. Post-war QC circles and TQC programs fit this paradigm. TQC programs, in particular, with their emphases on continual improvement, nothing less than perfection, and full employee participation, represent structured efforts to mobilize corporate-wide resources for pan-corporate benefits. Factory campaigns, like the notion of negotiated hierarchies, are another means to clarify, structure, and make goals operational.[24]

The cooperative structure of labor–management relations in post-war Japan has undoubtedly encouraged localized knowledge, particularly what is called trial-and-error learning and vicarious learning. An open and supportive workplace (favoring local knowledge) in the context of massive technology flows from overseas (general knowledge) resulted in dynamic and positive cycles of organizational learning. The interactive aspects of the process cannot be denied, while consensus and consent among employees in large firms in the post-war period provided the institutional and social bases for initiating positive feedback cycles.

However, the cooperative aspects of the Japanese firm, that is a joining of labor and management in a largely negotiated hierarchy, is not in any way a foregone conclusion. A full implementation of Toyota's acclaimed just-in-time (JIT) system of inventory control and small-lot manufacturing took fully twenty-five years; another fifteen years may have been required before first-tier Toyota suppliers followed suit.[25] Other manufacturing innovations, such as U-line layout and multiple-model flow-processing, have likewise demanded considerable time and effort for implementation. A mechanistic and deterministic model of how JIT and FMS have created harmonious shop-floor relations misses the point, and such errors are compounded more often than not by ascribing the successful implementation of JIT and FMS solely to managerial initiative.

The process of acquiring a more egalitarian, negotiated, and participatory hierarchy was not simply a top-down, managerial triumph. If that was the dynamic, Japanese firms would be characterized by the same lack of incentives and general flaccidity of purpose and responsiveness found in too many Western firms. Instead, a veritable partnership in goals, methods, and means has been negotiated and renegotiated during the past quarter-century, and this accomplishment has depended on contributions and initiatives from both labor and management. Enterprise unionism, therefore, is the key institutional innovation on which labor–management cooperativeness rests.

A frank recognition that hierarchical control is a managerial function while horizontal coordination is best accomplished by workers undergirds the post-war industrial-relations system. Both are necessary and neither is to be preferred. Such shared inclinations have been described by Robert Smith under the heading of 'order and diffuseness', as basic cultural values attributable to the Japanese.[26]

Interaction and interdependence, that is a division of labor and specialization of tasks both within and between firms, are particularly important in the mechanical, electrical, and transportation equipment industries which have spearheaded Japan's post-war recovery. Order and diffuseness may be more characteristic of some industries and companies than others, affirming that opportunities for interaction and interdependence are more readily available in certain industrial circumstances.

In short, value creation on the part of employees results not only in enhanced corporate performance but also in relatively equal recognition and reward according to value-added contributions. All romantic notions aside and disregarding the supposed Japanese preference for group activity and reward, there is no doubt that honest assessment and fair reward are what sustain the new system of labor–management relations in post-war Japan. Nevertheless, the interactive dynamics of a hierarchical order are not fixed in any final sense, and, as a result, the cycles of performance, reward, and recognition that currently characterize shop-floor organization in Japan may be altered, incrementally in the short run and permanently in the long run. It is this recognition that drives frequent factory campaigns, TQC contests, JIT promotion, product-development efforts, and the emphasis on in-company education. It is this recognition that ultimately drives the transactional-cost structures of Japanese firms, embedded in systems of social relations and in structures of social interaction substantially different in the post-war as compared with the pre-war era.

In any firm the costs of normal operation as well as of product and process innovation depend on what has been called the x-efficiency of the firm, namely the summed effort position of an organization's many employees.[27] Even though a one-to-one correspondence in structures and attitudes cannot be assumed, joint decision-making presumes a reciprocity in structures and meanings for large firms in post-war Japan.[28] Reciprocity hinges on balance, equity, and fair recognition; these can be encouraged and enhanced but they cannot be mandated or legislated. Expressed differently, the post-war environment of industrial relations has evolved in the direction of a kind of organic solidarity between labor and management. Interdependencies bind the two. Interdependencies that are rooted in a tacit agreement about how performance will be evaluated, rewards distributed, and profits invested. Interdependence assumes that while power corrupts, responsibilities motivate.[29]

And though motives joining corporate members may not be identical, conflicts of interest may be minimized through a common sharing of information and outcomes and a common vision of what the corporation means and how it should be run. The belief that these interdependencies will endure sustains employees in their efforts to overcome short-run differences of opinion and position in the interest of long-run performance.[30] The belief is buttressed by an irreversible fact: given an internalized labor market with premium wages, employees will lose everything if firms fail.

Finally, the new pattern of labor–management relations has been in place for a quarter-century or more and it would seem that the broad agreement reached will be preserved, even if the high rates of economic growth under which the agreement was reached are not sustained. Indeed, the system works well, perhaps even better, since the 1970s in an era of moderate economic growth. Reciprocity, equity, and distributive justice have become part and parcel of the post-war system of industrial relations.[31] These norms have been anchored in the structures of the Japanese enterprise system, securing the institutional foundations of a capitalist, democratic, and competitive industrial order. In effect, a fundamental renegotiation of the human side of industrial organization in large post-war Japanese firms has occurred and it is not likely to be reversed.

Accordingly, the corporation in Japan has been the institution providing the main arena of deliberation and decision on basic questions affecting the national livelihood, distribution of income, and social well-being, and in doing so, the corporation has become an institution devoted to the advancement of social as well as economic progress. For many Japanese, the modern corporation is credited with raising the standard of living to international levels before the Pacific War, with rescuing the country from the utter devastation of that war, and with restoring Japan to a position of social and economic pre-eminence in world affairs.

While the government's part in promoting social and economic development cannot be denied, the corporation has been the institution most responsible for the day-to-day, step-by-step betterment of the livelihood of the people. Also, the ideologies of individualism, egalitarianism, and democracy have been worked out within the context of the post-war corporation for the most part. The modern sense of self and identity as well as Japanese sensibilities towards participation, motivation, and recognition have been framed by a national experience of recruitment, education, and reward in corporate enterprise.[32]

The Adaptive as Opposed to Innovative Enterprise

A re-emergence of underlying macro-economic forces, the diffuseness of government regulations, combined with the micro-organizational reformation of industrial relations outlined above encouraged corporations to improve past practices rather than to experiment and innovate radically new lines. An ongoing if gradual adaptation of corporate structure was the result. Joint decision-making was accommodated in large part by limiting the domain of the new employment system (long-term employment, seniority-based compensation, and enterprise unions) to regular employees of large corporations. Without limitation, the expense and effort of sustaining a new employment system could have easily become socially and institutionally unmanageable.[33] For such adaptive reasons, corporations extended either the basic U-Form organization which had been established before the war into elaborated but still functional organizations, or they nudged U-Form organizations into emergent but incomplete multidivisional enterprises.

In general, large corporations can reorganize for growth in one of two ways: (1) extending a functional structure which localizes production responsibilities at the factory level while sales, financial, and planning functions are divided between factory and head-office organizations, or (2) devolving the full range of operational responsibilities to divisional management structures organized according to products and markets. In a U-Form organization, the former model, production and sales are not integrated into units organized by product and market, as in the multidivisional form of business organization, the second option.

Multidivisionalization spread throughout the Western world during the 1950s and 1960s and finally to Japan in the 1960s and 1970s. The economic assumptions behind the multidivisional model were allocative efficiencies in capital and in the transferability of managerial resources across product boundaries. But as Japanese companies became world-wide competitors in shipbuilding, machinery, steel, textiles, and electrical and optical equipment, they did not adopt a mature, Western-style multidivisional form of organization. Instead, most Japanese companies stuck with the basic U-Form organization but modified it in two important ways.

First, during the 1960s and 1970s, many Japanese companies moved towards what might be called incomplete divisionalization through the creation of product-focused, functional units within their organizations. These divisions rarely achieved the independence of action and the full profit-center responsibility of divisions in major Western firms. Instead, many personnel, financial, and managerial decisions were still made at the corporate level while important operational decisions, having to do with the management of specific product lines and of the product-development process, were delegated to factories. As a result, divisions were sandwiched between emergent head offices and powerful factory-level organizations, and were left without the autonomy and authority that one normally associates with multidivisional organizations.

Second, a well-established tactic of the inter-war period, the creation of corporate federations and combinations for the segmentation and specialization of economic tasks among independent but interrelated business entities, was extended and improved significantly. There was an accompanying shift in the nature of alliance bonding, away from financially based interdependence and towards interdependencies characterized by relational or long-term contracting. Such alliances minimized the managerial role of divisions by attenuating the authority of divisional managers. In part, alliances and coalitions superseded divisional roles and functions. Accordingly, divisions were embedded in upper- and lower-level organizational structures which powerfully affected their autonomy and performance.

These two developments, constrained divisionalization and interfirm network elaboration, represent a corporate response to economic growth and product/market proliferation in post-war Japan. In either case, the structures and processes of large firms in Japan are decidedly different than those of their Western counterparts, even while the adoption and diffusion of the multidivisional model of organization in Japan suggest similarities in corporate structure and function. Instead, large

Japanese firms tend to follow one of two organizational variants on the U-Form model. A few firms found ingenious ways to combine both. Matsushita Electric Industrial and Hitachi, two electrical-goods giants followed in the last chapter, illustrate corporate alternatives to multidivisionalization in Japan.

Matsushita and Hitachi: Structural Change and Post-war Strategy

In the electrical-equipment industry, Matsushita Electric Industrial has a form of business organization wherein major product groups are organized into divisions which are responsible for product design, engineering, production, and sales forecasting. But the actual selling and marketing of divisional products are handled by corporate-level sales offices, and for financial, legal, and cost-of-labor considerations, so-called divisions are often spun off as independent business units. Such plasticity in divisional form and function suggests that divisions in Matsushita Electric Industrial are not the actual basis of product and market operations.

Hitachi is similarly organized with a divisionalized structure, except that large production facilities, called factory works, are the loci of product planning and production. In fact, Hitachi factory works operate as profit centers, juxtaposing 26 powerful product-centered factory organizations with the head offices centralized, functional capabilities. Product information is summed at the divisional level but divisions themselves are not the meaningful level of product-performance measurement and analysis.[34]

In the case of both Matsushita and Hitachi, sales, distribution, and marketing functions are not localized in either divisions or factories. These are carried out in field offices or offices attached to the head office. In short, production and sales are not integrated within divisions, and, as a result, divisions are not given comprehensive authority and responsibility for related product areas, as the logic of the multidivisional form would dictate. The rationale leading to incomplete divisionalization is clearly evident in the historical evolution of both Matsushita Electric Industrial and Hitachi. In the case of MEI, a marketing strategy of promoting and distributing a full line of Matsushita branded products in exclusive chain stores across the nation dictated the subordination of product and market responsibilities to centralized, head-office control. Hitachi took another route. It delegated product and market responsibilities to factory-level organizations wherein by the addition of R & D, design, and marketing capabilities, factory-level organizations became analogous in function to Western product divisions. This followed the focal-factory pattern detailed in Chapter 6. Descriptions of Matsushita Electric Industrial's and Hitachi's evolution towards these solutions as extended, large modern corporations are considered below.[35]

Matsushita's Post-war Revival

In 1949, a year of economic crisis exacerbated by the adoption of the Dodge deflationary line in Japan, Matsushita Electric Industrial restructured its headquarters into six functional divisions: personnel, general affairs, sales, production, technological development, and finance. The production division located the responsibility for financial performance in five factories manufacturing dry-cell batteries, vacuum tubes, radios, telecommunications equipment, heating, and other electric appliances. In 1949 MEI was a classic U-Form firm.

In the same year, Matsushita revived its distributor network by forming a mutual betterment association and resuscitating its federation of retail-sales outlets. Exclusive sales shops were served by 240 distributors, and they were able to buy Matsushita products at predetermined wholesale prices. Matsushita signed up 16,000 retail stores and welded them into an exclusive sales network. This approach minimized competition among distributors for retail-store affiliations and ultimately resulted in a formidable national-sales force of 9 regional-sales offices, 19 branch-sales offices, 620 distributors, and 33,000 federated retail outlets by 1952.[36]

Consumer Electronics and Household Electrical Appliances

The market for consumer electronics and household electrical appliances grew tremendously during the 1950s. In 1955 the value of production was 73 billion yen, in 1960 450 billion, and by 1964 830 billion—a growth rate of 1,140 percent. Radios, made before World War Two but largely devoted to military uses then, were the first hit products of the post-war consumer electronics age. The most popular radios in the late 1940s were four-tube, recycled war-surplus models, while larger five-tube 'super' sets were highly prized. In 1948, 200 companies, large and small, were making radios, and sales climbed to over 800,000 sets.

Civil radio broadcasts resumed in 1951 at the close of the Occupation, and these created a demand for radio sets with a finer tuning capability. In 1952 the first portable radio sets appeared and in 1955, Tokyo Tsushin Kogyo (today's Sony) brought out a transistorized radio which caught on overseas, especially in the United States. Transistorized Sonys were high-priced radios, selling for more than 10,000 yen ($28.00 at 360 = $1). Export sales boosted Sony's growth fantastically.[37]

Household electrical appliances, such as irons, fans, and washing machines, increased at a somewhat less frantic pace than radios. The first electric washing machines were agitation-type machines with long washing cycles. Then Toshiba imported a water-jet type of washing mechanism from the Hoover Company in England, and in 1953 Sanyo succeeded in producing this type of machine domestically. The water-jet machine quickly dominated the market.

Refrigerators were another household appliance which witnessed tremendous increase in demand, and established heavy industrial goods producers like Toshiba and Hitachi with experience in electrical-motor design and manufacture were the first to bring out popularly priced models. However, smaller, quicker-moving, light electrical-goods manufacturers, like Sanyo and Matsushita, were the companies that best capitalized on these markets.

The growth rate in sales of black and white televisions and radios, the core of the consumer electrical-goods industry, reached nearly 60 percent per year during the late 1950s and early 1960s. But by the second half of the 1960s sales growth slowed, although a decline in black and white televisions was offset by a growth in the sale of color televisions. Electric washing-machine sales spread rapidly but with a slight annual decline during the entire ten-year period from 1955 to 1964 while refrigerator sales started low but grew steadily. Sales of air conditioners during the late 1960s were especially brisk and they compensated for the slower sales growth of black and white televisions, washing machines, and refrigerators by this time.

Overall sales of washing machines, televisions, and refrigerators, the so-called three household treasures of the early post-war period, were remarkable (see Table 5.2).

Strengthening the Marketing Structure: 1955–1965

In 1957, in order to respond more effectively to the explosive growth in household electrical goods and appliances, Matsushita reorganized its sales network. The reorganization was also in response to competition, especially from heavy electrical-machinery makers, like Hitachi, Mitsubishi Electric, and Toshiba.[38] First, Matsushita strengthened its chain of retail shops by clarifying the distinction between large exclusive dealers, large representative dealers, and smaller shops. Second, in order to bolster sales at the wholesale level, a national sales company was formed and turned into a distribution company for major wholesalers while regional sales organizations were created to supplement the national distribution company. Third, a system of rebates to support and encourage sales was established. Fourth, after 1958 a collection company was formed to receive monthly

TABLE 5.2. *Washing Machines, Televisions, and Refrigerators in the Total Production of Electrical Goods* (in %)

	1955	1957	1959	1961	1963	Diffusion rate in 1964
Washing machines	21.4	12.5	7.2	6.9	6.6	61.4
Televisions (B & W)	25.7	26.4	43.7	36.9	29.1	87.8
Refrigerators	5.7	9.9	8.8	13.3	21.0	38.2
3 main products	52.8	48.8	59.7	57.1	56.7	
TOTAL PRODUCTION	100	100	100	100	100	

Source: Yasuo Okamoto, *Hitachi to Matsushita*, ii (Tokyo: Chuo Koronsha, 1979), 41–3.

credit payments, and this allowed sales shops to concentrate on selling without worrying about collections. Finally, as a back-up to sales at the retail and wholesale levels, showrooms and display centers were established at major sales offices in order to promote public relations for Matsushita.

In sum, the core of Matsushita's strategy for overhauling its marketing at this time was to review and strengthen its sales network while making a full line of products after other companies, like Sony, Sanyo, Hitachi, and Toshiba, pioneered the problems of manufacturing a new generation of consumer electrical goods. Matsushita's strategy was not to compete at the front-end of the market by being the first to introduce products. Instead it chose to improve on pre-existing models of rival firms by adding more features and by aggressively marketing its broader model range through its nation-wide chain of retail outlets. So, while Matsushita was not first into the market, it was first in its efforts to exploit its superior market position.[39]

Becoming an All-Around Consumer Electronics Manufacturer

The timing of Matsushita's entry into the markets for televisions, washing machines, and even air conditioners, relative to the maturation of the market and to the production of heavy electrical-machinery makers with their superior capital resources, was critical. Had larger, more resource-rich companies, like Toshiba and Hitachi, sought to commit themselves more fully to consumer-goods industries at an earlier point in time, companies like Matsushita would have had great difficulty in building up economies of scale in manufacturing and distribution. For late-comers, like Matsushita, the opportunity to conduct research, refine manufacturing techniques, acquire and invest capital resources, establish a market reputation, and otherwise reach a competitive level of production without a great deal of competitive pressure was fortuitous.

But ultimately, the high rate of diffusion for major consumer-electronic goods (in 1962, 79 percent of households had televisions and 58 percent had washing machines) meant that annual rates of sales increase averaged only 9.6 percent in the first half of the 1960s, and this ushered in an era of relative stagnation. Matsushita balanced sluggish sales in its electronic-parts division making radios and black and white televisions by strengthening its electrical-appliances division. In the early 1960s Matsushita bolstered its hand by forming a joint venture with the Nakagawa Electric Company, which was renamed Matsushita Refrigerator (Reiki) in 1966.

This was the first of a number of Matsushita product divisions that were spun out as independent manufacturing affiliates but without independent marketing capabilities. Using the model of Matsushita Refrigerator, namely the establishment of a separately incorporated manufacturing subsidiary, Matsushita Electric Industrial undertook a major program of corporate and strategic restructuring during the late 1960s. In order to insulate itself from fluctuations in demand for products, from rapid shifts in product life cycles, and from the attrition of competitive position brought about by the introduction of substitute products by rival firms, MEI split off many of its production divisions into a dozen different U-Form companies.[40] Matsushita affiliates produced washing machines, electric vacuum cleaners, air conditioners, and other products in one after another newly built factories.

While each was separately incorporated, each sold its products exclusively to Matsushita Electric Industrial which marketed and distributed them. In one radical maneuver, MEI minimized its cost structure by displacing its fixed-cost overhead in facilities and personnel to less expensive areas of Japan, and it maximized its cash flow by broadening the flow and mix of products that it marketed through its particularly dense retail-distribution system in Japan. By this move MEI distanced itself from the difficulties of competing head-to-head with a dozen different, aggressive rival firms. Matsushita Electric Industrial was becoming more a marketing than manufacturing enterprise.

Hitachi's Response to Matsushita

From the mid-1950s Hitachi undertook a fundamental reorientation of its strategic direction. The basic move was away from heavy electrical equipment to electronics as the latter field was believed justifiably to offer greater growth potential. In the shift from heavy equipment to electronics, Hitachi began to make consumer and household electrical goods as well, although Hitachi never emphasized these products in its strategic planning. But in the drive to be a general electronics/ electrical-goods maker, Hitachi felt compelled to enter certain markets in the interest of developing a full line of products and of maintaining good faith with its customers. These decisions did not always make good economic sense, and some were later regretted. Indeed by the 1980s Hitachi was abandoning markets where it did not have the wherewithal to persevere.

Hitachi: 1955–1964

From 1955 to 1964, during a period of very rapid economic growth in Japan, Hitachi's investment strategy evolved in the following ways: while participating in the production of home electrical appliances, especially refrigerators, Hitachi moved strongly into the manufacture of televisions and other electronic goods. In 1957 a television-picture-tube plant was established, and in 1958 a transistor research group was set up in the Central Research Laboratories. In 1959 part of the transistor research group left the research lab to found a transistor production facility in Musashi. Another, even larger, picture-tube plant opened in 1959, and in 1960 factories for electrical parts and components, radios, and televisions were erected.

In the field of household electric goods, in 1956 Hitachi spent around 4 billion yen to expand refrigerator production in a Tochigi facility devoted especially to manufacturing small refrigerators and air conditioners. In the same year and with roughly the same amount of investment, the Taga Works opened to make washing machines and electric fans. Hitachi's consumer goods were not as attractively marketed as, say, Matsushita's, but benefiting from its heavy electrical-goods background, Hitachi's products were reliable, sensible, and good value for the money.

Hitachi's energies were increasingly directed towards the electronics revolution. And for this reason, research efforts were strengthened by a series of actions in the latter half of the 1950s and early 1960s. In 1955 a technology management division was located in the corporate headquarters to coordinate company-wide research efforts. In 1957 the Central Research Laboratories became independent of operational management, and by 1960 Hitachi was investing the equivalent of 2.9 percent of total sales in R & D. Only the relatively slow sales growth of Hitachi consumer goods curbed the absolute amount of R & D funds.

Hitachi: 1965–1974

Hitachi's investment strategy during this period was to capitalize on economies of scale, modernize plant and equipment, rationalize production, and contain energy costs—all at a time of unprecedented economic growth. As part of the company's overall business plan, investment in heavy electrical machinery and industrial equipment was scaled back in favor of electronic parts and equipment.

Following a pattern already apparent from the previous decade, promising new technologies and young researchers investigating those technologies were hived off from Central R & D as catalysts for new production facilities. This gave Hitachi's factories a strongly technical bent, similar in most respects to Toshiba's 'focal factories', described in Chapter 6. The Yokohama Works, for example, was split off from Central R & D in 1965 to focus on increasing Hitachi's output of color televisions. In 1966 a factory was started in Odawara for computer input–output devices, and in 1969 for software development. These, too, were extensions of Central R & D projects into production facilities.

In order to better organize and redirect the strategic thrust of the company at this time, a modified multidivisional form of organization was adopted in 1967. In this reorganization, factories became independent profit centers, and production as well as marketing functions were subsumed under factory facilities. In order for factories to become 'divisional-like' in this way, the first half of 1968 was spent in tallying factory-specific investment and in allocating costs to different factories. Such 'factories' were anything but small and narrow in their activities. Instead, several branch factories might be subordinated to a lead factory, and in each lead factory, a variety of technically related products would be manufactured. Achieving economies of scale and scope were the targets.

About the same time that the company was reorganized in the above manner, four division-level research labs were established: one for household electrical goods in 1965, one for electrical machinery in 1966, another for computer systems in 1969, and the Yokohama facility for television, electronic devices, and communications in 1970. Division-level labs were given the assignment to worry about product and process development with a 3–6-year time horizon while other laboratories, with time horizons in the 5–10-year category, were initiated in three areas of basic research: atomic power generation, large-scale electric machinery, and semiconductors. Most importantly, divisional-level labs were sited at lead factories in a pattern of organizational evolution called herein, focal factories: multi-product, multi-function, fully integrated production facilities. Ultimately, this results in a manufacturing structure of many plants within a plant (PWP) plus complementary assets (R & D, design, managerial, and marketing functions) and a negotiated hierarchy (discussed above in the section on the Shop-floor Reformation).

While concentrating more R & D and planning functions on select manufacturing sites, large electrical/electronics makers simultaneously and systematically began to subcontract and outsource 'dried-out' (*kareta*) products during the 1960s. Dried-out products were volume products where the manufacturing process was stabilized, the defect rate calculated in parts per 1,000 or 10,000, and the value-added contribution to manufacturing output not especially high. As focal factories accumulated multi-function, multi-product capabilities, related but less integrated aspects of the manufacturing process could be outsourced to a network of suppliers.

Large industrial firms already had such networks from before the war, but during an era of intense competitive pressures predicated by double-digit rates of annual growth, the value of networks could be greatly extended if they could be reliably transformed from mere subcontractors into relational networks of suppliers. The transformation implied intimate knowledge of each others capabilities, a willingness to invest in learning and building those capabilities, and the capacity to work together closely, effectively, and interdependently. The success of Toshiba and of Toyota Motor, discussed in detail in Chapters 6 and 7, depends today on the management of their relational networks with suppliers.

Matsushita and Hitachi in Review

In the case of either MEI or Hitachi, their corporate structures were and are constrained with reference to the multidivisional model. As for Hitachi, factory-level organizations, akin to either U-Form divisions or multi-function, multi-product factories, accumulated the resources and authority needed to run smoothly and effectively without divisional-level control and oversight. In Matsushita's case, product-focused organizations were sometimes spun off as independent but affiliated (interdependent) enterprises.

Matsushita offers an especially apt example of this latter strategy: it grew rapidly in the post-war era from a limited organizational base, and many of its U-Form production divisions were spun out as independent companies. This was a sensible solution to the problems of joining mass production with mass distribution because sales, marketing, and distribution functions were already highly centralized for Matsushita. It was far simpler to disaggregate production to allied firms and retain distribution and marketing within Matsushita's centrally controlled sales organization than it was to decentralize most but not all sales responsibilities to some but not all factories.

Hitachi, already a large and highly successful heavy-equipment manufacturer in the pre-war era, strengthened its existing structure by promoting the evolution of some of its factory-works into focal factories, that is full-function, integrated production environments. Like Matsushita, Hitachi attempted to create a chain of exclusive sales shops across the country, but unlike Matsushita, Hitachi's network peaked at less than 10,000 outlets during the 1950s and only several thousand more have been added subsequently.[41] As a consequence, Hitachi was never able to achieve the same economies of scope and scale in distribution that it mastered in production. Hitachi retained and extended its production focus by further differentiating manufacturing facilities into mass-production sites with limited non-production capabilities and full function, multi-product sites.

The organizational consequences of the two patterns of corporate development and strategy followed by MEI and Hitachi are revealed in a comparison of non-union managers (staff *kacho*, *bucho*, and above) working for the two firms. It is manifest that MEI has relatively fewer managers in its so-called operational divisions, while Hitachi's are more numerous and concentrated lower in the organizational hierarchy (see Table 5.3).

Organizational Interdependence in Post-war Japan

The salience of interfirm networks and focal factories have altered the structure and strategy of corporations in post-war Japan. In fact, the central argument of this book is that factories, firms, and networks must be considered together to comprehend the institutional foundations of industrial capitalism in modern Japan. The existence of interfirm networks carries the realm of business activities far beyond the borders of any particular divisional boundary, deep into what is generally called the task environment.[42] In the case of Matsushita Electric Industrial, thirteen subsidiary enterprises make or sell products for it, turning it more into a distributor and trading company than a manufacturer. In the case of Hitachi, a basic emphasis on developing proprietary technology created a low center of gravity in the firm. Factories rather than divisions are the loci of product development and responsibility with the result that core technologies are clearly identified, carefully nurtured, and effectively exploited. In the case of either MEI or Hitachi, longstanding precedents within patterns of enterprise development have significantly altered the Western model of multidivisionalization.

However, within the electrical-equipment industry, there are some companies, post-war companies for the most part, which diverged from traditional patterns of enterprise organization and which achieved levels of corporate divisionalization comparable to many Western firms. Consumer-electronics firms, like Sony, Sanyo, and Sharp, were all founded after the war, and they specialize in catering to the changing tastes and whims of increasingly affluent and restless cosmopolitans.

TABLE 5.3. *A Comparison of Managerial Hierarchies in 1984*

	No. of Non-Union Managers at	
	Hitachi	MEI
Executive level	214	84
Operational level	921	225
Total managers	1,135	309
Total employees	80,000	62,000
Ratio of managers to employees	1:70	1:206
Executive level managers (%)	23.2	37.3

Source: Kaisha Shokuin-roku (Tokyo: Diamondo, 1985).

Especially close coordination between market research, sales, and product design are essential for such firms, and they are exceptional in post-war Japan in that they have adopted multidivisional organizations that maximize the connection between manufacturing, distribution, and marketing within single divisions.

In spite of the emergence of multidivisionalization in some post-war firms, Japanese enterprises rarely attain the size and internal complexity of their Western counterparts. In the case of companies like Sony, Sanyo, and Sharp, their history may simply be too brief to allow them to challenge the likes of General Electric, Siemens, or Philips. But in the case of firms with a pre-war legacy and already established patterns of structured interaction, post-war choices to keep the size of firms small allows them to maximize four important kinds of economies: economies of scale, scope, learning, and transaction cost.

By focusing manufacturing activities in relatively narrow product areas, firms achieve high-volume production by maximizing economies of scale. They focus on doing a few things and doing them well, as demonstrated by the phenomenal rates of output and productivity achieved by Toyota Motor and Matsushita Electric Industrial. At the same time, learning-curve data suggest that costs per unit of production are a partial function of accumulated experience, especially when efforts to apply learning are continued above and beyond initial experience with new knowledge and technique. The difficulty, as always, is in translating experience into value, yet that is a partial function of the post-war structure and meaning of work: the evolution of focal factories and the transformation of industrial relations, detailed earlier in this chapter.

Localized knowledge, a positive shop-floor environment, and well-managed production resources drive costs down the learning curve. In short, high-quantity production can result in high-quality production, if sufficient attention is directed to improving learning, the design and throughput of the manufacturing process, and if everyone involved in the process participates in and benefits from incremental and adaptive efforts to enhance productivity. Efforts to achieve scale economies were and are often transferable to related technologies and products/ markets, adding even more emphasis on the scope economies so characteristic of Japanese industrial firms. The order of the progression is important. Scope economies grow out of scale economies in production because fundamental manufacturing issues, like quality, stability, dependability, and reliability, are effectively resolved sequentially and in a hierarchical fashion. As a result, scope economies follow scale economies in production.[43]

Yet high-volume, focused, and learning-oriented methods of manufacturing are not enough in themselves. Complex products require high-precision parts and assemblies involving overlapping technologies and multiple spheres of R & D competency. Many goods demand a marketing approach based on a matrix of financial, distribution, and market-specific resources that few firms can muster entirely on their own. Japanese industrial firms attack these obstacles by forming business confederations which in combination provide a complete range of business services and which offer *interfirm* scope and transactional economies.

Post-war Enterprise Groups

Interfirm networks, as argued previously, are nothing new to Japan. Since the late nineteenth century, in the case of *zaibatsu* groupings, and since the inter-war period for many other federations, interfirm networks have been accepted as tried and true means of conducting business. The post-war period has witnessed a great elaboration and specialization of functions and activities in interfirm federations in response to a tremendous growth in the economy and a concomitant evolution elaboration of the means of coordinating through interfirm networks. Interfirm relations have become more rather than less important, even while financial ties between interdependent firms have diminished (discussed below).

Most simply, an interfirm network is a coalition of firms wherein companies or subsets of companies coordinate their activities, cooperating in various ways for various reasons. Cooperation might consist of the sharing of resources, such as warehouses and wharves, an agreed-upon allocation of raw or intermediate materials, such as differential shares to the output of a petroleum refinery, or consecutive and alternative uses of the same resource, such as scheduled access to a wind-tunnel testing site, to a three-quarter million dollar electron microscope, or to seaside recreational facilities.[44] Aligned companies might agree to share development costs of a new product and they may even constitute an internal market for a product that does not yet have, and perhaps never will, sufficient demand to succeed on the open market.

In short, the reasons for cooperation, alliance-building, and coalition-formation among firms may be many, including historical, financial, technical, and managerial reasons. Because the forms of cooperation are numerous and the reasons for cooperation equally numerous, companies that cluster together in an interfirm group vary enormously in their degree of integration, interrelation, and 'fit'.[45]

Broadly speaking, the notion of 'fit' or the degree of interdependence that characterizes a single enterprise's involvement in group activities can be illustrated by dividing member companies into *inner* and *outer* tiers. The inner tier are companies with substantial financial, technical, and contractual ties to core activities while the outer tier are companies with less substantial ties. Core activities are defined as those business activities that contribute substantially to the overall sales volume and market share of the enterprise group. Thus, from the standpoint of the core activities of the group, member firms are distributed along two dimensions that are, in fact, continuums: one where ties are substantial and concrete, requiring close coordination of activities within, between, and among core firms, and another where ties are less clear-cut and demanding.

For individual companies, the picture is simpler. Single firms depend on numerous others for coordination and cooperation in such matters as development, design, production, marketing, purchasing, and finance. While some firms may have ties of business interaction with hundreds or thousands of other firms, witness Toyota Motor, most firms operate in an environment where several dozen key alliances are the rule. When interactions are more numerous, organizational devices, such as Toyota's methods of disaggregating inter-level transactions and parts pricing, are employed.

The Japanese sometimes categorize corporate relations by such terms as *chokkei*, *bokkei*, and *shitauke*, or as 'wholly/substantially owned', 'partly owned', and 'subcontractors', but this scheme focuses too narrowly on the matter of ownership. Interfirm networks may involve hundreds of closely interacting enterprises where interfirm cooperation does not necessarily involve interfirm shareholding. Indeed, the quality of interfirm relations is more akin to a kind of competitive cooperation: firms are always trying to make the best deals for themselves while they are in the midst of close cooperation with others. An overwhelming number of interfirm coalitions—a guess might go higher than 90 percent—depend little on financial ties to hold firms together. Instead, firms choose to follow strategies of interdependence and at the same time to retain financial, organizational, and managerial independence.

Types of Interfirm Groupings

Having given a general statement of the rationale for interfirm groupings, it is important to recognize that most people have specific sets of groupings in mind when they refer to enterprise groups in Japan. There are six major enterprise groups recognized today: three derive from pre-war *zaibatsu* groupings (Mitsubishi, Mitsui, and Sumitomo) and three from the post-war regrouping of firms, called *kigyo shudan*, around important city (private) banks (Daiichi Kangin, Fuji (Fuyo), and Sanwa).

Recall that the pre-war *zaibatsu* were largely commercially focused groups capitalizing on interfirm economies of scope. They were capped vertically by family-dominated holding companies which maintained majority ownership in operating companies by direct shareholding control and by indirect financial and managerial policies exercised through group banks, trading companies, industrial firms, and insurance and investment companies. During the inter-war period, *zaibatsu* federations increasingly extended their activities into manufacturing.

The post-war *kigyo shudan* include revived and restructured *zaibatsu* groupings but also reconstituted new *zaibatsu*, such as Nissan, Toyota, and Kawasaki, and newer, vertically integrated industrial groupings, such as Idemitsu Kosan, Yamaha Motor, NEC, and Matsushita Electric Industrial. Most of the post-war groupings are less commercial in character than the pre-war *zaibatsu*, they are often tied together by financial links through main, so-called city or private banks, and they are more complex and better organized in two ways: first, individual firms are larger but nevertheless specialized in their activities, so that post-war firms may be represented as substantial bundles of managerial, technical, and organizational capabilities focused around particular product lines; second, the overall breadth of business activities conducted by post-war groupings has been enlarged.

Post-war *kigyo shudan*, including pre-war *zaibatsu*, have expanded to be active in most every field of business endeavor. The drive to compete across-the-board by having at least one member company in each business is termed the 'one-set' principle in Japan. As a principle, it works best for the older, better developed interfirm networks. Instead of the 'one-set' principle, however, Makoto Usami, President of Mitsui Bank and later President of the Bank of Japan, called it 'the principle of getting set control'. 'I think that the truth is not that we have the idea of getting a complete set of everything there is, but that these things happen out of the necessities of business.'[46] Accordingly, the post-war scale and scope of enterprise groups has expanded dramatically. Not only did traditional *zaibatsu* combines seek the principle of set control but also inter-war and post-war groupings grew greatly as the economy expanded.

Once engaged in a number of different businesses, enterprise groups evaluated their own performance and were often assessed in turn by government and private agencies on the basis of aggregate sales. Aggregate sales thereby became a widely used measure of group performance and status. The Bank of Japan's formula for the supply of funds to city banks and government policies for the encouragement of industry and foreign-exchange control, among other initiatives, also encouraged interfirm groupings to expand by measuring their performance in terms of overall output and capacity.[47] Thus, expansion of sales and market share were widely regarded measures of performance that led to even greater investment in new interfirm ventures, pushing the levels of post-war economic performance even higher.

Changing Financial Relations in Kigyo Shudan Groupings

The degree of interfirm shareholding varies significantly on whether or not the group was reconstituted around a city bank in the post-war period, as the figure below suggests. Groups derived directly from pre-war *zaibatsu* may have as much

TABLE 5.4.　Kigyo Shudan *Intergroup Shareholding, 1961–1977*
(percentages, odd years only)[a]

Year	Mitsui	Mitsubishi	Sumitomo	Daiichi	Fuji
1961	11.23	21.27	22.94	14.70	13.10
1963	9.63	17.75	19.19	10.14	10.34
1965	10.04	17.20	18.79	10.26	10.85
1967	11.58	16.94	19.03	12.62	12.33
1969	13.10	19.47	21.26	15.66	15.47
1971	14.65	22.74	22.62	15.21	16.99
1973	17.25	26.04	24.39	15.23	18.76
1975	17.23	26.41	24.71	16.76	19.23
1977	17.47	26.78	24.79	16.79	18.64

[a] Kobayashi's data were calculated in the following manner: (1) Intergroup shareholding was calculated on the basis of outstanding, publicly listed shares; (2) Shares held by group trust and savings banks were included; (3) The following seven companies were not included in figures given for the Fuji Group (Nisshin Seifun, Toa Nenryo, Kubota Tekko, Hitachi, Tobu Tetsudo, Nissan, and Keihin Kyuko); (4) Kobayashi's sources were annual volumes on enterprise-group activities published by the Keizai Chosa Kyokai, *Keiretsu no Kenkyu: Daiichi Jojo Kigyohen.*

Source: Yoshihiro Kobayashi, *Kigyo Shudan no Bunseki* (Sapporo: Hokkaido University Press, 1980), 132.

as a 50 percent higher level of intergroup shareholding. This occurs for the most because of the outlawing of holding companies during the Occupation era. Shares were redistributed among a larger group of corporate players resulting in the dilution of core companies' control (see Table 5.4).

Since the oil shocks of the mid-1970s, the ways in which companies raise capital have changed noticeably. Self-financing through retained earnings and share participations has increased. With the liberalization of capital markets at home and abroad from the early 1970s, Japanese companies have gone directly to financial markets with increasing frequency. They now have much more latitude than in the past as to what capital instruments and currencies to use, where to raise funds, and in general how to increase capital. Companies, even those enmeshed within an interfirm network, are now more than ever free to choose their own financial future.[48]

In 1978 the debt-to-equity ratio for Japanese companies as a whole was 75 percent, but by the succeeding decade it had fallen to 61 percent and was still falling. The phenomenon of reduced bank borrowing, so-called *ginko-banare*, is a phenomenon associated with large firms after the mid-1980s, especially the 1 percent of firms represented on the first and second sections of the Tokyo Stock

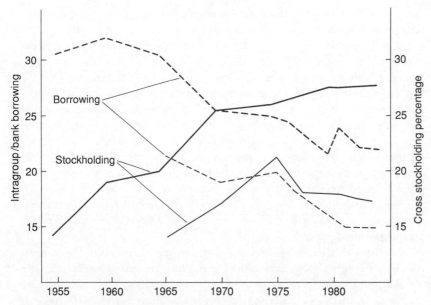

FIG. 5.2. *Trends in Intragroup Relations: Stockholding and Bank Borrowing*

Notes: Data were not available for all groups in early years.

Source: Kosei Torihiki Iinkai (FTC), *Kigyo Shudan no Jittai Chosa ni Tsuite (An Empirical Enquiry concerning Interfirm Groupings)* (Tokyo: FTC, 1977 and 1989), 7, 15, 14, 24.

The upper solid and dotted lines depict the Mitsubishi, Mitsui, and Sumitomo groups; the lower solid and dotted lines depict three bank-centred groups, Dai-Ichi, Fuji, and Sanwa.

Exchange.[49] The debt-equity ratios of large Japanese industrial firms are moving much closer to the ratios found in Western countries.

Even while companies have become more independent financially, they have not become independent of other companies in the way they do business. Indeed, greater financial independence has allowed companies to invest more fully in the creation and maintenance of non-financial interfirm alliances that buttress the production and distribution of their core technologies and main product lines. Financial independence has led to greater interdependencies of other kinds (see Fig. 5.2).

Accordingly, cooperation and coordination among firms occur for a number of reasons, only a few of which could be said to be directly connected to issues of ownership and control. Ownership, in today's mammoth and far-flung interfirm networks is hard to pinpoint, and even after the ultimate sources of equity and debt have been identified, it would be more difficult to determine what role ownership plays in industry structure and decision-making. Given the dispersion of shareholding among major members of the Big Six, it is safe to say that some degree of risk aversion characterizes equity crossholding. This may reduce profits which accrue to one or a smaller number of firms if shares were less widely held, and it also reduces the risk that one firm or a subset of firms have to be prepared to accept.

Indeed, new research findings by American and Japanese business economists have shown that since the 1960s, companies affiliated with the Big Six enterprise groups have not realized as high a rate of average profit as comparable independent companies. Iwao Nakatani found that the rate of profit before interest payments to total assets was 1.1−2.7 percent lower for companies enmeshed in one of the traditional business groupings. However, he and others also found that these companies pay higher and more stable average wages and that they enjoy somewhat lower rates of interest on borrowed capital than non-member firms do.[50] In addition, Makoto Usami's 'one-set principle' might lead to lower profits if enterprise groups happen to take on or carry unprofitable product lines 'out of the necessities of business'.

In a sense, higher wages and lower profits may be explained as surrogate insurance payments to general-trading companies, insurance companies, group commercial and savings banks for their financial, strategic, and market-planning functions. In this view, traditional, financially focused enterprise networks may form an internalized capital market for risk-sharing, market stabilization, and cross-subsidization.[51] While profits for group members may be lower than for non-group members, as a whole companies have more stable growth and profit levels. Stability encourages investment in new technologies and markets.

The attractiveness of group membership from a financial point of view varies according to the perceived financial risk, therefore. Under conditions of information asymmetry and market uncertainty, the value of interfirm membership increases. So while membership may lower profits, transaction costs associated with interfirm relations are seemingly lower due to reduced monitoring costs based on the stability of long-term contracting.

Nakatani further believes that the relatively high capacity of the Japanese economy to adjust to variable market conditions, not just the oil crises of the 1970s but also the shocks of yen revaluation in the 1980s, is quite clearly related to the structure of interfirm networks. Corporate performance can be steadied by risk-sharing within an alliance, and, at the same time, it can be enhanced by pursuing all possible internal economies, knowing full well that numerous other firms stand ready to support and align themselves with your efforts. Group affiliation is obviously advantageous, although the advantages should not be exaggerated. A recent Fair Trade Commission study found that about 15 percent of the total business conducted by enterprise groups (*kigyo shudan*) was transacted internally. In other words, even within groups that are linked financially and with some degree of interlocking directorates, the internal market for goods and services is not larger than about 15 percent.[52]

If it were not the case, it would be surprising. Joining an enterprise alliance is, in part, a risk-reducing strategy that predictably limits new investment opportunities and channels existing ones. An alliance attenuates the need (and perhaps the opportunity) for one company to increase greatly the diversity of its operations, especially outside of the technical and market boundaries where it is contextually situated within the group. As a result, a good alliance citizen expands output within its product specialty, narrowly defined. This directly amplifies single-firm performance while spillover effects may benefit other enterprises in the network.

This risk-limiting (scope-limiting) element was most evident before the mid-1970's oil shocks when the astonishing pace of business expansion eliminated the need for aligned companies to seek non-group, alternative uses for corporate resources as a guarantee of acceptable levels of profitability. Especially in the six major enterprise groups, which have had a history of being full-service, well-integrated, and diversified concerns, with financial, shipping, marketing, as well as manufacturing resources in many different product areas, the large size of the interfirm group itself may have resulted in some intergroup/subgroup sectionalism, low performance (sub-goal pursuit), inertia, and in somewhat less efficient strategies by which to maximize firm-specific advantages. During the high-growth era, however, such maladaptive aspects of group membership were not salient. But these have led to post-1970s fissures within traditional enterprise groups, which some observers see as the beginning of the end of the Japanese interfirm system. Yet loosening of ties within financially based enterprise networks is simply mirroring what is already happening in less financially oriented interfirm groups: companies are pursuing more self-serving alliances to maximize opportunities for growth and profit.

The structure of interfirm groups has important consequences for new investment in start-up ventures as well as for the manufacturing and marketing of new products by already established companies. In the case of start-ups, capital is likely to be raised or, more likely than not, allocated among member firms in the group, so that no single firm contributes an unusually large share of the investment. The current product lines or future product streams of group companies are not jeopardized by the need to invest large sums in new projects. In pooled investment situations, no single firm has to invest that much in a new venture, although it is also true that profits are distributed in line with the level of investment.[53]

One of the clearest historical examples of the group-investment/allocation process would be the building of numerous integrated petrochemical complexes, called *kombinato*, by virtually all of the major enterprise groups during the latter part of the 1950s and early 1960s. The capital requirements were so huge and the time horizons for profitability so long that no single company or even small group of companies could afford the investment and risk on their own. Indeed, Nihon Soda left the Mitsui group of companies because it did not want to participate in a required investment allocation of this sort. But this may be the exception that proves the rule. By allocating investment shares among interrelated firms, the problems of raising and risking capital for individual firms are minimized, especially when many analysts agree that petrochemical combinations were not so profitable.

Firms in a coalition that have invested in a new venture will have access to its market intelligence, R & D, product planning, intermediate and final products, so that the business strategy of the group as a whole can be hopefully consolidated and integrated. New business formations, either start-ups or spin-offs, within a network should not endanger the flow of capital, information, or personnel to already established firms in the group. However, by the same token, single firms within an interfirm alliance may not have the ability, resources, or independence to integrate and diversify as they desire. Individual firms may not have the autonomy to move in desired directions, either for lack of wherewithal (capital, technical, and organizational resources) or for lack of political leverage. Within the Mitsubishi group, for example, a good half-dozen companies manufacture a range of fairly similar petrochemical products. Working out a mutually agreeable strategy of growth for so many cooperating but competing companies has proven to be a vexing and conflicting issue.

The structure of older enterprise groups puts an emphasis on increasing yields more than reducing costs, since maximizing the *flow* of resources through well-established interdependence relationships, such as ties between banks, insurance companies, trading firms, and large manufacturing units, has become a basis for ongoing business interactions. This is necessary in order to keep the group as a whole, with its high sunk costs in existing resources, functioning properly. But this also strains the leadership capacity of core firms to maintain high levels of resource flows, especially for firms requiring rapid resource replenishment. Within the Sumitomo Group, for example, the resource needs of high-flyers like Sumitomo Light Metal and NEC may distort resource allocation and mobilization patterns. So, even though older coalitions seek ways to reduce costs as well as maximize flows, their very size, traditional core technologies, older plant and equipment, and entrenched patterns of interdependence, make this difficult to accomplish.

New Enterprise Groups

There are other enterprise groups (other than the Big Six just described) for which history is not so important, either because they were established recently or because their history is not significant for understanding their contemporary operations. Among such enterprise groups would be found some of Japan's most famous international firms, like Sony, Toyota, Honda, Kao, and Canon, as well as other companies that are less well known overseas but which are no less important domestically.

These firms are also coalitions of companies in the aggregate, often numbering in the dozens, hundreds, or even thousands of enterprises, and these conglomerations coordinate their activities in ways that are similar to, but not necessarily identical with, the methods of older, more established interfirm groups. By and large, financial ties and legally enforceable contractual arrangements are less important in these groups than are mutually binding production and distribution activities. In short, the new groups tend to cluster around activities that provide goods and services to end-user markets, hence market-oriented activities and performance are keys to network development and effectiveness. The new enterprise groups may be divided into three according to the goods they produce and the markets they serve: intermediate industrial goods, final industrial goods, and consumer goods.

Intermediate Industrial Goods. These are groups that cooperate and coordinate activities to achieve economies of scale in intermediate industrial goods, and to take limited advantage of opportunities to diversify such products towards end-users. The best examples of specialized producer goods makers are the five groups of firms clustered in the post-war steel industry: Nippon Steel (ranked No. 11 by assets in 1987), NKK (No. 22), Kobe Steel (No. 25), Kawasaki Steel (No. 26), and Sumitomo Metals (No. 29). Each steel major leads combinations of a half-dozen to a dozen companies that are highly integrated vertically but with limited product or service differentiation.

Since the 1980s, however, the efforts of major steel companies to diversify their product lines have been notable.[54] Not surprisingly, they diversify by creating affiliated companies within their interfirm group and, as a result, the coalitions of firms around major steel companies are expanding. Although some of the companies in these steel combinations may have evolved from pre-war *zaibatsu* groups, they belong neither to the successor groups of the *zaibatsu* nor to the newer, product-service or consumer-goods companies of the post-war era. These are groups organized to achieve economies of scale and, to some lesser extent, scope in manufacturing.

Final Industrial Goods. A second type of new enterprise group also concentrates on industrial goods but their strength and cohesion are derived less from economies of scale and scope than from the provision of specialized marketing and technical services. Obviously, this does not mean that manufacturing costs are unimportant for these producers. The best examples of firms in this category are those that offer data-processing services, like Hitachi, Fujitsu, and IBM Japan, or specialized machinery for factory and office automation, like Fanuc, Toshiba, Omron, and Hitachi. This is an area where hardware must be combined with specialized software, customized installation, service and repair contracts, and perhaps tailored credit arrangements.

The process-control devices, ATM machines, and traffic/factory control systems manufactured by the Omron Tateishi Company are representative products of this type of group. Fuji-Xerox, Canon, or Mita photocopiers and other office-automation equipment are additional examples. These are neither the producers' goods of old nor the customers' goods of today. Companies in this group emphasize high-volume throughput in order to achieve minimum efficient scale but they depend strongly on specialized marketing services to win and retain a pool of well-defined customers.

Consumer Goods. The third, most noteworthy and conspicuous of the new enterprise groups are those that make branded consumer goods in large volume and which have created sales and distribution channels to handle those items. Because consumer, mass-marketed goods are new to post-war Japan and because brand image and development are key to success in this group, enterprise groups that specialize in these goods have been unable to rely on the sales and distribution networks for older, industrial goods or on the marketing channels for such retail items as foods, bolt cloth, and paper supplies. As a result, new distribution channels, including new ways to deliver products to market (principally by truck rather than by train), new product and credit financing, as well as new sales and servicing arrangements have been forged and promoted.

In all cases, leading firms within the new interfirm groups are smaller than comparable leading firms within Western industries. But because they are smaller, they tend to be more focused and have less slack. Less attention is paid to alternative uses of company resources because companies rarely build up significant internal resources that are not fully committed. If slack resources do emerge, however, it is common to create an affiliated firm to focus on new market opportunities rather than to diversify resources within firms.

The newer enterprise groups organized around batch-processing technologies rely heavily on original equipment manufacturing (OEM) arrangements. Because of the importance of general and specialized trading firms in Japan and because of entrenched marketing and distribution channel control, OEM contracting is quite common in Japan. It is difficult for most companies, no matter how good their product, to break into the well-established distributing and marketing channels of post-war Japan. There is no particular stigma attached to the OEM status, however. Indeed, by becoming a supplier to a Toyota or a Toshiba, a firm actually gains status in Japan. And, at the same time, OEM firms strive to expand the size and breadth of their product runs so that they can enlarge their business: not just contracted or outside business but their own brand-name business.

By concentrating resources on fewer products and more specialized markets, Japanese firms, especially the leading firms within interfirm networks, often achieve astonishing rates of growth in sales and profits. Some of the high-flying Japanese firms of recent years, such as Kyocera, Fanuc, Canon, and Matsushita Electric Industrial, are essentially single-product companies where a single-product line, be it IC ceramic packages, NC devices, photocopiers, or VCRs, can account for 40–70 percent of sales.[55] These are focused technology companies, highly geared in particular product lines and with very little margin for error.

But what was big for Canon or Matsushita Electric Industry in 1960, for example, may not be such a big seller in 1965, 1970, 1975, or 1990. MEI, in particular, can shift its product focus and therefore its profitability quickly because it is not an integrated, mammoth corporation. Instead, it is rather small (62,000 employees is small in a world of General Electric, Siemens, or Philips), more akin to a trading company than a manufacturer, since its disaggregation of manufacturing divisions into separate, independent enterprises in the late 1960s (discussed in the last chapter). Of course, disaggregation does not eliminate the need for good management.

The Utility of Interfirm Networks

Mitsubishi Motors

An interfirm network provides an organizational framework of great adaptability and flexibility. In 1988 Mitsubishi Motors' Galant won the Japanese Car of the Year award for the first time in the company's history. A full complement of high-technology features, including four-wheel steering, four-wheel drive, integrated transmission, an active, electronically controlled suspension system, anti-skid brakes (ABS), and a multi-valve, turbo-charged, high-rev engine, catapulted the automobile into the public's eye. Sales of the new Galant were up 50 percent between 1987 and 1988.[56]

Mitsubishi Motors' R & D staff numbers no more than 3,500 which is less than half of Toyota's and Nissan's. But MMC's R & D staff was augmented by borrowed engineers and technicians from two of the Mitsubishi groups' most important enterprises: Mitsubishi Electric and Mitsubishi Heavy Industries. Mitsubishi Electric contributed valuable process-control technology, designing the sensor and relay systems for the steering, suspension, integrated transmission, and engine control systems. Not only are these complicated systems in their own right but the integration of various electronically controlled sub-assemblies within each system and the overall coordination of each subsystem into a responsive, effective whole, were technical matters beyond the reach of MMC's R & D staff. Likewise, motor-design proficiency, incorporating emission-control know-how with turbo-power performance, was not a resident capability within MMC. Mitsubishi Heavy Industry, one of the most advanced engineering firms in the world with aircraft-engine design experience, contributed its expertise in these areas. The combined talents of Mitsubishi Electric and Mitsubishi Heavy Industry gave Mitsubishi Motors a leading edge in designing and producing the automotive subsystems that are still on the drawing board of rival firms. The utility of interfirm cooperation in this instance is beyond question.

The leading edge that Mitsubishi Electric and Mitsubishi Heavy Industry gave Mitsubishi Motors was not financial in character. Lead-time savings are far more important than cost savings in development and design activities, especially when a new model can reconfigure industry standards in rapidly changing markets. Where costs are well known or fairly estimated in advance, that is when sourcing parts and components is a low-risk activity, group affiliation means little or nothing at all. In such instances, Mitsubishi Motors or any other major manufacturer simply buys from the lowest cost producer.

However, when close coordination between different steps in the development sequence is critical and, therefore, when ease and speed of effective communication in product development are of primary importance, the tacit, implicit, and sometimes explicit ties of cooperation based on interfirm affiliation are irreplaceable.[57] Coalitions like the one binding MMC, MHI, and MELCO offer a more rapid, less costly, and less irreversible response to market and technological innovation than internal development, provided that coalitional partners do not waste resources in excessive monitoring and governing activities.[58]

The utility of interfirm alliances for Mitsubishi Motors was to lower the risk of an unacceptable delay in product development when high value-added products were being sourced. The complexity of developing a new Galant model demanded considerable asset interspecificity between MMC and its two sister firms. Brainstorming, clarification and verification of specifications, team-building, and strict product-development deadlines, are not easily accomplished across corporate boundaries. But the already established, ongoing, and enduring quality of intercorporate relations within firms in the Mitsubishi group enabled Mitsubishi Motors to produce an automobile of high quality and ingenuity several years before rival and larger companies did so. (Note well that until 1970 Mitsubishi Motors was a product division within Mitsubishi Heavy Industry.)

Tokyo Electron

A further example of and the utility function of interfirm alliances comes from a recent start-up in the electronics industry. Tokyo Electron was founded in 1963 as a trading company, exporting VTRs and importing electronic parts. From the beginning the company increased the value-added component of its electronic-parts sales business by doing some assembly in Japan. In 1965 manufacturing was added to the original trading functions of the firm.

Three years later Tokyo Electron formed its first subsidiary, Tele-Samuco, a manufacturing joint-venture with a small maker of electronic components. In two more years Tokyo Electron established a second manufacturing subsidiary, Telemek, as a 100-percent-owned subsidiary. During the 1970s as VTR–VCR exports boomed at a 20–50 percent annual growth rate, Tokyo Electron merged its three organizations to strengthen its import–export capabilities. In order to raise enough money to float the expansion and integration of the three organizations, Tokyo Electron went public on the second section of the Tokyo Stock Exchange in June 1980. At this time, all trading and manufacturing functions were rolled into one company.

However, in 1981 in order to delegate responsibility for pell-mell expansion in production, again two manufacturing subsidiaries were formed. But the rate of expansion was so rapid that the manufacturing subsidiaries were not able to employ enough young, talented technicians and engineers. So, in February 1984, the manufacturing subsidiaries were reintegrated into the parent company, adding 600 persons, mostly engineers, to the 400-person parent firm. In March the company went back to the equity market, floating a new offering of shares on the first section of the Tokyo Stock Exchange.

Flush with cash and orders, six new manufacturing subsidiaries were established between 1986 and 1988 in local areas of Japan, giving the production function sufficient independence and resources to adapt successfully to market demand, product development pressures, and local labor conditions. As a result, Tokyo Electron is today a major semiconductor-equipment manufacturer and has concluded an agreement with Varian to market its products in the United States. Once again, the need for organizational flexibility resulted in the decentralization of corporate resources by way of a network of affiliated firms rather than by creating competing divisions within the parent company.

In short, during the course of twenty-five years, Tokyo Electron had gone through three cycles of integration and two of devolution in order to adjust its corporate structure to strategic and market needs. Whether as an integrated, functionally organized, single enterprise or as an alliance of specialized but interrelated firms, Tokyo Electron had complete managerial control over the present and future course of its organizational form and function. The choice of which structure to pursue was a strategic one. When growth was rapid and technical advantages needed to be emphasized, an alliance structure efficiently mobilized resources. When consolidation for financial, organizational, or managerial reasons appeared desirable, a more unified corporate form was established.[59]

Toso (Tokuyama Soda)

Another example of interfirm adaptability and utility is found in the recent history of Tokuyama Soda. Tokuyama Soda, one of the largest synthetic chemical manufacturers in Japan, decided in June of 1986 to revamp its finished veneer-products business. It did so by merging a raw materials subsidiary of its veneer-products division, Shunan Chemical, with another subsidiary specializing in manufacturing veneers, Sun Arrow. To this new combination, Tokuyama Soda added its own veneer-products sales department, creating a new company encompassing raw-materials acquisition, production, and sales. The new structure is expected to lower transaction costs between functions and to provide a more unified and focused structure for product development and R & D.[60]

The important point is that Tokuyama Soda decided to create an independent enterprise specializing in purchasing, production, and sales rather than fold these activities as a reconstituted division into Tokuyama Soda. It could have done so of course, but from the perspective of Japanese organizational practice, the monitoring and coordinating efficiencies to be derived by integrating a new division within an existing corporate structure are offset by additional organizational rigidities in the parent structure and by a loss of organizational flexibility on part of the subsidiary.

In fact, there is often an oscillation between the functions of integration and devolution in Japan. Firms have a choice to fold in or spin out business activities according to their transactional needs and strategies. The choice is made by the top management of core and concerned firms in light of market, hierarchical (interfirm), and historical conditions. Choices are framed by what is known and what worked well before.

By striving for scale *and* scope economies within interfirm-network structures, Japanese companies can transform some unusual products and markets into high-volume, national industries. The lumber industry, for example, is usually populated by large numbers of small mills that compete on the edge of bankruptcy with other companies producing undifferentiated, highly standardized, cuts of lumber. But Dicel Industries and Sumitomo Ringyo (the 215th and 103rd largest Japanese industrial firms in 1987, respectively) have become national companies in Japan by providing a wide range of highly specialized cuts of lumber, specified according to the needs of large industrial and residential builders.[61]

Misawa Homes and National Home Industries (No. 158 and No. 189, in 1987) have taken high volume but highly specialized cuts of wood provided by Dicel and Sumitomo, and combined them with a range of plastic, ceramic, and cement materials to provide affordable, modular, diversified homes and apartments. These companies are not home builders but home fabricators, and although they may work in conjunction with an affiliated home-building company, companies like Misawa Homes and National Home Industries essentially design, make, and deliver home-construction kits. Because Japanese consumers will not buy faceless, undifferentiated housing, economies of scope at the point of manufacture become key to successful home marketing and sales.

The epitome of how to market products through economies of scope are the numerous fashion goods that have become hit products in Japan. These goods go beyond standard advertising and branding, by promoting fashion, color, variety, and personal taste. Sony's Walkman as an item of personalized leisure and recreation as well as a fashion accessory illustrates this point. Exercise/athletic shoes offer another case in point. Economies of scope provide consumers with variety, and marketing propels the shoes into new realms of comfort, color, softness, and style. In such instances, economies of scope are achieved through the development of focused intrafirm competencies linked to structured sets of interfirm-dependent capabilities. The key is the speed with which products can be designed, developed, made, and marketed. In interdependent organizations, speed to market is most often a function of low transaction costs. Low transaction costs rest ultimately on organizational learning, that is the ability to join efficiency and learning in elaborated, specialized structures. Needless to say, interfirm alliances of this sort result in firms with structures and strategies quite different from those of Western firms that try to be completely independent in design, manufacturing, distribution, and management activities.

In the cases of Mitsubishi Motors, Tokyo Electron, Tokuyama Soda, Misawa Homes, and Sony, the malleability and permeability of corporate boundaries within interfirm networks offers significant opportunities for shortening product-development cycles, focusing corporate resources by function and by product, mobilizing human and financial resources, and otherwise molding corporate structures to tactical and strategic needs. The utility of interfirm alliances in such instances can hardly be doubted.

The Modern Corporation and Enterprise System in Post-war Japan

The modern Japanese corporation follows predictable patterns of strategy, structure, and behavior. These are consonant with an institutional legacy worked out largely before World War Two even while such patterns have been adapted and modified since then. Before or after the war, Japanese industrial companies are inclined to have a focused set of core technologies while less closely related technologies are delegated to outside, affiliated firms (interfirm networks). To the extent that firms maintain this focus, the need for elaborate portfolio and strategic planning exercises diminishes. Instead of trying to allocate capital efficiently among scores and perhaps hundreds of different divisions (the American multi-divisional model), Japanese companies concern themselves with several to perhaps a half-dozen core business. Thus, enterprises can be categorized as single-product and dominant-product firms for the most part.[62] This structural focus results in its own strategy, namely digging deeper and deeper into what you do best and finding ways to use firm-specific resources more flexibly.

Strengths are always integrated within a network of affiliated and related firms which can be mobilized by strategies based on economies of scale and scope. Because such economies are dynamic, the boundaries of interfirm transactions are likewise dynamic. While competitive advantages founded on cooperative structures may be realized (or not) for any number of reasons, ranging from similarities and dissimilarities in intention, planning, implementation, and execution, inter-dependencies are initiated with high expectations of cooperation and reciprocity.[63]

A reliance on cooperative structures and alignments means that Japanese companies can focus even more on depth than breadth. As a result, firms are relatively small, functionally organized, constrained in the nature and degree of divisionaliza-tion, and embedded in interfirm alliances. Constrained divisionalization refers to the forging of division-like structures which are responsible for some but not all of the major decisions affecting particular products and markets. Another variant, selective divisionalization, occurs when certain businesses within large enterprises are given relatively more autonomy than other businesses. In almost all instances, however, financial, personnel, and long-range planning functions are *not* entirely delegated or divisionalized.

Of course, there are always exceptions to the rule and some firms follow patterns of enterprise growth based on full divisionalization. Fujikoshi Machine Tool Company, mentioned in the previous chapter, is one such example. Recall that in 1937, Fujikoshi had created a U-Form corporation with employees divided between manufacturing and sales. By 1956 the sales department had moved from Fukuyama to Tokyo in order to better follow national market trends as well as to participate in the emergence of the Japan Engineering Standards (JES) and Japan Industrial Standards (JIS) as national standards. Four years later, the Tokyo sales department subdivided into six according to type of product or activity (domestic versus foreign sales, for example) and the manufacturing department divided into three for machine tools, bearings, and machinery product lines.

Fujikoshi's restructuring occurred in the same year, 1960, that the Industrial Council for Rationalization held its annual congress under the theme of 'Profit Management in the Multidivisional System'. Fujikoshi's Sales Manager, Ken Imura, attended the congress and had toured in the United States a year earlier studying the advantages of decentralized management in the multidivisional system as compared with the *ringi* system of centralized management practiced in Fujikoshi.[64] In February 1962 Fujikoshi established an M-Form management structure, creating three divisions (machine tools, bearings, and machinery), and attaching sales, manufacturing, and management departments to each of them. In October purchasing departments were added to the divisions. These structures have remained intact and withstood considerable increase in organizational size and complexity. By 1988 Fujikoshi was tied with Toshiba as the fourth largest industrial-robot makers in Japan with 1.1 billion yen in sales.[65]

In considering interfirm networks as alternatives to M-Form structures, it is important to re-emphasize that the contemporary sense of common purpose and action within interfirm networks is not based principally on ties of ownership. Among the six major enterprise groups today, the degree of interfirm shareholding is not especially high, and since the oil shocks of the mid-1970s, credit dependency on group banks, financial institutions, and trading companies has been declining while interfirm shareholding among manufacturing and marketing companies within groups is rising. And it could be argued that much of the debt owed to member financial institutions was not really debt in that loans were rarely called in or paid off. Thus, debt was closer to equity: it represented an investment in the ongoing and future earnings of borrowing firms.

The most obvious difference between pre-war and post-war interfirm groupings is size but size is a function of history and structure. The pre-war *zaibatsu* groups that have persisted into the post-war period or the post-war, city-bank *kigyo shudan* groups are conglomerations of many firms, some with more than a century of history and others with just a few years of operation. In the case of older *kigyo shudan* groups, they have had time to develop resources, elaborate forms, and integrate and diversify activities. The newer and more product-focused groups of the post-war period, however, have not had the same amount of time to grow and mature and they are less encumbered by ties to established financial institutions. As a result, they are sometimes called 'independent enterprise groups' (*dokuritsu kigyo gurupu*).

Thus, significant differences exist within Japan between the successors to the pre-war interfirm combines and the newer, post-war interfirm groups like Sony, Kyocera, or Sharp. Most significantly, the structure of the older enterprise groups, centered on banking, trading, real estate, and heavy-industrial functions at the core, tend to put more emphasis on *interfirm* economies of scale and scope. Such groups with high fixed costs concentrated in core functions emphasize the maximization of cash flow through banks, trading companies, and manufacturing affiliates. The coordination of this flow is what keeps the older-style groups functioning properly.

By contrast, an emphasis either on vertical integration or functional specialization and segmentation within the newer interfirm groups underscores the importance of intrafirm cost reductions in production and distribution. These groups more closely approximate the Western multidivisional corporation in structure and strategy. Nevertheless, Japanese companies and groups of companies prefer to grow by accretion, affiliation, alliance-building, that is by adding new business units to existing interfirm groupings or by restructuring transactions within a group of essentially single-product/dominant-product firms.

Newer, post-war interfirm groupings are smaller, less integrated and less diversified, and thus more focused in their competitive strategies. This also means that they are less able to muster a wide range of resources of various sorts. For example, if they have their own trading companies, they are noticeably smaller than the general-trading companies of older groups. They rarely have their own banks, shipping companies, and insurance firms. As a consequence, they are more focused in their activities—in the types of manufacturing processes employed and in the range of products made.

In some ways, the smaller size of the newer groups can be an advantage, since it may reduce the bureaucratic impediments and sub-goal pursuits that result from long-established institutional practices. Because production and distribution are more closely coordinated in newer groups and often combined in the same firm, firms in newer enterprise groups more closely approximate their Western counterparts in structure. Firms in newer groups are also likely to seek intrafirm economies of scope based on company-specific learning as a way to differentiate their product lines. For these reasons, size differentials between older and newer groups may simply be a shorthand for suggesting a range of basic differences, historical, financial, and organizational, that divide and distinguish the two sorts of groups. However, as the very size of older groups has led to internal fissures and reorganizations, subsets of firms are restructuring their activities and interactions around strategies that resemble those of newer groups. In such cases, there is little to distinguish old groups from new.

NOTES

1. Takafusa Nakamura, *The Postwar Japanese Economy* (Tokyo: University of Tokyo Press, 1981), 78, 139; Johannes Hirschmeier and Tsunehiko Yui (eds.), *The Development of Japanese Business*, 2nd edn. (London: George Allen & Unwin, 1981), 298, 342; Richard J. Samuels, *The Business of the Japanese State* (Ithaca, NY: Cornell University Press,

1987), 198–204. The transportation revolution is closely connected with the post-war distribution revolution in Japan. New forms of transportation, such as the use of trucks as opposed to railroads, allowed manufacturers to bypass entrenched wholesalers that were bunched around nodes in the railroad network. New forms of packaging played a role in the transport revolution. The use of bottles instead of kegs, for example, allowed *shoyu* and *sake* makers to streamline and rationalize distribution facilities. Finally, the growth of new marketing outlets, such as chain and supermarket stores, allowed manufacturers to distribute directly in bulk, shifting control of distribution towards manufacturers, allowing them to develop more integrated corporate organizations.

2. The measure of diversification used is 20 percent of total sales falling within a single SIC category at the three-digit level. When the data is aggregated at the two-digit level, however, product lines that fall within the same two-digit category are characterized as representing a 'full-line' strategy rather than a 'diversification' strategy. The confusion as to whether 40 or 50 percent ('41 to 52 percent') of diversification should be treated as a full-line strategy occurs because the American SIC code classifies computers and computer-related equipment in a different category from electrical equipment.

3. Peter Duus, 'The Reaction of Japanese Big Business to a State-Controlled Economy in the 1930s', *Rivista Internazionale di Scienze Economiche e Commerciali*, 31/9 (Sept. 1984). Samuels, *Business of the Japanese State*, finds a general agreement on goals between industry, firms, and the state in energy markets.

4. Eleanor M. Hadley, *Antitrust in Japan* (Princeton, NJ: Princeton University Press, 1970).

5. See Table 1.4, for a test of which SIC categories are more sales or asset sensitive.

6. Richard Vietor, 'Energy Markets and Policy', in Thomas K. McCraw (ed.), *American vs. Japan* (Boston: Harvard Business School Press, 1986).

7. For an argument of Government's leading role in industrial development, esp. of the post-war steel industry, see Thomas K. McCraw (ed.), *America vs. Japan* (Boston: Harvard Business School Press, 1986). For a counter-argument, see Seiichiro Yonekura, 'Sengo Nihon Seitetsu ni okeru Kawasaki Seitetsu no Kakushinsei', *Hitotsubashi Ronso* (The Annals of Hitotsubashi University), 90/3: 387–410. Yonekura provides a detailed discussion of the background to the capacity competition between the major steel firms in the mid-1950s. The story about the initial involvement of MITI in the post-war steel industry was related to me by Professor Keiichiro Nakagawa who heard it, first hand, from a MITI official directly responsible for developing the first 3-year plan.

   Writings that argue against industrial policy effectiveness include: 'Limited Effectiveness of the Government's Industrial Adjustment Policies', *Nihon Keizai Shinbun*, 7 June 1984: 15; Dennis J. Encarnation and Mark Mason, 'Neither MITI nor America: The Political Economy of Capitai Liberalization in Japan', *International Organization*, 44/1 (Winter 1990), 25–54.

8. James C. Abegglen and George Stalk, *Kaisha: The Japanese Corporation* (New York: Basic Books, 1985).

9. Robert E. Cole, 'Issues in Skill Formation and Training in Japanese Manufacturing Approaches to Automation', mimeo, Technology and the Future of Work Conference, Stanford University, 28–31 Mar. 1990: 18.

10. The best history of the pre-war industrial-union movement is Andrew Gordon, *The Evolution of Labor Relations in Japan: Heavy Industry, 1853–1955* (Cambridge, Mass:

Council on East Asian Studies, Harvard University Press, 1985). The term 'active consent' comes from Roberto Camagni, 'Functional Integration and Locational Shifts in New Technology Industry', in Philippe Aydalot and David Keeble (eds.), *High Technology Industry and Innovative Environments* (London: Routledge, 1988).

11. Here I am borrowing from the title of Masahiko Aoki's book, *Information, Incentives, and Bargaining in the Japanese Economy* (Cambridge: Cambridge University Press, 1988).

12. Andrew Gordon, 'Cultures of the Workplace in Postwar Japan', paper given at the Conference on Postwar Japan as History, 14–16 Apr. 1988: 6.

13. e.g. in 1984, there were 309 managers out of 40,000 MEI employees who did not belong to the union. Or, in the same year, 525 managers out of 45,000 employees at Mitsubishi Heavy Industry were not union members.

14. Hiroyuki Itami, *Jinponshugi Kigyo* (Human Resources as a Foundation) (Tokyo: Tsukuba Shobo, 1987); Masashi Wakabayashi, *Nihonteki Keieiron kara Nihonteki Kaisharon e* (From Japanese-Style Management to Japanese-Style Corporations) (Tokyo: Chuo Keizaisha, 1989). Also, Robert S. Ozaki uses the phrase 'enterpriser sovereignty' in his writings on the Japanese firm.

15. Masahiko Aoki, *The Co-operative Game Theory of the Firm* (Oxford: Oxford University Press, 1986); Wakabayashi, *Nihonteki Keieiron kara Nihonteki Kaisharon e*.

16. Robert E. Cole, *Work, Mobility, and Participation* (Berkeley: University of California Press, 1979), chs. 5 and 6. Also see his *Strategies for Learning* (Berkeley: University of California Press, 1989).

17. Paul Lillrank and Noriaki Kano, *Continuous Improvement: Quality Control Circles in Japanese Industry* (Ann Arbor: Center for Japanese Studies, University of Michigan, 1989). Actually Lillrank and Kano state that TQC was introduced in 1962 whereas Ono and Odaka document its introduction into Nippondenso in 1957.

18. Masahiko Aoki, 'Horizontal vs. Vertical Information Structure of the Firm', *American Economic Review*, Dec. 1986.

19. The extension of hierarchy as a means of gaining participation, recognizing merit, and stretching out the career ladder for long-term employees has been found by a number of researchers, including Robert Cole, Koya Azumi, and Ronald Dore: Cole, *Work, Mobility and Participation*; Koya Azumi, David Hickson, Dezso Horvath, and Charles McMillan, 'Bureaucratic Structures in Cross-National Perspective: A Study of British, Japanese, and Swedish firms', in G. Dlugos and K. Weiermair (eds.), *Management under Differing Value Systems* (New York: Walter de Gruyter, 1981); Ronald Dore, *British Factory—Japanese Factory* (Berkeley: University of California Press, 1973). For a suggestive approach, different from these, however, see Carol R. Snodgrass and John R. Grant, 'Cultural Influences on Strategic Planning and Control Systems', paper presented at the Strategic Management Society Conference, Philadelphia, Oct. 1984: 31.

20. Harvey Shaiken, *Work Transformed* (New York: Holt, Reinhardt & Winston, 1984).

21. Margaret Graham and Stephen Rosenthal, 'Flexible Manufacturing Systems Require Flexible People', Manufacturing Roundtable, School of Management, Boston University, 1985.

22. Bala Chakravarthy and Seog K. Kwun, 'The Strategy Process: An Organizational Learning Perspective', discussion paper, The Carlson School of Management, University of Minnesota, 1987.

23. W. Mark Fruin, 'Factory-to-Factory Organization and Technology Transfer', paper given at the 2nd Mitsubishi Bank Foundation Conference on Internationalization of the

Japanese Firm, held at the University of Michigan, 26–9 Aug. 1988.

24. See Chakravarthy and Kwun, 'The Strategy Process', n. 16.

25. Taiichi Ono and Yasuhiro Monden, *Toyota Seisan Hoshiki no Shintenkai* (New Developments in the Toyota Production System) (Tokyo: Nihon Nortisu Kyokai, 1983), sect. 5; W. Mark Fruin and Toshihiro Nishiguchi, 'The Toyota Production System: Its Organizational Definition and Diffusion in Japan', paper presented at the EIASM conference on country competitiveness, Brussels, 1 June 1990.

26. *Japanese Society* (Cambridge: Cambridge University Press, 1983), ch. 2.

27. Harvey Leibenstein, 'Aspects of the X-efficiency Theory of the Firm', *Bell Journal of Economics*, 6/2 (Autumn 1975), 580–606.

28. Paul Willman, *Technological Change, Collective Bargaining, and Industrial Efficiency* (Oxford: Oxford University Press, 1986), 103–6.

29. I want to thank Robert S. Ozaki for these words.

30. Huseyin Leblebici and Avi Fiegenbaum, 'Managers as Agents without Principles: An Empirical Examination of Agency and Constituency Perspectives', *Journal of Management*, 12/4 (1986), 485–98.

31. Peter Smith Ring and Andrew H. Van den Ven, 'Structures and Processes of Transaction', discussion paper No. 86, Strategic Management Research Center, University of Minnesota, May 1988.

32. Christena L. Turner, *Breaking the Silence: Consciousness, Commitment and Action in Japanese Unions* (Berkeley: University of California Press, forthcoming).

33. A detailed case-study of the evolution of the Japanese employment system is contained in W. Mark Fruin, 'The Japanese Company Controversy: Ideology and Organization in Historical Perspective', *Journal of Japanese Studies*, 4/2 (Summer 1978).

34. *Nikkei Business*, 'Hitachi Seisakusho, Part III', 24 Apr. 1989: 17–21.

35. Most of this information on Hitachi and Matsushita Electrical Industrial comes from Yasuo Okamoto's encyclopaedic *Hitachi to Matsushita* (2 vols.) (Tokyo: Chuo Koronsha, 1979).

36. Ibid. ii. 40–60.

37. Market shares of major radio producers before the appearance of transistorized, portable sets.

Market Shares of Major Radio Makers (%)

	1949	1950	1955
Matsushita	16	27	31.7
Shichibo	13	—	—
Sanyo	—	—	11.0
Hayakawa	13	14	7.7
Yamanaka	11	9	—
Hachibo	—	7	7.2
Hakutsuna	—	—	5.9
Toshiba	—	—	5.7

Source: Yasuo Okamoto, *Hitachi to Matsushita*, ii. 17.

Before the war Matsushita was the major radio-set maker in Japan but did not manufacture radio tubes itself, purchasing them instead from Toshiba and Tokyo Denki. After the war, Matsushita began to make tubes itself with the help of licenses from RCA and GE. In 1952 Matsushita established Matsushita Electronics Industry, a joint venture with Philips, capitalized at 660 million yen, which was 70 percent owned by Matsushita and 30 percent by Philips. The importance of this new company to Matsushita's management was considerable. First, Matsushita gained basic electronics technology in a field in which it had previously no knowledge. Second, Matsushita studied the budgeting system employed by Philips management and adopted this to its own organizational structure, thereby strengthening its management capabilities. After 1953 the radio tubes used in Matsushita radio sets were supplied internally by Matsushita Electronics Industry. Later, picture tubes and after 1956 transistors, integrated circuits, and semiconductors were all supplied by Matsushita Electronics Industry.

38. *Growth Rates in the Sale of Selected Electrical Goods in Japan* (%)

Growth Rates in the Sale of Selected Electrical Goods

	1955–9	1960–4	1965–9
All electrical goods	57.6	9.6	28.1
Washing machines	27.9	6.5	17.4
Televisions (B & W)	69.4	3.1	0.7
Refrigerators	77.2	18.9	3.4
Air conditioners	—	12.2	33.3

Source: Yasuo Okamoto, *Hitachi to Matsushita*, ii, 41–3.

39. Matsushita Electric Industrial has often been accused of being non-innovative. In Japan during the 1960s and early 1970s, Matsushita was derisively called *manneshita denki-sangyo* or 'copy-cat electric industrial'. However, by the late 1970s Matsushita's development and manufacturing capabilites were catching up with its marketing strengths, and it is rare now to hear Matsushita referred to as an imitative firm.

40. The major subsidiaries of MEI include: Matsushita Industrial Equipment (100% owned by MEI), Matsushita Housing Products (100%), Matsushita Electronic Components (96.2%), Matsushita Battery Industrial (95.4%), Matsushita Electronics (65.0%), Matsushita Communication Industrial (61.3%), Matsushita Graphic Communication Systems (60.0%), Matsushita Kotobuki Electronics Industries (56.9%), Matsushita Refrigeration (50.5%), Matsushita Seiko (50.4%), Victor Company of Japan (50.4%), Matsushita Electric Trading (50.3%), Kyushu Matsushita Electric (50.1%). These were ownership figures for the mid-1980s; they may vary from year to year. See Toyo Keizai, *Kaisha Shikiho*, annual volume, or any other standard company reference.

41. *Nikkei Business*, 'Hitachi Seisakusho, Part I', 24 Apr. 1989: 8–12. Yasuo, *Hitachi to Matsushita*, ii, 95–133.

42. P. J. McDermott and M. J. Taylor, *Industrial Organization and Location* (Cambridge: Cambridge University Press, 1982), 146–8.

43. I have asserted in earlier chapters that scale economies followed scope economies; this

may appear contradictory with what is indicated in this chapter. However, I was tracing the rise of interfirm economies of scope in non-manufacturing industries earlier. Here, I am describing the rise of firm-specific (really plant-specific) scale economies in manufacturing which broadened into scope economies, again at the level of the firm.

44. The electron-microscope example comes from Nissan's Central Engineering Laboratories. Interview with Mr. Hiroshi Takao, 2 Mar. 1990.

45. These are issues developed more fully in Ch. 8 but it is important to emphasize at this point that different contracting cultures exist where world-view, values, and ethos affect economic logic and outcomes. Neo-classical, Western economics holds that economic and social efficiencies are substitutes, so that social and cultural differences are discounted by a logic of economic rationality and efficiency.

46. Usami Makoto, 'Zaibatsu kaitai no kozai', *Ekonomisuto*, 18 Aug. 1964; quoted by Yoshikazu Miyazaki, 'Rapid Economic Growth in Post-War Japan', *Developing Economies*, 5/2 (1967), 337.

47. R. Komiya, S. Okuno, and K. Suzumura (eds.), *Nihon no Sangyo Seisaku* (Japan's Industrial Policy) (Tokyo: Tokyo University Press, 1984), esp. chs. 2, 8, and 9. See also Yoshikazu Miyazaki, *Sengo Nihon no Kigyo Shudan* (Enterprise Groups in Post-War Japan) (Tokyo: Nihon Keizai Shinbunsha, 1976), for a left-leaning interpretation of how government measures affected financial performance.

48. Yutaka Inoue, 'The Many Forms of Financial Maneuvering by Big Business in Japan', *Nihon Keizai Shimbun*, 20 Dec. 1984: 6.

49. Tom Roehl, 'Japanese Industrial Groupings: A Strategic Response to Rapid Industrial Growth', mimeo, unpublished, 1988. Also, Jennifer Corbett, 'Patterns of Finance and Government Lending to Industry in Japan', mimeo, Apr. 1990, delivered at the Euro-Asia Centre, INSEAD, Fontainebleau, France, 4 May 1990.

50. 'The Economic Role of Financial Corporate Groupings', in Masahiko Aoki, *The Economic Analysis of the Japanese Firm* (Amsterdam: North-Holland, 1984), 246. See also, Hiroyuki Odagiri, 'Kigyo Shudan no Riron,' *Kikan Riron Keizaigaku*, 26 (1975); Richard E. Caves and Masu Uekusa, *Industrial Organization in Japan* (Washington, DC: Brookings Institution, 1976).

51. Paul Sheard, 'Financial Corporate Grouping, Cross-Subsidization in the Private Sector and the Industrial Adjustment Process in Japan', Discussion Paper Series, Faculty of Economics, Osaka University, 1984. See also, Paul Sheard, 'Intercorporate Shareholdings and Structural Adjustments in Japan', *Pacific Economic Papers*, No. 151 (1987).

52. Fair Trade Commission, *The Actual Conditions of the Six Major Corporate Groups*, No. 7, pamphlet (Tokyo: External Affairs Office, Aug. 1989). See ch. 2, pp. 74–5, n. 6, where representatives of the Mitsubishi group of companies are quoted as claiming: (1) the manufactured products of members of the Mitsubishi group account for 6% of the total sales of the Mitsubishi Trading Company, and (2) internal buying and selling within the Mitsubishi group account for 16–18% of total group sales. *Nihon Keizai Shimbun*, 'Tomadou Gyokai' (Perplexing Industry), 24 Feb. 1990: 3.

53. This represents only one of the cooperative strategies detailed by Richard P. Nielsen. The cooperative strategies he considers in addition to pool are exchange, de-escalate, and experiment/contingency. Richard P. Nielsen, 'Cooperative Strategy', *Strategic Management Journal*, 9 (1988), 475–92.

54. Kazumi Kenmochi, 'The Hollowing', *AMPO Japan–Asia Quarterly Review*, 19/1: 30–3; *The Economist*, 'Japan's Steelmakers Recast Themselves, 29 Aug. 1987: 59–60; *Asiaweek*, 'The Hard Facts about Steel', 5 Apr. 1987: 50–1.

55. Sumantra Ghoshal and Christopher A. Bartlett, *Matsushita Electric Industrial*, INSEAD–CEDEP Case, Fontainebleau, France, Exhibit 8, 1987: 28.
56. *Far Eastern Economic Review*, 'Dowdy Galant Reborn', 19 Jan. 1989: 62.
57. Interview with Mr. Koichi Hashimoto, Manager, Mitsubishi Motors, 2 Mar. 1989, Paris, France. For another detailed example of the importance of the same sort of relational network approach to product development, see Bunteru Kurahara, Kiyoshi Uchimaru, and Susumu Okamoto, *Gijutsu Shudan no TQC* (Tokyo: Nikajiren, 1990).
58. Michael Porter and M. B. Fuller, 'Coalitions and Global Strategy', in M. Porter (ed.), *Competition in Global Industries* (Boston: Harvard Business School Press, 1987).
59. 'Saigo wa Kigyonai Kigyoka—Kogaisha Senryaku Jitsurei Kenkyu sonohimitsu', *Nikkei Business*, 18 July 1988: 17–18. As an aside, Tokyo Electron is the TEL of the *Computervision—Japan* 1985 case of Harvard Business School.
60. *Nihon Keizai Shimbun*, 'Tokuyama Soda Restructures Its Veneer Products Division', 16 June 1986: 10.
61. 'Saigo wa Kigyonai Kigyoka', *Nikkei Business*, 18 July 1988.
62. Leonard Wrigley classified the strategies employed by manufacturing firms into several, stair-stepping categories. First came the single-product firm, then the dominant-product firm (with non-basic businesses accounting for no more than one-fifth of sales), then the related-product yet diversified firm, and finally the unrelated-product, diversified firm. See his 'Divisional Autonomy and Diversification', DBA thesis (Harvard University, Harvard Business School, 1970). Wrigley's categories were further refined by Richard Rumelt, *Strategy, Structure, and Economic Performance* (Boston: Harvard Business School Press, 1986).
63. Nielsen, 'Cooperative Strategy', 475–92.
64. Fujikoshi Machine Tool, *Fujikoshi Gojunenshi* (50 years of Fujikoshi) (Tokyo: Dainippon, 1978), 45–6.
65. *Nihon Keizai Shimbun*, 14 Apr. 1989: 10.

6

Focal Factories

I
Product Development and Strategic Management at Toshiba

Multi-function and often multi-product, focal factories are categorically different in concept and purpose from mass-production factories with distinctive management styles and structures devised to integrate planning, design, and product and process engineering. Focal factories mirror the industrial history of modern Japan: an acceleration of institutional receptivity to knowledge and technique that culminates ultimately in unprecedented rates of organizational learning and economic performance.[1]

Organizational flexibility, technological adaptation, and mental more than manual labor are institutional traits of focal factories while liveliness, productivity, and a negotiated hierarchy in the workplace are some behavioral and social consequences.[2] A wealth of factory-based managerial functions transforms focal factories into one leg of the organizational prism known as the Japanese enterprise system. In contrast to widely held notions of factories as labor-intensive production sites, removed from top- and middle-level management, employing standardized and narrowly specialized work routines for high-volume manufacture of a limited range of products, focal factories are management-intensive organizations that contain standardization, limit specialization, and instead emphasize learning, creativity, and resource transformation.

While this chapter follows these developments in one industry and company, the appearance and maturation of focal factories, a component architecture of the Japanese enterprise system, occurred widely, whenever and wherever companies responded effectively to the rapidity of economic and technical change as well as to swings in market and customer preferences by endowing certain manufacturing facilities with the capabilities to respond quickly, constructively, and well to change.[3] Such factories first appeared during the inter-war period when the level of economic development did not permit nation-wide coordination of output but it did demand local and regional centralization of business functions. Balkanization of markets yielded smallish corporate head offices, incomplete divisionalization, and robust manufacturing works. Hitachi has been followed as one example of this. Toshiba is another.

In the post-World War Two era, especially during the high-growth era spanning the 1950s, 1960s, and 1970s, managers recognized the difficulties of combining routine, stability, and predictability along with adaptability, flexibility, and innovation in one manufacturing site. Rather than attempt to merge what does not mix well, development-intensive activities were distinguished from more routine operations and hived off. At a minimum, the distinction was conceptual—a recognition of the need for such a distinction—and recognition often led to a differentiation of facilities. Sometimes this was seen in an internal specialization of personnel and projects within existing facilities; otherwise, it was expressed in the physical, locational, and strategic differentiation of production sites.

A push towards differentiation of manufacturing facilities happened for a number of reasons. First, the thrust of technology transfer, as argued earlier, was felt most in manufacturing. Production facilities had to arm themselves with sufficient resources to absorb, analyze, and adapt foreign technology of various sorts to local circumstances. This required a concentration of resources in factories and an entitlement of factory managers with considerable strategic discretion. Key production sites were charged with responsibilities for gaining and maintaining technical advantage. Focal factories in some ways approximated strategic business units (SBUs) in function and significance. This was a second force endowing manufacturing facilities with unusual significance.

Finally, given the limited size of some markets and attendant difficulties of stabilizing long production runs, the crucial link between production and distribution was made often in factories rather than in more operationally remote administrative offices. Coordination was articulated close to the market. For such reasons, functionally integrated manufacturing facilities with notable operational and strategic leeway appeared. Fully matured factories of this sort are called focal factories—multi-function and multi-product factories—in this study.[4] They represent an amalgamation of several distinct interests: the R & D activities of specialized research laboratories, the market and product-planning functions of divisions, and the manufacturing know-how of production sites, all combined in a single organizational entity.

It is important to remember that full-bodied, full product-line, manufacturing sites emerged in response to a crisis of industrial catch-up over which managers had little control. What control they had was exercised in endowing manufacturing plants with available resources. Because such factories are an interconnected part of the Japanese enterprise system, they are linked directly with corporations and interfirm networks in upstream and downstream activities. Hence, choices in one part of the system become progressively linked with choices made elsewhere, strengthening the operational and strategic interdependence of the whole system.

Three circumstances define the structure of a focal factory and these, in turn, facilitate the process of organizational learning which leads to multi-functionality. First, all the distinct functions underpinning manufacturing are *localized* to create an integrated production environment. These include applied technology research, product and process research, market research, product design, design engineering, product planning, engineering feasibility studies, trial manufacture, scaled-up manufacture, and sales coordination functions. In some sites, many of these functions were already localized during the inter-war era.

Second, the manufacture of a *number of products* in widely varying amounts. Some products may be mature and some may not, some may be primarily producer goods while others are more for consumers. While some products may be related technologically, the degree of technological relatedness, by itself and within limits, is not a compelling reason to manufacture a particular product in a particular focal factory. Instead, the choice of product lines serves primarily as a means of exploiting the past, that is taking advantage of the history of manufacturing that defines different facilities, reinforcing the functional and managerial integration of that past (the first circumstance above), and creating product-related springboards for encouraging cross-pollination of manufacturing and managerial patterns, procedures, and routines between different departments and sections. Manufacturing strategies of this sort are sometimes called unbalanced product specialization.[5]

Finally, the building of a stair-step process of give-and-take, interaction, and integration between various production functions, and the welding of this *interactive, feedback process* into a product-development system. For high-technology industries, well suited to the focal-factory architecture, variability within and between products/models is desirable. Variability results in learning and learning is the basis of a strategy based on functional integration, innovation, and continual improvement in manufacturing.[6]

In concert, these three circumstances define a dynamic environment of organizational specialization and integration that may lead to a cascade of product and process innovation. The timing and emergence of these circumstances and, thus, the rate of innovation was varied by industry and by company, but factories as architectures of innovation appeared no earlier than the inter-war period and no later than the last quarter of the twentieth century. The decision to consciously organize a factory for functional integration and product/process innovation rather than mass production, as evidenced in steps one through three above, is a *managerial* one, and it rests on a conviction that institutions can think, learn, and act for the purposes of self-improvement and self-renewal.[7]

Institutions do this most vividly when managers create strategies which link and exploit organizational resources through processes of organizational learning. But institutions can also do this unconsciously, naturally, as a consequence of the force of change. The degree of conscious choice is a question of how and when managers realized the advantages of a focal-factory organization, namely endowing and integrating multi-function, multi-product capabilities in certain manufacturing facilities. Such a cumulative, iterative, and ultimately transformational outcome embodies much of the history of the modern corporation in Japan as well as organizational experience of the Yanagicho Works, one of the Toshiba Corporation's focal factories. The Yanagicho Factory is the prototype for the third leg of the institutional prism that constitutes the Japanese enterprise system, and it is the main subject of this chapter.[8]

A History of Late Development

The history of the Yanagicho Works is a story of an emerging strategy, which evolved over time, in response to the relative backwardness of Japan as compared to more industrially advanced Western nations, and which involved processes of differentiating, combining, and refining organizational and managerial resources at every level of corporate organization, but especially at the level of the factory and shop-floor. Because the relationship between strategy and outcome is not one-to-one, the history of organizational response to industrial opportunity is necessarily piecemeal, sequential, and cumulative.

As argued earlier, the push-and-pull behind Japanese macro-economic growth has been the effective transfer to technology from abroad and its transformation into useful, attractive, and affordable products. That transfer and transformation occurred at the micro-organizational level in factories like the Yanagicho Works, where workers and managers have learned how to cooperate together in the acquisition of resources, skills, and competencies, and, above all else, how to innovate in combining these factors. For these reasons, it can be fairly said that focal factories have been and continue to be the cutting edge of strategic management in Japan.[9]

Historically, factories were perhaps the most consciously modelled part of the organizational triad which forms the Japanese enterprise system. Interfirm networks and large industrial enterprises came after the first manufacturing facilities were already established, and thus factories were the most widespread institutions of learning, especially foreign learning in Meiji Japan (1868–1911). Since almost everything learned from the West was considered greater, higher, more important, and useful than anything Japan had to offer, the potency of Western learning was especially apparent where no indigenous institutions and ideas collided with foreign ones. The modern factory system was without native imitation and it quickly flourished.

The modern factory system and Western corporations were already well developed and endowed by the time of their introduction into Japan, and their later interjection in Japan touched off an organizational revolution, culminating in less than a half-century in manufacturing and managerial structures comparable in sophistication to what had required several centuries of organizational development in the West. (See Chapters 2 and 3.) The highly compressed, reflexive aspects of the process of institutional transfer and transformation help explain the salience of factories among the modern institutions of Japanese capitalism.

Institutional Consequences of Late Development

Critical elements in structure and strategy, interdependent at every level of Japanese enterprise organization, were closely connected to Japan's late development, and the overriding need to learn, and learn quickly, from the West. The implicit linking of factory and corporate structure with the need to learn quickly in the context of late development can be seen most clearly at the top and bottom of the corporation: in how Japanese corporations define their general spheres of organizational endeavor and in how they act upon that definition for planning and manufacturing activities.

The Modern Corporation

The smaller size of Japanese corporations, as discussed already, stems from several causes, only one of which has to do with the size of the market.[10] Otherwise, the preference of Japanese industrial firms to confine their activities to well-defined spheres of competence means that they are not highly integrated vertically or widely diversified in product line. Vertical integration and broad diversification are most often left to an accompanying complement of related firms. The strategic decision to concentrate effort on well-defined internal spheres of competence imparts a crucial significance to manufacturing activities as one of the principal areas where Japanese firms can differentiate themselves from rivals.

The prime concept behind these structural differences in the patterns of Japanese enterprise development has been a managerial strategy of organizational learning. Organizational learning became a strategic necessity as Western knowledge, both practical as well as theoretical, confronted Japanese industrial and political leaders with high risk and uncertainty in achieving developmental aims. Given the limited capabilities of entrepreneurs to identify, implement, and evaluate Western learning, it was strategically sound to focus enterprise efforts in well-defined spheres of activity while encouraging other institutions to do the same, especially in complementary areas of endeavor.

Interfirm networks as well as focal factories in this sense were strategic responses to the need to know and, at the same time, to minimize the risks of not knowing. In this vein, the strategic importance of creating an interlocking organizational framework rests on the overriding significance of knowing, learning from each other, and concentrating the practical value of what you do know. The slack in this system of organizational interdependence is found in the permeable boundaries joining factory, firm, and network.

The Focal Factory

In the case of the modern factory system, one can argue for an early differentiation in manufacturing functions and, as a consequence, in manufacturing facilities. The relevant distinction is between high-volume and low-volume manufacturing, coupled with a related distinction between mature and immature products. Notwithstanding the recent world-wide success of Japanese manufacturers with high-volume, mature products, like cameras, photocopiers, audio equipment, automobiles, and motorcycles, the history of manufacturing in Japan is more enmeshed with low-volume, immature or, better put, incipient and embryonic products.

The logic for the historical importance of low-volume manufacturing in Japan is clear-cut. First, an overwhelming reliance on Western technology has meant that far more effort has gone into experimental, limited, and prototype manufacturing than high-volume manufacturing. Acquiring technology, fiddling with it, producing a limited run of prototypes, selecting from among them, and then fine-tuning products for the market-place has captured the attention of far more workers, technicians, engineers, and managers than high-volume manufacturing.

Second, until the 1960s, there were very few products that could be sold in volume. Per capita income and government budgets were simply not sufficient to purchase large amounts of any product, save the most ordinary, like bulk foods, soaps, outer garments, school and military uniforms, agricultural fertilizers, light bulbs, and ceramic tableware. The consumer revolution and highly customized producer goods came late to Japan.

Finally, there is a certain cohesiveness and stickiness in the manufacturing processes. While it is possible to produce, say, computers without any prior manufacturing experience in electrical equipment and electronics, the process of designing and producing computers goes a lot smoother with such experience. Familiarity with calculators and mechanical typewriters should make it easier to produce electronic typewriters and word processors. Yet late-developers can ill afford to recapitulate the product histories of more advanced rivals. So, late development coupled with limited demand and the small size of the domestic market have mandated that manufacturing skills are managed with a sticky flexibility in mind. This stickiness in capabilities, concentrated in focal factories, goes far in explaining the emphasis on a full-line product strategy in Japan.

Japanese and other latecomers to industrial development are not really able to leapfrog the production technologies and product lines of already industrialized nations. But neither are they required to repeat their entire industrial history. What they can and must do instead is to produce far fewer, perhaps only a handful, of the key transition products linking immature and mature technologies. This interim production is low volume but absolutely necessary and, more likely than not, it occurs in some production facilities analogous to focal factories.[11] That is, design, development, and manufacturing arise as interdependent functions in focused facilities.

Cost economies steeped in the learning curve, that is in the reduction of average cost as a function of accumulated experience, are not always available in such low-volume production. But a large portion of learning benefits accrue only by doing, so the importance of building up a repertoire of firm-specific know-how and experience cannot be underestimated, especially when firms consciously set out to capture learning economies. In short, learning is costly, so organizations should capture as much of it as soon as they can.

The role of focal factories (or the role of multi-function, multi-product departments within ordinary factories) is to take the lead in identifying useful production technologies, experiment with them, mock up products, solve design problems, run limited volumes of many different products, and, above all else, learn the problems and promises associated with a variety of products and production processes. In this sense, such factories are the ultimate stage of effective technology transfer.[12] And, as Japan moves to become a net exporter of technology by the close of the twentieth century, focal factories will undoubtedly be the engine of discovery and innovation behind much of the new technology transfer from Asia to the West. Already, the export of Japanese technical know-how increased threefold during 1970–85, improving considerably the percentage of expenditures to payments for new technology.[13]

Toshiba: The Role of Strategic Manufacturing

This chapter attempts to analyze the process of product development in factories and the nature of the linkages between factories and higher level managerial units within Toshiba in order to identify organizational incentives and obstacles which have characterized the emergence of multi-function focal factories. Product development is highlighted because quantity and quality of products are direct measures of effectiveness in linking corporate strategy and structure.

The strength of these organizational linkages have delimited and propelled Toshiba's competitive edge, and this chapter explores this hypothesis by following the history of one of Toshiba's twenty-seven manufacturing facilities, the Yanagicho Works, an archetypical focal factory. In brief, the history of product development at the Yanagicho Works can be broken down into four phases, each exhibiting ever higher levels of factory productivity based on the successful linking of organizational learning with strategic planning. The four phases are:

1. 1936–53, a period characterized by small-batch production of a considerable number of different products and by more labor-intensive than capital-intensive manufacturing technique; emergent scale economies.
2. 1953–68, larger batch production of a more limited product line employing increasingly capital-intensive production technologies; scale economies.
3. 1968–81, capital-intensive, high-volume production characterized by low cost yet highly specific automation and by mixed-model, small-lot manufacturing systems; product differentiation; emergent scope economies.
4. 1981–90, increasingly capital-intensive, flexible and automated manufacturing systems geared towards small-lot production of a highly varied product line, offering numerous models and options; scope economies.

In general, it could be proposed that these stages of development result in threshold effects with regard to the efficacy of matching organizational resources with technological requirements, and that Stages 3 and especially 4 correspond with a model of high-output firms in high-technology industries proposed by

Abernathy and Utterback.[14] The tempo of change is noteworthy: while nearly twenty years separate Stages 1 and 2, fifteen years separate Stages 2 from 3, and only thirteen divide 3 and 4. Also, the direction of change is clear: higher value-added manufacturing by accelerated throughput. Accelerated throughput depends on better product and process design, fuller exploitation of learning and scope economies, plus extensive outsourcing of parts, components, and sub-assemblies.

History and Organizational Patterns

The Toshiba Corporation, the second largest general manufacturer of electrical equipment and electronic goods in Japan, originates from a pre-World War Two combination of Shibaura Engineering Works (begun as Tanaka Electric Works in 1875) and Tokyo Electric Company (established as the Hakunetsu-sha in 1890). These companies merged in 1939 to form Tokyo Shibaura Electric which was renamed the Toshiba Corporation in 1978. In 1983 Toshiba's sales reached $16.4 billion on a consolidated basis and were almost evenly divided between heavy electrical goods (29 percent), communications and electronics (30 percent), and consumer-goods/electronics (30 percent). Materials, machinery, and other products accounted for 11 percent. By 1987 the shift in Toshiba's product mix towards industrial electronics and electronic components was unmistakable with that sector of Toshiba's $22.6 billion annual sales accounting for 36 percent of net sales, consumer products 28 percent, heavy electrical apparatus 26 percent, and materials, machinery, and other products 10 percent.

Toshiba has a proud history of technological accomplishment and product development. Toshiba was the first company in the world to develop 16-inch color television sets, television phones, fully automated computer-controlled thermal power plants, both-sides-of-the-page printing facsimile, super-conducting magnets for magnetic levitation trains and nuclear fusion, cartridge-type VCR instavision, 64-bit and 256-bit CMOS static RAM.

Within Japan, Toshiba was first to manufacture, among other things, a water-powered electrical generator (1894), electric-hoist crane (1903), X-ray tubes (1915), double-coil light bulbs (1921), radio reception tubes (1921), radio receiving sets (1924), electric washing machines and refrigerators (1930), television-broadcasting equipment (1933), fluorescent lamps (1940), radar (1942), electronic calculators (1954), fully transistorized television sets (1960), automatic mail-sorting equipment (1967), 12-bit microcomputers (1973), high-resolution, high-speed CAT scan equipment (1977), space communications transmitting equipment (1981), ultra-high voltage transformers (1981), magnetic resonance imaging systems (1982), high-capacity IC cards for cashless shopping (1985).

Toshiba's product cornucopia reflects a century-long process of organizational learning as the company has adapted with fluidity to circumstances of technology transfer, market development, government regulation, and rival company maneuvering. The cumulative and contemporary result of Toshiba's history of organizational learning is a company with flexible manufacturing and managerial structures well poised to take advantage of high-technology applications and markets. Devleopment factories are key to this positioning.

Organizational Boundaries and the Focal Factory

As one of the oldest, most successful, and most structurally elaborated firms in Japan, Toshiba may be considered representative of a pattern of enterprise development characteristic of major Japanese industrials: a core firm with well-established spheres of product and technology competence developed before and after World War Two; a divisional management structure defining these core activities surrounded by a phalanx of interrelated firms which are connected to the core firm and to each other financially through interfirm shareholding, through limited rotation of senior-level personnel and the 'retirement' of some of the same to affiliates and subsidiaries, through sequencing in the processes of backward and forward integration in production and distribution, and through coordinating business activities in research, product development, manufacturing, and sales. In short, Toshiba is the hub of an enterprise system comprising a full set of manufacturing and service facilities that are differentiated along functional, cost, and strategic lines.

Because of the interconnections between the core firm and its surrounding cast of affiliated firms, Toshiba is neither as large nor as internally differentiated and managerially decentralized as comparably advanced multidivisional firms in the United States. As argued throughout, much of what would be done inside a large American firm is typically delegated to subsidiaries and affiliates in Japan, in keeping with a strategy of focusing corporate resources in order to maximize the effectiveness of organizational learning. This is especially true of business activities which are not considered central to the strategic thrust of the core firm. Rather than keep peripheral activities within the firm or sell them away, however, the choices in most large American corporations, Japanese firms prefer to localize such business activities in a cluster of enterprises orbiting the core firm.

Affiliates and subsidiaries are related genealogically to the core firm in two ways. Either they were acquired or bought into, and may be characterized, therefore, as being financially related to the core firm. In the case of the Toshiba Corporation, this reflects the relationship, for example, between Toshiba, the parent firm, and Toshiba Machine Company, a subsidiary acquired originally in 1962. Toshiba Machine was itself the result of a merger in 1961 between Shibaura Machine Company and Shibaura Machine Tool Company. Toshiba owned 40.2 percent of the former and 99.9 percent of the latter, leaving Toshiba with 50.01 percent of the Toshiba Machine Co.[15]

Because Toshiba Machine Company is a major machine-tool maker and, thus, a supplier of machine tools to companies like the Toshiba Corporation, Toshiba never sought to actually incorporate or integrate Toshiba Machine into its own corporate structure. Their lines of business endeavor were complementary, but not so complementary as to warrant a takeover. Instead, Toshiba was content to hold a bare majority of Toshiba Machine's stock, and to enjoy the accompanying rights of appointing Board members or of receiving dividends from its investment in Toshiba Machine.

Or, another sort of genealogical relationship between core and peripheral firms occurs when affiliates and subsidiaries have been separated from or spun off, as the expression goes, from the core firm. This happens when it is decided that the parent company and one of its divisions or departments (the soon-to-be-separated firm) would be better off legally independent of each other. This characterizes the relationship between Toshiba and Toshiba Chemical, for example, which was spun off as an independent entity in 1974. Toshiba Chemical is a leading company in the manufacture of veneers, varnishes, and other chemical substances used in cabinetwork and casings for electrical appliances and equipment. Although Toshiba is the major buyer of Toshiba Chemical's products, the two companies serve considerably different markets and concentrate on different manufacturing technologies, so by the mid-1970s it made more sense to separate their spheres of business effort and responsibility.[16]

In Japan, the process of spinning off firms is not a process of selling firms or of divestiture. Aside from the obvious desire to diversify managerial resources, the most common reasons for spinning off enterprises from core companies, according to a 1976 survey, were the wish to group together products with similar technological, manufacturing, purchasing, and sales requirements, and the desire to rationalize distribution channels.[17] Spun-off firms, therefore, remain part of the parent firm's group of companies, and the degree to which its business and that of the parent overlap are matters of strategic as well as practical choice.

In these ways, the interconnections between core and outer firms have arisen rationally for the most part, as a consequence of economic and strategic decision-making. The fundamental issues for decision revolve around the identification, development, and retention of spheres of technological competence which allow for the timely introduction of cost-effective products by the core firm and its affiliates. The allocation of these spheres between the core firm and its related enterprises becomes top management's most critical function: namely, the exploitation of the advantages of permeable boundaries or organizational interdependence.

As a consequence, the sinews knitting Toshiba with its affiliates are logical outcomes of a process that seeks to maximize corporate resources while minimizing corporate risks. This process is worked out first for the core firm and then, through time and in consultation with the management of affiliates, for related enterprises. The determination and delegation of spheres of technology/product responsibility within a network of related firms may be conceptualized as a product/market map where the position of firms along lines of related business activity can be calibrated and, if necessary, measured by degrees of interrelatedness from each other.

Initially, this may be represented graphically by a two-dimensional map where firms may be positioned along axes of technological competencies running from the core firm. However, over time new centers of competence develop within enterprise groups and from these emerging centers, new forms of product/market interrelatedness grow. As a consequence, clusters of interrelated firms evolve which are not related to each other through the core firm but rather have their own dynamic centers of technological competence. However, it should be possible still, if one chooses to do so in three-dimensional space, to relate all firms in an enterprise group to historical and logical patterns of development based on the original business of the core firm, allowing for the processes of merger, acquisition, and division along the way.

As of 1988 there were thirty-three consolidated subsidiaries, where Toshiba's financial stake exceeded 50 percent, and over one hundred more where Toshiba's financial interests were not so great. It is not possible here to trace out the particularistic history which binds Toshiba to each of these entities, but Fig. 6.1 suggests something of the accordion-like process by which firms are merged into and spun out of the parent company's trajectory of structural and strategic evolution.

An evolved enterprise group may be conceptualized as a kind of matrix organization with many planning and control functions carried out for the group as a whole by corporate management and technology boards. Below the strategic level, however, divisions within large corporations and affiliated companies enjoy operational independence, although divisions and firms may choose to operate interdependently.

This characterization of the strategy and structure of the Toshiba enterprise group must be contrasted with the more popular notions of *zaibatsu* enterprise groups. The pre-war *zaibatsu* groups were only loosely linked in structure and strategy. Fiscal and political exigencies as much as economic forces in the nation-building process prompted the formation of *zaibatsu* enterprise groups during the Meiji period. Thereafter, during the Taisho and Showa eras, a somewhat greater coherence in the alignment of *zaibatsu* affairs became noteworthy but this process was impeded by the rise of a military-led economy after 1931 and by the final disaster of World War Two.

Japanese firms do not parallel the structural and strategic features of American firms which evolved in vastly different legal, economic, social, and political circumstances. Accordingly, in 1969 it was found that 75 percent of the largest American industrial firms had adopted the multidivisional structure, whereas more than ten years later in 1980, only 41 percent of the largest Japanese firms had adopted a similar structure.[18] Furthermore, even where Japanese firms have adopted the multidivisional form, they are far less diversified than their American counterparts. Incomplete or constrained divisionalization was the result (as detailed elsewhere).

To return to the original point, namely an organizational definition of the focal factory within the context of the Toshiba Corporation, one can identify a core set of business endeavors characterizing the main thrust of Toshiba activities during the

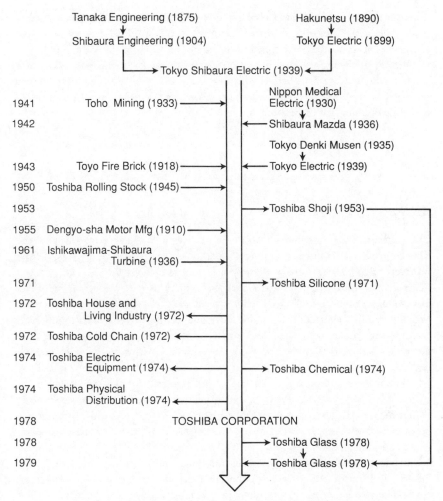

FIG. 6.1. *Major Mergers and Devolutions: The Toshiba Corporation*

Note: Parenthetical dates are Toshiba investment years.
Source: Toshiba Corporation, *Electronics and Energy*, Brochure, Tokyo, 1987.

last half-century, and this thrust is reflected in the manufacturing and product-development activities of Toshiba's production facilities, like the Yanagicho Works. Within Toshiba, much of the responsibility for new product development has been pushed way down the organizational hierarchy, to the level of focal factories. Outside the firm, a constellation of companies orbits Toshiba, each of which is related in various ways to the activities and competencies that characterize the Toshiba Corporation.

Indeed, because of the intersecting yet highly differentiated functions of companies, interfirm networks, and focal factories, the managerial process in a large Japanese industrial firm, like Toshiba, is far more concerned with the problem of organizational definition, that is where to draw corporate boundaries, than comparable American firms. Precisely because boundaries are permeable and easily redefined in the Japanese context, a great deal of attention must be given to problems of boundary delineation and definition.

II
Pre-war and Post-war Reorganization at Toshiba and Yanagicho

Pre-war Patterns

The concentration of corporate effort in relatively well-defined areas and the delegation of related business activities to affiliated enterprises are reflected in the relatively small size of corporate head offices in Japan, including that of Toshiba. Compared to head offices and divisional level offices in large American industrial firms, Japanese head offices and divisional level offices are smaller, less functionally and structurally elaborate. In addition, many of the divisional planning and coordinating functions—what are usually referred to as middle managerial functions—are carried out within factories, especially within multi-function focal factories, where product and market responsibilities for entire lines of business activity are highly localized. (Obviously, the reasons why Japanese firms, head offices, and divisions *were* smaller and why they *remain* smaller may be different.)

In pre-war Toshiba as well as in other major industrial firms, connections between the head office and its manufacturing facilities were, for the most part, direct and unmediated. This was possible because of the small size of the company overall, just 6,300 persons in 1930 (combining the employees of both Tokyo Electric and Shibaura Engineering), but in particular the small numbers of the head office as opposed to factory-based personnel was significant. In 1930, out of 6,300 employees, 4,250 were factory workers, leaving 2,050 as researchers, engineers, higher level technicians, and managers in factories, sales and service offices, overseas branches, as well as in the head office.[19] My estimate of head-office employees would be no less than 400 and no more than 600; taking a mean of 500 would mean that just 7.9 percent of personnel were in the head office. Indeed, considering that most manufacturing facilities had their own accounting, personnel, and sales offices, as well as substantial numbers of manufacturing engineering specialists a mean of 500 in the head office may be high. (Recall the earlier estimate that only 1.3 percent of Toyobo Spinning's 36,215 personnel worked in the head office in 1914. As few as 5 percent of Tokyo Shibaura's employees may have been head-office personnel in 1930.)

Before the war and indeed for more than a decade after World War Two, in keeping with the small size of the head office, Toshiba was functionally organized, meaning that the corporate manufacturing department was responsible for all products and production processes and was in close contact with its production facilities, concentrated for the most part along the lower reaches of Tokyo Bay in the vicinity of Shibaura, Kawasaki, and Tsurumi. In addition to the manufacturing department, the largest head-office department, other departments would include accounting, finance, legal, purchasing, and a small personnel office for head-office employees.

In short, Toshiba was a U-Form corporation: simple, unified, and functionally organized. This form of organization reflected the limited number of product lines made by the firm as well as a series of decisions about how those product lines were organized and managed. By and large, product and process decisions were delegated to factories. Both of these features of the pre-war management of Toshiba are reflected in the pre-war and early post-war history of the Yanagicho Works.

The Yanagicho Works in the Pre-war Period

The Yanagicho Works, established in 1936, began as the manufacturing arm of a subsidiary of Tokyo Electric, one of the two firms which merged in 1939 to form Tokyo Shibaura Electric. During World War One, as early as August 1916, Tokyo Electric had begun work on vacuum-tube development, a critical component for wireless communications equipment, and in the next year, Tokyo Electric successfully produced the first vacuum tube designed and manufactured in Japan. After the war, as the electrical-equipment industry burgeoned in Japan, wireless radio and communications equipment became nearly indispensable from a cultural and recreational point of view and absolutely obligatory from a military standpoint.[20] Tokyo Electric's success with volume manufacture of vacuum tubes placed it in the forefront of this rapidly growing and highly profitable industry.

In 1924 the Tokyo Broadcasting Company, the forerunner of today's publicly owned National Broadcasting Company, was established, escalating demand for radio broadcasting and receiving equipment. The Tokyo Electric Company which had been concentrating development efforts on vacuum tubes for wireless sets until this time, now broadened its product range to include the radio body itself as well as a full complement of radio parts. In 1928 the company began research and development in the field of wireless transmission and completed in 1930, in cooperation with the Wireless Transmitter Company of Japan, a 40-kilowatt, short-wave transmitter. Since Japan had depended almost completely on imported radio equipment until this time, the domestic design and manufacture of transmission and receiving equipment were accomplishments of considerable strategic and patriotic significance.

Radio Nationalism and Preparations for War

In September 1931 the Manchurian Incident erupted, boosting even more the domestic demand for developing and manufacturing radio transmission and receiving sets. Radio equipment was made for the most part by civilian contractors, even though the Imperial Japanese Army operated some eight arsenals and forty-six factories for the production of defense-related goods while the Japanese Navy had arsenals at Yokosuka and Kure. As Japan edged towards an increasingly militaristic footing, orders for radio equipment from civilian suppliers jumped significantly. In order to cope effectively with heightened demand, the Tokyo Electric Company consolidated all radio-related development and production in a new radio division created in January 1934.

The newly hived radio division had no more than thirty employees when it was first established in 1934 but within a year, it had metamorphosed into an independent corporation with a considerably larger number of employees. The Tokyo Electric Company had been associated with the General Electric Company of the United States since 1903 in a broadly gauged, across-the-board process of technology transfer which in the estimation of Japan's military-minded leaders of the 1930s was inimical to Japan's strategic position. As a result, GE's financial interests in Tokyo Electric as well as the engineers which GE had sent to Japan to assist in research and development were forcibly reduced in importance to the point of ineffectiveness. In October 1935 a new enterprise, the Tokyo Electric Wireless Company, was forged to make radio equipment without any foreign financial, research, or production ties, and to manufacture small arms and ammunition for the military.

Tokyo Electric Wireless began operations in November 1935 on a 10,600-square-meter plot in Kawasaki City (current site of Toshiba's Horikawa Plant) leased from the Tokyo Electric Company, taking over all the equipment, assets, and personnel concerned with radio research, production, and sales of Tokyo Electric. At this point. Tokyo Electric Wireless swelled with a capitalization of 6 million yen, 800 employees, and two executives from Tokyo Electric, President Yoshichiro Shimizu and Vice President Kisaburo Yamaguchi. Shimizu was a graduate of Tokyo University, had spent some time in the Telecommunications Ministry's research laboratories, entered Tokyo Electric Company in 1919, and worked as the head of production and sales before shifting to Tokyo Electric Wireless Company. His experience in a variety of positions in the maturing electrical-instruments industry would prove invaluable to the company in its efforts to develop its product line.

Breaking Ground, Taking Root, and Bearing Fruit

In June of 1936, the executives of Tokyo Electric Wireless authorized the building of a new wireless production facility in the northern half of a mammoth 120,000-square-meter parcel which had been purchased by Tokyo Electric three years earlier in the Yanagicho district of Kawasaki City. Although the plant was only partially operational by the end of the year, the Yanagicho Plant was officially opened on 25 October 1936. It was brought on line quickly to coincide with the commemoration of the founding of the parent firm a year earlier. The outbreak of the

Sino-Japanese War in 1937 spurred completion of the plant and until April 1945, the Yanagicho Works was a major fabricator of vacuum tubes, radios, and radio parts for the Japanese war effort.

By 1938, after four buildings had been erected at the Yanagicho site, the headquarters of Tokyo Electric Wireless was likewise moved to Yanagicho. This decision not only signified the centrality of Yanagicho as the main operational location for Tokyo Electric Wireless but also it indicated the strategic and logistical importance of proximity between manufacturing and corporate planning. None the less, the coincidence of strategic and operational activities at the Yanagicho Works was fairly common. Similar practices for Hitachi, Toyo Spinning, Kurabo, Kureha, Fujibo, Nitchitsu, Dainippon Artificial Fertilizer, Teikoku Sugar, Nihon Cereal Milling, Niigata Engineering, among others, were documented in earlier chapters.

At the Horikawa Works, close by Kawasaki City railroad station, for example, Tokyo Electric produced light bulbs in volume and some variety. After the merger of Tokyo Electric with Shibaura Engineering to form Tokyo Shibaura Electric in 1939, the Horikawa Works continued to manufacture light bulbs as well as a number of different electric products as the head office of the Matsuda Corporation. Matsuda was the largest light-bulb maker in Japan, a subsidiary of Tokyo Shibaura, and headquartered at the Horikawa Works. In the case of the Horikawa Works as well as that of the Yanagicho Works, factories were directly attached to corporate head offices without any organizational and, often, spatial intermediation. Factories and headquarters were one.[21]

At Yanagicho, after the establishment of Tokyo Shibaura Electric in 1939, Tokyo Electric Wireless remained independent in its management, consolidated in its facilities, and focused in its strategic thrust into wireless communications. In this regard, therefore, Tokyo Electric Wireless was like many other technologically intensive firms of the pre-war period: strategic, managerial, and operational activities were all joined at the same site.

Although some degree of cost-savings in land and facilities may have been achieved by such a combination, more important rationale for the move include the advantages of proximity for the speed of decision-making, new product development and product planning activities, and most importantly, the ease of transfer of technology from overseas to the shop-floor. The process of technology transfer demanded frequent adjustments in the methods of manufacture, the products themselves, the means of distribution, and the modes of marketing. Anything less than proximity in corporate and operational activities was a competitive disadvantage during a time when quite a number of domestic rivals vied to secure business in growing defense industries.

With the outbreak of the Pacific War, demand for Yanagicho's products jumped dizzingly. Comparing half-year totals in size (floor area) of company facilities, sales, and number of employees, for the latter half of the 1935–6 and 1942–3 fiscal years respectively, size of plant increased thirteenfold, sales seventeenfold, and number of employees twentyfold. The rapid expansion of plant capacity, sales, and employees fostered an atmosphere of cooperation, interdependence, and *esprit de corps.* A tremendous sense of urgency, learning, and accomplishment enveloped the Yanagicho plant as one after another prototype was brought into production.

The plant developed new materials for the chassis and frames of communication devices, wireless radios for naval and aviation applications, short-, medium-, and long-wave receivers and transmitters, vacuum tubes for sound and picture transmission, televideo equipment, microphones, and mimeograph machines. Product proliferation transformed the character of the plant by replacing the humdrum routine of making a few things in large amounts with the excitement of discovery, creation, and realization. Yanagicho was becoming a development works, one where existing production was not jeopardized (but was instead enhanced) by new product and process development. Wartime necessitated speed and scope in both design and manufacturing activities.

A measure of this transformation can be calibrated by tracing the fortunes of the metals-fabrication department. It was established in the Yanagicho Works early in 1937 as the plant opened. It had been appended previously to Tokyo Electric as a research laboratory for the development of specialty metals for use in vacuum tubes, tools, and communications equipment. Continued study of the properties of tungsten, molybdenum, and other metals, plus research on metallurgy adapted from steel development, when coupled with Tokyo Electric Wireless's product diversification, led to the establishment of a special research section for tungsten in June 1937. Shorter term product-development research in the metals-fabrication department and longer term, purer research in the tungsten-research section were carried on side by side. After the introduction of a 150-kilowatt, high-powered induction blast-furnace on 15 December 1937, the Yanagicho Works was able to manufacture specialty metals for its own use as well as for that of affiliated firms.

Not content simply to make these metals, the metals-fabrication department perfected methods of oxygen reduction, drawing, rolling, pressing, and punching. Within two years, the Yanagicho Works had developed the capacity to make, shape, and produce in volume the metals it required for its expanding line of precision communication devices. Success in developing new materials and new products was transforming the spirit and body of the Yanagicho Works.

Fusing Strategic and Operational Management

By the 1940s the Yanagicho Works emerged locomotive-like, as a strategic and operational driving force behind the appearance of Tokyo Electric Wireless as one of Japan's pre-war, high-technology firms. By siting corporate-level and operational-level activities together, product planning, development, and manufacturing stages were better integrated, resulting in less loss of time, energy, and investment in new product and process development. Also, Yanagicho brought together manufacturing efforts for two types of products, precision machinery and electrical devices, that represented the opening wedge of what was to become the major growth industry of the late twentieth century—electronics.

By the outbreak of the Pacific War, the Yanagicho Works had taken on many of the characteristics of a focal factory, that is, a single manufacturing organization which integrates all the stages of planning, development, production, and distribution (up to the point of shipping) for a number of different product lines. At the time, however, the interlaced character of product and process engineering and the combination of strategic and operational functions were just beginning to bear fruit. It was doubtful that anyone completely understood the social and technical implications of this emerging form of factory organization.

In circumstances of rapid mobilization and deployment of resources, multi-function factories offered a great deal: more than higher level organizational units whose utility was marginal during a period of urgency. None the less, those at Yanagicho were simply giving their utmost to supply products from their factory/headquarters for urgent wartime needs. In spite of everybody's best efforts, Yanagicho could not keep up with demand. Tokyo Electric Wireless' Komukai Works was established in another area of Kawasaki in 1937 to supply Yanagicho with parts. Within a year, it had become a producer of machine parts in its own right. In 1939 a six-story, reinforced concrete factory was completed at Komukai, actually eclipsing Yanagicho to become the main mass-production facility for radios and radio parts for Tokyo Electric Wireless. At the height of its pre-war production, 10,000 employees labored at the Komukai Works.

To meet more localized production needs, Tokyo Electric Wireless established small branch factories in Kobe, in Hyogo Prefecture near Himeji, and in Tientsin, China. These plants were primarily repair facilities although they produced limited volumes of some specialized parts as well. Back at the headquarters of Tokyo Electric Wireless in Kawasaki, the other half of the large company plot at Yanagicho was used by Tokyo Electric, the parent company of Tokyo Electric Wireless, for the production of water and electric utility meters and for specialty metals research and development.

At the outbreak of the Pacific War in 1941, Tokyo Electric Wireless had its headquarters and main development factory in Yanagicho in Kawasaki City, a mass-production factory at Komukai also in Kawasaki, two branch and repair factories in Western Japan, and an overseas facility in Tientsin, China. Together the plants, shops, and offices of Tokyo Electric Wireless employed nearly 20,000. Tokyo Electric Wireless' swift ascent to prominence ended even more rapidly and climactically. An air raid on 15 April 1945 destroyed 80 percent of the Yanagicho Works. Other raids levelled most of the Komukai Works and the branch factories in western Japan.

Post-war Revival and Product Diversity

On 15 August 1945, the remaining workforce at the Yanagicho Works was assembled to hear the emperor's capitulation speech. Ironically enough for a factory that produced microphones and speakers, there was not enough functioning equipment to broadcast the emperor's speech without a hasty repair of the public-address system. The end of the war meant an end to the pre-war plant with its heavy involvement in manufacturing vacuum tubes and communication devices for the Japanese military. On 1 October the company announced a total overhaul of the firm, one that would point the way for the next forty years.

Vacuum tubes, the original product of the Yanagicho Works, were moved to the Horikawa plant, next to the Kawasaki railroad station. Yanagicho was restructured to manufacture five main product-lines with three technical-support departments. The product lines were communications equipment, measuring devices (meters and gauges), electrical fixtures, precision instruments, and fabricated metal. However, in 1945 these product lines existed more on paper than in fact because of a shortage of materials and demand constriction.

It is noteworthy that technical-support sections were not appended to the communications equipment, instruments, and fabricated-metal departments. Notwithstanding that technical-support groups were created to help product-line departments improve the design and manufacture of their goods, they were organized independently of the product-line departments at this time. Somewhat later, under pressure to become more actively involved with product and process engineering, technical-support sections were appended directly to product-line departments but this would come after a reorganization in 1971 (see Fig. 6.2).

The end of the war came abruptly and dramatically enough, severing the orderly flow of activities and forcing factory employees to grow vegetables in the plant compound and to refine salt in Zushi, near the seashore. Works Director Ikeda, the first post-war plant manager, elected to mark the passage from wartime footing to civilian production with a ritual ceremony on 8 December 1945—four years to the day (Tokyo time) after the attack on Pearl Harbor. In a formal shinto ritual ablating the past and anointing the present, Ikeda spiritually joined and pledged the efforts of all employees of the new Yanagicho Works to peaceful and productive purposes. Exactly one month later with the receipt of an official operating license, the Yanagicho Works began post-war production.

Within eight months, the value of the plant's output topped 10 million yen with electrical meters and water-immersion lights the leading products. Bombed and partially destroyed plant and facilities were restored and new buildings were erected for magnetic die-casting and electroplating. But the recovery was based less on a physical rebuilding of plant and equipment than a renewal of human knowledge and experience. Ironically enough, therefore, the successful rejuvenation of Yanagicho was shattered by a 55-day general strike from 1 October 1946, bringing Toshiba's post-war recovery efforts to a sudden and total stop.

The locus of conflict was rooted in a frightful escalation of consumer prices while at the same time Toshiba attempted to hoard as much profit as possible for rebuilding and regrouping. Employees were hard-pressed to make ends meet and in the political and economic turmoil of the immediate post-war period, all sorts of radical, untraditional, and sometimes impractical solutions to the problems of the day were aired. The company sought and successfully isolated the more militant workers from the union and the remaining workers were by no means united in their grievances or in the settlements they sought. By the end of November, the strike ended, as much from internal union dissention as from corporate compromise.

In 1947 the communications-equipment line was moved from Yanagicho to the Komukai Works where production of all communication devices was consolidated. This marked the end (at least temporarily) to what had been the beginning for the Yanagicho Works, namely the manufacture of wireless communications equipment. However in 1947 the manufacture of wireless sets was no longer a strategic enterprise and Yanagicho's cumulative experience and know-how with precision-equipment manufacture were to be put to better use.

In June 1947 Yanagicho was reorganized into three product lines: machinery, machine parts, and fabricated metal. For a brief while, Yanagicho would become a maker of precision machinery and parts without any clear product-line focus. However, because of the post-war amalgamation of Tokyo Electric Company and the Tokyo Electric Wireless Company facilities, located on the same property, electric-meter production became the main product of the Yanagicho Works in late 1947. Given the sorry condition of the country's electric power-grid following the war, demand for electrical power meters was extraordinary. Running production day and night, on the basis of this product alone, Yanagicho's operating profits were in the black by year's end.[22]

Post-war Product Diversity, Factory Organization and Management

Post-war Patterns

The post-war evolution of the structure and strategy of the Toshiba Corporation reveals two waves in the process of redrawing the borders which differentiate the activities of the core firm from those of affiliates and subsidiaries and which distinguish product and market responsibilities of principal manufacturing facilities from one another. The first of these occurred during the 1950s and 1960s, an era of rapid economic growth. The second followed, covering the 1970s and continuing until the end of the 1980s, a period of much lower rates of economic growth. The second period coincides with an accompanying emphasis on quality rather than quantity. In either period, changing economies of scale and scope as well as new strategic imperatives required a reshuffling of which activities were best carried out in the core firm as opposed to affiliates and a reconsideration of which manufacturing responsibilities will be carried out at what production facilities.

During the post-war era, as Toshiba adopted and experimented with the multi-divisional form of organization, a divisional level of organization and control was juxtaposed between the head office and production facilities. This represented the first administrative intermediation of operational and strategic planning since the company was founded in 1875/1890 (depending on which half of the company is

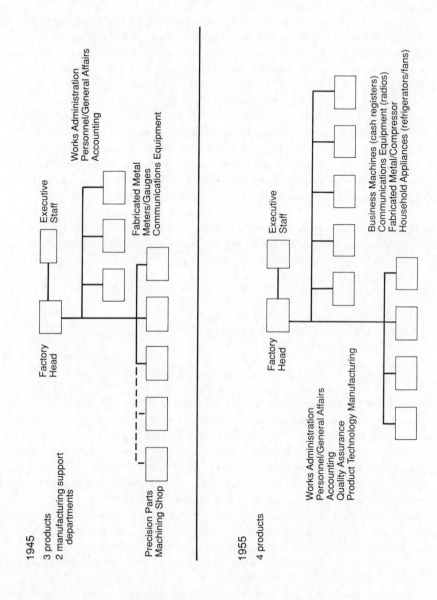

1945

3 products
2 manufacturing support
departments

Factory
Head

Executive
Staff

Works Administration
Personnel/General Affairs
Accounting

Fabricated Metal
Meters/Gauges
Communications Equipment

Precision Parts
Machining Shop

1955

4 products

Factory
Head

Executive
Staff

Works Administration
Personnel/General Affairs
Accounting
Quality Assurance
Product Technology Manufacturing

Business Machines (cash registers)
Communications Equipment (radios)
Fabricated Metal/Compressor
Household Appliances (refrigerators/fans)

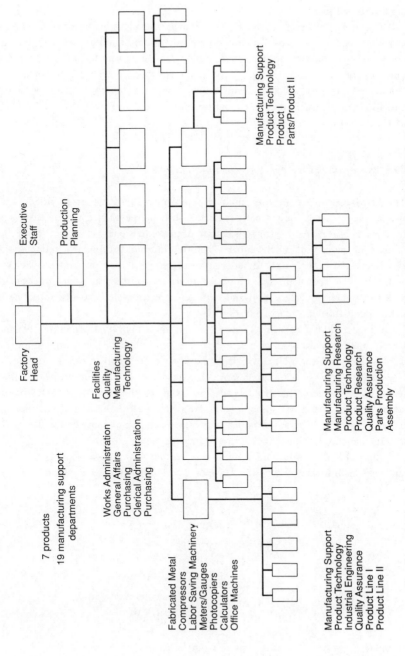

FIG. 6.2. *Technical Support and Organizational Structure: The Yanagicho Works in 1945, 1955 and 1971*

tracked). Later, higher order business elements, such as strategic business units (SBU), product groups and sectors, were introduced, further complicating the organizational picture.

The factory, however, remained the strategic nexus of organizational performance and promise. In Toshiba's case, post-war macro-organizational restructuring appeared with some regularity above the level of the factory from the mid-1960s, but for the most part it served to reinforce the fundamental importance of manufacturing, production planning and design, and thus the salience of factory-based management and organizational learning. Speed and complexity of economic and technical changes were the primary reasons why.

The Appearance of the Multidivisional Structure

The first recasting of Toshiba unfolded in August 1949 under President Taizo Ishida. He replaced a functionally organized firm composed of two product groups, light and heavy electrical goods, with a multidivisional structure, comprised of four divisions: tubes, machinery, communications equipment, and electrical machinery. In order to coordinate activities between these expanded spheres of endeavor, a divisional management council was established, an audit function was added to the headquarters staff, and sales departments were appended to the newly inaugurated tube and machinery divisions.[23]

During the 1950s Toshiba's newly hewn multidivisional structure remained largely unaltered although two new divisions, turbines and measuring equipment, were added, and the point of balance between central and divisional managerial responsibilities was recalibrated more than once. After half a century of unitary management under centralized head-office control, the multidivisional structure adopted in 1949 did not signal a complete break with the past. Indeed, the most difficult part of the transformation was the separation of powers for day-to-day management from long-range, strategic management.

In July 1962 Toshiba undertook a much more thorough separation of powers and responsibilities. What were formerly six divisions were transformed into eleven:

Old Division	New Division
electronic tubes	illumination equipment
	electronics
machinery	machinery
	household electronics
electrical machinery	electrical machinery
	electrical materials
	electrical parts
turbines	turbines

communication devices

measuring equipment

communication devices
televisions

measuring equipment

This was an obvious effort to broaden the scope of the firm's activities but, at the same time, to decentralize authority over the lines of expanded business activity. It was believed that a more decentralized mode of organization, based on the model of General Electric—Toshiba's mentor in all things managerial—would result in better performance during a period of extremely rapid economic growth. Eleven Vice Presidents were appointed as Divisional Managers, and each division was given clearly defined budgets as well as product and market responsibilities. Also, some previously independent companies, most importantly Ishikawajima Turbine, were reintegrated into Toshiba Corporation in October 1961, creating a Japanese version of the American multidivisional enterprise.[24]

At the divisional level, the newly defined 1962 organizational form has remained surprisingly stable with new additions being appended to the divisional roster but without serious attempt to reform the overall role of divisions within the corporation. Subsequent efforts at reforging structure have occurred primarily in two ways: (1) below divisions at the level of the factory and above divisions at the level of divisional groups and strategic business units (SBUs); (2) at the boundaries of Toshiba itself within the structure of Toshiba's network of affiliated enterprises. From a managerial point of view, the 1960s' divisions have remained the structural backbone around which other units of the corporation have been consciously calibrated.

Other changes in the 1962 overhaul included the replacement the President's 'executive staff' (*shachoshitsu*) with a 'general planning office' (*sogo kikakubu*), the movement of the design department from 'manufacturing' (*kiki jigyobu*) to 'sales' (*eigyo kanribu*), the establishment of a 'public relations department' (*fukyubu*) and its location in the Toshiba Science Museum, and finally the collapsing of the tripartite division of manufacturing—purchasing, manufacturing processing, and products—into two halves: materials, including purchasing, and production, including processes and products. The thrust of these changes was to clarify fundamental distinctions between product and market planning at the business-unit level and between manufacturing and non-manufacturing activities at the level of the factory.

The keel, girders, and staves having been laid, two years later, an electronic-calculator division was established and two departments, overseas contracts and trade promotion, were combined into an international division. Two years after that, in 1966, an even finer separation of business activities into distinct product lines resulted in thirteen new divisions, bringing the total divisional count up to twenty-six. At the same time a number of special project and task-force structures were created in the firm. The latter initiative was particularly important because it recognized the need to combine forces within the firm for relatively short-range purposes without altering the basic structure and strategy of the company.[25]

In 1969, to round out the fundamental changes which transformed the organization of Toshiba during this decade, the Research and Development Center was reorganized as the Central Research and Development Laboratory comprising five sub-units specializing in electronic materials, electronic parts, electronic devices, electrical machinery, and precision manufacturing. Also, additional divisional units were added in order to fine-tune organizational capabilities in response to changing market needs. As always, however, the implementation of corporate-level strategy was reflected in the definition of organizational boundaries and activities at the level of production, in this case at the Yanagicho Works.

Mass Production at Yanagicho: Consumer Goods Lead the Way

In 1951 production at Yanagicho took a new turn. Before the war, the plant utilized small-batch production technology and little of that was for consumers. But as the Korean War boosted the economy with badly needed demand, Toshiba among other electrical-equipment makers began to respond to the needs of Japanese consumers for relatively simple home electric appliances, like irons, fans, refrigerators, and air conditioners.[26]

The plant's first home appliance was an air conditioner, the RAC 101 (Room Air Cooler). The first experimental model was tested during the summer of 1952, prototypes were made in September of 1952, and by 1953 the coolers were being manufactured in volume. Ramping up to volume production proved arduous because it was much easier to design an air conditioner than to make one. The closest product to air coolers with which Yanagicho had previous experience were electrical meters, and these were a poor preparation for dealing with practical matters of how to make coolers which did not leak gas, had sufficient compression torque, and did not break down in Tokyo's sweltering summer stickiness. The product base of Yanagicho was not yet sufficiently broad for significant cross-over learning in this product area.

About the same time, the Yanagicho Works began production of residential and railroad-car lighting fixtures. The technology for these products came from the American firm Day Brite with which Toshiba had entered a technology-transfer licensing agreement. Before long, the manufacture of Day Brite lighting fixtures was consolidated with the making of vacuum tubes and other glass products in the Horikawa Works; the spray-painting technology which had been learned for Day Brite products at Yanagicho was later applied with success to the painting of refrigerators and washing machines there. This is perhaps the earliest example of cross-product learning at Yanagicho.

In May 1952, near the end of the Allied Occupation of Japan, Toshiba concluded its first agreement for the export, as opposed to the import, of technology. An Indian firm, Remco, bought Toshiba's electric-meter manufacturing technology. This was Yanagicho's oldest continuing line of products. The welcoming of Indian engineers to the Yanagicho Works as well as the consultations and deliberations surrounding the technology-transfer agreement with a foreign firm gave many at Yanagicho a sense of accomplishment and recognition for their long labors.

In August 1953 most of Toshiba's refrigerator production was moved to the Nagoya Works, while Yanagicho concentrated on making compressors for refrigerators (modeled on the Tecumseh line of American compressors), assembling a few refrigerators to retain the know-how and experience that had been accumulated in this product area, and manufacturing the P-model washing machine. By March 1954, when factory facilities had been fully converted to these new uses, production was running at 2,000 washing machines and 400 refrigerators per month. And in June a newer model washing machine, VB-3, began production as well. By this time, during the mid-1950s, the Japanese economy had recovered fully from the devastation of the war and disposable income was running at an all-time high. Televisions, refrigerators, and washing machines were all the rage, so much so that they were known as the Three Sacred Treasures. The Yanagicho Works made two of these three indispensable items, so factory output and profits grew enormously.

In April 1954 the manufacture of radios was switched from the Komukai Works back to Yanagicho, returning Yanagicho to the roots of its original product line. The reasons for this were related to Yanagicho's metalworking and metal-fabricating capabilities which were becoming strategically important in developing and producing bimetal parts and electronic capacitors for transistor radios. The evolving technology of radio reception made a transfer back to Yanagicho for the manufacture of radio sets, a logical and effective use of Yanagicho's inbred, core capabilities.

In June 1954 a household products department was formed within the plant. With the establishment of these two new departments, radios and household products, the output of the Yanagicho Works climbed markedly. Output for the latter half of 1955 was 50 percent ahead of output for the same period in 1953. Even so, the factory was running at a loss on a manufacturing cost basis. The paradox was that profits were falling as output climbed. This initiated a factory-wide effort to cut costs, eliminate waste, and improve productivity which, by the end of 1956, put the factory in the black.

The thrust of the cost-cutting effort involved manufacturing organization and practice on the shop-floor. QC methods among a host of small-group activities were introduced and diffused, emphasizing the importance of labor–management accord, participative management, intensifying the managerial and skill-based content of shop-floor routine, creating employment practices that involved a high measure of consent with regard to questions of authority, control, autonomy, and equity in the production function. From this point onward, the history of the Yanagicho Works is one of increasing output with increasing profitability.

In December 1956 the production of washing machines was consolidated in Toshiba's Nagoya Works, leaving Yanagicho with departments that produced electric-power meters (models 1–15), various kinds of radios, the GR-820 refrigerator, a cold-foods display-locker, and the metalworking/fabricated-metals department. These products combined to take the plant's monthly output over the 10-million-yen mark on a manufacturing-cost basis in August 1957.

Until 1961 two product lines—refrigeration equipment and radios—formed the core of Yanagicho's activities and energies. As the export market for Japanese transistor radios grew overseas, the radio department grabbed an 80 percent share of the factory's output by value. The refrigeration department meanwhile continued to expand its products, bringing out air conditioners for cars as well as for trains and developing a number of food display-lockers. Many of the new refrigeration products were born from the difficulties of manufacturing compressors, the heart and soul of Toshiba's refrigerator line.

These troubles bore splendid fruit when Yanagicho was awarded the contract to build and install air conditioning and heating equipment for the *shinkansen*, Japan's new high-speed railway, which was scheduled for completion by the opening of the Tokyo Olympics in 1964. By 1963 prototypes of the equipment were being tested and improved at a branch factory established at the Totsuka railroad station for those purposes. By the opening of the new line between Tokyo and Osaka, the air conditioning/heating equipment was fully installed, and it has continued to operate during the next quarter century with an extremely low rate of failure and service. The success of Yanagicho with this showcase project, like the overall success of the Tokyo Olympiad for the nation, became a symbolic victory for the plant and its employees.

In short, from the mid-1950s through the mid-1960s the Yanagicho Works prospered largely on the strength of two product lines, household/industrial electric appliances, especially refrigeration and air-conditioning equipment, and radios. These products put the plant in the black, forced an introduction of new methods of manufacturing organization and management, and, at the peak of production in March 1962, employed 7,538 personnel. The factory continued to do what it had done so well for so long, all of this apart from the divisional reshuffling at corporate headquarters.

The Maturation of the Multidivisional Structure

Toshiba's efforts to mimic the organization of General Electric in its own structural transformation were quickened with the appointment of Toshio Doko as President in 1965. Doko's tenure as Toshiba's President is a convenient watershed for dating the transition from the early multidivisional structure of the 1950s and mid-1960s to a later multidivisional structure of great complexity and strategic sophistication. It could be said that under Doko, Toshiba's experience with the multidivisional form evolved beyond the stage of trial-and-error to a more advanced stage of trial-and-success. Both at the corporate and operational levels, organizational learning was key to the advance.

Doko is one of the best-known managers and business leaders of the post-war era. He succeeded in pushing Ishikawajima Harima to the top of Japan's ship-building industry in the early 1960s, moved to revamp the Toshiba Corporation during the last half of the 1960s, and finally reigned as the head of the Keidanren, Japan's influential Federation of Economic Organizations, after leaving Toshiba in 1972. As President of Toshiba, Doko moved to rationalize its structure in three ways. He continued to follow the structural differentiation of Toshiba modeled on General Electric's experience, adding a level of divisional groups between the corporate and divisional spheres of activity. Toshiba created seven divisional groups in 1970. These were:

1. industrial electronics
2. calculation devices
3. household electronics
4. atomic power
5. heavy industrial equipment
6. materials
7. international business

Each divisional group encompassed several divisional lines of business activity in an effort to group together products and markets. As before, however, there were additions and subtractions to as well as combinations of the divisional-level structures created within the firm. A single individual was usually named to coordinate and promote business endeavors covered by the divisional group designation, and accordingly seven group managers were named in 1970. Additional measures enacted by this time included the creation of divisional management committees to strengthen overall managerial activities within divisions, and the standardization of accounting and auditing procedures across divisions. By May 1970 the seven group managers were overseeing the activities of twenty-seven different product divisions.

Doko next moved to unify top management. Separate Boards for Managing and Executive Directors were disbanded in favor of a single Board of Directors. Corporate-level executives were freed from all responsibilities for divisions or divisional groups, and they were given instead functional responsibilities covering the corporation as a whole. Again, following the example of General Electric, Doko took Toshiba to the logical extension of the multidivisional structure: a clear separation of function, authority, and responsibility between corporate and divisional level management. Of course, the anticipated end-results were higher levels of corporate performance.

As higher order reshuffling progressed, Doko sought to reduce the number of divisions as well as to spin off some divisions and departments into independent enterprises. This was in conscious opposition to the earlier effort to centralize more activities and lines of business within Toshiba's corporate umbrella. In an apparent recognition of the limits to organizational effectiveness as well as a frank appraisal of the rising power of rival electrical-equipment makers, like consumer-goods oriented Sanyo and Matsushita Electric Industrial, Toshiba began in the early 1970s to hive off as independent firms those endeavors which by their capital requirements, unique organizational demands, or special marketing requirements were best suited to an independent managerial existence.[27]

In April 1971 Toshiba Silicon was spun off as a specialty maker of semiconductor materials. In June 1973 Toshiba Home Industries was likewise separated from the parent company. In May 1974 Toshiba Electronic Materials was formed, and in October of the same year Toshiba Chemical was established, resulting in the closure of two Toshiba factories and in the amalgamation of another. Finally, in October of 1974, Toshiba Distribution and Materials Handling was formed. In the case of Toshiba Distribution and Materials Handling as well as in the case of other newly established firms, previously existing divisions within Toshiba were discontinued when independent enterprises were founded to carry on these lines of business, and the production facilities associated with these business lines were either recombined with existing production units within Toshiba or separated off with the newly established enterprises.

The changing divisional boundaries within Toshiba as well as the boundary interface between Toshiba and its affiliates were related to new research activities inaugurated during the 1970s. In April 1970 a Manufacturing Technology Institute and a Consumer Electronics Research Institute were opened. The latter was appended to the consumer and home electrical appliances division. In December 1972 a High- Low-Temperature Research Center was opened within the heating and cooling devices division, and in July of the same year a Product Reliability Technology Center was established.

A new Central Research Laboratory was founded in 1972, amalgamating the activities of numerous existing research efforts. At first, Central R & D divided its activities between three areas of research: consumer electronics, integrated circuits–micro-electronics, and information systems. A year later, in 1973, the Electrical Equipment Research Institute changed its name to Energy Devices Research Institute and in 1974 the Electronic Materials Research Institute was divided between the Light Metals–Ceramics Research Center and the Electro-Chemical Research Institute. Finally, in March 1976 a Machinery Research Institute was established.[28]

The intended result of these organizational initiatives was a clarification of which activities were best carried out inside and outside Toshiba's corporate boundaries. Within Toshiba, further determinations clarified where research activities would be conducted and to which product group and division the activities would be appended. But, because of the volatility of markets and changing technological developments, the determination of where a particular line of business activity fits is problematic at best.

Nevertheless, the rationale for such determinations are both economic and strategic. On the economic side of the calculation, economies of scale, scope, transaction, and labor costs must be balanced against strategies of market entry, new product development, and risk minimization. It is a laborious, troublesome, and nearly unending task, to match corporate organization and enterprise strategy in a world of rapidly changing markets, technologies, and products. While the changing product mix of the Yanagicho Works captures the efforts of top managers of the Toshiba Corporation to align strategy and structure during post-war decades of Japan's most rapid economic growth, the danger was that the restructuring efforts of Doko and other corporate executives might actually insulate planners at the top from workers at the bottom of the hierarchy.

Towards Industrial Electronics and a New Future at Yanagicho

From the early to mid-1960s, when Doko moved to restructure Toshiba at the top, the character of the Yanagicho Works changed yet again. Yanagicho's labors to develop household electrical appliances had paid handsome dividends for a decade or more, but in April 1961 the manufacture of small- and medium-sized refrigerators was moved to mass-production facility in Osaka, and in June of the same year most of the air-conditioner production was likewise shifted to the Fuji Works. Larger refrigerator units were also consolidated in the Osaka Works in 1969. By June of 1970, when a new rotary-compressor line was opened elsewhere, only reciprocal compressors remained in the once formidable line of refrigeration and air-conditioning equipment manufactured at the Yanagicho Works.[29]

But by combining experience in designing, making, and marketing various product lines with new market opportunities, the Yanagicho Works was able to adapt, expand, and diversify. Yanagicho was being groomed as Toshiba's principal factory for the production of precision industrial and office electrical equipment. In 1962 the old radio, metalworking, and fabricated-metal departments were rolled into one, comprising a new electro-mechanical products department. It was given a mandate to develop a new line of business and office-machinery products. Under a technical licensing agreement with Remington Univac, the first card-punch sorters appeared by the end of the year.

There were some precedents for this rather drastic reorganization. Twenty years earlier when the Yanagicho Works was Tokyo Electric Wireless' main factory, it had played a principal role in the successful development of a television prototype. Also, during the wartime period, the Yanagicho plant was given the maintenance contract for government-seized International Business Machine card-punching and sorting equipment. But even with these earlier accomplishments, it took a year or two before the Yanagicho Works had geared up for any substantial levels of business-machinery production.

The breakthrough came in 1966, when Yanagicho was chosen as the site for manufacturing Toshiba Type's typewriter. Toshiba Type, an affiliated firm within the group of Toshiba companies, had no manufacturing facilities of its own while Yanagicho's management was looking for projects in the new area of business and office machinery. Starting with typewriters, Yanagicho soon produced a series of new office products, including facsimiles, photocopiers, card readers and sorters, and, of course, the ubiquitous desktop calculator.

Calculator production was the breeding ground for training a whole new generation of Japanese firms in electrical mechanical process engineering and product development. In the late 1960s the market for calculators seemed unlimited as costs were halved and output doubled every year. In the long run only a handful of firms stayed in the calculator business but of those that dropped out, most avoided bankruptcy by switching their efforts to alternative product lines. In this way, the manufacture of calculators was the basis for much of today's electronics industry.

Yanagicho's first calculator was the RCD-071, an electrical relay model, which came out in August 1964. This was replaced in December of the next year by the BC-1001, the plant's first all-electronic calculator. Unbelievably, this initial model of the Toscal series of calculators required over a thousand parts and manufacturing steps to complete. But new semiconductor developments in integrated circuitry and large-scale integration quickly simplified the processes of design, development, and manufacture, while simultaneously reducing size and increasing functions. The SC-7100 calculator, which went into production in January 1965, dramatized these amazing developments by halving the size, tripling the functions, and quadrupling the plant's manufacturing productivity, compared to the BC-1001, in fourteen months.

In November 1966 an office-equipment department was newly established within the Yanagicho Works to consolidate the organizational gains already realized with calculator production. This department designed and manufactured desktop and larger business equipment, such as typewriters, card sorters and readers. The breakthrough product for this department was *photocopiers* which became the single most important export from Yanagicho by the 1970s. Toshiba's initial photocopiers were developed at the Tamagawa Works in 1962, and the first commercial models, the AF Series, appeared from 1963. But until the photocopier line was moved to Yanagicho in 1966, the technical problems of volume manufacture were not entirely solved.

In 1968 Yanagicho introduced its high performance (BD-21) and custom (BD-11) lines of direct electrostatic photocopiers, the leading technology of the day. The BD-21 was the world's first commercial photocopier with enlarging and reducing capabilities. In 1970 the BD-32 was shipped, quickly earning high marks for reliability and functionality in both domestic and overseas markets. From the early 1970s, however, as consumer preference shifted to plain paper copiers (PPC), Yanagicho was forced to develop a new line of photocopiers. The first of these, the BD-720, appeared in 1973, but it was not until 1975 that Yanagicho produced a commercially successful machine, the BD-703. At the end of that year, the Yanagicho Works pulled its 250,000th plant-manufactured photocopier off the line and ceremoniously shelved it in a show of factory spirit and community pride.

Yanagicho had solved the Tamagawa Work's problems with the production of special-paper copiers (AF series) and originated its own plain-paper copier based on the AF line. Given the optical, mechanical, electro-mechanical, paper sorting, manufacturing, and process-engineering complexities of the BD photocopier series, 1975 could be considered Yanagicho's coming of age year. Only this would not do justice to another stream of product development that looms forth during the 1970s.

Labor-Saving Equipment: The Disappearing Postman?

During the 1960s the Japanese economy, growing at two to three times the rate of other industrial economies, began to outstrip the demographic resources of the nation. Historically, a large push of people, especially from the countryside, had propelled the Japanese economy forward, but as couples had fewer children and as the economy continued to prosper in the post-war period, the large numbers of educated, experienced, and relatively inexpensive workers who had shouldered much of the burden of economic development in Japan during the first half of the century began to disappear. Engineers and technicians at Yanagicho realized that much of their experience in coping with production bottlenecks and manpower shortages in the manufacture of calculators and photocopiers might be turned into new products for a new Japan.

In 1963 the Yanagicho Works developed a coffee-dispensing machine and in the next year an automatic change-making and ticket-dispensing machine for the Hankyu Railroad in Osaka. But the big push into labor-saving equipment came when the Ministry of Post and Telecommunications asked Toshiba in the early autumn of 1965 to develop postal-sorting equipment. For this effort. Yanagicho teamed with the company's Central Research Laboratory. Yanagicho worked on designing and developing the mechanical parts and components for the letter-sorting and paper-handling equipment while Central R & D contributed pattern-recognition technology reading mail addresses and zip codes. The importance of pattern-information recognition and processing technology was recognized at the national level with the creation of a National Research and Development Project for this technology by MITI (Ministry of International Trade and Industry) in 1971.[30]

In October 1965 a letter-handling (LH) section had formed within the factory. In competition with other companies for the Postal Ministry's contract, Yanagicho's LH section worked day and night for a year, producing an automatic letter-sorting machine with pattern-recognition capabilities by late November 1966. At this point, the prototype stage of product development, Toshiba along with NEC was chosen to share in the next stage of the government's contract to develop LH equipment. Ultimately, Toshiba secured a lion's share of the domestic market for LH equipment and shipped its first machine to the American postal service in 1970. In 1972 the Australian postal service took delivery of fifteen automatic letter sorters, and in 1976 the entire Hungarian postal system was redesigned around Yanagicho-made LH equipment. More recently, the British post office took delivery of 120 card, letter, and package-sorters of Yanagicho design and manufacture.

LH equipment not only reads handwritten postal codes but also prints postal codes on envelopes in bar-code format. Code conversion of this sort greatly simplifies the mail-sorting process because it requires only a simple code reader at mail-sorting sub-stations to distribute the mail. While simplifying the process of mail sorting, Yanagicho's LH equipment is anything but simple. For optical character recognition (OCR), the address must be written within 2–12 cm from the bottom line of the evelope. Letters culled by the LH feeder are sent to the optical scanner which is composed of a prescanning unit and a main-scanning unit.

OCR occurs in four stages: segmentation, normalization, recognition, and answer edition. In the segmentation stage, character signals sent from the scanning unit are separated one by one. Segmented character signals are normalized using the Gaussian sampling method. In the normalization stage, the normalized character pattern is compared to patterns stored in the LH microcomputer memory and the degree of similarity is compared by a statistical pattern-matching technique. The digit with the highest degree of similarity is chosen, the recognition stage, and sent to the microcomputer of the main system, the answer edition stage. Bar codes are printed on envelopes according to data sent by the LH microcomputer, and mail is sent for pre-sorting. Processing capacity by the mid-1980s reached 28,000 letters/hour.

The competition to develop LH equipment catalyzed a great deal of applied research in the area of pattern recognition which was then easily extended to other sorts of labor-saving equipment. In 1967 Yanagicho formed a department of special machinery for this purpose. In 1968 the Yanagicho Works began shipping automatic ticket-vending machines to railroads across the country. In February 1969 Hankyu Railroad took possession of a Yanagicho designed laser-printing, ticket-vending machine, and in the next year, the world's first fully electronic, ticket-printing and vending machine was delivered to the Japan National Railroad. By 1970 every Hankyu and Hanshin station in Western Japan boasted automatic ticket-vending and ticket-taking machinery designed and developed in the Yanagicho Works.

In 1972 Yanagicho developed a cash-handling machine for the Bank of Japan which sorted bogus bills from the real thing. This was another world's first—a commercially available device for cash-counting and counterfeit detection. In a 1975 Keidanren-sponsored exposition of labor-saving equipment for the financial world, Yanagicho again scored a first with an ATM machine which read any major bank card and dispensed cash in varying amounts and varying denominations at the rate of 600 bills per minute.

Within a decade, in short, Yanagicho pioneered a new field of labor-saving devices with applications in banking, postal services, ticket sales, printing, and ticket-taking. In terms of general product areas, the technological interrelationships underlying this entire line of products is shown in Fig. 6.3.

The applications, of course, extend well beyond these initial areas, and the demand for labor-saving devices has proved steady and strong, even if the payback in terms of cost-savings is quite variable depending on local wage rates. Neverthe-

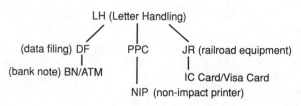

FIG. 6.3. *Product Lineage at the Yanagicho Works: Labor-Saving Products*

less, the reliability, versatility, and speed of operation of the labor-saving devices developed by Yanagicho have won national and international attention. Recall that success with labor-saving devices began with the triumphant production of the BD series of photocopiers, resulting in 250,000 BD-703s being made by 1975. Automatic mail-sorting equipment, cash-handling devices, ATMs, train-ticket validation equipment, and PPC came later: these products attest to Yanagicho's design and production capabilities.

The technical interrelationships linking Yanagicho's labor-saving products reveal economies of scope may be realized when a number of closely related products are designed, developed, and manufactured in tandem. Table 6.1 demonstrates these interrelationships quite clearly.

Corporate Strategy and Factory Response at Toshiba

Within the Toshiba Corporation, it is the day-to-day operation of divisions and of factories within divisions that drive the main thrust of Toshiba's business activities. However, a number of cross-divisional projects were initiated in the early to mid-1970s to join the resources of numerous different divisions and factories for new product development. In 1970, for example, a Manufacturing Engineering Research Center was founded along with a Consumer Electronics Technical Research Center. These new institutes distributed the results of research efforts across a wide spectrum of Toshiba units. In June 1975 probably the most significant of these pan-enterprise endeavors was the establishment of the Very-Large-Scale-Integration Project (VLSI) to develop high-capacity microchip designs within the electronic-devices division.

In 1972 Toshio Doko was elevated to the office of Chairman of the Board, a position he held for four years while serving simultaneously as the head of the Keidanren. He was succeeded by Keizo Tamaki, former Director of MITI, whose accomplishment was to implement more fully the policies and strategies laid down by Doko. He was replaced in June 1976, the trough between the two oil crises, by Futao Iwata, a specialist in finance. Iwata's promotion marked the beginning of the second century of Toshiba's history, and it signalled a desire to do something

TABLE 6.1. *Basic Technologies Incorporated in Labor-Saving Equipment*

	Banking	Mail sorting	Railroad	Data storage
Paper transmission	XX	XX	XX	X
Electronic controls	XX	XX	XX	X
Image processing	XX	XX	XX	XX
Electromagnetism	XX	X	XX	—
Printing technologies	XX	X	XX	XX
Coin counting/sorting	XX	—	XX	—
Telecommunications	XX	X	XX	XX
Software engineering	XX	X	XX	XX
Precision machining	X	X	X	XX
Production engineering	XX	X	XX	X

Note: X = some overlap
    XX = considerable overlap
    — = no relationship

positive about Toshiba's sluggish performance since 1970.[31] Essentially, Toshiba's sales, earnings, and dividends for the five-year period between 1970 and 1975 were flat and unencouraging.

The Emergence of Strategic Business Planning

Iwata took office with an ambitious three-part strategy which emphasized selectivity in management, the strengthening of affiliates and subsidiaries, and the international-ization of business activity. These goals were crystallized by drawing up the company's first medium-range three-year plan. Note that it took a hundred years before Toshiba introduced such planning exercises. The impetus and model for achieving Iwata's goals came from General Electric, once again, and they materialized in the form of introducing the concept and practice of strategic business units (SBUs). SBUs were areas of business activity, usually running across several of the more traditional product areas, that were deemed to have unusual business potential.[32] Initially, SBUs were localized both above and below the divisional level of organization, although in time they came to be mostly concentrated above the level of divisions.

SBUs were formed with several purposes in mind. One was to correct problems of alignment between R & D, products, and markets. If, for example, research and development in the area of optical character recognition (OCR) technology did not noticeably improve the quality of imaging for photocopiers but did uncover potentially large and lucrative markets in such areas as letter- and cash-handling equipment, then an SBU designed to exploit these possibilities might be created. Another use for SBUs would be in joining the resources of several divisions in order to create new business endeavors. A power systems SBU, for example, might combine turbines from the turbine division, electrical equipment from the machinery division, power measuring and metering devices from the heavy apparatus division, software from the industrial electronics division, and finally service personnel from a regional sales office. Without SBUs, it is quite troublesome to combine personnel and activities across divisional, product, and factory boundaries.

A final use for SBUs, more conceptual than structural, was the effective introduction of new and more powerful techniques of business analysis. As a group of techniques, they are called strategic business planning, and at each level of product and market planning, different methods are employed. There are five principally: product market analysis (PMA), profit improvement program (PIP), product portfolio management (PPM), product planning process (PPP), and product market strategy (PMS).[33] The thrust of these new planning tools was to force Toshiba's management to be much more discriminating about its products and their market potential. In gross terms, divisions were designated as either growth centers or profit centers, with more resources flowing to the former.

At first, SBUs were separate from the normal line and staff structure of Toshiba. They stood apart and initially they were considered more palliative than normative. However, in time, because of the importance of their strategic and structural purposes and because of the powerful planning tools they employed, they were gradually integrated into the routine structure of Toshiba. Strategic business planning became part of the normal activities of business units, divisions, and divisional groups, and as this occurred, SBUs came to be localized higher and higher in the corporate hierarchy. In a sense their very success in creating a closer alignment and better use of resources at lower levels of the organization, obviated their purpose there while it opened up new opportunities for higher level strategic planning.

Ultimately, by the early 1980s there was very little difference between the traditional line and staff structure of Toshiba and the structure of SBUs introduced in the mid-1970s. SBUs, which had begun as something to aim for, that is a kind of ambition or direction, had evolved into something to be accomplished, a measure of organizational capability. The absorption and integration of strategic planning methods by sectorial and divisional business units heralded the success of the original SBU effort while, at the same time, they marked the end of their independent utility and value.

By 1982 SBUs of the original sort had disappeared, and instead, seven corporate-wide new projects were identified. These were:

ultra-high capacity information systems,
new media/home electronics,
office automation systems,
factory automation systems,
large-scale integration/microchip systems,
key system components, and
software systems.

Top-level executive directors were put in charge of each project area with a mandate to integrate resources across the full spectrum of corporate competencies.

While the new corporate-wide projects imitate the spirit of the original SBUs, they are different in some fundamental ways. First, they are not designed to realign mismatches in existing technologies, products, and markets, and as such, they have no goal of restructuring the firm. Instead, they define a direction for the future and they imply a recognition that the current alignment of resources may not be the best use of resources in the future. However, in the mean time, SBUs do not compete with existing business units as had been the case during the late 1970s. A rethinking of Toshiba's competitive strengths and of the organizational foundations of those strengths, like the Yanagicho Works, distinguish Toshiba's strategic direction from the 1980s.

The Impact of SBUs on the Yanagicho Works

The consolidation of Toshiba's strategic thrust within seven different company-wide projects by the 1980s was reflected in the development of three new product lines at the Yanagicho Works (see Fig. 6.2). These were optoelectronic data-storage systems, non-impact printers, and IC (integrated circuit) cards. The first two of these, like many of the current products manufactured at Yanagicho, are related historically to the efforts, initiated in 1965, to build the first automatic mail-sorting equipment in Japan.

What distinguishes these two products was a rather complicated cross-factory sourcing of needed materials and technology. On one hand, laser-disk production facilities were developed on-site while the laser heads for reading laser disks were acquired outside the factory. On the other hand, the transfer of thermal printer technology from another Toshiba factory was combined with the purchase of laser-printing devices from firms outside Toshiba. In both cases, the product-development process at Yanagicho had evolved to the point where Yanagicho could rather easily combine its resources with those of other manufacturing facilities both within and without Toshiba. Recall that cross-product fusion within the firm had been among the original aims of the SBU.

Heretofore, product-development activities at the factory level were carried out in-house, for the most part. In the 1980s, however, Yanagicho has become more and more a fulcrum for organizational leverage by combining the resources of many different business units within and without Toshiba.[34] This new direction reflects a sophisticated sense of when it is best to buy and when it is best to make the parts, components, and sub-assemblies that go into today's high-technology products. Moreover, the decision to buy or make subsumes a number of other decisions involving R & D, production planning, manufacturing, and marketing.

Deciding to develop new components in-house is a frank recognition of the value of organizational learning. In the case of either Yanagicho or Toshiba, this critical question has become a cornerstone of company policy. On 27 December 1984, President Saba announced that seven of Toshiba's focal factories (there are currently twenty-seven Toshiba factories in Japan) were embarking on a plan to exchange factory-level know-how that had been accumulated in each plant over the years. Factories were writing technology 'guidebooks' incorporating the wisdom that had been acquired in various fields. Some factories were writing on automation systems while others were concentrating on parts-packaging know-how. Once the guidebooks were written, a factory-to-factory technology-transfer seminar for 700 Toshiba employees was planned. At least the first phase of the project was successful with a company-wide planning conference held in the spring of 1986.

The commercial potential of IC cards is perhaps the largest among the Yanagicho product-development projects begun at least in partial response to the SBUs initiatives of the late 1970s. IC cards are credit cards with an embedded integrated circuit which, in contrast to today's magnetic-stripe card, should minimize or entirely eliminate millions of dollars of annual loss due to fraud, counterfeiting, and credit overcharges.

Yanagicho's IC card project began formally in December 1985, although it was based on earlier efforts within Toshiba, such as the development of a magnetic-stripe bank card for Mitsui Bank in 1984, a telephone credit card for NTT in 1986, as well as various LSI, CPU, and memory-development projects. From December 1985 until December 1987, during a two-year period, the IC card section of the Yanagicho Works working in tandem with other Toshiba factories, divisions, and research units, as well as with companies within and without the Toshiba enterprise group, pioneered a number of interrelated technological breakthroughs, innovative design concepts, and trial-and-error successes.

The most notable of these, all accomplished at the Yanagicho Works, include:

 1. flexible liquid crystal display
 2. thin-film battery
 3. low-loop wire bonding
 4. multi-color printing on steel
 5. raised embossing on steel
 6. operations and applications software
 7. laser welding technology
 8. automatic assembly production technology
 9. heat-seal technology
10. thin tuning fork
11. two-sided, through-hole, high-density printed circuit board
12. smart card system, including card, software, card read/write technology, and card-issuing machine

The capability of pulling together in two years the distinct but interlocking technological innovations that underpin the IC card project at Yanagicho offers perhaps the best evidence of the benefits of structuring a manufacturing corporation around its product-development capabilities.[35] This may be regarded as a factory equivalent of designating certain divisions as growth centers and others as profit centers. The conscious structuring of factories to accomplish innovative purposes is based on an appreciation of the benefits that may be achieved through organizational learning, especially when the skills of business units within and without Toshiba may be mobilized to those ends. In developing the IC card, for example, the Yanagicho Works enlisted the cooperation of 138 managerial/ technical personnel from other units within Toshiba and from five outside companies: Toshiba Battery, Toshiba Chemical, Toshiba Silicon, Marucon, and Hattori Seiko.[36]

Within Toshiba, the emphasis on SBUs from the late 1970s facilitated the process of factory-to-factory technology transfer, and the willingness of Toshiba affiliates and other companies to cooperate within a framework provided by Toshiba's Yanagicho Works. And lest it be overlooked, that cooperation is based on Toshiba's ability to deliver the goods: to design, develop, and deliver new products that will not only sustain Toshiba's competitive edge but also those of its partners and allies.

Disappearing SBUs: Back to Basics?

In a somewhat surprising reversal, in April 1987 the Toshiba Corporation aborted the sector-level of organization or what had been known as Strategic Business Units (SBUs). Apparently, the thinking was that the concept of SBUs had become so thoroughly internalized within the major divisions of Toshiba that a separate organizational hierarchy to accomplish SBU objectives was no longer necessary. At the same time, however, Toshiba has emphasized the importance of cross-divisional and cross-factory integrated activities while renewing the importance of groups and divisions as profit centers, and these ambitious goals and redefinitions certainly reflect the legacy of SBUs for the firm.

The elimination of SBUs at Toshiba has resulted in a five-tiered organizational structure, when viewed from the level of the factory: factories, business units (BU), divisions, divisional groups (sectors), and corporate offices.[37] Lately, the importance of heavy industry within the divisions and group structures of Toshiba has noticeably lessened. Although Toshiba remains one of the world's premier makers of heavy industrial equipment, along with Hitachi, Fuji, and Mitsubishi Electric in Japan, nevertheless Toshiba has come to rely less and less on heavy electrical machinery and parts, once the mainstay of the company. In 1984 the heavy electric side of the business accounted for one-third of Toshiba's sales. Since then, heavy electric equipment has slipped to less than one-third of Toshiba's sales—a historic low which heralds a basic, probably irreversible, shift from what was once the original business of the company.

In fact, by March 1989, computers, information systems, and industrial electronics accounted for 53 percent of Toshiba's sales, relegating heavy electric goods and consumer electronics to a minor position in the company's earning stream. The restructuring of Toshiba, catalyzed in part by the introduction of SBUs, had been successful. Of the Big Three comprehensive electric-equipment makers, Hitachi, Mitsubishi Electric, and Toshiba, only Toshiba garnered more than 50 percent of its sales from businesses other than heavy equipment and consumer goods by 1989.[38]

Toshiba's four 'business sectors' (*honbu* in Toshiba talk) had become rarefied SBUs in effect. They were strategic units where matters of planning and positioning for entire product families occurred, and they were the organizational units where resources were mobilized and aligned. *Honbu* managed products. Factories managed the process of making products. The capabilities and know-how to convert resources into products linked factories to *honbu* in a direct and unequivocal way. *Honbu*, rarefied SBUs, were analogous, interdependent, and symbiotic with factories. Neither one could do without the other.

Because multi-function, multi-product factories produce for many BUs and several divisions within a *honbu*, they harbor the organizational capabilities underlying product planning across the firm; they effect crucial transfers of technology and personnel; they capitalize on experience, converting manufacturing running time into organizational learning. If it could be fairly said that SBUs were brought down to earth by having divisions and sectors absorb their strategic promise, by the same token focal factories were raised up high as omnibus sites where strategic visions are implemented. They are the systems-converters in today's world of complex, intermingled technologies. The interdependence of factory and firm, a primary thesis of this study, was graphically revealed in an organization chart drawn by the head of the (IC) Card Systems Department at Yanagicho in February 1990 (see Fig. 6.4).

Conclusion: Focal Factories

This chapter has sought to describe and analyze the process by which the Toshiba Corporation, including its affiliates and subsidiaries, has grown and restructured itself during this century while recognizing the ongoing and crucial importance of manufacturing. The recognition is based upon a seemingly paradoxical conviction that while factories cannot be in a constant state of flux, and for this reason predictability in structure, routine, and behavior is desirable, the necessity and desirability of change, both incremental and substantial, must be built into factory organization and management.

The focal factory embodies an institutional response to this paradox. It represents an institutional response to a set of historical contingencies, such as the pre-war fragmentation of markets, extremely high rates of post-war economic growth, rapidly shifting, maturing, and segmenting product markets, dramatic improvements in engineering and manufacturing know-how, and the intensification of market rivalries across a broad spectrum of industries. A managerial riposte to these contingencies was to choose and act in behalf of endowing certain manufacturing organizations with special qualities: sufficient resources to respond systematically to new market and technical opportunities and an urgent mission to

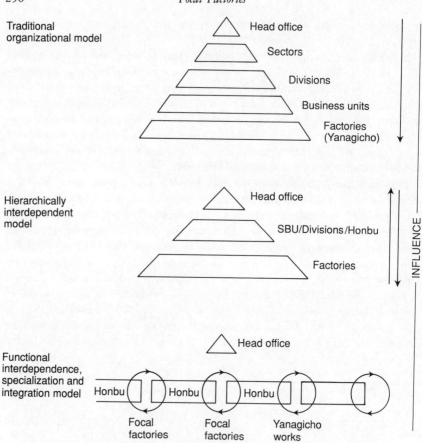

F I G. 6.4. *The Toshiba Corporation and the Yanagicho Works: Functional Interdependence*

do so, quickly and repeatedly. To the extent that these choices and actions were reiterated and accumulated, experience piled atop experience, specific and divergent institutional values and practices became possible.

Focal factories appeared as a culmination of this pattern of induced, reflective choice and action. The widespread existence of such factories in Japan but their relative scarcity or non-existence elsewhere offers a powerful explanation for the increasingly competitive edge enjoyed by Japanese firms in established product markets and for their ability to respond quickly, even pre-emptively, to new markets. Manufacturing of this sort is a formidable competitive advantage.

The argument of this chapter and indeed of this book is that the historic circumstances of technology transfer and the speed of economic development in Japan have underscored the significance of the link between manufacturing and corporate operations. This strategic connection has been nourished and maintained by devolving responsibility for new-product development, design and planning, as well as some sales coordination to integrated production sites, focal factories.

While devolving functional responsibilities to focal factories, strategic planning has remained in the hands of divisional and corporate-level managers, so that the importance of long-term, rewarding ties linking all levels of corporate activity are underscored. This may suggest why non-competitive bidding between business units and factories and between business units and divisions appears to be such an important aspect of intrafirm transactions in Japan. Adjustments in structure and strategy at corporate and operational levels constitute a kind of collective-bargaining activity that promotes organizational adaptation and effectiveness, if not efficiency.[39]

A functional emphasis on manufacturing and a focused concentration of resources in production are not recent developments, as the pre-war history of Yanagicho attests. And to recapitulate briefly post-war developments, the Works produced a variety of electrical devices and gradually concentrated on mass producing electric meters, motors, and then consumer appliances. Yanagicho manufactured a half-dozen different consumer and industrial product-lines, including coolers, refrigerators, washing machines, fans, and compressors.

Then in 1954 Yanagicho went back to one of its original products, the radio. However, it was not the vacuum-tube radio but a brand new product, the transistor radio. Before long, mass production of transistors accounted for 80 percent of the plant's income. The transistor was the most important of the new semiconductors and through its volume production and use, Toshiba gained competitively in a number of emerging electronics-based industries.

By 1971 three of Toshiba's seven divisions were producers of semiconductor-driven, electronic goods. The extraordinary coincidence of one of the most important new technologies of the second half of the twentieth century with one of the most basic organizational forms to harness such technologies explains Toshiba's spectacular rise as an international electronics company.[40] In the case of the Yanagicho Works, the marriage of new technologies with new organizational capabilities appears convincingly in such world-class products as high-speed, automatic mail-sorting equipment, Visa International and Toshiba SuperSmart cards, Toshiba's PageLaser 12 and other laser beam printers, and TOS File 4550SD, currently the best-selling, mass storage, opto-electric system sold in Japan.

On a conceptual level, various arguments may be advanced for the effectiveness of the focal factory's architecture of manufacturing organization. First, economies of scope may be realized when the costs of manufacturing two or more products in the same facility are lower than the costs of making each separately. It is not coincidental that non-impact printers and photocopiers are assembled in the same department or that water, gas, and electric meters are produced in the same industrial instruments department at Yanagicho. The scope of manufacturing activities allows for plant-specific economies of scale in multiple product-lines.

Second, economies of scope may be well suited to the size of Japanese industrials, which are small alongside comparable American firms and focused in the manufacture of a limited number of product families. Because of learning economies realized in focused assembly operations, however, opportunities to improve products, fine-tune processes, and cut costs seem almost unending.[41] Also, scope economies appear because asset-specific investments in personnel, technology, plant, and equipment are spread out between Yanagicho's product departments and a network of affiliates, suppliers, and subcontractors. The sharing of intangible know-how as well as more tangible physical assets, such as jigs, molds, dies, NC and CNC tools, across a product range but within an interfirm network suggests why per unit costs of production and assembly fall. As long as transaction costs do not offset production costs, the focal factory model of manufacturing yields a concentration of high-value-added activities in core sites combined with a distribution of complementary activities in lower cost, high productivity, affiliated sites.

Finally, there appears to be significant cross-over learning effects associated with manufacturing multiple product-lines. These may be found in greater capacity utilization of plant and equipment, the transfer of learning in product/process design and engineering, cross-shop transferability of superior organizational methods, and the actual movement of personnel between product departments and manufacturing functions.

The history of product and process developments at the Yanagicho Works indicates that learning and experience effects, while primarily product-related, may be expandable to the level of plant-wide effects, especially when on-the-job training is coupled with off-the-job learning.[42] At Toshiba, the search for high-value-added manufacturing has led to an increasing differentiation of manufacturing facilities into two sorts: routine-based, volume production factories and learning oriented, multiproduct, multifunction factories.[43] At first, focal factories appeared as an efficient organizational solution to problems of rapid technology transfer. Later they became effective institutions for organizing R & D, engineering and manufacturing activities. What was a solution to the developmental problems of one age became an answer to the needs of another.

NOTES

1. For at least the last decade, Japan has been a leader in the quantity and quality of patent registrations. According to studies which count the frequency of patent citations and from that figure infer their importance, as early as 1976 patents awarded Japanese inventors were cited more frequently than those awarded Americans, and the gap between Japanese and American patent-citation frequency appears to be growing.

   These findings indicate the long-standing importance of innovation for Japanese firms, and that, in turn, reflects a Japanese emphasis on organizational learning and on focal factories as sites for technology transfer and technological innovation. For further information on the studies of patent registrations, see 'Novel Technique Shows Japanese Outpace Americans in Innovation', *New York Times*, 7 Mar. 1988, 1.

2. Desirable institutional traits such as these are sometimes discussed under the heading of flexible manufacturing systems (FMS). While the concept of FMS is useful for describing some aspects of a focal factory, it does not convey many of the important themes and overtones that interlace this concept. Most importantly, the literature on FMS is not greatly concerned with such issues as the social and technical history of factory organization and product development, the strategic management process as it evolved through an interactive dialogue between head office division and manufacturing facility, the significance of institutional learning as a precondition for product planning, design, and manufacturing control, and, most critically, the prior necessity of organizational culture, managerial leadership, and human-resource flexibility if a FMS strategy is pursued.

3. For a complete ethnographic description of the Yanagicho Works and an analysis of the historical importance as well as future implications of focal factories in Japan, see W. Mark Fruin, *Knowledge Works* (Oxford University Press, forthcoming).

4. In the forthcoming study, cited above, I use the term development factory instead of focal factory. I have avoided the development-factory term in this study because I wish to emphasize that the role of focal or lead factories is more than simply development. While the development function has become increasingly important during the postwar years, it is by no means the only important function performed by focal factories.

5. Alan R. Beckenstein, 'Scale Economies in the Multiplant Firm: Theory and Empirical Evidence', *Bell Journal of Economics*, 6/2 (Autumn 1975), 644–57.

6. Nathan Rosenberg and W. Edward Steinmueller, 'Why are Americans such Poor Imitators?', *American Economic Review*, 78/2 (May 1988), 229–34.

7. Mary Douglas, *How Institutions Think* (Syracuse, NY: Syracuse University Press, 1986).

8. The conceptual foundations of the focal factory as a new architecture for manufacturing innovation and productivity may be found in the reference in n. 2 above.

9. See Wickham Skinner, *Manufacturing: The Formidable Competitive Weapon* (New York: John Wiley & Sons, 1985); Steven C. Wheelwright, 'Japan: Where Operations Really Are Strategic', 67–74, and Robert H. Hayes, 'Why Japanese Factories Work', 57–66, both appearing in the *Harvard Business Review*, July/Aug. 1981.

10. Kenneth Flamm's study of the development of computers in Japan verifies the importance of a handful of developmental laboratories and factories for the formative stages of computer manufacture in Japan. See his *Creating the Computer* (Washington, DC: The Brookings Institution, 1988), ch. 6.

11. *Tokyo Shibaura Denki Kabushiki Kaisha Hachijugonenshi* (85 Years of the Tokyo Shibaura Electric Corporation) (Tokyo: Daiyamondo, 1963), 895–9.

12. The average periods required to perfect products in the R & D stage when borrowed as opposed to self-developed technology is employed in Japan are considerably shorter. Across all industries, the R & D incubation period using borrowed technology is 2.36 years as opposed to 3.54 years. In some industries, the contrast is even sharper: pulp and paper, 1.39 to 4.00; chemicals, 2.74 to 5.45; pharmaceuticals, 5.38 to 8.08; oil and coal products, 2.21 to 4.57; industrial machinery, 1.63 to 2.96; communications, electronics, and electrical instruments, 1.83 to 3.43; and transportation, communications, and utilities, 2.80 to 3.59 years. See *Japan Economic Survey*, 10/5 (May 1986), 8–9.

13. National Science Foundation, *The Science and Technology Resources of Japan: A Comparison with the United States* (Washington, DC: NSF 88–318, 1988), pp. x, 7–8.

14. William J. Abernathy and J. M. Utterback, 'A Dynamic Model of Process and Product Innovation', *Omega*, 3/6 (1975), 639.

15. Mudge, Rose, Guthrie, Alexander, and Ferdon, 'Investigation into Sales of Propeller Milling Machines to the Soviet Union by Toshiba Machine Co., Ltd.', in *Report to the President and Directors of Toshiba Corporation* (Washington, DC, 1987).

16. Tokyo Shibaura Denki, *Toshiba Hyakunenshi* (Tokyo: Daiyamondo, 1977), 301–2.

17. Masahiro Shimotani, 'Gendai Kigyo-gurupu no kozo to kino', in Kazuichi Sakamoto (ed.), *Gijutsu Kakushin to Kigyo Kozo* (Technological Innovation and Comparison, Structure) (Kyoto: Minerva Press, 1986), 214. A more recent statement of Shimotani's ideas may be found in Kazuichi Sakamoto and Masahiro Shimotani (eds.), *Gendai Nippon no Kigyo Gurupu* (Contemporary Japanese Enterprise groups) (Tokyo: Toyo Keizai, 1987).

18. Akitake Taniguchi, 'Gigyobusei soshiki no gendankai', in Sakamoto (ed.), *Gijutsu Kakushin to Kigyo Kozo*, 149–51.

19. Tokyo Shibaura Denki, *Toshiba Hyakunenshi*, 624–5.

20. The product history sections of this paper are drawn from two sources. Tokyo Shibaura Denki, *Toshiba Yanagicho Yonjunen no Ayumi* (40 Years of Toshiba's Yanagicho Works) (Kawasaki, 1976), and Toshiba, *Sozo: Toshiba Yanagicho Kojo Gojunenshi* (Create: 50 years of Toshiba Yanagicho Works) (Kawasaki, 1987).

21. Tokyo Shibaura Denki, *Kabushiki Kaisha Hachijugonenshi* (85 years of Tokyo Shibaura Electric Corporation) (Tokyo: Daiyamondo, 1963), 247–52.

22. Also in 1947, a sports as well as a cultural pavilion were constructed and tennis courts were laid out. The plant's management was attempting to wipe away the physical evidence of bombings from the factory grounds and the psychological remnants from factory employees. The women's basketball team from Yanagicho has been particularly successful. It won the All Japan Industrial League in 1950 and 1954. When I visited the factory for the second time in 1986, the Yanagicho women were third in Japan.

23. Taniguchi, 'Gigyobusei', in Sakamoto (ed.) *Gijutsu Kakushin*, 151.

24. Tokyo Shibaura Denki, *Toshiba Hyakunenshi*, 215–18.

25. Taniguchi, 'Gigyobusei', in Sakamoto (ed.) *Gijutsu Kakushin*, 155–6.

26. Again, my sources for the product history of the Yanagicho Works are found in n. 20 above.

27. Taniguchi, 'Gigyobusei', in Sakamoto (ed.), *Gijutsu Kakushin*, 159, 162, and 170.

28. Tokyo Shibaura Denki, *Toshiba Hyakunenshi*, 216–17.

29. Again, I am relying on the sources cited in n. 20 above.

30. MITI, *Agency of Industrial Science and Technology*, pamphlet (Tokyo, 1987), 9.

31. Tokyo Shibaura Denki, *Toshiba Hyakunenshi*, 214.

32. Taniguchi, 'Gigyobusei', in Sakamoto (ed.), *Gijutsu Kakushin*, 155.

33. Ibid. 157–8.

34. See my paper on the supplier network for the Yanagicho Works, entitled 'Cooperation and Competition: Supplier Networks in the Japanese Electronics Industry', UC Berkeley, Japan Seminar, 4 Nov. 1987.

35. An in-depth case-study of the IC card development project will be part of another book, *Knowledge Works* (Oxford University Press, forthcoming).

36. This information was obtained through interviews with the managers of the card-

systems department of the Yanagicho Works during the summer of 1987.
37. *Nikkei Business*, 11 May 1987, 38–41. The reshuffling of organizational boundaries, sectors or groups within sectors for heavy electrical equipment occurred as below:

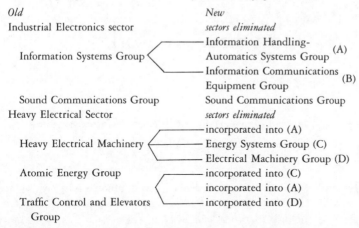

Old	*New*
Industrial Electronics sector	*sectors eliminated*
Information Systems Group	Information Handling-Automatics Systems Group (A)
	Information Communications Equipment Group (B)
Sound Communications Group	Sound Communications Group
Heavy Electrical Sector	*sectors eliminated*
Heavy Electrical Machinery	incorporated into (A)
	Energy Systems Group (C)
	Electrical Machinery Group (D)
Atomic Energy Group	incorporated into (C)
	incorporated into (A)
Traffic Control and Elevators Group	incorporated into (D)

38. 'Toshiba: Kiso Kenkyu no Tsugi ni Itte', *Trigger*, 9/3 (Feb. 1990), 7.
39. Paul Willman, *Technological Change, Collective Bargaining, and Industrial Efficiency* (Oxford: Oxford University Press, 1986), 87–8.
40. See James C. Abegglen and George Stalk, *Kaisha: The Japanese Corporation* (New York: Basic Books, 1985), for a discussion of how conditions of rapid economic growth affect corporate-level strategy and structure in Japan.
41. Learning environments like Yanagicho's seem analogous to the wet-rice agriculture that flourished in pre-industrial Japan: marginal labor inputs almost always boosted marginal grain outputs. For a full discussion of the point, see the source cited in n. 3 above. Also see Thomas C. Smith, *The Agrarian Origins of Modern Japan* (Stanford, Calif.: Stanford University Press, 1959), for a discussion of wet-rice agriculture and marginal returns.
42. See e.g. Nathan Rosenberg's many writings on technological innovation, from 'The Direction of Technological Change: Inducement Mechanisms and Focusing Devices', *Economic Development and Cultural Change*, 18/1 (Oct. 1969), to *Inside the Black Box: Technology and Economics* (Cambridge: Cambridge University Press, 1982). For a suggestion of possible plant-wide effects, see Graham Hall and Sydney Howell, 'The Experience Curve from the Economist's Perspective', *Strategic Management Journal*, 6/6 (1985). Also, Henry A. Glick and Michael J. Feuer, 'Employer-Sponsored Training and Governance of Specific Human Capital Investments', *Quarterly Review of Economics and Business*, 24/2 (Summer 1984), and Ann P. Bartel and Frank R. Lichtenberg, 'The Comparative Advantage of Educated Workers in Implementing New Technology', *Review of Economics and Statistics*, 69/1 (Feb. 1987).
43. This is true not only at Toshiba but also at various other leading electrical-equipment makers. In Japan, Professor Banri Asanuma has written of this fundamental distinction in Japanese manufacturing. See his 'Setsubi Toshi Kettei no Prosesu to Kijun (2)' (Decision-making Processes and Standards for Plant and Equipment Investments), *Keizai Ronso* (Economic Papers), Kyoto University, Department of Economics, 130–5/6 (Nov.–Dec. 1982), 44–5.

7

Interfirm Networks

I

Multi-layered Managerial Coordination and the Toyota
Enterprise Group

The Toyota production system, which defines Toyota Motor Company's approach
to automobile design, manufacture, and distribution is composed broadly of two
parts: what goes on inside Toyota, and what occurs outside Toyota within the
network of firms supporting Toyota. The success of this combined system is
noteworthy. Measured by sales, the Toyota Motor Company is the largest industrial company in Japan, and the third largest automobile and truck maker in the
world. Measured by the number of employees, however, it is a relatively small
company compared with its Western competitors. Toyota's 65,000 employees
produced over 4.5 million vehicles a year, while General Motors' 750,000 employees made closer to 7.9 million in 1989. Even a specialty car maker like
Daimler-Benz employed 370,000 in 1989 when cars and trucks accounted for 75
percent of sales and 90 percent of profits.[1]

Inside Toyota, clockwork-like meshings of just-in-time production have been
described in far greater detail than the workings of a highly articulated supplier
network outside Toyota. Yet, the internal and external dynamics of the Toyota
production system are intimately wedded and equally significant to Toyota's
success. Considered separately and together, the history and integration of these
inner and outer dimensions of the Toyota production system reaffirm a number of
basic themes of this book—the importance of organizational learning, the significance of economies of scope as well as of scale for corporate performance, the
utility of interfirm networks, and the progressive linking of intrafirm/interfirm
organizational capabilities. These organizational features have enabled Toyota
Motor to become one of the world's most successful companies without becoming a
particularly large one.

Types of Interfirm Networks

Toyota's interfirm network of suppliers is an example of vertical task-force coalitions as opposed to other sorts of interfirm networks which emphasize ties of a
financial or historical nature, or which may exist for purposes of research and

development and information exchange. Generally speaking, there are as many different ways to affiliate in networks as there are reasons to collaborate in business. More narrowly conceived, however, business combinations may be grouped into loosely coupled and tightly coupled networks. And these, in turn, lend themselves to further discrimination.

The former, for example, include companies that share little more than a common point of origin and, thus, some history; in this book, such combinations are called namesake groups, and include many of the companies bearing the illustrious Mitsubishi, Yasuda, Mitsui, or Sumitomo prefix in their company names. Today, Mitsubishi Heavy Industry has little to do with Mitsubishi Paper although in the past the two companies may have had a close business relationship, and both were part of a wider coalition of Mitsubishi companies under the direction of the Iwasaki family holding company and its financial representatives. But, in contemporary Japan, even though dozens of companies carry the Mitsubishi name, a minority of them are actually interdependent in business transactions.

Other loosely coupled business associations are Presidents' Councils, where chief executive officers exchange business intelligence, discuss trends, debate the feasibility and desirability of business projects, and in general share and shape viewpoints. Nevertheless, in spite of the abundant discussion and debate at Presidents' Councils, few issues of substance are decided there. They are left instead to the deliberations of those parties most directly affected by the proposed activities; such parties may or may not sit together on Presidents' Councils.

Intermediate between loosely and tightly coupled networks are companies joined financially, by considerations of interfirm shareholding. Depending upon the degree of cross-firm shareholding, financial sinews can dictate, if not determine, the kind and frequency of business transactions. It does not require anything like majority ownership to have a prominent voice in a company's strategic direction. Often, a single block representing 10 percent or less of a firm's outstanding shares can exert considerable influence, particularly if such shareholding is coupled with other group shareholdings and buttressed by other business relationships.

The latter condition is especially important in the case of banks where the law dictates a 5 percent limit on shareholding in other firms. However, the days when finances alone could induce a cooperative attitude among the member companies of an interfirm network have passed, as family holding companies were disbanded during the post-war Occupation era, as closely held intergroup shareholding has declined, as financial markets have been liberalized, and as a heavy reliance on bank debt rather than corporate financing through equity issues, publicly traded debentures, and retained earnings has declined. In general, financially oriented groups, once the core of Japan's industrial order, have diminished remarkably in importance and solidarity in recent decades, moving them from the tightly coupled to loosely coupled category of business coalitions.

Tightly coupled, non-financial combinations of companies have grown in significance as opportunities for economies of scale and scope have gained ground during the past half-century. Companies only somewhat related by history, financial ties, or other weakly articulated business links, have decided to work more closely together for their mutual advantage. In the post-war era, tightly coupled combinations for large-scale developmental projects, such as petrochemical refineries, communication satellite systems, and long-distance telephone service have been noteworthy. Also, tightly coupled constellations of firms are increasingly common in manufacturing industries producing intricate, high-value-added equipment and machinery with many parts and sub-assemblies. These products permit a highly specialized division of labor where a number of different companies can produce components and subsystems for a larger whole.

Yet even within tightly coupled groupings, extremes exist. Tightly coupled relationships may be governed by ongoing contractual negotiations on one hand, or by considerations of lineage, long-term relationship, and hierarchy on the other. In terms of relations with Toyota Motor, Daihatsu falls more into the former type and Nippondenso into the latter. Today, however, Daihatsu is moving towards a more hierarchical relationship with Toyota while Nippondenso is exploring a more reciprocal relationship with Toyota.

This chapter focuses on what happens within firms supplying goods and services to Toyota. Arguably, what happens in the outer shell of the Toyota production system is more important than what happens inside, because Toyota is more a designer and assembler than a manufacturer of trucks and automobiles. Toyota is not exceptional in this regard; all nine automotive companies in Japan emphasize design and assembly over manufacture. Such emphases make Toyota what it is: a global company designing and selling motor vehicles largely made by others. Toyota illustrates perfectly the constituent elements of the Japanese enterprise system: the interdependency of multi-function factories, strategy coordinating firms, production and distribution networks.

Hence, the reasons for Toyota's smaller size but greater output (in 1984 Toyota produced an amazing 66.7 cars per employee while General Motors managed 11.5) are readily apparent: it is much less vertically integrated and diversified by product line than its American counterpart. In these ways, Toyota fits the general model of the Japanese firm as described in this volume. Seen alone, Japanese enterprises are specialized in form and function; seen as parts of a wider association of related firms, Japanese companies are formidable building-blocks of macro-organizational diversity and integration.

Toyota, in fact, buys about 75 percent of the sales value of its cars in the form of parts, components, and services supplied by other companies. General Motors' purchase-to-sales ratio is about 50 percent.[2] Thus, Toyota is around 50 percent less vertically integrated than General Motors, indicating that Toyota is much more specialized and focused than GM. In addition, General Motors owns GM Hughes Electronics, Allison Gas Turbine, Electronic Data Systems, Military Vehicle Operations, Saturn Corporation, and a successful locomotive group as well as fourteen associated companies in which GM's stake is less than 51 percent—all businesses, except for Saturn, somewhat afield from its core motor vehicle business.

Toyota Motor, by contrast, has nearly cut itself free of the prefabricated housing business, one of its rare ventures outside of motor vehicles.

Specialization and its concomitant, the division of labor, are so pronounced in Toyota's case because more than 30,000 suppliers fuel Toyota's factories on a 24-hour, precisely scheduled basis. This colossal supporting cast, described in this chapter, enables Toyota to buy much more than it makes, and thereby to concentrate on design and assembly rather than manufacture.

Toyota's Strategy of Interdependence

Toyota Motor Corporation offers perhaps the most outstanding example of a tightly coupled interfirm network. Toyota's interfirm alliance is in fact a mammoth, largely externalized, managerial hierarchy to integrate, coordinate, plan, procure, produce, and distribute. Toyota's strategy was to align these many functions among dozens, even hundreds, of production units organized in multi-layered and multi-tiered structures. Toyota aimed to control directly only the first-tier of this network, relying on first-tier companies to control second-tier units and so on down the hierarchy of suppliers.

Toyota did not begin with this strategy. Instead, starting in the late 1950s, Toyota converted its suppliers, already numerous, into contract assemblers and systems-component manufacturers. They, in turn, reorganized lower tiers of suppliers in the same manner. Organizational control functions were clustered at the interstices of these tiers or levels, so that Toyota did not control the whole system itself even though it provided functional leadership and strategic direction.[3]

The amount and degree of coordination between companies in Toyota's network are truly remarkable, and this extraordinary interdependence is the main subject of this chapter. Task-force networks represent the epitome of tightly coupled interfirm systems. Such systems benefit Toyota Motor in two ways. They permit Toyota to gain most of the advantages of vertical integration in production and distribution without the disadvantages (high risk and high cost). Toyota can offer a full-line of trucks and automobiles to satisfy every consumer need and whim without investing itself fully in the people, plant, and facilities necessary to do so. However, such a strategy does require Toyota to invest in and manage institutional relationships with suppliers.

This strategy evolved from Toyota's limited resources in the face of formidable challenges: the historical weaknesses (of technical capability and of demand) of the automobile industry at home and a global oligopoly in the automobile industry abroad. Toyota's success with this strategy has become a model for other automobile makers in Japan and in the West. Reportedly, Western makers have been moving towards disaggregating their production systems and corporate resources. In short, they are beginning to buy more than they make in the production of automobiles and trucks.[4]

The strategic strength of Toyota is largely the strength of its supporting cast of firms. Toyota's greatest success, therefore, may not be what it has accomplished on its own as much as what it has encouraged, allowed, and required others to do. Toyota sits astride the world's most effectively coordinated interfirm network to achieve economies of scale in manufacturing, while offering a full-line of automobiles and trucks and a wide selection of models, options, styles, and accessories.

This organization revolution—comprising the intricate coordination of a far-reaching and multi-layered network of interrelated enterprises focused in a single product-line—is the essence of the Toyota production system, and this chapter will concentrate on relating how Toyota accomplished this, both by describing the history of Toyota and some of its major affiliates, and by analyzing the organizational methods employed by Toyota to achieve effective coordination among tens of thousands of supporting firms.

However, this chapter should be read in conjunction with Chapter 6 where Toshiba's structures and strategies of production are characterized. No less revolutionary, the Toshiba production system relies less on outside affiliates and more on internal resources. This approach, epitomized by Toshiba's differentiation of its production facilities into focal and mass-production factories, is consonant with the fungibility of the underlying technologies found in the electrical-equipment/electronics industry as opposed to the automobile industry. It also illustrates a different sort of organizational learning, one more appropriate to the nature of enterprises in the electrical-equipment/electronics industry.

To understand Toyota's interfirm network approach to managerial coordination, three descriptive concepts are employed. It is the *intensity* (from loosely to tightly coupled), the *density* (from several dozens to hundreds of independent enterprises), and the *duration* (from intermittent to recurring) of ties among the Toyota family of firms which needs to be understood. History reveals the ways in which Toyota's interfirm network evolved and how intensity, density, and duration describe the ties that bind Toyota to its suppliers.

A Short History of Toyota Motor

From Looms to Automobiles

Toyota Motor history begins as another Toyoda story ends. In 1930, at the age of 63 and on his deathbed, Sakichi Toyoda reportedly confided in his son Kiichiro:

The automatic loom business was my life's work. I had nothing but ideas and my two hands when I first started out. You should have your own life's work.

I believe in the automobile. It will become indispensable in the future. Why not make it your life's work?[5]

Sakichi gave Kiichiro a million yen to get started. This represented the royalty income that Sakichi had received from the Platt Brothers Ind., the leading

British loom maker, for the sale of Toyoda patents to the English firm. Father and son had actually worked together on the technology found in the patents, and it seemed somehow fitting that the income, effort, and experience of one generation and one technology should now become the seedbed for another age and technology.

Toyoda Automatic Loom Works Ltd., the parent company of what would become the Toyota enterprise group, had been incorporated by Sakichi in 1926 in order to supply the booming cotton-spinning and weaving companies in Japan with machinery of domestic manufacture. As the largest maker of specialized textile machinery in a country where textiles were the most important industry, Toyoda Automatic Loom grew to one of Japan's largest industrial firms (the 191st largest, ranked by assets, in 1930, just four years after its founding), providing yet another successful example of the adaptation and domestication of foreign technology to Japanese economic and market conditions.[6]

Kiichiro was well prepared to tackle his father's challenge. He had graduated in mechanical engineering from the University of Tokyo, the most prestigious university in Japan. He had spent nearly two decades refining his engineering, production, and managerial know-how in his father's automatic loom company. But Kiichiro's vision was more far-reaching than his father's. He had foreseen the promise of the automobile even before Sakichi's last words. Kiichiro had already decided to create an automobile of Japanese design and manufacture.[7]

At the time, motor cars in Japan were almost entirely American-made but locally assembled from knockdown kits. (Fifty years later, the tables have turned. Japanese motor-vehicle makers now export knockdown kits world-wide.) General Motors and Ford had assembly plants in Osaka and Yokohama respectively, while a handful of European vehicles were imported fully assembled. Three struggling Japanese makers, Ishikawajima Industries, Tokyo Electric-Gas Industries, and DAT Motors, together managed a meager output of several thousand cars per year in the early 1930s. In short, the domestic market for automobiles was not large and it was dominated by General Motors and Ford.

As Managing Director in charge of production and technology at Toyoda Automatic Loom Works, Kiichiro enjoyed great freedom in his activities. He used this leeway to purchase on company account his first automobile in 1931 and to educate himself and his staff in its use. Deciding to take the car apart and reverse-engineer its parts, he began to import high-quality machine tools from Germany and the United States; he rearranged the layout of one of the loom factories in order to accommodate chrome-plating equipment, molding machinery, and an electric furnace; he added a conveyor assembly-line, bought a small French-made engine, disassembled it, sketched it, and reassembled the parts.[8]

By the late summer of 1931, Kiichiro's copies of the French engine were mounted on bicycles and run in the factory compound. So far, Kiichiro's dream of domestic auto manufacture had been kept to himself and close associates. When Kiichiro decided to repeat the reverse-engineering process on a 1933 Chevrolet sedan and he needed more sophisticated tools, a larger place, and more personnel, it became impossible to hide the project any longer.

At the close of 1933 Toyoda Automatic Loom Works authorized 3 million yen for the establishment of an automobile division and dedicated a 9,000-square-meter plot for the new venture. Kiichiro sent men to Europe and the United States to buy equipment, visit auto and auto-parts makers, study foreign manufacturing techniques, and in general absorb as much as possible about the design, production, and distribution of automobiles abroad.

Kiichiro put up the flimsiest plant possible, funnelling every last yen towards the purchase of machine tools, testing and manufacturing equipment, as well as towards applied research and development. He decided not to waste valuable time and money on developing his own designs, and instead he simply copied selected American models. Engine design was taken from Chevrolet, transmissions, axles, and chassis from Ford, and body style from Desoto/Chrysler.[9] Determined to distance the new effort from past business, Kiichiro named the new product 'Toyota' rather than Toyoda.

Simply put, Kiichiro had neither the manpower nor the know-how to produce an automobile of Japanese manufacture, even if the basic designs were reverse-engineered from American models. And unlike some other Japanese firms, Toyota could not rely on technology transfers from overseas to ease the start-up process. Both General Motors and Ford were producing in Japan and thus disinclined to help Toyota in any fashion. Later, around 1938–9, when Ford was being forced out of the Japanese market by a military-dominated Government, the Army twice nixed a friendly sale to Toyota.[10]

For auto parts, Kiichiro turned to domestic sources of supply, of which there were three. First, there were established automobile- and truck-parts makers serving the quite limited replacement-parts market, mostly for foreign vehicles. Second, there were a handful of parts makers currently producing for other domestic manufacturers, like Isuzu, Hino, and Nissan (which by the late 1930s had absorbed the auto manufacturing efforts of Ishikawajima Industries, Tokyo Electric-Gas Industries, and DAT Motors). These makers could be wooed by Kiichiro because they were producing at low volumes. Finally, Kiichiro could find and hopefully convince non-auto companies to make parts according to his specifications.

At first Kiichiro employed all three channels of domestic supply, as he was intent on producing his car in the shortest time possible. It was obvious, however, that the last alternative of creating his own supply network, was the most certain means of securing a dependable source of supply. Yet this choice would require the greatest effort, most money, and time of the three. Nevertheless, Kiichiro scoured the Nagoya countryside and eventually succeeded in recruiting a number of supporting parts makers to supplement his internal efforts.

A few of the enterprises that allied themselves with Kiichiro in the early days included Kayadokoro Industries (founded in March 1935), Kyowai Leather (August 1935), Koito Engineering (April 1936), Nippon Specialty Ceramics (October 1936), and in 1938, Aisan Industries, Aichi Steel, Kawashima Weaving, Shiga Chassis Industries, and, finally, in 1939, Sugiura Engineering, Daido Metal,

Otomo Industries, Chuo Precision Tools, Imperial Piston Ring, and Shiko Industries. All of these were local firms with strong ties to Toyota Motor.

In November 1936 when only 200 vehicles were produced, 51 percent of the manufacturing cost of the vehicles came from purchased parts. And, in 1939 when 12,000 units were manufactured, 66 percent of the manufacturing cost were purchased parts. Already in a 1939 Board Meeting, only five years after the authorization of the motor vehicle manufacturing venture, the extent of Toyota's reliance on suppliers was an issue for discussion. It was decided that the number of parts and components sourced from suppliers should be reduced by one-third, from 570 to 380. A *Kyohokai* or 'Association of Toyota Suppliers' was established at the same time to gain some measure of control over suppliers which now accounted for 55 percent of all parts in Toyota vehicles.[11]

At this time the nature of the ties between Toyota Motor and its suppliers could be characterized as low-powered with reference to their intensity, density, and duration. Even so, by the outbreak of the Pacific War in 1941, Toyota Motor was regularly contracting with four to five dozen independent suppliers.[12] Two-thirds of the parts and components sourced from suppliers came from the Nagoya area, while one-third came from either Tokyo or Osaka, considerable distances away.[13]

A prototype passenger car was completed in May 1935 and a prototype truck in August of the same year. Though Kiichiro had aimed at producing for the domestic market, the military situation in China and a depressed economy at home dictated that trucks and not automobiles rolled from the newly completed assembly plant in 1936. As relations worsened between Japan and China, the government passed the Automobile Industry Act of 1936 and designated Toyoda Automatic Loom Works as one of the approved manufacturers of cars and trucks. The future of the enterprise seemed assured, even if it was a somewhat different future than Kiichiro had first dreamed.

The Birth of Toyota Motor Company

In 1937 the automobile division of Toyoda Automatic Loom Works was separately incorporated as the Toyota Motor Company. The new company started well, with paid-in capital of 9 million yen and 3,123 employees. These figures included neither the capital nor the workers of the firms providing parts and services to Kiichiro's company.[14]

The capacity of the new plant was considered enormous for the day, 2,000 units per year yet Kiichiro began construction of a new plant, the Koromo Works, almost immediately. Koromo would produce that many vehicles per month. Koromo was completed in 1938, and it represented the first motor vehicle plant in Japan with true economies of scale. General Motors and Ford together assembled 30,000 units per year at their pre-war peak.

The Koromo Works, Toyota's lead or focal factory well into the 1950s, was the site for many of Toyota's innovations in production engineering and manufacturing. In order to supply the plant's enormous appetite for fabricated metals,

ferrous and non-ferrous materials, and all manner of parts and components, Toyota
Motor stepped up its efforts to localize a network of suppliers around the
mammoth Koromo plant.

With the outbreak of war in 1937, it became more and more difficult to obtain
good quality steel for automobile and truck fabrication, and, as a result, Kiichiro
established the Toyoda Steel Works in 1940. Toyoda Automatic Loom had been
supplying some of Toyota Motors' needs from its own foundry, but its output was
too limited in the face of Kiichiro's move to increase vehicle production.

In the next year, 1941, Toyoda Machine Works, later renamed Toyota Engineering, was separated from Toyota Motor. It had supplied two sorts of
engineering services: the design of plant equipment and facilities enabling Toyota
to produce an astonishingly large 25,000 vehicles per year; the modification and
retooling of existing equipment to keep pace with production. In addition to these
in-house tasks, Toyota's machine shop had spent much of its time designing,
developing, and making tools for a growing number of local affiliates and suppliers. Separating the shop from the company and making it as profit center,
enabled Toyota Motor to establish cost controls over the use of the engineering
services. As the demand for engineering services could be expected to grow,
splitting off the function early would simplify the management of this important
service later.[15] Coordination between Toyota and Toyoda Machine Works as well
as between Toyota and Toyoda Steel Works and Toyoda Automatic Loom Works
was effected through a Planning Council established in 1941.[16]

At the end of World War Two, nearly 10,000 persons were working for Toyota
Motor. This figure does not include those employed by Toyoda Steel, Toyoda
Engineering, or any supplier affiliated with Toyota Motor. Many of those laboring
at Toyota Motor were students and young girls sent to work there under military
orders. Even so, 3,700 regular workers depended on Toyota Motor for employment
when the Occupation Government, Supreme Command of the Allied Powers or
SCAP for short, placed a total production limit of 1,500 vehicles per month on the
domestic motor-vehicle industry.

At this point, Kiichiro decided to disintegrate production facilities and to
decentralize operations as far as it was possible. This was done in order to reduce
costs, lessen risks, and free workers to find whatever work available. Indeed,
Toyota's highly skilled machinists and engineers made anything and everything,
producing cooking ware, furniture, electrical appliances, and farming implements.

Disaggregation and Reorganization

In August 1945 Toyota's truck-body plant was spun off as Toyota Auto Body
Company. In June 1946 the aircraft-parts production facilities were sold to Aichi
Industries, and later merged in 1965 with Shinkawa Industries to become Aisin
Seiki, one of Toyota Motor's most important suppliers. According to the economic
policies of SCAP, holding companies with a capitalization in excess of 5 million
yen were to be dissolved. Accordingly Toyoda Industries Company, the holding

company for the Toyoda group, was dismembered. The trading functions performed by the holding company, however, were continued with the establishment of the Nisshin Tsucho Company in July 1948, later renamed as the Toyoda Trading Company. In the last month of 1949 the electrical department of Toyota Motor was hived off as Nippondenso, the enameled ironware division became Aichi Horo Company, and in May 1950 the spinning and weaving department was separated as Toyoda Spinning and Weaving.[17]

While the company has been busily devolving various departments, the Occupation Government had been reconsidering some of its earlier policies. In October 1949 restrictions on the number and kinds of vehicles that could be manufactured in Japan were removed, and Toyota could again consider designing and producing passenger cars. However, the lifting of the ban occurred shortly after the initiation of the so-called Dodge Line (so named after J. M. Dodge, a Detroit banker sent to Japan to recommend measures to control hyper-inflation) that called for a balanced budget, elimination of government subsidies to industries, and an initiation of a fixed exchange rate (360 yen = $1.00).

Tightening-up economic controls did not stimulate passenger-car production, and in 1950 Toyota faced a ten-month labor strike over issues of working conditions and low wages. While the strike stalled production, the marketing department of Toyota Motor was separated as an independent firm in order to allow Toyota to sell vehicles. Toyota was dangerously close to bankruptcy. A local banking syndicate was willing to bankroll a sales company using the unsold inventory of automobiles as collateral, but only if the vehicles could be protected from Toyota Motor's debts. The bank syndicate further demanded accelerated rationalization of production facilities and the dismissal of surplus workers.[18]

Kiichiro Toyoda resigned from the presidency of Toyota Motor just as war erupted across the Korean Peninsula in the summer of 1950. He is thought to have taken this action because of the company's disappointing post-war performance. Taizo Ishida, President of Toyoda Automatic Loom, succeeded Kiichiro, implementing with just a few changes the five-year plan that Kiichiro had developed. It called for a doubling of the company's monthly production, to 3,000 units, without increasing the number of employees. This could be accomplished only by rationalizing and modernizing the company facilities.[19] At the time in 1950, the entire output of the Japanese automobile and truck industry, at some 31,597 units, amounted to little more than one day's output for the American auto industry.[20]

1950 found Toyota Motor in serious straits. Production was down, the payroll could not be met, the president had resigned, and the company had been split up in an attempt to lower costs, simplify management, and reduce risk. Nine major units had been cleaved from the firm. They were:

Toyoda Steel Works	separated in 1940
Toyota Engineering	1941
Toyota Auto Body	1945
Aichi Industries	1945

Toyoda Trading (Nisshin Tsucho)	1949
Nippondenso	1949
Aichi Horo	1949
Toyoda Spinning and Weaving	1950
Toyota Motor Sales	1950

Toyota Motor and the Japanese automobile industry were on the ropes.

The desire to decentralize operations, to dis-integrate production, and to dis-aggregate distribution from production was not based on a far-sighted strategy of corporate restructuring. Instead, the actions were designed to allow Toyota Motor a little more breathing space and a bit more time before the company would have to fold up and close down.

Korean War Revival

The outbreak of the Korean War in June 1950 kicked-off the post-war recovery of Japan. To Toyota it brought orders for military vehicles and special machinery, and it swelled the depressed Japanese economy with millions of badly needed dollars.

At this point, the Government offered to sell a large number of high-quality machine tools that had been owned by military arsenals during the war. Toyota Motor was able to pick up 200 of these. The new machine tools made it possible to increase production without increasing the size of the workforce. Wartime demand considerably eased Taizo Ishida's task of implementing Kiichiro's five-year plan. Rationalization and modernization were being accomplished simultaneously.[21]

Inside Toyota, the production-line layout and materials-handling efficiency of the Toyota plants were enhanced and factory lighting, sanitation, and safety standards were all upgraded. For the first time, automatic-inspection equipment was introduced on the line, necessitating improvements in the organization of production. Rather than attempt to direct change from above, Ishida chose to reduce administrative overhead by pushing production responsibilities downward and outward.

In 1954 a prototype *kanban-shiki* or 'action-plate' system of production was introduced in Toyota's main engine-assembly plant. Products were 'pulled' rather than 'pushed' through the factory. Toyota called this the 'supermarket system' because it stored parts and components in standardized containers at designated locations along the production line—in the same way that supermarkets replenish their shelves. The system was improved, reworked and introduced into all of Toyota's factories by 1963.[22]

At the same time, outside Toyota, Toyota Motor was organizing its suppliers into an association designed to improve the quality of production, management, and communication. The original Association of Toyota Suppliers, the *Kyohokai*, was founded in November 1939, but as wartime controls on the purchase and sale of raw and intermediate goods made it nearly impossible for suppliers to get what they needed, the Association was more akin to that of a black market clearinghouse than a management improvement association. Shortages, deficiencies, and horse-trading were the story.

In 1946 and 1947 *Kyohokai*, which had been disbanded by the war's end, were reformed in eastern, central, and western Japan. They numbered 155 firms: 108 in the central region around Nagoya where Toyota Motor was located, 31 to the east including Tokyo, and 16 in the west. Three years later, in 1950, only 16 firms had been added, indicating the slow pace of production during the Occupation years.[23]

But Toyota Motor could not respond to Korean War demand without bolstering and advancing the capabilities of suppliers. In 1951 Toyota offered Management Training Programs (MTP) and Training Within Industry Programs (TWI) to suppliers. Toyota offered these without charge and although voluntary, it was expected that suppliers would attend and excel.[24]

A simultaneous strengthening of the production and managerial systems within Toyota along with a renewal of the linkages between Toyota and its suppliers led to the evolution of a corporation where inner and outer dimensions of design, development, and production cannot be disentangled. The intricacy of this inter-dependence is both the strength and the weakness of the system. Efforts to raise production, production know-how, and operations management within Toyota Motor and its Association of Suppliers materialized most clearly in 1955 with the production of the 'Crown', a 1,500 cc model that was the first mass-produced passenger car in Japan. Introducing a second model, the 1,000 cc 'Corona' in 1957, Toyota's output reached 30,000 units per month. This was far, far in excess of production before or during the Pacific War years. During the 1960s, new model followed new model, pushing Toyota's monthly output to over 100,000 units in 1968.

As a result of a decade of hothouse expansion from the mid-1950s to mid-1960s, Toyota learned how to assemble many different kinds of vehicles on the same production lines. This marvelous feat of manufacturing, which permits full and steady production of an impressive range or vehicles, was reared from the marriage of the Toyota production system with the factory-automation technologies of such companies as Mitsubishi Electric and Omron Tateishi Electric. Electronic sensors detect changes in the types of vehicles moving down the line, automatically supplying the needed parts and accessories for each model as they move through the production process. There are limits to this capability of course; large trucks cannot be assembled on lines designed to handle small cars and light vans.

Reaching the Top

By pioneering managerial and technical innovations during the 1950s and 1960s, Toyota pushed itself to the top of the automotive industry in Japan by the 1970s. In 1960 Toyota made 480,000 cars and trucks. Ten years later in 1970, it produced ten times as many, reaching the astonishing annual total of 5,290,000 vehicles.

The rapid expansion of Toyota can be credited to numerous causes. First, and most importantly, the company continually reinvested profits in modernizing plant and equipment, improving labor productivity, upgrading inspection and control systems, reducing costs, and enhancing management. Also, Toyota aimed to achieve not only manufacturing economies of scale but also economies of scope and transaction-cost economies through the creation of an interfirm network.

The latter two economies were realized by forging of a system of managerial coordination that joined the production and distribution facilities of hundreds of firms associated with Toyota. This lowered operating costs per transaction for each company as well as for the group as a whole. The localization and integration of many supplier firms in the vicinity of Nagoya allowed firms to deal directly with one another without imposing an intermediating layer of bureaucratic organization. Proximity promoted the quantity and quality of business transactions.

By the 1970s, Toyota's production and supply systems gave it three significant advantages over its rivals. First, it had achieved minimum efficient scale in manufacturing without internalizing much of the production process. Most of the parts and components that went into Toyota's automobiles were made instead by affiliated firms, reducing Toyota's direct costs of production. Second, as a result, Toyota could offer a full line of vehicles—some two dozen auto and truck models in the 1970s and more since then. Toyota is perhaps the world's most systematic developer of 'contract assemblers'.

Finally, Toyota could offer its customers several thousand possible combinations of colors, engines, shapes, sizes, and fittings per model. Most cars in Japan are customized according to a buyer's specifications *after* its purchase. This is made possible through the computerization of dealers' orders and Toyota's no-inventory, just-in-time system of production and supply. Customers get their cars in a timely fashion because suppliers respond quickly and effectively to Toyota's orders.[25]

Toyota's strategy, a full-line, full-option, volume production of vehicles without vertical integration in production and distribution, is uncommonly successful. Economies of scale and scope were realized without internalizing most of the production and supply process. In short, Toyota Motor realized scale economies without scale, transforming the logistical and technical problems that such a strategy demands into matters of manageable proportion.

The Cottage Industry Analogy

Toyota has been likened to the world's largest cottage industry. However true this may seem because of the extraordinary division of labor within the Toyota group of companies, it fails to comprehend the sophistication and complexity of Toyota's unique production and procurement system which can be likened to a structured hierarchy of interwoven firms.[26] Hierarchy, interrelated coordination, and operational sophistication do not characterize cottage industries.

The progressive shortening of the time frame within which parts and components are delivered to Toyota is a good illustration of the intergroup coordina-

TABLE 7.1. *Time Periods Used in Delivery Schedules for Parts and Components Supplied to Toyota Motor, 1979 and 1982 (in %)*

	Weekly/monthly	Daily	Hourly	Other
Ferrous/non-ferrous metals				
1979	59.0	40.0	1.0	0.0
1982	38.4	56.7	4.8	0.0
Electrical equipment				
1979	55.5	43.4	0.0	0.0
1982	40.4	55.7	2.5	1.4
Automobile parts/components				
1979	28.3	58.9	10.5	2.3
1982	16.3	51.7	30.5	1.7

Source: Based on original survey research by Prof. Shiomi, partially reproduced in a different format in H. Shiomi, 'The Structure of Production Logistics: The Case of Toyota', in K. Sakamoto (ed.), *Technical Innovation and Enterprise Structure (Gijutsu Kakushin to Kigyo Kozo)* (Kyoto: Minerva Books, 1985), 105.

tion. Table 7.1 details a shift from longer to shorter delivery periods between 1979 and 1982. Since the second oil embargo of 1978, Toyota group companies have improved considerably their terms of delivery and interindustry coordination.

Delivery times and terms are significant because Toyota has some 170 closely affiliated parts manufacturers and several dozen others, from which it regularly buys batteries, tires, and the like. Between 1979 and 1982, the number of suppliers delivering on an hourly as opposed to a daily or weekly basis jumped by 200 percent. The intensity of interfirm ties have been strengthened, by more tightly coupling suppliers to Toyota; rates of productivity and throughput for suppliers have improved by increasing the frequency of their transactions with Toyota. Higher rates of capacity utilization represent a huge saving in the costs of land, labor, and capital as well as in transportation and inventory costs.

Types of Suppliers

As to types of suppliers, there are a few firms that make parts and perform services only for Toyota. These might be called *subcontractors*. There are relatively few first-tier suppliers that are dedicated wholly to production for Toyota. If subcontracting is defined as supplying only firms in the Toyota group, a minority of firms, probably 10–15 percent, fall in this category.

There are other firms that supply automotive parts and components to Toyota and make and market their own non-automotive products. These may be termed *affiliates*. Toyoda Automatic Loom Works and Yamaha Motors are examples. In common Japanese usage, 'affiliates' (*kanren kaisha*) have a financial relationship with a parent company; corporate financial statements, such as *zaimu shohyo kisoku*, spell out the capital requirements for being considered an affiliate or a subsidiary.

There are companies that make auto parts, components, and finished vehicles for Toyota and also market similar or identical products under their own brand names, such as Hino Motors, Daihatsu Motors, and Nippondenso. Companies in this category might be called *independent suppliers*. They are independent companies even though they may be partially owned by Toyota. Nippondenso, about 25 percent owned by Toyota, sold 60 percent of its auto components to Toyota in 1986. The remaining 40 percent was sold to other final-assemblers, except Nissan Motor; Nippondenso's non-auto sales included integrated circuits and residential space heaters.[27]

Finally, there are a number of independent or semi-independent suppliers which are financially independent of capital investment by one final assembler; instead they are partially or equally owned by a number of competing assemblers. Diesel Kiki and Akebono Brake are examples of this sort of independent supplier.

Companies, like Nippondenso, that have achieved independent or semi-independent status illustrate what might be termed the logic of intercorporate evolution in Japan. While all companies do not follow this path, some do and many aspire to:

- They begin as an internal shop or department, and they move up to the status of a division;
- They evolve from a division into a subsidiary or affiliate;
- Finally, they achieve the status of an independent enterprise, if they have acquired sufficient wherewithal to separate themselves from a parent firm.

Of course, not all departments or shops have the resources, leadership, and independence to climb the ladder of intercorporate evolution. Even so-called independent enterprises, it should be pointed out, may remain dependent for a large share of their business on one or several other companies.

Three-Tiered Hierarchy of Suppliers

Japanese auto makers have been increasing the number of models and the range of trim level and mechanical choices per model. How can Japanese motor vehicle manufacturers manage such complexity, both for current and forthcoming models, in a world which is itself so uncertain; Toyota does this, and does it very well, by decentralizing its production, inventory control, purchasing, sub-assembly and, in some cases, even R & D and design activities to a nested hierarchy of interrelated enterprises. There are three (or more) layers or tiers to the hierarchy, resulting in a very large span of control.

TABLE 7.2. *Division of Labor in the Automobile Industry: Toyota Motor Suppliers by Level*[a]

	First-level	Second-level	Third-level	Total
Engine parts	25	912	4,960	5,897
Electrical/electronics	1	34	352	387
Transmission, gears, steering	31	609	7,354	7,994
Brakes, suspension	18	792	6,204	7,014
Brake and suspension parts	18	926	5,936	6,880
Chassis and parts	3	27	85	115
Body and pressing	41	1,213	8,221	9,475
Other	31	924	8,591	9,546
TOTALS	168	5,437	41,703	47,308

[a] In the original MITI study, Toyota Motors is identified as Firm A.

Source: Small- and Medium-Sized Enterprise Agency, MITI, 'An Investigation into the Current Level of the Division of Labor (Automobiles)', mimeograph, 1977. Also cited by H. Shiomi, 'Structure of Production Logistics', in Sakamoto (ed.), *Gijutsu Kakushin to Kigyo Kozo*, 81.

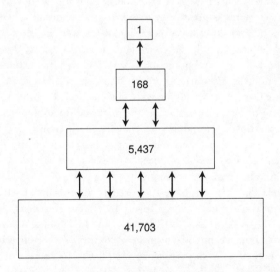

FIG. 7.1. *Toyota Motor Supplier Network: Inter-Level Decentralization of Transactions*

Note: The figures represent the numbers of business units transacting at each level.

The numbers of affiliated makers, both the 'close' or recurrent suppliers and the more 'distant' or periodic suppliers, are large because Toyota usually opts for 'dual' sourcing, that is Toyota rarely relies on one source of supply. Instead, several make *nearly* the same part and this serves as a means of comparative cost and quality control.[28] Toyota does this in two ways, by dealing directly with about 170 of its largest suppliers, and by dealing indirectly with the hundreds and thousands of others. In sharp contrast, traditional practice in the American automobile industry outsourced exactly the same part numbers to at least two suppliers and sometimes more, negotiating single-year contracts with each.[29]

Toyota's relations with the first-tier affiliates and suppliers are based on many considerations. Financial, historical, technical, organizational, and managerial considerations, all play a part. But, in the final analysis, the basic consideration is the technical complexity of the modern automobile. In order to offer a wide selection of colors, styles, interior and mechanical options to customers, a major manufacturer today may need some 15,000 to 20,000 different parts and components on hand for each car and thousands more for each model series. The organizational problems of managing such a sprawling breadth of auto parts, components, and sub-assemblies along with attendant services are vastly minimized by separating the issues of coordination and control at each level of the hierarchy. So, there is an extremely close interface between buyers and sellers at points of inter-level transaction. That is each layer of transactions for the buying and selling of auto parts and services is greatly separated from any and all others. Toshihiro Nishiguchi calls the inter-level decentralization of transactions 'cluster control'.

This principle allows highly specific transactions to occur throughout the supplier network without any appreciable degree of overall control exercised by Toyota, even though the amount of coordination between Toyota and its suppliers as well as between and among suppliers is obviously great. Moreover, the separation of transactions by level permits the intensity and duration of transactions to grow without the density or number of transactions becoming so large at any one point that managerial or operational control is lost. In short, decentralized coordination is maximized and centralized control is minimized even if Toyota Motor sets the overall direction for the group.

Face-to-face relations between buyers and sellers when coupled with inter-level decentralization of transactions, allows Toyota to achieve enormous organizational size and complexity without managerial breakdown. Face-to-face relations patterns also economize on transaction costs by having companies deal directly with each other without internalizing various managerial levels to coordinate, plan, and schedule the flows between steps in production, delivery, and assembly. According to a 1977 study by the Medium- and Small-Sized Enterprise Agency of MITI, Toyota's pyramid of affiliates, suppliers, subcontractors, and sub-subcontractors number some 36,000–47,000 (the variation in number depending upon whether suppliers are counted only once even if they supply auto parts in more than one parts category), which is divided in the manner shown in Table 7.2.

Second-level suppliers work for front-line firms, while third- and fourth-level concerns—often no more than family-sized workshops—supply upper-level firms. The astonishingly large number of enterprises in the extended Toyota group tallies only what might be called separate business units or enterprises; they do *not* include a large number of subordinated shops which do not keep independent business records. As one moves down the levels of suppliers, the number of medium- and small-sized companies and the ratio of female to male employees increases. Sixty-nine percent of the business units below Toyota have less than 300 employees and one-third of these are female.[30]

Obviously, the Toyota hierarchy of interrelated enterprises is huge—much too large for Toyota Motor itself to manage directly. Instead, it confines its activities to the management of the first tier of related firms, and, in turn, the first tier manages the second, and so forth down the line. In this way, the span of control at any one level never becomes too large while the division of labor can be developed in the extreme (see Fig. 7.1).

Another aspect of this division of labor is that Toyota does not attempt to control directly the process of work in thousands of affiliates and suppliers. It does demand and achieve, instead, a high level of standardization of work outputs. Focusing on what is made rather than on how something is made frees Toyota and its first-tier affiliates from internal problems of management and coordination at lower levels in its multi-level pyramid of suppliers. The diffusion of the Toyota production system from Toyota Motor to first-tier companies (during the 1960s) and to lower-tier companies (during the 1970s) does represent a form of indirect control, however.[31] Yet, the diffusion of Toyota's production system was not simply imposed by Toyota Motor. First- and lower-tier companies followed Toyota's lead as a way of enlarging and enhancing their own business opportunities.

Toyota has been anxious to teach its methods of production management, inventory, and cost control to those firms in the Toyota group that are willing to learn. It does this through the Toyota Supplier Association as well as through its methods of management with first-tier suppliers. They, in turn, are expected to apply the methods in their dealings with second-tier supplier, and so on down the line. Toyota Auto Body (Toyota Shatai), to take an example, assembled more than 400,000 trucks and automobiles for Toyota Motor in 1980. This was in addition to 300,000 light trucks and two-door sedans that Toyota Auto Body produced on its own under the Toyota brand name. So, four-sevenths of Toyota Auto Body's output was as a contract assembler for Toyota Motor and three-sevenths was as an independent maker of Toyota badge vehicles. There is no reason to assume a difference in quality between the two although Toyota Motor directly controlled only the former output rather than the latter. Toyota Auto Body's 700,000 unit output was produced not only in its own plants but also in the plants of its lower-tier affiliates and subcontractors, all of which had direct contact with Toyota Auto Body but very few of which had much contact with Toyota Motor.[32]

Toyota's Supply System

In spite of its obviously close relationship with Toyota Motor, Toyota Auto Body has no long-term contract (more than 12–16 months' duration) with Toyota Motor. Instead short-term agreements that specify Toyota Auto Body's costs, their composition, and their method of calculation are used to determine the pricing of goods purchased by Toyota Motor. Instead of fixed-price contracts of a lengthy duration, there is a mutually understood dependence of one company upon the other, and this is expressed in the tightly coupled transactions that bind company to company rather than in tightly worded contracts of good-faith performance.

Because the volume of flow (of parts, people, information, and money) between the two firms is so large, both sides are obviously locked into a long-term relationship with each other. Agreements on costs and prices are effective as long as the delivery of the same model continues, irrespective of quantity fluctuations that might unavoidably occur. Costs and prices are subject to *ex post* adjustments made at six-month intervals. The complexity, intensity, and interdependency of such contracting relationships cannot be easily written down. In fact, this seems unimportant to both parties.

Yet the fact that Toyota Auto Body and Toyota Motor have no long-term contract as practiced in the Western automobile industry is critical. During the 36-month period that it takes to design, fabricate, sub-assemble, and complete a new chassis model, thousands of engineering drawings, plans, and alterations, and hundreds of engineering and management decisions have to be undertaken not only within Toyota Auto Body but also between Toyota Auto Body and Toyota Motor. A vortex of such contingency could not possibly be covered by contracts which assume simple, fixed prices for production runs of lengthy duration.[33]

Of course, some contract-like groundwork is laid for the short-term. Toyota has four levels of production planning: annual estimates, monthly targets, inter-month adjustments (on the 8th, 18th, and 28th of the month), and dealer custom orders (for low-volume models). Thus, expected quantities of a certain part or component are adjusted monthly and prices for such items are negotiated semi-annually. Production targets are fixed from six to nine months in advance of actual production. Prices for finished goods are set according to the cost of raw materials, the cost of parts sourced elsewhere, production costs, a model-specific piece rate, plus an agreed upon mark-up or margin.[34] Obviously, all prices are subject to change— changes in models, specifications, levels of specification, and order volume.

Increases in the costs of labor or energy are absorbed by the sub-assembler or parts maker in Japan. To counteract a rise in these or other costs, there is an agreement that although the price of parts and components to the final assembler will drop over time, decreases in price are matched by labor-saving, productivity-raising investment on the part of suppliers and sub-assemblers. Their profitability, therefore, depends on their ability to lower production and transaction costs, and on an understanding that cost savings will not be transferred immediately to the final assemblers. There is evidence that this mode of bilateral price determination has increased dramatically in Japan since the 1960s, not only in the motor-vehicle industry but throughout the industrial sector. By 1983, 83.4 percent of pricing agreements were of this bilateral sort.[35]

Also, because final assemblers want to eliminate as many sub-assembly steps as possible, they expect suppliers to improve product designs in order to incorporate more features and value in the same unit, such as microprocessors instead of contact fuses in the electrical control panel. Ultimately this results in greater profitability for sub-assemblers as well as in time and labor savings for final assemblers. Bilateral price determination and bilateral design coordination (co-engineering) result in collaborative rather than contentious relations between final and sub-assemblers. The template for negotiating purchase contracts with parts suppliers for Toyota Motor is as follows.

Pricing for Parts Suppliers at Toyota Motor: An Example[36]

a = cost of raw materials

b = cost of purchased materials

c = cost of purchased intermediate goods

d = production costs

$a + b + c + d = A$ = manufacturing costs

e = assembly margin

f = administrative costs

$A + e + f = B$ = per unit manufacturing costs

g = reward for lowering costs

$B + g = C$ = actual per unit price

In addition, quality-control inspection of parts and components is the responsibility of sub-assemblers rather than the final assembler. Toyota Motor does not generally inspect incoming parts, and because of this, Toyota can employ its famous just-in-time manufacturing system of low inventory but high throughput. Toyota knows that the parts and components will fit, and fit well, because parts makers and sub-assemblers do not want to lose Toyota's business. Toyota is the second or third largest truck and automobile manufacturer in the world and therefore a highly desirable long-term customer; parts makers and sub-assemblers invest heavily in their relationship with Toyota and they will continue to do so.

For its part, Toyota Motor cannot succeed without its suppliers. The Toyota production system has become rooted in principles of bilateral, collaborative relations and mutuality of interests binding firms participating in the system. Plant sites, equipment specifications, worker skills, management plans, the pace and flow of work—all these and more are based on the relationship between Toyota and its affiliates. Toyota Motor and its affiliates are interdependent operationally as well as strategically.

By being so closely aligned with Toyota Motor, there is only one way for affiliates and suppliers to profit handsomely from this situation: it's up or out. You either make the grade—meet the quality control, price, reliability, and delivery terms set by Toyota—or you are demoted and possibly expelled from the Toyota family of companies. Suppliers not only fight to stay in the family but they struggle, scheme, and strive to clamber up the supplier hierarchy as well.[37]

Rising in the hierarchy means more money and status. There is a fundamental distinction between those suppliers and subcontractors who simply take plans and specifications provided by Toyota Motor or some first-level affiliate and make parts and components to order, and those suppliers who have the design skills and technical know-how to take an idea or suggestion from Toyota or some other front-line firms and then create, design, modify, and execute the production of needed parts on their own. An example of the first type of supplier would be outfits engaged in body-press and metal-fabrication work, while the latter type is found in bearing manufacture, brake assembly, engine design, and electrical-systems production.

Companies want to move up the supplier hierarchy for several reasons: first, there is more money to be made (the value-added component is greater) in designing your own parts and components; second, high-level parts makers and suppliers have more work since they design components and provide sub-assemblies for many different models and types of vehicles. The more Toyota Motor depends on Toyota Auto Body or Nippondenso, for example, the more work and profit these affiliates can guarantee for themselves. The more their stock rises in Toyota's esteem, the greater their status and power within the Toyota family of enterprises.

The crowning success for a subcontractor is when a subcontractor is no longer a subcontractor. Such firms as Nippondenso, Aisin Seiki, Hino Motors, and Daihatsu are considered Toyota affiliates rather than Toyota subcontractors. Their products may be largely manufactured under their own name, they may have their own distribution channels for after-market service and sales, and usually they have higher production know-how and sophistication in their own specialties than do final assemblers. Their self-developed technologies and proprietary know-how set them apart; they are recognized leaders in what they do.

Moreover, because of the considerable investment in people, design equipment, and manufacturing facilities that affiliates must shoulder in order to fashion as well as produce auto parts, it is obviously desirable for affiliates to spread their risk over as many models and vehicles as possible. This gives them the incentive to push ahead with R & D, to invest in labor-saving and step-saving production systems, to review continuously every feature of their operations, so that they will be able to do more for Toyota.[38]

Therefore, and this is crucial, large Japanese auto-parts suppliers like Toyota Auto Body or Nippondenso are not considered as specialized divisions of the final assembler. They have grown from a dependent auto-body maker into an independent contract assembler. Strictly speaking, they are neither independent companies nor dependent divisions. They are not independent because, in most cases, they are strategically tied to the operations of Toyota. But they are not dependent either, because the profits they realize are largely their own.

In most cases, Toyota's financial interest in its suppliers never exceeds a minority share. Unlike American divisions of a large multidivisional firm, Japanese affiliates do not simply move cash (profits) back to parent firms. Toyota does own between 11 and 49 percent of fifteen key, first-tier firms that along with Toyota Motor are known as the Toyota Group. Outside this group, however, Toyota's financial ties with affiliates are not substantial, generally less than 10 percent. And, even this figure extends only to first-tier firms.

More generally, the front-rank of Toyota affiliates and suppliers raise much of their own capital, hire their own people, prepare, organize, and execute their own production plans and budgets, and design and make their own parts. In these ways and others, they are independent. In other ways, they are not. Overall group strategy and long-term planning are the responsibility of Toyota Motor. Key technical and financial decisions about car propulsion and control systems as well as about where major investment capital will be raised or borrowed are Toyota Motor decisions. Nevertheless, such strategic decisions as these must be carried out by the actions of hundreds of companies supplying components and related services to Toyota, and each of these companies has its own past, present, and future.

It would be a mistake, however, to suggest that the power balance between final assemblers and suppliers is equal. From the final assembler's point of view, there are always alternative sources of supply. Toyota Motor always determines when and how many parts and components are needed. Nevertheless, suppliers have advantages of their own which Toyota would be foolish to ignore. They usually have lower labor and overhead costs, greater productivity in their specialized areas of manufacture, possible advantages of location relative to alternative sources of supply, less bureaucracy and formalism in keeping with their smaller size. Most importantly, if they have been in the Toyota family for years and if they have been able to survive and improve their position, they are likely to be among the best at what they do. Toyota depends on that excellence.

II
On the Nature of Interfirm Relations with Toyota Motor

The Toyota interfirm network is a system of organized interdependence. The interdependence in this case is unusually large and complex. There are three levels subordinate to Toyota Motor and three different sorts of companies in the hierarchy of interdependence. All of these are interrelated in various ways. Because of this complexity and degree of interdependence, it should not be assumed that there is only one dependent/paternalistic dynamic operating within the system. There is a whole range of ways in which companies are related and interact, and there is great scope in action and choice within the network.

Owners and managers of enterprises within the network are constantly deciding how much effort, how much time, and how much money to put into new and existing lines of business. And once such decisions are made, they have to be negotiated with other firms in the system because there are limits to what can be accomplished on one's own. Some managers, frustrated by such interactive limits, seek to reduce their network business activities. Others, enjoying the challenge of succeeding in the system, put all their energy into network-linked activities. Rising to higher levels in the network puts firms closer to Toyota, the source for the group's strategy. But rising in the network requires constant effort, ever greater systems integration and asset interdependence.

Opportunities to be increasingly involved or disengaged are largely delimited by history. Firms enter the network in particular ways and with specific strategies. While in the abstract, there is a limitless range of action and choice, in fact each firm defines its own course of action and direction. When thousands of firms are all doing so, there is an incredible range of choice and action available in the aggregate.

The following section follows the course of two companies' interactions within the Toyota interfirm network. It is meant to illustrate some of the range of action and choice available to suppliers within the Toyota production system. One company, Nippondenso, began as the electrical shop within a fledgling Toyota Motor, while the other, Daihatsu Motors, was a well-established diesel-engine manufacturer long before Toyoda Automatic Loom Company and Toyota Motor were founded. The history of both Nippondenso's and Daihatsu's involvement and interaction with Toyota demonstrates that while hierarchy defines the structure of firms within the network, hierarchy itself does not define interdependence. Instead it is the structure within which firms act, choose, and negotiate their own futures.

Nippondenso: From Dependence to Interdependence

Nippondenso epitomizes the tradition of corporate evolution within an enterprise group: it grew from a shop to a department within Toyota; from a department to a division, was then separated as a subsidiary, moved up to become an affiliate, and finally arrived as an independent company. (Independence, in this case, refers to Nippondenso's strategic autonomy in spite of being 20 percent owned by Toyota and selling 60 percent of its output to Toyota.) It is this logic of upward mobility which motivates firms to stay within the enterprise group while striving to climb to the top. The rewards of moving up within a growing network of enterprises are greater than those from spinning off on one's own. Nippondenso illustrates this principle well.

Nippondenso is the third largest firm in the Japanese automobile industry in spite of being a parts maker and not a final assembler. In 1983 it produced 10 percent of all the auto parts and components made in Japan, 60 percent of which went to Toyota Motor.[39] Not content with this substantial measure of domestic success, Nippondenso is already international. By 1989 Nippondenso had opened manufacturing facilities in Michigan and Tennessee for making starters and generators, and it is expected that the major purchasers will include General Motors, Chrysler, and Ford, along with Toyota. (Toyota's wholly-owned plant opened in 1988 in Georgetown, Kentucky.)

Nippondenso began as the electrical parts and repairs shop of Toyota Motor before the Pacific War and was not hived off as an independent firm until 1949. Its rapid growth since then has outstripped even that of Toyota, yet it is a Toyota company—a central and crucial member of the Toyota group—even though it supplies other automobile makers such as Mitsubishi Motors, Isuzu, Hino, Matsuda (Mazda), Fuji Heavy Industries (Subaru), Honda, Suzuki, and Daihatsu. Everyone, in fact, except Nissan—and, outside Japan, even Nissan.

When Kiichiro began in earnest in 1933 to build a Japanese automobile, the only electrical parts readily available on the open market were batteries. Everything else, starters, distributors, timers, and even internal and external lighting fixtures, had to be developed in-house. A task force was assembled in 1936 and assigned to produce 250 sets of starters, distributors, dynamos, and ignition coils. The project took most of a year to complete and it taught the project team as much or more about what materials and methods not to use as which were appropriate. Even Hitachi Ltd., which had been asked to supply electrical parts as an outside contractor, had difficulties, and Toyota resolved to abandon its purchasing relationship with Hitachi as soon as it could reliably manufacture its own electrical parts.[40]

Gradually, Toyota's electrical-parts group gathered the experience and technique to produce dependable and durable parts although most of its early output went into military trucks and aircraft instead of automobiles. When the electrical-parts department was separated from Toyota Motor in December 1949 as part of Kiichiro's desperate strategy of disintegration and decentralization, it faced major management and financial problems. Like Toyota Motor, Nippondenso had to fight a labor strike which erupted for the wholly understandable reason that workers, whose wages were being whipsawed by inflation and erratic work schedules, objected to management's efforts to cut costs by reducing wages. In addition, Nippondenso inherited from Toyota an accumulated deficit amounting to about ten times the size of its capital resources when it was split off in December 1949.[41]

For Nippondenso, as for Toyota Motor, the Korean War saved the day. Social Orders poured in from the United Nations' forces as well as from the newly formed Police Reserve Force in Japan. In December 1951, two years after its separation from Toyota Motor, Nippondenso went public with an offering on the Nagoya Stock Exchange, and within a month had tripled its capital from 15 to 45 million yen.

While the Korean War brought orders, it brought problems as well. Meeting the increasing volume of orders, given the limited scale and advanced age of Nippondenso's plant and equipment, was difficult enough, but producing a full line of needed electrical parts and components was beyond the technical know-how accumulated by Nippondenso. Fortunately, Robert Bosch Company, Germany's premier auto electrical-parts maker, was looking for overseas outlets for its products and technology.

Kiichiro Toyoda seized the opportunity and pressed home Nippondenso's case. In May 1953 an initial contract between Nippondenso and Robert Bosch was signed, and it gave Nippondenso exclusive rights to the importation as well as manufacture of Bosch products in Japan. More importantly, it provided Nippondenso with badly needed Bosch manufacturing technology and know-how, as well as the right to export Nippondenso-made products of Bosch design in overseas markets not already covered by Bosch licenses. In exchange, Bosch received 800,000 shares of Nippondenso stock, a lump-sum payment of 40 million yen, royalty payments, and the right to renew the contract after an initial ten-year period.[42]

In 1954 Nippondenso replaced the old-style car-heaters and windshield-wiper units that it had been supplying to Toyota with new ones of Bosch-design, and it has continued to upgrade and introduce new products every year since signing with Bosch. But according to Nippondenso's management, even more important than Bosch products, were Bosch's management systems and production methods. Every department, branch, and office benefited from new ideas on plant layout, choice of equipment and machinery, accounting tools and practices, R & D management, and product design and development.

Nippondenso had already introduced statistical quality control (QC) techniques in 1950 with the outbreak of the Korean War when it was designated as a parts supplier for the United States Army. These practices were reinforced and enhanced by Nippondenso's contract with Bosch which led to the standardization of production management and parts procurement. In 1957 Nippondenso embraced total quality control (TQC) and rationalized its systems of production, distribution, and management. In 1961 Nippondenso won the Deming Prize for outstanding QC performance.[43]

Nippondenso illustrates a basic element of Toyota's strategy. Toyota concentrates on the final assembly of automobiles and on the manufacture of a few highly critical parts, such as engines and transmissions. It depends on local suppliers for the rest. Ancillary firms have to expand at least at Toyota's rate, and sometimes faster, since Toyota may decide to discontinue in-house production of some parts and components, and these lines may be picked up by suppliers.

Of course, the reverse can occur as well, namely Toyota can choose to begin anew in-house manufacture of some parts and components that were supplied by affiliates and subcontractors. The choice to 'buy' or to 'make' carries strategic overtones for the future of Toyota and its network of related enterprises. Toyota would like to control the manufacture of the most important automobile parts. For the vitality of the group as a whole as well as its own bottom line, Toyota retains the sourcing of the most critical parts and assemblies and it determines the future direction of automobile design and development. The success of the group as a whole depends on Toyota Motor's leadership and authority on these matters.

But what is strategic and important at one time may not be so at another. The reasons why Toyota Motor has chosen to invest recently in car electronics illustrate the point of strategic leadership. Nippondenso has been Toyota's primary supplier of car electrical/electronic components since the firm was separated from Toyota in 1949. By hiving off electrical and electronic-systems development and production, Toyota was able to concentrate its own resources on other aspects of automobile design and manufacture without concerning itself with what was in 1949 a sideline to car production. At the same time, while Toyota sought to secure a reliable and efficient supply of electrical parts, Nippondenso sought to make the most of its opportunities by taking responsibility for its own financial and organizational future.

But times have changed and car electronics are now a crucial, some would say the crucial, element in any automobile company's strategy. By 1992 as compared to 1985, some analysts contend that the value-added contribution of electronics to automobile assembly will quadruple. Car electronics is now the key to product differentiation in such areas as engine and operating-systems efficiency, safety-sensing devices, suspension control, braking and steering, car communications, and passenger-compartment environment control. Not only are previously independent car-component systems increasingly interrelated within an on-board information-handling system but the timing and efficiency with which each independent system is controlled as well as integrated with other on-board systems are being speeded up considerably.

Electronics will add new dimensions to future automobiles. On-board navigation systems will appear soon. Mazda is offering one in its new Eunos flagship coupé from the spring of 1990. Integrated diagnostic and preventive maintenance systems are possible with the advent of centralized electronics systems. In addition, electronics are already indispensable for the manufacture of automobiles. In short, car electronics have become an ever more crucial element in car design and production, and a manufacturer without electronic design and development capabilities will lag in an industry characterized by extremely rapid technological change. More importantly, it will be unable to lead effectively a network of affiliates and subcontractors that depends on it.

Strategic issues such as these have prompted Toyota to invest in its own in-house car-electronics design and development capability, even though it has a guaranteed source of supply from the leading car-electronics firm in Japan, Nippondenso. This is in spite of the fact that Nippondenso will produce integrated circuits and other sophisticated electronic parts entirely according to Toyota Motor design and sales forecasts; something which Nissan Motors' main electronics-parts supplier, Hitachi, is not so apt to do.[44] Toyota wants to assure an alternate source of supply and to develop in-house technical capability by creating its own electronics arm; such maneuvers only make sense when Nippondenso's independence is recognized and accepted, affirming that Toyota does not control even its most strategic affiliates.

Daihatsu Motor: From Independence to Interdependence

Daihatsu Motor is another example of a large, well-capitalized, and effectively managed independent company which cooperates with Toyota in a number of ways and which coordinates its production according to Toyota specifications and schedules. Daihatsu, unlike Nippondenso, joined forces with Toyota after a long and illustrious history of independent manufacture and operations.

Founded in March 1907 as the 'Engine Manufacturing Company', Daihatsu was an early example of university—company cooperation in Japan; local businessmen and some of the engineering faculty from Osaka University set up the enterprise to produce diesel engines of Japanese design and manufacture for locomotives, public-transportation systems, and shipping vessels. Their first product was a 500 cc motor.[45]

In 1918, at the close of World War One, Daihatsu was appointed a civilian supplier of vehicles to the military and produced two prototype truck models in the next year. But the end of the war brought a stop to the military-procurement program and for a dozen years Daihatsu did not manufacture any motor vehicles.[46]

Daihatsu entered the automobile market with a three-wheeled, open-cab, light truck model in 1930 and a four-wheeler in 1937. These early vehicles were designed for delivery work, with engines displacing 250–300 cc and a pay-load of about 650 lb (in addition to the driver). In 1937 production peaked at just over 5,000 units and did not reach this level again until the post-war period. In 1948 Daihatsu produced 3,882 three-wheeled, light trucks, double the number of units (1,903) produced in the previous year. That number was nearly doubled when production reached to 7,206 units in 1949, 9,283 in 1950, and finally topped the 10,000-unit barrier with 12,446 units in 1951. In that year the company name was changed to Daihatsu Motor. All of these early post-war vehicles were light trucks, essentially identical to the models of the pre-war era.[47]

During the 1960s, however, the strategy and structure of Daihatsu Motor underwent dramatic revision. Since its establishment in 1907, Daihatsu had concentrated for a half-century on the manufacture of internal-combustion engines, primarily large diesel motors for land and water transportation. This was in keeping with the highly developed railroad and coastal-shipping services of the pre-war period. The transportation revolution of the post-war era, however, accelerated the development of a paved, national network of roads and highways and an attendant diffusion of light trucks and passenger vehicles. The implications of this fundamental shift in the mode of transportation for distributing of all manner of consumer goods was a major thrust of Chapter 5 which concerned itself in part with the post-war consumer goods—distribution revolution.

Daihatsu correctly foresaw the direction of this basic shift in how people and goods would be moved, and between 1958 and 1959, the company jumped its annual production from 38,000 to 70,000 units, most of the increase coming in the manufacture of small trucks with more power and capacity than earlier models. In 1963 Daihatsu produced a meager 498 passenger cars but multiplied this tenfold in the following year. As the number of passenger cars and small trucks increased, Daihatsu shifted more and more of its production to four-wheeled rather than three-wheeled vehicles. By 1964 the company was making 170,000 cars and trucks a year, of which only 36,000 were of three-wheeled design. In the same year, Daihatsu topped the million-car barrier, having produced a total of 1,058,209 vehicles in its 57-year history.

By the Tokyo Olympiad in 1964 Daihatsu was growing at a rate of about 20 percent per year, adding some 200,000 units annually to its base production of 1 million vehicles. The company was in the right industry and was pursuing the right strategy but, incomprehensibly, it was being overwhelmed by success. The company's growth was so rapid that it faced a myriad of problems ranging from production management, accounting controls, purchasing bottlenecks, cash-flow difficulties, to engineering and design insufficiencies and inefficiencies.[48]

Also, the passenger car and truck market was changing drastically as a result of government intervention and regulation. Throughout the 1950s the government had encouraged the automotive industry by both direct and indirect means. These had included export subsidies, import tariffs, foreign-exchange regulation, low-interest loans to manufacturers, and restrictions on foreign investment. Then in 1961 the Japanese government began removing restrictions on the importation of foreign-made trucks and buses and in 1965 on the importation of passenger cars. In 1966 new regulations concerning auto emissions were enacted and other safety and pollution-control requirements were to follow.[49]

Even more importantly, as the Japanese government removed restrictions on the importation of foreign-made vehicles, it sought to strengthen the position of domestic Japanese vehicle manufacturers by encouraging mergers in the industry. It was the view of the Japanese government, particularly of MITI, that Japanese car and truck manufacturers could not compete successively against much larger American and European auto firms without significant economies of scale, and these could be realized only with vertical and horizontal integration.

Integration occurred but not in the way MITI envisioned. Independent firms with long histories in spite of their small size, such as Daihatsu and Isuzu, refused to be merged or bought out. Among the smaller makers only Prince Motors (Fuji Precision Machinery) disappeared entirely, becoming a division of Nissan Motor in August 1966. Otherwise, from 1966 to 1971, Japanese auto and truck makers formed into a series of semi-exclusive alliances which offered the promise of economies of scale through vertical integration without sacrificing long-established identities and strategies. Resource and organizational interdependence were chosen over managerial independence and production autonomy. Interfirm networks, a basic organizational form of the Japanese enterprise system, were fashioned in the motor vehicle industry.

Daihatsu's Strategic Ties to Toyota

Daihatsu allied itself with Toyota in November 1967 as did Hino Motors a year earlier in October 1966. Thus, three independent manufacturers combined with twelve others to form what is commonly called today the Toyota Group.[50] Daihatsu's agreement with Toyota in November 1967 was straight forward enough: Toyota bought 12.6 percent of Daihatsu's shares, promised not to move into the manufacture of light or mini-cars (Daihatsu's forte), and, in exchange, Daihatsu obtained a few percent of Toyota's stock and agreed to make small cars, vans, and trucks for Toyota. The logic of the agreement was more complex than it would appear on the surface, however.

Toyota benefited by being able to offer a full line of automobiles and trucks to potential customers. Toyota could become, as a result, the largest one-stop auto maker/seller in Japan, offering customers a greater variety of models for trade-in, lease, or purchase than any other manufacturer. Moreover, the cost (12.6 percent of Daihatsu's equity shares) of adding the extra models supplied by Daihatsu to Toyota's line-up was incurred for far less money than if Toyota had to invest itself in new plant and equipment in order to make the vehicles.

Also, the risk of adding capacity in this way, that is through a joint production agreement with an already established manufacturer, was considerably less than if Toyota took on the complex tasks of financing, designing, developing, producing, and marketing a new series of small autos and trucks by itself. This is a concrete illustration of the advantages accruing from economies of scope within an interfirm network: per unit costs of production and distribution for Toyota Motor are lowered through joint production and distribution arrangements.

Further, in keeping with Toyota's usual policy of not relying on a single supplier, by contracting with Daihatsu (as well as Hino Motors), Toyota could obtain sources of manufacturing cost comparison with its own captured sub-contractors. 'Friendly competition' of this sort keeps costs low for Toyota as well as for Daihatsu. A final benefit for Toyota was Daihatsu's location in western Japan. By supplying the western portion of the country with Toyota vehicles made in Daihatsu's Ikeda factory outside of Osaka, Toyota could respond more quickly and effectively to changing market conditions in that part of the country.

Daihatsu benefited as well. First, it could run its own facilities at higher capacity reducing its per unit cost in the process (economies of scale). In 1985 Daihatsu was running its plants at 93 percent capacity—nearly full bore.[51] The 7 percent differential represented occasional stopping of the line for late deliveries from suppliers, mechanical problems with assembly operations, and other unforeseen events (mostly acts of God). Furthermore, it could lower the cost of many parts and components by procuring them in greater volume but lower cost through its own hierarchy of related enterprises (economies of scope). This was possible because certain Toyota and Daihatsu models shared up to 80 percent of their parts and components in common.

Second, it protected its market niche in light cars and trucks from competition by aligning itself with the most formidable auto maker in Japan. (In fact, by the middle of the 1980s, some overlap in the companies' two product lines was apparent, but this was the result of Daihatsu's encroachment into Toyota's territory rather than the reverse.) Third, and most importantly, Daihatsu received proven design and production technology without which it could not have maintained its rapid pace of expansion into the 1970s (just-in-time methods of manufacturing, purchasing, and delivery as well as value engineering benefits garnered from Toyota). As a consequence, Daihatsu could claim by the 1980s that their cars were just as good as Toyota's and know, for a fact, that it was true.[52]

Recall that Daihatsu was growing at the rate of 20 percent a year in the early 1960s. The strain this put on the company's financial, managerial, labor, and production engineering resources was considerable, and it was mounting year by year. Almost paradoxically, success was overwhelming Daihatsu. By joining forces with Toyota, Daihatsu relieved the financial pinch, protected its flank, spread its costs over a much expanded production, climbed to the position of the number five auto maker in Japan by 1985 (in terms of the number of vehicles produced), and learned vital production and management techniques that were essential to continued success in the industry, such as Toyota's just-in-time/*kanban-shiki* system of delivery, production, and purchasing.

A concrete manifestation of these interwoven advantages for Daihatsu was the introduction of a new four-wheel drive model, the Rugger (known as Rocky in American markets), in 1984. Daihatsu had neither sufficient demand nor adequate know-how to produce a jeep-like recreation vehicle on its own, but by capitalizing on Toyota's proven Land Cruiser technology and by counting on Toyota Motors to take a large share of its production, Daihatsu was able to design, manufacture, and introduce a new vehicle for domestic and overseas markets.

The beneficial effects of the Toyota system of production management was felt immediately. Daihatsu reduced the number of firms directly supplying it with parts, components, and services from 440 to 167 within a year of adopting the *kanban* system in 1969. Suppliers that did not measure up in that exacting system were weeded out. Others were encouraged to combine in order to minimize organizational and operational overlap, and still others were positioned lower in the hierarchy of suppliers. In this way, the number of suppliers with which Daihatsu directly transacted was noticeably reduced. As in Toyota Motor's experience, coordination of the flow of parts, services, and sub-assemblies improved without increasing centralization and bureaucracy for Daihatsu.

The former Chairman and past President of Daihatsu, Tomonaru Eguchi, came to Daihatsu from Toyota in 1969 as a specialist in purchasing management, and it was his leadership which raised the level of technology, quality control, and production know-how among Daihatsu's suppliers. He followed ten top Toyota executives who had moved over to Daihatsu in 1967. As a result of the weeding and upgrading process based on Toyota know-how, Daihatsu is now able to involve its major suppliers in car-design and car-conceptualization activities at the start of the design and development cycle.[53] It is much easier, more effective, and less costly to do so before the design is finalized.

The reasons why Daihatsu has to depend on the quality and reliability of its parts suppliers are simple and compelling: Daihatsu buys 67–75 percent (depending on the vehicle model) of the manufacturing cost of its cars, and it

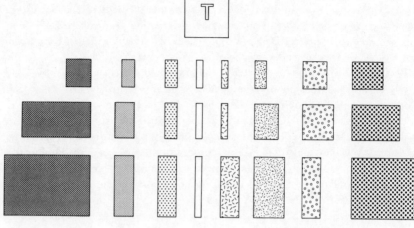

FIG. 7.2. *Toyota Motor Supplier Network: Cross-Level Functional Groups*

TABLE 7.3. *Numbers of Suppliers Appended to Major Firms in the Toyota Group, 1982*

Sub-group	No. of suppliers	No. in which major firms own shares
Hino Motors	246	20
Daihatsu Motor	143	6
Kanto Auto Works	84	12
Toyota Auto Body	79	11
Toyoda Automatic Loom Works	51	3
Nippondenso	66	13
Aishin Precision Machinery	95	6
Aichi Steel	48	1
Toyoda Machine Works	65	1
Toyoda Synthetic	73	2
Central Motor	64	2
Aisan Industry	25	1
TOTALS	1,039	78

Source: H. Shiomi, 'Structure of Production Logistics', in Sakamoto (ed.), *Gijutsu Kakushin to Kigyo Kozo*, 87

operates its final assembly plants at 93 percent capacity. Figures, incidentally, which are higher than Toyota's.[54] In other words, Daihatsu has direct manufacturing control over less than one-third of the parts and components that go into its cars, and it has less than 7 percent down time on its production line. The defect rate from suppliers is never higher than 0.4 percent, and usually far lower than that.[55] Daihatsu can concentrate on running at full capacity with very little inventory because it has evolved a highly complex, integrated system of quality parts manufacture and supply—a system it learned from Toyota.

It must be stressed that Daihatsu's system, and Toyota's for that matter, does not depend on Daihatsu direct investment in its affiliate suppliers. In 1985, for example, Daihatsu owned shares in only 7 out of 168 current sub-assemblers, and most of the investments were made to bolster firms having difficulties of one sort or another. In short, Daihatsu intervenes financially in its suppliers only as a last resort.[56]

Level I–Level II Interactions: Daihatsu's Supplier Network

Daihatsu, like Toyota, whose example served to encourage the refinement of its supplier network, depends on functional subgroupings among its suppliers and affiliates. Functional subgroupings typically include sets of companies making suspension parts, brake components, electrical sub-assemblies, or any of the parts and components that go into a vehicle's major subsystems. Specialized, cross-level connections between functionally interrelated firms play a crucial role in Japan's outsized automobile networks.[57]

Functional, cross-level networks provide:

1. an important channel of information exchange on market and technology matters between large and small firms in the same area of development and production;
2. an arena, both formal and informal, within which managers, engineers, and high-level production workers can get to know each other; acquaintance becomes a basis for work cooperation;
3. a forum wherein production targets, new-product development, and interfirm coordination can be discussed, and where the terms of performance can be hammered out to mutual satisfaction; matters of design, production, management are clarified through the participation of specialized suppliers along with Daihatsu delegates;
4. a means for extending and expanding sales channels not only for Daihatsu Motor but also for its suppliers.

Using Toyota's supplier network as an example, the functional interrelations between levels may be illustrated as is shown in Fig. 7.2. Daihatsu's functional subsystems are no different in character than those of Toyota's but because the number and variety of firms in Daihatsu's subsystems are fewer, it is easier to describe and analyze this aspect of enterprise networking by looking at Daihatsu rather than Toyota. Daihatsu can lay claim to the second largest number of sub-contractors and suppliers in the Toyota group (see Table 7.3).

Within the Daihatsu supplier group of 143 companies in 1982, there were four subgroupings according to the type of parts or assembly manufacture. The largest group with 49 firms made chassis and chassis parts, and of these under half, 45 percent, had less than 500 employees. The next largest group with 42 firms made specialized components for functional subsystems, like steering, electrical, or brake subsystems; only 31 percent of these had less than 500 employees. The body panel press group with 22 companies, and the die- and mold-casting group with 29 firms were mostly small: 59 percent of the former and 76 percent of the latter fell into the under-500 employee category.[58]

In short, there is a significant degree of differentiation among Daihatsu's suppliers in terms of their number of employees and the value of their physical assets. These parameters, it must be remembered, are not disturbed to any significant degree by Daihatsu's investment in its suppliers, as Daihatsu owns shares in only seven or 4 percent of the members of the Daihatsu *Kyoyukai* or 'Supplier Association'. And Daihatsu has been doing business with these firms for many decades in some cases. Indeed, of the 142 *Kyoyukai* companies in 1980, only five had been established since 1960. Better than 95 percent of the *Kyoyukai* companies, in short, had been carrying on their own business, including buying and selling with Daihatsu, for years without any significant degree of financial interdependence with Daihatsu or each other. In fact, twenty of Daihatsu's suppliers had been wholly aligned with the Toyota supplier network before Toyota's alliance with Daihatsu, and another 49 had been partly so. So, nearly half of Daihatsu's current suppliers came over from Toyota. This was another benefit of Daihatsu's alliance with Toyota.

Obviously, managerial coordination is not based on ownership within Daihatsu's interfirm system of supply. It is based instead on the utility of organizational interdependence, that is on the mutual recognition of the value of making money together. Although the power and position of companies within Daihatsu's inter-firm network, or within Toyota's for that matter, are not equal, such differences do not deter a positive attitude of cooperation and coordination among firms. Inequality does not imply inequity. Instead, organized interdependence defines a structured context for expanding business opportunities.

Choice and Interdependence

The reason for Toyota's marked dependency on suppliers is that the domestic manufacture of automobiles began, like so much of Japanese industrial production, with the importation and imitation of foreign manufacturing technology. The choice of whether 'to buy' or 'to make' was, in fact, no choice. Aside from a few foreign cars that were imported in the late 1930s, quickly stripped, studied piece by piece, and reverse engineered, Toyota and the Japanese automobile industry had no choice but to make themselves what was needed. Foreign cars were extraordinarily expensive to buy and difficult to maintain. Foreign auto-parts were likewise expensive and hard to come by. If Toyota was to build a car for the mass market, it would have to do so alone.

But it could not do so alone. Toyota Motor, and its parent company Toyoda Automatic Loom, were lacking in engineering and technical know-how, strapped for capital, short of needed tools, without sufficient managerial skill and an experienced labor force. On its own, Toyota Motor could do very little.

Furthermore, in 1950, Toyota Motor tottered on the edge of bankruptcy. To prevent a free fall into the abyss, Toyota cut away many of its core departments, making them into separate companies and responsible for their own operating expenses. Economic necessity dictated this unorthodox maneuver, not some grand design of corporate devolution. By force of circumstances, Toyota came to rely on a network of affiliated companies for parts, components, assemblies, engineering, and even labor. Toyota looked outside for help. It had to work closely and constantly with outsiders because what Toyota needed—parts, components, and services appropriate to a domestic automobile industry—were not available. So, Toyota and dozens of independent companies joined forces and worked together in a spirit of mutual self-interest to secure the foundations of a modern Japanese automobile industry.

Financial Ties are not the Answer

The financial relations between Toyota Motor and its first-tier companies are transparent, and in most cases Toyota Motor's investment is not overwhelming. Financial ties are not the answer as to why these companies work closely together. Shareholding is simply one expression of the interaction between Toyota and its major affiliates. It is definitive in only a few cases. Kanto Auto Works (48 percent owned by Toyota) built, for example, 18 percent of the top-selling Corolla bodies in 1980, while Toyoda Automatic Loom, from which Toyota Motor evolved and which is owned 20 percent by Toyota, built 9 percent of the Corollas.

So far so good, which is to say, that there is some correspondence between Toyota's equity ownership and the number of vehicles assembled by Toyota affiliates. But Hino Motors, a heavy-truck manufacturer in which Toyota has only an 8.5 percent stake, built 230,000 light trucks and 18,500 Carina cars for Toyota in 1980. And Daihatsu Motors, building an assortment of light trucks, vans, four-wheel-drive recreation vehicles, and passenger cars for Toyota, was only 12.6 percent owned by Toyota.[59]

Likewise, Toyota Motor's investment in other sub-assemblers and component makers, such as Arakawa Shatai, Akebono Brake, and Aisin Seiki, is not sufficient to determine the nature of the relationship between them. In all but a few instances Toyota's investment in its approximately 170 first-tier suppliers is a minority stake. According to 1986 data, among seventy-seven of Toyota's largest suppliers, the average level of Toyota shareholding was 20.7 percent. Excluding

TABLE 7.4. *Toyota Motor Intragroup Shareholding, 1982*

	1	2	3	4	5	6	7	8	9	10	11	12	13	14	15	16	Total No.	% of Outstanding Shares
1		13,700	3,455	1,335	4,950			7,195	16,359	89,571	5,847	3,020	4,167	4,071			153,670	8.7
2	210,072		1,155	38	170		38	550	7,653	4,111	3,016	270					227,073	47.4
3	35,198	819		290	1,428		243	330	959	20,749	255	122					60,393	41.6
4	27,257		1,130		903		33	1,430	9,570	787	33					4,500	41,143	34.3
5	15,345		1,102				28	147	193	1,377	93						18,285	28.5
6	700		750							3,000						18,361	22,811	45.6
7	27,120		1,000		36		50										28,231	54.3
8	31,997	3,361	1,100		267	15	107	395		10,272	206	33				4,930	48,855	27.0
9	67,585	1,383	1,102		431	23	74	651	1,782	31,440	332	237	203				105,462	27.8
10	37,621	350	1,423		731		35	180			431	107					44,555	22.8
11	30,512	2,205	1,000		180		35			6,370							38,662	50.5
12	15,910	15,269	999				30										32,213	50.6
13	30,047		1,103	105								42					33,532	10.9
14	36,819	7,000	930				100	150	1,045								46,044	12.6
15	26,400	6,000	1,200	3,600	3,600	1,800		3,600	4,200	6,000	3,600						60,000	100.0
16	49,000		3,000	1,000	6,000	1,000		6,000	11,000	17,000	4,000	1,000					99,000	99.0
TOTALS	641,583	50,087	20,445	6,951	18,696	2,838	773	19,198	44,621	199,460	18,606	4,935	4,370	4,071		27,791	1,059,929	24.1

1. Toyota Motor Manufacturing
2. Toyota Motor Sales
3. Toyoda Tsusho Trading
4. Aichi Steel Works
5. Toyoda Machinery
6. Toyoda Spinning and Weaving
7. Toyoda Synthetics
8. Aishin Machinery
9. Nippondenso
10. Toyota Automatic Loom Works
11. Toyota Auto Body
12. Kanto Auto Works
13. Hinode Motors
14. Daihatsu Motor
15. Toyoda Central Research Institute
16. TOWA Real Estate

Source: H. Shiomi, 'Structure of Production Logistics', in Sakamoto (ed.), *Gijutsu Kakushin to Kigyo Kozo*, 36.

the fifteen largest of these, either firms controlled directly by Toyota such as Toyoda Tsucho Trading or Toyoda Central Research Institute, or firms that were spun-out of Toyota such as Nippondenso or Toyoda Synthetics, drops the figure to 13.7 percent.[60]

While cross-holdings between first-tier firms in the Toyota group may raise these figures, most shares are publicly held and traded (see Table 7.4). Moreover, in second- and third-tier companies, Toyota rarely, if ever, invests anything at all. Financial relations would appear to buttress rather than to determine group interactions. Intragroup shareholding also reflects the financial attractiveness of holding shares in major auto-parts suppliers. Their rates of growth in profits and dividends are among the best of all publicly traded firms in Japan. And not surprisingly, among early entrants to the motor vehicle industry—Nissan, Isuzu, and Toyota—interfirm shareholding is most pronounced.

In other words, companies do not supply Toyota and Toyota does not buy from them for financial reasons alone. Financial relations may induce and abet but they do not dictate transactions between firms. More likely to do so are the buying and selling of fifteen to twenty thousand parts, components, sub-assemblies, and assemblies that go into today's medium-sized, passenger automobile.

Interfirm Coordination: Not Financial Ties

Japanese automobile makers, on average, buy some 75 percent of all parts and components for the final assembly of cars, while American manufacturers purchase just over half (roughly 52 percent). Expressed arithmetically, American car producers are about 50 percent more integrated than Japanese auto makers. Less integration for Japanese auto companies, like Toyota Motor, means they are characterized by smaller size, lower fixed and variable costs, and less bureaucratic inertia. Lower levels of vertical integration give Toyota greater flexibility in management decisions, production operations, and cost control, and these advantages appear decisive in Toyota's competition with other car-manufacturing companies overseas.[61]

But Toyota's advantages today were Toyota's disadvantages yesterday. Neither in the 1930s nor in the decades following World War Two, did any motor-car manufacturer in Japan have the capital, engineering skill, labor force, production facilities, and management know-how, to produce the thousands of high quality, precision parts and components that are needed to mass produce automobiles and trucks. Even the space to house a multi-line production facility, as obvious as that may seem, was not always available. Making an automobile of domestic design seemed an unreachable and unreasonable goal. Certainly the Japanese government had come to that conclusion.

Buying the needed parts, assemblies, and services to make a car, however, appeared equally unrealistic. The cost of imported parts was prohibitively high and they were generally unavailable. The uncertainties of shipping and delivery, importation and customs regulations, and foreign-exchange controls also made reliance on imported parts decidedly impractical. Although both 'making' and 'buying' appeared untenable, making was slightly more feasible in that thousands of firms had excess capacity, unused human resources, and a desire to work hard and long for minimal compensation. In the depressed economy of rural Nagoya during the 1930s or in the hard luck circumstances of post-war Japan, business opportunities were rarely scorned. Necessity required that firms were found, enlisted, trained, and, if necessary, cajoled, in order to secure parts and components. Otherwise, Toyota could not produce a single car or truck on its own.

So, Toyota Motor set out to develop an interfirm network of suppliers through which an automobile of domestic design, development and production could be realized. At first, the design of the automobile as well as the organization of suppliers were basic, rough hewn. The process of creating and promoting ancillary firms for parts and components supply took years to complete, and there were always entries and exits from the group of suppliers. The start-up costs associated with this form of interfirm organization were considerable. Good suppliers are hard to find and harder to train. The development of effective interfirm linkages underpinned by high levels of information exchange, product and technology transfer, and personnel movement, presupposes large transaction-cost expenses. However, the ongoing costs of monitoring and maintaining a supplier network should fall relative to start-up costs and as a result of organizational learning.

Ancillary firms generally organized themselves into cooperative associations to share information on how to rationalize production, how to make use of new technology, and how to coordinate delivery and purchasing arrangements. The largest ancillary firms grew so rapidly that they created their own sub-hierarchies of related firms and subcontractors. Together, Toyota and its leading affiliates invested to continuously upgrade facilities and personnel in order to keep pace with the rapid growth of the automotive industry in Japan.

As the complexity of this argument illustrates, the Toyota family of firms is much more than a simple production cartel which sets prices and quotas for member enterprises; likewise, it cannot be defined satisfactorily by financial models of interfirm behavior; although managers and workers move among subsets of firms in the Toyota group, such movement is not particularly large, important, or permanent, and it does not entail a significant means of control within the network; differentials in wages, turnover, investment, and facilities between large and small firms in the group do not come close to explaining the dynamics that motivate and propel the group forward. In short, traditional explanations of interfirm behavior based on models of profit maximizing, financial capitalism, monopolistic/monopsonistic dual economies, and the like, are simply not convincing explanations as to why the Toyota production system works and how the group of companies sustaining Toyota evolved into the world's most elaborated supplier network. Self-interest and a recognition of interdependence as the best means to promote self-interest offer the only persuasive explanations for the social dynamism that underpins the Toyota production system. Simply put, organizational interdependence provides a dynamic framework of incentive and opportunity.

No doubt financial sinews run through the skein of interdependence. The borrowing and lending of credit, interfirm shareholding, and common banking relationships buttress and reinforce trading patterns based on incentive and opportunity. Financial ties complement organizational learning processes. They help channel and lubricate the volume, content, and direction of the flow of goods and services, resulting in ever tauter and tighter, day-to-day transactions within the group. In sum, Toyota sits astride a pyramid of some 170 first-tier affiliates with which it has regular and direct relationships. These firms, in turn, contract with their own suppliers and sub-assemblers, so that the swell of Toyota-related companies builds in number to several tens-of-thousands.

The management of such a nested hierarchy of interrelated enterprises demands a high degree of information exchange and a constant coordination of production estimates, product flows, cost figures, model changes, technological advances, and so forth. Because the volume of the flow is so vast and because each firm in the system retains some degree of independence, relations between firms are kept as specific as possible and information flows are separated at each level in the hierarchy. Toyota seeks to control the quality of the work output by product specification rather than attempting to oversee the nature of the work process itself. Of course, if affiliated firms request help from Toyota Motor in designing work flow and content, Toyota Motor will help. Indeed, under the guidance of Toyota Motor, many firms have adopted Toyota-style production, purchasing, and delivery systems. But Toyota Motor does not impose its systems on affiliated enterprises. Instead functionally specialized firms in related product areas are integrated by the creation and maintenance of cooperative association-networks of interrelated, functionally specialized firms—such as those grouped under Nippondenso and Daihatsu Motors.

In sum, through four principles of organization—specification of work output and quality, firm-to-firm specific interaction, inter-level decentralization of transactions, and the formation of specialized networks of closely interrelated firms—the livelihood of each firm and the coordination of the enterprise group as a whole are intertwined. In these ways, low-frequency decisions of strategy and financing, such as those associated with introducing new models are completely separated from high-frequency decisions of hourly, daily, and monthly duration which bind together the hundreds and thousands of suppliers. Toyota Motor retains control over low-frequency decisions of great importance while it delegates the rest to the network.

Incentives are clear-cut. Each firm strives to do its best, that is to make more and better quality goods for less, in the hope that it will improve its own position in the group as well as add to the general prosperity of the group. Each company is relatively small and specialized, and the consequences of its actions in terms of operational performance are easily known. Pursuing the twin objectives of individual profit and group reciprocity, companies exhibit high levels of adaptation and adjustment to market circumstances and technological change. In sum, Toyota Motor and the Toyota group of companies have combined advantages of size—

economies of scale and scope—with benefits of organizational learning, local specialization, a highly developed division of labor, and small-firm motivation.[62]

Conclusion: Interfirm Networks

One of the most astonishing aspects of Japan's post-war economic recovery has been a surprisingly rapid penetration of the world oligopoly in such capital-intensive industries as automobiles and in the related industries of steel, glass, and tires. In each of these industries, there were and are formidable barriers to entry in the form of huge capital-investment requirements and daunting thresholds of minimum efficient scale in manufacturing. But the biggest difficulties for potential motor-vehicle producers in Japan were the technologies of modern mass production and distribution. In this sense, the largest barriers to entry were ones of knowledge, learning, and experience. Nevertheless, during a ten- to twenty-year period or within the same length of time that it took American and German firms to establish global oligopolies in rubber, machinery, and chemicals at about the time of World War One, Japanese companies cracked the established world oligopoly in automobiles. By 1980 Japan was the largest automobile-producing nation in the world.

Japanese firms gained this power primarily on the basis of organizational learning. One day at a time, one step at a time, one decision at a time, corporate managers moved the structure and strategy of automobile companies in a trajectory towards global competitiveness. In the case of Toyota Motor, this effort took more than fifty years and involved tens of thousands of direct employees and even larger numbers of persons employed in affiliated and supplier firms.

In each company and in every way possible, new methods and routines were tried, tested, and, ultimately, adopted or discarded. Within Toyota as well as within the hierarchy of firms supplying Toyota, an uncountable number of individual actions, decisions, and negotiations have moved firms inexorably closer together. The movement towards interdependence, a movement involving thousands of firms and tens of thousands of workers and managers, graphically describes the processes of organizational learning. This can be seen in one instance as the diffusion of the Toyota production system, but the spread of this system is only one obvious example of organizational learning.

Organizational learning explains why transaction costs associated with the management of a mammoth interfirm system of manufacture do not overwhelm production cost-savings. Learning economies have been achieved by consciously choosing a strategy based on an intricate, well-defined and managed network of suppliers, most of which are only indirectly tied to Toyota in financial matters. The size, complexity, mutually beneficial and interdependent nature of this network go far beyond the production systems found elsewhere, and for such reasons the Toyota system is not really analogous to the zones of interrelated small- and medium-sized enterprises found in northern Italy, for example.[63]

The strategy of multi-layered managerial coordination through interfirm alliances has been one of Toyota's creation, even though choice to affiliate with and supply Toyota has been made by thousands of independent enterprises. Individual firms and individuals in firms are motivated by the opportunities that appear within a structured hierarchy of suppliers. Decisions and actions to work with Toyota describe the contemporary structure of Toyota's interfirm network. That self-interest motivates interfirm relations can hardly be doubted. Suppliers accounted for about 50 percent of the manufacturing and other operating costs borne by Nissan and Toyota in the production of small cars in 1983 while paying wages equal to 80 percent of those received by Nissan and Toyota workers. So while costs and wages were lower, productivity gains were not.[64]

The effectiveness of Toyota's decentralized system of management and the strengthening of intergroup coordination within Japan have been especially evident since the mid-1970s' oil shocks. Since then, Toyota and Japanese companies have redoubled their efforts to increase efficiency and productivity, and they have done so without vertically integrating and centralizing their operations. In fact, they have tended to do just the opposite. This would not be possible without the extraordinarily tight scheduling, quality of parts supplied, and fail-safe reliability in delivery, production, and distribution that characterize the world of Toyota and its interfirm network of suppliers.

NOTES

1. Information on GM and Toyota from the *Financial Times*, 5 Jun. 1990, 1, and on Daimler-Benz from the *New York Times*, 20 Aug. 1990, C8.
2. Michael A. Cusumano, *The Japanese Automobile Industry* (Cambridge, Mass.: The Council on East Asian Studies, Harvard University, 1985), 190.
3. This chapter has benefited from a close reading by Dr. Toshihiro Nishiguchi, a recent graduate from the University of Oxford. Nishiguchi's thesis on supplier networks in the automobile and electronics industries in Japan has proven a valuable resource and supplement for my own work.
4. Banri Asanuma, 'Transactional Structures of Parts Supply in the Japanese Automobile and Electric Machinery Industries: A Comparative Analysis', Technical Report No. 1, Socio-Economic Systems Research Project, Kyoto University, Jul. 1985. See also Michael J. Smitka, 'The Invisible Handshake: The Development of the Japanese Automotive Parts Industry', *Business and Economic History*, 2nd ser., 19 (1990), 1–9. And, in working-paper form, a newer analysis by Banri Asanuma, 'Japanese Manufacturer–Supplier Relationships in International Perspective: The Automobile Industry Case', Working Papaer No. 8, Faculty of Economics, Kyoto University, 1988.
5. Keinosuke Ono and Konosuke Odaka, *Ancillary Firm Development in the Japanese Automobile Industry: Selected Case Studies (1)* (Kunitachi: Institute of Economic Research, Hitotsubashi University, 1979), 15. Ono and Odaka's work in revised form appeared as Konosuke Odaka, Keinosuke Ono, and Fumihiko Adachi, *The Automobile Industry in*

Japan: A Study of Ancillary Firm Development (Tokyo: Kinokuniya, 1988). My citations refer to the earlier version of their work.

6. I characterize the institutional capacity to borrow, imitate, learn, and innovate as organizational learning, and it is in my opinion the fundamental strength of the Japanese enterprise system. This chapter and the previous one are essentially case-studies in the process of organizational learning. Toyota's case is an example of interfirm organizational learning, Toshiba's intrafirm organizational learning.

7. Ono and Odaka, *Ancillary Firm Development*, 16.

8. Ibid. 16–18.

9. Ibid. 19.

10. Mr. John Eby, Executive Director of Corporate Strategy at Ford, told me in Dearborn, Mich. on 10 Aug. 1990 that he had documents that detailed a Ford–Toyota joint venture for production in Japan during the early post-war period. The project was vetoed by the Japanese Government.

11. Nishiguchi, 'Strategic Dualism', 58.

12. Tetsuo Minato, 'Ryo-daisenkan ni okeru Nihongata Shitauke Seisan-shisutemu no Hensei Katei' (The Formation of the Japanese Subcontracting System between the Two World Wars), *Aoyama Kokusai Seikei Ronshu* (Aoyama Papers on International Political Economy), 7 (Jun. 1987), 102. Fujita Akihisa, 'Seisan Koritsuka e no Jakkan no Kosatsu', 1/5 *Kansai Daigaku Shogakubu Ronshu* (Kansai University Papers on Business, 26/5 to 28/5 (1981–3). The 55 per cent figure comes from Toyota Motor Corporation, *Toyota: A History of the First 50 Years* (Tokyo: Dainippon Printing, 1988), 99.

13. Nikkan Kogyo Shimbun, *Toyota o Sasaeru Kigyogun* (The Enterprise Group Supporting Toyota) (Tokyo: Nikkan Kogyo Shimbunsha, 1980), 179–348. This volume contains short histories of the association between Toyota Motor and most of its major suppliers.

14. 'Formation of the Japanese Subcontracting System', 102.

15. Cusumano, *Japanese Automobile Industry*, 59–60; Ono and Odaka, *Ancillary Firm Development*, 20.

16. Toyota Motor Corporation, *Toyota*, 77–8.

17. Ono and Odaka, *Ancillary Firm Development*, 24.

18. Ibid. 27–8.

19. Ibid. 29. For a detailed discussion of labor relations at this time, see Reiko Okayama, 'Industrial Relations in the Japanese Automobile Industry 1945–70: The Case of Toyota', in Steve Tolliday and Jonathan Zeitlin (eds.), *The Automobile Industry and Its Workers: Between Fordism and Flexibility* (Oxford: Polity Press, 1986).

20. Ono and Odaka, *Ancillary Firm Development*, 31.

21. Michael Cusumano, 'Manufacturing Innovation and Competitive Advantage: Reflections on the Japanese Automobile Industry', paper draft, 9 May 1988, 6.

22. Ono and Odaka, *Ancillary Firm Development*, 30–1.

23. Cusumano, *Japanese Automobile Industry*, 265, 275, 293, 295–8.

24. Nikkan Kogyo Shimbun, *Toyota o Sasaeru Kigyogun*, 86–7.

25. Ibid. 161–4.

26. 'The World's Biggest Cottage Industry', *Economist*, 26 Jul. 1980, 65–6.

27. Banri Asanuma characterizes the differences between types of suppliers somewhat differently. He writes, 'The conventional view dichotomizes parts into "shihaihin" and "shitaukenhin" . . . and batteries, tires, and bearings are treated as "marketed goods" or *shihaihin*. However, the fact is that these items are also customized to some degree and, correspondingly, firms like Nippon Denchi, Bridgestone, and Nihon Seiko have been

members of Toyota's *Kyohokai* for a long time. There are suppliers which do not belong to the *Kyohokai* and still keep longstanding supply relations with Toyota: First, suppliers of jigs, dies, equipment, and construction services. Core members of such firms have been organized into *Eihokai*. They number 61 as of 1986 (52, if those which also belong to *Kyohokai* are excluded). Second, suppliers of raw materials, which have not formed any association.' Personal communication, letter dated, 19 Apr. 1990.

28. I thank Toshihiro Nishiguchi for this crucial distinction.

29. Banri Asanuma, 'Yasashi Keizaigaku (Easy Economics)', *Nihon Keizai Shimbun*, 21–5 Feb. 1984.

30. Annual reports of the Small- and Medium-Sized Business Agency of MITI, 1983–8.

31. Ohno Taiichi, *Toyota Seisan Hoshiki* (The Toyota Production System) (Tokyo: Daiyamondo, 1978), 60–1.

32. A discussion of Toyota's production system in the organizational context of its suppliers is found in W. Mark Fruin and Toshihiro Nishiguchi, 'The Toyota Production System: Its Organizational Definition and Diffusion in Japan', paper presented at the EIASM conference on country competitiveness, Brussels, 1 Jun. 1990.

33. A most enlightening analysis of the institutional underpinning of Toyota's supplier network is H. Shiomi, 'Seisan rojisutikkusu no kozo', in Kazuichi Sakamoto (ed.), *Gijutsu Kakushin to Kigyo Kozo* (Kyoto: Minerva Books, 1985), 77–113. A later work by Sakamoto and Shimotani Masahiro (eds.), *Gendai Nippon no Kigyo Gurupu* (Tokyo: Toyo Keizai Shinposha, 1987), is also available. Another recent work is Aichi Rodo Mondai Kenkyusho, *Toyota Gurupu no Shinsenryaku* (The New Strategy of the Toyota Group) (Tokyo: Shin-Nihon Shuppansha, 1990).

34. The information on pricing practices comes from a series of papers written by Professor Banri Asanuma of Kyoto University. See items cited above in n. 4 as well as 'The Structure of Parts Transactions in the Automotive Industry: The Mechanisms of Adjustment and Innovative Adaptation' (in Japanese), *Gendai Keizai*, 59 (Summer 1984).

35. Nishiguchi, 'Strategic Dualism', 199–201.

36. Banri Asanuma, 'Jidosha Sangyo ni okeru Buhin Torihiki no Kozo' (The Structure of Parts Supply in the Automotive Industry), *Gendai Keizai* (Modern Economics), 59 (Summer 1984), 42.

37. W. Mark Fruin, 'Cooperation and Competition: Supplier Networks in the Japanese Electronics Industry', a paper presented at the Center for Japanese Studies, University of California, Berkeley, 4 Nov. 1987.

38. This is basically the insight of Professor Banri Asanuma. Asanuma's work has focused for the moment on the relationship between parts suppliers and Toyota. The relationship between vehicle assembly and subcontractors, such as Toyota and Toyota Auto Body, may reasonably differ in its contractual terms.

39. ' "Ichiokuen kigyo" e Daiichi Kanmon wa "Toyota-hazure" ' ('In Order to Become a One-Oku Yen company, The First Order of Business is to Break Away from Toyota'), *Nikkei Business*, 21 Jan. 1985.

40. Ono and Odaka, *Ancillary Firm Development*, 77–8.

41. Ibid. 80.

42. Ibid. 85–7.

43. Ibid. 92.

44. 'Toyota Shifts to In-House Supply', *Nihon Keizai Shimbun*, 13 Jan. 1985, 5; 'The Key to High-Technology Diffusion', *Nihon Keizai Shimbun*, 16 Jan. 1985, 11; ' "Ichiokuen

kigyo" e Daiichi Kanmon wa "Toyota-hazure" ', *Nikkei Business*, 39; 'Toyota will develop a High-Performance Passenger Car Microcomputer', *Nihon Keizai Shimbun*, 14 Feb. 1985, 9; 'The Spring Sales Offensive in New Cars', *Nihon Keizai Shimbun*, 19 Feb. 1985.

45. Daihatsu Kogyo Kabushiki Kaisha, *Rokujunenshi* (A Sixty Year History) (Osaka: Daihatsu Kogyo, 1967), 2–3.
46. Ibid. 11–12.
47. Ibid. 50–4.
48. Ibid. 97–103.
49. Shogo Amagai, *Nihon Jidosha Kogyo no Shiteki Tenkai* (The Historical Development of the Japanese Automobile Industry) (Tokyo: Aki Shobo, 1982), 247–52.
50. The Nissan Group is likewise a composite of three independent manufacturers, not including Prince Motors which was merged into Nissan in 1966: Nissan Motor, Nissan Diesel (which had been known as Minsei Diesel previously), and Fuji Heavy Industries (Subaru automobiles). Nissan Diesel's links to Nissan Motor go back to 1950 while Fuji Heavy Industry's ties were forged in Aug. 1968.

Of the five remaining independent auto makers in Japan, Isuzu Motors has been the most active in pursuing alliances with domestic manufacturers at first and later with foreign firms. In 1968, Isuzu arranged a short-lived alliance with Fuji Heavy Industries before Fuji joined with Nissan Motor, and at the same time forged another brief year-long encounter with Mitsubishi Motors. Although both of these aborted prematurely, Isuzu was the second Japanese auto producer, after Mitsubishi Motors, to align itself with a foreign manufacturer. In Jul. 1971 General Motors bought into Isuzu Motors as part of its unfolding global strategy of making and marketing a world car.

Mitsubishi Motors, however, had beaten Isuzu to the international line-up. It had formed a sales agreement with Chrysler Corporation in Feb. 1970 and this resulted in Chrysler's purchase of 15 percent of Mitsubishi's outstanding shares in Sept. 1971. (Actually, during the 1950s, Mitsubishi had a licensing agreement with Wyllis Jeep, Nissan with Austin Motors, and Isuzu with Hillman; these ties became attenuated by the 1960s as much because these foreign firms were failing as because Japanese firms were succeeding.) A few months later, Toyo Kogyo ('Mazda' after the early 1980s), the Hiroshima-based maker of Mazda automobiles, joined with Ford Motor in an agreement which resulted eventually, as in the Mitsubishi case, with Ford buying 25 percent of Mazda in 1979. Thus, Isuzu, Mitsubishi, and Mazda, all forged new links with foreign makers in the early 1970s although each retained its managerial independence and manufacturing autonomy.

The final two auto makers, Honda Motor and Suzuki, were mavericks from Hamamatsu City in Central Japan. Both started as motorcycle manufacturers and both preferred to rely on their own wits and wherewithal as they husbanded resources to move up from motorcycle to automobile production. Only after each had established its reputation and particular market niche did they link-up with other makers: Honda with British Leyland (BL) in Dec. 1979 and Suzuki with General Motors (GM) in Aug. 1981.
51. Interviews with K. Nishi of the Public Relations Dep. of Daihatsu Motor on 18 and 22 Feb. 1985. His estimate of annual capacity utilization.
52. Daihatsu Kogyo, *Rokujunenshi*, 165–75. Interviews with Mr. K. Nishi of the Public Relations Dep. of Daihatsu, on 18 and 22 Feb. 1985.
53. Personal communication with Mr. K. Nishi of the Public Relations Dep. of Daihatsu,

22 Feb. 1985.

54. According to Daihatsu's Yukashoken Hokokusho for the 1976–89 period. Toyota's outsourcing percentage hovers around 70 percent.

55. Interview with Mr. Nishi of Daihatsu at the company headquarters in Ikeda City, 18 Feb. 1985.

56. This is clearly seen in the records of the annual transactions between Daihatsu and its suppliers. See Daihatsu Kogyo, *Kaisha Meikan* (Company Register) (Osaka: Daihatsu Kyoyukai, 1980).

57. Functionally specialized interfirm networks attempt to maintain a state-of-the-art approach to the problems of production and management within a relatively narrowly defined field of activity. The parameters are largely delimited by the relevant technology defining such fields as automobile suspension or transmission. Nevertheless, each major field of activity is composed of numerous minor fields of activity, and in order to stay on the cutting edge of development and production in each subfield, functionally specialized interfirm networks play a crucial role in promoting education, technology diffusion, and management improvement, and in stimulating the motivation of managers to do business within the context of specialized enterprise subgroupings.

58. Daihatsu Kogyo, *Kaisha Meikan*, 11–160. In 1980, when there were 142 companies in Daihatsu's core group of suppliers, the breakdown of member firms by number of employees and asset capitalization was as follows. The low level of capitalization reflects the lower value of the yen in 1980 as well as the low valuation of land in Japanese accounting practices; land holdings are carried at the historical cost of purchase rather than at current or recent market value.

	No.	%
1. more than 5,000 employees and more than $200,000 in assets	11	8
2. 2,000 to 4,999 employees and $60,000 to $199,999 in assets	24	17
3. 500 to 1999 employees and $8,000 to $59,999 in assets	37	26
4. less than 500 employees and less than $8,000 in assets	70	49

59. Intragroup shareholding within the major firms of the Toyota Group (consisting of 16 firms) for 1982 is detailed in Table 7.4. The major change between 1982 and today is that Toyota Motor and Toyota Motor Sales merged in 1986. It should be noted that firms which were spun out of Toyota Motor, such as Nippondenso, or which are closely tied to marketing and sales for Toyota Motor, such as Toyoda Tsusho Trading or Tokyo Real Estate, have higher levels of intergroup shareholding. Among the fifteen major firms detailed below, the average level of intergroup shareholding is 24.1 percent. For the approximately 170 firms in the first-tier of the Toyota Motor's supplier network, the average level of intergroup shareholding is no more than a few percent. In Daihatsu's case, Toyota's initial shareholding amounted to 12.5 percent but that has climbed slightly to 15.2 percent. This reflects the joining of Toyota Motor's shares with those of Toyota Motor Sales after the merging of the two firms.

60. The Nomura Securities Company, Japan's largest securities investment firm, comes to the same conclusion of limited financial ties between Toyota Motor and most of its suppliers. See its report, 'Toyota Motor Corporation', Investment Note Memorandum, 18 May 1983, 11. Financial relationships are reported in Industry Research System, *Toyota Jidosha*, Nagoya: Industry Research System, 1986: 25–9. Also, see Michael J. Smitka, *Competitive Ties: Subcontracting in Japanese Manufacturing* (New York: Columbia

University Press, forthcoming 1991).

61. Cusumano, *Japanese Automobile Industry*, 189–90.

62. There remains the question of how different is Toyota's system of interdependent, decentralized production. A few numbers can be offered. General Motors is 50 percent more integrated than Toyota in terms of value-added content. Fiat has approximately 4,000 suppliers to Toyota's 40,000. Volvo began a strategy of decentralized production in the 1920s and 1930s which was presented by Volvo's founder, Assar Gabrielsson, as unique to Volvo. However, the number of suppliers was never over 100 at any time during the 1920s and 1930s and, during these years, Volvo acquired many of its important suppliers.

    Conceptually, the purchase of suppliers, removing the residual rights of control from management of the supplying company, can seriously distort management incentives and lead quickly to sub-optimization. Thus, the size and the nature of interfirm transactions in Volo's network were substantially, even fundamentally, different than Toyota's. Nils Kinch, 'Emerging Strategies in a Network Context: The Volvo Case', *Scandinavian Journal of Management Studies*, May 1987, 167–84. Sanford J. Grossman and Oliver D. Hart, 'The Costs and Benefits of Ownership: A Theory of Vertical and Lateral Integration', *Journal of Political Economy*, 94/4 (Aug. 1986), 691–719.

63. Charles F. Sabel and Michael J. Piore, *The Second Industrial Divide* (New York: Basic Books, 1984). Basically, Sabel and Piore's argument is that the market has evolved beyond scale economies and, as a result, smaller sized organizations, specialized in particular market niches but cooperating together (because of technical complementarities as well as the desire to reduce risks) represent the wave of the future.

    The flaw in the argument is obvious. Toyota competes on the basis of scale and scope. Indeed, scope economies are thought to depend on increasing returns to scale. The Toyota production system emphasizes the rationalization of production on a gigantic scale by (1) reducing waste throughout the system; inventories are not simply shifted to suppliers; (2) motivating and rewarding suppliers to do their best by working with Toyota. Thus, rationalization of the system remains rooted in principles of scale and scope economies. What is different is the intensity, density, and frequency of transactions in the system, and the levels of these achieved are on the basis of extremely high levels of organizational learning. For a descriptive treatment in English of the history of Toyota Motor, see Toyota Motor Corporation, *Toyota*.

64. Cusumano, 'Manufacturing Innovation and Competitive Advantage', 12–13. Between 1960 and 1983, value-added productivity tripled among suppliers, a higher rate than for Nissan and Toyota. A recent book that deals directly with this theme is Yoshinobu Sato, *Toyota Gurupu no Senryaku to Jissho Bunseki* (An Empirical Analysis of the Strategy of the Toyota Group) (Tokyo: Shirakaba Shobo, 1988). While Sato documents the interfirm relationships that characterize the Toyota Group in great detail, he does not do so from the perspective of organizational learning, the basic framework of this chapter for interpreting not only the means but also the ends of the interfirm network model of organization.

8

Dynamic and Structured Interdependence

The Making of the Japanese Enterprise System

Three themes undergird and unify this study of the Japanese enterprise system. First, history describes what was possible and practical in the institutional development of the modern Japanese economy. To these ends, the origins, emergence, and evolution of the constituent elements of the Japanese enterprise system have been examined as interwoven historical themes, and the connections securing factory, firm, and network have been analyzed and characterized. Without this history, it is precipitate and quixotic to generalize about the Japanese corporation and business system.[1]

Second, the history of the firm, any firm, is inextricably linked with the social, economic, and political circumstances that co-evolve with the firm. Corporate history traces an institutional evolution in which the firm transforms and is transformed by environmental circumstances. These tracings, that is the process of institutional embedding, demarcate conceptual limits to any treatment of the firm.[2] Tracings also delimit institutional choice: the past channels a range of choices by which business structures and strategies are molded and managed now and in the future. Yet the process of institutional embedding is not once-and-for-all, even while sense-making and action-taking tend to be cumulative, interactive, and difficult to reverse.

Because of this indigenous history of choices, actions, and outcomes, the Japanese enterprise system should not be interpreted solely in light of economic and organizational theories based on Western experience. While it is seemingly obvious that history may beget social-science theory in this case (and many others), the study of Japanese business institutions is too often disassociated from Japanese history, yielding data without credible boundaries, sightings, and judgements.[3]

Third, if the Japanese business system cannot be fitted to an abstraction based on Western experience, a paradigm grounded in local knowledge should be fashioned and, ideally, joined with a general model of the firm. This study has concentrated on the former task in order to establish that the outstanding record of the Japanese enterprise system is grounded in history and a progressive interdependence of factory, firm, and network.

The interactive dynamic of the Japanese enterprise system must be emphasized in unifying particular and general models of the firm because the achievements of the system cannot be disassociated from a history of competitive strategies and cooperative structures binding factories, firms, and networks, and of these being tempered and honed in light of experience and becoming implicit, general, and effective.[4] These arrangements are sufficiently different from those found in the West to constitute a basis for a different economic system—a system that is becoming a world-class model.

Thus the approach taken here is a rather complicated one, for I take the long view and I combine social science theory with local history and culture. I have sought to understand the history of Japanese corporations in terms of what we know about corporations world-wide, but I am equally interested in the special-ness of the Japanese experience and in how that specialness may inform and perhaps transform a general theory of the firm. By studying history and by building economic and organizational models, particular and general streams of knowledge about the firm may be joined. Merging the two styles of enquiry is possible if one recognizes that industrial firms have become large in just three ways and that these correspond more or less to industrial developments in three leading regions of advanced capitalism.

The American, M-Form model internalizes transactions in the interest of efficiency, separating out operational from strategic decisions, applying a uniform set of performance criteria and allocative guidelines. The model assumes that divisions are operationally independent but strategically and financially dependent. The European, H-Form (holding company) model is less sanguine concerning organizational and allocative efficiencies. It grants substantial autonomy to its companies managing them more like investments than related businesses. Operations and strategies are not centrally coordinated, only finances are uniformly evaluated.

Finally, the Japanese enterprise system offers a model of operational and strategic interdependence coupled with financial independence. The model assumes no organizational or allocative efficiencies. Individual companies are responsible to no one but themselves, even while their futures (operational as well as strategic) are tied to countless other firms over which they have only limited influence. Influence is exercised by being independent, autonomous, excellent, available. Companies that choose to act together may evolve allocative efficiencies through mechanisms that emphasize an internal division of labor based on organizational learning. The stylized features of these models are highlighted below (Table 8.1).

An overarching insight of this study is that choices concerning the size, scope, and structure of enterprises as generalized in M-Form, H-Form, and JES patterns and practices have strategic and behavioral consequences. In relatively small and specialized Japanese firms, growth by acquisition is rare and strategic control is focused in the development of firm-specific resources leading to high levels of internal innovation as well as to a dynamic forging of interfirm networks of complementary specialization. Single-firm resources are developed in tandem with other firms and become positively and intricately interrelated.[5]

The Corporation and its Environment

The interrelated histories of many firms in Japan have culminated in general patterns of enterprise activities that are clearly different from Western, especially American, corporations in terms of structure, function, conduct, performance as well as meaning. These numerous points of difference emerged early on, that is from the initial motivations for bringing the corporate form of organization to Japan and during the myriad moments of incremental adjustment and advancement thereafter.

Questions of corporate form and process hinge on issues of strategy, that is on managerial models and cycles of reflection, decision, and action that motivate predictable patterns of resource allocation, organizational governance, and enterprise performance. Not only are single Japanese firms different in size, structure, and activity from their Western counterparts, but also they differ in their partial and overall configurations or in the ways single units join and detach the whole of the system.

High levels of organizational interdependence in Japan promote gradual, incremental change because organizations need to be cognizant of and responsive to countless other firms. The duration, density, and intensity of interactions within this context does not appear to deaden organizations. Quite the opposite seems true: organizations are enlivened by an interactive dynamic, perhaps validating Granovetter's thesis of the strength of weak ties.[6]

Such micro- and macro-organizational differences are grounded in history and in the efforts of managers to respond to history. The Japanese enterprise system is rooted in two distinct features of that country's industrial experience and in a sequence of structural and strategic adjustments to those features: agreement that the firm was a primary means of economic and political progress; and more importantly, a scarcity of every imaginable resource to achieve these ends.

TABLE 8.1. *Three Pathways to Modern Industrial Organization*

	M-Form	H-Form	JES
Operations	O	O	X
Finances	*	*	O
Strategy	*	O	X

O = independence
* = dependence
X = interdependence

The resulting conflict of means and ends dictated a strategy of combining, aligning, and sharing resources. In spite of false starts, failures, confusion and conflict, this was done with government promotion at national and local levels and with an entrepreneurial rush by businessmen from every social class and region. As described earlier, the monetized, urbanized, and generally commercialized character of Japan's pre-industrial economy may be regarded as *sine qua non* for this strategy.

The institutional means to organize and exploit resources appeared in two forms: interfirm and intrafirm coalitions. Both sorts of coalitions were piecemeal and imperfect at first, but they became more elaborated, extensive, and effective in time. In either case, there was a recognition that cooperation was a means of economic competition. Without cooperation, given scale and knowledge requirements for industrial competition, enterprises were unlikely to garner sufficient resources, take hold, and survive.

Even with cooperation, scarce resources were squandered, poor decisions taken, and greedy, self-serving behavior apparent. Strategies of cooperative development merely reduced waste and excess. Fortunately, legal barriers to cooperation were low. Social, political, and economic circumstances promoted cooperation. Cooperation evolved and became tacit, implicit, a necessary part of doing business.

A number of considerations made this possible. Institutional boundaries separating markets and firms were not always clear-cut. For example, government-founded enterprises were sold at a fraction of cost in the 1880s, transferring valuable organizational resources from public to private hands at below market value.[7] Government-assisted trade associations set market prices, production quotas, and investment schedules in key industries, like textiles, cement, paper, and marine shipping.[8] Also, government-backed banks sometimes extended credit without adequate collateral, and credit was often employed in ways closer to equity than debt. Notes were rarely called in or came due.[9]

Policy, in general, was bent to the promotion and protection of domestic economic activity. Across every spectrum and sector of business endeavor, entrepreneurial ambitions joined with national aspirations to encourage cooperative economic actions without specifying contractual contingencies in much detail and depth. Expediency more than market efficiency was the rule. Expediency reflected both the late-development effect and strategic purpose. Japanese corporations were molded by industry and government leaders who gainsaid the example of Western firms by interposing public purpose and vision in what were essentially private-interest organizations.[10] Thus, the firm in Japan carries a legacy of innovativeness, of new institutional consciousness and purpose, based on its origins and premeditated evolution. The corporation was an agent of progress: a large-scale, profit-making institution that joined powerful production and organizational techniques with risk-taking managers devoted to personal, institutional, and national gain.

Voluntary and managed effort became the key to firm and interfirm effectiveness. Effectiveness, in turn, was related to predictability and gain, that is to the likelihood of profiting through repeated transaction. This definition of effectiveness depends on coalition-building, that is a process of creating institutional correspondence and integration, expressed today in such everyday practices as collaborative R & D efforts and export-limitation agreements among rival firms.[11]

Companies joined in coalitions are marked by an avoidance of vertical integration as a preferred means of enterprise growth. A lack of vertical integration leads to a distribution of incentives, investments, and rewards all along the value chain, creating a business system characterized by many points of independence, autonomy, and ambition. Economic success requires coordination among many such points of specialization (product and market specialization), and ultimately repeated acts of coordination may lead to institutional practices distinguished by elevated levels of organizational interdependence, information flow, and multilateral coalition-building.[12] Enterprise dynamics of this sort are contingent on low transaction costs, high organizational learning, and, non-trivially, the absence of a market for acquisitions. The division of labor, as a consequence, is limited as much by the degree of organizational interdependence as by the extent of the market.

Bases for Coalition-Building

Alexander Gerschenkron's assertions that later developing countries have to be more calculating and organized in the push towards industrialization and that centripetal forces of planning and ordering result in higher levels of political, economic, and social interdependence are generally persuasive for Japan. Gerschenkron rings true in the sense that institutional cooperation was less an expression of altruistic motivation than a frank appreciation of the need to join entrepreneurial efforts within a context of severely limited resources.[13]

Where Gerschenkron is less convincing is in assuming that greater economies of scale in later industrializing economies naturally result in larger sized institutions. Optimal size is a question of the size of organizational units, such as production and distribution units, relative to available technology and market demand.[14] Smaller Japanese firms do not suffer productivity or throughput deficiencies relative to Western competitors because organizational learning, a central feature of the Japanese enterprise system, is closely tied to organizational size. If smaller sized organizations, that is factories and firms, can capture learning in more focused and effective ways than would otherwise be the case, economies of scale, scope, and transaction cost are realized because of, and not in spite of, smaller size.

The tension between competition and cooperation that characterizes economic institutions in Japan did not arise without precedent, however. An exceptional willingness to cooperate and form coalitions can be found in a number of circumstances, the *sum* of which exemplify the distinctive trading and transacting cultures that characterize the Japanese enterprise system.

Epistemological Basis

Expediency appears within a specific social and philosophical context. In neither Buddhism nor neo-Confucianism, the major philosophical traditions of pre-industrial Japan, was self-interest enshrined with Adam Smith-like universality. From the early seventeenth century, a highly regarded Confucian philosophy posited a natural order of things, a diffuse hierarchical notion that integrated cosmic and social forces and that reasoned in behalf of cooperation in social and economic affairs. This philosophy was espoused in many schools of 'warrior' or *bushi* education as well as in the official and unofficial policies of the Tokugawa regime.

In this epistemology, hierarchy was not imposed on the world but was part of the world. Thus, a Confucian notion of social hierarchy linked human endeavor in an orderly, predictable, and reciprocal fashion within strata of structured and complementary interaction, achieving an idealized and harmonious blending of economic activities and institutions. In the Confucian world-view, social interest rather than self-interest was the basis for economic existence and achievement, and this suggests, a priori, a profoundly cooperative outlook on social order, institutional purpose, and individual effort.[15]

Historical Basis

To the notion of a pre-existing foundation for structured social interaction, add a climate of national emergency over a Western incursion and a widespread recognition of the need to do something credible, convincing, and in concert in order to forestall an attempted colonization of the country. Realize also that the early owners of industrial enterprises lacked production and managerial know-how, while engineers possessed know-how but lacked land, labor, and capital, and workers, without productive assets other than their labor, were resistant to industrial time, regimen, and ways of working. A successful mobilization of resources for industrial development in this disjointed environment would require structured cooperation and agreement that other courses of action were unattractive, and impractical.

Cultural Basis

The rooting of life in an experience of interdependence cannot be entirely derived from circumstances of epistemology and resource scarcity, however. Ronald Dore deduces a distinctive capitalist milieu in Japan which he terms the spirit of 'mutual goodwill'. It is colored by a long-term, future orientation and moralized commercial transactions wherein honesty in business affairs is expected, perhaps even dutiful. Non-opportunism in economic transactions transcends narrow self-interest, although non-opportunism occurs within a specific context of contingent, long-standing institutional relations.[16]

As a normative representation of business activities in Japan, Dore's description has validity, especially when one considers that cultural values such as these, are the result of historical processes of adjustment, adaptation, and reaction to industrial development. Nineteenth-century Japanese did not begin with these values, even if twentieth-century Japanese promote them.[17]

Kinship may be another cultural factor holding firms together. Rather than adhere to strict genealogical definitions of family, household members are those who contribute to the economic welfare of the group in *ie* or traditional stem households. The *ie* has been called an economic organization dressed up in family trim.[18] Because of this generous notion of kinship and widespread use of adoption, Japanese stem families have been likened to firms. And because Japanese firms purposely incorporate family symbolism, language, and customs into their managerial practices, they have been likened to families.[19] 'Kinship', in this dual sense of family as firm and of firm as family, helps hold firms together. Hence, goodwill and kinship affect the cultural contours of cooperation.

Organizational Basis

Given minimal efficient scale requirements in manufacturing and distribution and given formidable barriers to entry for industrial late developers, cooperation lessened risk and lowered return-to-scale requirements. Hence, cooperation was upheld as socially acceptable and economically pragmatic, even though the nature, limits, and meanings of cooperation were ambiguous. So while cooperative structures were encouraged, the uses of such structures for competitive advantage were still emerging.[20]

The historical record suggests that what began as an experimental and contingent approach to enterprise cooperation under circumstances of extreme environmental stress was transformed by the test of time and the efforts of untold individuals into an expected, commonplace, and positive framework for mutual enterprise gain.[21] Cooperation promoted competition. People learned this lesson and through experience, cooperation became institutionalized.

In circumstances of risk avoidance and resource scarcity, the nature of cooperation was to stress promises of performance rather than agreements on price. That is, agreements on price were often *ex post* rather than *ex ante* and they emphasized long-term relationships between enterprises. Organized interdependence of this sort not only reduced risks but also minimized the problem of adverse selection.[22] Adverse selection, that is ignorance about probable outcomes, was diminished by transacting within a set of finite trading partners. Cooperative, interdependent relations *became* an efficient means to organize.

This was possible, even probable, because information and information processing are costly. As organizations develop, they evolve dedicated channels of information flow and decision making to reduce costs. These are expensive to reverse and, hence, information-processing costs become deeply ingrained in organizational structure. From this perspective, organized interdependence among firms was a means to expand information choices and information-handling capacity without incurring the full costs for doing so.[23]

Economic Basis

Economic growth spurred interdependence. Across-the-board increases in rates of throughput, productivity, efficiency, and compensation in large firms in post-World War Two Japan are best explained by organized cooperation, that is by the structured interdependencies that describe intrafirm and interfirm coalitions.

The speed and effectiveness with which coalitions can be mobilized depend on low switching costs and high equity. Low switching costs are mostly transactional costs. That is, if interorganizational coalitions require excessive monitoring, evaluation, and supervision, they cannot offer a cost-effective means for accomplishing work. On the other hand, if coalition members benefit in some direct proportion to their contribution, transaction costs will be low and benefits high.[24] The likelihood of continued, high rates of enterprise growth reduces opportunism and moral hazard because organizational coalitions face larger losses in the future by shirking and soldiering in the present. As employees gained stability of tenure in large firms in post-war Japan, organizational coalitions of a dense, durable, and personal sort became possible.[25]

Also, contracts and acquisitions are *not* alternative means of securing coalitional relations in Japan because almost no market for corporate control exists. Since financial markets are *not* an efficient means to allocate risk, given that substantial shares in most firms are closely held and thinly traded, organizational interdependence—a form of indirect but none the less shared ownership and asset control—became prevalent.[26]

The economic logic of cooperation requires long-term equity.[27] The choice to be mutually, reciprocally bound together, enables firms to achieve coordination without a great deal of centralization. And because companies remain independent even while they are interdependent, they are not tied by several levels of management devoted to organizational integration. Less time and fewer resources are devoted to compliance monitoring as a result.

Political Basis

Industrial enterprises in Japan started with national, avowedly political purposes. As a partial consequence of Japan's resource-constrained, late-development industrialization, many functions and activities that were government responsibilities in the West were relegated to private firms in Japan. By default, private firms became vehicles of public progress.

High levels of in-company education and company-related social-welfare benefits, such as housing, medical coverage, commuting subsidies, cost of living supplements, retirement assistance, and the like, can be traced historically to the inability of local and national governments to muster adequate resources for social welfare and community benefits.[28] The Kikkoman Corporation, for example, financed railroads, grammar schools, cultural centers, water works, fire departments and town halls in Noda City for exactly these reasons.[29]

Yet politics were and are important for other reasons. Cooperative strategies are action plans that are endorsed, furthered, and sometimes subsidized by banks, insurance, industrial, and trading companies associated with interfirm groups. The mustering and allocation of economic resources within such groups necessarily involves the exercise of politics since power relations emerge whenever and wherever transaction-specific investments are made.[30] Politics also drives the building of sub-unit coalitions. A capacity to mobilize resources quickly and repeatedly hinges on institutional as well as personal reputations for fairness and equity. Hence, politics affects the degree of organized interdependence (permeability) joining factory, firm, and network.[31]

The Sum is Greater than the Parts: Theoretical Implications

The special qualities of interorganizational cooperation in Japan are not found simply in notions of coordination, cooperation, and interdependence. These exist elsewhere, indeed everywhere in the world of economic organizations. The specialness is derived from several differences that characterize the Japanese enterprise system.

First, cooperation and interdependence are assumed to be effective. This may be because the risks of what economists call hold-up and moral hazard—the costs of opportunism in a non-judgemental sense—have not been especially pronounced in Japan for the reasons outlined above. Second, coordination and cooperation, both formal and informal, take place within a much larger group of directly and indirectly affiliated firms. Toyota's 40,000 suppliers have to be contrasted with Fiat's 4,000 and Volvo's 1,500.[32]

Within interfirm groups, a breach of acceptable business practices can result in a kind of network ostracism (perhaps a modern form of 'village ostracism' *mura hachibu*) with disastrous results for offending firms. So while opportunism may infect interorganizational relations in Japan as elsewhere, what Oliver E. Williamson calls 'opportunism with guile' may be less pronounced. Firms that mislead, distort, and disguise with calculation will be forced out of trading networks due to the excessive monitoring costs incurred by such behavior.

Even when there is no intent to confuse or deceive, firms must guard their reputation: they must try to match the best buys available in the market-place and be responsive in their dealings with network members. Without such efforts, network membership is questioned. Finally, firms not only recognize but also value their investment in interdependence: it represents a sunk cost in an intangible but critical asset. Organizational interdependence creates momentum, builds focus, mobilizes resources, and sustains a kind of creative tension.[34]

Hierarchical Origins and Outcomes

A rationale for systemic constraints on the behavior of individual firms within interfirm groups may be found in the epistemological, historical, and cultural dimensions of a cooperative *and* competitive hierarchy, as outlined above. These have been fortified by a logic of equity in efforts and rewards. The range and pervasiveness of intrafirm/interfirm relations in Japan demands a vastly different view of economic and organizational behavior from either the transactional or marginalist point of view.[35]

Instead of beginning with self-interest, bounded rationality, and opportunism as starting-points for theorizing about the firm, begin instead with a notion of dynamic, structured, and reciprocal hierarchy. Through hierarchy, self-interest and opportunism are minimized while dynamic yet structured incentives lessen sub-goal pursuit and satisficing behavior. Long-term contracting and enduring intrafirm/interfirm relations are sustained without high levels of asset-specific investment because organizational interdependence promotes and encourages such behavior.

While a 'given' in contemporary Japan, dynamic and equitable hierarchies of this sort emerged only in this century through the efforts and ingenuity of tens of thousands of Japanese workers and managers. Joining a hierarchy and participating therein are just the *beginning* of a strategic process of negotiating hierarchical position and power that culminates in gaining competitive advantage. One begins with hierarchy as an established social fact and, from there, hierarchy is extended, elaborated, and managed. This view of hierarchy characterizes Toyota's structured supplier relations and, for that matter, Toshiba's integrated production environments, like the Yanagicho Works.

Participation, recognition, and reward are enhanced through an expansion and refinement of hierarchy. Such a notion of hierarchy accommodates not only the beginnings of the modern corporation and enterprise system in Japan but it includes a concept of hierarchical continuity through organizational learning, strategic interfirm positioning, network entry and exit.

Organized interdependence, that is relations characterized by competitive-cooperative tension between organizational units, allows Japanese companies to reduce firm-specific bounded rationality and, at the same time, to guard against opportunism. Unless the costs of doing business interdependently, and these are mainly transaction costs, become larger than the costs of doing business independently, then the weight of history and strategy favors the continuation, adaptation, and intensification of intrafirm/interfirm relations. Interdependence has its own built-in rewards and penalties and these will not easily be displaced or replaced.[36]

Interdependence: Order and Reciprocity

The flexibility and resiliency of interorganizational combinations in Japan (involving factory, firm, and network) constitute a basic strength of the modern Japanese economy, and they anchor a sustained and unrivalled capacity for heightened use of intrafirm and interfirm resources. In the case of either intrafirm or interfirm coalitions, it is the *intensity* (frequency), *density* (number), and *duration* (stability) of transactions that distinguish interactions. Increasingly, the distinctiveness of these patterns are being recognized.[37]

Conceptually, two stylized forms of interfirm networks may be distinguished: hierarchical and reciprocal. These differ in degree, the degree to which a predetermined order characterizes bilateral and multilateral interorganizational relations. Financially oriented networks display hierarchical tendencies to the degree that interfirm lending patterns are intense, dense, and durable as well as predictable. *Zaibatsu* and *keiretsu* groups are more inclined toward the hierarchical network model while product-centered and task-force groups are more reciprocal in character. In Toshiba's case, for example, interfirm relations are less predictably structured, due to a greater diffusion and decentralization of technological know-how, including product design and development capabilities, among affiliates and suppliers.[38]

In either type of network (and countless hybrids in between), networks presuppose social, political, and economic frameworks for their existence. Such frameworks are outcomes of prior network experience.[39] Given the strong arguments in favor of hierarchy, already outlined, and given relatively higher degrees of resource scarcity before the 1960s and 1970s, it would appear that networks were more commonly hierarchical than reciprocal until recently in Japan. However, heightened competitive pressures have pushed networks towards more reciprocal modalities since then.

There is a financial dimension as well. Recall that large, traditional *kigyo shudan* (discussed in Chapter 5) have lower rates of return on capital than smaller, more reciprocal, product-focused groups. Recently, growing pressures for enhanced financial performance push traditional groups in a more reciprocal direction as a means of increasing incentives, opportunities and revenues for firms. At the same time, however, it should be emphasized that both dynamics may co-exist within and between firms, since organizational and environmental contingencies do not necessarily have uniform effects. Like the variable speed transmission of a modern automobile, an entire range of dynamic principles are possible within multi-tiered, multi-hierarchical, multi-nodal, networked organizations, such as Toyota and Toshiba.

Reliance on long-term relationships to bind organizations together is a critical feature of network effectiveness. Long-term contracting allows for the specification of contingent claims in order to adapt to fluctuations in supply and demand, even though it is virtually impossible to specify all the contingencies that affect the distribution of resources and rewards.[40] Instead of attempting to define every contingency, stable contracting relationships promote reciprocity, fair play, a profitable partnership. Reciprocity simplifies the process of ordering economic relations, resting transactions on a bedrock of cumulative experience, mutual effort, organizational learning, a common and dynamic institutional culture.

It may be argued that the idea and practice of 'fairness' as a constraint on profit-seeking is not confined to the Japanese business environment. Yet it seems clear that in the course of Japan's modern economic growth various notions of fairness have operated within interfirm networks to constrain both excessive profit-seeking and profit-taking by firms. The rapid growth of the Japanese economy, before and after the Pacific War, may have been a necessary condition for the emergence and evolution of such high levels of cooperation, fairness, and organizational interdependence, however.

The Enterprise System in Japan: Development and Evolution

Between firms, patterns of interfirm resource-allocation have proven remarkably durable, adaptable, and effective. Beginning with business combinations that coalesced around *zaibatsu* interests at the turn of the twentieth century, patterns of interfirm cooperation and collaboration emerged in behalf of generating interfirm economies of scope and, eventually, scale.[41] Specialization, brought about by technology acquisition and application, drove both kinds of economies.

Scope economies were important in the acquisition of raw and intermediate products and in their eventual processing and distribution. For such purposes, an alignment of banking, trading, shipping, warehousing, and marketing services along with manufacturing activities were important, and often financial ties joined such activities. By the inter-war period, none the less, interfirm alliances for production and distribution in the absence of substantial equity ties became more and more common. Over time, financial ties became less important, others more so. Product-based interfirm networks without substantial equity pooling, such as Hitachi and Toyota Motor's supplier networks, emerged. Often, such enterprises were organized to serve regional markets with well endowed, multifunction factories, that is focal factories.[42]

Two common strategies of business growth, horizontal combination and vertical integration, appeared at this time in electrochemicals, petrochemicals, machinery, and transportation-equipment industries. Vertical alliances were formed in the interest of achieving minimal efficient scale in industries where intermediate products were the outputs of some firms and the inputs of others. Horizontal coordination avoided duplicate investment, utilized existing facilities more fully, and propelled firms along lines of established competency.

The commercial emphasis that originally characterized *zaibatsu* groupings was transformed by a structural shift in the economy. Within the light industrial sector, for example, as cotton-textile firms moved into the manufacture of woolen and worsted goods and as synthetic-fiber products began to appear, interfirm coalitions were the mechanisms by which new products were brought on stream and existing ones broadened. Trading companies imported feed stock or raw materials, textile and chemical companies produced fiber, weaving companies wove it, and specialized trading firms distributed cloth to wholesalers, apparel manufacturers, and retailers. Interfirm networks were not only a way to organize resources but also a means to exploit resources.

Historically, the weight of so many examples of the efficacy and reliability of interfirm combinations has resulted in substantial demonstration and modeling effects. It is virtually unthinkable for firms to attempt to succeed entirely on their own. And given interfirm network dynamics, access to and positioning in a network may be as important as the anticipated value-added share in network output.[43] Recently formed businesses in international service industries, such as database Value-Added Networks (VANs) and telecommunications transmission carriers (for example, Dai-Ni Denden Kosha, Japan's second long-distance telecommunications company), adopt highly interdependent forms of cooperative organization at the start. The value of network affiliation is more akin to potential than kinetic energy: firms maximize opportunities by use of network-based resources.

Access, transaction frequency and intensity likewise affect issues of *intrafirm* organization, governance, and performance. A post-war reorganization of firms accelerated a pre-war trend in the direction of separating ownership and control and the professionalization of management. All employees in major firms, and not just certain key employees as in the pre-war period, were vested with rights of long-term employment, seniority-based compensation, and in-company training. Compensation was geared toward length of service and work-group contribution, so that consistency and intensity of effort were rewarded. The cost-benefit calculus of corporate membership has shifted upward for all employees although this is especially true for line workers and lower-level managers, traditionally the most numerous but least well paid employees.

Expanded opportunities for participation, an emphasis on training both on the job and off the job, a general professionalization of work, increasingly refined performance standards and rewards—these are rewards of an elaborated internal hierarchy. Greater equality of opportunity, reflected in a conscious effort to balance inputs (effort) and outputs (recognition and reward) has been realized. High firm-specific learning rates are one result.

The rapidity of technical progress in post-war Japan has lead to a general foreshortening of product life-cycles. High levels of company-specific learning and doing based on technological developments creates substantial entry barriers for competitors. The juxtaposition of these elements means that proprietary learning within firms builds barriers to entry for a limited time only, generally for a single-generation of the product life-cycle. During this brief window of technological advantage, superior firms maximize sales and revenues on the basis of managerial and marketing capabilities.[44]

Accelerated cycles of organizational learning (tied to product life-cycles) have been particularly noteworthy since the mid-1970s. Firms that have lost out in the race to be first to commercialize a new product do not abandon the competition. Instead, they redouble their efforts in R & D, design, manufacturing, and marketing to be the first out with the next generation of products, thereby intensifying the conditions of successful product innovation and introduction. In the microelectronics industry today, product life-cycles of less than a year are normal. Substantial resources have to be continually invested in product and process innovation in order to ensure competitive advantages in subsequent product generations, where, once again, because of information diffusion, organizational learning, and enhanced intrafirm/interfirm cooperation, first-mover advantages can be sustained only by additional investments in learning, training, and across-the-board exploitation of experience.

'Excessive competition' and a 'torrential downpour' (*shuchu go-u*) of products, often seen abroad as 'dumping', may be consequences of the deepening of intrafirm/ interfirm capabilities and the need to exploit these advantages fully and promptly when they appear. When annual growth rates of over 100 percent in some markets occurred during the 1960s and 1970s, companies had to double their physical plant capacity every year just in order to survive. The 'de-maturation' of what were once considered stable industries is another consequence of the intensification of interdependencies progressively linking of factory, firm, and network.[45]

The coupling of competitive strategies and cooperative structures through intrafirm/interfirm coalitions and networks encourages investment in learning in spite of brevity of proprietary learning advantages. Outside Japan, the strategic belief is that learning diffusion cancels out the desirability of ongoing investment in organizational learning. In Japan, however, long-term employment, seniority-weighted compensation, and performance bonuses have provided sufficient contextual incentives for employees of large firms to deepen their organizational commitment and levels of performance.

A positive cycle of network expansion and enterprise growth results. Hence, post-war economic conditions and a modern social contract imbue Japanese firms with a distinctive post-war spirit and culture, and these reinforce a movement toward building firm-specific, employee-based coalitions and competencies.[46] These become key rate-limiting factors in the growth of single enterprises and, more generally, of the Japanese enterprise system.[47]

To summarize, Japanese firms appeared in the midst of resource scarcity, international rivalry, and a certain irreducible exigency: being competitive in a world of minimum efficient scale. In the context of late development, cooperative arrangements between firms to achieve economies of scope and scale and, eventually, intrafirm learning economies evolved. Even so, there were no labels or recipes for such strategies. There were no guarantees that any strategies, economies, or policies, cooperative or not, would succeed.

TABLE 8.2. *Towards the Modern Corporation and Enterprise System in Japan:*
A Progressive and Hierarchical Model

	Intrafirm Resources	*Interfirm Resources*
Stage I to 1918 The Firm in its Parts	• Minimum Efficient Scale (MES) in only one industry: cotton textiles • towards functional focus and excellence	• economies of scope in finance, transport & distribution • loosely-coupled, non- manufacturing networks
Stage II 1918–1954 The Firm its Whole	• economies of scale in products of the Second Industrial Revolution • towards systems excellence in an expanded hierarchy	• emerging product-based interfirm groupings • product/market specialization without much vertical integration
Stage III 1954–1990 The Firm in its Environment	• economies of scale and scope based on task-force coalitions • towards network excellence with multiple nodes and hierarchies; intrafirm and interfirm resources increasingly aligned	• transaction cost economies based on interfirm organizational learning • tightly-coupled coalitions/ networks with high entry & exit barriers; 'enacted' environment

These lines of organizational development are represented in Table 8.2, recognizing that a table cannot capture the complexity and interdependence of Toshiba's Yanagicho Factory depicted in Chapter 6 or the Toyota supplier network described in Chapter 7.

Consider that in 1989 Yanagicho was upwardly and horizontally connected to 137 different corporate sub-units while it was supplied by 242 independent business units.[48] Thus, one factory was simultaneously and frequently transacting with 379 other organizational units and these, in turn, were linked internally and externally to even larger numbers of units. In fact, Yanagicho's purchasing department issues some 30–40,000 bids per month, resulting in several hundred intrafirm/interfirm transactions per hour.[49]

The complexity of such organized interdependence may be illustrated by a lattice-like, three-dimensional figure below (left-hand side) that links making, creating/coordinating, and selling functions through intrafirm/interfirm coalition-building at three discrete levels. Figure 8.1 is a better representation of organ-

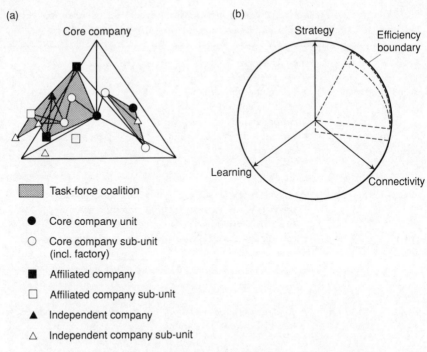

(a)

Core company

Task-force coalition

● Core company unit

○ Core company sub-unit
  (incl. factory)

■ Affiliated company

□ Affiliated company sub-unit

▲ Independent company

△ Independent company sub-unit

(b)

Strategy

Efficiency boundary

Learning

Connectivity

FIG. 8.1. *Organizational and Functional Interdependence in the Japanese Enterprise System*

Product-Centered, Task-Oriented Coalition: A Three-Dimensional View of Functional Interdependencies and Efficiency Boundaries

izational interdependence than Figure 1.1, the introductory, two-dimensional illustration of the Japanese enterprise system in Chapter 1.

A more abstract representation of the dynamics joining intrafirm/interfirm resources is found on the right-hand side of the figure. In this illustration (which may be overlaid on the left-hand side), three axes are important: strategy or the policies that motivate organizational relations; connectivity or the numbers of spokes, hubs and junctions (organizational units) that define an interorganizational system and the intensity, density, and duration of their interactions; learning or the degree to which interorganizational relations are effective and efficient. These axes, time- as well as transaction-dependent, may be thought of as pie slices; each slice depicts potentialities associated with parts of the Japanese enterprise system.

How much potential exists or how much pie is consumable is a question of the efficiency boundaries defining relationships between strategy and connectivity, connectivity and learning, learning and strategy. The first relationship is governed by the degree to which product strategies effectively mobilize the resources of interorganizational units (factories and firms); the second is driven by transaction-costs joining those units; the last is related to the experience of acting inter-dependently and advantageously. Defining the pie in this fashion lays bare an anatomy of Japanese economic power—the organizational interdependencies that interlace and energize the Japanese enterprise system.

Lines of Divergent Development: Japan and the West

Economic theory does not discriminate well between cultural, historical, and organizational circumstances as outlined above, although notions of managerial strategy offer a means to understand a set of progressive decisions that exploit institutional goals, based on an assessment of environmental risk and cultural resources. Strategy embodies a stream of intentional choices where historical circumstances are consciously incorporated in oversight, planning, and reward systems.

Succeeding in a world of severely constrained resources required a kind of coherence in world-view and practice that emphasized organizational connections and interdependencies. The dominant strategy of enterprise growth under these circumstances was to specialize in a limited range of products within a larger framework of multiple-firm interdependence. Firms specialized in one or a few business lines. Outside of this specialization, instead of internalizing managerial, planning, and coordinating functions required by vertical integration and product diversification strategies, managers preferred to 'externalize' those functions.

Japanese firms grew by specialization and by associating unneeded functions and activities with an expanding enterprise group. Coordination between organiza-tional units emphasized matters of reciprocity and fair exchange, resulting in a type of control which was not so much financial as organizational. Obviously, internal as well as external growth strategies can be exercised simultaneously. A study of the shipbuilding industry during the post-war years, for example, reveals exactly that. As divisional structures were adopted internally by firms to cope with expanding lines of business, 63 affiliated companies were established between 1955–64, 107 between 1965–74, 103 between 1975–84, and 124 since 1985.[50] That averages to 57 affiliates per shipbuilder or about two formed per year.

Such patterned interdependence between firms has been characterized in a number of ways. The Japanese have written voluminously on the dual economic structure, *zaibatsu*, *keiretsu*, *kigyo shudan*, subcontracting, and other forms of firm interdependence. The tone of this outpouring has been negative for the most part: either Marxian tracts on the political and economic exploitation of small firms by large firms or cultural apologies as to why Japanese economic organization does not conform to Western models of industrial organization.

A few authors have argued for functional equivalency, namely that the culturally specific patterns of organizational interdependence in Japan make good economic sense as functional equivalents to Western notions of how markets and hierarchies should be organized. Accordingly, the advantages of flexible specialization, good-will, and 'strong' corporate culture, based on the Japanese experience, can be offered as remedies for the arteriosclerosis and shortsightedness of Western corporations gone awry.[51] This Panglossian view may be good advice, but only if Western and Japanese companies are indeed functional equivalents.

The arguments presented herein, however, are that modern industrial firms in Japan look different, behave differently, are engendered by and engender different institutional values than Western firms. If structure, behavior, and values differ, and if these are embedded features, then arguments based on functional equivalency are trivial, even contentious. Prevailing Western paradigms of corporate structure and behavior can only be misapplied to Japanese firms in such instances.

Of the largest 200 Japanese industrial firms, only 40 percent engaged in limited diversification in 1987. And their efforts were quite constrained; 41 percent of these made goods in the same two-digit SIC category. (Actually, the figure would be higher—46 percent—if the American SIC code did not classify computers in a different category, 35, from other electrical devices, 36 and 38.) No major Japanese firms were highly diversified, and only a handful, 9 or 6, depending on how one counts computer-equipment firms, were relatively diversified (with three different product lines, each accounting for at least 20 percent of sales).

Without a massive reorganization of intrafirm/interfirm networks and realloca-tion of business resources, companies in the Japanese enterprise system could not hope to follow strategies of vertical integration and unrelated product diversifica-tion as *primary* means of corporate growth. While in some instances spin-offs from core companies by affiliates may be considered a form of diversification and growth, the autonomy experienced by Japanese spin-offs within larger interfirm networks is greater than that enjoyed by divisions in M-Form corporations. Japanese spin-offs are *not* operational profit-centers, the logic of the multidivisional firm. When crucial matters of organizational autonomy and control are so differently structured and evaluated, functional equivalency arguments are beside the point.[52]

Japanese industrial firms, even the so-called diversified ones, are closer to business-unit than multidivisional forms of organization. Of course, Japanese firms can and do diversify their product lines but they simply do not diversify to the extent and in the way that Western, particularly North American firms do. And they are unlikely to do so in the future. Though some performance advantages may be attributed to M-Form structures, for companies already in the Japanese enter-prise system the risks of switching to evolved multidivisional structures far out-weigh the rewards.

Likewise, the performance benefits of M-Form structures may not surpass the advantages inherent in focused, business-unit forms of organization.[53] The con-centration of Japanese firms in well-defined product lines and its concomitant strategy of organizational interdependence appear almost prescient in a world where 'sticking to the knitting' and 'a long-term relationship with suppliers' are popularly heralded in commission reports, management seminars, and the business media.[54]

Concluding Thoughts

This book began with simple questions: what are the reasons for the smaller size of Japanese industrial firms, their generally higher levels of performance, and their notable interorganizational dependencies in contrast to comparable Western firms.

The answers are partly historical—industrialization began later and market maturation was slower; partly economic and technical—rapid economic growth hastened nearly continuous and intense organizational learning based on technology transfer and acquisition; and partly organizational—after a certain size and beyond a certain degree of business relatedness, functions and activities are divided among discrete yet interdependent organizations. Smaller firms, even those embedded in colossal interfirm networks, are flexible and adaptable. They are responsive to market signals because few resources are hoarded internally and these are activated more on the basis of reciprocity and equity than by managerial fiat.

Accordingly, relatively small and specialized firms are dynamically aligned with networks of affiliated firms and integrated, production sites, creating a business potential limited only by the information, incentives, and bargaining that couple factory, firm, and network. Competitive strategies and cooperative structures binding the Japanese enterprise system are my answers to the questions asked years ago.

However, in some scalar dimensions Japanese firms are less different than they used to be, resulting in a congruence of industrial firms world-wide along similar structural lines. Increasingly Japanese corporations share certain characteristics with firms anywhere, an abstraction of corporate features that has little to do with space and time. Similarities are found in basic patterns of industrial organization and economic change within the limited range of options available to profit-seeking companies.[55]

Nevertheless, differences are apparent in the timing, scale, rates, and magnitudes of those basic patterns and in the ways that organizations are segmented, ordered, and managed to accommodate change. And once strategic patterns are established, radical changes in structures, boundaries, and processes are unlikely.[56] In Japan these patterns and practices were appearing and coalescing six to seven decades ago. Hence, it is necessary to recognize a plurality of pathways and a certain plasticity of form and function in the institutional patterns of modern industrial capitalism.

So, while certain size differentials may be lessening among the world's major industrial firms, differences with respect to organizational strategy and structure and to efficiency and learning may be growing. The basic strength of the Japanese enterprise system is a process of increasingly differentiating strategy, structure, and managerial systems at discrete levels of organization on the basis of effective learning. All evidence points to an expanding importance of interorganizational learning in gaining competitive advantage, and hence to an ongoing differentiation of enterprise structure, strategy, and systems along established lines.

On various levels the triad of factory, firm, and network have shaped the course and content of organizational economics in Japan. On a descriptive level, the histories of dozens of firms during the last century have been traced in this volume. It is apparent that while major firms, like Toyota, Mitsubishi Motor, Kikkoman, Kirin, Tokyo Electron, Matsushita Electric Industrial, and Toshiba have been reducing their financial dependence on banks, trading companies, and other financial intermediaries, they have been advancing non-financial ties with other firms that complement their technical and marketing strengths. In such instances, company-specific advantages are worked and reworked within a nexus of inter-organizational opportunities by devoting considerable resources to the management of interorganizational relations.

Analytically, the course and content of industrial change have been pursued by examining interrelationships binding factory, firm, and network. In the beginning, cooperation between firms was contingent on a crash-dive towards economic development. Later, as firms exhausted sources of historically inexpensive technology from abroad and financing at home, they moved towards interfirm collaboration on bigger ticket, technology-intensive, longer lead-time projects. Cooperation evolved, became increasingly strategic, and should intensify as cross-industrial/interdisciplinary coordination quickens.

At the level of the factory, this has meant a continuing differentiation of facilities and functions, allowing firms to cut costs, promote innovation, and maintain a cascade of high-quality goods. Between firms and factories, specialization of tasks and tighter coordination of efforts builds lattices of interdependence linking functions, products, and markets in numerous positive feedback loops.

On a conceptual level, the adaptability and performance of the Japanese enterprise system requires a reconsideration of organizational theory and business strategy. Competitive strategies and cooperative structures, that is the certainty of permeable boundaries joining factory, firm, and network, represent a new and convincing model of interorganizational action, one that differs from prevailing industrial policy explanations for Japan's economic success and one that offers an example of organizational correspondence, reciprocity and resonance in the midst of rapid change. The strategic consequence is to move whole sets and subsets of interrelated firms in patterns of coalition and network coordination that maximize firm-specific competencies while building network-specific competitiveness and interdependence.

Competitiveness emerges as a network-embedded capacity activated by the ambitions and initiatives of countless corporate managers in countless institutional settings. Competitive strategies and cooperative structures thread through the Japanese enterprise system with subtlety, resilience, concurrence, and ambition. Such qualities are more often ascribed to works of art than to industrial organizations even though the intricacy, vitality, and long-term performance of the Japanese enterprise system are truly impressive. The Japanese enterprise system is an interorganizational innovation of local design, major proportions, and global significance.

NOTES

1. As Japan has become increasingly important in the world economy, it is more and more common to find analyses that are rooted in something other than the study of history and country-specific patterns of social, economic, political, legal, and cultural development. While certain aspects of Japan's development may be universal in character, it seems rather problematic to distinguish the general from the particular without a thorough understanding of history and of country-level institutional and behavioral patterns.

   While few studies explicitly endorse a 'generalist' view in place of a 'culturalist' one, not reading and reporting on the valuable work of anthropologists, psychologists, lawyers, economists, and historians that might support a cultural, historical, and institutional view as opposed to a 'culturalist' one is regrettable. It would certainly inform a 'generalist' view with valuable cultural and historical insights. To mention a few of the often uncited but valuable studies that exist in English: Harumi Befu's work on gift-giving and social organization; DeVos on social achievement; Dan Fenno Henderson on legal and institutional development; Sugiyama Lebra on patterns of Japanese behavior; David Plath on social aspects of work and after-work; Robert Smith on social order; Kawashima Takeyoshi on law and social order; Christena Turner on industrial relations and social consciousness; Thomas C. Smith on family and state in pre-industrial and industrial times; Gary Allinson on urban politics and industrial development; Andrew Gordon on industrial relations in heavy industries; Michael Cusumano on the automobile and software industries; Koji Taira on labor markets; Solomon Levine and Hisashi Kawada on human resources in industrial development; and the list goes on. James R. Lincoln and Kerry McBride, 'Japanese Industrial Organization in Comparative Perspective', *Annual Review of Sociology*, 13 (1987), 289–312.

2. Mark Granovetter, 'Economic Action and Social Structure: The Problem of Embeddedness', *American Journal of Sociology*, 91 (Nov. 1985), 481–510. Granovetter tries to find the high ground between what he calls over- and under-socialized behavior, namely people who act solely for either social or economic reasons. Stated starkly in this way, everyone will opt for something in between and this Granovetter calls 'the problem of embeddedness'. The real problem is to define that something in between, recognizing that it moves in time and space and that there are infinite degrees of in-betweenness.

   A slightly different formulation of this problem is found in Paul David's writings on 'path dependency' which discusses how history matters in social science, particularly in economics; see Paul A. David, 'Path-Dependence: Putting the Past into the Future of Economics', Technical Report 533, Economics Series, Institute for Mathematical Studies in the Social Sciences, Stanford University, Nov. 1988. Here, as in the Granovetter article, choices are not determinative. However, choices have consequences, and when consequences are pursued to their logical ends, it becomes increasingly difficult to reverse, abandon, or alter choices. This is especially true when technical choices require substantial investment in physical and human resources.

3. For an impassioned statement on the need to ground theory in history, see Friedrich August von Hayek, 'The Pretense of Knowledge', Nobel Memorial Lecture, 11 Dec. 1974, repr. *American Economic Review*, 79/6 (Dec. 1989), 3–7.

4. In the process, both social and political rules and the structure of political institutions have become endogenized in organizational forms and institutional arrangements. Thrainn Eggertsson, *Economic Behavior and Institutions* (Cambridge: Cambridge University Press, 1990), p. xiii.

5. The workings of the Japanese enterprise system illustrate an almost perfect reversal of the suggested consequences of a business system populated with acquisitive, M-Form firms. See Michael A. Hitt, R. E. Hoskisson, and R. D. Ireland, 'Mergers and Acquisitions and Managerial Commitment to Innovation in M-Form Firms', *Strategic Management Journal*, 11/Special Issue (Summer 1990), 29–48.

6. Mark Granovetter, 'The Strength of Weak Ties', *American Journal of Sociology*, 78/6 (May 1973).

7. Too much has been made to my way of thinking of the apparent lack of an obvious profit motive among Japan's early industrial ventures. See e.g. Byron K. Marshall, *Capitalism and Nationalism in Prewar Japan: The Ideology of the Business Elite, 1864–1941* (Stanford, Calif.: Stanford University Press, 1967). Some have even argued that a policy of devolving productive assets among a number of favored enterprises was followed, in order to maximize gain and spread risk for the nation.

8. Takeo Kikkawa, 'Functions of Japanese Trade Associations before World War II', paper, 14th Fuji Business History Conference, Gotenba, Shizuoka, Japan, 5–8 Jan. 1987. See also, Juro Hashimoto and Haruhito Takeda, *Ryodaisenkanki Nihon no Karuteru* (Cartels between the Two World Wars) (Tokyo: Ochanomizu Shobo, 1985).

9. Takafusa Nakamura, *The Post-war Japanese Economy* (Tokyo: University of Tokyo Press, 1981), 141. Shunsaku Nishikawa, 'Ginko: Kyoso to sono Kisei', in T. Kumatani (ed.), *Nihon no Sangyo Soshiki* (Japanese Industrial Structure) (Tokyo: Chuo Koron, 1973).

10. Although the point of community-centered entrepreneurship can be exaggerated, there was widespread support for the concept of the corporation as a vehicle of national progress. See Gustav Ranis, 'The Community Centered Entrepreneur in Japanese Development', *Explorations in Entrepreneurial History*, 13 (1955), who first raised the issue as well as Johannes Hirschmeier, *The Origins of Entrepreneurship in Meiji Japan* (Cambridge, Mass.: Harvard University Press, 1964); Johannes Hirschmeier and Tsunehiko Yui (eds.), *The Development of Japanese Business*, 2nd edn. (London: George Allen & Unwin, 1981), and my own, 'From Philanthropy to Paternalism in the Noda Soy Sauce Industry: Pre-Corporate and Corporate Charity in Japan', *Business History Review*, 56/2 (Summer 1982), 168–91.

11. The promise of such arrangements is reflected in the current world-wide concern with strategic alliances. Yet the Western concept of strategic alliances does not capture the rich multiplicity of institutional roles and purposes in Japan, that has been cleverly captured in the contemporary Japanese phrase '3C companies'. 3C companies are simultaneously the customer, co-producer, and competitor of other companies. The process of getting to be a '3C company' and of having an enterprise system of '3C companies' was long, difficult, and uncertain.

12. The distinction between specific rights and residual rights comes from Sanford J. Grossman and Oliver D. Hart, 'The Costs and Benefits of Ownership: A Theory of Vertical and Lateral Integration', *Journal of Political Economy*, 94/4 (Aug. 1986), 691–719.

13. Richard P. Nielsen, 'Cooperative Strategy', *Strategic Management Journal*, 9 (1988), 475–92.

14. Chandler, *Scale and Scope*, 27.

15. Confucianism is undoubtedly the greatest civil tradition of philosophy and political economy in East Asia. Furthermore, it was vigorously promoted by the Japanese Government as a formal basis for the social and political development of modern Japan. As a world-view and a coherent set of values, therefore, Confucianism has had more impact on the development of Japanese business institutions than any other system of thought. Buddhism, in addition, is thought to have contributed notably to the Japanese business tradition. See Robert Bellah, *Tokugawa Religion* (Glencoe, Ill.: Free Press, 1957).

    Also see, Ronald Dore, *Taking Japan Seriously* (Stanford, Calif.: Stanford University Press, 1987), see esp. chs. 1 and 9. Takie Sugiyama Lebra discusses social relativism as a basic cultural pattern in *Japanese Patterns of Behavior* (Honolulu: University of Hawaii Press, 1976); my study of the Kikkoman Corporation documents a long and intimate association between corporate and community interests within the context of a Confucian point of view. See *Kikkoman: Company, Clan and Community* (Cambridge, Mass.: Harvard University Press, 1983).

16. Koji Taira, 'Factory Legislation and Management Modernization during Japan's Industrialization 1886–1916', *Business History Review*, 44/1 (Spring 1970); Thomas C. Smith, 'Landlords' Sons in the Business Elite', *Economic Development and Cultural Change*, 9/1, Part II (Oct. 1960).

17. See the work cited in n. 6 above as well as Dore's *Flexible Rigidities* (Stanford, Calif.: Stanford University Press, 1986).

18. The historical studies of Koji Taira, Hiroshi Hazama, Andrew Gordon, and myself, among others, have established beyond a doubt that nineteenth-century Japanese workers and work organizations were completely unlike those of the twentieth century, esp. those of the post-World War Two era.

19. Harumi Befu, *Japan: An Anthropological Introduction* (San Francisco: Chandler, 1971), 38–9.

20. W. Mark Fruin, 'The Firm as Family and the Family as Firm in Japan', *Journal of Family History*, 5/4 (Winter 1980).

21. David Plath's studies of pearl-diving communities confirms that pearl-diving beds are community controlled. The maintenance of community resources and the assignment of family diving-areas are set by community organizations; within this framework, however, individual diving families are profit-maximizers.

22. Kahneman, Kretsch, and Thaler, 'Fairness as a Constraint on Profit Seeking: Entitlements in the Market', *American Economic Review*, 74/6 (Sept. 1986), 728–41.

23. Marvin B. Lieberman, 'The Learning Curve, Diffusion, and Competitive Strategy', *Strategic Management Journal*, 8 (1987), 441–52. I am grateful to Mitchell Koza for the insight concerning adverse selection. He deals with adverse selection and the valuation problem in Mitchell Koza and Srinivasan Balakrishnan, 'Organization Costs and a Theory of Joint Ventures', INSEAD Working Paper, Fall 1989.

24. I am borrowing the perspective of Kenneth J. Arrow, *The Limits of Organization* (New York: W. W. Norton, 1974).

25. The flexible wage agreements of large Japanese firms provide a case in point. Here I am reaffirming a point made some time ago by economists who were not specialists on Japan. Benjamin Klein, Robert G. Crawford, and Armen A. Alchian, 'Vertical Integration, Appropriable Rents, and the Competitive Contracting Process', *Journal of Law and Economics*, 21/2 (1978); repr. in Jay B. Barney and William G. Ouchi, *Organizational Economics* (San Francisco: Jossey-Bass, 1986), 55.

26. There is a long and distinguished literature on this point, beginning perhaps with George Homans, *The Human Group* (New York: Harcourt Brace Jovanovich, 1950), with many others, including Harvey Leibenstein, *Beyond Economic Man* (Cambridge, Mass.: Harvard University Press, 1976); E. P. Thomson, *The Making of the English Working Class* (New York: Vintage, 1963); James Lincoln, 'Intra- (and Inter-) Organizational Networks', in S. Bacharach (ed.), *Research in the Sociology of Organizations*, i (Greenwich, Conn.: JAI, 1982).

27. I am indebted to Mitchell Koza for pointing out why various forms of equity pooling as a means of securing interorganizational cooperation are not common in Japan. See two papers by Mitchell Koza and Srinivasan Balakrishnan, 'Organizational Costs and a Theory of Joint Ventures', and 'Information Asymmetry, Market Failure, and Joint-Ventures: Theory and Evidence', both unpublished working papers.

28. However, Satoshi Kamata, *Japan in the Passing Lane* (New York: Penguin Books, 1982), argues otherwise.

29. Solomon B. Levine and Hisashi Kawada, *Human Resources in Japanese Industrial Development* (Princeton, NJ.: Princeton University Press, 1980).

30. A partial treatment of some of these issues is contained in my article, 'From Philanthropy to Paternalism in the Noda Soy Sauce Industry: Pre-Corporate and Corporate Charity in Japan', *Business History Review*, 62/2 (Summer 1982).

31. This argument recalls the resource-dependency perspective of Jeffrey Pfeffer and G. R. Salancik, *The External Control of Organizations* (New York: Harper & Row, 1978); Jeffrey Pfeffer, *Power in Organizations* (Cambridge, Mass.: Ballinger, 1981). Michael Yoshino and Thomas Lifson treat issues of interpersonal relations and information exchange within general trading companies by employing a largely political framework. See *The Invisible Link* (Cambridge, Mass.: MIT Press, 1986).

32. Hakan Hakansson (ed.), *Industrial Technological Development: A Network Approach* (London: Croom Helm, 1987); Nils Kinch, 'Emerging Strategies in a Network Context: The Volvo Case', *Scandinavian Journal of Management Studies*, May 1987, 167–84. The 4,000 figure for Fiat was heard during fieldwork interviews in northern Italy, during 25 April to 5 May 1990.

33. Ronald Dore, 'Goodwill and the Spirit of Market Capitalism', *British Journal of Sociology*, 34 (1983).

34. This is the perspective of many industrial economists at Hitotsubashi University, perhaps Japan's leading university for business and economic studies. See, in particular, Hiroyuki Itami with Thomas W. Roehl, *Mobilizing Invisible Assets* (Cambridge, Mass.: Harvard University Press, 1987). The benefits of interdependence are extrapolated from Itami and Roehl, 144–53.

35. This is basically Herbert Simon's point of view, as expressed in *Administrative Behavior* (New York: Macmillan, 1957). But Simon's point of view has to be juxtaposed with many other frameworks and traditions of organizational analysis in the West, including the economic–rational, power and authority, transaction-cost, and resource-dependency models. In Japan, however, there is unanimity of thought and action favoring hierarchical views of life.

36. Walter W. Powell, 'Hybrid Organizational Arrangements: New Form or Transitional Development?', *California Management Review*, Fall 1987, 78–9; Richard Walton, 'From Control to Commitment in the Workplace', *Harvard Business Review*, 85/2 (1985), 76–84.

37. Japanese as well as American professors are studying interfirm flexibility, alliance

structure, and competitive behavior in Japan. Some depict how government policies facilitate the mobilization of interfirm resources. Masahiko Aoki describes the horizontal (as opposed to vertical) flows of information and authority in the Japanese firm and ascribes important advantages to the Japanese firm as a result. Others, including myself, write on factories as laboratories, integrated development sites, negotiated hierarchies, and as transaction-cost structures of supplier–purchaser interdependence.

See, Michael Gerlach, 'Business Alliances and the Strategy of the Japanese Firm', *California Management Review*, 30 (Fall 1987), 126–42; Ken'ichi Imai and Hiroyuki Imai, 'Interpretations of Organization and Market: Japan's Firm and Market in Comparison with the US', *International Journal of Industrial Organization*, 2 (1984); Iwao Nakatani, 'The Role of Intermarket *keiretsu* Business Groups in Japan', *Pacific Economic Papers*, 97 (1982); Odagiri Hiroyuki, 'Kigyo Shudan no Riron', *Kikan Riron Keizaigaku*, 26 (1975).

Teranishi Juro, 'A Model of the Relationship between Regulated and Unregulated Financial Markets: Credit Rationing in a Japanese Context', *Hitotsubashi Journal of Economics*, 23 (1982); Kozo Yamamura, 'Success that Soured: Administrative Guidance and Cartels in Japan', in Kozo Yamamura (ed.), *Policy and Trade Issues of the Japanese Economy: American and Japanese Perspectives* (Seattle: University of Washington Press, 1982); Daniel Okimoto, Takuo Sugano, and Franklin B. Weinstein, *Competitive Edge: The Semiconductor Industry in the U.S. and Japan* (Stanford, Calif.: Stanford University Press, 1984); Chalmers Johnson, *MITI and the Japanese Miracle* (Stanford, Calif.: Stanford University Press, 1982); Daniel I. Okimoto, *Between MITI and the Market* (Stanford, Calif.: Stanford University Press, 1989).

Masahiko Aoki, 'Horizontal vs. Vertical Information Structure of the Firm', *American Economic Review*, Dec. 1986; id., *The Co-operative Game Theory of the Firm* (Oxford: Oxford University Press, 1984); id., *Information, Incentives, and Bargaining in the Japanese Economy* (Cambridge: Cambridge University Press, 1988).

Yasunori Baba, 'Sokatsu Komento 1', in Ryutaro Komiya, Masahiro Okuno, Taro Suzuki, *Nihon no Sangyo Seisaku* (Japan's Industrial Policy) (Tokyo: University of Tokyo Press, 1985); Yasunori Baba, 'The Dynamics of Continuous Innovation in Scale-Intensive Industries', *Strategic Management Journal*, 10 (1989); Banri Asanuma, 'Transactional Structure of Parts Supply in the Japanese Automobile and Electric Machinery Industries: A Comparative Analysis', Faculty of Economics, Kyoto University, paper prepared for Rokko Conference, 16 July 1985. This has been revised and enlarged, and appeared as 'Manufacturer–Supplier Relationships in Japan and the Concept of Relation-Specific Skill', *Journal of the Japanese and International Economies*, 3 (1989), 1–30. Also, see Robert E. Cole's new book, *Strategies for Learning* (Berkeley: University of California Press, 1989); Tom Roehl, 'A Transactions Cost Approach to International Trading Structures: the case of Japanese General Trading Companies', *Hitotsubashi Journal of Economics*, 24 (Dec. 1983), 119–35; Tom Roehl, 'Japanese Industrial Groupings: A Strategic Response is Rapid Industrial Growth', unpublished paper, University of Washington, 1988.

38. These two types and many variations in between could be classified according to various schemes based on information technology, transaction-control mechanisms, authority relations, and so forth. Although I have not attempted to do so here, I will look at this issue in the future. For one classification scheme, see John Child, 'Information Technology, Organization, and the Response to Strategic Challenges', *California Management Review*, Fall 1987. Another is offered by Ken'ichi Imai in 'Kigyo Gurupu', in Ken'ichi

Imai and Ryutaro Komiya (eds.), *Nihon no Kigyo* (The Japanese Enterprise) (Tokyo: Tokyo University Press, 1989).

39. The failure of US Memories to enlist a coalition of American semiconductor firms to build a state-of-the-art, computer-memory manufacturing facility represents a failure of American firms to build a history of cooperative relations. Firms cannot cooperate on billion-dollar investments without a history of less ambitious and expensive interactions.

40. Scott E. Masten and Keith J. Crocker, 'Efficient Adaptation in Long-Term Contracts: Take-or-Pay Provisions for Natural Gas', *American Economic Review*, 75/5 (Dec. 1985), 1083–93.

41. W. Mark Fruin, 'Jumyo no mijikai Nihon no kigyo' (Corporate Life-Cycles in the United States and Japan: A Hundred Year Comparison), *Nikkei Business*, 10/12 (1985). A shift away from financial-based relations is a theme developed most fully in Chs. 4 and 5.

42. My source here and in Ch. 5 is Yoshitaka Suzuki, 'The Formation of Management Structure in Japanese Industrials 1920–40', lecture notes, Tohoku University, Sendai, 1983. See also, Tsunehiko Yui, 'Development and Organization of Large Industrial Enterprises in Japan', *Bulletin of Social Science of Meiji University*, 25/1 (1987).

43. Robert Axelrod, *The Evolution of Cooperation* (New York: Basic Books, 1984), 122–5. H. B. Thorelli, 'Networks: Between Markets and Hierarchies', *Strategic Management Journal*, 7 (1986), 38. Koichiro Hayashi, *Nettowakingu no Keizaigaku* (The Economics of Networking) (Tokyo: NTT Press, 1989). Access is likewise a key feature of the industrial district argument concerning the network form of organization. See Walter W. Powell, 'Neither Market nor Hierarchy: Network Forms of Organization', *Research in Organizational Behavior*, 12 (1990), 295–336.

44. James Abegglen was one of the first Westerners to link the internal features of the Japanese firm to the competitiveness of the Japanese domestic economy. He did not pursue the links, however, between individual firms, interfirm networks, and domestic competition. Besides *Kaisha: The Japanese Corporation* which he wrote with George Stalk, Jr. in 1985, Abegglen was developing this point of view as early as 1970 in an article he wrote with William V. Rapp, 'Japanese Managerial Behavior and "Excessive Competition"', *Developing Economies*, 8/4 (Dec. 1970), 427–44. George Stalk has continued to develop some of these themes in a new book on time-based management: George Stalk, Jr. and Thomas M. Hout, *Competing Against Time* (New York: Free Press, 1990).

45. Kotaro Kuwada, 'Strategic Learning in a Mature Industry', Faculty of Economics, Tokyo Metropolitan University, paper presented at TIMS XXIX, Osaka, Japan, 25 July 1989. Also, Shigeru Asaba and Kotaro Kuwada, 'The Continuous Side of Discontinuity', *Keizai to Shakaigaku*, 63 (Feb. 1989).

On de-maturation, see 'A New Perspective on Globalization', a paper presented by Yoshikazu Shusa and Kotaro Kuwada at the conference mentioned in the note above as well as another paper, 'Technological Innovation and Global Strategy', given at the 2nd Mitsubishi Bank Foundation Conference held at the University of Michigan, 29–31 Aug. 1988.

46. Robert E. Cole considers some of these issues in 'The Macropolitics of Organizational Change: A Comparative Analysis of the Spread of Small Group Activities', *Administrative Science Quarterly*, 30 (1985). What I have in mind, however, is far more than small-group activities although they are undoubtedly important. I am thinking more broadly

of the politics of production and the role of enterprise unions, company campaigns, internal labor markets, and extensive in-company training, in creating an enterprise-based society. Cole's article has now been expanded in book form, *Strategies for Learning* (Berkeley: University of California Press, 1989). Also, Keith Thurley, 'Japanese Direct Investment in the United Kingdom and its Social Implications', paper, 3rd Mitsubishi Bank Foundation Conference on Japanese Overseas Investment, Cumberland Lodge, Windsor Great Park, 15–17 Sept. 1989.

47. At the macro-economic level, coalition-building can be correlated with two 'effects', the learning effect and the price effect. The learning effect occurs when output growth enhances productivity increase through the accumulation of experience while the price effect occurs when productivity increase stimulates growth in output through declining prices. These effects as well as the extent and rate of organizational learning are all dependent on the effectiveness of coalition-building. See Hiroyuki Odagiri, 'Research Activity, Output Growth, and Productivity Increase in Japanese Manufacturing Industries', *Research Policy*, 14 (1985); Hiroyuki Odagiri and Hitoshi Iwata, 'The Impact of R & D on Productivity Increase in Japanese Manufacturing Companies', *Research Policy*, 15 (1986).

48. 242 is the number of suppliers of Toshiba designed parts. About 800 more suppliers provide off-the-shelf parts to Yanagicho.

49. Personal communication from the section head of the purchasing department, Yanagicho Works, Aug. 1988. If both factory-specified and off-the-shelf products are counted, the factory had some 987 suppliers as of 1989.

50. Seigo Mizoda, 'Zosen', in Shin'ichi Yonekawa, Shimokawa Koichi, and Hiroaki Yamazaki (eds.), *Sengo Nihon Keizaishi* (Japanese Post-War Economic History) (Tokyo: Toyo Keizai, 1991), 239–41. It should be noted that the process of forming affiliates begins before the Pacific War and grows. Before 1945, the seven major shipbuilders had established 25 affiliate companies, 38 between 1945–54, and 397 thereafter.

51. William G. Ouchi's *Theory Z* (Reading, Mass.: Addison Wesley, 1981) is a well-known example of this effort. Apples and oranges cannot be compared and neither should American and Japanese firms, not even by analogy, at least not without careful qualification and definition of the standards for comparison.

52. 'Equal playing field' and 'unfair competition' criticisms of Japan keep appearing based on a fallacy that Japanese and Western corporations are comparable one-to-one.

53. These findings are based on American data and would, if anything, be reconfirmed and reinforced by Japanese data. Richard P. Rumelt, 'How Much Does Industry Matter?', *Strategic Management Journal*, 12 (Mar. 1991), 67–85. Gary S. Hansen and Birger Wernerfelt, 'Determinants of Firm Performance: The Relative Importance of Economic and Organizational Factors', *Strategic Management Journal*, 10/5 (Sept.–Oct. 1989). Vijay Mahajan, Subhash Sharma, and Richard A. Bettis, 'The Adoption of the M-Form Organizational Structure: A Test of the Imitation Hypothesis', *Management Science*, 34/10 (Oct. 1988).

54. Admittedly, the emphasis on 'sticking to the knitting' may only be rhetorical. Strong support can be found in such articles as: D. Kahneman, J. L. Knetsch, and R. Thaler, 'Fairness as a Constraint on Profit Seeking', 728–41. Richard P. Nielsen, 'Cooperative Strategy', *Strategic Management Journal*, 9 (1988). In the latter piece, it is argued that a tit-for-tat strategy works best in cooperative environments.

Jeffrey L. Bradach and Robert G. Eccles in their review article argue for plural systems of control combining price, authority, and trust mechanisms for governing economic transactions. 'Price, Authority, and Trust: From Ideal Types to Plural Forms', *Annual Review of Sociology*, 15 (1989). In the context of interfirm networks in Japan, trust and authority are always paired with price mechanisms. My intuition would be that authority is most salient in what I am calling hierarchical networks and trust in reciprocal networks.

55. Although the spread of multidivisionalization has been used as one measure of structural development for Western firms throughout the book, it is important to recognize that not all firms, even the large ones, adopt multidivisional forms. By the mid-1950s half of the largest American manufacturing firms had adopted the multidivisional form. Is that a lot or a little? Certainly, it suggests that as industrial firms grew larger in the United States, they were increasingly likely to adopt the multidivisional form, although this tendency was less pronounced in certain industries, less widespread in manager-controlled firms, and less common in highly diversified firms. See N. Fligstein, *State and Markets* (Cambridge, Mass.: Harvard University Press, 1989); D. Palmer, R. Friedland, R. Jennings, and P. D. Powers, 'The Economics and Politics of Structure: The Multidivisional Form and the Large U.S. Corporation', *Administrative Science Quarterly*, 32 (Mar. 1987), 25–48.

56. M. Hannan and J. Freeman, 'Structural Inertia and Organizational Change', *American Sociological Review*, 49 (Apr. 1984), 149–64.

Appendix

A.1. *The 200 Largest Industrial Firms In Japan: 1918*

Rank	Company name	Assets[a]	Capital[b]	Sales[c]	Profit[d]	Employees[e]	SIC1[f]	SIC2
1	Kawasaki Shipyards	140,347	45,000	50,125	29,368	15,167	373	
2	Kuhara Mining[g]	103,610	41,250	63,636	17,116	2,475	333	
3	Mitsubishi Shipyards	89,327	30,000	—	13,116	24,065	373	
4	Kanegafuchi Spinning	69,936	15,787	189,839	19,089	33,247	228	
5	Toyo Spinning	61,705	18,550	42,908	18,774	23,538	228	221
6	Dai-Nihon Spinning	59,209	22,580	98,741	17,365	28,454	228	221
7	Taiwan Sugar Manufacturing	55,930	20,835	37,295	6,841	206	206	
8	Mitsubishi Steel	46,942	30,000	15,461	2,139	2,315	331	
9	Fuji Gas Spinning	40,057	13,000	69,171	10,893	18,648	228	
10	Japan Steel (Kokan)	39,374	9,400	25,993	5,945	3,320	331	
11	Dai-Nihon Sugar Manufacturing	38,219	18,000	51,231	5,231	597	206	
12	Furukawa Mining[g]	36,938	20,000	22,634	4,198	1,435	333	
13	Japan Oil	36,665	25,000	21,479	8,138	135	291	
14	Oji Paper	35,928	15,250	27,370	6,260	3,797	262	
15	Japan Steel Works	35,863	15,000	9,224	4,050	3,445	332	348
16	Ensuiko Sugar	35,782	11,250	18,500	5,287	—	206	
17	Japan Wool Textiles	34,722	10,000	36,982	4,975	5,673	223	
18	Fuji Paper	32,826	17,425	35,307	6,662	2,519	262	
19	Uraga Dock	32,708	10,000	26,551	3,747	4,808	373	
20	Houden Petroleum	32,153	16,250	—	6,198	245	291	
21	Osaka Works	29,932	10,500	*17,495*	9,122	5,754	373	
22	Harima Shipyards	29,824	10,000	—	—	5,937	373	
23	Tanaka Mining[g]	28,774	20,000	—	412	626	331	
24	Meiji Sugar Manufacturing	28,337	8,925	26,048	3,160	221	206	
25	Kobe Steel Works	26,143	10,000	23,177	4,895	3,740	331	
26	Tokyo Wire	25,639	7,000	25,034	5,827	659	349	322
27	Teikoku Sugar Manufacturing	25,476	9,375	16,580	3,867	214	206	
28	Osaka Godo Spinning	25,382	8,738	*17,776*	11,393	8,667	228	
29	Asano Cement	25,363	9,135	18,201	2,809	2,013	324	
30	Katakura Gumi	24,794	—	—	—	4,694	228	
31	Shibaura Electric	24,189	5,000	32,857	5,912	2,795	361	362
32	Toyo Sugar Manufacturing	23,896	10,110	*10,043*	8,268	121	206	

A.1. Continued

Rank Company name	Assets[a]	Capital[b]	Sales[c]	Profit[d]	Employees[e]	SIC1[f]	SIC2
33 Ishikawajima Shipyards	21,318	2,868	26,204	3,139	3,314	373	
34 Tokyo Wool	21,060	14,000	22,676	3,615	6,850	223	
35 Synthetic Fertilizer	20,423	10,375	5,283	2,148	857	287	
36 Yokohama Dock	20,274	5,313	20,127	4,022	6,720	373	
37 Teikoku Linen	19,540	8,000	19,679	4,825	2,152	226	229
38 Tainan Sugar	17,537	8,985	8,137	1,098	695	206	
39 Dai-Nihon Beer	17,194	8,800	30,798	4,031	1,628	208	
40 Naigai Cotton	15,612	3,750	43,894	3,530	1,900	228	221
41 Nitrogen Fertilizer	15,333	7,600	10,667	3,026	3,523	287	
42 Fujita Mining[g]	15,300	15,000	—	—	159	333	
43 Hokkaido Steel	15,000	15,000	—	—	1,615	331	
44 Tokyo Gas Electric Industry	14,901	4,750	953	977	144	354	353
45 Niitaka Sugar Manufacturing	14,581	5,000	6,287	2,261	133	206	
46 Osaka Zinc	13,796	5,000	9,518	2,234	1,857	333	
47 Kurashiki Spinning	13,697	4,120	32,136	4,636	6,220	228	
48 Muslin Spinning	13,047	7,500	50,845	2,419	4,570	221	
49 Kawakita Electric	12,668	9,000	1,962	815	—	362	
50 Fukushima Spinning	12,494	4,000	10,054	3,553	5,715	228	
51 Tokyo Muslin Spinning	12,123	5,500	15,126	1,924	1,915	221	
52 Dai-Nihon Salt	12,070	3,803	12,278	264	75	289	
53 Kishiwada Spinning	11,602	3,025	30,237	4,321	3,512	228	
54 Toa Tobacco	11,579	2,500	—	649	—	213	
55 Osaka Alkalies	11,328	3,413	1,948	518	525	281	
56 Fuji Steel	11,176	5,884	5,273	1,036	1,120	331	
57 Osaka Ceramics	10,942	5,088	7,856	1,940	2,234	324	325
58 Toyo Steel	10,855	10,317	401	264	925	331	
59 Karafuto Pulp and Paper	10,064	2,000	4,769	1,888	1,888	261	262
60 Tokyo Electric	9,486	6,000	13,646	1,843	1,843	363	364
61 Mitsubishi Paper	9,348	5,000	717	1,106	1,774	262	
62 Nisshin Spinning	9,347	4,000	16,235	3,473	3,763	228	
63 Sumitomo Foundry	9,185	4,500	5,013	1,352	1,628	336	
64 Asahi Glass	9,069	3,050	13,199	1,539	2,982	321	
65 Toyota Spinning	9,058	5,000	—	209	2,147	221	
66 Rasato Phosphate	9,020	6,000	7,455	1,390	42	287	
67 Akita Lumber	8,729	2,750	1,601	1,380	435	242	
68 Electro-Chemical Industry	8,323	5,000	8,992	2,757	746	287	
69 Kanto Soda	8,169	3,250	11,762	1,316	1,021	281	

A.1. Continued

Rank	Company name	Assets[a]	Capital[b]	Sales[c]	Profit[d]	Employees[e]	SIC1[f]	SIC2
70	Uchida Shipyard	8,130	2,000	—	—	1,103	373	
71	Railroad Car Manufacturing	8,095	2,212	2,272	624	2,403	374	
72	Osaka Shipyard	7,978	2,375	2,430	1,777	534	373	
73	Japan Flour Mills	7,664	1,913	3,323	974	348	204	
74	Japan Linen	7,543	3,500	12,109	2,299	800	226	229
75	Jomo Muslin	7,435	2,800	9,049	798	2,032	221	
76	Japan Printed Cotton	7,260	2,250	14,357	616	487	226	
77	Kiso Electro-Metallurgy	7,233	4,250	208	130	65	331	
78	Onoda Cement	7,063	2,700	5,554	746	1,018	324	
79	Nippon Electric (NEC)	7,010	2,500	—	1,400	574	366	
80	Noda Soy Sauce	7,000	7,000	—	—	1,009	209	
81	Japan Chemical Manufacturing	6,979	2,600	5,047	1,482	664	281	
82	Sankyo	6,968	3,125	2,398	589	—	283	
83	Hattori Textiles	6,950	4,000	—	—	3,198	228	221
84	Japan Glycerin	6,872	3,750	5,242	613	251	207	
85	Wakayama Textiles	6,868	2,600	15,640	3,580	4,404	228	221
86	Tokyo Steel Products	6,813	2,000	6,406	1,051	779	331	
87	Yokohama Electric Wire	6,703	1,875	13,489	495	1,663	335	
88	Nichiro Fishing[h]	6,672	3,000	5,374	425	—	209	
89	Kirin Beer	6,652	3,750	5,344	492	397	208	
90	Japan Pigment Manufacturing	6,619	6,400	6,350	104	639	281	
91	Toyo Muslin	6,599	3,420	10,568	1,669	2,086	221	
92	Nisshin Flour Mills	6,567	2,275	2,891	902	445	204	
93	Nikka Spinning	6,509	4,000	6,337	316	—	228	
94	Osaka Electro-Metallurgy	6,413	3,750	14,981	1,115	768	333	
95	Hinode Textiles	6,398	2,700	7,497	617	1,481	228	
96	Asano Shipyard	6,250	3,750	15,000	5,000	3,645	373	
97	Tokyo Calico	6,100	2,750	5,814	1,040	2,199	226	228
98	Japan Arms Manufacturing	6,065	2,375	3,797	−2,355	1,131	348	
99	Yokohama Fish Oil	6,040	2,800	1,947	890	594	207	
100	Japan Leather	6,012	2,500	1,205	952	440	311	
101	Asano Steel	6,000	6,000	—	—	371	331	
102	Oshima Steel	5,918	2,400	715	449	1,036	331	
103	Okamura Electric	5,832	3,500	—	852	1,190	362	
104	Nisshin Oil Products	5,758	3,000	789	458	40	207	
105	Osaka Steel	5,715	2,328	4,098	1,006	502	331	

A.1. Continued

Rank	Company name	Assets[a]	Capital[b]	Sales[c]	Profit[d]	Employees[e]	SIC1[f]	SIC2
106	Minami Manshu Sugar	5,703	3,500	3,112	311	—	206	
107	Gunze Silk Mills	5,698	1,721	29,913	567	3,902	228	
108	Teikoku Beer	5,548	4,000	645	324	255	208	
109	Tosa Paper	5,545	1,750	2,855	701	982	262	
110	Tenma Textiles	5,451	2,750	12,356	1,004	936	221	228
111	Japan Paint	5,426	2,375	1,841	1,376	899	285	
112	Japan Chemical Industries	5,262	2,060	2,846	1,055	666	281	
113	Yasuda and Company	5,189	1,125	—	362	393	345	
114	Omi Sail	5,048	600	1,189	610	1,565	239	228
115	Shinagawa Fire Brick	5,045	2,474	4,800	681	1,105	325	
116	Toyo Paper	5,038	2,450	4,747	1,494	338	262	
117	Hattori Clock and Watch	5,000	5,000	—	—	1,933	387	
118	Hakodate Dock	4,979	2,000	7,916	1,536	1,240	373	
119	Toyo Ice	4,586	2,695	1,547	535	73	209	
120	Osaka Textiles	4,566	1,800	11,121	1,901	2,304	221	228
121	Japan Glass Industries	4,561	2,565	2,212	248	576	321	
122	Oita Spinning	4,557	1,875	7,165	1,094	2,092	228	
123	Yamaju Gumi	4,500	—	—	—	7,266	228	
124	Yokohama Wire	4,488	1,250	7,350	1,682	438	349	322
125	Izumi Spinning	4,468	2,250	3,149	1,838	1,110	228	
126	Korea Leather	4,442	600	—	—	—	311	
127	Tokai Steel	4,434	2,240	3,385	328	193	331	
128	Japan Paper Products	4,413	4,375	—	383	592	262	
129	Sakai Celluloid	4,403	2,000	4,845	1,387	698	282	
130	Japan Ice	4,359	2,933	2,102	755	266	209	
131	Kabuto Beer	4,303	2,490	4,658	458	141	208	
132	Japan Synthetic Fiber	4,114	1,800	3,017	342	383	222	
133	Toyo Match	4,100	2,000	—	—	5,389	399	
134	Toyo Wool Spinning	4,012	3,000	13	—	612	223	228
135	Japan Rolling Stock	3,756	1,650	2,988	346	951	374	
136	Fujikura Electric Wire	3,691	2,000	7,143	302	688	335	
137	Manshu Flour Mills	3,681	1,500	1,456	821	—	204	
138	Ikegai Works	3,600	1,750	—	—	649	354	
139	Osaka Chemical Fertilizer	3,544	1,000	1,298	712	74	287	
140	Nitto Steel	3,527	3,000	—	603	226	331	
141	Japan Linen	3,520	2,600	615	350	615	229	
142	Teikoku Thread and Fabric	3,510	1,050	1,764	443	1,813	226	

A.1. Continued

Rank	Company name	Assets[a]	Capital[b]	Sales[c]	Profit[d]	Employees[e]	SIC1[f]	SIC2
143	Toa Mills	3,491	1,250	1,327	577	65	204	
144	Meiji Foundry	3,474	1,275	2,938	263	266	333	
145	Kyoto Textiles	3,465	2,500	6,273	691	1,358	226	
146	Oki Electric	3,465	1,288	3,594	482	761	366	
147	Niigata Engineering	3,448	2,000	5,776	702	1,407	353	
148	Yokkaichi Paper	3,420	1,950	3,321	892	395	262	
149	Hayashi Gumi	3,400	2,275	—	40	3,147	228	
150	Taito Sugar	3,382	2,275	37,295	172	206	206	
151	Toyo Corrugated Paper	3,373	1,200	—	705	126	262	265
152	Osaka Bleach	3,266	1,500	1,528	317	389	281	
153	Sulfate Fertilizer	3,206	1,200	2,724	173	150	287	
154	Nagasaki Spinning	3,203	1,500	6,592	525	1,725	228	
155	Meiji Confectionary	3,193	1,200	—	255	—	206	
156	Japan Cement	3,050	1,450	1,986	518	752	324	
157	Korea Paper	3,040	1,250	29	13	—	262	
158	Noritake (Nihon Toki)	3,018	2,000	881	156	2,904	326	
159	Yushutsu Foods	2,966	1,560	957	958	—	209	
160	Nangoku Foods	2,897	2,750	229	120	—	206	
161	Dai-Nihon Wooden Pipe	2,855	1,875	2,128	272	784	249	
162	Osaka Chemical Industries	2,837	1,125	4,130	1,166	322	281	
163	Osaka Chain Manufacturing	2,825	1,500	—	858	271	349	
164	Suzuki Shoten/ Ajinomoto	2,795	1,200	3,931	202	495	209	
165	Hoshi Pharmaceutical	2,772	1,250	1,329	724	411	283	
166	Japan Optical Industry	2,718	2,400	1,656	216	698	383	
167	Japan Silk Goods	2,706	2,500	—	114	68	228	
168	Aichi Electric Clock	2,568	825	2,159	249	702	387	
169	Settsu Oil	2,556	750	8,549	501	326	207	
170	Osaka Wool	2,529	1,000	3,768	511	847	223	
171	Morinaga Confectionary	2,447	900	5,499	53	1,065	206	
172	Meidensha	2,391	2,000	1,139	516	345	362	
173	Toyota Weaving Machinery	2,390	1,080	1,553	819	644	355	
174	Naniwa Spinning	2,318	750	6,348	379	1,521	221	228
175	Saga Spinning	2,301	1,200	1,131	166	738	221	228
176	Tokyo Silk and Wool	2,300	1,500	509	200	393	223	
177	Dai-Nihon Petroleum Industry	2,300	1,250	260	51	—	291	
178	Odawara Spinning	2,295	1,500	1,214	47	1,170	221	228

A.1. Continued

Rank	Company name	Assets[a]	Capital[b]	Sales[c]	Profit[d]	Employees[e]	SIC1[f]	SIC2
179	Sanyo Spinning	2,288	1,250	5,189	530	1,183	221	228
180	Nanyo Sugar	2,266	1,500	420	144	—	206	
181	Chuo Paper	2,232	750	—	660	219	262	
182	Aichi Cement	2,183	1,650	*2,511*	214	1,056	324	
183	Japan Dyeing	2,147	1,100	4,396	216	272	226	
184	Sakura Cement	2,146	800	*2,674*	704	439	324	
185	Tobata Foundry	2,120	2,000	*690*	128	1,293	332	
186	Engine Manufacturing	2,114	625	*202*	157	529	362	
187	Zinc Electro-Magnetic	2,069	1,498	210	50	—	331	
188	Saga Cement	2,064	800	1,503	215	248	324	
189	Dai-Nihon Pharmaceutical	2,040	700	*513*	463	116	283	
190	Chuo Oil	2,037	1,000	—	505	—	291	
191	Kyokuto Glass	2,031	750	1,718	93	140	321	
192	Kiyo Spinning	1,965	1,060	3,725	657	957	221	228
193	Japan Musical Instrument	1,962	900	4,178	224	868	393	
194	Kiso Pulp	1,961	825	2,610	389	185	261	
195	Yasuki Steel	1,845	750	*2,194*	198	253	331	
196	Sagami Spinning	1,797	625	9,990	467	—	228	
197	Senshu Weaving	1,792	1,422	—	79	—	221	228
198	Japan Explosives Manufacturing	1,776	1,000	*1,126*	—	210	289	
199	Mie Cement	1,705	1,375	—	−23	—	324	
200	Osaka Kitsugawa Cement	1,688	945	—	152	—	324	

Notes: Sumitomo Sohoten, the holding company for the pre-war Sumitomo group of companies, does not appear in the listing as it is impossible to separate manufacturing from non-manufacturing assets owned by Sumitomo Sohoten. Monetary figures are in 1000s of yen.

[a] Losses, if existing, have been deducted from total assets.

[b] Not-yet-paid-in-capital has been subtracted from total capitalization.

[c] Italicized figures represent revenues instead of sales.

[d] Figures preceded by a minus represent losses for the year.

[e] Both blue-collar and white-collar employees are counted where known; before World War Two, however, most companies reported blue-collar workers only.

[f] SIC columns represent product lines that account for at least 20 percent of sales.

[g] These companies engaged in mining as well as metals manufacture; it is not practical or even possible to distinguish one activity from the other, even though mining should not be included in a listing of industrial firms.

[h] Fishing and marine foodstuffs companies are like mining and metals manufacturers in

A.1. Continued

that it is difficult to distinguish between raw-materials acquisition, which is not a manufacturing activity, and raw-materials processing, which is.

Sources: Nomura Shoten Chosabu, *Kabushiki Nenkan* (Company Annual Reports) (Osaka: Osaka Kobunsha, 1919, 1920); Tsunehiko Yui (ed.), *Eigyo Hokokusho Nenkan* (Annual Company Reports), microfilm (Tokyo: Yuihikaku, 1918, 1919); about ten privately held companies were investigated by speaking directly with principals from those companies.

A.2. The 200 Largest Industrial Firms in Japan: 1930

Rank	Company name	Assets[a]	Paid in capital[b]	Revenue sales[c]	Profit[d]	Employees[e]	SIC1[f]	SIC2
1	Kawasaki Shipyards	252,045	74,250	*15,123*	−6,966	11,023	373	
2	Fuji Paper	156,277	58,925	107,386	5,010	8,270	262	
3	Oji Paper	154,473	48,683	90,378	7,345	5,190	262	
4	Kanegafuchi Spinning	129,572	28,596	149,924	8,999	—	221	
5	Karafuto Pulp and Paper	125,208	53,389	36,570	2,711	—	262	
6	Japan Nitrogen Fertilizer	122,924	39,248	18,077	4,958	1,200	287	
7	Dai-Nihon Spinning	113,087	52,000	102,384	4,721	27,913	221	
8	Dai-Nihon Sugar	111,537	34,749	98,477	4,456	3,300	206	
9	Japan Oil	107,705	56,000	44,658	3,479	5,309	291	
10	Toyo Spinning	106,111	36,850	30,550	8,782	22,791	221	228
11	Taiwan Sugar	103,723	43,080	62,469	5,686	2,289	222	
12	Mitsubishi Shipyards	96,369	30,000	61,124	1,571	15,500	373	
13	Asano Cement	90,242	53,988	32,487	1,909	1,500	324	
14	Ensuiko Sugar Manufacturing	89,354	17,438	28,865	−13	3,565	206	
15	Dai-Nihon Beer	82,660	50,000	46,500	9,153	3,022	208	
16	Korea Nitrogen Fertilizer	81,344	30,000	—	—	—	287	
17	Japan Wool	77,484	27,500	66,409	4,407	12,645	223	
18	Dainihon Synthetic Fertilizer	75,021	26,800	*15,662*	1,586	1,300	287	
19	Fuji Gas Spinning	69,795	34,000	47,214	−3,363	18,885	221	228
20	Meiji Sugar	67,269	34,800	77,539	6,062	1,900	206	
21	Katakura Silk Spinning	61,618	26,375	73,960	3,527	27,500	228	
22	Japan Mining[g]	59,477	50,000	21,554	−2,603	8,991	333	
23	Nichiryo Fishery	56,874	22,750	25,054	−1,680	—	209	
24	Japan Steel Products	50,001	30,000	*1,051*	1,052	4,364	332	331
25	Kobe Steel	48,910	20,000	23,217	218	4,849	331	
26	Naigai Cotton	46,548	16,000	45,150	2,824	33,900	221	228
27	Osaka Godo Spinning	45,031	18,750	*17,585*	7,989	17,000	228	221
28	Dai-Nihon Ice	44,481	28,676	11,856	2,700	—	209	
29	Mitsubishi Steel	41,622	25,000	5,582	—	1,056	331	
30	Yamaju Silk Mills	41,263	12,500	—	−5,551	17,584	228	
31	Electro-Chemical Industry	39,307	17,500	17,180	723	1,286	287	
32	Japan Steel	37,726	15,225	—	−352	2,665	331	

A.2. Continued

Rank	Company name	Assets[a]	Paid in capital[b]	Revenue sales[c]	Profit[d]	Employees[e]	SIC1[f]	SIC2
33	Furukawa Mining	37,535	22,500	33,213	1,376	4,678	333	
34	Kamaishi Mining	37,336	20,000	—	−93	2,827	331	
35	Tokyo Electric	36,312	21,000	33,305	9,391	1,790	363	364
36	Onoda Cement	35,944	21,815	*19,257*	1,571	4,180	324	
37	Asano Shipyard	35,821	25,000	6,607	172	—	373	
38	Teikoku Linen	35,724	10,675	10,601	−148	4,184	226	229
39	Tokyo Gas Electric Industry	35,454	5,250	*1,012*	−15	1,200	354	371
40	Nissin Spinning	35,408	18,300	29,790	3,064	11,312	228	221
41	Teikoku Rayon	35,401	21,000	20,133	6,648	—	222	
42	Hoshi Pharmaceutical	35,397	6,000	1,874	−961	2,284	283	
43	Kurashiki Spinning	35,311	12,350	*5,399*	−1,366	5,407	228	221
44	Teikoku Sugar	34,584	13,500	13,718	1,712	1,946	206	
45	Toyo Steel	33,739	30,600	*418*	342	—	331	
46	Tokyo Muslin Spinning	33,287	10,381	27,189	154	8,892	221	
47	Noda Soy Sauce	33,110	26,250	18,763	931	2,097	209	
48	Osaka Works	32,027	10,500	*3,086*	363	4,667	373	
49	Japan Paper Industry	31,797	9,496	22,604	−653	2,741	262	
50	Godo Wool	31,603	25,000	*1,395*	−10,043	—	223	
51	Japan Flour Mills	29,746	3,938	*4,885*	385	550	204	
52	Shibaura Electric Works	29,510	20,000	13,478	−1,685	2,379	361	362
53	Gunze Silk Mills	29,218	11,717	50,747	1,279	12,000	228	
54	Sumitomo Besshi Mining	28,919	15,000	10,733	−13	4,475	333	
55	Nikka Spinning	28,164	8,800	5,537	963	7,800	228	221
56	Nisshin Flour Mills	27,903	9,402	*7,188*	1,501	980	204	
57	Shanghai Silk Mills	27,644	10,000	*2,568*	2,344	11,560	228	221
58	Japan Beer Kosen	27,614	13,994	15,226	1,483	700	208	
59	Furukawa Electric Works	27,440	12,500	37,045	1,612	2,200	335	
60	NEC	25,510	15,000	*7,818*	1,450	908	336	
61	Showa Steel	25,420	25,000	*1,229*	189	—	331	
62	Hitaohi Ltd.	24,654	10,000	19,226	1,257	4,100	361	362
63	Asahi Glass	24,017	6,875	14,261	694	2,040	321	
64	Kawasaki Railroad Car	23,633	12,000	2,790	968	3,056	374	
65	Fukushima Spinning	23,490	5,600	8,021	1,078	—	228	221
66	Fujita Mining	22,648	5,000	—	−90	4,300	333	
67	Honen Oil	22,520	10,000	*1,343*	−46	300	207	

A.2. Continued

Rank	Company name	Assets[a]	Paid in capital[b]	Revenue sales[c]	Profit[d]	Employees[e]	SIC1[f]	SIC2
68	Mitsubishi Aircraft	22,005	5,000	8,802	612	2,274	372	
69	Tokyo Steel	21,874	8,500	9,692	828	1,838	349	229
70	Yokohama Dock	21,795	5,000	*1,650*	623	5,081	373	
71	Kirin Beer	21,656	8,300	23,009	2,188	783	208	
72	Tainan Sugar	21,762	10,000	6,597	−198	500	206	
73	Sumitomo Rolling Mills	21,196	12,000	7,789	154	1,605	335	
74	Toyo Rayon	21,166	10,000	*2,289*	165	2,973	222	
75	Toyo Muslin	20,906	11,785	17,462	−406	9,451	228	221
76	Niitaka Sugar	20,872	10,750	8,076	577	1,000	206	
77	Morinaga Confectionary	20,575	13,800	12,436	806	1,472	206	
78	Mitsubishi Electric	20,378	10,500	11,406	59	2,650	361	362
79	Sumitomo Electric Wire	20,048	10,000	17,980	1,485	1,278	335	
80	Kishiwada Spinning	19,880	6,186	16,256	−519	8,062	228	221
81	Sankyo	18,388	7,840	*4,831*	1,411	875	283	
82	Iwaki Cement	17,858	9,062	6,291	258	831	324	
83	Mitsubishi Paper	17,762	8,000	9,237	358	1,564	262	
84	Rasato Phosphate	17,283	5,550	5,092	−1,714	1,470	287	
85	Showa Fertilizer	17,190	10,000	5,569	−3	300	287	
86	Oita Cement	17,075	9,300	5,571	−348	1,430	324	
87	Kinka Spinning	17,050	7,875	18,163	280	6,500	228	221
88	Ajinomoto	17,004	11,000	11,029	1,165	368	209	
89	Uraga Dock	15,969	5,250	*1,176*	380	1,600	373	
90	Dai-Nihon Celluloid	15,864	10,000	*6,467*	1,005	1,300	282	
91	Asano Kokura Steel	15,647	6,300	8,752	37	491	331	
92	Hattori Textiles	14,992	6,240	2,449	−1,407	3,122	221	228
93	Fujinagata Shipyard	14,891	5,000	487	−56	1,761	373	
94	Shanghai Mills	14,793	4,793	*1,894*	1,660	10,250	228	
95	Asahi Rayon	14,349	6,000	*1,368*	868	2,700	222	
96	Harima Shipyard	14,107	5,000	4,876	−96	1,920	373	
97	Yasuda & Company	13,984	5,844	3,529	95	450	345	
98	Godo Yushi Glycerin	13,798	5,000	13,476	−113	380	207	
99	Sumitomo Steel	13,741	9,000	5,409	305	1,480	331	
100	Doko Spinning	13,714	10,500	*4,149*	2,154	3,715	228	
101	Fuji Electric	13,644	8,300	6,815	−170	610	362	
102	Hokoku Cement	13,607	7,500	*4,617*	−169	—	324	
103	Toyoda Spinning	13,432	7,100	—	−25	1,060	221	

A.2. Continued

Rank	Company name	Assets[a]	Paid in capital[b]	Revenue sales[c]	Profit[d]	Employees[e]	SIC1[f]	SIC2
104	Hattori Clock and Watch	13,431	10,000	—	1,479	1,500	387	
105	Tokyo Ishikawajima Shipyard	13,175	3,000	9,672	−84	2,323	373	
106	Nagasaki Spinning	13,029	5,380	8,664	271	—	228	
107	Tenma Textiles	12,956	6,250	9,620	124	3,050	228	226
108	Minami Manshu Sugar	12,921	8,500	*52*	5	103	206	
109	Kawakita Electric	12,824	5,400	*282*	−219	—	363	362
110	Akita Lumber	12,390	5,550	*1,289*	−192	950	242	
111	Hokkaido Sugar	12,381	2,500	2,537	12	—	206	
112	Hinode Textiles	12,359	5,250	10,783	−165	—	228	
113	Kyushu Steel	12,212	5,000	*228*	−82	—	331	
114	Railroad Car Manufacturing	11,834	3,525	3,686	495	1,855	374	
115	Toyota Mills (Shanghai)	11,813	5,850	—	276	3,710	228	
116	Kita Karafuto Oil	11,623	7,997	8,588	1418	—	291	
117	Sakura Beer	11,228	2,440	*1,450*	−169	—	208	
118	Tobata Foundry	11,219	6,250	*2,157*	702	1,610	332	
119	Toa Tobacco	10,902	7,300	*1,163*	11	—	213	
120	Nagoya Spinning	10,740	5,574	7,816	10	2,965	228	
121	Omi Sail	10,715	4,875	8,350	−146	4,300	239	228
122	Japan Rayon	10,670	7,500	3,482	330	2,050	222	
123	Takeda Chemical Industries	10,557	5,300	16,642	1,060	290	283	
124	Wakayama Spinning	10,893	5,200	8,571	−2,787	4,760	228	
125	Japan Synthetic Fiber	10,505	6,000	*3,080*	−1,899	3,321	222	
126	Japan Camphor	10,080	6,750	3,495	554	214	287	
127	Chichibu Cement	10,001	4,750	3,951	256	—	324	
128	Japan Cement	9,772	5,688	3,916	129	—	324	
129	Chuo Wool Spinning	9,748	4,000	11,178	525	1,500	228	223
130	Showa Rayon	9,412	7,800	*2,911*	605	1,400	222	
131	Utsumi Spinning	9,364	2,500	9,308	8	—	228	
132	Tosa Cement	9,299	6,400	2,362	−73	370	324	
133	Japan Rolling Stock	9,210	6,250	1,452	859	3,320	374	
134	Showa Wool Spinning	9,204	8,000	3,847	256	1,700	228	223
135	Japan Printed Cotton	9,048	1,500	936	−331	400	226	

A.2. Continued

Rank	Company name	Assets[a]	Paid in capital[b]	Revenue sales[c]	Profit[d]	Employees[e]	SIC1[f]	SIC2
136	Japan Dyes	8,923	7,000	11,136	456	—	281	
137	Japan Leather	8,721	5,000	1,095	765	635	311	
138	Izumi Spinning	8,562	4,500	*11,500*	1,145	2,718	228	
139	Kiyo Spinning	8,558	4,875	1,945	−862	2,482	221	228
140	Izumo Paper	8,530	6,000	*1,770*	83	2,300	262	
141	Hokuetsu Paper	8,492	4,050	6,673	368	553	262	
142	Ube Cement	8,429	5,075	3,879	46	165	324	
143	Korea Mills	8,426	5,000	*574*	5	2,180	228	221
144	Fukusuke Tabi	8,420	5,000	4,269	691	2,754	225	
145	Fujikura Electric Wire	8,076	5,000	—	408	950	335	
146	Osaka Knitting Mills	7,839	2,720	2,177	164	2,971	228	221
147	Yuho Spinning	7,834	5,000	1,758	847	3,850	228	
148	Nikka Oil	7,730	4,000	427	8	233	207	
149	Aichi Electric Clock	7,494	2,275	6,526	435	1,689	387	
150	Shinchiku Sugar	7,460	2,175	1,667	14	1,000	206	
151	Sano Spinning	7,187	3,750	*1,371*	−167	970	228	221
152	Nisshin Oil	7,154	3,750	*1,322*	−324	—	207	
153	Kikui Spinning	6,999	4,500	*1,338*	−176	1,711	228	221
154	Nitto Spinning	6,889	3,925	8,085	31	3,417	228	
155	Oshima Steel	6,779	5,438	*1,224*	−70	300	331	
156	Niigata Engineering	6,689	4,000	5,806	539	1,500	353	
157	Osake Ceramic and Cement	6,652	4,500	3,860	659	420	324	
158	Toyo Can Manufacturing	6,497	2,290	6,293	533	2,500	341	
159	Kyoritsu Muslin	6,454	4,000	1,010	−101	1,740	221	
160	Taki Fertilizer	6,326	3,500	*851*	136	—	287	
161	Shionogi	6,216	2,700	10,630	279	479	283	
162	Meidensha	6,095	3,500	1,891	33	670	362	
163	Hayashi Gumi	6,066	2,500	—	−177	—	228	
164	Toppan Printing	6,060	3,375	3,942	359	—	274	
165	Osaka Weaving	6,050	3,000	4,957	18	1,600	228	221
166	Oki Electric	6,046	3,500	3,885	219	850	366	
167	Japan Flat Glass	5,953	3,250	3,905	276	350	321	
168	Itami Carpet	5,922	2,625	9,266	429	1,380	227	
169	Kubota Works	5,919	3,550	4,600	366	1,200	352	349
170	Japan Music Instrument	5,901	3,740	7,807	296	1,194	393	
171	Ikegai Works	5,873	3,400	*1,483*	339	630	354	

A.2. Continued

Rank	Company name	Assets[a]	Paid in capital[b]	Revenue sales[c]	Profit[d]	Employees[e]	SIC1[f]	SIC2
172	Shueisha	5,840	3,000	3,117	366	1,253	274	
173	Nanao Cement	5,836	2,750	2,486	5	98	324	
174	Kurashiki Rayon	5,834	3,500	4,898	248	—	222	
175	Chuo Sugar	5,832	3,700	10,099	106	—	206	
176	Japan Paint	5,643	3,600	877	390	370	285	
177	Yoshimi Spinning	5,619	4,250	508	−1,290	1,708	228	221
178	Fuji Steel	5,594	3,100	2,236	−96	300	331	
179	Sagami Spinning	5,589	2,035	3,895	−132	1,588	228	
180	Kao Soap Company	5,517	3,000	4,535	615	353	284	
181	Asahi Spinning	5,504	2,640	881	56	2,700	228	221
182	Shinagawa Fire Brick	5,443	3,500	2,021	137	966	325	
183	Tsuji Spinning	5,296	3,000	731	−134	1,940	228	221
184	Tokyo Meter and Gauge	5,216	2,700	3,825	576	600	382	
185	Shinko Wool	5,174	2,500	11,155	468	—	223	
186	Dai-Nihon Salt	5,028	3,803	3,963	238	60	289	
187	Japan Rubber Shoe	5,000	5,000	—	—	—	306	
188	Kotobukiya (Suntory)	4,963	1,600	—	—	250	208	
189	Japan Motor Vehicle Manufacturing	4,962	1,710	163	109	—	371	
190	Osaka Wool	4,912	2,000	6,337	−49	1,000	223	
191	Toyota Textile Machine	4,781	2,175	1,233	291	1,350	355	
192	Tokai Steel	4,780	2,250	3,194	99	230	331	
193	Manmo Wool	4,763	1,950	2,388	−52	—	223	
194	Osaka Light Bulb	4,756	3,000	2,814	533	185	364	
195	Tokka Spinning	4,725	2,400	1,255	334	2,000	228	
196	Japan Copper Rolling Mill	4,720	2,250	6,819	−56	430	335	
197	Osaka Spinning	4,653	2,802	544	−216	1,100	228	
198	Teikoku Refrigeration	4,625	2,883	448	404	43	209	
199	Sumitomo Fertilizer	4,569	1,800	5,415	64	833	287	
200	Hakodate Dock	4,554	3,200	2,111	165	670	373	

Note: See Table A.1 for notes.

Sources: Nomura Shoten Chosabu, *Kabushiki Nenkan* (Company Annual Reports) (Osaka: Osaka Kobunsha, 1931, 1932); Tsunehiko Yui (ed.), *Eigyo Hokokusho Nenkan* (Annual Company Reports), microfilm (Tokyo: Yuihikaku, 1931, 1932); about ten privately held companies were investigated by speaking directly with principals from those companies.

A.3. The 200 Largest Industrial Firms in Japan: 1954

Rank	Company name	Assets[a]	Paid in capital[b]	Revenue sales[c]	Profit[d]	Employees[e]	SIC1[f]	SIC2	SIC3
1	Yawata Steel	105,544	9,600	71,687	1,633	35,971	331		
2	Fuji Steel	85,415	8,400	56,403	1,335	22,847	331		
3	Japan Steel	66,671	5,000	46,424	1,805	25,316	331		
4	Hitachi Ltd.	49,420	6,600	41,018	2,494	28,738	362	361	
5	Toyo Boseki	44,690	4,300	54,362	1,662	23,743	228	221	
6	Tokyo Shibaura Electric	41,799	6,000	32,943	2,812	23,701	362	361	364
7	New Mitsubishi Heavy Industries	35,895	5,600	30,642	2,081	22,631	373	351	371
8	Kanegafuchi Spinning	34,827	1,780	74,665	439	24,605	228	221	
9	Dai-Nihon Spinning	34,321	5,250	31,957	1,105	20,322	228	221	226
10	Sumitomo Kinzoku Industries	34,199	5,000	26,388	730	13,037	331		
11	Kawasaki Steel	33,617	4,000	25,041	433	15,745	331		
12	Mitsubishi Electric	28,387	2,400	24,139	830	17,952	362	361	
13	Mitsubishi Shipbuilding	27,902	2,800	19,493	958	16,738	373	351	
14	Toyo Rayon	24,468	3,000	29,759	2,653	18,994	222		
15	Onoda Cement	23,483	5,120	18,729	2,667	4,346	324		
16	Nissan Motor	23,210	1,400	14,247	1,025	6,696	371		
17	Nippon Mining[g]	22,931	2,100	20,946	979	13,959	333	291	
18	Japan Oil	22,500	4,500	50,376	2,064	2,628	291		
19	Showa Denko	22,459	2,200	15,592	588	9,850	336	287	336
20	Kobe Steel	21,401	3,600	22,248	379	8,386	331		
21	Sumitomo Chemical Industries	21,273	2,000	19,313	898	11,186	287	286	283
22	Asahi Chemical Industries	21,058	2,450	21,614	2,382	16,418	222	282	289
23	Hitachi Shipbuilding	20,517	3,160	12,668	−224	13,365	373		
24	Kureha Spinning	19,711	1,750	14,932	177	9,134	228	221	
25	Taiyo Fishery	19,087	2,000	22,879	541	7,819	209		
26	Japan Cement	19,053	2,500	16,545	2,770	4,698	324		
27	Japan Wool	18,806	1,280	16,556	1,269	11,555	223		
28	Ube Kosan	18,451	2,400	20,406	1,274	17,638	286	287	324

A.3. Continued

Rank	Company name	Assets[a]	Paid in capital[b]	Revenue sales[c]	Profit[d]	Employees[e]	SIC1[f]	SIC2	SIC3
29	Mitsubishi Japan Heavy Industries	18,408	3,000	14,323	834	11,951	373	371	351
30	Kurashiki Spinning	18,287	2,000	15,963	573	9,732	228	221	
31	Asahi Glass	18,281	3,100	15,771	933	6,730	321		
32	Mitsui Kinzoku Industries[g]	17,468	2,400	16,970	1,244	9,419	333		
33	Mitsubishi Kinzoku Industries	17,377	2,100	17,850	672	15,971	333		
34	Kurashiki Rayon	17,174	1,500	11,903	403	10,257	222		
35	Teikoku Synthetic Fiber	16,735	3,200	15,269	1,828	12,947	222		
36	Furukawa Electric	16,284	3,000	14,398	523	6,292	335		
37	Kawasaki Heavy Industries	16,214	3,360	9,513	468	8,932	373	351	362
38	Jujo Paper	15,648	1,120	19,594	1,320	5,633	262		
39	Fuji Spinning	15,633	2,000	14,619	780	8,731	228	221	226
40	Nitto Spinning	15,102	1350	11,405	−45	8,665	228	221	
41	Furukawa Mining	14,704	1,300	15,279	64	14,979	333	335	
42	Kohkoku Jinken Pulp	14,395	3,000	12,008	620	3,835	261	262	282
43	Ishikawajima Heavy Industries	14,365	1,300	8,532	369	6,795	373		
44	Daiwa Spinning	14,060	960	16,068	622	7,648	228	221	
45	Matsushita Electric Industrial	14,054	3,000	19,053	1,658	7,935	363	365	
46	Nissan Chemical Industries	14,015	2,000	16,147	871	6,582	287		
47	Honshu Paper	13,726	2,000	10,824	391	4,478	262		
48	Takeda Chemical Industries	13,722	2,100	13,144	1,003	5,123	283		
49	Oji Paper	13,646	1,600	13,205	1,624	4,348	262		
50	Japan Oil Refining	13,174	4,000	5,533	439	1,816	291		
51	Kirin Beer	13,111	1,230	27,221	1,221	2,574	208		

A.3. Continued

Rank	Company name	Assets[a]	Paid in capital[b]	Revenue sales[c]	Profit[d]	Employees[e]	SIC1[f]	SIC2	SIC3
52	Sumitomo Kinzoku Industries[g]	13,060	1,300	11,800	347	8,655	333		
53	Nisshin Spinning	13,040	1,040	14,712	810	7,239	228	221	
54	Mitsubishi Chemical Industries	12,988	2,384	11,474	411	5,760	226	282	287
55	Toyo Koatsu Industries	12,935	1,800	15,636	1,187	6,993	287		
56	Japan Keikinzoku	12,923	2,046	6,346	913	3,571	335		
57	Sanyo Pulp	12,891	2,175	9,374	853	2,096	261		
58	Maruzen Oil	12,594	1,050	19,878	1,069	2,420	291		
59	Mitsubishi Oil	12,280	2,400	17,330	1,689	1,461	291		
60	Shikishima Spinning	12,157	800	12,655	316	5,169	221	228	
61	Nippon Suisan	12,111	2,800	13,098	730	3,544	209		
62	Japan Steel Works	12,104	840	4,613		5,467	332	349	
63	Isuzu Motors	11,981	2,000	13,261	857	4,765	371		
64	Asahi Beer	11,839	1,460	26,547	994	2,304	208		
65	Sumitomo Electric Industries	11,561	2,000	11,779	365	4,353	335		
66	Idemitsu Kosan	11,381	400		967	1,896	291		
67	Japan Beer	11,305	1,460	23,464	909	2,275	208		
68	Ajinomoto	11,266	1,640	19,867	2,210	2,838	209	281	
69	Harima Shipbuilding	11,245	1,000	5,307	−153	5,809	373		
70	Iwaki Cement	11,185	750	13,981	1,851	3,412	324		
71	Showa Oil	11,114	1,700	14,396	1,312	2,068	291		
72	Toyota Motor	10,888	1,672	16,887	1,386	5,162	371		
73	Kubota Works	10,402	2,520	11,363	1,184	4,323	352	353	
74	Nitto Chemical Industries	10,254	2,000	9,225	762	3,195	287		
75	Bridgestone Tire	10,149	2,000	—	334	—	301		
76	Kokusaku Pulp Industries	10,120	1,200	7,583	425	2,635	261		

A.3. Continued

Rank	Company name	Assets[a]	Paid in capital[b]	Revenue sales[c]	Profit[d]	Employees[e]	SIC1[f]	SIC2	SIC3
77	Tohoku Pulp	10,077	1,040	7,490	541	1,962	261		
78	Mitsubishi Rayon	10,050	1,500	7,848	437	6,078	222		
79	Nichia Seiko	10,049	1,600	8,453	546	2,050	331		
80	Toyo Kogyo	9,968	300	12,674	943	2,911	371		
81	Fuji Electric Manufacturing	9,830	1,500	9,950	671	6,738	362	361	
82	Omi Silk Spinning	9,815	1,000	9,590	821	9,759	228	222	
83	NEC	9,648	1,000	8,170	529	6,875	366		
84	Fuji Film	9,500	2,000	9,579	1,293	4,727	386		
85	Katakura	9,371	1,000	12,062	369	9,928	228		
86	Mitsui Shipbuilding	9,327	1,120	7,268	505	6,091	373		
87	Hino Diesel	9,200	1,000	8,335	801	1,962	351		
88	Toa Fertilizer Manufacturing	9,188	3,159	15,865	1,730	1,916	291		
89	Komatsu	8,973	1,500	8,558	456	4,550	352	353	
90	Japan Oils and Fats	8,810	1,000	10,554	130	3,758	207		
91	Electro-Chemical Industries	8,776	510	5,461	406	5,201	287	286	282
92	Toyo Can	8,758	400	9,462	319	1,212	341		
93	Japan Pulp Industries	8,708	1,600	6,498	487	1,589	261		
94	Mitsui Chemical Industries	8,682	800	7,445	289	5,471	299	282	281
95	Japan Refrigeration	8,613	1,000	11,165	738	2,733	203		
96	Dai-Nihon Celluloid	8,360	1,000	7,633	454	4,126	282		
97	Dowa Mining	8,317	1,000	6,793	516	6,625	333	335	
98	Shin-Nihon Chisso Fertilizer	8,253	1,200	4,766	374	4,031	287		
99	Fuji Heavy Industries	7,921	831	1,979		5,163	371		
100	Yokohama Rubber	7,843	770	8,585	519	3,274	301		
101	Uraga Dock	7,777	1,000	5,664	151	·5,142	373		

A.3. Continued

Rank	Company name	Assets[a]	Paid in capital[b]	Revenue sales[c]	Profit[d]	Employees[e]	SIC1[f]	SIC2	SIC3
102	Nakayama Steel Works	7,757	240	9,736	198	2,564	331		
103	Toho Rayon	7,747	1,500	6,978	544	4,161	222		
104	Dakyo Oil	7,746	1,200	10,086	1,410	723	291		
105	Toa Spinning	7,533	1,200	8,184	632	5,044	223		
106	Nisshin Flour Mills	7,300	800	32,346	534	1,633	204		
107	Daito Spinning	7,272	1,200	5,877	592	3,858	223		
108	Japan Teppan	7,210	800	12,237	355	1,953	331		
109	Japan Yakkin Industries	7,134	1,185	4,465	374	2,415	331		
110	Japan Soda	7,092	1,160	6,622	339	4,491	281	335	
111	Kyowa Hakko Industries	7,058	1,150	5,395	743	1,554	208	286	202
112	Japan Rayon	6,910	1,200	6,751	376	5,081	222		
113	Toyo Fiber	6,773	1,200	4,677	218	5,357	229	226	
114	Sankyo	6,569	520	6,740	528	2,822	283		
115	Morinaga Seika	6,554	500	13,902	692	4,282	206		
116	Japan Flour Mills	6,539	720	23,602	403	1,256	204		
117	Toa Synthetic Chemicals	6,526	1,200	5,634	541	3,595	282	281	287
118	Meidensha	6,488	1,050	5,437	321	3,380	362	361	
119	Osaka Yogyo Cement	6,485	1,375	6,397	1,037	1,595	324		
120	Tekkosha	6,457	720	3,490	216	2,320	331	281	288
121	Daido Steel	6,431	840	5,001	7	4,415	331		
122	Nagoya Sugar	6,338	1,200	13,200	921	592	206		
123	Dai-Nihon Sugar	6,216	720	16,546	1,096	907	206		
124	Daihatsu Industries	6,208	600	9,521	644	3,391	371		
125	Japan Flat Glass	6,115	1,200	6,374	707	2,880	321		
126	Noda Soy Sauce	6,082	800	10,340	492	3,522	209		
127	Ishihara Industries	5,954	1,357	4,684	161	3,236	287	335	
128	Mitsubishi Paper	5,926	900	6,658	128	2,828	262		
129	Hokuetsu Paper	5,868	900	5,217	236	3,144	262	261	

A.3. Continued

Rank	Company name	Assets[a]	Paid in capital[b]	Revenue sales[c]	Profit[d]	Employees[e]	SIC1[f]	SIC2	SIC3
130	Takara Distillery	5,829	2,380	13,727	1,302	2,243	208		
131	Fujikura Densen	5,758	1,056	5,480	209	1,910	335		
132	Gunze	5,684	500	7,390	190	7,871	228		
133	Dai-Showa Paper	5,593	480	6,751	354	2,870	262	261	
134	Toyo Soda Industries	5,423	1,000	5,777	424	1,518	281	324	
135	Fujikoshi Kozai Industries	5,306	1,100	2,934	20	3,540	331	356	
136	Daido Wool	5,277	400	3,681	90	2,030	223		
137	Japan Rolling Stock	5,234	440	4,574	317	5,189	374		
138	Showa Elect. Wire & Cable	5,051	1,000	5,729	216	1,686	335		
139	Nichiro Fishery	4,987	1,100	4,611	202	1,483	209		
140	Meiji Confectionary	4,940	560	9,973	605	3,501	206	283	
141	Shimazu Seisakusho	4,927	600	3,584	256	3,650	382	384	369
142	Tokuyama Soda	4,867	400	6,140	533	2,124	281	324	
143	Kowa Spinning	4,794	500	6,647	312	3,678	228	221	
144	Yanmar Diesel	4,746	300	—	—	—	352	351	
145	Toyo Kohan	4,727	240	5,442	122	1,429	331		
146	Konishiroku Film	4,710	800	5,130	410	3,360	386		
147	Yodogawa Steel Works	4,690	500	4,737	213	1,758	331		
148	Koa Oil	4,660	660	6,636	858	583	291		
149	Shionogi	4,647	720	5,638	295	2,338	283		
150	Toyoda Automatic Loom	4,617	700	4,171	178	3,564	355	371	
151	Kotobukiya (Suntori)	4,602	58	—	—	—	208		
152	Teikoku Hemp	4,566	720	2,993	263	3,431	229	228	
153	Amigasaki Steel	4,557	570	2,800	155	1,362	331		
154	Mitsubishi Steel Products	4,501	400	2,606	185	1,728	331	371	

A.3. Continued

Rank	Company name	Assets[a]	Paid in capital[b]	Revenue sales[c]	Profit[d]	Employees[e]	SIC1[f]	SIC2	SIC3
155	Otani Heavy Industries	4,450	86	5,771	34	2,111	331		
156	Niso Steel	4,418	416	3,768		1,441	331		
157	Sanki Industries	4,407	200	6,895	82	1,406	331		
158	Fuji Seimitsu	4,380	667	2,279	255	—	371	351	382
159	Niigata Engineering	4,379	600	4,107	231	4,308	351	353	
160	Amigasaki Steel Works	4,361	960	397	1,205	—	331		
161	Chuo Synthetic Fiber	4,301	500	3,024	66	3,356	229	228	
162	Japan Seiko	4,270	400	3,448	384	2,486	356		
163	Japan Special Steel Products	4,259	600	2,234	164	1,484	331		
164	Japan Synthetic Fiber	4,245	1,000	2,828	113	2,781	229	228	
165	Kanzaki Paper	4,224	250	3,355	215	1,047	262		
166	Central Wool Weaving	4,147	570	3,867	228	1,799	228	223	
167	Teikoku Manufacturing	4,144	600	5,175	279	3,619	228	229	324
168	Sanraku Distillery	4,091	735	3,825	298	949	208		
169	Osaka Shipbuilding	4,077	11	8,639	92	1,800	373	331	
170	Shinko Kinzoku Manufacturing	4,034	480	4,983	71	2,004	335		
171	Taito	4,015	200	11,789	651	516	206		
172	Kanegafuchi Chemical Industries	3,984	400	6,106	129	679	286	282	281
173	Meiji Milk Products	3,958	600	8,775	154	2,355	202		
174	Showa Manufacturing	3,952	500	11,783	293	898	207		
175	Fukusuke Tabi	3,898	140	4,602	184	3,022	239	232	
176	Honda Giken Manufacturing	3,898	60	5,979	68	—	375	351	
177	Japan Kagaku	3,884	500	4,521	326	4,120	289	281	

A.3. Continued

Rank	Company name	Assets[a]	Paid in capital[b]	Revenue sales[c]	Profit[d]	Employees[e]	SIC1[f]	SIC2	SIC3
178	Chichibu Cement	3,841	192	6,024	348	1,267	324		
179	Howa Industries	3,805	360	4,196	98	1,963	355		
180	Sanyo Electric	3,761	792	6,382	1,038	2,874	364	365	
181	Toto Seiko	3,736	400	3,868	54	1,445	331		
182	Oki Electric	3,721	360	3,348	291	3,586	366		
183	Morinaga Milk Products	3,711	465	9,090	294	1,613	202		
184	Chuetsu Pulp	3,711	600	2,151	159	634	261	262	
185	Dainichi Electric Wire	3,710	400	4,079	101	1,291	335		
186	Ibigawa Electric Manufacturing	3,664	480	1,332	148	121	287	281	362
187	Japan Chemical Industries	3,585	480	3,635	210	1,608	281	287	
188	Shinetsu Chemical Industries	3,473	480	2,964	158	2,413	287	281	
189	Ube Soda Industries	3,462	500	2,854	−586	1,355	281		
190	Japan Carbide Manufacturing	3,457	340	2,427	82	1,662	287	281	
191	Fuji Automotive	3,435	520	4,559	136	5,153	371		
192	Japan Hydrogen Manufacturing	3,423	300	3,549	143	1,709	287	281	
193	Kawasaki Aircraft Manufacturing	3,421	876	2,609	16	3,465	371		
194	Honen Oil	3,418	600	5,312	444	541	207		
195	Kanematsu Wool Industries	3,405	250	1,269	2,285	43	228	223	
196	Japan Synthetic Chemical	3,351	420	2,200	197	1,732	286	281	282
197	Toho Zinc	3,327	800	2,600	292	1,483	333		

A.3. Continued

Rank Company name	Assets[a]	Paid in capital[b]	Revenue sales[c]	Profit[d]	Employees[e]	SIC1[f]	SIC2	SIC3
198 Konoshima Chemical Industries	3,324	640	4,879	217	1,282	287		
199 Yukijirushi Milk Products	3,314	480	7,236	67	2,662	202		
200 Osaka Kiko	3,310	300	3,395	42	1,935	355	354	

Note: See Table A.1 for notes.

[i] Nippon Mining, by 1954, was a primary metals and petroleum products firm.

Sources: Publicly listed companies, *Yukashoken Hokokusho* (Tokyo, 1954, 1955); Daiyamondo, *Kaisha Yoran* (Tokyo: Daiyamondo, 1954, 1955); about ten privately held companies were investigated by speaking directly with principals from those companies.

A.4. *The 200 Largest Industrial Firms in Japan: 1973*

Rank	Company name	Assets[a]	Paid in capital[b]	Sales[c]	Profits[d]	Employees[e]	SIC1[f]	SIC2	SIC3
1	Shin-Nihon Steel	2,270,889	230,000	1,855,833	50,776	78,616	331		
2	Mitsubishi Heavy Industry	1,891,257	105,708	906,591	16,083	80,183	353	362	373
3	Japan Steel	1,371,319	101,846	868,822	18,046	39,348	331	373	
4	Hitachi Ltd.	1,198,053	126,860	1,000,929	32,996	80,908	362	363	367
5	Ishikawajima Harima	1,111,154	41,390	480,391	8,368	36,319	373	356	
6	Sumitomo Kinzoku Industry	1,084,556	82,976	725,216	14,807	30,615	331	334	
7	Kawasaki Steel	1,033,610	89,250	589,237	18,842	38,057	331		
8	Nissan Motor	1,005,063	53,462	1,270,833	41,422	52,819	371		
9	Toshiba	1,001,285	96,311	762,763	19,000	17,474	363	362	
10	Kobe Steel	887,039	76,154	612,485	10,452	34,888	331	351	
11	Mitsubishi Electric	726,430	58,459	573,027	11,819	55,535	362	363	
12	Matsushita Electric Industrial	723,048	45,750	1,143,031	44,058	46,360	365	363	
13	Toyota Motor	721,674	48,759	1,355,021	39,146	42,892	371		
14	Kawasaki Heavy Industry	652,716	43,379	436,025	9,155	34,616	373	351	
15	Hitachi Shipbuilding	572,818	30,149	234,594	4,870	23,816	373		
16	Toyo Industry (Mazda)	566,045	25,704	506,700	8,065	36,891	371		
17	Idemitsu Kosan	550,343	1,000	741,293	1,300	7,956	291		
18	Mitsubishi Chemical Industry	494,071	38,851	339,257	5,555	8,655	282	287	
19	Japan Petroleum Refining	465,685	8,000	265,772	3,675	2,749	291		
20	NEC	460,141	40,150	343,796	10,212	33,125	366	367	
21	Komatsu	459,415	24,960	274,665	12,751	17,675	353		
22	Japan Oil	440,226	22,500	841,624	5,044	3,005	291		
23	Asahi Chemical Industry	434,798	34,355	392,677	16,129	18,042	222	282	
24	Toray	433,873	47,901	362,547	18,803	23,101	222		
25	Mitsui Shipbuilding	420,926	20,222	207,064	11,838	15,703	373	356	
26	Nippon Mining	404,689	24,600	427,662	2,692	6,987	299	333	

A.4. Continued

Rank	Company name	Assets[a]	Paid in capital[b]	Sales[c]	Profits[d]	Emp- loyees[e]	SIC1[f]	SIC2	SIC3
27	Sumitomo Chemical Industry	403,643	44,973	336,125	5,569	14,233	281	282	333
28	Maruzen Oil	391,457	16,425	449,430	2,075	4,972	291		
29	Teijin	353,429	31,289	291,314	16,353	12,202	222		
30	Sumitomo Heavy Industry	351,167	15,747	174,036	4,100	12,527	373	356	
31	Ube Kosan	349,187	30,600	231,548	5,777	10,558	324		
32	Showa Denko	334,087	42,200	235,313	2,056	9,109	299	335	
33	Mitsubishi Oil	332,172	15,000	365,380	535	2,964	291		
34	Honda Jiken	300,723	19,480	366,777	11,308	18,287	375	371	
35	Mitsui Toastu Chemical	297,452	21,952	223,077	2,717	8,121	281	282	
36	Kubota Works	294,637	41,389	336,021	15,127	15,838	352	349	353
37	Mitsubishi Kinzoku	285,630	22,500	214,988	2,927	8,845	333	335	
38	Kanebo	275,234	14,360	392,915	6,659	20,231	222	223	
39	Isuzu Motors	270,706	38,000	288,515	2,530	11,156	371		
40	Fujitsu	267,809	28,443	209,343	9,308	29,820	357	366	
41	Asahi Glass	265,018	28,881	199,427	13,192	11,433	321		
42	Toyo Spinning	261,947	29,202	311,648	7,964	23,325	222	221	
43	Nisshin Steel	257,340	32,400	215,993	6,780	9,887	331	334	
44	Fuji Electric	252,679	21,039	168,800	3,175	20,395	361	362	
45	Takeda Chemical Industries	252,252	24,860	224,720	8389	12,426	283	209	
46	Unitika	246,018	22,325	261,838	7,400	16,379	222		
47	Furukawa Electric	237,557	16,107	257,896	3,654	5,964	335		
48	Showa Oil	236,866	4,500	223,798	983	2,183	291		
49	Mitsubishi Petrochemical	232,180	15,625	148,936	5,659	5,008	282		
50	Mitsubishi Rayon	226,920	16,353	180,417	4,889	8,907	222		
51	Sony	223,928	6,625	294,869	19,844	10,969	365		
52	Sumitomo Electric	222,543	18,064	238,487	6,381	11,322	355		
53	Toa Fuels	220,845	18,400	207,606	7,597	2556	291		
54	Sanyo Electric	216,313	25,159	343,251	6,350	15,537	367	363	
55	Kirin Beer	215,608	28,800	481,802	9,492	7,891	208		
56	Hino Motors	210,692	12,522	194,855	4,152	6,954	371		
57	Bridgestone	206,125	11,587	225,751	11,841	18,143	301		

A.4. Continued

Rank	Company name	Assets[a]	Paid in capital[b]	Sales[c]	Profits[d]	Employees[e]	SIC1[f]	SIC2	SIC3
58	Sanyo Kokusaku Pulp	204,841	12,300	158,204	2,765	5,803	261		
59	Mitsui Kinzoku	199,892	16,200	202,691	1,915	7,846	333		
60	Japan Keikinzoku	199,255	15,691	88,498	1,516	4,970	335		
61	Oji Paper	198,919	10,943	166,230	4,064	4,755	262		
62	Mitsubishi Mining and Cement	197,042	17,500	135,607	2,352	2,366	324		
63	Jujo Paper	196,562	8,234	154,561	2,521	6,913	262		
64	Kuraray	189,792	10,000	170,598	5,161	11,207	222		
65	Taiyo Fishery	189,504	15,000	331,116	1,380	11,070	209		
66	Sumitomo Metal and Mining	187,956	13,539	165,749	2,145	3,996	333	335	
67	Suntory	187,827	2,200	234,929	3,639	3,807	208		
68	Honshu Paper	181,069	5,882	149,832	2,034	5,391	262		
69	Onoda Cement	179,263	20,000	122,288	4,296	3,606	324		
70	Dai-Nihon Ink Chemicals	178,701	10,813	176,772	3,636	5,281	289		
71	Dai-Showa Paper	177,258	8,500	118,344	2,691	4,669	262		
72	Kajima Oil	170,218	10,000	107,063	2,121	798	291		
73	Sekisui Chemical Industry	167,308	5,730	161,782	4,169	6,133	282	353	
74	Eidai Industry	165,301	6,989	149,862	7,635	4,182	243		
75	Mitsui Petrochemical Industry	165,086	11,025	110,205	6,224	3,976	286		
76	Matsushita Electric Works	164,219	12,000	288,653	12,549	11,704	364		
77	IBM-Japan	162,680	50,000	—	22,410	7,636	357	367	
78	Toa Oil	159,569	4,725	143,769	897	774	291		
79	Sasebo Heavy Industry	158,613	3,000	58,123	316	6,655	373		
80	Sharp	158,062	11,767	164,367	3,312	11,307	365	363	
81	Dai-Nihon Printing	154,926	14,038	21,503	8,867	12,788	274		
82	Dakyo Oil	154,210	6,033	301,342	554	1,915	291		
83	Japan Cement	153,956	10,500	90,389	4,086	3,937	324		
84	Fuji Film	152,564	13,476	161,912	7,694	10,286	386		

A.4. Continued

Rank	Company name	Assets[a]	Paid in capital[b]	Sales[c]	Profits[d]	Emp-loyees[e]	SIC1[f]	SIC2	SIC3
85	Japan Steel Works	151,515	12,712	80,920	2,076	8,479	358	332	
86	Kyowa Oil	151,256	4,800	145,211	1,403	1,345	291		
87	Niigata Engineering	149,192	10,731	96,772	2,130	6,152	353	351	
88	Fuji Heavy Industry	148,705	10,000	154,740	1,399	14,649	371		
89	YKK (Yoshida Kogyo)	147,826	5,600	89,490	3,626	16,000	349		
90	Ajinomoto	143,781	10,467	200,455	5,264	5,764	209	207	
91	Daido Steel	141,367	12,500	116,808	1,455	8,570	331		
92	Hakodate Dock	133,365	1,547	38,486	228	3,274	373		
93	Nippondenso	131,415	6,602	165,310	5,818	15,508	371	358	
94	Electro-Chemical Industry	129,492	10,608	92,619	2,167	4,204	282		
95	Mitsubishi Gas Chemical	127,822	11,559	80,866	3,143	3,809	281		
96	Kohjin	126,537	5,384	70,058	944	3,719	245	222	
97	Suzuki Motors	126,230	12,000	166,617	2,421	9,723	371	375	
98	Asia Oil	124,255	5,630	151,495	14	985	291		
99	Nissan Diesel	123,760	6,082	101,721	2,264	4,202	371		
100	Nichiro Fishery	121,564	7,471	109,584	1,628	6,387	209		
101	Dowa Mining	120,301	10,000	112,628	3,302	3,218	333		
102	Toyo Soda Industry	117,980	8,000	77,826	2,391	3,185	281	324	
103	Toppan Printing	117,843	10,900	175,392	5,769	9,490	274		
104	Oki Electric	115,629	11,722	106,653	2,878	15,115	366	382	
105	Toyo Can	114,981	8,000	135,147	2,909	4,848	341		
106	Japan Kinzoku Industry	114,801	6,500	62,210	1,862	1,708	341		
107	Koyo Seiko	114,638	8,148	85,051	2,613	7,122	356		
108	Japan Synthetic Rubber	113,186	4,494	74,510	1,879	2,410	307		
109	Hitachi Electric Wire	113,037	11,160	149,667	4,595	5,142	335		
110	Fuji Sash Industry	112,774	4,803	70,505	802	4,276	344		
111	Shiseido	110,251	5,400	167,243	7,063	12,206	284		
112	Yukijirushi Milk Products	109,383	7,500	235,364	1,876	10,643	202		

A.4. Continued

Rank	Company name	Assets[a]	Paid in capital[b]	Sales[c]	Profits[d]	Employees[e]	SIC1[f]	SIC2	SIC3
113	Kanegafuchi Chemical Industry	106,849	7,183	91,369	2,214	3,191	282	222	
114	Sumitomo Keikinzoku	104,868	8,400	86,434	1,930	3,803	335		
115	Central Glass	103,742	5,580	72,682	1,032	3,791	321		
116	Yokohama Rubber	103,072	5,602	97,400	2,316	9,505	301		
117	Hitachi Kinzoku	102,925	7,950	12,7184	4,286	9,294	331	339	
118	Japan Suisan	102,834	10,000	156,184	4,013	6,872	209		
119	Mitsubishi Paper	102,283	6,191	78,439	1,458	3,948	262	261	
120	Japan Flat Glass	102,198	12,000	64,867	1,306	6,115	321		
121	Sumitomo Cement	99,839	10,000	74,152	2,538	3,961	324		
122	Kawatetsu Chemical	97,438	3,750	125,999	537	1,930	282		
123	Japan Petrochemical	95,555	4,000	94,993	965	1,809	299 283		
124	Sankyo	95,022	8,280	71,258	3,638	5,833			
125	Kurashiki Spinning	94,943	6,223	116,695	5,271	7,865	226		
126	Japan Seiko Bearings	94,860	7,960	95,037	2,716	7,170	356		
127	Kyowa Hakko	94,601	7,574	79,145	1,496	4,377	286		
128	Yanmar Diesel	94,417	1,200	88,641	1,580	5,411	351		
129	Japan Yakkin Industry	94,151	4,860	69,732	1,959	2,926	331		
130	Daihatsu Industry	93,016	18,300	118,940	1,841	7,671	371		
131	Tokuyama Soda	91,906	3,250	65,191	3,694	2,421	324	281	
132	Fujikura Electric Wire	91,452	7,528	89,930	2,422	4,563	335		
133	Sapporo Beer	90,964	10,080	162,887	1,387	4,215	208		
134	Japan Musical Instrument	89,118	4,483	165,502	5,721	14,746	393		
135	Toyoda Automatic Loom	88,489	3,948	110,435	2,757	55,71	355	353	
136	Japan Zeon	88,459	6,912	66,605	1,180	2,717	307	306	
137	Sanoyasu Dock	88,164	1,430	20,134	328	1,974	373		
138	Daiken Industry	87,993	4,085	63,605	2,865	2,408	324		

A.4. Continued

Rank	Company name	Assets[a]	Paid in capital[b]	Sales[c]	Profits[d]	Employees[e]	SIC1[f]	SIC2	SIC3
139	NTN Toyo Bearing	87,940	8,273	84,011	1,550	3,899	356		
140	Meiji Confectionary	87,388	7,680	100,215	1,890	6,879	206	283	
141	Asahi Beer	87,105	10,084	124,702	1,374	3,770	208		
142	Fuji Oil	86,438	7,500	98,505	1,001	572	291		
143	Nissan Chemical Industry	85,586	4,326	70,910	1,749	2,094	282	287	
144	Matsushita Electronics	85,377	10,000	94,804	6,889	8,150	367		
145	Dai-Nichi Japan Wire	83,570	6,000	90,163	1,037	3,879	335		
146	Rengo	83,562	3,000	111,881	2,611	3,165	265		
147	Daikin Industry	83,028	8,280	90,913	1,831	6,085	358		
148	Ricoh	81,594	6,908	106,034	3,448	7,654	382	386	
149	Kyushu Oil	80,857	3,000	112,663	2,373	514	291		
150	Aishin Seiki	80,694	4,007	89,676	1,326	7,082	371		
151	Nakayama Steel	79,481	2,000	72,142	1,641	3,290	331		
152	Nisshin Flour Mills	79,186	6,059	134,561	1,804	2,966	204		
153	Morinaga Milk Products	78,407	6,000	143,186	525	5,073	202		
154	Nisshin Spinning	78,073	6,000	112,976	7,941	8,765	226	228	
155	Fuji Xerox	77,738	5,200	54,251	4,347	7,076	382		
156	Nissan Auto Body	77,300	4,800	203,013	2,311	7,490	371		
157	Shin-Nihon Steel and Chemical	76,909	6,000	61,257	464	2,256			
158	Yasukawa Electric Manufacturing	76,840	7,401	55,938	1,829	6,897	362	382	
159	General Oil Refining	76,663	9,000	113,524	931	822	291		
160	Shinetsu Chemical Industry	76,178	9,928	76,103	2518	2,962	281		
161	Sumitomo Forestry	75,949	2,500	94,765	1,996	532	242	245	
162	Ebara Manufacturing	75,670	6,000	83,177	2,925	4,894	358	356	

A.4. Continued

Rank	Company name	Assets[a]	Paid in capital[b]	Sales[c]	Profits[d]	Employees[e]	SIC1[f]	SIC2	SIC3
163	Tokyo Toyo Electric	75,308	7,254	121,733	2,814	7,756	363	365	
164	Fuji Kosan	74,912	3,235	65,739	655	944	299		
165	Meiji Milk Products	74,815	7,195	159,114	1,301	6,294	202		
166	Daicel	74,434	7,000	63,794	1,654	3,677	282		
167	Japan Reizo	74,290	9,010	129,952	2,285	3,770	209		
168	Japan Soda	74,115	3,000	43,865	530	2,692	281	287	
169	Furukawa Mining	73,175	8,500	80,062	1,694	3,010	358	333	
170	Topy Industry	73,024	4,450	75,566	959	3,396	331	371	
171	Yamaha Motors	72,896	3,241	148,403	3,610	7,330	375		
172	Nikkei Aluminum	72,733	3,030	63,061	682	4,195	344		
173	Toki Machinery	72,446	8,000	90,862	6,888	8,682	325	326	
174	Shionogi	72,402	7,290	70,089	4,602	7,190	283		
175	Japan Victor	71,035	5,400	108,512	1,677	8,307	365		
176	Japan Pulp Industry	70,193	3,210	57,760	1,139	2,354	261		
177	Hitachi Chemicals	70,031	3,716	100,846	1,275	4,693	329	364	
178	Daiwa Spinning	68,793	4,654	80,864	3,583	7,811	228	222	221
179	Kurimoto Works	68,286	3380	68,402	831	3,868	349	353	
180	Japan Rolling Stock	67,817	3,100	61,448	656	4,133	374		
181	Shimazu Works	67,619	6,528	50,641	714	4,524	382		
182	Fuji Spinning	67,427	3,600	93,774	2,032	7,479	222	221	
183	Chisso	67,087	7,813	59,204	7,595	1,475	282	299	
184	Meidensha	66,754	7,200	57,985	903	5,473	361	362	
185	Kureha Chemical Industry	66,545	8,000	41,961	671	2,343	282	281	
186	Chichibu Cement	66,243	600	47,971	2,255	1,879	324		
187	Morinaga	66,143	5,019	76,156	1,070	5,445	206		
188	Gunze	65,706	5,556	77,609	2,125	7,261	225	226	
189	Yodogawa Steel Works	65,361	4,135	69,340	2,828	2,493	331	344	
190	Shinko Electric	65,319	6,000	43,741	363	6,072	362		
191	Japan Wool	64,953	4,103	58,680	1,227	7,248	223		

A.4. Continued

Rank	Company name	Assets[a]	Paid in capital[b]	Sales[c]	Profits[d]	Emp-loyees[e]	SIC1[f]	SIC2	SIC3
192	Japan Sanso	64,565	7,500	45,075	2,169	1,878	281	355	
193	Fujikoshi	63,971	6,423	57,610	1,543	5,454	356		
194	Tanabe Drug	63,794	8,000	68,946	2,631	5,343	283		
195	Kao Soap	63,608	2,751	116,189	2,254	3,993	284		
196	Showa Electric Wire	63,576	5,000	101,942	2,097	2,999	335		
197	Hayashi Spinning	63,535	3,345	47,482	733	4,221	223		
198	Mitsubishi Steel	63,129	7,200	55,046	3,129	3,740	331	349	
199	Omron Tateishi Electronic	63,011	3,218	81,116	4,237	5,373	382		
200	Konishiroku Film	62,984	5,000	64,853	2,359	4,008	386		

Note: See Table A.1 for notes.

Sources: Publicly listed companies, *Yukashoken Hokokusho* (Tokyo, 1973, 1974); Daiyamondo, *Kaisha Yoran* (Tokyo: Daiyamondo, 1973, 1974); about ten privately held companies were investigated by speaking directly with principals from those companies.

A.5. *The 200 Largest Industrial Firms in Japan:* 1987

Rank	Company name	Assets	Paid in capital	Sales	Income	Employees	SIC1[a]	SIC2	SIC3
1	Toyota Motor	6,024,909	200,208	4,307,201	2,657,338	64,329	371		
2	Nissan Motor	3,418,671	38,584	2,907,113	1,338,881	51,237	371		
3	Matsushita Electric Industrial	3,277,613	85,343	2,538,978	1,439,666	39,707	365	357	363
4	Japan Tabacco Industry	2,946,881	106,680	1,793,669	947,339	32,000	211		
5	Hitachi	2,919,539	65,138	2,838,109	975,555	76,210	357	362	
6	Toshiba	2,682,781	37,040	2,419,325	700,384	70,288	357	363	362
7	Honda	2,650,077	47,273	1,231,521	542,823	29,640	371		
8	NEC	2,304,392	37,477	2,064,156	608,112	38,004	357	366	
9	Nippon Steel (Shin Nippon Sei)	2,147,038	31,883	3,145,722	600,367	61,423	331		
10	Mitsubishi Electric	1,954,187	19,818	1,668,848	473,665	48,562	357	362	363
11	Mitsubishi Motors[b]	1,753,000	—	1,110,086	142,672	22,997	371		
12	Nippon Oil	1,725,814	16,739	1,186,272	309,433	2,734	291		
13	Fujitsu	1,714,424	32,066	1,789,853	666,131	50,617	357		
14	Mitsubishi Heavy Industries	1,708,256	21,152	2,611,722	530,829	45,363	361	362	
15	Mazda Motor	1,602,293	4,438	870,863	289,457	28,423	371		
16	Idemitsu Kosan[c]	1,529,101	7,295	1,244,715	40,807	5,792	291		
17	Cosmo Oil[d]	1,297,593	6,944	966,382	51,901	3,062	291		
18	Kirin Brewery	1,266,349	34,059	813,499	323,038	7,557	208		
19	Showa Shell Sekiyu	1,265,622	7,372	750,352	54,719	2,578	291		
20	NKK (Nippon Kokan)	1,050,325	12,665	2,300,510	266,723	25,193	331		
21	Sony	1,029,891	30,681	1,140,906	515,811	15,858	365		
22	Nippondenso	994,007	27,889	835,084	444,071	36,109	371		
23	Kobe Steel	975,932	7,640	1,671,860	217,679	22,741	331	366	
24	Kawasaki Steel	936,372	6,916	1,692,143	331,853	20,803	331		
25	Isuzu Motors	909,915	9,385	675,840	152,304	13,757	371		
26	Sanyo Electric	909,393	14,128	1,070,361	559,261	34,754	363		
27	Sumitomo Metal Industries	909,271	1,317	1,899,047	318,922	23,108	331		
28	IBM Japan[c]	878,539	118,883	578,781	259,494	20,421	357	357	
29	Sharp	872,707	18,857	1,131,426	453,334	22,845	357		
30	Asahi Chemical Industry	763,483	20,146	768,679	240,912	15,595	282		
31	Suzuki Motor	759,550	5,872	432,946	99,944	12,912	371	367	363
32	Dainippon Printing	754,720	26,584	684,291	354,933	10,594	275	289	
33	Suntory	749,506	14,051	591,799	157,946	4,789	208		
34	Asahi Glass	721,234	32,518	744,152	373,081	9,555	321	278	
35	Ishikawajima-Harima Heavy Industry	714,714	1,514	954,355	106,883	15,873	353		

A.5. Continued

Rank	Company name	Assets	Paid in capital	Sales	Income	Employees	SIC1[a]	SIC2	SIC3
36	Nippon Mining	709,905	4,745	607,929	86,760	5,540	291	281	
37	Fuji Heavy Industries	686,238	10,430	597,227	172,625	14,997	371		
38	Fuji Film	680,052	61,838	794,109	523,869	11,067	386	335	
39	Mitsubishi Oil	671,719	5,196	436,968	37,809	2,411	291		
40	Matsushita Electric Works	662,710	17,216	553,188	249,386	13,735	363	367	
41	Mitsubishi Metal	656,440	5,345	513,070	77,396	6,919	335		
42	Mitsubishi Chemical Industries	623,010	12,911	858,424	165,557	8,751	286	364	
43	Kawasaki Heavy Industries	579,731	1,016	878,437	79,287	16,587	353		
44	Japan Victor[e]	578,904	5,595	380,674	181,006	13,286	365	281	
45	Canon	578,644	8,853	683,957	109,439	15,572	357	372	
46	Toppan Printing	577,026	17,073	561,465	265,194	10,729	275		
47	Ricoh	560,017	13,054	505,910	263,985	11,982	386	368	
48	Kubota	557,979	14,068	632,497	302,671	15,519	352	278	273
49	Daihatsu Motor	557,627	5,103	334,671	98,901	11,226	371	357	
50	Bridgestone	557,243	29,277	609,396	309,637	16,077	301	331	
51	Taiyo Fishery	550,445	363	306,879	29,437	3,685	209		
52	Sumitomo Electric Industries	550,115	12,517	482,201	196,876	12,992	335	307	
53	Toray Industries	541,511	16,223	718,784	287,136	10,143	282		
54	Takeda Chemical	539,754	31,387	675,909	313,728	10,771	283		
55	Komatsu	539,038	9,067	782,940	374,184	15,707	353	307	
56	Toa Nenryo Kogyo	532,571	32,559	461,776	273,472	2,322	291		
57	Sumitomo Chemical	515,762	11,236	659,434	124,764	7,707	286		
58	Kao	490,019	13,247	420,224	193,976	6,697	284		
59	Nippon Suisan	481,136	3,102	230,896	65,323	3,772	209		
60	Furukawa Electric	470,068	4,476	392,015	118,562	7,008	335		
61	Sapporo Breweries	467,046	5,250	365,830	108,557	3,791	208		
62	Snow Brand Milk Products (Yukijirushi)	460,657	4,059	225,335	58,976	8,213	202	334	
63	Hino Motors	448,412	4,054	245,481	82,264	8,095	371		
64	General Sekiyu	446,018	7,463	304,464	78,473	1,427	291		
65	Sekisui Chemical	441,488	12,092	339,682	119,633	5,150	282		
66	Toyo Seikan	437,690	16,070	312,482	140,499	6,107	341		
67	Ajinomoto	432,524	14,079	495,680	267,812	5,438	209		
68	Sumitomo Metal Mining	429,239	2,287	306,666	63,727	3,197	335		203
69	Dainippon Ink and Chemical	417,697	14,508	480,405	124,804	6,468	286		

A.5. Continued

Rank	Company name	Assets	Paid in capital	Sales	Income	Employees	SIC1[a]	SIC2	SIC3
70	Oki Electric Industry	416,203	4,107	473,332	112,637	13,813	357		
71	Showa Denko	415,608	5,550	554,641	68,684	5,002	291	289	
72	Fuji Electric	402,301	5,020	503,443	104,657	12,066	361	366	367
73	Nippon Meat Packers (Ham)	398,630	8,882	211,689	104,831	3,359	201	281	286
74	Nissan Auto Body	395,133	2,051	137,674	60,279	5,533	371	382	
75	Yamaha (music)	391,852	5,411	290,236	112,831	12,709	393		
76	Oji Paper	387,758	15,738	451,681	175,193	5,454	262		
77	Kanebo	381,819	2,334	478,464	49,155	8,821	282		
78	Aisin Seiki	370,040	7,718	257,333	136,036	9,348	371		
79	Yamaha Motor	367,119	3,811	238,057	56,942	7,157	375	284	
80	Honshu Paper	366,974	3,979	513,213	42,307	6,450	262		
81	Ube Industries	364,989	3,739	605,995	72,444	7,309	324	373	
82	Toyoda Automatic Loom	367,828	10,598	247,660	145,279	6,697	371		
83	Yamazaki Baking	367,317	9,530	225,654	120,045	13,581	205		
84	Nisshin Steel	363,555	12,267	496,732	116,640	7,450	331		
85	Mitsui Toastsu Chemicals	363,388	6,211	491,382	46,172	5,291	287	282	284
86	Meiji Milk Products	360,898	2,494	142,910	48,745	5,586	202		
87	Itoham Foods	357,593	6,364	186,244	101,320	4,208	201		
88	TDK	352,210	15,709	402,610	238,946	7,826	367	366	
89	Asahi Breweries	345,112	2,509	266,235	79,851	2,944	208		
90	Jujo Paper	342,619	9,391	428,534	95,731	4,441	262		
91	Konica	329,326	6,804	333,427	186,656	4,938	386	383	
92	Kanto Auto Works	320,980	2,557	84,987	24,182	5,761	371		
93	Shiseido	320,228	9,622	361,176	198,792	13,802	284		
94	Morinaga Milk Industry	315,167	1,952	159,246	45,909	4,290	202		
95	Daishowa Paper	313,026	9,216	481,709	48,816	5,050	262		
96	Teijin	309,666	15,602	492,034	190,328	5,964	282	286	
97	Alps Electric	304,059	6,416	301,298	118,937	6,401	357	367	
98	Lion	303,231	5,070	206,637	74,028	3,994	284		
99	Toyobo	298,378	5,603	325,913	80,601	8,466	228	282	
100	Nisshin Flour Milling	298,265	5,642	172,066	73,617	3,073	204		
101	Sumitomo Ringyo	293,560	1,132	188,041	31,138	2,304	243		
102	Sankyo	291,724	10,473	288,127	146,136	5,822	283		
103	Toyoda Auto Body	289,147	2,333	94,449	29,196	6,787	371		
104	Mitsubishi Petrochemical	288,920	9,242	406,307	89,344	2,782	286	282	
105	Nichirei	284,213	2,602	147,405	53,727	2,315	209	204	
106	Sanyo Kokusaku Pulp	279,701	7,835	318,268	77,671	4,298	262		

A.5. Continued

Rank	Company name	Assets	Paid in capital	Sales	Income	Employees	SIC1[a]	SIC2	SIC3
107	Omron Tateisi Electronics	277,962	6,905	236,290	134,101	6,174	382	357	
108	Kyocera	271,165	19,882	415,773	310,369	12,397	367	386	
109	Mitsui Mining & Smelting	268,933	1,266	249,921	22,475	3,305	333	334	
110	Pioneer Electronic	266,177	7,123	224,348	174,115	7,129	365	366	
111	Nissan Diesel Motor	260,586	284	277,134	50,385	5,404	371		
112	Hitachi Zosen	256,318	8,386	559,077	59,344	4,639	351	356	353
113	Mitsui Mining	251,163	589	253,226	31,062	1,330	291	325	
114	Hitachi Chemical Industries[f]	249,753	2,953	158,259	47,490	4,915	281	353	
115	Unitika	248,183	447	289,360	27,465	4,508	282	228	
116	Nippon Light Metal	248,023	10,016	272,762	31,964	3,735	344		
117	Nippon Seiko	246,243	3,771	337,503	138,572	8,285	356		
118	Toto	235,108	10,210	245,866	112,836	8,004	326	325	
119	Daido Steel	234,082	2,257	256,133	59,613	7,802	331		
120	Hitachi Cable[f]	232,971	7,912	219,729	110,052	5,271	335		
121	Mitsui Petrochemical Industries	232,465	7,319	378,515	84,128	4,291	286	282	
122	Kyowa Hakko	231,496	7,035	276,280	105,161	5,133	283	208	
123	Toyo Sash	231,129	7,114	237,255	104,387	4,355	344		
124	Arabian Oil	227,476	2,207	112,812	51,031	2,177	291		
125	Prima Meat Packers	227,084	589	90,540	18,106	3,332	201		
126	Yokohama Rubber	226,344	3,668	231,723	40,179	6,380	301	306	
127	NTN Toyo Bearing	225,745	4,874	295,049	110,550	7,062	356		
128	Daikin Industries	225,267	5,696	177,166	60,147	6,443	358		
129	Aichi Machine Industry	223,078	2,047	89,227	27,936	4,313	371		
130	Nichiro Gyogyo	214,592	355	117,839	11,624	1,935	209		
131	Casio Computer	211,147	4,332	213,179	113,237	3,557	357	387	
132	Taio Paper	210,903	6,215	259,222	65,772	2,787	262		
133	Tosoh (Toyo Soda)	210,254	2,758	339,916	57,701	4,381	282	281	
134	Matsushita Kotobukiya[e]	209,314	8,442	185,200	131,075	4,962	365		
135	Shin-Etsu Chemical	207,028	8,879	247,207	102,698	3,394	282	281	

A.5. Continued

Rank	Company name	Assets	Paid in capital	Sales	Income	Employees	SIC1[a]	SIC2	SIC3
136	Shionogi	206,118	10,326	241,050	144,330	6,410	283		
137	YKK (Yoshida Kogyo)	205,293	21,108	105,278	—	13,916	396	344	
138	Nippon Sheet Glass	203,918	6,392	254,980	96,014	3,653	321	329	
139	Shinnitsu Tekkagaku[g]	202,575	2,031	183,213	32,177	3,029	291	286	
140	Rengo	101,337	1,476	126,808	33,966	2,900	263		
141	Sumitomo Heavy Industries	200,026	305	330,487	63,053	5,970	353		
142	Diesel Kiki	199,733	2,355	161,795	50,588	5,766	358	371	
143	Kuraray	198,795	2,219	230,803	49,163	5,169	282	228	
144	Sumitomo Rubber	198,718	2,819	191,604	23,636	4,912	301	394	
145	Minolta Camera	196,939	2,837	201,056	85,058	6,687	386		
146	Kyokuyo Fishery	194,741	475	78,848	8,349	1,110	209		
147	Mitsubishi Rayon	193,973	3,682	263,718	83,441	4,298	282	228	
148	Denki Kagaku Kogyo	192,519	5,186	290,256	80,386	3,927	286	324	
149	Meiji Seika	191,077	3,275	173,995	102,128	5,315	206	283	
150	Fujisawa Pharmaceutical	190,293	8,364	330,143	171,446	5,436	283		
151	Murata Manufacturing	189,855	11,317	268,134	166,600	2,734	367		
152	Shueisha	188,700	11,547	—	—	600	272	273	
153	Nisshinbo Industries	188,603	5,528	196,595	106,373	6,287	221	228	
154	Kokuyo	187,146	7,157	198,464	75,840	2,440	252	264	
155	Onoda Cement	186,887	8,424	283,114	67,401	1,460	324	329	
156	Misawa Homes	185,098	4,001	168,021	43,975	1,229	245		
157	Kanegafuchi Chemical Industry	183,544	7,279	198,426	86,496	3,304	286	282	
158	Koa Oil	183,335	1,544	177,984	38,296	1,131	291		
159	Sankyo Aluminum	182,827	1,860	182,977	39,409	4,758	344		
160	Mitsui Engineering and Shipbuilding	182,354	856	427,623	88,190	6,770	373	353	
161	Mitsubishi Gas Chemical	182,104	4,947	240,577	91,281	3,744	281	282	283
162	Koyo Bearing	181,766	3,326	213,011	85,581	6,478	356	344	
163	Toyo Tire and Rubber	180,832	2,599	161,089	24,230	3,586	301		
164	Matsushita Refrigerator[e]	180,465	7,384	117,353	75,463	4,341	358		

A.5. Continued

Rank	Company name	Assets	Paid in capital	Sales	Income	Employees	SIC1[a]	SIC2	SIC3
165	Kyushu Matsushita Electric[e]	179,502	6,516	148,366	66,698	5,271	365	367	
166	Marudai Foods	175,513	6,305	120,592	93,176	3,911	201		
167	Nihon Synthetic Rubber	174,627	3,669	215,516	68,511	2,744	282		
168	Toyo Ink Manufacturing	174,314	5,105	149,126	79,532	2,984	289	286	
169	Mitsubishi Mining and Cement	173,406	4,768	263,401	67,592	2,063	324		
170	Hitachi Construction Equipment[f]	173,255	2,849	147,754	35,066	3,962	356		
171	Sumitomo Light Metals	173,222	1,783	292,358	7,193	2,905	344		
172	Toa Steel	172,954	−13,577	186,060	6,046	1,769	331		
173	NGK Insulators (Nihon Gaishi)	171,514	14,279	211,924	93,597	4,941	326		
174	Mitsubishi Paper	170,712	7,024	209,289	69,276	3,649	262		
175	Nikon	170,347	2,313	218,976	111,598	6,670	386	383	
176	Nippon Electric Glass[h]	169,005	3,355	209,033	67,417	4,493	367	322	
177	Tokyo Electric[i]	168,233	2,829	176,386	79,469	5,051	357		
178	Fujikura Cable	168,203	3,622	208,371	66,581	3,656	335	367	
179	Tanabe Pharmaceuticals	167,231	8,210	184,692	94,449	5,126	283		
180	Eisai	167,063	9,938	211,299	116,268	3,692	283		
181	Brother Industries	166,502	4,370	164,262	90,859	5,165	357	363	
182	INAX	164,093	5,173	145,022	69,487	4,865	325		
183	Yamanouchi Pharmaceuticals	164,053	16,745	265,712	138,854	3,164	283		
184	Citizen Watch	162,123	3,037	162,900	88,685	3,301	387		
185	Tokyo Steel	162,067	14,310	120,991	60,991	1,430	331		
186	Yokogawa Electric	161,777	5,254	213,659	115,392	6,359	382		
187	National Homes Industry[e]	155,802	4,460	104,220	34,672	2,558	245	249	
188	Nihon Cement	155,138	4,292	271,865	73,571	2,204	324		
189	Showa Sangyo	154,236	2,063	105,691	32,706	1,556	204	207	
190	Central Glass	151,359	3,323	186,066	31,822	2,613	322	281	
191	Nissin Foods	150,587	9,309	183,824	142,675	1,049	204		
192	House Food Industrial	149,789	14,523	145,959	83,939	2,824	203	205	
193	Ebara	147,698	7,083	178,359	77,822	3,483	356		
194	Toyoda Gosei	147,544	2,564	93,898	43,788	5,297	306	307	
195	Daiichi Pharmaceuticals	147,450	15,311	232,872	106,389	3,230	283		

A.5. *Continued*

Rank	Company name	Assets	Paid in capital	Sales	Income	Employees	SIC1[a]	SIC2	SIC3
196	Yodogawa Steel Works	147,114	7,396	147,924	72,495	1,683	331		
197	Nihon Flour Mills	146,847	2,428	80,407	44,196	1,445	204		
198	Kodansha	145,800	7,589	98,074	48,048	1,052	273		
199	NOK	144,636	2,914	78,072	32,194	3,216	306		
200	Q.P.	143,469	3,442	106,451	41,728	2,013	203		

Note: Monetary figures are in 1,000s of yen.

[a] SIC columns represent product lines that account for at least 20 percent of sales.

[b] Company affiliated with Mitsubishi group through shareholding; recently listed company.

[c] Privately controlled companies.

[d] Formed in 1986 as a result of the merger of Maruzen Oil and Daikyo Oil.

[e] Companies that are affiliated with Matsushita Electric Industrial through shareholding.

[f] Companies that are affiliated with Hitachi Ltd. through shareholding.

[g] Company affiliated with Shin-Nitetsu through shareholding.

[h] Company affiliated with NEC through shareholding.

[i] Company affiliated with Toshiba Corporation through shareholding.

Sources: Publicly listed companies, *Yukashoken Hokokusho* (Annual Reports filed with the Government) (Tokyo: 1987, 1988); Daiyamondo, *Kaisha Yoran* (Tokyo: Daiyamondo, 1987, 1988).

Bibliography

WORKS IN JAPANESE LANGUAGE

AICHI RODO MONDAI KENKYUSHO, *Toyota Gurupu no Shinsenryaku* (The New Strategy of the Toyota Group) (Tokyo: Shin-Nihon Shuppansha, 1990).

AMAGAI, SHOGO, *Nihon Jidosha Kogyo no Shiteki Tenkai* (The Historical Development of the Japanese Automobile Industry) (Tokyo: Aki Shobo, 1982).

ASABA, SHIGERU, and KUWADA, KOTARU, 'The Continuous Side of Discontinuity', *Keizai to Shakaigaku*, 63 (Feb. 1989).

ASAJIMA, SHOICHI, *Senkanki Sumitomo Zaibatsu Keieishi* (The Business History of the Sumitomo *Zaibatsu* between the Two World Wars) (Tokyo: Tokyo University, 1983).

ASANUMA, BANRI, 'Setsubi Toshi Kettei no Prosesu to Kijun (2)' (Decision-Making Processes and Standards for Plant and Equipment Investments), *Keizai Ronso* (Economic Papers), Kyoto University, Department of Economics, 130–5/6 (Nov.–Dec. 1982).

—— 'Yasashi Keizaigaku' (Economics Made Easy), *Nihon Keizai Shimbun*, 21–5 Feb. 1984.

—— 'Jidosha Sangyo ni okeru Buhin Torihiki no Kozo' (The Structure of Parts Transactions in the Automotive Industry: the Mechanisms of Adjustment and Innovative Adaptation), *Gendai Keizai* (Modern Economics), 59 (Summer 1984).

—— 'Manufacturer–Supplier Relationships in Japan and the Concept of Relation-Specific Skill', *Journal of the Japanese and International Economies*, 3–1 (Mar. 1989), 1–30.

BABA, YASUNORI, 'Sokatsu Komento 1' (General Comments), in Ryutaro Komiya, Masahiro Okuno, Taro Suzuki (eds.), *Nihon no Sangyo Seisaku* (Japan's Industrial Policy) (Tokyo: University of Tokyo Press, 1985).

DAIDO, KEORI, *Ito Hitosuji* (The Thread of Our Existence and Enterprise) (Tokyo: Bunshodo, 1960).

Daihatsu Kogyo, *Rokujunenshi* (A 60 Year History) (Osaka: Daihatsu Kogyo, 1967).

—— *Kaisha Meikan* (Company Affiliates Roster) (Osaka: Daihatsu Kyoyukai, 1980).

FRUIN, W. MARK, 'Jumyo no mijikai Nihon no kigyo' (Corporate Life-Cycles in the United States and Japan: A Hundred Year Comparison), *Nikkei Business*, 10/12 (1985).

Fujikoshi Machine Tool Company, *Fujikoshi Gojunenshi* (50 Years of Fujikoshi) (Tokyo: Dainippon, 1978).

FUJITA, AKIHISA, 'Seisan Koritsuka e no Jakkan no Kosatsu' (Some Thoughts on the Rationalization of Production), 1/5, *Kansai Daigaku Shogakubu Ronshu* (Kansai University Papers on Business), 26/5 to 28/5, 1981–3.

HANLEY, SUSAN, 'Zenkogyokaki Nihon no Toshi ni Okeru Koshu Eisei' (Public Health in Japanese Cities Before Industrialization), in Hayami Akira, Saito Osamu, and Sugiyama Shinya (eds.), *Tokugawa Shakai kara no Tenbo* (Perspectives from Tokugawa Society) (Tokyo: Dobunkan, 1988), 216–37.

HASHIMOTO, JURO, and TAKEDA, HARUHITO, *Ryodaisenkanki Nihon no Karuteru* (Cartels Between the Two World Wars) (Tokyo: Ochanomizu Shobo, 1985).

HATATE, ISAO, *Nihon no Zaibatsu to Mitsubishi* (Mitsubishi and Japanese *Zaibatsu*) (Tokyo: Rakuyu Shobo, 1978).

HAYAMI, AKIRA, *Kinsei Noson no Rekishijinkogakuteki Kenkyu* (The Historical Demography of Early Modern Agricultural Villages) (Tokyo: Toyo Keizai Shinposha, 1973).

—— *Nihon Keizaishi e no Shikaku* (Perspectives on Japanese Economic History) (Tokyo: Toyo Keizai Shinposha, 1986).

HAZAMA, HIROSHI, *Nihon ni okeru Roshi Kyowa no Teiryu* (Undercurrents in Japanese Labor Relations) (Tokyo: Waseda University Press, 1978).

HIGETA, SHOYU, *Shashi* (Company History) (Tokyo: Toppan, 1972).

HIRANO, HISAO, *Seikosha Shiwa* (Tales of Seiko) (Tokyo: Seikosha, 1968).

—— *Hattori Kintaro* (Mr. Kintaro Hattori) (Tokyo: Jijitsushin, 1972).

Hitachi Ltd., *Hitachi Seisakushoshi* (A History of Hitachi, Ltd.), 3 vols. (Tokyo: Hitachi, 1949–71).

IGARASHI, A. (ed.), *Kojo Kosto Daun Jiten* (A Dictionary of Factory Cost Reduction Terms) (Tokyo: Nikkan Kogyo, 1990).

IMAI, KEN'ICHI, 'Kigyo Gurupu' (Enterprise Groups), in Imai Ken'ichi and Komiya Ryutaro (eds.), *Nihon no Kigyo* (Japan's Enterprise) (Tokyo: Tokyo University Press, 1989).

—— and KOMIYA, RYUTARO (eds.), *Nihon no Kigyo* (Japan's Enterprise) (Tokyo: University of Tokyo Press, 1989).

INOUE, YUTAKA, 'The Many Forms of Financial Manœuvring by Big Business in Japan', *Nihon Keizai Shimbun*, 20 Dec. 1984, 6.

ITAMI, HIROYUKI, *Jinponshugi Kigyo* (Human Resources as a Foundation) (Tokyo: Tsukuba Shobo, 1987).

ITO, TAIKICHI, 'Kikai kogyo no hattatsu: Tokuni menboshoku kikai kogyo no hattatsu o chushin to shite' (The Development of Machinery Industries: With Special Reference to the Development of the Cotton Spinning Machinery Industry), in Arisawa Hiromi, et al. (eds.), *Chusho Kigyo Kenkyu I: Chusho Kigyo no Hattatsu* (Research on Small- and Medium-Sized Business I: The Development of Small- and Medium-Sized Companies) (Tokyo: Toyo Keizai Shinposha, 1960).

KANNO, WATARO, *Nihon Kaisha Kigyo Hasseishi no Kenkyu* (Research on the Origins of Japan's Joint-Stock Companies) (Tokyo: Keizai Hyoronsha, 1966).

Kao Corporation, *Kao Sekken Gojunenshi* (A 50 Year History of Kao) (Tokyo: Kao Corporation, 1940).

—— *Kao Sekken Nanajunenshi* (A 70 Year History of Kao) (Tokyo: Toppan, 1960).

—— *Kao Kyujunen no Ayumi* (90 Years of Kao) (Tokyo: Kao Corporation, 1980).

KAWAKAMI, GENICHI, *Ongaku Fukyu no Shiso* (Thoughts on the Diffusion of Music) (Tokyo: Yamaha Ongaku Shinkokai, 1977).

Keizai Chosa Kyokai, *Keiretsu no Kenkyu: Daiichi Jojo Kigyohen* (Research on *Keiretsu*: The First Section of the Tokyo Stock Exchange) (Tokyo: Ministry of Finance, annual).

Kirin Beer, *Kirin Biiru Gojunenshi* (50 years of Kirin Beer) (Tokyo: 1957).

—— *Kirin Biiru no Rekishi* (A History of Kirin) (Tokyo: Toppan, 1969).

—— *Kaisha Gaiyo* (Company Profile) (Tokyo: 1981).

Kokuyo Company, *Kokuyo: Nanajunen no Ayumi* (70 Years of Kokuyo), (Tokyo: Dainippon Insatsu, 1975).

KOMIYA, R., OKUNO, S., and SUZUMURA, K. (eds.), *Nihon no Sangyo Seisaku* (Japan's Industrial Policy) (Tokyo: Tokyo University Press, 1984).

KUNITOMO, RYUICHI, *Kyocera Ameba Hoshiki* (Kyocera's Amoeba Management System) (Tokyo: Paru Shuppan, 1985).

KURAHARA, BUNTERU, UCHIMARU, KIYOSHI, and OKAMOTO, SUSUMU, *Gijutsu Shudan no TQC* (TQC for Engineers) (Tokyo: Nikajiren, 1990).

Matsushita Electric Industrial, *Matsushita Denki Gojunen no Rekishi* (A 50 Year History of Matsushita Electric Industrial) (Kyoto: Nihon Shashin Insatsu, 1968).

Meidiya, *Meidiya Nanajusannenshi* (73 Years of Meidiya) (Tokyo: Toppan, 1961).

MINAMI, RYOSHIN, *Nihon no Keizai Hatten* (Japan's Economic Development) (Tokyo: Toyo Keizai Shinposha, 1981).

MINATO, TETSUO, 'Ryo-daisenkan ni okeru Nihongata Shitauke Seisan-shisutemu no Hensei Katei' (The Formation of the Japanese Subcontracting System between the Two World Wars), *Aoyama Kokusai Seikeironshu* (Aoyama Papers on International Political Economy), 7 (June 1987).

Ministry of Commerce and Industry, *Kikai Kigukogyo Gaichu Jokyo Chosa* (Report on Suppliers in the Machine Tool Industry) (Tokyo: November 1936).

MISHIMA, YASUO, *Mitsubishi Zaibatsushi* (A History of Mitsubishi *Zaibatsu*) (Tokyo: Kyoikusha, 1979).

—— *Nihon Zaibatsu Keieishi: Mitsubishi Zaibatsu* (A Business History of Japanese *Zaibatsu*: The Mitsubishi *Zaibatsu*) (Tokyo: Nihon Keizai Shinbunsha, 1981).

Mitsubishi Company, *Mitsubishi no Hyakunen* (100 Years of Mitsubishi) (Tokyo: Toppan, 1970).

Mitsubishi Corporation, *Mitsubishi Shashi* (A Gazette of Mitsubishi Companies' History) (Tokyo: University of Tokyo Press, 1981).

Mitsubishi Electric, *Kengyo Kaiko* (Reflections on Business) (Tokyo: Toppan, 1951).

Mitsubishi Electric Company, *Mitsubishi Denki Shashi* (A History of Mitsubishi Electric Company) (Tokyo: Toppan, 1982).

Mitsubishi Research Institute, *Mitsubishi Shashi: Sosakuin* (An Index to the History of Mitsubishi) (Tokyo: Tokyo University Press, 1982).

MIYAMOTO, MATAJI, and SAKUDO, YOTARO (eds.), *Sumitomo no Keieishiteki Kenkyu* (Research on the Business History of Sumitomo) (Tokyo: Jikkyo Shuppan, 1979).

MIYAMOTO, MATAO, *Kinsei Nihon no Shijo Keizai* (Market Economics in Early Modern Japan) (Tokyo: Yuihikaku, 1988).

MIYAZAKI, YOSHIKAZU, *Sengo Nihon no Keizai Kiko* (The Structure of Japan's. Post-war Economy) (Tokyo: Shinhyoron, 1966).

—— *Sengo Nihon no Kigyo Shudan* (Japan's Post-war Enterprise Groups) (Tokyo: Nihon Keizai Shinbunsha, 1976).

MIZODA, SEIGO, 'Zosen' (Shipbuilding), in Shin'ichi Yonekawa, Koichi Shimokawa, and Hiroaki Yamazaki (eds.), *Sengo Nihon Keizaishi* (Post-war Economic History of Japan) (Tokyo: Toyo Keizai, 1991).

MORIKAWA, HIDEMASA, *Gijutsusha: Nihon Kindaika no Katsugite* (Technicians: Japan's Modernizers) (Tokyo: Nihon Keizai Shinbun, 1975).

—— *Nihon Zaibatsu-shi* (A History of Japanese *Zaibatsu*) (Tokyo: Kyoiku-sha, 1978).

—— *Zaibatsu no Keieishiteki Kenkyu* (A Business History of the *Zaibatsu*) (Tokyo: Toyo Keizai, 1980).

—— *Zaibatsu: The Rise and Fall of Family Enterprise Groups in Japan* (Tokyo: The University of Tokyo Press, 1992).

NAKANO, TAKASHI, *Shitauke Kogyo no Dozoku to Oyakata Kokata* (Clan-like Households and Fictive Kinship in Subcontracting Industries) (Tokyo: Ochanomizu Shobo, 1978).

—— *Shoka Dozokudan no Kenkyu* (Research on Business Clans and Households) (Tokyo: Miraisha, 1978).

NEC, *Nihon Denki Kabushiki Kaisha Nanajunenshi* (70 Years of NEC) (Tokyo: Dai-Nihon Insatsu, 1972).

Nihon Keieishi Kenkyujo, *Chosen to Sozo: Mitsui Bussan Hyakunen no Ayumi* (Challenge and Creativity: A Century of Mitsui & Company) (Tokyo: Toppan, 1976).

Nihon Keizai Shimbun (Japan Economic Journal) 'The Limited Effectiveness of the Government's Industrial Adjustment Policies', 7 June 1984, 15.

—— 'Tokuyama Soda Restructures Its Veneer Products Division', 16 June 1986, 10.

—— 'Toyota Shifts to In-House Supply', 13 Jan. 1985.

—— 'The Key to High-Technology Diffusion', 16 Jan. 1985.

—— 'Toyota will develop a High-Performance Passenger Car Microcomputer', 14 Feb. 1985, 9.

—— 'The Spring Sales Offensive in New Cars', 19 Feb. 1985.

—— 'Tokuyama Soda Restructures Its Veneer Products Division', 16 June 1986, 10.

—— 'Tomadou Gyokai' (Perplexing Industry), 24 Feb. 1990, 3.

Nihon Seifun Company, *Nihon Seifun Kabushiki kaisha* (Nihon Seifun) (Tokyo: 1955).

—— *Nihon Seifun 70 Nenshi* (70 Years of Nihon Seifun) (Tokyo: 1968).

Nikkan Kogyo Shimbun, *Toyota o Sasaeru Kigyogun* (The Enterprise Group Supporting Toyota) (Tokyo: Nikkan Kogyo Shinbunsha, 1980).

Nikkei Business, ' "Ichiokuen kigyo" e Daiichi Kanmon wa "Toyota-hazure" ' (In order to Become a One-Okuyen company, The First order of Business is to Break Away from Toyota), 21 Jan. 1985.

—— 'Saigo wa Kigyonai kigyoka: kogaisha senryaku jitsurei kenkyu sono himitsu' (Intrapreneuring: Secrets culled from Research on the Strategies of Subsidiaries), 18 July 1988, 17–18.

—— 'Hitachi Seisakusho' (Hitachi Ltd.), Parts I and III, 14 Apr. 1989.

Nippon Gakki (Yamaha Musical Instruments), *Shashi* (A History) (Nagoya: Bunposha, 1977).

NISHIKAWA, SHUNSAKU, 'Ginko: Kyoso to sono Kisei' (Banking: Competition and Regulation), in T. Kumatani (ed.), *Nihon no Sangyo Soshiki* (The Organization of Japanese Industry) (Tokyo: Chuo Koron, 1973).

Nisshin Seifun Company, *Nisshin Seifun Kabushiki Kaisha Nanajunenshi* (70 Years of Nisshin Seifun) (Tokyo: Toppan, 1970).

ODAGIRI, HIROYUKI, 'Kigyo shudan no riron' (A Theory of Enterprise Groups), *Kikan Riron Keizaigaku*, 26 (1975).

OHNO, TAIICHI, *Toyota Seisan Hoshiki* (The Toyota Production System) (Tokyo: Daiyamondo, 1978).

—— and MONDEN, YASUHIRO, *Toyota Seisan Hoshiki no Shintenkai* (New Developments in the Toyota Production System) (Tokyo: Nihon Noritsu Kyokai, 1983).

OKAMOTO, YASUO, *Hitachi to Matsushita* (Hitachi and Matsushita), 2 vols. (Tokyo: Chuo Koronsha, 1979).

SAITO, OSAMU, *Puroto kogyoka no jidai: Seio to Nihon no hikaku* (The Age of Proto-industrialization: A Comparison of the West and Japan) (Tokyo: Hyoronsha, 1985).

SAKAMOTO, KAZUICHI, and SHIMOTANI, MASAHIRO (eds.), *Gendai Nippon no Kigyo Gurupu* (Contemporary Japanese Enterprise Groups) (Tokyo: Toyo Keizai, 1987).

SAKUMA, YOTARO, *Sumitomo Zaibatsushi* (A History of the Sumitomo *Zaibatsu*) (Tokyo: Kyoikusha, 1979).

Sangyo Kenkyu Shisutemu (Industry Research System), Toyota Jidosha (Toyota Motor Vehicles), Nagoya: Industry Research System, 1986.

SATO, YOSHINOBU, *Toyota Gurupu no Senryaku to Jissho Bunseki* (Strategy and Analysis of the Toyota Enterprise Group) (Tokyo: Shirakaba Shobo, 1988).

Seiko Company, *Hattori & Co*, mimeographed in Japanese, undated.

Shibaura Seisakusho, *Shibaura Seisakusho Rokujugonenshi* (A 65 Year History of Shibaura Engineering) (Tokyo: Bunshodo, 1940).

SHIOMI, HIROSHI, 'Seisan rogisuteikusu no kozo' (The Structure of Production Logistics), in Kazuichi Sakamoto (ed.), *Gijutsu Kakushin to Kigyo Kozo* (Technical Innovation and Enterprise Organization) (Kyoto: Minerva Books, 1985), 77–113.

SHIMOTANI, MASAHIRO, 'Gendai kigyo-gurupu no kozo to kino', in Kazuichi Sakamoto (ed.), *Gijutsu Kakushin to Kigyo Kozo* (Technical Innovation and Enterprise Organization) (Kyoto: Minerva Press, 1986).

Shiseido, *Shiseidoshi* (A History of Shiseido) (Tokyo: Kyodo Insatsu, 1957).

Showa Musen, *Gojunen no Ayumi* (50 Years of History) (Tokyo: Daiyamondo, 1975).

SUDO, MEGUMI, 'Shokengyo no Haba no Keizai' (Economies of Scope in the Securities Business), *Kinyu Gakkai Hokoku*, 65 (1988).

SUGIYAMA, SHIN'YA, 'Jukyuseiki Kohanki ni okeru Higashi Ajia Seito-shijo no Kozo' (The Structure of the Spinning Thread Industry in East Asia during the Latter Half of the Nineteenth Century), in Akira Hayami, Osamu Saito, and Shin'ya Sugiyama (eds.), *Tokugawa Shakai kara no Tenbo* (Observations from Tokugawa Society) (Tokyo: Dobunkan, 1989).

SUMIYA, MIKIO, *Showa Kyoko* (The Showa Crisis) (Tokyo: Yuikaku, 1974).

Suntory Corporation, *Suntory Hachijunen no Ayumi* (80 Years of History) (Tokyo: Suntory, 1979).

TAKAHASHI, KAMEKICHI, *Nihon Keizai Toseiron* (The Control of the Japanese Economy) (Tokyo: Kaizosha, 1933).

Takeda Yakuhin Kogyo, *Takeda Yakuhin Sanbyakunenshi* (300 Years of Takeda Pharmaceuticals), 1985.

TANIGUCHI, AKITAKE, 'Gigyobusei soshiki no gendaidei' (Contemporary Forms of the Multidivisional Structure), in Kazuichi Sakamoto (ed.), *Gijutsu Kakushin to Kigyo Kozo* (Technical Innovation and Enterprise Organization) (Kyoto: Minerva Press, 1986).

TATEISHI, KAZUMASA, *Tsukuru Sodateru Watakushi no Rirekisho* (Make and Nurture: My History) (Tokyo: Nihon Keizai Shinbunsha, 1975).

TOGAI, YOSHIO, *Mitsui Bussan Kaisha no Keieishiteki Kenkyu* (A Business History of Mitsui & Co.) (Tokyo: Toyo Keizai Shinposha, 1974).

—— *Mitsui Zaibatsushi* (A History of Mitsui *Zaibatsu*) (Tokyo: Kyoikusha, 1978).

Tokyo Electric Company, *Tokyo Denki Gojunenshi* (50 Years of Tokyo Electric) (Tokyo: Dainippon, 1940).

Tokyo Shibaura Denki, *Kabushiki Kaisha Hachijugonenshi* (85 Years of the Tokyo Shibaura Electric Corporation) (Tokyo: Daiyamondo, 1963).

—— *Toshiba Yanagicho Yonjunen no Ayumi* (40 Years of Toshiba's Yanagicho Works) (Kawasaki: 1976).

—— *Toshiba Hyakunenshi* (A Century of Toshiba) (Tokyo: Daiyamondo, 1977).

Toshiba Rodo Kumiai Yanagicho Shibu, *Kumiai Undoshi* (Labor Movement History) (Tokyo: Puresu Sabisu, 1986).

Toshiba Corporation, *Sozo: Toshiba Yanagicho Kojo Gojunenshi* (Create: 50 Years of Toshiba's Yanagicho Works) (Kawasaki: 1987).

Toyobo Company, *Hyakunenshi* (A Century of History) (Tokyo: Toppan, 1986).

Trigger, 'Toshiba—Kiso Kenkyu no Tsugi no Itte' (Toshiba—Towards Basic R & D) 9/3 (Feb. 1990).

UDAGAWA, MASAHARU, *Shinko Zaibatsu* (The New *Zaibatsu*) (Tokyo: Nihon Keizai Shinbunsha, 1984).

UMEZU, KAZURO, *Zaibatsu Kaitai* (Breakup of the *Zaibatsu*) (Tokyo: Kyoikusha, 1978).

USAMI, MAKOTO, 'Zaibatsu kaitai no kozai' (*Zaibatsu* Breakup), *Ekonomisuto*, 18 Aug. 1964.

Wacoal, *Wakoru Monogatari* (The Story of Wacoal) (Kyoto: Terada Kuzutani, 1979).

WAKABAYASHI, MASASHI, *Nihonteki Keieiron Kara Nihonteki Kaisharon e* (From Japanese-style Management to Japanese-style Corporations) (Tokyo: Chuo Keizaisha, 1989).

Yamasa Shoyu Company Archive, *Shokko Sagyo Bunryocho* (Employee Work Records), handwritten, Choshi City: 1923–4.

—— *Kojo Getsubetsu Moromi Motokoku-zandaka* (Monthly Production of *Moromi* by Factory), handwritten, Choshi City: 1930–7.

—— *Shoyugyo Jozo ni Tsuite* (Concerning *Shoyu* Production), typed, Choshi City, May 1929.

YASUOKA, SHIGEAKI (ed.), *Zaibatsu Kenkyu* (*Zaibatsu* Research) (Tokyo: Nihon Keizai Shimbun, 1979).

—— *Nihon Zaibatsu Keieishi: Mitsui Zaibatsu* (A Business History of Japanese *Zaibatsu*: Mitsui *Zaibatsu*) (Tokyo: Nihon Keizai Shinbunsha, 1982).

—— *et al.*, *Zaibatsu no Hikakushiteki Kenkyu* (Historical and Comparative Research on *Zaibatsu*) (Kyoto: Minerva Shobo, 1985).

Yomiuri Newspaper, *Matsushita Kigyo Renpo* (The Matsushita Enterprise Group) (Tokyo: Yomiuri Shinbun, 1984).

YONEKAWA, SHIN'ICHI, 'Meijiki Daiboseki Kigyo no Shokuinso' (Managers in Large Textile Companies during the Meiji Period), *Shakai Keizaishigaku* (Social Economic History), 51/4 (Fall 1986).

YONEKURA, SEIICHIRO, 'Sengo Nihon Seitetsu ni okeru Kawasaki Seitetsu no Kakushinsei' (Kawasaki Steel's Innovations in the Post-war Japanese Steel Industry), *Hitotsubashi Ronso* (The Annals of Hitotsubashi University), 90/3: 387–410.

YOSHIHARA, HIDEKI, SAKUMA, AKIMITSU, ITAMI, HIROYUKI, and KAGONO, TADAO, *Nihon Kigyo no Takakuka Senryaku* (The Diversification of Japanese Firms) (Tokyo: Nihon Keizai Shimbun, 1981).

YUI, TSUNEHIKO, 'Meiji Jidai ni okeru Juyaku Soshiki no Keisei' (The Formation of Boards of Directors during the Meiji Period), *Keiei Shigaku* (Business History), 14/1 (Winter 1982).

—— (ed.), *Yasuda Zaibatsu* (A History of Yasuda *Zaibatsu*) (Tokyo: Nihon Keizai Shimbunsha, 1986), 118–21, 283–4, 325.

WORKS IN ENGLISH LANGUAGE

ABEGGLEN, JAMES C., *The Japanese Factory* (Glencoe. Ill.: Free Press, 1958).

—— and RAPP, WILLIAM V., 'Japanese Managerial Behavior and "Excessive Competition"', *Developing Economies*, 8/4 (Dec. 1970), 427–44.

—— and STALK, GEORGE, *Kaisha: The Japanese Corporation* (New York: Basic Books, 1985).

ABERNATHY, WILLIAM J., and UTTERBACK, J. M., 'A Dynamic Model of Process and Product Innovation', *Omega*, 3/6 (1975), 639–56.

ABRAMOWITZ, J. G., and SHOTLUCK, G. A., JR., 'The Learning Curve: A Technique for Planning, Measurement and Control', IBM Report No. 31. 101, 1970.

AMSDEN, ALICE H., *Asia's Next Giant* (New York: Oxford University Press, 1989).

AOKI, MASAHIKO, *The Co-operative Game Theory of the Firm* (Oxford: Oxford University Press, 1986).

—— 'Horizontal vs. Vertical Information Structure of the Firm', *American Economic Review*, 76/5 (Dec. 1986), 971–83.

AOKI, MASAHIKO, *Information, Incentives, and Bargaining in the Japanese Economy* (Cambridge: Cambridge University Press, 1988).

ARROW, KENNETH, 'The Economic Implications of Learning by Doing', *Review of Economic Studies*, 1962, 155–7.

—— *The Limits of Organization* (New York: W. W. Norton, 1974).

ASANUMA, BANRI, 'Transactional Structure of Parts Supply in the Japanese Automobile and Electric Machinery Industries: A Comparative Analysis', Technical Report No. 1, Socio-Economic Systems Research Project, Kyoto University, July 1985.

—— 'Japanese Manufacturer–Supplier Relationships in International Perspective: The Automobile Industry Case', Working Paper No. 8, Faculty of Economics, Kyoto University, 1988.

—— 'Manufacturer–Supplier Relationships in Japan and the Concept of Relation-Specific Skill', *Journal of the Japanese and International Economics*, 3 (1989), 1–30.

Asiaweek, 'The Hard Facts about Steel', 5 Apr. 1987, 50–1.

AXELROD, ROBERT, *The Evolution of Cooperation* (New York: Basic Books, 1984).

AYDALOT, PHILIPPE, and KEEBLE, DAVID (eds.), *High Technology Industry and Innovative Environments* (London: Routledge, 1988).

AZUMI, KOYA, HICKSON, DAVID, HORVATH, DEZSO, and MCMILLAN, CHARLES, 'Bureaucratic Structures in Cross-National Perspective: A Study of British, Japanese and Swedish Firms', in G. Dlugos and K. Weiermair (eds.), *Management Under Differing Value Systems* (New York: Walter de Gruyter, 1981), 537–64.

BABA, YASUNORI, 'The Dynamics of Continuous Innovation in Scale-Intensive Industries', *Strategic Management Journal*, 10/1 (1989), 89–100.

BARNEY, JAY B., and OUCHI, WILLIAM G., *Organizational Economics* (San Francisco: Jossey-Bass, 1986).

BARTEL, ANN P., and LICHTENBERG, FRANK R., 'The Comparative Advantage of Educated Workers in Implementing New Technology', *Review of Economics and Statistics*, 69/1 (Feb. 1987), 1–11.

BAUMOL, WILLIAM J., PANZAR, JOHN C., and WILLIG, ROBERT D., *Contestable Markets and the Theory of Industry Structure* (San Diego: Harcourt Brace Jovanovich, 1988).

BECKENSTEIN, ALAN R., 'Scale Economies in the Multiplant Firm: Theory and Empirical Evidence', *Bell Journal of Economics*, 6/2 (Autumn 1975), 644–57.

BEFU, HARUMI, *Japan: An Anthropological Introduction* (San Francisco: Chandler, 1971).

BELLAH, ROBERT, *Tokugawa Religion* (Glencoe, Ill.: Free Press, 1957).

BOISOT, MAX, and CHILD, JOHN, 'The Iron Law of Fiefs: Bureaucratic Failure and the Problem of Governance in the Chinese Economic Reforms', *Administrative Science Quarterly*, 33/4 (Dec. 1988), 507–27.

BRADACH, JEFFREY L., and ECCLES, ROBERT G., 'Price, Authority, and Trust: From Ideal Types to Plural Forms', *Annual Review of Sociology*, 15 (1989), 97–117.

BRENNER, REUVEN, *Rivalry: In Business, Science Among Nations* (Cambridge: Cambridge University Press, 1987).

CABLE, J., and DIRRHEIMER, M. J., 'Hierarchies and Markets: An Empirical Test of the Multidivisional Hypothesis in West Germany', *International Journal of Industrial Organization*, 1: 43–62.

—— and YASUKI, H., 'Internal Organization, Business Groups and Corporate Performance: An Empirical Test of the Multidivisional Hypothesis in Japan', *International Journal of Industrial Organization*, 3 (1985), 401–20.

CAMAGNI, ROBERTO, 'Functional Integration and Locational Shifts in New Technology

Industry', in Philippe Aydalot and David Keeble (eds.), *High Technology Industry and Innovative Environments* (London: Routledge, 1988).

CARROLL, GLENN R., 'On the Organizational Ecology of Chester I. Barnard', in Oliver E. Williamson (ed.), *Organization Theory* (New York: Oxford University Press, 1990), 56–71.

CAVES, RICHARD E., and UEKUSA, MASU, 'Industrial Organization', in Hugh Patrick and Henry Rosovsky (eds.), *Asia's New Giant* (Washington, DC: Brookings Institution, 1976).

—— —— *Industrial Organization in Japan* (Washington, DC: Brookings Institution, 1976).

CHAKRAVARTHY, BALA, and KWUN, SEOG K., 'The Strategy Process: An Organizational Learning Perspective', working paper, Carlson School of Management, University of Minnesota, 1987.

CHANDLER, ALFRED D., Jr., *Strategy and Structure* (Cambridge, Mass.: MIT Press, 1962).

—— *The Visible Hand: The Management Revolution in American Business* (Boston: Harvard University Press, 1977).

—— 'Government Versus Business: An American Phenomenon', in John T. Dunlop (ed.), *Business and Public Policy* (Cambridge, Mass.: Harvard University Press, 1980).

—— *Scale and Scope* (Boston: Harvard University Press, 1990).

CHANG, SEA JIN, and CHOI, UNGHWAN, 'Strategy, Structure and Performance of Korean Business Groups: A Transactions Cost Approach', *Journal of Industrial Economics*, 37/2 (Dec. 1988), 141–58.

CHANNON, DEREK F., *The Strategy and Structure of British Enterprise* (Boston: Harvard Business School Press, 1973).

CHILD, JOHN., 'Information Technology, Organization, and the Response to Strategic Challenges', *California Management Review* (Fall 1987), 33–50.

CLARK, PETER, *Anglo-American Innovation* (London: Methuen, 1987).

CLARK, RODNEY, *The Japanese Company* (New Haven, Conn.: Yale University Press, 1979).

COLE, ROBERT E., *Japanese Blue Collar* (Berkeley: University of California Press, 1971).

—— 'Permanent Employment in Japan: Facts and Fantasies', *Industrial and Labor Relations Review*, 26 1972, 615–30.

—— *Work, Mobility, and Participation* (Berkeley: University of California Press, 1979).

—— 'The Macropolitics of Organizational Change: A Comparative Analysis of the Spread of Small Group Activities', *Administrative Science Quarterly*, 30 (1985), 560–85.

—— *Strategies for Learning* (Berkeley: University of California Press, 1989).

—— 'Issues in Skill Formation and Training in Japanese Manufacturing Approaches to Automation', mimeo, Technology and the Future of Work Conference, Stanford University, Stanford, Calif., 28–31 Mar. 1990, 18.

COOL, KAREL, and DIERICKX, INGEMAR, 'Strategic groups, Rivalry and Firm Performance', mimeo, INSEAD, Mar. 1990.

—— and SCHENDEL, D., 'Strategic Group Formation and Performance: The Case of the U.S. Pharmaceutical Industry, 1963–1982', *Management Science*, 33/9 (Sept. 1987), 1102–24.

—— —— 'Performance Differences among Strategic Group Members', *Strategic Management Journal*, 9/3 (1988), 207–23.

CORBETT, JENNIFER, 'Patterns of Finance and Government Lending to Industry in Japan', Apr. 1990, paper delivered at the Euro-Asia Centre, INSEAD, Fontainebleau, France, 4 May 1990.

CRAWCOUR, SIDNEY, 'The Development of a Credit System in Seventeenth-Century Japan',

Journal of Economic History, 21 (Sept. 1961).

CUSUMANO, MICHAEL A., *The Japanese Automobile Industry* (Cambridge, Mass.: Council on East Asian Studies, Harvard University, 1985).

—— 'Manufacturing Innovation and Competitive Advantage: Reflections on the Japanese Automobile Industry', draft paper, MIT, 9 May 1988.

—— *Japan's Software Factories* (New York: Oxford University Press, 1991).

DAEMS, HERMAN, *The Holding Company and Corporate Control* (Leiden: Nijhoff, Martinus, 1978).

DAITO, EISUKE, 'Industrial Training and Factory Management in Japan, 1990–1930', in Keiichiro Nakagawa and Tsunehiko Yui (eds.), *Organization and Management* (Tokyo: Japan Business History Institute, 1983), 65–6.

—— 'Railroad and Scientific Management in Japan, 1900–1930', paper presented at the U.C. Intercampus Group in Economic History Conference, University of California, Santa Cruz, 29 Apr. 1988.

DAVID, PAUL A., 'Path-Dependence: Putting the Past into the Future of Economics', Technical Report 533, Economics Series, Institute for Mathematical Studies in the Social Sciences, Stanford University, Nov. 1988.

DAVIS, LANCE E., AND NORTH, DOUGLASS C., *Institutional Change and American Economic Growth* (Cambridge: Cambridge University Press, 1971).

DERTOUZOS, MICHAEL L., LESTER, RICHARD K., SOLOW, ROBERT M., and the MIT Commission on Industrial Productivity, *Made in America: Regaining the Productivity Edge* (Cambridge, Mass.: MIT Press, 1989).

DLUGOS, G., and WEIERMAIR, K. (eds.), *Management Under Differing Value Systems* (New York: de Gruyter, Walter, 1981).

DORE, RONALD, *Education in Tokugawa Japan* (Berkeley: University of California Press, 1965).

—— *British Factory—Japanese Factory* (Berkeley: University of California Press, 1973).

—— 'Goodwill and the Spirit of Market Capitalism', *British Journal of Sociology*, 34/4 (1983), 459–82.

—— *Flexible Rigidities* (Stanford, Calif.: Stanford University Press, 1986).

—— *Taking Japan Seriously* (Stanford, Calif.: Stanford University Press, 1987).

DOUGLAS, MARY, *How Institutions Think* (Syracuse, NY: Syracuse University Press, 1986).

DOWER, JOHN (ed.), *Origins of the Modern Japanese State: Selected Writings of E. H. Norman* (New York: Pantheon Press, Random House, 1975).

DOZ, YVES, and LEHMANN, JEAN-PIERRE, 'The Strategic Management Process: The Japanese Example', *Bonner Zeitschrift für Japonologie*, 8 (1986), 263–83.

DUDLEY, LEONARD, 'Learning and Productivity Change in Metal Products', *American Economic Review*, 62 (Sept. 1972), 662–9.

DUUS, PETER, 'The Reaction of Japanese Big Business to a State-Controlled Economy in the 1930s', *Rivista Internazionale di Science Economiche e Commerciali*, 31/9 (Sept. 1984).

DYAS, GARETH, and THANHEISER, HEINZ, *Emerging European Enterprise* (London: Macmillan, 1976).

The Economist, 'The World's Biggest Cottage Industry', 26 July, 1980: 65–6.

—— 'Japan's steelmakers recast themselves', 29 Aug. 1987, 59–60.

EGGERTSSON, THRAINN, *Economic Behavior and Institutions* (Cambridge: Cambridge University Press, 1990).

ENCARNATION, DENNIS J., and MASON, MARK, 'Neither MITI Nor America: The Political Economy of Capital Liberalization in Japan', *International Organization*, 44/1 (Winter 1990), 25–54.

ERICKSON, STEVE, 'Private Railroads in the Meiji Era: Forerunners of Modern Japanese Management?', in Keiichiro Nakagawa and Tsunehiko Yui (eds.), *Japanese Management in Historical Perspective* (Tokyo: University of Tokyo Press, 1989).

Fair Trade Commission (Japan), *The Actual Conditions of the Six Major Corporate Groups*, No. 7, pamphlet (Tokyo: External Affairs Office, Aug. 1989).

FAMA, EUGENE F., 'Agency Problems and the Theory of the Firm', *Journal of Political Economy* (1980), 288–307.

Far Eastern Economic Review, 'Dowdy Galant Reborn', 19 Jan. 1989.

FLAMM, KENNETH, *Creating the Computer* (Washington, DC: Brookings Institution, 1988).

FLIGSTEIN, NEIL, 'The Spread of the Multidivisional Form Among Large Firms, 1919–1979', *American Sociological Review*, 50/3 (June 1985).

—— *State and Markets* (Cambridge, Mass.: Harvard University Press, 1989).

FRIEDMAN, DAVID, *The Misunderstood Miracle* (Ithaca, NY: Cornell University Press, 1988).

FRUIN, W. MARK, 'Labor Migration in Nineteenth-Century Japan: A Study Based on Echizen *Han*', Ph.D. dissertation, Stanford University, Ann Arbor, Mich.: University Microfilms, 1973.

—— 'The Japanese Company Controversy: Ideology and Organization in Historical Perspective', *Journal of Japanese Studies*, 4/2 (Summer 1978).

—— 'The Firm as a Family and the Family as a Firm in Japan', *Journal of Family History*, 5/4 (Winter 1980).

—— 'Pre-Corporate and Corporate Charity in Japan: From Philanthropy to Paternalism in the Noda Soy Sauce Industry', *Business History Review*, 56/2 (Summer 1982).

—— *Kikkoman—Company, Clan, and Community* (Cambridge, Mass.: Harvard University Press, 1983).

—— 'Cooperation and Competition: Supplier Networks in the Japanese Electronics Industry', paper given at the Center for Japanese Studies, UC Berkeley, 4 Nov. 1987.

—— 'Factory-to-Factory Organization and Technology Transfer', paper given at 2nd. Mitsubishi Bank Foundation Conference on Internationalization and the Japanese Firm, University of Michigan, Ann Arbor, Mich., 26–9 Aug. 1988.

—— 'Instead of Management—Internal Contracting and the Genesis of Modern Labor Management', in Tsunehiko Yui and Keiichiro Nakagawa (eds.), *Japanese Management in Historical Perspective* (Fuji Business History Conference XV) (Tokyo: University of Tokyo Press, 1989).

—— *Knowledge Works* (New York: Oxford University Press, forthcoming).

—— and NISHIGUCHI, TOSHIHIRO, 'The Toyota Production System: Its Organizational Definition and Diffusion in Japan', paper given at the EIASM conference on country competitiveness, Brussels, 1 June 1990.

———— 'Supplying the Toyota Production System: Making a Molehill Out of a Mountain', in Bruce Kogut (ed.), *Country Competitiveness and Organizing at Work* (New York: Oxford University Press, 1992).

GEERTZ, CLIFFORD, *Local Knowledge* (New York: Basic Books, 1983).

GERLACH, MICHAEL, 'Business Alliances and the Strategy of the Japanese Firm', *California Management Review*, 30 (Fall 1987), 126–42.

—— *Alliance Capitalism* (Berkeley: University of California Press, forthcoming).

GERSCHENKRON, ALEXANDER, *Economic Backwardness in Historical Perspective* (Cambridge, Mass.: Harvard University Press, 1962).

GHOSHAL, SUMANTRA, 'Global Strategy: An Organizing Framework', *Strategic Management Journal*, 8 (1987) 425–40.

—— and BARTLETT, CHRISTOPHER A., *Matsushita Electric Industrial*, INSEAD–CEDEP

Case, Fontainebleau, France, 1987.

GIDDENS, ANTHONY, *Central Problems in Social Theory* (Berkeley: University of California Press, 1983).

GLICK, HENRY A., and FEUER MICHAEL J., 'Employer-Sponsored Training and Governance of Specific Human Capital Investments', *Quarterly Review of Economics and Business*, 24/2 (Summer 1984).

GORDON, ANDREW, *The Evolution of Labor Relations in Japan: Heavy Industry, 1853–1955* (Cambridge, Mass.: Council on East Asian Studies, Harvard University Press, 1985).

—— 'Cultures of the Workplace in Post-war Japan', paper given at the Conference on Post-war Japan as History, 14–16 Apr. 1988, 6–11.

GOTO, AKIRA, 'Statistical Evidence on the Diversification of Large Japanese Firms', *Journal of Industrial Economics*, 29/3 (Mar. 1981), 271–9.

—— 'Business Groups in a Market Economy', *European Economic Review* (1982), 53–70.

GRAHAM, MARGARET, and ROSENTHAL, STEPHEN, 'Flexible Manufacturing Systems Require Flexible People', Manufacturing Roundtable, School of Management, Boston University, 1985.

GRANOVETTER, MARK, 'The Strength of Weak Ties', *American Journal of Sociology*, 78/6 (May 1973), 1360–80.

—— 'Economic Action and Social Structure: The problem of Embeddedness', *American Journal of Sociology*, 91 (Nov. 1985), 481–510.

GROSSMAN, SANFORD J., and HART, OLIVER D., 'The Costs and Benefits of Ownership: A Theory of Vertical and Lateral Integration', *Journal of Political Economy*, 94/4 (Aug. 1986), 691–719.

HADLEY, ELEANOR, *Anti-trust in Japan* (Princeton, NJ: Princeton University Press, 1970).

HAKANSSON, HAKAN (ed.), *Industrial Technological Development: A Network Approach* (London: Croom Helm, 1987).

HALL, GRAHAM, and HOWELL, SIDNEY, 'The Experience Curve from the Economist's Perspective', *Strategic Management Journal*, 6/6 (1985).

HANNAN, M., and FREEMAN, J., 'Structural Inertia and Organizational Change', *American Sociological Review*, 49 (Apr. 1984), 149–64.

HANSEN, G. S., and WERNERFELT, B., 'Determinants of Firm Performance: The Relative Importance of Economic and Organizational Factors', *Strategic Management Journal*, 10/5 (Sept.–Oct. 1989).

Harvard Business School Case, *Computervision Japan*, 1985.

HASHIMOTO, KOICHI, Manager, Mitsubishi Motors, interview, 2 Mar. 1989, Paris, France.

HAYES, ROBERT H., 'Why Japanese Factories Work', *Harvard Business Review*, 59/4 (July–Aug. 1981), 57–66.

—— and YUI, TSUNEHIKO (eds.), *The Development of Japanese Business*, 2nd edn. (London: Allen, George, & Unwin, 1981).

HIRSCHMEIER, JOHANNES, *The Origins of Entrepreneurship in Meiji Japan* (Cambridge, Mass.: Harvard University Press, 1964).

HITT, MICHAEL A., HOSKISSON, R. E., and IRELAND, R. D., 'Mergers and Acquisitions and Managerial Commitment to Innovation in M-Form Firms', *Strategic Management Journal*, 11/Special Issue (Summer 1990), 29–48.

HOMANS, GEORGE, *The Human Group* (New York: Harcourt Brace Jovanovich, 1950).

HOSKISSON, ROBERT E., and HITT, MICHAEL A., 'Strategic Control Systems and Relative R & D Investment in Large Multiproduct Firms', *Strategic Management Journal*, 9 (1988), 605–21.

IMAI, KEN'ICHI, 'The Corporate Network in Japan', *Japanese Economic Studies*, 16 (Winter 1988).

—— 'Japanese Patterns of Innovation and its Commercialization Process', Discussion Paper 136, Institute of Business Research, Hitosubashi University, Aug. 1989.

—— and ITAMI, HIROYUKI, 'Interpretations of Organization and Market: Japan's Firm and Market in Comparison with the U.S.', *International Journal of Industrial Organization*, 2 (1984).

ITAMI, HIROYUKI, and ROEHL, THOMAS W., *Mobilizing Invisible Assets* (Cambridge, Mass.: Harvard University Press, 1987).

IWAUCHI, RYOICHI, 'The Growth of White-Collar Employment in Relation to the Education System', in Keiichiro Nakagawa and Tsunehiko Yui (eds.), *Japanese Management in Historical Perspective* (Tokyo: University of Tokyo Press, 1989).

JANNETTA, ANN B., *Epidemics and Mortality in Early Modern Japan* (Princeton, NJ: Princeton University Press, 1987).

JARILLO, J. CARLOS, 'When Small is not Enough', *European Management Journal*, 6/4 (Nov. 1988), 325–9.

JOHNSON, CHALMERS, *MITI and the Japanese Miracle* (Stanford, Calif.: Stanford University Press, 1982).

JOHNSON, H. THOMAS, and KAPLAN, ROBERT S., *Relevance Lost: The Rise and Fall of Management Accounting* (Boston: Harvard Business School Press, 1987).

JOVANOVIC, BOYAN, and LACH, SAUL, 'Entry, Exit, and Diffusion with Learning by Doing', *American Economic Review*, 79/4 (Sept. 1989), 690–9.

JURO, TERANISHI, 'A Model of the Relationship between Regulated and Unregulated Financial Markets: Credit Rationing in a Japanese Context', *Hitotsubashi Journal of Economics*, 23 (1982).

KAHNEMAN, D., KNETSCH, J. L., and THALER, R., 'Fairness as a Constraint on Profit Seeking: Entitlements in the Market', *American Economic Review*, 74/6 (Sept. 1986), 728–41.

KAMATA, H., *Japan in the Passing Lane* (New York: Penguin Books, 1982).

KANTROW, ALAN M., *The Constraints of Corporate Tradition* (New York: Harper & Row, 1987).

KAWASAKI, SEIICHI, and McMILLAN, JOHN, 'The Design of Contracts: Evidence from Japanese Subcontracting', *Journal of the Japanese and International Economies*, 1 (1987).

KAZUMI, KENMOCHI, 'The Hollowing', *AMPO Japan–Asia Quarterly Review*, 19/1: 30–3.

KIKKAWA, TAKEO, 'Functions of Japanese Trade Associations before World War II', paper, Fuji Business History Conference XIV, Gotenba, Shizuoka, Japan, 5–8 Jan. 1987.

KINCH, NILS, 'Emerging Strategies in a Network Context: The Volvo Case', *Scandinavian Journal of Management Studies*, May 1987, 167–84.

KOIKE, KAZUO, *Understanding Industrial Relations in Modern Japan* (New York: St. Martins Press, 1988).

KONO, TOYOHIRO, *Strategy and Structure of Japanese Enterprises* (London: Macmillan, 1984).

KOTZ, DAVID M., *Bank Control of Large Corporations in the United States* (Berkeley: University of California Press, 1978).

KOZA, MITCHELL, and BALAKRISHNAN, SRINIVASAN, 'Information Asymmetry, Market Failure, and Joint-Ventures: Theory and Evidence', INSEAD working paper, 1989.

—— —— 'Organization Costs and a Theory of Joint Ventures', INSEAD Working Paper, Fall 1989.

KUWADA, KOTARO, 'Strategic Learning in a Mature Industry', paper presented at TIMS

XXIX, Faculty of Economics, Tokyo Metropolitan University, Osaka, Japan, 25 July, 1989.

KUZNETS, SIMON, 'Notes on the Pattern of U.S. Economic Growth', in Edgar O. Edwards (ed.), *The Nation's Economic Objectives* (Chicago: University of Chicago Press, 1964).

LAUX, JAMES M., 'Managerial Structures in France', in Harold F. Williamson (ed.), *Evolution of International Management Structures* (Newark, NJ: University of Delaware Press, 1975).

LEBLEBICI, HUSEYIN, and FIEGENBAUM, AVI, 'Managers as Agents without Principles: An Empirical Examination of Agency and Constituency Perspectives', *Journal of Management*, 12/4 (1986), 485–98.

LEBRA, TAKIE SUGIYAMA, *Japanese Patterns of Behavior* (Honolulu: University of Hawaii Press, 1976).

LEIBENSTEIN, HARVEY, 'Aspects of the X-efficiency Theory of the Firm', *Bell Journal of Economics*, 6/2 (Autumn 1975), 580–606.

—— *Beyond Economic Man* (Cambridge, Mass.: Harvard University Press, 1976).

LEVINE, SOLOMON B., and KAWADA, HISASHI, *Human Resources in Japanese Industrial Development* (Princeton, NJ: Princeton University Press, 1980).

LEVITT, B., and MARSH, J., 'Organizational Learning', *Annual Review of Sociology*, 14 (1988), 319–40.

LEWIS, DAVID L., *The Public Image of Henry Ford* (Detroit: Wayne State University Press, 1976).

LIEBERMAN, MARVIN B., 'The Learning Curve, Diffusion, and Competitive Strategy', *Strategic Management Journal*, 8 (1987), 441–52.

LILLRANK, PAUL, and KANO, NORIAKI, *Continuous Improvement: Quality Control Circles in Japanese Industry* (Ann Arbor, Mich.: Center for Japanese Studies, University of Michigan Press, 1989).

LINCOLN, JAMES R., 'Intra- (and Inter-) Organizational Networks', in S. Bacharach (ed.), *Research in the Sociology of Organizations*, i (Greenwich, Conn.: JAI, 1982).

—— and MCBRIDE, KERRY, 'Japanese Industrial Organization in Comparative Perspective', *Annual Review of Sociology*, 13 (1987), 289–312.

MAHAJAN, VIJAY, SHARMA, SUBHASH, and BETTIS, RICHARD A., 'The Adoption of the M-Form Organizational Structure: A Test of Imitation Hypothesis', *Management Science*, 34/10 (Oct. 1988).

MAITLAND, IAN, and DEFILLIPPI, BOB, 'The Scope of the Firm: An Efficiency Critique of Resource Dependency Theory', Discussion Paper No. 61, Strategic Management Research Center, University of Minnesota, Oct. 1986.

MANNARI, HIROSHI, *The Japanese Business Leaders* (Tokyo: University of Tokyo Press, 1974).

MARCH, J., *Handbook of Organizations* (Chicago: Rand McNally, 1965).

MARSHALL, BYRON K., *Capitalism and Nationalism in Pre-war Japan: the Ideology of the Business Elite, 1864–1941* (Stanford: Stanford University Press, 1967).

MASCARENHAS, BRIANCE, and AAKER, DAVID A., 'Mobility Barriers and Strategic Groups', *Strategic Management Journal*, 10 (1989), 475–85.

MASTEN, SCOTT E., and CROCKER, KEITH J., 'Efficient Adaptation in Long-Term Contracts: Take-or-Pay Provisions for Natural Gas', *American Economic Review*, 75/5 (Dec. 1985), 1083–93.

MCCRAW, THOMAS K. (ed.), *America Versus Japan* (Boston: Harvard Business School Press, 1986).

MCDERMOTT, P. J., and TAYLOR, M. J., *Industrial Organization and Location* (Cambridge: Cambridge University Press, 1982).

MITI, *Agency of Industrial Science and Technology*, pamphlet, Tokyo, 1987.

Mitsubishi Corporation, *An Outline of Mitsubishi Enterprise* (Tokyo: Dainippon Printing, 1942).

MIYAMOTO, MATAO, 'The Position and Role of Family Business in the Development of the Japanese Company System', in Akio Okochi and Shigeaki Yasuoka (eds.), *Family Business in the Era of Industrial Growth* (Tokyo: University of Tokyo Press, 1982).

—— 'The Products and Market Strategies of the Osaka Cotton Spinning Company: 1883–1914', in Shigeaki Yasuoka and Hidemasa Morikawa (eds.), *Japanese Yearbook on Business History*, 5 (Tokyo: Japanese Business History Institute, 1988).

MIYAZAKI, YOSHIKAZU, 'Rapid Economic Growth in Post-War Japan', *Developing Economies*, 5/2 (1967).

MOLONY, BARBARA, 'Innovation and Business Strategy in the Prewar Chemical Industry', in Keiichiro Nakagawa and Tsunehiko Yui (eds.), *Japanese Management in Historical Perspective* (Tokyo: University of Tokyo Press, 1989), 150–1.

MORIKAWA, HIDEMASA, 'Significance and Development of Middle Management in Japan', in Keiichiro Nakagawa and Tsunehiko Yui (eds.), *Organization and Management* (Proceedings of the Japan–Germany Business History Conference) (Tokyo: Japanese Business History Institute, 1983).

MOWERY, DAVID C., and ROSENBERG, NATHAN, *Technology and the Pursuit of Economic Growth* (Cambridge: Cambridge University Press, 1989).

MUDGE, ROSE, GUTHRIE, ALEXANDER, and FERDON, 'Investigation into Sales of Propeller Milling Machines to the Soviet Union by Toshiba Machine Co., Ltd.', in Report to the President and Directors of Toshiba Corporation, Washington, DC, 1987.

NAKAGAWA, KEIICHIRO, 'Learning Industrial Revolution', in Keiichiro Nakagawa and Tsunehiko Yui (eds.), *Japanese Management in Historical Perspective* (Fuji Business History Conference XV) (Tokyo: University of Tokyo Press, 1989).

—— and DAITO, EISUKE, 'Business Management in Historical Perspective: Lifetime Employment in Japan', mimeo, 1990.

—— and YUI, TSUNEHIKO (eds.), *Organization and Management* (Proceedings of the Japan–Germany Business History Conference) (Tokyo: Japanese Business History Institute, 1983).

NAKAMURA, TAKAFUSA, *The Postwar Japanese Economy* (Tokyo: University of Tokyo Press, 1981).

—— *Economic Growth in Pre-war Japan* (New Haven, Conn.: Yale University Press, 1983).

NAKATANI, IWAO, 'The Role of Intermarket *Keiretsu* Business Groups in Japan', *Pacific Economic Papers*, 97 (1982).

—— 'The Economic Role of Financial Corporate Groupings', in Masahiko Aoki, *The Economic Analysis of the Japanese Firm* (Amsterdam: North Holland, 1984), 227–58.

National Science Foundation, *The Science and Technology Resources of Japan: A Comparison with the United States* (Washington, DC: National Science Foundation 88–318, 1988), 1–8.

NELSON, RICHARD R., and WINTER, SIDNEY G., *An Evolutionary Theory of Economic Change* (Cambridge, Mass.: Harvard University Press, 1982).

New York Times, 'Novel Technique Shows Japanese Outpace Americans in Innovation', 7 Mar. 1988, 1.

New York Times, 'Is the New Villain Going to be Japan? It Works on Paper', 18 June 1990, B1.

NIELSEN, RICHARD P., 'Cooperative Strategy', *Strategic Management Journal*, 9 (1988), 475–92.

NISHIGUCHI, TOSHIHIRO, 'Strategic Dualism: An Alternative in Industrial Societies',

D.Phil. thesis, Oxford University, 1990.

Nomura Securities Company report, 'Toyota Motor Corporation', Investment Note Memorandum, 18 May 1983.

NORTH, DOUGLASS C., *Institutions, Institutional Change and Economic Performance* (Cambridge: Cambridge University Press, 1990).

ODAGIRI, HIROYUKI, 'Research Activity, Output Growth, and Productivity Increase in Japanese Manufacturing Industries', *Research Policy*, 14 (1985), 117–30.

—— and IWATA, HITOSHI, 'The Impact of R & D on Productivity Increase in Japanese Manufacturing Companies', *Research Policy*, 15 (1986), 13–19.

ODAKA, KONOSUKE, ONO, KEINOSUKE, and ADACHI, FUMIHIKO, *The Automobile Industry in Japan: A study of Ancillary Firm Development* (Tokyo: Kinokuniya, 1988).

OECD, *Comparative Economic Performance in OECD Nations* (Paris, 1989), 66.

OHKAWA, KAZUSHI, and SHINOHARA, MIYOHEI (eds.), *Patterns of Japanese Economic Development* (New Haven, Conn.: Yale University Press, 1979).

OI, W. Y., 'Heterogeneous Firms and the Organization of Production', *Economic Inquiry*, 21 (Apr. 1983).

OKAYAMA, REIKO, 'Industrial Relations in the Japanese Automobile Industry 1945–70: the Case of Toyota', in Steve Tolliday and Jonathan Zeitlin (eds.), *The Automobile Industry and its Workers: Between Fordism and Flexibility* (Oxford: Polity Press, 1986).

OKIMOTO, DANIEL I., *Between MITI and the Market* (Stanford, Calif.: Stanford University Press, 1989).

OKIMOTO, DANIEL, SUGANO, TAKUO, and WEINSTEIN, FRANKLIN B., *Competitive Edge: The Semiconductor Industry in the U.S. and Japan* (Stanford, Calif.: Stanford University Press, 1984).

OKOCHI, K., KARSH, B., and LEVINE, S. B. (eds.), *Workers and Employers in Japan* (Princeton, NJ, and Tokyo: Princeton University Press and University of Tokyo Press, 1973).

OLIVER, CHRISTINE, 'The Collective Strategy Framework: An Application to Competing Predictions of Isomorphism', *Administrative Science Quarterly*, 33 (1988), 543–61.

ONO, KEINOSUKE, and ODAKA, KONOSUKE, *Ancillary Firm Development in the Japanese Automobile Industry: Selected Case Studies (1)* (Kunitachi: Institute of Economic Research, Hitotsubashi University, 1979).

OUCHI, WILLIAM G., *Theory Z* (Reading, Mass.: Addison-Wesley, 1982).

—— *The M-Form Society* (New York: Avon Books, 1984).

OZAKI, ROBERT S., 'Japanese Views of Industrial Organization', *Asian Survey*, Oct. 1970.

PALMER, DONALD, FRIEDLAND, ROGER, DEVEREAUX JENNINGS, P., and POWERS, MELANIE E., 'The Economics and Politics of Structure: The Multidivisional Form and the Large U.S. Corporation', *Administrative Science Quarterly*, 32 (Mar. 1987), 25–48.

PATRICK, HUGH, and ROSOVSKY, HENRY, *Asia's New Giant* (Washington, DC: Brookings Institution, 1976).

PENROSE, EDITH T., *The Growth of the Firm*, rev. edn. (White Plains, NY: M.E. Sharpe, 1980), 260–5.

PETERS, T., and WATERMAN, R. H., Jr., *In Search of Excellence* (New York: Harper & Row, 1982).

PFEFFER, JEFFREY, *Power in Organizations* (Cambridge, Mass.: Ballinger, 1981).

—— and SALANCIK, G. R., *The External Control of Organizations* (New York: Harper & Row, 1978).

PIORE, MICHAEL J., and SABEL, CHARLES F., *The Second Industrial Divide: Possibilities for*

Prosperity (New York: Basic Books, 1984).

PLATH, DAVID W., *Long Engagement: Maturity in Modern Japan* (Stanford, Calif.: Stanford University Press, 1980).

PORTER, MICHAEL, *Competitive Strategy* (New York: Free Press, 1980).

—— and FULLER, M. B., 'Coalitions and Global Strategy', in M. Porter (ed.), *Competition in Global Industries* (Boston: Harvard Business School Press, 1987).

POWELL, WALTER W., 'Hybrid Organizational Arrangements: New Form or Transitional Development?', *California Management Review*, Fall 1987, 67–87.

—— 'Neither Market nor Hierarchy: Network Forms of Organization', *Research in Organizational Behavior*, 12 (1990), 295–336.

RANIS, GUSTAV, 'The Community Centered Entrepreneur in Japanese Development', *Explorations in Entrepreneurial History*, 13 (1955).

RAPPING, LEONARD, 'Learning and World War II Production Functions', *Review of Economics and Statistics*, 47 (Feb. 1965), 81–6.

REID, GAVIN, *Theories of Industrial Organization* (Oxford: Basil Blackwell, 1987).

RING, PETER SMITH, and VAN DEN VEN, ANDREW H., 'Structures and Processes of Transaction', discussion paper No. 86, Strategic Management Research Center, University of Minnesota, May 1988.

ROBERTS, JOHN G., *Mitsui* (Tokyo: Weatherhill, 1973).

ROBINS, JAMES A., 'Organizational Economics: Notes on the Use of Transaction Cost Theory in the Study of Organizations', *Administrative Science Quarterly*, 32/1 (Mar. 1987), 68–86.

ROEHL, TOM, 'A Transactions Cost Approach to International Trading Structures: The Case of Japanese General Trading Companies', *Hitotsubashi Journal of Economics*, 24 (Dec. 1983), 119–35.

—— 'Japanese Industrial Groupings: A Strategic Response to Rapid Industrial Growth', unpublished paper, School of Business Administration, University of Washington, 1988.

ROSENBERG, NATHAN, 'The Direction of Technological Change: Inducement Mechanisms and Focusing Devices', *Economic Development and Cultural Change*, 18/1 (Oct. 1969), 1–24.

—— *Inside the Black Box: Technology and Economics* (Cambridge: Cambridge University Press, 1982).

—— and STEINMUELLER, W. EDWARD, 'Why are Americans Such Poor Imitators?', *American Economic Review*, 78/2 (May 1988), 229–34.

ROSTOW, W. W., *The Stages of Economic Growth*, (Cambridge, Mass.: Harvard University Press, 1961).

ROZMAN, GILBERT, *Urban Networks in Ch'ing China and Tokugawa Japan* (Princeton, NJ: Princeton University Press, 1973).

RUMELT, RICHARD P., *Strategy, Structure, and Economic Performance* (Boston: Harvard Business School Press, 1986).

—— 'How Much Does Industry Matter?', *Strategic Management Journal*, 12/3 (Mar. 1991), 167–86.

SABEL, CHARLES F., and PIORE, MICHAEL J., *The Second Industrial Divide* (New York: Basic Books, 1984).

SALTHE, STANLEY N., *Evolving Hierarchical Systems* (New York: Columbia University Press, 1985).

SAMUELS, RICHARD J., *The Business of the Japanese State* (Ithaca, NY: Cornell University Press, 1987).

SAWAI, MINORU, 'The Development of Machine Industries and the Evolution of Production and Labor Management', in Keiichiro Nakagawa and Tsunehiko Yui (eds.), *Japanese Management in Historical Perspective* (Tokyo: University of Tokyo Press, 1989).

SAXONHOUSE, GARY R., and YAMAMURA, KOZO (eds.), *Law and Trade Issues of the Japanese Economy* (Seattle: University of Washington Press, 1986).

SCHEIN, EDGAR H., *Organizational Culture and Leadership* (San Francisco: Jossey-Bass, 1985).

SCHERER, F. M., *Industrial Market Structure and Economic Performance* (Boston: Houghton Mifflin Co., 1980).

SHAIKEN, HARVEY, *Work Transformed* (New York: Holt, Reinhardt & Winston, 1984).

SHEARD, PAUL, 'Financial Corporate Grouping, Cross-Subsidization in the Private Sector and the Industrial Adjustment Process in Japan', Discussion Paper Series, Faculty of Economics, Osaka University, 1984.

—— 'Intercorporate Shareholdings and Structural Adjustments in Japan', *Pacific Economic Papers*, No. 151, 1987.

SHINOHARA, MIYOHEI, 'MITI's Industrial Policy and Japanese Industrial Organization: A Retrospective Evaluation', *Developing Economies*, 14 (Dec. 1976).

—— *Industrial Growth, Trade and Dynamic Patterns in the Japanese Economy* (Tokyo: University of Tokyo Press, 1982).

SHIRAI, TAISHIRO (ed.), *Contemporary Industrial Relations in Japan* (Madison: University of Wisconsin Press, 1983).

SHUSA, YOSHIKAZU, and KUWADA, KOTARO, 'Technological Innovation and Global Strategy', paper given at 2nd. Mitsubishi Bank Foundation Conference, University of Michigan, 29–31 Aug. 1988.

—— —— 'A New Perspective on Globalization', background paper, Third Mitsubishi Bank Foundation Conference on Japanese Overseas Investment, Cumberland Lodge, Windsor Great Park, 15–17 Sept. 1989.

SIMON, HERBERT, *Administrative Behavior* (New York: Macmillan, 1957).

—— 'The Architecture of Complexity', *Proceedings of the American Philosophical Society*, 106 (Dec. 1962), 467–82.

—— *The Sciences of the Artificial* (Cambridge, Mass.: MIT Press, 1969).

SKINNER, WICKHAM, *Manufacturing: The Formidable Competitive Weapon* (New York: John Wiley & Sons, 1985).

SMITH, ROBERT J., *Japanese Society* (Cambridge: Cambridge University Press, 1983).

SMITH, THOMAS C., *Political Change and Industrial Development in Japan: Government Enterprise 1868–80* (Stanford, Calif.: Stanford University Press, 1955).

—— *The Agrarian Origins of Modern Japan* (Stanford, Calif.: Stanford University Press, 1959).

—— 'Landlords' Sons in the Business Elite', *Economic Development and Cultural Change*, 9/1, Part II (Oct. 1960).

—— 'Pre-Modern Economic Growth: Japan and the West', *Past and Present*, 60 (Aug. 1973).

—— *Nakahara: Family Farming and Population in a Japanese Village, 1717–1830* (Stanford, Calif.: Stanford University Press, 1977).

—— 'The Right to Benevolence: Dignity and Japanese Workers, 1890–1920', *Comparative Studies in Society and History*, 26/4 (Oct. 1984), 587–613.

—— *Native Sources of Japanese Industrialization* (Berkeley: University of California Press, 1987).

SMITKA, MICHAEL J., 'The Invisible Handshake: The Development of the Japanese

Automotive Parts Industry', *Business and Economic History*, 2nd. ser. 19 (1990), 1–9.

—— *Competitive Ties: Subcontracting in Japanese Manufacturing* (New York: Columbia University Press, 1991).

SNODGRASS, CAROL R., and GRANT, JOHN R., 'Cultural Influences on Strategic Planning and Control Systems', paper given at Strategic Management Society Conference, Philadelphia, Pa., Oct. 1984.

STALK, GEORGE, 'Technological Innovation and Global Strategy', paper given at Second Mitsubishi Bank Foundation Conference, University of Michigan, 29–31 Aug. 1988.

STIGLER, GEORGE J., *The Organization of Industry* (Chicago: University of Chicago Press, 1983).

STINCHCOMBE, ARTHUR L., 'Social Structure and Organizations', in J. Mar. (ed.), *Handbook of Organizations* (Chicago: Rand McNally, 1965).

—— *Creating Efficient Industrial Administrations* (New York: Academic Press, 1973).

SUZUKI, YOSHITAKA, 'Strategy and Structure of the Top One Hundred Japanese Industrial Enterprises, 1950–1980', lecture notes, Tohoku University, Sendai, 1982.

—— 'The Formation of Management Structure in Japanese Industrials 1920–40', lecture notes, Tohoku University, Sendai, 1983.

—— *Japanese Management Structures, 1920–80* (London: Macmillan, 1991).

TAIRA, KOJI, 'Factory Legislation and Management Modernization during Japan's Industrialization 1886–1916', *Business History Review*, 44/1 (Spring 1970).

—— *Economic Development and the Labor Market in Japan* (New York: Columbia University Press, 1970).

TAKAO, HIROSHI, Manager, Nissan Motor, interview, Mar. 2 1990, Oppama, Japan.

TEECE, DAVID J., 'Economies of Scope and the Scope of the Enterprise', *Journal of Economic Behavior and Organization*, 1 (Sept. 1980), 223–47.

—— 'Towards an Economic Theory of the Multiproduct Firm', *Journal of Economic Behavior and Organization*, 3 (Mar. 1982), 39–63.

—— (ed.), *The Competitive Challenge* (New York: Harper & Row, 1987).

THOMSON, E. P., *The Making of the English Working Class* (New York: Vintage, 1963).

THORELLI, H. B., 'Networks: Between Markets and Hierarchies', *Strategic Management Journal*, 7/1 (1986), 37–51.

THURLEY, KEITH, 'Japanese Direct Investment in the United Kingdom and its Social Implications', background paper, 3rd. Mitsubishi Bank Foundation Conference on Japanese Overseas Investment, Cumberland Lodge, Windsor Great Park, 15–17 Sept. 1989.

Toyota Motor Corporation, *Toyota: A History of the First 50 Years* (Tokyo: Dainippon Printing, 1988).

TURNER, CHRISTENA L., *Breaking the Silence: Consciousness, Commitment, and Action in Japanese Unions* (Berkeley: University of California Press, forthcoming).

UCHIDA, HOSHIMI, 'Comment on Professor Nakagawa's Paper', Fuji International Conference on Business History, 5–8 Jan. 1987.

ULRICH, DAVID, and BARNEY, JAY, 'Perspectives in Organizations: Resource Dependency, Efficiency, and Population', *Academy of Management Review*, 9 (1984), 471–81.

VAN WOLFEREN, KAREL, *The Enigma of Japanese Power* (New York: Basic Books, 1989).

VIETOR, RICHARD, 'Energy Markets and Policy', in Thomas K. McCraw (ed.), *American vs. Japan* (Boston: Harvard Business School Press, 1986), 193–228.

VON GLINOW, MARY ANN, and MOHRMAN, SUSAN ALBERS, *Managing Complexity in High Technology Organizations* (New York: Oxford University Press, 1990).

VON HAYEK, FRIEDRICH AUGUST, 'The Pretense of Knowledge', Nobel Memorial Lecture, 11 Dec. 1974, repr. *American Economic Review*, 79/6 (Dec. 1989), 3–7.

VON HIPPEL, ERIC, *The Sources of Innovation* (Oxford: Oxford University Press, 1988).

VOTAW, DOW, *Modern Corporations* (Englewood Cliffs, NJ: Prentice Hall, 1965).

WALTON, RICHARD, 'From Control to Commitment in the Workplace', *Harvard Business Review*, 63/2 (1985), 77–84.

WESTNEY, ELEANOR, *Imitation and Innovation* (Cambridge, Mass.: Harvard University Press, 1987).

WHEELWRIGHT, STEVEN C., 'Japan—Where Operations Really are Strategic', *Harvard Business Review*, July–Aug. 1981, 67–74.

WILLIAMSON, HAROLD F. (ed.), *Evolution of International Management Structures* (Newark, NJ: University of Delaware Press, 1975).

WILLIAMSON, OLIVER E., *Corporate Control and Business Behavior: An Inquiry into the Effects of Organizational Form on Enterprise Behavior* (Englewood Cliffs, NJ: Prentice Hall, 1970).

—— *Markets and Hierarchies: Analysis and Anti-trust Implications* (New York: Free Press, 1975).

—— 'The Economics of Organization: The Transaction Cost Approach', *The American Journal of Sociology*, 87/3 (1981), 548–77.

—— *The Economic Institutions of Capitalism* (New York: Free Press, 1985).

—— 'Comparative Economic Organization: The Analysis of Discrete Structural Alternatives', mimeo, University of California, Berkeley, Mar. 1990.

—— (ed.), *Organization Theory* (New York: Oxford University Press, 1990).

WILLMAN, PAUL, *Technological Change, Collective Bargaining, and Industrial Efficiency* (Oxford: Oxford University Press, 1986).

WRAY, WILLIAM D., *Mitsubishi and the N.Y.K., 1870–1914* (Cambridge, Mass.: Harvard University Press, 1984).

WRIGLEY, LEONARD, 'Divisional Autonomy and Diversification', unpublished DBA. thesis, Harvard University, Harvard Business School, Ann Arbor, Mich.: University Microfilms, 1970.

YAMAMURA, KOZO, 'Success that Soured: Administrative Guidance and Cartels in Japan', in Kozo Yamamura (ed.), *Policy and Trade Issues of the Japanese Economy: American and Japanese Perspectives* (Seattle: University of Washington Press, 1982).

YASUBA, YASUKICHI, 'The Evolution of Dualistic Wage Structure', in Hugh Patrick (ed.), *Japanese Industrialization and Its Social Consequences* (Berkeley: University of California Press, 1976).

YONEKAWA, SHIN'ICHI, 'University Graduates in Japanese Enterprises Before the Second World War', *Business History*, 26/2 (July 1984).

—— and YOSHIHARA, HIDEKI, *Business History of General Trading Companies* (Tokyo: University of Tokyo Press, 1987).

YOSHIHARA, KUNIO, *Sogo Shosha: The Vanguard of the Japanese Economy* (Oxford: Oxford University Press, 1981).

YOSHINO, MICHAEL Y., and LIFSON, THOMAS B., *The Invisible Link* (Cambridge, Mass.: MIT Press, 1986).

YUI, TSUNEHIKO, 'The Development of the Organizational Structure of Top Management in Meiji Japan', *Japanese Yearbook on Business History*, 1 (Tokyo: Japanese Business History Institute, 1984).

—— 'The Development of the Organizational Structure of Top Management in Meiji

Japan', *Japanese Yearbook on Business History* (Tokyo: Japanese Business History Institute, 1984).

—— 'Development and Organization of Large Industrial Enterprises in Japan', *Bulletin of Social Science of Meiji University*, 25/1 (1987).

—— 'Development, Organization, and International Competitiveness of Industrial Enterprises in Japan (1880–1915)', *Business and Economic History*, 2nd. ser. 17 (1988).

—— 'Development, Organization, and Business Strategy of Industrial Enterprises in Japan (1915–1935)', in Shigeaki Yasuoka and Hidemasa Morikawa (eds.), *Japanese Yearbook on Business History*, 5 (Tokyo: Japanese Business History Institute, 1988).

—— and NAKAGAWA (eds.), *Japanese Management in Historical Perspective*, Fuji Business History Conference XV (Tokyo: University of Tokyo Press, 1989).

Index of Names

Index of Subjects